Inside George Orwell

Also by Gordon Bowker

Pursued by Furies: A Life of Malcolm Lowry
Through the Dark Labyrinth: A Biography of Lawrence Durrell

INSIDE GEORGE ORWELL

Gordon Bowker

First published 2003 by PALGRAVE MACMILLAN™
175 Fifth Avenue, New York, N.Y. 10010 and
Houndmills, Basingstoke, Hampshire, England RG21 6XS.
Companies and representatives throughout the world.

PALGRAVE MACMILLAN is the global academic imprint of the
Palgrave Macmillan division of St. Martin's Press, LLC and of Palgrave
Macmillan Ltd. Macmillan® is a registered trademark in the United
States, United Kingdom and other countries. Palgrave is a registered
trademark in the European Union and other countries.

ISBN 0-312-23841-X

Library of Congress Cataloguing-in-Publication Data available from
the Library of Congress.

First published in Great Britain in 2003 by Little, Brown.

First PALGRAVE MACMILLAN edition: September 2003.

10 9 8 7 6 5 4 3 2 1

Printed in the United States of America.

*To my parents who survived these years and
to Rhoda who survived this book*

Contents

'Narcissism is a normal motive of novelists . . . and it is an unusual novel that does not contain somewhere or other a portrait of the author, thinly disguised as hero, saint, or martyr.'

Orwell, review of Colm Brogan's
The Democrat at the Supper Table, 1946

'A history constructed imaginatively would never be right about any single event, but it might come nearer to essential truth than a mere compilation of names and dates in which no one statement is demonstrably true.'

Orwell, review of Winwood Reade's
The Martyrdom of Man, 1946

'I don't think George ever knew what makes other people tick, because what made him tick was very different from what made most other people tick.'

Arthur Koestler, 'George Orwell',
BBC Third programme, November 1960

Preface

'Saints should always be judged guilty until they are proved innocent.'

Orwell, 'Reflections on Gandhi', 1949

Few can doubt that George Orwell was a writer of great power and imagination, and one of the greatest writers of the twentieth century, still widely read and greatly admired. He was one of those rare men – a bestselling novelist who also had a profound influence on the politics of his time. From a relatively obscure middle-class colonial background, an undistinguished career at Eton and with the Indian Imperial Police in Burma in the 1920s, he launched himself as a writer (first in Paris, then in London), supplementing his income by teaching, working in a bookshop, and running a village store in Hertfordshire. At the end of his comparatively short life his great literary stature was recognised, yet he became widely known only five years before he died.

He began intending to write poetry and 'enormous naturalistic novels . . . full of purple passages in which words were used partly for the sake of their sound'. But, as his social conscience developed, his fiction became sparse and sharply focused, and he also turned to writing non-fiction based on his own experiences. These early documentaries (for which he first took the name 'George Orwell') dealt with the lives of the marginal, exploited and dissident – the world of the poor and destitute (*Down and Out in Paris and London*), the grim conditions of the unemployed in the North of England (*The Road to Wigan Pier*), and the experience of fighting in the Spanish Civil War (*Homage to Catalonia*). Orwell wrote that, 'Good prose is like a window-pane,' and if we look through his prose in one direction we see the world as he saw it; from the other direction we can observe the inner man. It is not surprising, therefore, that the central characters in his pre-war fiction mirror his own life, his social and political concerns – a British colonial in Burma coming to hate imperialism (*Burmese Days*), a member of the middle class down and out among tramps (*A Clergyman's Daughter*), a struggling writer working in a bookshop (*Keep the Aspidistra Flying*), a lower-middle-class man searching for a political language to express his unease with modern capitalism and the threat of war (*Coming Up For Air*).

But was his 'true nature' confined to the ascetic intellectual we often think of him as being, or was it the passionate soul we sometimes glimpse in his less well-known writing? He wrote intensely enthusiastic letters about Joyce's *Ulysses*, and essays on Henry Miller and Salvador Dali, which tell us that inside the austere writer there was a romantic struggling to get out. All the protagonists in his novels, from John Flory in *Burmese Days* to Winston Smith in *Nineteen Eighty-Four*, are fired not only by social or political motives, but by frustrated passion. Orwell himself was a man with deep feelings, which he attempted as far as possible to conceal. Yet, as he admitted, it was emotion that provided the driving force of his creativity. The main thrust of this book will be to reach down as far as possible to the roots of that emotional life, to get as close as possible to the dark sources mirrored in his work.

Apart from passion, of course, Orwell also possessed peculiar mental qualities which helped form his distinctive perception of the world. For example, he was fascinated by how things work, from pieces of machinery to human societies, and, in whatever situation he found himself – among down-and-outs, working in a hotel kitchen, picking hops in Kent, teaching in schools, working in a bookshop, fighting in Spain – he quickly saw how the system worked. This intuitive grasp of social patterns and processes, his sociological imagination, enabled him to develop into a writer of vision. He saw present events in their wider contexts and also saw the future they implied. In many ways it was an eccentric vision, but a vision instantly recognisable to others through the fiction he wrote.

His distinctive mental powers and political imagination, which ultimately gave us his most outstanding works, were given direction by personal experience. Long before 1939, he saw the threat to individual liberty from totalitarianism of both left and right. His horror at what happened to him in Spain, his keen observations of country life and his close identification with animals, supplied the landscape and inspiration for his *Animal Farm* 'revolution-gone-wrong'. His involvement with bureaucracy and propaganda during his wartime years at the BBC gave him 'Newspeak', 'The Ministry of Truth' and 'Room 101' – the malevolent instruments of *Nineteen Eighty-Four*. But it would take the romantic, the poet inside Orwell, to transform such raw experiences into unforgettable fictions.

The post-war years brought Orwell his greatest success and lasting influence. A man who had laboured largely in the shadows emerged as a major author with the publication of *Animal Farm* in 1945, and then *Nineteen Eighty-Four* in 1949. Since publication they have sold in their millions (40 million is a recent estimate) and been translated into languages as disparate as Swahili and Serbo-Croat. The rhetoric of politics has been changed by Orwell's writing. Modern readers of his books are made more aware of the ease with which politicians can pervert language, and the ever-burgeoning school of cultural studies owes as much to Orwell's brilliant sociological literary essays as to the scholarship of Matthew Arnold, F. R. Leavis, Richard Hoggart or 'post-modern' theorists.

There have been three previous major biographies of Orwell: Bernard Crick's *George Orwell: A Life* (1980), Michael Shelden's *Orwell: The Authorized Biography* (1991) and Jeffrey Meyers' more recent *Orwell: Wintry Conscience of a Generation* (2000) – different biographers, different readings, different portraits. Crick's book stressed the political context of Orwell's life; Shelden's concentrated on Orwell the literary man, Meyers' acknowledged more the inner man.

New material (especially the recently published *Complete Works of George Orwell*) and new witnesses offer the opportunity to go even further in trying to reconstruct the evolving consciousness of this writer of genius. It is now possible for more attention to be directed to Orwell's quite complex sexuality and strangely deceptive nature, to explore the motives which drove him to Burma and thence into the underground world of the poor, dispossessed and deviant, and left a legacy of disgruntlement which fuelled much of his writing. And recently available KGB archives supply a clearer picture of how he was hunted and spied on in Spain, an experience that ultimately gave birth to his last two great novels. Taking in the broad sweep of his life also throws light on the story of Orwell's collaboration with the covert Information Research Department of the Foreign Office, which has aroused such controversy on the political left.

In some circles Orwell has been canonised, but it is now evident that as a man he had certain crucial weaknesses. For example, despite his reputation for crystalline honesty, he had a deceptive streak. He deceived fellow tramps about his identity and true circumstances; he kept his family ignorant of what he was doing; he deliberately kept some of his friends apart in order to present them with different faces; he was deceptive in his sexual relationships; he concealed his true feelings behind a mask of reserve. The revelation that he co-operated with the IRD left some of his old friends feeling badly deceived as to his true nature. He deliberately concealed himself behind a pseudonym, and argued that 'a writer's literary personality has little or nothing to do with his private character'. But elsewhere he wrote that in order to understand a writer's motives we need to understand his early life. His writing, especially about his childhood, provides sharper insights into Orwell's private character than has been previously recognised.

Some aspects of the inner Orwell were probably meant to remain obscure. The intention is to try to illuminate that shadowy self lying concealed behind a façade of dour irony and self-denial. The way he wrote about women, for example, betrays a fundamental, if repressed, sybaritic and chauvinistic nature; his political passions reveal a religious temperament acquired in his youth which survived his conversion to atheism; his feeling for animals and country life show him to have been a committed conservationist, and his love of French literature and culture reveals an exotic side not fully portrayed in previous accounts of his life.

Through that mass of detail now available, the human face of Orwell emerges. He was often painfully honest about his prejudices and self-contradictions. So while he was against private schools, disliked Scots, and was a staunch atheist, he put his adopted son down for Westminster, chose to live among Scots on Jura, and asked to be buried according to the rites of the Church of England. And although he was a rationalist he was superstitious enough to take ghosts and poltergeists seriously, and ask Rayner Heppenstall to cast his son's horoscope. And those who believe he lacked humour should look at his essay on seaside postcards and his poem about a man besotted by a Burmese girl:

> I said 'For twenty silver pieces,
> Maiden sleep with me.'
> She looked at me, so pure, so sad,
> The loveliest thing alive,
> And in her virgin lisping voice,
> Stood out for twenty-five.

Like his fictional heroes, he had difficulty approaching women. In his teens he was rebuffed by a childhood sweetheart; in Burma he indulged with prostitutes and is said to have had a child by a Burmese girl; in Paris in 1928 he lived for a while with a 'trollop'. Back in England, even though he managed the occasional liaison and was familiar with London prostitutes, recurring illness and self-induced poverty made sustaining a love life difficult. As a lover he lacked sophistication, but he certainly had powerful and unsatisfied sexual feelings and a sadistic streak to complement the masochism that drove him to self-punishment. Although part of him wished to emulate sexually unbridled writers like D. H. Lawrence, James Joyce and Henry Miller, the social and political climate of his age and the harsh obscenity laws propelled him towards literary puritanism.

Only when he met a young psychology student, Eileen O'Shaughnessy, in 1935, did he find a woman prepared to share his spartan lifestyle. Their marriage, though a success, became a fairly open one. To some extent each tolerated the other's occasional infidelities, although Eileen probably knew nothing of a secret liaison he began with one of her friends soon after they married. It is also now clear that a woman thought to be just an old friend was in fact a great obsession in his life and he attempted unsuccessfully to establish a *ménage à trois* with her and Eileen. Orwell's various sexual encounters may reflect his desperate desire for children and his fear of having become sterile. In 1944 the couple finally adopted a child, and George became a devoted father. When Eileen died suddenly in 1945 he felt shattered, but, like a good Etonian, concealed his true feelings from others. ('She was a good old stick,' he told a friend.) Thereafter he sought out young women and, after only the barest preliminaries, proposed marriage, offering the prospect of a lucrative literary inheritance in the event of his early death. This approach failed but, despite looking increasingly haggard, some – often wealthy – women were drawn by his strange, ascetic charisma. Shortly before his death in January 1950, the beautiful young editor Sonia Brownell was persuaded to marry him. She inherited the Orwell estate and became keeper of the flame until her death in 1980.

Illness stalked him from childhood and became a dark, malignant presence in his life. He was cursed with a weak chest, and careless living only worsened his condition. By the end of the war he was worn out and by the time he came to write *Nineteen Eighty-Four* TB had him in a deadly grip. There can be no doubt that this last novel became infused with the gloom cast over him by his fatal illness. But that same feeling reaches back to earlier novels in which his characters are smothered by convention, suffocating in suburban boredom and striving always to 'come up for air'. The general lack of sunlight in Orwell's fiction suggests that the shadow cast upon his lungs was also cast over the landscape of his imagination.

Another key aspect of Orwell rarely considered is the extent to which his intellectual life was affected by European ideas and events. He began publishing in France, and Paris gave him half the material for his first book. Spain transformed him politically and events in Germany and the Soviet Union dominated the last fifteen years of his life. To that extent he was a great European writer. And yet he had a profound sense of Englishness, which comes through in the best of his essays. This duality needs to be seen as central to his life as does the duality between the inner man and the literary-political man, the visionary romantic and the man for whom crystalline prose was an imperative.

What has been all too often neglected is the way Orwell's works mirror the shape of his own life. In book after book, freedom is achieved at great risk and sacrifice, then lost again through deception or cheating, or under the crushing weight of convention or state despotism – Orwell's version of *Paradise Gained* and *Paradise Lost*. (The reversal of an established form was characteristic of him.) This overarching metaphor of his life and work also reflects his sense of a lost 'Golden Age', the pre-1914 years of his childhood. In conveying to us key images of our times and in warning us of our futures, there is something of the secular priest, reminding us that his grandfather was a missionary bishop.

He saw himself as somehow chosen to live and endure by the pen. 'There is a minority of gifted, wilful people,' he wrote, 'who are determined to live their own lives to the end, and writers belong to this class.' While many writers and poets of Orwell's generation chose to express their inner lives through the seductive fog of poetry or the jargon of political sects, he chose rather the window pane of transpicuous prose. Despite his commitment to truth, however, his inner life was shrouded. Nevertheless, through the psychological depths of his fictional characters, in his autobiographical essays, and between the lines of his letters and diary entries, the shroud may be lifted sufficiently for the secret self to be revealed.

Most biographers like to think that they have turned up new and important information and been able thereby to cast their subject in a new light. The ground of Orwell's life has been well dug over in the past, so it is surprising how much fresh material is still to be found. Here, details of his mother's family history seem to have been overlooked by previous biographers, especially details of interracial liaisons and marriages; the fact of Eric Blair's early Catholic education has not previously been uncovered; his obsession with black magic and the true story of his dabbling in sympathetic magic as a schoolboy has never before been told, and the full influence of Eton, his public school, has not previously been fully explored and understood. Themes established at that time can be seen to have lasted and experiences undergone there continued to haunt him. There were new leads casting fresh light on his liaisons in Burma and, thanks to newly discovered letters, the extent of his involvement with one of his early girlfriends, before and throughout his married life, has finally come to light. Most extraordinary, perhaps, from the unearthing of KGB files, is just how firmly Orwell was in the sights of the Soviet authorities even while he was in Spain, and how some of those around him were themselves implicated. It is not always appreciated just how paranoid his Spanish experience left Orwell, but the evidence of a man who knew him in London after the war confirms the fact that he thought himself to be in great danger from Stalin's hit-men. Much of this new material enables Orwell to be seen in a somewhat different light from the way in which he has been hitherto viewed, and helps make greater sense of some of his later, seemingly contradictory, behaviour. His relationship with women can now be seen in better focus and the unfettered homophobia with which he has long been credited can be at least questioned, thanks to new testimony from a pre-war flatmate. In other words there is much that is new to be written about and reflected upon in reassessing Orwell, not only as a man, but as a man writing very much against the odds.

Chapter 1

The Inheritance

'It is probably true that you can't give a really revealing history of a man's life without saying something about his parents and probably his grand-parents.'

Orwell, BBC radio talk, 1945

As a young man Eric Blair was fascinated by ghost stories and intrigued by black magic. Once, seemingly to deadly effect, he laid a curse on a schoolboy who had offended him. On another occasion he reported seeing a ghost. Later, he told a friend that he used a pseudonym so that no enemy could take his name and work magic against him. In dreams he looked for symbols and interpretations, and more than once had highly prophetic visions. None of this quite fits with the widely held image of a man who transformed himself into the writer of clear-headed, rational and lucid prose, George Orwell. But behind every bearer of a pseudonym there stands an individual life, an individual who can appear in various guises and a life which can come to us in different versions. That is because personalities and lives are kaleidoscopic – records, images glimpsed behind words or lodged in reminiscence, fragments viewed and re-viewed through the mirrors of memory and conscious reflection, all projected in turn in new configurations through the eyes of biographers.

In a strange vision, at the age of twenty-six, Eric Blair (not yet 'George Orwell') seems to have foreseen his own death. Lying ill with pneumonia in a squalid Paris hospital ward in 1929, he saw in a bed opposite a man who had just died – pale, wasted, lifeless.

> *Numéro* 57's eyes were still open, his mouth also open, his small face
> contorted into an expression of agony. What most impressed me
> however was the whiteness of his face. It had been pale before, but now
> it was little darker than the sheets. As I gazed at the tiny, screwed-up

face, it struck me that this disgusting piece of refuse, waiting to be
carted away and dumped on a slab in the dissecting room, was an
example of 'natural' death, one of the things you pray for in the Litany.
There you are, then . . . that's what is waiting for you, 20, 30, 40 years
hence.[1]

Just over twenty years later, Orwell himself, wizened and enfeebled by
tuberculosis, lay at the brink of death in a hospital bed, the very image of
the old Frenchman he had once watched die. As his time approached, in his
solitary remorseless way, he observed his own slow deterioration. In 1948,
having caught sight of his naked reflection in a sanatorium mirror, he projected his own horrifying likeness on to Winston Smith, the persecuted
protagonist of his final novel, *Nineteen Eighty-Four*. Smith, too, is confronted by the ravaged spectre of a tortured man seemingly close to death:

A bowed, grey coloured, skeleton-like thing was coming towards him.
Its actual appearance was frightening, and not merely the fact that he
knew it to be himself. He moved closer to the glass. The creature's face
seemed to be protruded, because of its bent carriage. A forlorn,
jailbird's face . . . cheekbones above which his eyes were fierce and
watchful. The cheeks were seamed, the mouth had a drawn-in look.
Certainly it was his own face, but it seemed to him that it had changed
more than he had changed inside. The emotions it registered would be
different from the ones he felt . . . But the truly frightening thing was
the emaciation of his body. The barrel of the ribs was as narrow as that
of a skeleton: the legs had shrunk so that the knees were thicker than
the thighs . . . The curvature of the spine was astonishing. The thin
shoulders were hunched forward so as to make a cavity of the chest, the
scraggy neck seemed to be bending double under the weight of the
skull. At a guess he would have said that it was the body of a man of
sixty, suffering from some malignant disease.[2]

This was *The Picture of Dorian Gray* reversed. The cruel self-portrait, the
emaciated wreck, was the reality; the man he longed to be – handsome and
attractive to women – lay hidden in the attic, or at least in a secretive corner
of his imagination. The reality on his deathbed testified to a harsh life of
self-denial and self-mortification for sins both real and imagined. It is
tempting to see in O'Brien, Winston's torturer, the sadistic alter ego of
George Orwell, intent on rendering him less than human, and in Winston
himself the masochistic alter ego, the mirror-image self of the same complex character. This picture of the crushed and beaten man is Orwell,
transforming personal suffering into art. The passage quoted embodies

two other significant characteristics of the man – an impulse towards prophecy and a compulsion to be candid, the latter a quality he both valued and feared. So, while in many ways he could be brutally honest about himself, some aspects of him remained concealed behind a carefully constructed persona, secret sides of himself he seems to have feared and which he may have hoped would remain hidden, even beyond the grave.

The ancestry of this strange, guilt-ridden ascetic, with English, French and long-obscure Scottish connections, has been chronicled previously, though details remain somewhat sketchy, and therefore difficult to vivify. Some hints and clues and new revelations, however, do bring some life to names inscribed in dusty records.

Two geographical axes enable us to map the family inheritance. One links Hardy's Dorset to Kipling's India; the other connects a town in central France, celebrated for its delicate enamel paintings, to a bustling port in Burma. In his first work of fiction, *Burmese Days*, Orwell sets out to debunk the Kiplingesque myth of the 'white man's burden', the story unfolding with all the tragic inevitability of a Hardy novel. In no other work of his would these diverse strands of his distant heritage come together quite so evidently, except perhaps in the autobiographical sections of *The Road to Wigan Pier*, and a long work, a family saga projected before his death, which died with him.

On his father's side there were West Indian slave-owners, minor aristocrats and upstanding servants of Empire; on his mother's were French colonials, shipbuilders and timber merchants. He would come, as a young man, to despise those who profited from colonialism, as he found himself doing for a time, even though he sneakingly admired the people who made the system work. He poured scorn on Anglo-Indian imperialists, even while admiring their bard, Kipling, for portraying them so honestly. He was ashamed of what Europeans like his maternal ancestors had done in Burma, yet he embraced his Gallic heritage and immersed himself in French literature. Despite attending the most prestigious school in England, he rejected the easy path to wealth and privilege, and denied himself the many comforts which conformity would have brought. The rest of his life is a story of adventures, often reckless adventures, invariably destined to fail, as he was only too ready to admit. As he wrote, 'Any life when viewed from the inside is simply a series of defeats.'[3] The one adventure which did succeed for him was his venture into literature, though even that path, too, was strewn with disasters, and lasting success eluded him until the very end of his life.

A taste for adventure marks his family history on both sides – in colonial exploits and exploitations. In the eighteenth century the enterprise of the Blairs led to wealth and marriage into the nobility, only to be followed by slow decline into respectable obscurity. Charles Blair, Eric's great-grandfather, was born in 1743, probably of Scottish ancestry. By way of Jamaican sugar plantations and the slave trade he became sufficiently prosperous to be an acceptable husband for Lady Mary Fane, youngest daughter of the Earl of Westmoreland, to whom he was married in 1765. The Fanes were enthusiastic field sportsmen. Their ranks include Masters of Hounds and army cavalry officers as well as a Commander of the British Army in Burma. Eric was keenly aware of his Blair ancestry – the procession of ghostly forebears, their names inscribed in the Blair family Bible inherited from his father, an oil painting of Lady Mary Blair and a set of leather-bound volumes once owned by his great-uncle, Captain Horatio Blair, to which he became sentimentally attached. Unlike the worthy captain, he never developed a yen for the sea, but field sports, especially shooting and fishing, became lifelong passions. In novels such as *A Clergyman's Daughter* and *Coming Up For Air* he wrote knowingly about the fate of worn-out aristocrats and their declining families, and in his wartime call-to-arms, *The Lion and the Unicorn*, he observed that 'England was ruled by an aristocracy constantly recruited from parvenus' which nevertheless 'somehow . . . decayed [and] lost its ability, its daring, finally its ruthlessness.'[4]

However, back in the eighteenth century, at least, Blairs were thriving. The parvenu Charles Blair and Jane, his Lady wife, produced at least nine children, four of whom died young – Henry Charles was killed at nineteen while serving as captain in the 23rd Regiment of Foot in St Domingo. Of the surviving five, last in the line was Thomas Richard Arthur Blair, Eric's paternal grandfather. There were Blair cousins, too, including the first Horatio, born in 1808 and named, presumably, in honour of the great Nelson, killed at Trafalgar just three years earlier.

Thomas Richard was born in the year of his father's death, 1802, and grew up with his siblings and widowed mother at Ensbury in Dorset. In accordance with family tradition, the children were educated privately, though not entirely ineffectually. Thomas gained entrance to Pembroke College, Oxford, where for a year he read Theology as a Fellow Commoner with high-table privileges, before setting off for the colonies as an acolyte of the Anglican Church. Why he failed to complete his Oxford years and disappeared so precipitately to the colonies is unknown, but he was first ordained a deacon of the Church of England in Calcutta in 1839, then in 1843 as a priest in Tasmania. Legend has it that in the 1830s, sailing home on leave from India, his ship called at Cape Town where he met and proposed to Emily Hare, intending to marry her on his return. However, on arrival, he found her already married. Apparently unconcerned, he simply said, 'Well, never mind, I'll have Fanny' – Francis Hare, her fifteen-year-old sister. His first child, Horatio, was born in Calcutta in 1838. There followed a daughter,

Augusta Michel and two sons, Dawson, and Richard Walmsley Blair, born nine months apart in 1857.

Three years earlier, Thomas had returned to England and, through his Westmorland connections, was handed the vicarage of Milborne St Andrew, a small village in his home county of Dorset. Milborne stands a few miles north of Tolpuddle, where in 1834 six farm labourers attempted to set up a union and were transported to Australia – a martyrdom still celebrated by English socialists. The parish included the hamlet of Dewlish, where Fanes formed the squirearchy, and in this essentially feudal setting, Thomas remained vicar for thirteen years, until his death in 1867.

There was a touch of arrogance in old Thomas, and the village retains one controversial memorial to him. In 1856, considering the existing vicarage not quite dignified enough for the grandson of an earl, he excited great local hostility by building a new one at considerable cost to the parish. Although Eric would turn atheist and spend his life attacking institutional religions, he always had a lingering affection for the Anglican Church, identifying with its dissenting martyrs and allowing it to confirm, marry and ultimately to bury him. And, while he declared war on the capitalist class and embraced the basic philosophy of socialism there was a lingering streak of the nineteenth-century Tory in his make-up. No doubt it was with the High Church Blairs in mind that he commended his favourite eighteenth-century novelist, Smollett, for writing mostly about 'the kind of people who are cousins to a landowner, and take their manners from the aristocracy'.[5] The nineteenth-century industrial middle classes, on the other hand, who were catered for by the Low and Nonconformist Churches, and engineered the rise of capitalism, could be happily despised.

Like the rest of his brothers, Richard was privately tutored, in his case at Bath in neighbouring Somerset, continuing there until he was eighteen. As with most upper-middle-class families of the time there was great emphasis on public service. Thomas's cousin Horatio (son of the first Horatio Blair), not surprisingly perhaps, was destined for the Navy, Richard for the far more humdrum life of colonial civil servant. Horatio became a Royal Navy captain, and would be buried with full naval honours at Portsmouth in 1908, when Eric was five and Britain was building up its formidable fleet of dreadnoughts. It was he who left behind the much-valued set of leather-bound volumes kept in a wooden travelling-case which Eric was to inherit. But there were also unusual, unpredictable and unstable relations who brought a dash of drama to the family. On 13 January 1911, Richard Charles Blair, another of his father's cousins, a captain in the 6th Gurkha Rifles, sailing home from India through the Red Sea, and suffering from depression, walked up on deck one night and quietly jumped overboard. The family kept the newspaper cutting of the story, another scrap of Blair history retained, and one is reminded of Eric's alter ego, John Flory in *Burmese Days*, who did away with himself in Burma in similarly melancholic circumstances.

The aristocratic connection had weakened by the time Richard Walmsley Blair was born. What took him to India is unclear, but he is said to have had an unhappy love affair, and this may be what led him, at the age of nineteen, to take on one of the most obscure and least heroic roles in the whole colonial system. In 1875 he entered the Opium Department of the Province of Bengal, an uncovenanted member of the Indian Civil Service. As Assistant Sub-Deputy Opium Agent, grade 5 on 500 rupees per month, he could hardly have found a more remote and less exalted position at the lowest level in the order of precedence in the complex hierarchy of the Empire. His job was to oversee the growing of opium, mainly for export to China. It was a lucrative trade monopolised by Britain, but one which the Chinese Government was actively seeking to have banned. By 1897, Richard, still stuck on his lowly grade 5 and his poor starting salary, was serving in Tehta, in the Gaya district in Upper Bengal. He was thirty-nine, unmarried, and employed in a job that seemed to have a distinctly limited future.

Eric's mother, Ida Mabel Limouzin, grew up in Moulmein in Lower Burma. Her father, Francis Mathew Limouzin (known as Frank), was a timber merchant from Limoges, in central France, a region, according to the playwright Jean Giraudoux, 'which has bred more popes and fewer lovers than any other in the world'.[6] The town, which stands between Poitiers and Périgueux, was an early centre of French civilisation, the birthplace of the painter Auguste Renoir and Etienne de Silhouette, the man after whom the outline drawing was named. 'Limouzin' was the name applied to natives of the ancient French province of Limougeauds, and the first saloon car was christened 'the limousine' because it mimicked the enclosing warmth of the shepherd's cloak worn in those parts. One of Eric's childhood jokes was to refer to his mother's family as 'the automobiles' or 'the lemonskins'.[7] The ancient Limouzins of Limoges, however, were and remain celebrated painters of enamel, a craft which, by the mid-nineteenth century, it seems, had temporarily collapsed.

Frank emigrated to Burma, with his wife Eliza (née Fallon) and his brothers William Eugene and Joseph Edmund, sometime in the late 1850s. Joseph also took a wife, Mary, with him; William Eugene was single. The brothers settled in Moulmein, one of the most picturesque ports in the East, perched at the mouth of the Salween River. As well as a busy trading station, it was a centre for shipbuilding. William found work as a shipwright and Joseph as a general merchant, while Frank was employed in the offices of a large shipping company. Shortly after arriving in Burma, William produced a child by an Indian woman called Sooma.

By 1864, Frank, aged twenty-nine, and Eliza, twenty-three, had two young children – two-year-old Arthur, and Emily, just one. Then quite suddenly the young family was engulfed by tragedy and in less than three months Frank found himself not only a widower but childless. First Emily, the youngest, died of croup, then, two months later, Eliza died from dysentery, and within the following two weeks Arthur also succumbed to croup. Frank, however, did not remain single for long. In August 1865, just six months after Eliza's death, he married a 22-year-old English woman, Thérèse Catherine Halliley, by special licence in Moulmein, with members of his dead wife's family present. Within three years he had set up as a timber merchant, was settled into a large house, proudly named 'Franconia', in the fashionable riverside district of Salween Park, and was busily creating a second family. Frank and Thérèse were to produce eight children – Norah (born 1866), Charles, known as Chills (1868), Frank (1869), Helène Kate, known as Nellie (1870), Blanche (1872), Ida (1875), Mina (1880) and George (1881). Frank's brother William had died in 1863, aged thirty-nine, leaving just one child, Aimée, while Joseph and Mary produced four – Elizabeth, Minnie, Agatha and May. By the end of the century, Frank stood proudly at the head of his own firm, Limouzin and Co., and was the local consular agent for Italy, a country with which he did a good deal of business, while Joseph ran the local Phoenix distillery. The Limouzins of Moulmein were a thriving and much respected local family.

Ida Mabel was born in Penge, close to the Crystal Palace on the southern outskirts of London on 18 May 1875, while Frank and Thérèse were on leave visiting the Hallileys there. Although born in England, Ida was regarded as a French national, and, until she married, carried a French passport. The Limouzin children grew up in Moulmein and attended school there. The boys mostly went into the timber business, and at least two of the girls became teachers – Helène at the Diocesan School for Girls in Rangoon and Ida, more adventurously, as assistant mistress in the girls' department of a boys' school in Naini Tal, a hill station over six thousand feet above sea level in the North West Province of India. Beautifully situated in the hills between Rampur and Srinagar, Naini Tal was a popular summer resort for Europeans and a retreat for the provincial government during the hot season. Why Ida should have travelled so far from home to work is unclear, but it is said that as a young woman she was jilted, and it is possible that it was in Naini Tal that her lover had abandoned her, or where she had gone to try to forget. In Naini Tal she was destined to meet and marry Richard Walmsley Blair, also, it seems, the sad casualty of an earlier disappointment.

They were an ill-matched pair – ill-matched in age as much as character. At thirty-nine, Richard was still a lowly Sub-Deputy Opium Agent, Ida was just twenty-two; he was a staid, somewhat philistine British colonial, while she was a high-spirited vivacious woman with a lively intelligence. He was over six feet tall with clear blue eyes and rather chubby cheeks; she was dark and pretty, with a ready smile and a slightly exotic taste in dress. Ironically perhaps, they were married at the Church of St John in the Wilderness on 15 June 1897, with Ida's sister Blanche as bridesmaid. Francis Limouzin's name is absent from the marriage certificate, suggesting that he may not have approved his young daughter marrying a man old enough to be her father. Richard's best man was a lawyer also from Gaya, with whom he was probably taking summer leave when he met the woman he would take back as his wife.

The move from the attractive hill town of Naini Tal to the sweltering disease-ridden district of Gaya, at the heart of the Bengal opium trade, was no doubt something of a shock for Ida, who soon became pregnant with her first child, Marjorie Frances Blair, born on 21 April 1898. What sort of social life was possible in such a posting is difficult to imagine. The town of Gaya stands some eighty-one miles south of Patna. Named after a pagan monster once trapped under a stone there, it was a place of pilgrimage to both Hindus and Buddhists, with a high proportion of priestly Brahmins living well off taxes extorted from pilgrims. As was normal in British India, the Europeans lived separately from the native Indians and existed largely in ignorance of the local culture, cultivating among themselves a sense of exclusion and superiority – what George Orwell called 'the pukka sahib pose', living the lie that in exploiting the country and robbing its people they were solely committed to benefiting them.[8]

The Indian colonial life could be agreeable enough for those prepared to put up with a certain amount of discomfort and isolation. Even so, carrying the 'white man's burden' in an out-of-the-way place like Gaya must have been rather more of a burden than usual. Apart from certain government offices, mostly connected with the opium trade, the European quarter boasted little more than a government high school, a hospital and a branch of the Lady Elgin association for women. The Blairs, of course, would have had the usual compliment of servants, including an ayah for Marjorie, and there would have been the inevitable whites-only club where they could enjoy endless rubbers of bridge and endless rounds of *chota pegs* in the company of other Anglo-Indians. And for Richard there was the faint prospect of advancement. By 1902 he had inched his way from Sub-Deputy Opium Agent 5th class to Sub-Deputy Opium Agent 4th class, on a salary of 600 rupees a month.

Eric followed Marjorie on 25 June 1903, a Thursday's child with 'far to go'. By this time Richard, again promoted, to Sub-Deputy Opium Agent 3rd class on an income of 700 rupees, had been posted north to oversee the opium fields around Motihari, a spectacular part of the world, veined by rivers and a lacework of lakes and with inspiring views towards the forested heights of the Nepalese Himalayas. But it was far more remote and even less populous than Gaya, this time well beyond Patna, where the opium was distilled before being exported to China.

The years 1902 and 1903, the years of Eric's conception and birth, saw the publication of significant works by authors who were to greatly influence him as a writer – Rudyard Kipling's *Just So Stories*, Arthur Conan Doyle's *The Hound of the Baskervilles*, H. G. Wells's *The Discovery of the Future*, Joseph Conrad's *Heart of Darkness*, Samuel Butler's *The Way of All Flesh*, Charles Booth's *Life and Labour of the People of London* and Jack London's *The People of the Abyss*.

In January 1903, in Delhi, the recently-crowned Edward VII made a widely publicised tour of India where he proclaimed himself Emperor. The Edwardian age had been inaugurated and age of Empire was at its zenith, the fleet was expanding, and a third of the world's map was red. From the British point of view, there may have been pogroms in distant Russia and atrocities in the far-off Balkans, but for the moment there was peace in Western Europe and an *Entente Cordiale* between Britain and France would soon be signed as a guarantee of its continuity.

There were, however, intimations of change and turbulent times ahead. In the same year the Ford Car Company was established in Detroit, the dangerous Italian socialist Benito Mussolini was under police surveillance in Switzerland, and, in the American film *The Great Train Robbery*, the spectacular gunplay was causing a sensation in packed London cinemas. A new element of change and vicarious violence had entered British life. Labour increased its presence in the House of Commons to three, there were strikes and social unrest in Russia, and when Eric was four months old, Emmeline Pankhurst's Women's Social and Political Movement was launched in London. In August Lenin's Bolsheviks broke away from the other Russian socialists to form a party dedicated to revolution led by an inner core of dedicated fanatics. Two months later the Wright brothers made their first flight at Kitty Hawk, a miracle that within his lifetime Eric would see turned into the nightmare of aerial warfare. The era of mass communications came closer in 1904 with the invention of the radio valve, and Freud, now working on a theory of infantile sexuality, occupied a Chair in Neurology in Vienna. An age of probing into the human mind aimed at changing human behaviour and human thought had dawned.

The progress from Naini Tal to the small town of Gaya to the isolation of Motihari must have been less than inspiring. Yet despite its remoteness, life for a young mother like Ida might have been just bearable, with a new family to think about, another child on the way, and servants to take care of the routine chores. But then the district was struck by an outbreak of plague, and, not surprisingly, shortly after Eric's birth, she persuaded Richard to bring her and their children to settle permanently in England. Richard's name is temporarily absent from the India List of 1903, which seems to confirm that he took leave to accompany his young family on the long homeward voyage. Surviving photographs of the infant Eric in the arms of his mother and his ayah, were most likely taken at the time of his baptism on 30 October, just before their departure.

It was not unusual for British colonials to bring their children home to be educated. This happened to Thackeray, Kipling and Lawrence Durrell, all of whom were born and spent their early years in India, and to the short-story writer 'Saki' (Hector Hugh Munro), who was born in Burma. Normally, parents would then return to their comfortable colonial lives, grand houses and plentiful supply of cheap native servants. Ida, however, at twenty-eight, was probably all too happy to get away from the heat, the dust, the narrow circle of Anglo-Indian society, and the ever-present threat of deadly infection. In England, too, she was well away from her decidedly middle-aged husband and the risk of yet more restrictive and burdensome pregnancies.

Meanwhile, the Limouzins of Moulmein had fallen on hard times. The boat-building industry had collapsed by the end of the century, and Frank was said to have gone into the rice business, losing much of his money in the process. His long-deceased brother William had cohabited with an Indian woman; now, in 1899, his second eldest son, Ida's brother Frank, fathered a child by a Burmese girl, Mah Hlim. There could well have been a scandal over this, because Frank appears to have fled the country. The Limouzins were popular in the Anglo-Indian society of Moulmein and, perhaps to spare their blushes and save his own face, he disappeared to Siam to find work as a forester. However, by 1907 he had returned to face up to his responsibilities, to have his young daughter baptised, and at last stand by her mother. The records give only the bare bones of this drama and one can do little but spec-ulate about exactly what happened. In fact the Limouzin family was in the process of disintegrating. By 1904, most of Frank's children had left Burma and were settled in England – at least Ida, Charlie, Norah and Nellie were. George, the youngest, took a slightly different exit, emigrating to Cape Town. Frank was to die of old age in 1915, aged eighty-two; Thérèse is said to have dropped out of Anglo-Indian society and 'gone native', dying in Moulmein ten years later, also aged eighty-two. Strangely, there is no trace of her death in the official records, leaving open the possibility that she died something of an outcast, at least from the Anglican communion. In Burma in the early

1920s, Eric was to meet his grandmother Limouzin, and presumably his Eurasian relatives – his Aunt Aimée, daughter of William and Sooma, and his cousin, Kathleen, daughter of Frank and Mah Hlim, just four years older than himself. On this feature of his mother's family he remained silent, but in his first novel, *Burmese Days,* he gave the name Ma Hla May to the Burmese mistress of his tragic hero John Flory, and wrote knowingly of Eurasians in Burma, one of them, interestingly enough, called 'Francis':

> He thought of Rosa McFee, the Eurasian girl he had seduced in Mandalay in 1913. The way he used to sneak down to the house in a gharry with the shutters drawn; Rosa's corkscrew curls; her withered old Burmese mother, giving him tea in the dark living-room with the fern pots and the wicker divan. And afterwards, when he had chucked Rosa, those dreadful, imploring letters on scented notepaper, which, in the end, he had ceased opening.
>
> Elizabeth reverted to the subject of Francis and Samuel after tennis.
>
> 'Those two Eurasians – does anyone here have anything to do with them? Invite them to their houses or anything?'
>
> 'Good gracious, no. They're complete outcasts. It's not considered quite the thing to talk to them, in fact.'[9]

One of his favourite poets, Kipling, had adopted an observer's pose, had deliberately chosen the role of 'outsider' in British India, a position with which Eric could fully sympathise. 'While in India he tended to mix with "the wrong" people,' he wrote, 'and because of his dark complexion he was wrongly suspected of having a streak of Asiatic blood.' Mixing with 'the wrong people' and becoming 'suspect' was to become a focus of his own early writing.[10]

Later, even when transformed by a pseudonym, he acknowledged that few can ever entirely escape their family history. In his case his work reveals just how his family past moulded the consciousness of the author-to-be. A strong sense of Englishness, of course, marked the man who became 'George Orwell', a name with powerful English connotations. His feeling for the soil and the natural world, his fascination with traditional field sports, and his highly refined sense of social class stratification, were drawn directly from his paternal English roots. From the Blairs, too, he imbibed a heightened sense of public service, and, from the spirit of his parsonical grandfather a tradition of religious awareness and moral commitment. One of his few good poems begins, 'A happy vicar I might have been, a hundred years ago', and he was always wrestling with the question of how one creates a moral code in a godless age.

From his French ancestry he acquired the distinctly eccentric and obstinate edge to his character, and an intellectual curiosity which encompassed the great French writers and the whole European dimension. The Limouzins included their own nonconformists such as William and Frank who formed liaisons outside their caste, and aunts who in England were active Suffragettes and moved in Fabian circles. One of these independently minded women, Aunt Nellie Limouzin, would have more influence on his literary and political development than any other member of his family, and perhaps more than the teachers he encountered at his various schools. However, it seems also that it was from the Limouzins that he inherited his susceptibility to lung infections – a weakness which did for his grandfather's two firstborn, contributed to his mother's death and finally ended his own, well before his time.

While he left too young to remember India consciously or be influenced by it directly, he grew up in a decidedly Anglo-Indian family. His mother, though born on a fleeting visit to London, spent all her early life in British India, and his father spent most of his working life in Bengal. All that carried with it mental baggage and specific cultural assumptions, including a keen sense of caste, which he could hardly escape inheriting. He was very conscious of having been born in India, and throughout his adult life was fascinated first by the romance of the East – inspired and sustained by a youthful passion for Kipling – and then driven by the conviction that the British presence in India was morally wrong. Here, from among these disparate strands of history and ancestry the basis of this unique personality was constructed. There were, however, crucial elements still to be put into place, and England was the setting in which the other deep structures of his personality would finally be laid.

Chapter 2

'The Golden Age'

'A human being is what he is largely because he comes from certain surroundings, and no one ever fully escapes from the things that have
happened to him in early childhood.'

Orwell, BBC radio talk, 1945

'Guilt had, I think, been implanted in him at an early age.'

Anthony Powell, *Infants of the Spring*

By 1904, Richard was back in Motihari tending his opium fields, and Ida
was living with her two children at a rented house in the Oxfordshire
town of Henley-on-Thames. There, Marjorie, aged nine, was sent to the
local convent school while for Eric there was a series of nursemaids –
Louise, Violet, Edith and Mabel all in one year. It is evident from Ida's surviving diary for 1905 that she was by that time well-established in Henley
society, and settled into a comfortably decorous middle-class Edwardian
existence. Life for her was a continual round of churchgoing, country rambles, picnics with her children, afternoon teas, and evenings of bridge – a life
measured out by both tea- and coffee-spoons and perhaps the odd clink of
glasses. But Ida's life was by no means confined to coffee, cards and pic-
nicking. In the summer she played tennis and croquet, indulged a minor
passion for photography, spent time on the river and even on occasion
dared to bathe in it. She took Marjorie to dancing classes and arranged tea
parties for her and her friends, one of which Eric was permitted to attend
and did not, it seems, disgrace himself. Forty years on he recalled the
embarrassing party-going etiquette insisted upon by his mother. 'As a child
I was taught to say "Thank you for having me" after a party, and it seemed
to me such an awful phrase.' In fact, as he admitted, he was not a particularly gregarious little boy and, as an adult, found small-talk impossible.

Henley-on-Thames, an old market town nestling on a horseshoe bend of the Oxfordshire Thames between Marlow and Reading, was just sixty-five miles downstream from London Bridge and fifty minutes by train from Paddington. The town dated back to the fourteenth century and boasted a parish church said to have been built partly by Cardinal Wolsey. During the Civil War it fell first to Royalists then Parliamentarians, was used as a stopover by William of Orange on his march on London during the Glorious Revolution, and had once been the social centre of the county. Passing through on his *Tour Through the Whole Island of Great Britain* in 1778, Daniel Defoe recorded nothing more remarkable about the town than its trade in malt, meal and timber.[1] But in 1851 it attracted the attention of the Prince Consort, and Henley Regatta became Henley *Royal* Regatta. In 1905, with a population of little more than six thousand, photographs show a town still largely dominated by the horse. On market days farm wagons and merchants' carts jostled for parking space with the smart carriages and gigs of the local notables. In the marketplace the horse-trough was a focal point, and with its mix of people, farm animals and feedstuffs, Henley was a good place for a boy with such keen senses as Eric Blair to acquire a highly refined awareness of the touch, taste and smell of country life.

This Edwardian age into which Eric was born became for him his Golden Age – a world seemingly unchanged and unchanging, fixed in its certainties and sense of continuity. It was a period of considerable confidence and, for the moneyed classes, one of great affluence – of country house living and conspicuous indulgence, one aspect of the time he regarded with distaste. 'There never was . . . in the history of the world,' he wrote, 'a time when the sheer vulgar fatness of wealth, without any kind of aristocratic elegance to redeem it, was so obtrusive.'[2] A channel separated Britain from the quarrelsome Continentals, and its people stood self-sufficient and proud at the heart of a great trading Empire. It was a world at peace, secure behind its iron wall of dreadnoughts and a standing army steeped in centuries-old traditions. Jingoism was at its height, Europe could be ignored, and King and Empire were ideals glorious enough to die for. Foreigners were considered funny if not dangerous, and unquestionably inferior. The coming of the motorcar and telephone had barely disturbed the tranquillity of the age, the heavier-than-air machine (despite that twelve-minute flight at Kitty Hawk) was still considered a distant dream.

Edwardian Britain was a stable, highly structured, highly differentiated society, a class system of subtle gradations defining exactly to whom one deferred and to whom one condescended. In this still largely feudal system, prestige and power were carefully distributed. At its apex stood the titled upper class of mostly landowners, now rivalled by the newly enriched commercial classes who had risen on a tide of Victorian prosperity. Then came the middle class, the petite bourgeoisie, rooted in the professions or in trade. At the bottom of the heap lay the working class or proletariat, manual workers who survived by selling their labour on the open market. Within these broad bands were fine distinctions of rank, placing individuals more precisely in order of precedence.

These subtle nuances of class were readily identified and strictly observed, and little boys like Eric were expected to recognise them and play their part in the elaborate charade of etiquette and manners which sustained them. As he wrote, 'the social status of nearly everyone in England could be determined from his appearance, even at two hundred yards' distance. The working classes all wore ready-made clothes, ill-fitting poor reflections of outdated upper-class fashions. For men, the cloth cap was practically a badge of status. It was universal among the working class, while the upper classes wore it only for golf and shooting.'[3] Despite the recent formation of the Independent Labour Party and the increasing power of the trade unions, by and large the working class still 'knew its place', and women's suffrage was still considered a huge joke by readers of *Punch*. Great aristocratic figures dominated politics and the law, and enjoyed feudal power over their retainers. The Empire was ruled and run by men imbued with the public school ethos of service, motivated by pious loyalty and characterised by self-sacrifice.

Culturally, the age was still dominated by a generation that had grown up with Thackeray and Dickens, Tennyson and Browning, George Eliot and Mrs Gaskell. Eric would absorb them all, especially Dickens, whose work he loved on first reading, but the writers who best conveyed the spirit of those years for him were Kipling, Wells, Shaw, Ibsen and Chesterton, while, in a slightly different mode, Conan Doyle's Sherlock Holmes epitomised the genius and solidity which typified the new age of scientific curiosity.

On 7 February 1905, Eric, a little more than eighteen months old, was stricken with bronchitis, and confined to bed for a week. After five days, no doubt frustrated at being bed-bound, he uttered his first recorded word – 'beastly'. In fact he was, Ida recorded, calling *everything* 'beastly'. It must have been a word much on the lips of his mother, and no doubt what she called 'beastly', Eric called 'beastly', although his idea of what was or was not 'beastly' would eventually differ greatly from that of both his parents. However, the word 'beastly' stayed with him, and occurs in every one of his books, except, perhaps understandably, in *Animal Farm*.

That same year, Ida attended the Regatta, and visited Wimbledon for the annual tennis championships – two high-spots in the English social calendar. With Marjorie at the convent and Eric at home with his nanny, there were shopping excursions to Reading and Winchester. On trips to London, she took in Hampton Court Palace, went to concerts and theatres (to see Sarah Bernhardt on one occasion), to Kew Gardens with sisters Nellie and Norah, and to swim at Paddington Baths, close to Nellie's flat in Notting Hill. Nellie, the most bohemian of the Limouzins, is said to have enjoyed a brief career on the music-hall stage, and ran what amounted to an artistic salon at her flat in Ladbroke Grove. The sisters also attended Suffragette meetings and moved in Fabian circles, hobnobbing with writers such as Wells, Chesterton and E. Nesbit (author of not just *The Railway Children* and *The Would-be Goods*, but also *The Ballads and Lyrics of Socialism*), and radicals such as Conrad Noel, the famous vicar of Thaxted, who flew the red flag from his church tower, and was at that time Nellie's local curate in Paddington, a pioneer of Christian socialism who spent his spare time in London lodging houses among the down-and-outs.

Away from her husband, Ida developed a quite distinctive character. Ruth Pitter, the poet, who knew her later, recalled her as small and dark with a touch of French militancy in her make-up. 'She had dark eyes and hair, thin features . . . an acute mind [and] a very penetrating wit . . . Any satirical, any attacking moods in her son would have come from her rather than his old man.'[4] More than that, something of Ida's inquisitiveness and adventurous nature communicated itself to him very early. Shortly before his second birthday, on 14 June, she noted, 'Baby's latest feat was to go out in the garden by the drawing room window!' The natural world, the surface of the earth, the world at large and the urge to explore them he always found irresistible.

Eric's childhood was marred by further attacks of bronchitis that year, once when Ida was in London, probably visiting Nellie. On hearing he was ill she took the first train home, remaining with him till he recovered. Shortly afterwards, following a holiday at Frinton-on-Sea (where he paddled for the first time), Eric fell ill again. These recurrent illnesses must have been worrying, and, as her diary entries show, Ida was a watchful and caring mother, conscientiously recording the progress of each illness, and greeting signs of his recovery with evident relief. It seems certain that she had removed him from India in part from fear of infection – that outbreak of plague in Gaya must have been especially frightening to a young mother. And most likely, Eric's obsessive fear of rats (bearers of the Black Death) was learned at the knee of his anxious mother.

By September that year, the family had moved into a new house in Vicarage Road, Henley, for which Ida invented the name 'Ermadale' by combining the first two letters of 'Eric' and 'Marjorie'. The daily round was relieved by occasional visits from her sisters Nellie and Norah, and from her brother Charlie, who was not without money, and was busily engaged in managing and designing golf courses. He would later run a golf club in

Bournemouth where the Blair children sometimes spent their holidays. With Richard absent, Charlie was probably the first male on whom Eric could model himself.

By the spring of 1906, the family had moved to another Henley house, in Western Road, this one called 'Nutshell', after none of the children, one supposes. Eric, now almost three, was growing up surrounded by women. His mother, apparently, spoiled him and would not hear a word against him; there were nursemaids to care for him and a female servant always around the house. He developed a strange attitude towards women; on the one hand he enjoyed their company enormously, often preferring it to that of men, but he could also be quite indifferent, even cruel, towards them when he chose. This probably mirrors the ambivalent attitude towards his own sex which he detected in his mother and her friends. Men came into his life only infrequently. Apart from intermittent contact with Charlie, Ida formed attachments – one to a Henley magistrate called Simmons, who young Eric came to fear and dislike, and one to her neighbour, a local GP, Dr Dakin, who, according to his son Humphrey, was much smitten by the handsome young grass widow, seemingly abandoned by her elderly husband.

Eric's childhood was a happy retreat for him in later life, and a deep pool of memory from which to fish an occasional glimpse of a past he came to mourn. It was a vision retrievable only in fleeting memories, like those of George Bowling in *Coming Up For Air*, or in dreams, like Winston Smith's in *Nineteen Eighty-Four*. These are, of course, the memories of an author, surfacing in the course of his mature writing, often prompted not so much by the refined tastes of a Proust, but by a more diverse set of associations – a heap of junk, a newspaper headline, or, as with George Bowling, something as crude as a pungent smell.

> The past is a curious thing. It's with you all the time, I suppose an hour never passes without your thinking of things that happened ten or twenty years ago, and yet most of the time it's got no reality, it's just a set of facts that you've learned, like a lot of stuff in a history book. Then some chance sight or sound or smell, especially smell, sets you going, and the past doesn't merely come back to you, you're actually in the past.[5]

In one case, the sickly smell in a hospital ward recalled for him one of his many bouts of childhood illness and a grisly piece of Tennysonian verse read to him by an old Victorian nurse. 'The horrors and sufferings of the old-style hospitals were a vivid memory to her. We had shuddered over the poem together.'

> Our doctor had call'd in another, I never
>   had seen him before,
> But he sent a chill to my heart when I saw
>   him come in at the door . . .
>
> Wonderful cures he had done, O, yes, but
>   they said too of him
> He was happier using the knife than in trying
>   to save the limb . . .[6]

Needless to say, little Emmie, the patient, is killed by the cure, and the surgeon's 'ghastly tools'. It was just the poem to read to an ill child to give it a lifelong phobia about the medical profession. Clearly, this poem threw a shadow of nightmare across his mind, so much so that the memory and the horror it inspired returned to torment him more than twenty years afterwards. And at the age of thirty-five he told his wife that hospitals were 'institutions devised for murder'.

Recurring bouts of bronchitis and influenza were to plague his life. As an adult he liked to blame inept doctors and ignorant adults for the wretched state of his health. Six years after failing his army medical in 1940, he wrote to his old College tutor, explaining that he had not done much in the war partly because of 'a lesion in one lung which was never diagnosed when I was a boy'.[7] But his own antipathy to hospitals and doctors also played its part.

He recalled fragments of his Henley childhood, conjuring them up en passant in the course of his writings – a Victorian lady's bustle, found in a dusty cupboard when he was five; the annual cavalry ride through Henley and the strong manly physiques of the mounted soldiers; nursery rhymes learned ('See-saw Margerie Daw', 'Oranges and lemons'), ancient bits of 'churchyard wisdom' (such as 'Solomon Grundy'), and a memory evoked by John Flory, isolated in the Burmese jungle, of 'winter Sundays in his pew in the parish church at Home' watching 'the yellow leaves . . . drifting and fluttering against leaden skies'.[8] There were memories too, of old toys – rag-books, lead soldiers, German clockwork toys, kaleidoscopes, a hobby horse, plasticine and modelling wax, the Struwwelpeter and Beatrix Potter books, whip-tops, and ones which must have provoked a memorable event in the Blair household – 'clockwork mice to frighten your aunt'. Even more fascinating to him was 'a pond-water aquarium, for which one uses a small accumulator jar or a 7lb. pickle jar [and] the creatures that live in it – tadpoles, caddis flies and water fleas'.[9] And when he was given one of 'those agreeable little grocer's shops with scales, tin canisters and a wooden counter', there was no idea in the class-conscious Blair household that one day he would be reduced to the servile role of shopkeeper.

A conversation with a barmaid in wartime London prompted memories of 'the fallacies which were taught to me as a child . . . not as an old wives' tale but as a scientific fact'. He listed some in his notebook: 'That a swan can break your leg with a blow of its wing./That if you cut yourself between the thumb and forefinger you get lockjaw./That powdered glass is poisonous./ . . . /That bulls become infuriated at the sight of red.'[10] This reveals another favourite childhood diversion – compiling lists. It became for him a strange kind of addiction. He had, he admitted, 'the sort of mind that takes pleasure in dates, lists, catalogues, concrete details, descriptions of processes, junk-shop windows, and back numbers of *Exchange and Mart*'.[11] He made lists of books, redundant metaphors, jargon words, Kiplingesque epithets, poets who characterised the century, and 'sentimental writers'. At thirty-seven he produced a mental list remembered from an adventure story read when he was seven: 'Nearly thirty years after reading the book I can still remember more or less exactly what things the three heroes of Ballantyne's *Coral Island* possessed between them. (A telescope, six yards of whipcord, a pen-knife, a brass ring and a piece of hoop iron.)' List-making expressed what he called 'the jackdaw inside all of us, the instinct that makes a child hoard copper nails, clock springs, and glass marbles out of lemonade bottles'.[12] He was still constructing lists (and collecting junk) at the end of his life, most controversially the list of those he thought were suspected subversives.

Conversations between his mother and her friends, overheard as a child, had an important effect on how he came to regard himself. Men, they seemed to imply, were unattractive, uncouth smelly brutes who forced their attentions on women and were best kept at arm's length. In his famous essay on Dickens, Orwell wrote with compelling intensity about the terrifying, isolated and nightmarish world of the child, captured brilliantly, he thought, in *David Copperfield*, in passages which evoked his own feeling of deprivation as a fatherless boy with no one close enough to share his experiences. He later told a woman friend that he would have been far happier if he had had a brother. In his autobiographical essay 'Why I Write', he explored that childhood solitude and saw in it the beginnings of his creative life:

> I was the middle child of three, but there was a gap of five years on either side, and I barely saw my father before I was eight. For this and other reasons I was somewhat lonely, and I soon developed disagreeable mannerisms which made me unpopular throughout my schooldays. I had the lonely child's habit of making up stories and holding conversations with imaginary persons, and I think from the very start my literary ambitions were mixed up with the feeling of being isolated and undervalued . . . I felt that this created a sort of

private world in which I could get my own back for my failure in
everyday life.[13]

This 'inward eye/which is the bliss of solitude' he also invested in Julia in
Nineteen Eighty-Four – 'With another part of her mind she believed that it was
somehow possible to construct a secret world in which you could live as you
chose.'[14] The inner world of imagination was his sanctuary, the world in
which he could 'get his own back' on those who had offended him. Even in the
mature writer this revenge motif is evident and was clearly irresistible.

He had decided to become a writer, he said, at the age of five or six – the
age at which he must have begun to create that inner fictional life and the
age at which he must also have begun to read by himself. The earliest thing
he could recall having written was a poem composed at the age of four or
five, which his mother probably wrote down for him. 'I cannot remember
anything about it except that it was about a tiger and the tiger had "chair-
like teeth" – a good enough phrase, but I fancy the poem was a plagiarism
of Blake's "Tiger, Tiger".'[15] It suggests that India was never very far from his
childhood, even in the very English town of Henley-on-Thames.

The presence of India intensified in the summer of 1907, when Eric was
just four. His absent father returned on leave and left significant changes in his
wake. Richard, still no further up the promotion ladder, was now based at
Monghyr. By the time he returned to his opium fields, he had left Ida pregnant. When, on 6 April 1908 a second sister, Avril Norah, joined Eric, the
disappointment of not having a brother to help lessen his isolation must have
been acute.[16] Having a new child does not seem to have cramped Ida's style.
The following summer, no doubt having left the baby with her nanny, she took
the older children to the White City Exhibition in London, where Eric had
another unforgettable experience – 'the Wiggle-Woggle', 'a monster fairground
ride' – jolted back to mind thirty years later, while he was being driven to hospital in Spain inside a ramshackle ambulance over unmetalled roads.[17]

If the women who surrounded and indulged him as a boy left him feeling isolated, the harsh world of men was not always appealing to him either:

I am six years old, and I am walking along a street in our little town
with my mother and a wealthy local brewer, who is also a magistrate.
The tarred fence is covered with chalk drawings, some of which I have
made myself. The magistrate stops, points disapprovingly with his stick
and says, 'We are going to catch the boys who draw on these walls, and
we are going to order them Six Strokes of the Birch Rod'. (It was all in
capitals in my mind.) My knees knock together, my tongue cleaves to
the roof of my mouth . . . Not till many years later, perhaps twenty
years, did it occur to me that my fears had been groundless. No

magistrate would have condemned me to Six Strokes of the Birch Rod, even if I had been caught drawing on the wall. Such punishments were reserved for the Lower Orders.[18]

In fact, Blair here confuses a Reading brewer called Simmonds and a Henley magistrate called Simmons; it was the man of law who is said to have been paying more than platonic attention to Ida, and it was no doubt from a lingering sense of resentment towards this draconian rival for his mother's affections that he later gave the name Simmonds (whose name doubtless appeared on brewer's drays around Henley) to the man who drove Boxer, the carthorse hero of *Animal Farm*, off to the knacker's yard.

But rather than some little ruffian graffiti-artist in need of a thrashing, young Eric was in fact a very conformist little boy, and a budding jingo. 'Those were the great days of the Navy's popularity. Small boys wore sailor suits, and everyone belonged to something called the Navy League and had a bronze medal which cost a shilling, and the popular slogan was "We want eight (Dreadnoughts) and we won't wait!".'[19] Eric was no exception and wore his sailor's rig with 'HMS Invincible' on his cap as proudly as any boy.[20] A photograph from this time shows the very image of an obedient chubby-faced little Edwardian flag-wagger. But this smug-looking child felt desperately unattractive, as his alter ego, George Bowling in *Coming Up For Air*, reminds us: 'I was rather an ugly little boy, with butter-coloured hair which was always cropped short except for a quiff in front.'[21] He was also, according to the boy whose gang he joined around this time, a miserable little tale-teller into the bargain.

The shadow of the schoolroom fell across Eric at the age of five when he was sent as a day-boy to the convent which Marjorie attended – not an Anglican convent, as has been thought (no such convent existed in Henley), but a Catholic convent run by French Ursulines exiled from France after religious education was banned there in 1903. When they were able to return after eight or nine years, Marjorie, then fourteen, went with them to complete her education across the Channel, probably taking her young sister Avril with her.[22] Ida's 1905 diary records her visiting the place, no doubt to talk about Marjorie, which suggests that, although she was a regular Anglican churchgoer she had no anti-Catholic prejudice, and probably found French company more congenial than many others in Henley might have done. As Henley was mainly Protestant, non-Catholics were probably admitted and simply told others that the convent was Anglican.

If young Eric was first taught by Catholic nuns as a lone boy in a school of girls, it would explain two important and enduring aspects of his complex personality – his unremitting hostility towards Roman Catholicism and an acute sense of guilt. As he himself admitted, at the age of eight his consciousness of sin was never far away.[23] His Catholic friend at Eton, Christopher Hollis, recognised this in Blair and was puzzled by it; later friends Frederic Warburg and Anthony Powell felt his sense of guilt was implanted early, in a part of his past kept secret from others. And other personality traits of his could have had their roots among the cloistered Ursulines, such as his veritable Jansenist tendency to damn whole categories of people, his evermore complicated attitude towards women and sex, and his tendency to self-mortification, a characteristic not noticeably displayed by other members of his family. He never spoke of his earliest education, except for an occasional passing reference, but he had a gift for suffering in silence which enabled him to conceal his more extreme feelings. And even though he spoke of 'unnecessary torments' endured as a child,[24] and of feeling lonely and excluded, he wrote of his home as 'a place ruled by love rather than fear',[25] a 'warm nest' from which dislodgement was always going to strike him as a cruel blow.

If he was indulged at home, being disciplined by nuns was bound to come as something of a shock, though the presence of Marjorie, who helped teach the younger pupils and probably taught him to read, could have made it easier to bear. Two fleeting and sardonic references seem to evoke the shadowy Ursulines, one to 'nuns in convents, scrubbing floors and singing Ave Marias, secretly unbelieving',[26] the other more subversive:

> When we were children we had a story that after Robin Hood was done to death in the Priory, his men raped & murdered the nuns, & burned the priory to the ground. It seems this has no foundation in the ballads – we must have made it up. An instance of the human instinct for a happy ending.[27]

It was among the nuns that he was first smitten by a member of the opposite sex, a passionate if fleeting attachment. 'I fell deeply in love, a far more worshipping kind of love than I have ever felt for anyone since, with a girl named Elsie at the convent school which I attended. She seemed to me grown up, so I suppose she must have been fifteen.'[28] He saw her again years later and suddenly she seemed a grown woman, past her best. The delectable Elsie (renamed Katie Simmons) turns up in *Coming Up For Air*, when George Bowling rediscovers her married to a gypsy, 'a wrinkled-up hag of a woman . . . looking at least fifty years old' although she must have been no more than twenty-seven.[29]

Now old enough for school, Eric was also thought old enough to play out on his own. His sister Marjorie was friendly with Humphrey Dakin, the popular and assertive doctor's son, who led a small gang of local boys. They would go on expeditions into the surrounding countryside, bird-nesting, rabbit-hunting with their dogs, and, above all, fishing in the many pools hidden deep in the woods or in quiet stretches of the Thames at Henley Lock and beyond. Dakin disliked young Eric. He was more interested in Marjorie, and her wretched little brother simply got in the way. Furthermore, he didn't fit in with the gang who made their hostility clear to him, as Dakin recalled. 'Our gang of kids knocked him about in Henley. He was about the youngest member and he was an absolute nuisance. He was a little fat boy . . . always whining and sneaking, telling tales and so on . . . he was not a very nice little boy.'[30]

Unwanted by the Dakin gang, Eric sought companions elsewhere. A plumber and his family lived nearby and his children now became his play-mates. With them, not only did he get his first inklings of sex, but also his first lesson in class snobbery. 'We used sometimes to play games of a vaguely erotic kind. One was called "playing at doctors" and I remember getting a faint but definitely pleasant thrill from holding a toy trumpet, which was supposed to be a stethoscope, against a little girl's belly.'[31] But when Ida found out she put her foot down, and took the opportunity to teach Eric not so much the facts of life but the facts of English social life, and the sin-fulness of such contacts. Looking back, he understood that she was only doing what her class position required of her.

> I was forbidden to play with the plumber's children; they were 'common' and I was told to keep away from them. This was snobbish, if you like, but it was also necessary, for middle-class people cannot afford to let their children grow up with vulgar accents. So, very early, the working class ceased to be a race of friendly and wonderful beings and became a race of enemies. We realised that they hated us, but we could never understand why, and naturally we set it down to pure, vicious malignity.[32]

Not only was he taught that the plumber's children were 'common', but also that the lower classes smelt. If social distinctions depended in part on odour, this, in a boy as sensitive as Eric, was bound to cause problems for the future. The extent to which this lesson went home is seen in what he wrote in *The Road to Wigan Pier*, when he was thirty-three: 'You cannot have an affection for a man whose breath stinks – habitually stinks, I mean. However well you may wish him, however much you may admire his mind and character, if his breath stinks he is horrible and in your heart of hearts you will hate him.'[33] But that was not all; the lower orders were ugly and hostile: 'To me in my early boyhood, to nearly all children of families like mine, "common" people seemed almost sub-human. They had coarse faces, hideous accents and gross manners, they hated everyone who was not like themselves, and if they got half a chance they would insult you in brutal ways.'[34] And below this 'common' herd there lurked an even more frightful and threatening riff-raff – tramps, who he was taught were 'monsters' and 'blackguards'.[35] Now he was forbidden to play with the plumber's children, Ida insisted he be allowed to join Humphrey and his pals, and reluctantly they agreed to let sneaky little Eric, the snivelling tale-teller, string along.

Despite his unpopularity, with these boys he shared experiences that were to mark him and add an enduring dimension to his character. He had been on long country walks with his mother, gathering berries and mush-rooms on the way, and learning to recognise trees and flowers and various forms of wildlife. But in this new and rougher company he saw the natural world differently. For the gang, the woods were an adventure playground, where one could collect bird's eggs, use a catapult to knock down a nesting bird, chase rabbits, climb trees and, above all, fish! These experiences were lovingly retained as part of the landscape of memory to which he returned often and which came to symbolise something spiritual – a Garden of Eden from which moral corruption and the coming of war would expel everyone. It was a landscape far removed from the fake world of modernity with its false values, warped minds and perversion of the language.

But, even in this idyllic setting, there lurked cruelty. It was probably the Dakin gang he saw blow up a toad with a bicycle pump till it exploded, and who taught him that it was OK to steal and smash bird's eggs and kill sitting birds. As George Bowling reflects, 'The truth is that kids aren't in any way poetic, they're merely savage little animals, except that no animal is a quarter as selfish . . . Killing things – that's about as near to poetry as a boy gets.' Eric's childhood escapades clearly encouraged the sadistic streak to which he later confessed for example, the joy with which he contemplated bayoneting a Buddhist priest in 'Shooting the Elephant.' In 1940, reviewing Malcolm Muggeridge's book on *The Thirties*, a decade which he felt cut us off irretrievably from his idyllic Edwardian age, he wrote:

> I thought of a rather cruel trick I once played on a wasp. He was sucking jam on my plate, and I cut him in half. He paid no attention, merely went on with his meal, while a tiny stream of jam trickled out of his severed oesophagus. Only when he tried to fly away did he grasp the dreadful thing that had happened to him. It is the same with modern man. The thing that has been cut away is his soul, and there was a period – twenty years, perhaps – during which he did not notice it.[36]

In his mind, the crisis of the modern age was epitomised by the way he related to nature as a boy. Images from childhood recur throughout his work, suggesting how, by sleepwalking through history, not only had the

British jeopardised their stability and sense of continuity, their culture of decency and fair play, but also risked losing the freedom to be themselves.

Out with the gang, fishing became a sacred pastime, a symbolic ritual through which later some lost life could be reclaimed, just as flashes of past delight could be fished up from the dark reaches of memory. These recollections held more meaning for him as the pleasures of the period receded and the horrors of the new century closed in. Fishing, and his remembered delight in it, become a powerful metaphor in *Coming Up For Air*, the novel in which despair over lost childhood is at its most acute: 'Is it any use talking about it, I wonder – the sort of fairy light that fish and fishing tackle have in a kid's eyes? Some kids feel the same about guns and shooting, some feel it about motor-bikes or aeroplanes or horses. It's not a thing that you can explain or rationalise, it's merely magic.'[37] This 'magic' came to symbolise for him that Golden Country, so significant a feature of his fictional landscape, a country and age which were about to be swept away.

> The civilisation which I grew up in . . . is now, I suppose, just about at its last kick. And fishing is somehow typical of that civilisation. As soon as you think of fishing you think of things that don't belong to the modern world. The very idea of sitting all day under a willow tree beside a quiet pool – and being able to find a quiet pool to sit beside – belongs to the time before the war, before the radio, before aeroplanes, before Hitler. There's a kind of peacefulness even in the names of English coarse fish. Roach, rudd, dace, bleak, barbel, bream, gudgeon, pike, chub, carp, tench. They're solid kind of names. The people who made them up hadn't heard of machine-guns, they didn't live in terror of the sack or spend their time eating aspirins, going to the pictures and wondering how to keep out of the concentration camp.[38]

In his memory, those days remained days of perpetual sunshine, the rivers and pools always full of fish. Whenever possible, throughout his life, he tried to recreate that experience, staying as close to nature as he could, escaping whenever possible on fishing trips or excursions into the countryside.

The cruel streak which led Eric to cut up wasps or blow up toads shades into a fondness for guns and explosives. In his forties, recalling this youthful passion, he wrote about 'little brass cannons on wooden gun-carriages':

> The largest were six or eight inches long, cost ten shillings and went off with a noise like the Day of Judgment./To fire them you needed gunpowder, which the shops sometimes refused to sell you, but a resourceful boy could make gunpowder for himself if he took the precaution of buying the ingredients from three different chemists.

One of the advantages of being a child 30 years ago was the lighter-hearted attitude that then prevailed towards firearms. Up till not long before the other war you could walk into any bicycle shop and buy a revolver, and even when the authorities began to take an interest in revolvers, you could still buy for 7s. 6d. a fairly lethal weapon known as a Saloon Rifle. I bought my first Saloon Rifle at the age of 10, with no questions asked./Normal healthy children enjoy explosions.[39]

The spirit of Empire encouraged these violent predilections. Over-the-counter gun sales were only banned in 1919 when Irish terrorism and the Russian Revolution caused the authorities to clamp down. Orwell later came to regret this ban, especially when he thought that British workers should arm themselves in the event of a Second World War.[40]

The main rival for the attention of the young angler and explosives enthusiast was reading. After those rag-books, *Struwwelpeter* and E. Nesbit, he moved quickly on to sterner stuff, and fell in love with 'literature'. No Anglo-Indian home was without its Kipling: 'He was a sort of household god with whom one grew up and whom one took for granted whether one liked him or whether one did not . . . [he] was the story-teller who was so important to my childhood.'[41] With *Kim* he was able to revisit the northern India of his birth, with *The Jungle Book* he could enter a world where animals philosophised, and in *Stalky & Co.* he could anticipate the fun of boarding-school life. At eight, or so he said, he read Swift's *Gulliver's Travels*, a present discovered the night before his birthday and read straight through. At nine his birthday present was Wells's *The History of Mr Polly* and he discovered Dickens and read *David Copperfield* at the same age. These authors were certainly the most important discoveries of his childhood, authors he read and reread throughout his life. The Blair home was not especially bookish, but there was other reading-matter to hand to absorb a young boy – *Punch*, which his parents took, and the popular boys' comics, the *Boys' Own Paper*, the *Gem* and the *Magnet* ('the most consistently and cheerfully patriotic papers in England'), children's books about America, probably Marjorie's, and ghost stories, particularly R. H. Barham's Gothic parodies, *The Ingoldsby Legends*, with its tales of witchcraft, hideous hauntings and murder most foul. He loved Jack London's adventure stories and, as a humorous antidote to Kipling, Hilaire Belloc's gentle satire on British Imperialism, *The Modern Traveller*, including the immortal lines, 'Whatever happens, we have got/The maxim gun and they have not.'[42] 'There are books that one reads over and over again,' he wrote, 'books that become part of the furniture of one's mind and alter one's whole attitude to life . . .'[43] Swift, Dickens and Kipling, read and reread, were probably the most prominent of his mental furnishings, except perhaps Defoe. Gissing came later.

From his reading, too, he acquired what he called 'a false map of the world, a series of fabulous countries into which one can retreat at odd moments throughout the rest of one's life, and which in some cases can even survive a visit to the real countries which they are supposed to represent'.[44] His reading took him to the South American pampas, Transylvania among boyars and vampires, the China of nineteenth-century adventurers, George Du Maurier's gas-lit Paris, and the Americas of Mark Twain and Louisa M. Alcott. He would, of course, create his own maps, his own sordid Paris and London, a dramatically exotic Burma, a subterranean world of tramps and the dispossessed, a lost landscape of childhood, an imaginary world of animals and a fearful landscape of mental slavery. These were not all cosy worlds into which to escape the real world, more often they brought the real world closer and lent it new moral significance and more than a touch of nightmare.

There were other, more real worlds to explore. In 1910 Ida took the family on holiday to Looe in Cornwall – a sweltering summer, as Eric recalled it.[45] There he spent time not only playing with his sisters, seabathing and rock-climbing, and trailing off on country walks, but also making friends with local farmers; and it was from a Cornish farmhand that he learned his first swearword, 'bugger!'[46] Such men – labourers, blacksmiths and farmhands – were early heroes of his, and he retained a fascination with how things were made, how they worked and in particular how the land was farmed. But there were also occasions in Cornwall, perhaps, when, like John Betjeman, holidaying nearby, he could feel 'deliciously alone'.

A few weeks before Eric's seventh birthday his Golden Age ended officially with the death of Edward VII. It was a year that saw one of the great old-fashioned English domestic murders, ending in the trial and execution of Dr Crippen, the death of Count Leo Tolstoy at the railway station at Astopov, and Prime Minister Herbert Asquith harassed in the London streets by Suffragettes. The following year King George V was crowned, there was a shoot-out between police and anarchists in London's East End, revolution broke out in Mexico, and there were left-wing riots in Wales and Liverpool; the Russian Prime Minister was assassinated at the opera and Winston Churchill was given charge of Britain's navy. Meanwhile at Eton, a large demonstration of Old Etonians protested against the College's abolition of the birch. One might detect a wind of change in all this, but nothing much seemed to change in the small Thameside town of Henley, and, for the time being, Eric and his friends would continue to play and fish and do unspeakable things to little animals when he was not withdrawing into his own private fictional world of Dickens, Swift, Kipling and boys' comic books.

Chapter 3

Pathos and Nightmare

'Eric; or, Little by Little [was a] great drug . . . "Here we are," said M'Turk. "Corporal punishment produced on Eric the worst effects. He burned *not* with remorse or regret" – make a note o' that, Beetle – "but with shame and violent indignation. He glared" – oh, naughty Eric!'

Kipling, *Stalky & Co.*

The world of childhood, wrote George Orwell, was not just one of idyllic pleasures and imaginary wonderlands, it had another and far grimmer aspect. 'Childhood has its pathetic side, and also its nightmare side. A child lives a lot of its time in a terrifying world. And even seen from the outside a child is a very pathetic thing.'[1] As an adult he could observe his childhood self from without, but he also had the imagination to recreate the nightmare within. That nightmare world he might have experienced in some measure at the Ursuline convent, but he was to encounter something far more terrifying shortly after his eleventh birthday when the time came to leave the 'warm nest' of home to move to the cold-hearted domain of an English preparatory school. It was to leave him feeling, or so he claimed, intimidated, pathetic and forlorn.

In his family the belief was that Eric's education was more important than that of his sisters and so sacrifices had to be made to ensure him a good start in life. Ida was particularly ambitious for her only son, and her brother Charlie was asked to find the best possible school to prepare him for higher things. The choice would prove fateful.

Whatever his relation with the Henley Ursulines, Eric did well enough from his convent education to be thought sufficiently worthy to enter St Cyprian's, the prestigious preparatory school at Eastbourne in Sussex recommended by Charlie. David Ogilvy called it 'an aristocratic Dotheboys Hall' and Gavin Maxwell claimed it brought on his 'night horrors'.[2] And George Orwell, while warning against exaggeration and not wishing to draw the Dickensian parallel too closely, agreed in spades: 'I should be falsifying my own memories if I did not record that they are largely memories of disgust.'[3] Obviously, moving there was to be a scarifying experience for him, a baptism of fire which changed his emotional landscape for ever. The smug little eight-year-old jingo who entered the school would emerge five years later a rebellious young cynic, but that cynicism, he intimated, concealed a guilt-ridden and emotionally damaged child. However, this sense of guilt and failure was balanced, he said, by the instinct to survive and learn from whatever befell him. The mask of reserve concealed a highly intelligent boy brimming with curiosity.

Orwell's notorious memoir of the school, 'Such, Such Were the Joys', the product of over thirty years of brooding, is his own anatomy of melancholy, complemented only by *Nineteen Eighty-Four*. It is the recollection of a place and period viewed through a highly sensitive and complex mind, filtered through time and coloured by ideology, the account of a closed and oppressive world from the alter ego of Winston Smith, the last apostle of free thought. It is as much a polemic aimed at the English private school system as a piece of reflective self-analysis, and probably more revealing than intended. In a 1935 book review he described a study of the subjective life of a child as 'a marvel of imaginative reconstruction'. In similar mode, 'Such, Such Were the Joys' is an extraordinary piece of retrospective reinvention, an adult version of a childhood experience. Added to this is the dramatic force of a long-felt hurt coming from the pen of a master satirist who could be as savage as he could be inventive.

Whatever its shortcomings as history, this long-lingering 'childhood nightmare' provides the only glimpse we have into the interior world of this particular schoolboy. There is, of course, more than a hint of vengeance in it – after all, 'getting his own back' was one of his admitted motives for becoming a creative writer – and that no doubt contributed to the somewhat sinister caricatures he drew of the head and his wife and the exaggerated horror of the school he recreated.

St Cyprian's was probably not so very different from other schools of that period, but Eric Blair *was* different from most schoolboys of the time. He would, after all, develop into one of the great misfits of his generation, an outsider who made idiosyncrasy his hallmark. Even so, others recognised something of their own experience in Orwell's memoir. Cecil Beaton, a contemporary at St Cyprian's, thought that, despite some exaggeration, he had 'seen through all the layers of snobbery and pretence' of the couple who ran it and captured them both perfectly. 'How I loathed [them] and loathed every minute of the school regime,' he wrote, and as for the head's monstrous wife, 'I was fascinated by her, terrified, had absolutely no affection for her, in fact hated her almost as much as Orwell did.'[4] It may have been questionable history but its emotional resonances echoed the deep feelings of sympathetic contemporaries.

It was in late September 1911 that Eric exchanged his proudly-worn sailor suit for the St Cyprian's blue-collared green jersey, corduroy knee-breeches and blue cap with Maltese Cross. The cost of sending him to the school, £180 a year, was beyond his family's means. However, because they favoured Anglo-Indians and were impressed by his potential, the head, Leslie Vaughan Wilkes and his redoubtable wife Cecily took him for half the normal fee. High-flying pupils brought prestige by winning scholarships to great public schools.

Although Eric knew nothing of this reduced-fee arrangement when he began at St Cyprian's, he soon recognised that he was from a poorer home, seeing other boys arrive in smart chauffeur-driven cars with mothers dripping with furs and jewellery. And those other boys no doubt picked up quickly on these differences, too, especially as Mrs Wilkes oozed snobbery and treated such visitors like royalty. The cult of Scotland, with its military tradition and royal connections, was something she was also eager to promote. '[Her] face always beamed with innocent snobbishness when she spoke of Scotland,' wrote Orwell. For her, 'Scotland was a private paradise which a few initiates could talk about and make outsiders feel small.'[5] Not surprisingly, Eric grew to hate all things Scottish, but it was the snobbery of wealth that offended him most. 'Probably the greatest cruelty one can inflict on a child is to send it to a school among children richer than itself,' says Gordon Comstock in *Keep the Aspidistra Flying*. 'A child conscious of poverty will suffer snobbish agonies such as grown-ups can scarcely even imagine.'[6] He became aware of belonging to 'a kind of shabby-genteel family' with 'far more *consciousness* of poverty than in any working-class family above the level of the dole . . . [in which] . . . practically the whole family income goes in keeping up appearances . . .'[7] Keeping up appearances would never figure much in his life, and schools that promoted this kind of snobbery would become a special target for his hatred.

At that time, Eastbourne, a rather sedate Sussex coastal resort, was a centre for private education with more than eighty schools and dozens of private tutors listed in the local directory. St Cyprian's stood on the western edge of the town, on Summerdown Road, on a rise looking over the links of the Eastbourne Golf Club towards the broad sweep of sea beyond. Further west lay the South Downs leading to Beachy Head. The school was based in a large gabled Victorian house fronted by a wide sports field and a small parade-ground. When Blair arrived, it had some eighty boys aged from eight to thirteen, and a staff of a dozen teachers. The main aim at St

Cyprian's was to prepare boys for public school entrance, but especially through scholarships for Eton, Harrow, Wellington and Winchester. These were the schools from which the Establishment was mostly drawn, and on whose playing fields it was thought England's battles were destined to be won by future heroes of Empire. The ideals and values of imperial and public service were what the place was designed to instil. Ironically, St Cyprian, after whom this highly conformist school was named, was an early Christian martyr decapitated for heresy.

Half a mile to the north, and lending the local topography an allegorical character, stood a forbidding old Napoleonic War barracks, then the Eastbourne Union Workhouse – the local poorhouse. There the needy, the destitute, the outcast and the illegitimate worked for food and a roof over their heads. To its casual ward came the beggars and tramps who, through choice or necessity, haunted the twilight world of the down-and-out. So, at St Cyprian's, young Eric Blair found himself placed between the two extremes of English society – those with a privileged start and every expectation of position and wealth, and those cast out and stigmatised, destined to remain submerged in hopeless dereliction. And no doubt, he would sometimes see the vagrants on their way to the poorhouse, a stark warning of what awaited any boy who failed to conform.

In 1911 Mrs Wilkes was a vigorous woman of thirty-five, mother of four children, the school's undoubted matriarch and driving force. She insisted the boys call her 'Mum', a form of address used mostly by servants, but because of her waddling gait which set her oversized bosoms in motion, she was known to the boys as 'Flip'. In Orwell's haunted memory, Flip was 'a stocky square-built woman with hard red cheeks, a flat top to her head, prominent brows and deepset, suspicious eyes . . . full of false heartiness, jollying one along with mannish slang ("Buck up, old chap!" and so forth). It was very difficult to look her in the face without feeling guilty, even at moments when one was not guilty of anything in particular.'[8] Her husband Leslie, nicknamed 'Sambo', was 'a round-shouldered, curiously oafish-looking man, not large but shambling in gait, a chubby face which was like that of an overgrown baby, and which was capable of good-humour'.[9] When necessary, Sambo meted out the canings; Flip resorted to other forms of control. Apart from the accusing stare, like some capricious queen, she dispensed favours in a way that induced both apprehension and sycophancy. To be 'in favour' with Flip, wrote one pupil, Henry Longhurst, was to be in heaven, to be 'out of favour' was like hell; according to another, Edward Meyerstein, she was a woman 'of devastating female guile', a mistress of psychological manipulation, who left him distrustful of women for the rest of his life.[10] When Orwell wrote that as a child he found it difficult to trust or love anyone over thirty (apart from his mother), doubtless he had Flip Wilkes somewhere in mind. Seemingly he never attempted to understand or respond to the volatile mood of this woman, as some boys did, and thereby retained a certain moral integrity, though at a price.

The school ran along rigid lines, and daily rituals were strictly observed – a seven-thirty wake-up, a plunge in the school swimming pool, then physical training and chapel before breakfast. The food was monotonous – thick lumpy porridge served in pewter porringers, followed by a hefty slice of bread with butter and jam. According to David Ogilvy, the Wilkes profited greatly from serving their pupils inferior food while dining in style themselves. Boys in favour were sometimes allowed to wait at their high table, with the attractive prospect of being able to smuggle leftovers back to the dormitories for secret midnight feasts. After breakfast, Flip took Scripture and boys were expected to recite a prescribed collect or verse from the Bible on pain of punishment. One morning a week French alone was spoken, the only morning, it was said, when breakfast was eaten in silence. Later, as a teacher, Orwell himself tried the only-French method, and his ability to quote the Authorised Version from memory clearly owes something to the breakfast-time demands of Cecily Philadelphia Vaughan Wilkes.

Above all else the school encouraged 'character, character, character',[11] meaning asceticism, self-sacrifice, duty, public service and playing the game – all achieved through an emphasis on sport, military training, manliness reinforced by moral sermonising, shamings and beatings. The Wilkes believed that 'the public school ideal' which they aimed to inculcate would ensure the continuity of the great imperial order. They extolled the virtues of money, strength, beauty, charm, athleticism and something called 'guts' or 'character', all embodied in Haggard, Newbolt and, most explicitly, in Kipling's 'If'. Orwell reflected wryly that he possessed none of these qualities and, in any case, saw a contradiction at the heart of the system – 'Broadly, you were taught to be a good Christian and a social success, which is impossible.' By the age of ten or eleven he had concluded that you were no good unless you had £100,000 yielding £4,000 a year at 4 per cent. 'Going into the City' was how money was made. 'Top-notchers' were always rich when young. For one of the ambitious middle-class examination-sitters, like himself, 'only a bleak, laborious kind of success was possible . . . You scrambled upwards on a ladder of scholarships into the Home Civil Service or the Indian Civil Service, or possibly you became a barrister.' 'Slacking' or 'going off' and missing a rung (as Sambo warned), meant ending up 'a little office boy at forty pounds a year'. But even if you made it as high as you could, you could only ever hope to be 'an underling, a hanger-on of the people who really counted'.[12]

Sadly for homesick young Eric, on his very first day at the school he put himself completely out of favour with the awesome Mrs Wilkes, rebuffing all her attempts to comfort him and make him feel welcome – even a picnic on the Downs with one of her sons failing to melt him. 'He was,' she is reported saying, 'not an affectionate little boy. There was no warmth in him.'[13] Worse followed. Soon afterwards he began wetting the bed. Instead of this being regarded as a normal reaction in a young boy torn away from home, it was treated as a revolting crime, and he the guilty perpetrator. He was publicly humiliated, and beaten three times. Once, overheard by Flip saying that one beating had not hurt much, he was thrashed again until the cane broke and he was reduced to a snivelling heap, crying, he claimed, more from humiliation than pain.[14] It was possible, he had discovered, to commit a sin unwittingly and be unable to avoid doing so. That last double beating brought home to him the nature of the harsh world in which he now found himself. 'Life was more terrible, and I was more wicked, than I had imagined.' For the first time he felt convinced of his own sin, folly, weakness and guilt,[15] and it took him twenty or thirty years to see that he had been fooled. There was one more bed-wetting and one more beating and then it stopped, so he was left feeling that the Wilkes's method actually worked.

As far as the Blairs were concerned, Eric was in good hands and good spirits. Neither at home during the holidays nor in his (probably censored) letters to his mother did he betray any of the unhappiness he claimed to have suffered. To complain, he thought, was unforgivable. 'To write home and ask your parents to take you away would have been even less thinkable, since to do so would have been to admit yourself unhappy and unpopular, which a boy will never do. Boys are Erewhonians: they think that misfortune is disgraceful and must be concealed at all costs.' But his reticence went beyond his schoolboy miseries. *All* his thoughts and emotions belonged to his inner world and were therefore private. 'Not to expose your true feelings to an adult seems to be instinctive from the age of seven or eight onwards.'[16]

Yet, however much he felt compelled to conceal his woes, he could still think his own thoughts. Gradually he came to see the school as 'a system', a commercial enterprise dedicated to snobbery. It was Sambo's ambition to attract boys with titles and wealth that led boys to quiz each other about their parents' income and place of residence, something he found deeply annoying.[17] The titled boys were always addressed as 'Lord So-and-So' and all rich boys were openly favoured. 'I doubt,' he wrote, 'that Sambo ever caned any boys whose father's income was much above £2,000 a year.'

As a high-flyer, after three years of Latin and one of Greek, he was put into a scholarship class for special coaching in Classics. The teaching, he wrote, was intensive and aimed solely at passing examinations. 'Boys were crammed with learning as cynically as a goose is crammed for Christmas.' Marks were all that counted, examinations became 'a sort of confidence trick [to] give the examiner the impression that you knew more than you did'.[18] This 'evil' system on which a gifted boy's career was made to hang, produced cynical and empty teaching practices – the study of passages likely to be examined rather than whole books, a discouragement of science and nature study (things which interested Eric), books read with only the 'English paper' in mind and – this he especially disdained – the rote learning of dates which passed for History teaching.

However, Flip did shine as an English teacher and probably influenced him more than he admitted. Her more admiring pupils recalled her great insistence on simplicity and clarity in prose, the very qualities George Orwell later sought to emulate, and he had to admit that in certain ways she encouraged him. 'I was always tremendously proud when I succeeded in making Flip laugh. I have even, at her command, written *vers d'occasion*, comic verses to celebrate memorable events in the life of the school.'[19] On one occasion he was favoured by being allowed into her library and there discovered Thackeray's *Vanity Fair*, so something of her literary taste did communicate itself to him. However, her inspired teaching was often marred by an instinct to browbeat. One of her methods of spurring on scholarship boys was to pull their hair. Blair countered this by plastering his own blond locks with grease.

In Orwell's memory the most oppressive cramming was in advanced Classics, with Sambo 'always goading, threatening, exhorting . . . prodding away at one's mind to keep it up to the right pitch of concentration, as one might keep a sleepy person awake by sticking pins in him'. The goading sometimes turned physical – a tap on the skull from Sambo's heavy silver pencil, a tug on the short hairs around the ears or a kick on the shins under the table. Sometimes failure to learn meant being hauled off for a caning. As much as he detested Sambo's methods, Orwell admitted reluctantly that a classical education would probably be unfeasible without corporal punishment.[20] But at St Cyprian's these brutal methods were reserved for the poor scholarship boys whose brains were Sambo's 'gold-mine'. Their expectations were also lowered compared to the rich boys. They were not going to grow up with money, they were reminded. 'Your people aren't rich. Don't get above yourself!' And they were allocated less pocket money than the rich boys, whatever their parents had sent them. But what hurt Eric most was the fact that the traditional iced cake with candles for a boy to share around on his birthday was never provided for him, so the chance of gaining at least momentary popularity was lost.

He was made to feel that he must win a scholarship or be condemned to that grim little office stool. To avoid that dreaded fate he resorted to every kind of superstitious charm – fervent prayers over wishbones, horseshoes and wishing-wells, and under new moons – but at the same time he felt impelled by some inner demon to slack. Then Flip and Sambo would throw his reduced-fee status in his face, accusing him of 'not playing the game', of letting his mother down and being unfair to them, the Wilkes. Did he know what they had done for him? Was it very 'straight' of him? The more brutal Sambo would say, 'You are living on my bounty.' Not surprisingly, he spent his schooldays agonising about money and became, in his own words, 'a money snob'. 'Looking back, it is astonishing how intimately, intelligently snobbish we all were, how knowledgeable about names and addresses, how swift to detect small differences in accents and manners and the cut of clothes.'[21]

When he was able to circumvent school rules and steal out to buy sweets, he was overcome by paranoia, feeling he was being spied on – a feeling which was to plague him more as time went on. He was gripped by two powerful competing emotions, a deep hatred of the Wilkes, and an equally strong feeling of 'shame and dismay' at his lack of gratitude. 'All through my boyhood I had a profound conviction that I was no good, that I was wasting my time, wrecking my talents, behaving with monstrous folly and wickedness and ingratitude – and all this, it seemed, was inescapable, because I lived among laws which were absolute . . . but which it was not possible for me to keep.' In retrospect he hated the Wilkes even more because he had come to see that all he was to them was 'good speculation'.[22]

Having described in such detail his sufferings at St Cyprian's he then admitted having good times there. There were expeditions across the Downs and to Beachy Head, and 'nature walks' equipped with nets and jars in search of caterpillars, butterflies and newts dredged from dew-ponds. There were twilit wanderings in the school grounds in midsummer, followed by plunges in the pool, dawn risings to read alone for an hour in a sunlit dormitory from favourite authors such as Ian Hay, Thackeray, Kipling and Wells. The impact of Wells was considerable:

> Back in the nineteen-hundreds it was a wonderful experience for a boy
> to discover H. G. Wells. There you were, in a world of pedants,
> clergymen and golfers, with your future employers exhorting you to 'get
> on or get out', your parents systematically warping your sexual life, and
> your dull-witted schoolmasters sniggering over their Latin tags; and
> here was this wonderful man who could tell you about the inhabitants
> of the planets and the bottom of the sea, and who knew that the future
> was not going to be what respectable people imagined.[23]

Reading Wells encouraged an interest in science, a curiosity about how things worked and how mysteries were solved, which in turn led him to the exploits of the great fictional detectives – Conan Doyle's Sherlock Holmes, Ernest Brahma's Max Carados, Chesterton's Father Brown, and in particular, the crime stories of J. Austen Freeman featuring the forensic scientist Dr Thorndyke. Another hero was Raffles, the gentleman crook, with whom he shared an enthusiasm for cricket. His passion for reading was not just confined to great literature and he would always retain an attachment to what he called (after Chesterton) 'good bad books', from Doyle and Brahma to A. E. W. Mason and Leonard Merrick.

One teacher at St Cyprian's who won the undying affection of this small resentful child was the second master, Robert Sillar – a quiet, charismatic figure sporting the fashionable Kitchener moustache, who had been at the school from its beginning, and was not, it seems, at all beholden to the Wilkes. He conducted his own 'nature trips', encouraging his young enthusiasts with butterfly-collecting competitions and magic lantern shows. His philosophy, oft repeated, was, 'No one can understand difficult things like their own lives unless they understand simpler things like animals and birds first.'[24] His Christmastime readings from Dickens, illustrated with slides, were a highlight of the school year, and his readings from the Apocrypha something of a curiosity. He was a devotee of the gun, taught shooting, and once showed young Blair his treasured pearl-handled six-shooter. Flip ridiculed Sillars's nature excursions as 'bug-hunting', no help for passing exams. But Eric's love of nature was important to him. He had the true eye of a naturalist and his knowledge of plants and animals would become extensive. 'Most of the good memories of my childhood,' he said, 'are in some way connected with animals.'[25] His attitude to animals, however, was ambivalent, balancing a strong love of them with an equally powerful hunter's urge to destroy them.

There were other pleasures to which he only alluded – wandering off to small villages to buy fizzy drinks and wonderful sweets (Paradise Mixture, Farthing Everlastings, Caroway Comfits, Penny Monsters, sugar mice and liquorice pistols).[26] There were walks around Eastbourne, thronged in the summer with holidaymakers enjoying the promenade, the donkey-rides and end-of-the-pier entertainment, with minstrels singing the latest songs. In his forties he could still recall the hits of the day – 'Every nice girl loves a sailor', 'My little grey home in the west', 'The Turkey Trot', 'Gilbert the filbert, the knut with a K', and the sentimental Irish song of 1914, 'Tipperary'.[27] In Eastbourne, too, he discovered naughty seaside postcards, a source of delight and fascination for the rest of his life. Perhaps the caricatures of fat women dominating meek and puny husbands were comic reminders of Flip and Sambo, and his stirring libido was titillated by the depiction of scantily clad women and the risqué captions. He started a secret collection, keeping the rudest ones in a separate envelope. By 1914 he had acquired an albumful – a new hobby to replace a forgotten childhood passion for stamp-collecting.[28]

Like most children of his generation he was ignorant of sex. The Wilkes raged so furiously against what they called 'swinishness' and 'beastliness' (meaning masturbation and homosexuality) that he was left feeling sinful, depraved and destined for suicide or the lunatic asylum; sex and sin were associated early in his mind. Only at eleven was he told by a schoolfellow where babies came from, and even then had no idea how they got there in the first place. From those overheard conversations between his mother and her feminist friends (and her referring to men always as 'those brutes'), he gained the impression, which stayed with him until he was twenty, that only men derived pleasure from sexual intercourse. The picture left in his mind was of 'a man pursuing a woman, forcing her down & jumping on top of her', much as he had seen a cock do to a hen. Men, it seemed, were hateful and unattractive in women's eyes, an idea which would mar his sexual life for a long time afterwards.[29] If he raised the question with Ida or Richard he seems to have received no honest answer.

Music-hall songs, seaside postcards and thoughts of sex, of course, were passing pleasures gently subverting the moral proprieties for which St Cyprian's stood. For a deeper, more satisfying pleasure he could escape to the magic world of literature. He had already discovered Swift and Dickens; at St Cyprian's he was introduced to Shakespeare and Thackeray, and there were always the *Gem* and the *Magnet* and *Stalky & Co.* to transport him beyond St Cyprian's, to schools where japes and scrapes and hilarity predominated and thrashings were made fun of, especially when applied to the ample posterior of Billy Bunter.

'Such, Such Were The Joys' is the dark side of his famous essay on 'Boys' Weeklies'. Orwell's schooldays were recalled not in jolly adventures but savage canings, baleful glares from the Wilkes, choking Eton collars on Sundays, purgatorial football matches and disgusting food. The litany of horrors includes draughty dormitories, lumpy porridge with hairs floating in it, porringers with stale porridge caked under their rims, forks clogged with old food, slimy water in the swimming pool, towels with damp cheesy smells, filthy doorless lavatories, evil faecal smells in corridors, the clang of emptying chamber pots, and once, on a visit to a public swimming baths, a floating human turd – a truly Orwellian touch. To him, the age of seven to seventeen was 'the age of disgust' when 'one always seems to be walking the tightrope over a cesspool'. It was a feeling he never quite shook off, as his novels, especially *Nineteen Eighty-Four*, demonstrate. This sense of disgust was connected with his belief that he was ugly and unworthy, and that he smelt. And there was a further fact about him which set him apart and could account for his half-hearted attitude to games. It was a fashion in those days for upper-class boys to be circumcised. In the bath after sport Eric was quickly identified by the others as 'not one of us' and felt acutely embarrassed.[30]

On top of that was his chronic ill health. At St Cyprian's the emphasis was on health and vigour; illness was regarded as moral deficiency. What was called his 'wheeziness' or 'chestiness' was dismissed by Sambo as imagined or due to overeating. 'My cough was referred to as a "stomach cough", which made it sound both disgusting and reprehensible. The cure for it was hard running, which, if you kept it up long enough, ultimately "cleared your chest".' Rather than a cause of concern, it was treated as a source of annoyance. In a note he records the jibe of his school drill sergeant – 'Corf! Corf! Corf! Corf! We shall have to send you to Corfe Castle.' Thirty years later, after being told that he had bronchiectasis and TB, he blamed this primitive mentality for costing him his health. The shadow of illness weighed heavily upon him, marking him out as different – an unattractive solitary child and an irritant to others. 'By boyish standards, I was a poorer specimen,' he wrote, and it was against this perceived condition and those who deemed him unworthy that he rebelled.

For his first three years at the school he appears to have conformed. At Christmas 1912 he turned out for a Fancy Dress Dance dressed as a footman 'with a red velvet coat and a white flowered waistcoat, and red-silk trousers, and black stockings, and a lace frill and a wig'.[31] He was a member of the winning ten-a-side rugby team in the winter of 1913, and the following spring won first place in the Junior High Jump. In the August 1914 edition of the *St Cyprian's Chronicle* he was featured as a 'best bat' and a cricketing 'character'. But cricket carried no prestige at the school, he said, because 'boys only attach importance to a game if it requires strength or courage'. The sport which did bring prestige was football, a game he derided as 'a species of fighting'. 'The lovers of football are large, boisterous, nobbly boys who are good at knocking down and trampling on younger boys.' That was what the school celebrated – 'the continuous triumph of the strong over the weak'.[32] The one game he did enjoy was fives, a game one could play with a chosen friend, or even alone.

At home, meanwhile, things had changed. In January 1912, after thirty-seven years' service and at the age of fifty-five, Richard Blair retired from the Bengali Opium Service on a pension of just over £400 a year, probably with additions from contributions set aside and a family supplement.[33] While still at the very bottom of the British Indian Order of Precedence, and despite his obscure position and posting he had finally risen to the rank of Sub-Opium Agent Class 1. Now he returned to join his family in Henley. Determined not to fall pregnant yet again, Ida banished 'Dick', as she called him, to his own separate room. He was put firmly in his place around the house, which by now was her own domain.[34] His had not been a glittering career, and Ruth Pitter thought him a man with 'a deep-seated grudge against life'.[35]

With only distant memories of his father, Eric met this intimidating new arrival only on returning for his spring holidays just before his ninth birthday. Now instead of being spoiled at home he found himself confronted by 'a gruff elderly man forever saying "Don't!"'[36] By the beginning of 1913 his sisters were in France with the Ursulines, so Eric had to face up to this new situation alone. His feelings about his father are hinted at in what he wrote about how children view adults:

> The enormous size of grown-ups, their ungainly, rigid bodies, their coarse, wrinkled skins, their great relaxed eyelids, their yellow teeth, and the whiffs of musty clothes and beer and sweat and tobacco that disgorge from them at every movement! Part of the reason for the ugliness of adults, in a child's eyes, is that the child is usually looking upwards, and few faces are at their best when seen from below. Besides, being fresh and unmarked itself, the child has impossibly high standards in the matter of skin and teeth and complexion.[37]

One of his father's habits was to begin each meal by removing his false teeth and depositing them beside him on the table, replacing them after he had eaten.[38] The apparent horror with which he came to regard false teeth must have had its origins here. Even so, many of his father's favourite dishes became Eric's own – kippers, Gentleman's Relish, thick-cut marmalade, and, no doubt, very strong Indian tea.

However wretched St Cyprian's was and however unsettling his home had become, horrors of the modern external world were increasingly ready to intrude. In April 1912 news of the sinking of the 'unsinkable' *Titanic* left Eric feeling quite stricken.[39] In 1913 Eastbourne was riveted by a murder trial – a 'hooded man', a long-term criminal with numerous aliases, had shot and killed a local policeman, and reports of the case filled the *Eastbourne Gazette* for weeks. On 13 February it ran a minute-by-minute account of the hanging – the arrival of the executioner, Ellis, the prisoner's last meal, the walk to the scaffold, the thud of the long drop and the grave waiting beside the prison walls. Everyone at the school would have known of the case. Whether he read the report in the *Gazette* or not, he cannot have been unaware of the sensation the case of 'the hooded man' caused locally. He certainly developed a fascination with 'the English murder', later writing his own moving account of a hanging, and was sufficiently familiar with execution literature to produce thirty years later a list from memory for a newspaper column, including the final scene of *A Tale of Two Cities*, Byron's description of a guillotining, a beheading described by Horace Walpole, Jack London's story 'The Chinango' and Kipling's 'Danny Deever'.[40]

Because he was thought too clever and a bit strange he was often bullied at St Cyprian's, sometimes teased as 'Eric; or, Little by Little'. In a letter to his mother in February 1912 he casually reported that someone had torn up her last letter before he had had a chance to read it.[41] John Grotrian, a contemporary at the school recalled, 'His face was moon-shaped and all too often streaked with tears.'[42] Only once, it seems, did he react when turned upon by a bigger boy. Cliffy Burton, a hearty soccer player, an athlete, a marksman and a corporal in the Cadets, was a popular conformist, whose parents sponsored school prizes. To Flip he embodied the St Cyprian's ideal, and was much favoured. According to Orwell, when Burton grabbed him and twisted his arm, he decided on revenge. Next day, he sauntered up to his tormentor and without warning hit him in the face with all his might, sending him flying. When challenged to fight, he refused. He knew he was breaking an unwritten code of honour, but felt justified in the circumstances, and thereafter the bullying ceased. But that did not altogether assuage his thirst for vengeance. Twenty years later, while checking into casual wards and dosshouses around London and once when arrested for drunkenness, he gave the name Burton, and even suggested it as a pseudonym for the author of *Down and Out in Paris and London*. To bring the apple of Flip's eye down into the workhouse would have pleased him enormously.

'Getting his own back' through his writing was something he came to prefer to direct retribution. At St Cyprian's there was a teacher called Ellis who taught Maths and had a fearsome temper, as Gavin Maxwell recalled. 'Failure . . . to give the correct answer to a question was enough to start a ten-minute seeming manic hysteria, beginning with a terrific crash of his stick across the culprit's desk, a crash that would have broken bones unwise enough to be in the way.'[43] It may be no coincidence that 'Ellis' is the name Orwell gave to the most obnoxious character in *Burmese Days*, who blinds a boy with a stick, although a close friend of the hated Burton, also called Ellis, might have been the target in mind there.

By the end of 1912, the family had moved three or four miles upriver from Henley to a large detached house in Shiplake, a beautiful riverside hamlet perched on a chalk cliff overhanging one of the prettiest bends on the Thames, close to its confluence with the River Lodden. Alfred Lord Tennyson was married at the church there in 1850 and at Binfield, a few miles beyond Wargrave on the other bank, Alexander Pope was born and grew up. The river at Shiplake was a paradise for fishermen, the perfect place, as Jerome K. Jerome would have said, for 'messing about in boats'.[44]

Behind weirs and locks lay still stretches of the Thames, overhung with willow and teeming with fish, and hidden pools lying deep in woods bordering nearby Binfield Heath. This magical setting came to represent a spirit of place and time that would haunt Orwell's consciousness and reshape his imaginary world. It became, with Henley, the 'Lower Binfield' of *Coming Up For Air* while the countryside around inspired the visionary landscape of Winston Smith in *Nineteen Eighty-Four*. 'Lower Binfield', which also crops up as a place name in *Down and Out in Paris and London* and *A Clergyman's Daughter*, was a conflation of Binfield Heath and Lower Shiplake, where the Blairs' house, Rose Lawn, stood close to the station. It was also close to Harpesden where Richard had found a job to supplement his pension, as secretary to the Henley Golf Club.

Eighteen months after moving to Shiplake, next door to Rose Lawn, Eric discovered new friends. Part of the Blairs' back garden bordered part of the garden of Quarry House, where the Buddicoms lived with their three children – Jacintha (fourteen), Prosper (eleven) and eight-year-old Guinever. Seeing them playing there one day, Eric climbed through the hedge and, still keeping a polite distance, calmly stood on his head. The children were suitably impressed, and when they asked him what he was doing he replied, 'You're noticed more if you stand on your head than if you're the right way up.'[45] It could have been a scene from *Alice in Wonderland* with Eric acting the slightly Mad Hatter. The result was that they all became friends, and for the next seven years he spent most of his school holidays in their company. In Prosper Buddicom he found a friend with whom to hunt and fish, and share his new passion for explosives – anything that 'went off with a noise like the Day of Judgement'. The Buddicoms had a good spread of wooded land that he would roam with Prosper hunting for rabbits and birds.

In Jacintha, although two years older than him, Eric had discovered an intellectual companion, a nature-lover and bookworm like himself. She was a serious girl, a pupil at Oxford High School for Girls with a university career in mind, who clearly enjoyed his company. They shared books and he showed her some of his stories. 'He said that reading was a good preparation for writing; *any* book could teach you something, if only how not to write one. Of course, Eric was always going to write; not merely as an author, always as a FAMOUS AUTHOR in capitals.'[46] Among the Buddicoms he became known thereafter as 'Eric the FAMOUS AUTHOR'. And his future *Collected Works* became a favourite topic for discussion. 'It was to be a Uniform Edition, and we argued at length about the respective merits of rather small books bound in red leather with gold letters like my family's Kiplings, or rather larger in chaste blue with silver, to which Eric was finally more inclined.'[47] And the FAMOUS AUTHOR's name was always to be E. A. Blair. 'Eric', he told them, was not an author's name.

Together they read through all the children's favourites, Kenneth Grahame's *Golden Age*, Lewis Carroll's *Through the Looking Glass*, Harry Graham's *Ruthless Rhymes for Heartless Homes*, and a book from the Buddicoms' library which he borrowed again and again – Wells's *A Modern Utopia*. That, he told Jacintha, was the kind of book that he might write himself one day, a clear portent of *Nineteen Eighty-Four*, she thought later. And *Animal Farm*, she was sure, had its roots in Beatrix Potter's *Pigling Bland*, which they read aloud to cheer one another up.[48] It was no doubt in this same mood of levity that he played practical jokes on crooked advertisers, in one case pretending to be a woman troubled by obesity and anxious for a cure. Having haggled the fee down from two guineas to half a crown he then announced that the problem had been cured by a rival firm.[49]

The Buddicoms helped bring out another side of him, somewhat more dramatic and sinister. He was, Jacintha recalled, a very accomplished teller of ghost stories and loved especially *The Ingoldsby Legends*. He gave her copies of *The Turn of the Screw* and *Dracula*, plus a crucifix and clove of garlic to keep away vampires. But he did not always please her. When she discovered that he and Prosper had killed a hedgehog and shot a sitting bird, she was outraged. However, their friendship became extremely important to him and would play a significant part in determining the course of his later life.

The delight of getting away from the hated St Cyprian's at holidaytime probably explains why Jacintha remembered him always as a happy boy with a great sense of humour, and was amazed that he wrote so bitterly of his miserable childhood. They played French cricket, croquet and tennis together, and obviously he left the reclusive, morose little Eric behind at school, showing a very different face to the Buddicoms. It was a trick he would perfect over time, showing one face to one set of people and another to others.

If Eric's home life was marred by a coolness between his parents, by his dislike for his father and the distance between himself and his two sisters, the Buddicoms appear to have been extraordinarily normal and happy, even though the children's parents separated in 1915. In the Blairs' case an ill-assorted couple remained together. Jacintha remembered Ida Blair as 'vivacious and spirited', and Richard as gruff and elderly, calling through the hedge to summon Eric indoors to finish his homework – a man who thought children were better seen than heard, and best kept off the lawn.[50]

The outbreak of the Great War on 4 August that year would transform not just old England – and old Europe – for ever, but also the Blair family. Avril, only six at the time, recalled her brother on that day, down in Cornwall for their usual summer holiday, 'sitting cross-legged on the floor of my mother's bedroom, talking to her about [the outbreak of the war] in a very grown-up manner', while she knitted him a school scarf.[51] Eric himself had a veritable album of memories of the period – a cartoon of the Kaiser which shocked people unused to the guying of royalty; a cabman in tears in Henley marketplace as his old horse was taken for war service; at the railway station, 'a mob of young men . . . scrambling for the evening papers that had just arrived on the London train',[52] and the sight of soldiers, 'monstrous men with chests like barrels and moustaches like the wings of eagles who strode across my childhood's gaze', marching off to war that year 'when all soldiers seemed like giants to me'.[53] The memory of those giants marching off to a muddy death in Flanders remained to haunt him, as it did so many of his generation just too young themselves to join the parade.

One of the men to go marching off to war was Marjorie's old flame Humphrey Dakin, the doctor's son whose gang young Eric had tagged behind. Humphrey, now nineteen, had gone to America to seek his fortune. When war broke out he took the first ship home, and promptly signed up for the Royal Liverpool Regiment. By the following April he was gazetted Second Lieutenant and by the end of 1915 was out in France, no longer creeping through woods in search of rabbits but along trenches in search of Germans. Elderly, gruff old Richard, not to be outdone, joined the Henley Territorials. As George Orwell later wrote, he 'grew up in a military tradition'.

One effect of the war was that Eric the jingo was reborn. Inspired, no doubt, by the welter of blazing headlines, and perhaps encouraged by Flip, he penned a poem for the occasion, a call to arms, which was submitted to the *Henley and South Oxfordshire Standard*, no doubt by his proud parents. It was published at the beginning of October 1914, headed, 'The following verses were composed and written by Master Eric Blair, eleven-year-old son of Mr. R. W. Blair, of Rose Lawn, Shiplake.'

> Oh! give me the strength of the lion,
> The wisdom of Reynard the fox,
> And then I'll hurl troops at the Germans,
> And give them the hardest of knocks.
>
> Oh! think of the War lord's mailed fist,
> That is striking at England to-day;
> And think of the lives that our soldiers
> Are fearlessly throwing away.
>
> Awake! oh you young men of England,
> For if, when your Country's in need
> You do not enlist by the thousand,
> You truly are cowards indeed.[54]

His effort greatly pleased Mrs Wilkes and, briefly at least, he basked in her favour.

The image of 'sleeping England' recurred to him a quarter of a century later followed by a quite different call to arms. Later still he would compose a similar verse in more revolutionary vein to be sung to the strains of 'Clementine' or 'La Cucuracha',[55] not intended to inspire young humans to fight but for all animals to unite against human tyranny. He must have felt he knew a good deal about that, even as a child.

Master Blair's poem sat well beside such headlines as, 'Germans Driven Back', 'Turn of Tide', and (a little prematurely) 'Germans Defeated', and messages carried in most newspapers from the king, Lord Kitchener and other luminaries of the day, many of them Eric's writer-heroes. The *Henley and South Oxfordshire Standard* quoted Wells, invoking the aid of science and urging, 'Give our men only machines enough and support enough and they will do their work,' and Kipling, solemnly declaring that, 'If England fails the lights of Freedom will go out, and even the very tradition of Freedom will pass out of remembrance.'[56] Uncannily, these were phrases echoed almost exactly by Winston Churchill in 1940, and much the same sentiments about freedom inform Winston Smith's anguished thoughts in *Nineteen Eighty-Four*. And Eastbourne had visits and patriotic speeches from Conan Doyle and Hilaire Belloc. On the other hand, another of Eric's literary heroes, George Bernard Shaw, declared that England and Germany were 'a couple of extremely quarrelsome dogs', and advised soldiers on both sides to 'SHOOT THEIR OFFICERS AND GO HOME'. No newspaper would print this pearl of Shavian sagacity.[57]

The *St Cyprian's Chronicle* was in no mood for such cynicism either, and was not to be outdone at flag-waving. In its last edition of 1914 it ran a list of Old Boys who had rallied to the colours, including the half-dozen killed in the first battles. Above this list ran the rubric '*Dolce et decorum est pro patria mori*' ('Sweet and glorious it is to die for your country'), words which Wilfrid Owen later damned as 'the old Lie' that led men to choking deaths in gas-filled trenches.[58] Over the following four years the *Chronicle*'s lists of 'glorious dead' slowly grew to thirty-eight. Medals were won, legs, eyes and lives lost, but, declared the *Chronicle*, 'Their names will go down in glory etc. etc.' Obituaries extolled the virtues of courage, self-sacrifice and character of every fallen Old St Cyprian. One concluded, 'Donald was the whitest man I ever met,'[59] a revealing comment on the school's prevailing ethos.

While thousands flocked to the recruiting stations, under the stern gaze and pointed finger of Lord Kitchener, and the words 'Your Country Needs You!', St Cyprian's, too, mobilised for war. A map was posted showing the site of each new battle, boys knitted socks and scarves for soldiers and saved up to buy cigarettes to distribute to wounded men at the neighbouring

Summerdown Camp, an experience that Orwell gave to George Bowling in *Coming Up For Air*. School concerts were re-run to entertain troops, though what reception they gave to Cecil Beaton's 'Little Buttercup' in *HMS Pinafore* or Eric Blair's Farmer Wardle in a dramatised excerpt from *The Pickwick Papers*, is not reported. For Eric, Farmer Wardle was a good part – a hunting, shooting and fishing gentleman, who lived, interestingly enough, at Manor Farm.

Imbuing boys with the martial spirit was a significant part of St Cyprian's life. The Cadet Corps, in which Blair had one of the coveted roles of bugler, was run strictly according to the War Office Drill Book, aimed, among other things, 'to inculcate the military spirit to train the soldier to bear fatigue, privation and danger cheerfully'. Apart from the aim to instil 'obedience to orders', the Drill Book appeared to have done a good job on Cadet Blair. But whether it prepared boys suitably for modern warfare is questionable. In the summer before war broke out, the Corps was rehearsing scenes from the Zulu Wars. According to the *Chronicle*, at the bugle call of 'Form Square' 'a herd of savages . . . rushed at the astonished troops', but, after steady firing 'the barbarians had . . . been killed to a man'.[60] Such then-fashionable attitudes of course afforded a convenient rationale for British imperialism.

If Blair had few friends at St Cyprian's, he found one at last in September 1914 with the arrival of Cyril Connolly, a small, strangely brilliant boy of Irish ancestry, slightly younger but distinctly uglier than himself. Probably because they were 'different', these two were drawn to one another, although their backgrounds and tastes were not identical. Connolly left a telling image of Blair at St Cyprian's: 'Tall, pale, with his flaccid cheeks, large spatulate fingers, and supercilious voice, he was one of those boys who seem born old.'[61] Coming from an Irish military background, and a family rather more affluent than Blair's, Connolly was used to more travel and more exotic cuisine. However, both disliked games, shared a considerable aptitude for languages, especially French and Classics, and were voracious readers. One of the few ways in which Blair could get into Flip's favour was by winning her weekly prize for the best list of books read. Connolly claimed that between them he and Blair won it every week, rising early to plough through their latest discovery. According to Orwell, when Connolly produced a book of Wells's short stories, including 'The Country of the Blind', they kept borrowing and re-borrowing it by turns, often in the middle of the night, reading it again and again under the bedclothes without bothering to sleep.[62] But not all their reading met Flip's approval. When she found them with Compton Mackenzie's great *succès de scandale* of 1913, *Sinister Street*, they were promptly cast into disfavour – and, Orwell thought, may even have been caned for it.

It was not surprising that *Sinister Street* should so rivet young Eric. Its hero, Michael Fane, is studying Classics at a prep school, and moves with his mother from the countryside to Kensington (close to where Aunt Nellie lived). He spends holidays in Cornwall (as the Blairs did), visits Bournemouth (where Uncle Charlie lived), and meets a girl from an Anglo-Indian family whose father is away in Burma. He visits Eastbourne and thinks what a lovely place. (Hollow laughter from Blair and Connolly, no doubt.) Fane envies a wild-looking, unkempt boy he sees wandering down Kensington High Street and longs to be 'a raggle-taggle wanderer'. He is bullied on his first day at school but stands up to the bullies.[63]

To some Blair sounded older than his years, but often this was a borrowed erudition. Once, while they were meandering round Eastbourne, Connolly recalled him saying, 'in his flat, ageless voice', 'You know Connolly, there's only one cure for all diseases,' to which a slightly guilt-ridden Connolly replied, 'You mean going to the lavatory?' 'No,' said Blair, 'I mean Death!'[64] Connolly was deeply impressed, but this neat paradox was taken from Chesterton's *Manalive*: 'The only cure is an operation – an operation that is always successful: death.'[65] On a later Eastbourne perambulation Blair solemnly announced, 'Whatever happens in this war, Britain will emerge a second-rate power,' which left Connolly equally impressed. But most likely he had gleaned this remark from his worldly-wise Uncle Charlie, who, he told a school friend, treated him like a grown-up and had adult conversations with him.[66] By now he was lost to the superficial values extolled by the Wilkes. 'The remarkable thing about Orwell,' wrote Connolly, 'was that he alone among the boys was an intellectual, and not a parrot, for he thought for himself; read Shaw and Samuel Butler, and rejected not only [St Cyprian's], but the war, the Empire, Kipling, Sussex, and Character.'[67] As it happened, he was not yet quite ready to reject Kipling, but that day was not far off.

Connolly, while greatly disliking the Wilkes and their school, was more successful in concealing the fact. If it made life easier, he was prepared to act the role expected of him, which Blair was not. He went out of his way to attract Flip's approval, attempting to manipulate her affections just as she manipulated the fears of the boys, and anxiously charting the degree to which he was in or out of favour with her. Blair, on the other hand, was rarely in favour. With the Wilkes he found it difficult to pretend. Connolly recognised this difference between them. 'I was a stage rebel,' he wrote, 'Orwell a true one.'[68] As cramming for scholarships became more intense, the two friends found themselves in fierce competition with each other (alternately winning the so-called Harrow History Prize), and this probably helped them towards the high marks they eventually achieved.

With Avril's and Margerie's as well as Eric's education to be paid for, the large house at Shiplake had become too expensive. In Autumn 1915 the Blairs moved back to Henley, to a smaller semi-detached house at 36 St Mark's Road. However, there was little chance of him feeling lonely; his friends the Buddicoms were just a few miles away in Shiplake and he got into the habit of cycling over there during school holidays for hunting expeditions with Prosper and reading sessions with Jacintha. He gave her the book from which he had quoted to Connolly, Chesterton's *Manalive*, a strange book very much in tune with his odd way of regarding things, full of paradoxes and contradictions, which might also have supplied him with the seeds of 'Doublethink'. And he shared with her the short stories which were then absorbing him – Kipling's 'Baa Baa Black Sheep', Wells's 'A Slip under the Microscope', Poe's 'The Premature Burial' and 'The Pit and the Pendulum'. She was now fifteen and, with a place at Oxford in mind, working for her School Certificate.

It was in 1916, he wrote later, that he rejected war, sickened by the ever-more exaggerated propaganda and no doubt by the drum-beating nationalism of the Wilkes, and the spy-fever that swept Eastbourne from time to time. The 'reality' of propaganda reports, he decided, was a swindle. As the casualty lists grew, he cannot have been entirely unaware of the horror of what was happening across the Channel, where the boom of guns could be heard occasionally. His old gang leader, Humphrey Dakin, returned from Flanders that spring minus an eye and was sent to a London hospital to convalesce.

By May that year Blair and Connolly were ready to try for scholarships and were taken by Sambo to Wellington College to sit the necessary examinations. Afterwards, Connolly was driven back to London in his aunt's carriage and four, while Blair and Sambo returned to Eastbourne by train. A week later, Sambo took Blair to sit the examinations for Eton. He soon heard that he had won a scholarship to Wellington, and in June that he had won one for Eton. However, in the Eton examination, he had come fourteenth, and there were only twelve vacancies in the so-called Election of 1916. To gain entrance, he would have to wait until someone dropped out. The Wilkes were delighted, and a school holiday was declared in his honour. For once Blair was in favour, even popular, and perhaps, for the moment, memories of the iced-cake-that-never-was faded somewhat.

Despite his sense of alienation from the Wilkes and their school, even with the prospect of liberation in sight, he still had an impulse to please Flip. When Lord Kitchener was lost at sea on 7 June, she ran a competition for a poem to mark the occasion. Blair and Connolly, perhaps cynically in view of their opinions, each produced an elegy, then wrote critiques of the other's efforts. To Connolly Blair wrote, 'Dashed good. Slight repetition. Scansion excellent. Meaning a little ambiguous in places. Epithets for the most part well selected. The whole thing is neat, elegant and polished.' To this Connolly replied, 'My dear Blair! I am both surprised and shocked.'[69] There is no record of Connolly's opinion of Blair's effort, which began, 'No stone is set to mark this nation's loss,/No stately tomb enshrines his noble breast . . .', but the patriotic little jingle certainly appealed to the editor of the *Henley and South Oxfordshire Standard*, who published it on 21 July beneath a letter from the Mayor and beside an article on 'The Problem of the Tramp' in Henley.[70]

No doubt to celebrate his examination success, Eric was taken to London to see the hit show *Chu Chin Chow*. It gave him an alternative fictional image of the mysterious East from that of Kipling. The charm of it, he recalled, 'lay in the fantastic unreality of the whole thing, and the droves of women, practically naked and painted to an agreeable walnut-juice tint. It was a never-never land, the "gorgeous East", where, as is well-known, everyone has fifty wives and spends his time lying on a divan, eating pomegranates.'[71] It was a great hit with the audience of mostly young soldiers on leave from the battlefields of France, and no doubt had a great appeal to a boy on the very brink of adolescence.

In January, eager to escape St Cyprian's rather than wait for a place at Eton, he chose to go to Wellington. In view of his attitude to the war by that time, it was hardly his most rational decision to choose a College with a particularly strong military tradition. When he dutifully reported to Flip in his smart new Old Boys' tie, she shook his hand and for the first time called him 'Eric'. In his imagination she told him that he had not really been worth their while, that he had never been grateful for what they had done for him, and that he was bound to amount to nothing. Even if this was grossly unfair to her, the idea was fixed in his mind and no doubt went to fuel his terrific urge to succeed that those who knew him later acknowledged. In this case, success for him would be the best revenge.

With the exception of an occasional attempt to interpret his dreams, Orwell was never much impressed by psychoanalysis. He was not drawn, as many of his generation were, to self-analysis in the Freudian vein. W. H. Auden and Christopher Isherwood were ready to do this, and were able thereby to damn their parents as the villainous source of all their worldly woes.[72] Orwell never took that line and once surprised his friend Richard Rees by remarking, 'I hope you love your family.'[73] He blamed them only once in passing for 'screwing up' his sex life, and was far readier to blame an inequitable social system and the embodiments of injustice. So, St Cyprian's and 'Mum' Wilkes in particular, became the target of his vitriol – the mother he *could* happily hate. His own parents were thus acquitted by default. It may have been Ida's ambition for him which had led to his being 'cruelly crammed' at St Cyprian's, as Ruth Pitter believed,[74] but he found it difficult to blame the mother who spoiled him and stood by him. Even his father, for whom he had no real affection, was someone he respected, and for whose approval he yearned.

He hated St Cyprian's because there his sensibilities, his sense of self-worth and self-respect, had been traduced and distorted, leaving him with an intense sense of guilt and self-hatred. Later, as a socialist, he saw the place for what it was – a commercial venture, dedicated to profit, favouring the rich pupils and abusing the poor, imbuing him with an outlook on the world which would lead him to make serious mistakes and gravely jeopardise his future. Not only did it embody all the things he came to reject – imperialism, snobbery, the valuing the strong over the weak, the denigrating of his curiosity about the natural world – but helped to distort his normal feelings about sex. In trying to retrieve the inner anguish that lay behind his hatred of the place and its proprietors, he created what may be a Dickensian caricature, and yet it is not such a distorted picture if Gavin Maxwell, Cecil Beaton and Cyril Connolly are to be believed.

The long-term effects of his prep-school experiences were considerable, and an essay like 'Such, Such Were The Joys' suggests a recognition on Orwell's part that it went a long way to explaining what he became. Whatever it gave him as a writer, and whatever grounding it gave him in scholarship, he saw the effect mostly as crippling. 'The conviction that it was *not possible* for me to be a success went deep enough to influence my actions till far into adult life. Until I was about thirty I always planned my life not only on the assumption that any major undertaking was bound to fail, but that I could only expect to live a few years longer.'[75] He said that when he left St Cyprian's the very name of the place made him feel sick, and he was determined never to visit Eastbourne or Sussex again. Had he done so barely twelve years later as a tramp visiting the local spike (as he did in neighbouring counties), at the Eastbourne Union Workhouse he might have caught sight of one of the guardians. Cecily Vaughan Wilkes joined the committee in 1922 and by 1929 had become chairman of the sub-committee dealing with the adoption and fostering of pauper and illegitimate children. Having spent thirty years disposing of the children of the wealthy, now she was also disposing of the children of the poor.[76]

Blair carried into his adult life not only that sense of a rich secret inner life, and his love of nature, but such a range of other interests that some of his contemporaries came to regard him as a schoolboy who never quite grew up. His fascination with cultural mores – his passion for boys' comics and children's literature, seaside postcards and old-fashioned murders, how nature ticked and how the land was farmed – was acquired as a child and never left him. They form an essential part of the character of the man we know today as 'George Orwell'.

St Cyprian's gave him something to rebel against. The school and the Wilkes became a particular focus for his animosity. He left with a heightened sense of grievance, exceedingly sensitive to any unfairness or bullying, but with a defensive mask of cynicism that would be one of his most noticeable features at Eton. As for St Cyprian's he was mentioned just twice in the school *Chronicle* after his departure – reports from third parties no doubt – and there was no mention of his ever having contacted or visited the school again. The break was final.

But another pattern had been set – that of the intellectual who could read and absorb ideas and look at them askance, and the romantic adventurer looking for escape into unorthodox literature and dissident postures, into the natural world, and into dreams of derring-do.

Chapter 4

'Absorbing Wisdom Unawares'

'The chief virtue of the great public schools (with their traditions of High Anglicanism, cricket and Latin verses) . . . [is] . . . their atmosphere of literary scholarship . . . and . . . masters . . . the kind from whom one absorbs wisdom unawares.'

Orwell, *Burmese Days*, 1934

The Eric Blair who left St Cyprian's for the anticipated freedom of Wellington was not solely a well-educated cynic; he had also acquired a strong affinity for the supernatural. The Buddicom children had noticed this, and had shivered at his ghost stories. He had steeped himself in the literature of horror – Edgar Allan Poe, Bram Stoker, M. R. James, and at some point even dipped into Aleister Crowley. He had certainly read Oscar Wilde's *The Picture of Dorian Gray*, later lending a copy to Connolly who said he 'could not swallow it'.[1] The theme of the hidden identity would play an important part in his life. He told Jacintha that half the people you saw walking the streets were in fact ghosts and he had a fascination with the idea of sympathetic magic underlying Wilde's story and more starkly portrayed in R. H. Barham's 'The Leach of Folkestone' in *The Ingoldsby Legends*.

The martial spirit and sound of bugles to which St Cyprian's had accustomed him was even more evident at Wellington, the College established in 1859 in honour of the Iron Duke. In January 1917, when Blair arrived, the atmosphere must have been strange. Here was a great school fostering the military tradition of patriotism and service, and many of its Old Boys were fighting in a war with no end in sight. The previous July, the Battle of the Somme had claimed 60,000 British lives in one day and the subaltern's life expectancy was not more than three weeks. Within the Army the mood had swung from optimism through grim resignation to deep cynicism, a mood captured in the harrowing poetry of Wilfrid Owen and in soldiers' songs, the cheerfully sung 'Tipperary' now replaced by the lugubrious 'I Want to Go Home'. In the country at large the atmosphere of restlessness was gradually giving way to one of iconoclasm and near-revolution. The prospect for young public school men destined to go directly from the classroom into the trenches, must have seemed bleak. Even so, outward displays of patriotism continued, and the new Prime Minister, Lloyd George, declared emphatically that 'Defeat is impossible'.

Eric now had his own cubicle, but the freedom he had hoped for was not to be had. Wellington was a tough school; its regime was highly spartan and beatings were common. Conrad Noel, the Christian socialist friend of Nellie Limouzin and an Old Wellingtonian, called it 'indeed a place of blood and iron' and another, Sir Ian Hamilton, wrote of the 'zebra-like decoration on my back . . . the result of a succession of beatings at the hands of the Head'. It was an institution suitable perhaps for masochistic conformists, but certainly not for E. A. Blair, and when a place became available at Eton, he took it. Asked at his new school how he felt about changing, he replied, 'Well, it can't be worse than Wellington. That really was perfectly bloody.'[3] It was, said his friend Jacintha, 'a cold-douche disappointment to him'.[4] The only happy memory of the place he seems to have retained was of skating on the lake there.[5]

At Easter he spent a week with the Buddicom children at their grandfather's house, Ticklerton Court, at Church Stretton in Shropshire. Travelling there on the train, Eric, attempting to drive the only other passenger, a woman, from their carriage, tried out a few japes, loudly asking Prosper if his spots had come out, and swinging from the luggage rack pretending to be an orang-utan, until the woman threatened to hand him over to the guard.[6] It was at Ticklerton the following August that Jacintha's Aunt Lilian became aware of Eric's cough. 'He says it's chronic,' she wrote to Jacintha's mother, '*Is this really the case?* I don't remember it before.' Perhaps the 'chronic' cough was invented in the same mischievous spirit as the spots on the train, and, although he said he bought his first gun when he was ten, he told the Buddicoms that he had never fired a rifle before and then impressed them enormously by bagging a rabbit with his second shot.[7] Ticklerton Court was a huge country mansion lit by oil and candlelight, and Eric persuaded the other children that one of its bedrooms was haunted.[8] It was the perfect setting for him to scare them with more ghost stories.

The prospect of Eton College is best captured in Thomas Gray's celebrated lines, 'Ye distant spires, ye antique towers,/That crown the watery glade.'[9] On one bank of the Thames stands Windsor with its great castle, the town where Wells once worked as a draper's assistant. Across the river sits the historic town of Eton with the College as its magnificent centrepiece. The arches and pinnacles, the cloisters and towering chapel give the College a distinctly ecclesiastical air. In Blair's time the Provost was the son of a vicar and the headmaster was pastor to King George. These two sat at the apex of what Connolly depicted as an essentially feudal system, the headmaster being the Pope, the masters representing 'the church', and a Sixth Form of top boys acting as feudal lords. The Provost on this analysis would have been God, and the newly arrived Blair a mere vassal.

Not long after arriving at Eton Blair decided that he was no longer a Christian. 'Till the age of about fourteen,' he wrote, 'I believed in God, and believed that the accounts given of him were true. But I was well aware that I did not love him. On the contrary, I hated him, just as I hated Jesus and the Hebrew patriarchs.' He was on the other side, with Pontias Pilate, Caiaphas and the other High Priests. He even found the commandment to love his parents impossible to observe. 'The good and the possible,' he said, 'never seemed to coincide.'[10] For him it was an important discovery that he could renounce his religion and not be struck by thunderbolts. Unbelief sat well with ideas he was fast absorbing from Wells, Shaw and Butler – sadly for him none of them was 'required reading' at Eton. But what he valued most were the freedom to read what he liked and the chance to retreat into the fictional worlds absorbed from his reading. At Eton he would be far freer to do both.

If at St Cyprian's Blair had been a secret rebel, at Eton he unmasked. He was never to be known as Blair the 'sap' (Eton's term for 'swot'), but long remembered as Blair 'the young cynic', a type alluded to by one of the College clerics as 'a real stinker'. Now he had ceased to believe in God. Now *all* icons must fall – not just Sussex, Kipling, God and Empire, but parents, archbishops and the Hereafter. Despite this, he allowed himself to be prepared for confirmation, and, after openly affirming his belief in God the Creator, and with Ida in attendance, was duly blessed and admitted to the Communion of the Church of England by the Bishop of Oxford. Thereafter his relationship with the Anglican church would always be one of fond irreverence.

His manner, while anathema to certain masters, did not necessarily bring him kudos among his peers. In fact, he was not particularly popular, not seen as one of 'the golden boys' – well-connected, athletic and good-look-ing. According to his fellow Colleger, Denys King-Farlow, he had 'a large, rather fat face, with big jowls, a bit like a hamster', and a noticeably croaky voice. His best feature were his 'slightly protruding blue eyes'.[11] Another contemporary called him 'pretty awful [and] a bit of a bastard',[12] while others noted his aloofness and lack of sympathy.[13] However, most of Blair's Election, recognising him as something of a solitary, accepted him as such. Yet he did make some friends. King-Farlow thought him impressively out-spoken, prepared to make jeering comments about other boys' parents – something unheard of – and even to criticise his own. 'He thought his mother was a frivolous person who wasn't interested in any of the sort of things that he thought people should be interested in and his father wasn't apparently interested in anything.'[14] Steven Runciman, future historian of the Crusades, found him 'a character whose mind worked differently from other boys', and who didn't really *like* people. 'He liked their intellectual side, but friends didn't really mean anything to him.'[15] Runciman was more committed to the classics, but was impressed by Blair's knowledge of contemporary literature, even reading at his suggestion Butler's *The Way of All Flesh*. Connolly, his old St Cyprian's comrade, who had also won a scholarship to Eton, arrived a few months after him, but by that time Blair had already established a reputation in College.

In retrospect it must have made a strange sight – George Orwell, the gaunt socialist of later photographs, dressed for Eton in a tail-coat, striped trousers and black silk top hat – damned by him later as the 'symbol throughout half the world of British plutocracy'.[16] If there were in those days, as Orwell reported, gangs of working-class 'cads' lurking around English towns ever ready to set upon rich boys, he and his fellows must have made extremely tempting targets.

A very distinctive ambience had clung to Eton since its foundation in 1440. On his *Tour Through the Whole Island of Great Britain*, Defoe described it as 'the finest School for what we call Grammar Learning, for it extends only to the Humanity Class, that is in *Britain*, or, perhaps, in *Europe*,' and founded 'for the Encouragement of Learning, to Profusion'.[17] Its traditions had remained largely unchanged during the nineteenth century when it resisted the widely copied reforms of Dr Arnold's Rugby. It therefore retained, as Orwell admitted, a tolerance of oddity which suited him perfectly.[18] In fact there was scarcely a better school for young Blair than Eton – the College of Fielding, Shelley, Gray, Swinburne, John Aubrey and Izaak Walton. The library contained Caxton incunabula, early Shakespeare folios, first editions of *Paradise Lost* and the 'Elegy in a Country Churchyard', and an unpublished Shelley manuscript. Blair's Eton contemporaries included an excess of literary talent – not just Connolly and Runciman, but Anthony Powell, John Lehmann, Henry Green, Harold Acton and Ian and Peter Fleming. One of his teachers was Aldous Huxley, and the newly appointed Provost was M. R. ('Monty') James, the distinguished classicist, ghost story-writer and translator of fairy stories.

At Eton there are strange divisions and distinctions, and a terminology to match, which are found nowhere else. In 1917 there were around a thousand boys at the College, most paying the £165 annual fee. The seventy scholars paid £25. Fee-payers lived in houses located around Eton and were known as Oppidans ('town boys'). Scholars lived in College, wore distinctive gowns with toggles, were known as 'Tugs', and had the letters K. S. ('King's Scholar') placed after their names. Oppidans had once looked down on 'Tugs' who paid so much less, but over time this attitude had softened. Even so, the term 'Tug' still carried mild overtones of contempt, and many years afterwards Blair is said to have flinched when it was uttered casually by Richard Rees, an Oppidan-contemporary of Blair. The fact that at Eton he never met coevals such as Rees, shows how separate a life the Scholars lived. More than that, among Collegers themselves there was also a caste system which decreed that one kept one's distance from members of other Elections.

Ronnie Watkins, another Scholar-contemporary of Blair, was very struck by the cloistered life in College, isolated in what Connolly called an 'intensive intellectual forcing-house'.[19] Even today, the place has a monastic aura. The magnificent Chapel of Henry VI, the College's founder, whose bronze statue sits in the centre of a cobbled quad (School Yard), dominates the scene. On the north side stand Weston's Yard and the Long Chamber where new Scholars live. The Upper School is housed at the front of the College, and beyond School Yard, cloisters lead to the Provost's and headmaster's quarters through an archway above which a chiming tower-clock marks the passing Eton day. Behind the College lie the playing fields and the long wall where the famous Wall Game is played. Gardens and water meadows stretch off to the right down to the sedgy banks of the river.

As a Scholar, Blair lived in College under the supervision of a Matron, Miss Oughterson, and a Master-in-College, John Crace. He was assigned a personal tutor, the caustically witty Andrew ('Granny') Gow, a thirty-year-old Classicist and later Fellow of Trinity College, Cambridge, and took his place in the timber-beamed medieval Long Chamber, in which the members of the 1916 Election were each allocated a curtained-off wooden cubicle opening onto a communal sitting room. It afforded little privacy, but once Blair had made it clear that he was not the gregarious type he seems to have been mostly left alone.

Having arrived later than the others, he needed to adjust more quickly to customs and routines, and rules about dress (who could and who could not wear a coloured waistcoat or a scarf) and College bounds (who could walk on which side of the main road through Eton or cross the bridge into Windsor). He had also to submit to a minor ordeal known as Chamber Singing, in which new Scholars were required to entertain a Chamber full of Collegers sufficiently to escape a bombardment of shoes. Blair sang 'Riding Down from Bangor', an American song picked up probably from minstrels on Eastbourne promenade, and acquitted himself well enough to escape a pelting.

But far worse awaited him. For his first year, every new Colleger was required to 'fag', to be at the beck and call of members of the College Sixth Form, the top ten Scholars (distinguished by their colourful waistcoats and stick-up collars) who would summon boys with long cries of 'Here'. The wretched fag was expected to respond on pain of beating. The Sixth Form in power when Blair arrived in College had a reputation for cruelty and were extremely unpopular. Two members of that Sixth in particular drew venom from him – Edward Marjoribanks, the School Captain, noted for sadism, may well have offended Blair by a beating or some other form of humiliation. Godfrey Verrall, part of the same tyrannical clique, and Blair's 'fagmaster',[20] later showed him up badly in a football game. Orwell also told a friend that he was beaten for not scoring in a College cricket match in his first half (or term) at Eton and either the brutal Marjoribanks or keenly sporty Verrall was the likely beater. Another senior boy attracting Blair's disfavour was Philip Yorke, eldest brother of Henry Yorke (the novelist Henry Green). He had insulted Runciman by applying a particularly unpleasant name to him; Blair shared his friend's indignation and agreed to help him get his revenge.

Both boys were interested in the occult, and Blair suggested they retaliate through sympathetic magic. As Runciman recalled, they fashioned an image of Yorke from candle wax. Blair wanted to pierce it through with a pin, but Runciman thought that far too drastic. Instead they simply broke off a leg. To their horror, shortly afterwards, Yorke not only broke his leg but in July died of leukaemia.[21] The story of what had happened soon spread and, in somewhat garbled form, became legend. Blair and Runciman suddenly found themselves regarded as distinctly odd, and to be treated warily. Christopher Hollis, a boy from a senior Election, actually approached Blair addressing him respectfully by name – something unheard of among Collegers – and Runciman's elder brother, afraid that he might have offended one of them, grew nervous and became unusually friendly. But Yorke's younger brother, Gerald, became utterly fascinated by them and eager to pick their brains about magic and the black arts. He later became an acolyte of Aleister Crowley and, because of his scandalous behaviour, was all but disinherited.

Runciman, who lived to be ninety-eight, continued to feel deeply guilty about the Yorke affair, and a boy as prone to guilt-feelings as Blair must have felt it deeply too. Not long before he died, he wrote, 'The death of a child is the worst thing that most people are able to imagine,'[22] and in trying to understand his tendency towards self-mortification, together with what sense of sin the Ursulines and the Wilkes had instilled in him, this episode must play a part. No doubt the belief that he had caused a death left him feeling even more isolated and different, and fearful of the damage he could cause others. Now without religion, it was not easy to find absolution for sins, real or imagined; he would need to discover other ways to do this and to suffer punishment.

The Blair legend produced other strange and often amusing memories.

There is Blair informing a green young Colleger that he was collecting the religions of new boys. 'Are you Cyrenaic, Sceptic, Epicurean, Cynic, Neoplatonist, Confucian or Zoroastrian?' 'I'm a Christian,' came the reply. 'Oh,' said Blair. 'We haven't had that before.'[23] There was Blair's somewhat Wildean exchange with Crace, the Master-in-College, of whom he was not a little contemptuous. 'Well, Blair . . . Either you or I will have to go.' 'I'm afraid it will have to be you, sir.'[24] And there was Blair announcing that 'There are at least six masters on the staff who are making a very good living out of the Crucifixion.'[25]

All this time, 'Eric the FAMOUS AUTHOR' was filling notebooks with plays and stories. His earliest surviving story, 'The Vernon Murders', bears traces of Conan Doyle, a play called 'The Man and the Maid' suggests a recent reading of *The Tempest*. He also remembered producing semi-comic *vers d'occasion* at high speed, and, at fourteen, 'a whole rhyming play, in imitation of Aristophanes, in about a week', and helped edit little magazines – 'pitiful burlesque stuff', he called them. Short-lived magazines, usually satirical, known at Eton as 'ephemerals', were a feature of the College, bearing such titles as *Paunch*, *It* and *Bubble & Squeak*. In the Michaelmas half of 1917 he helped Roger Mynors edit a handwritten ephemeral, *Election Times*, circulated at a penny a time, and later contributed parodies and lampoons to *Bubble & Squeak* and *College Days* which he co-edited with King-Farlow. He shielded himself with anonymity, which suited his superstitious mood and the fear, now perhaps sharper than ever, that an enemy could take his name and work magic against him.[26]

The role of critical 'outsider' sat well on him, and he soon became known as a Socratic, challenging received ideas and drawing others into contentious dialogues. Roger Mynors recalled him 'endlessly arguing and . . . showing up other people's fallacies and so forth'.[27] Everything traditional and approved by so-called 'Vile Old Men' (Masters and Old Etonians) was fair game. Kipling and Empire, top hats and millionaires were definitely 'out'. He was anti most institutions, and saw a 'swindle' in all of them. John Wilkes, son of Flip and a member of the highly conformist Election above him, called him 'a boy with a permanent chip on the shoulder, always liking to find everything around him wrong, and giving the impression that he was there to put it right . . . Bernard Shaw was one of his favourite authors, and he saw himself a bit as a future Bernard Shaw.'[28]

After all that ferocious cramming from the Wilkes he had decided to slack off. During his first two or three years, although he failed to distinguish himself, at least he held his place in his Election – not quite bottom. Yet he was in no mood 'to Learn to Profusion', and like Gordon Comstock in *Keep the Aspidistra Flying*, worked simply as he pleased and 'managed to develop his brain along the lines that suited it. He read the books which the headmaster denounced from the pulpit, and developed unorthodox opinions about the C. of E., patriotism and the Old Boys' tie,'[29] and most probably, like Gordon, submitted poems to national periodicals which were invariably rejected.

At first he made some effort to conform on the sports field, coming second in the Election high jump and turning in a couple of good innings for the College cricket team. This made him what Etonians call a 'dry bob', a boy opting for summer sports on dry land. 'Wet bobs' spent their time on the river, and 'slack bobs' contrive to do neither. At the end of each school year, there was always the thrill of the annual Eton v Harrow match at Lord's, cricket's Holy of Holies, where he would share a picnic hamper with Jacintha and Prosper, now at Harrow.[30] At sixteen he faded from the cricket scene and confined himself to the gentler pursuits of river-bathing, fishing and fives.

Along the Thames at Eton there were blissful hidden places for swimming and angling where one could while away an afternoon memorising Theocritus or Gibbon and watch the river go by.[31] Fishing was a passion shared by the Yorke brothers, and probably from them he heard of one of their favourite fishing haunts at the confluence of the rivers Teme and Severn, just below Worcester, not far from their home near Tewkesbury. The father of another Etonian, Lord Beauchamp, owned the local manor, Madresfield, and the land around it near Callow End. This stretch of river would lure him some twenty-five years later for a summer holiday away from another war.

Not only did he get away from the College to fish alone, but to take long walks or bike rides along the Thames, occasionally to a favourite local beauty spot, Burnham Beeches, to which he later took girlfriends and which would feature in *A Clergyman's Daughter* and *Keep the Aspidistra Flying*. The sort of activities which Connolly favoured – aspiring to membership of the most exclusive societies at the College, such as the Eton Society (or Pop) – Blair considered derisory, a capitulation to all the snobberies Eton stood for. But to Anthony Powell, Connolly was 'one of those individuals – a recognizable genius – who seemed to have been sent into the world to be talked about'.[32] Blair was more of a mystery and by no means such a focus of attention. Only at the very end of his Eton career was he elected to any society, the College Debating Society, a suitable home, one might think, for the College Socrates. This was the Society that temporarily liberalised the College, breaking down barriers between Elections, a policy soon reversed by a later, more reactionary Sixth Form.

The theme of poor boy among the rich continued to obsess him, but while he may have been only relatively poor (as were Watkins and Hollis), he felt it more keenly than most. The idea of being a poor boy at the rich man's table would long persist. ('He was an awful bore about money,' recalled King-Farlow.)[33] His close friend Runciman was from an extremely wealthy and well-connected family. His grandfather was a shipping tycoon, his father had been President of the Board of Trade in the recent Asquith government, and he had already met most of the great politicians and eminences of the time. He admired Blair's mind and shared his antipathy to games, but was unaware of feeling at all superior. However, when he invited his friend home for the holidays Blair always made an excuse, probably thinking he would find the Runcimans' very formal and mannerly way of living uncomfortable. And yet Runciman was no snob. When he met Ida, who entertained her son's friends and bought them treats, he concluded that the Blairs' poverty was his own invention. Eric, on the other hand, found parents' days farcical and excruciating. In *Keep the Aspidistra Flying*, Gordon would actually pray for his parents not to turn up on such occasions.[34]

The war continued to devour men. In April 1917 America declared war on Germany, and in June the British commander, Haigh, was planning a massive offensive in Flanders, hoping to win the war before the 'Yankees' arrived. With no end to hostilities in sight, Blair and his contemporaries fully expected to go straight from school to the front. They were, after five years in the Officer Training Corps, to all intents and purposes, trained officers. During the war the OTC was compulsory, which annoyed Eric, having rejected the war and all it stood for. In particular he objected to the antiquated parade-ground drill, and managed to avoid much of it by joining the Signals section, which meant mostly being driven around in trucks.[35] 'To be as slack as you dared on OTC parades,' wrote Orwell, 'and to take no interest in the war, was considered a mark of enlightenment.' Connolly remembered Blair treating Corps field days (often replays of British defeats, such as the Retreat from Mons) as a joke, sneaking off to some convenient hideout and entertaining the others with hilarious readings of *Eric; or Little by Little* – a book he hated, for its fake piety and its image of 'Eric the goody-goody', about which he was teased at St Cyprian's.

Richard Blair was not so prone to cynicism. In September 1917, already over sixty and a Territorial, he volunteered for active service and was commissioned as a Temporary Second Lieutenant, supposedly the oldest subaltern in the Army. He was soon posted to France with the 51st (Ranchi) Indian Labour Company, and from November 1917 till May 1918 served 'in the field'. He oversaw the care of horses used for hauling gun carriages, and would have been close to the action during the great German spring offensive on the Western Front. After a brief spot of leave, as the war drew to a close, he was sent to Marseilles to serve with the Royal Artillery.[36] Eric never mentioned his father's war service, but may have been alluding to it when he wrote that, 'Of the middle years of the war, I remember chiefly the square shoulders, bulging calves and jingling spurs of the artillerymen, whose uniform I much preferred to that of the infantry.'[37] Meanwhile, Ida and Marjorie (now eighteen) also wanted to do their bit. The Blair's house at Henley was sub-let and the family moved to London, to 23 Cromwell Crescent in Earl's Court. Marjorie joined the Women's Legion as a dispatch rider, and Ida went to work as a civil servant at the Ministry of Pensions. The dogged Humphrey, despite his lost eye, had talked his way into the Royal Flying Corps, and was now back in touch with Marjorie.

Earl's Court was *Sinister Street* territory, where young Michael Fane once walked and from whence he had gone on to public school. Eric later wrote disdainfully about 'The foul . . . endless . . . "London fogs" of my child-hood',[38] and of 'the dreary wastes of Kensington and Earl's Court', home of the slowly expiring upper middle-class.[39] However, his new address placed him close to his lively Aunt Nellie at Notting Hill, and it must have been through her that he discovered London music halls. Runciman remembered that he was quite an aficionado, loved singing the comic songs and was a fan of such performers as Little Tich, George Robey and the legendary Marie Lloyd, who he always liked to boast having seen perform. Robey, one of the country's star comedians, was even persuaded to write a letter for *College Days*.[40] And although he had no ear for music, he certainly had an ear for bawdy music-hall songs, rich with sexual innuendo.[41]

The Great War was making it patently evident that science, so often linked with progress by writers such as Wells, was also potentially baleful. Evilly applied science now threatened man's future, bringing closer the night-mares foretold in dystopian novels such as M. P. Shiel's *The Purple Cloud* and *The Yellow Peril*.[42] As a sign of things to come, in June 1917, a few days before his fourteen birthday, the first-ever bombs were dropped over London from a squadron of German aeroplanes – a powerful image that was to haunt his novel *Coming Up For Air*. Far distant from bombs over London, and passing almost unnoticed at the time, the October Revolution overthrew the Provisional Government of Alexander Kerensky in Petrograd, bringing the Bolshevik Communists to power in Russia. An experiment in social engineering on a vast scale would come to grip the minds of many of Blair's heroes, including Wells and Shaw, and go to make a world which in time he would play his part in unmaking.

The old fascination with how things worked, encouraged by Mr Sillar at St Cyprian's, and by his attachment to Wells, had not left him. For a year (from Michaelmas 1918 to Michaelmas 1919), together with Roger Mynors, he dropped Classics to concentrate on Science for School Certificate, which meant switching tutors from Gow to John Christie, the man who later founded Glyndebourne. Eton was not without a science tradition. It had, after all, produced Robert Boyle, 'the father of modern chemistry'. Blair and Mynors shared a curiosity about the function of animal systems, and particularly enjoyed cutting things up. On one occasion they attempted to dissect a jackdaw, shot by Blair with his catapult on the Chapel roof. By mistake they cut open the gall bladder, which gave off such a stench that thenceforth all such experiments were abandoned. Even so, both went on to obtain School Certificates with matriculation that summer, just past their sixteenth birthdays. To hope for Oxford or Cambridge entrance, Eric now needed to specialise further for Higher School Certificate. But by the beginning of the 1919 Michaelmas half, he had abandoned Science and returned to Gow, who no longer listed him as a Classics specialist but as part of a General Studies group, not considered good enough for Classical Higher. Unintentionally perhaps, by allowing himself to be removed from the specialist group, Blair seems to have spoilt his chances of going to university. However, for the time being, with School Certificate out of the way, the scholastic atmosphere lightened and now he could indulge in wider interests.

French had been a passion since St Cyprian's. Until that summer Aldous Huxley had taught French at Eton, and both Blair and Runciman were greatly impressed by him, as was Lord David Cecil, a slightly older Oppidan. Cecil recalled the very strange excessively tall figure, with pebble glasses and bohemian dress, 'walking out . . . dressed in a delicate dove-grey, a black sombrero & round his neck a flowing scarf of flame-coloured silk which contrasted with his white countenance & waving dark hair, which he grew much longer than was common in those days'.[43] Runciman remembered him more as an inspiring teacher. Being almost blind, he could not see much beyond the first row, and some boys, knowing this, would misbehave, some even playing bridge at the back of the class. Blair thought it outrageous that a blind man should be treated in this way, but he and Runciman found Huxley's lessons riveting, especially his unusual use of language,[44] and Blair was also impressed by his familiarity with France and French literature.[45] He was reading a great deal of French fiction – Anatole France, Flaubert, Zola and Maupassant, whose stories 'Boule de Suif' and 'La Maison Tellier' he read and reread. Flaubert, like Dostoevsky, appealed probably because from him – and later from Joyce – he got 'the feeling that here was a country of the mind which one had always known to exist, but which one had never thought of as lying within the scope of fiction'.[46]

Now he took up Extra English with George Lyttelton. Unfortunately, in those days there were no Oxbridge English scholarships on offer at Eton.

English literature was an 'afterthought' and its teachers reflected a wide range of approaches. Hugh Macnaghten, for example, was in love with flowery language and believed, with Ford Maddox Ford, that prose was as good a vehicle for poetry as was verse. George Lyttelton's literary taste, according to Runciman, was not that of Blair, who was keen on American literature, especially Mark Twain, Walt Whitman and Jack London. (At his death Orwell still had a volume of Whitman's poems, a sixteenth birthday present from his father.) Twain was a particular favourite, especially *Roughing It*, a novel of tramping life, and *Huckleberry Finn*, from which he derived his 'fictional world' of the Deep South. Whatever he thought of Lyttelton, in Extra English he was at least studying a school subject that coincided with his literary ambitions.

Orwell was full of self-contradictions. Although he said later that he 'learned very little' at Eton,[47] elsewhere he implied otherwise, hinting at masters steeped in literary scholarship 'from whom one absorbs wisdom unawares'.[48] One example stands out. He complained that having to do Lyttelton's Extra English involved reading Milton, 'for whom he had no love',[49] yet the great Miltonian themes of *Paradise Lost* and *Paradise Regained* were to be echoed in every work of imagination he later produced, although, pessimistically, he reversed the sequence. And it was through reading *Paradise Lost*, he later said, that he suddenly discovered 'the joy of mere words', their 'sounds and associations'.[50]

Simply in terms of his studies, he absorbed a great deal as a Colleger, and surviving records, fragments and memoirs, chime with significant elements in his later life. For example, in his first few months at the College he read Aristophanes and La Fontaine, a classical and a medieval fabulist, progenitors of the talking animal, and in College he himself came to be known as a writer of fables, stories with a moral, often to be read aloud. It may have been on Lyttelton's desk that he once found a magazine open and for the first time read a poem by D. H. Lawrence.[51] And it was probably from Lyttelton that he learned about *Dialogues of the Dead,* composed by his illustrious ancestor, the first Lord Lyttelton, which included imaginary conversations with dead writers, such as Pope. Almost thirty years later, for radio, George Orwell would create a similar dialogue with Swift, though in his case there was the usual moral appended, namely, 'Consider history if you want to understand the present.'[52]

The *College Chronicle* ran editorials, often in the essay tradition of William Hazlitt, Charles Lamb and Robert Louis Stevenson on subjects such as 'Pub Signs', 'Food Psychology' and 'The Top Hat' – a tradition to which Orwell harked back later in his 'As I Please' column for *Tribune*, and in essays on aspects of English culture, such as boys' comics, seaside postcards and an imaginary pub. There was a reference in one *Chronicle* editorial to the 'morning hate' session of the Prussian family, which was held responsible for 'the type of mind which is convinced of its absolute infallibility and which therefore argues that "might is right"'[53] – not so far from 'Hate Week' and the Inner Party mind-set in *Nineteen Eighty-Four*. One anonymous essay in the *Chronicle*, when Blair's friend King-Farlow was editor, speculated on the life of the tramp in relation to the millionaire, and there was an attack on suburban respectability which could have come straight from the mouth of Gordon Comstock.[54] Blair's critical ruthlessness was doubtless boosted when a *Chronicle* article eulogised 'the critical spirit', maintaining that 'Great critics have often been the contemporaries of great poets and great historians . . . To be alive to the errors of others is often the starting-point for a great production either in literature or art.' 'Criticism to us,' it concluded, 'is the breath of life.'[55] An earlier *Chronicle* editorial had argued that pacifists merely gave ammunition to the enemy, the very argument Orwell used against pacifists in the Second World War; another warned against the 'delusive rumours of joys of a literary career' and attacked 'vulgar, pedantic, self-centred, conceited forms of exaggeration'.[56] These ideas, circulating at Eton during Blair's time, imbibed and slowly digested over the years, cannot be entirely disassociated from identifiable elements in the mature works of George Orwell. And in almost everything he later wrote there was the implied moral.

In Eton ephemerals the emphasis was satirical. Blair contributed amusing pieces on a masters' strike (with Lenin and Trotsky being discussed in the College), a revolution where science takes over Eton, the social snobbery of girls visiting the College, all bearing palpable traces of Wodehouse and *Punch*. In *College Days* he published a short story on spiritualism that reads like a sardonic reflection on the Yorke affair, suggesting that, like Runciman, it continued to haunt him. Purporting to be written by 'The Bishop of Borstall', it reflected in part on the devastating effect on a boy of taking part in a seance. Blair's ambivalence towards the supernatural is captured in his Shakespearean conclusion – 'There are more things in heaven and earth, Horatio . . .'[57] And although he himself never again ventured into sympathetic magic using wax effigies, he had by no means lost his fascination with it. However, the pen, he was to discover, was mightier than the pin and could be used to skewer one's victims, often with far greater satisfaction.

In addition to the ferment of ideas then current in the College, there was also an Eton tradition, no doubt also absorbed unconsciously, of dissent and deviation. One sixteenth-century Etonian, Greenhall, is said to have been hung, drawn and quartered at Tyburn for highway robbery, another is listed in Fox's *Book of Martyrs*, but the most celebrated Etonian deviant and dissenter before Orwell was Shelley. At his death Orwell still had a collection of Shelley's poems acquired at Eton, and was undoubtedly the inheritor of the Shelleyan spirit of revolution tinged with romance and not a little tragedy. This lesser-known Eton tradition of radical dissent was one with which Blair could readily identify.

By September 1918, just before the war ended, the Blairs had moved to 23 Mall Chambers, a low-rental apartment in Kensington, close to Notting Hill Gate. For young Eric it must have been a congenial area, with its many literary associations. Chesterton was born there, William Cobbett began and finished his rural rides there and Ford Maddox Ford lived close by. Mall Chambers was also just a short walk from Aunt Nellie's flat in Ladbroke Grove, where Chesterton, E. Nesbit, M. P. Shiel and Wells were said to attend her salons. Moving in such circles must have been a heady experience for the aspiring young author. Nellie would prove herself a great champion of 'Eric, the FAMOUS AUTHOR', and visiting her probably did much to keep the flame of authorship alive in him.

London also offered playhouses. He loved the theatre. Towards the end of the war, among a lively and appreciative audience of newly returned soldiers, he saw Shaw's *Arms and the Man* – a play which echoed the playwright's 1914 exhortation urging soldiers to shoot their officers and go home. At Christmas 1920 he saw two plays in two days – H. De Vere Stackpole's *The Blue Lagoon* and John Gay's *The Beggar's Opera*, the widely acclaimed Nigel Playfair production at the Lyric Theatre, Hammersmith. And there must have been numberless visits to music halls to savour the popular culture, the jokes and songs of the day, many recalled in a London *Evening Standard* essay a quarter of a century later.[58]

At Eton, Blair, the aloof cynic and Socratic disputer of all things sacred, enjoyed a reputation for strangeness, which gave him charisma in the eyes of some boys. He broke rules, and broke bounds from time to time – an elusive, almost romantic presence recalled by the slightly younger Harold Acton as 'a stork-like figure, prematurely adult, fluttering about the school yard in his black gown'.[59] In an Eton notebook full of gossip, Connolly offered another glimpse of the lofty cynic in his den: 'Blair amid a litter of cigarette ash drinks tea from a samovar which hisses insidiously to Eastwood and Watkins who try to run away but a horrible magnetism detains them – he oozes distrust from Miss Oughterson – tracts flutter round his head and in the seclusion of an upstairs room Connolly lies – not alone – in his armchair.'[60] Smoking, strictly forbidden at Eton, was a new habit for Eric. He had, he later told Prosper, discovered the delights of Turkish tobacco,[61] and no doubt his cigarettes were hand-rolled. And on a quaintly domestic note, Watkins recalled that he obtained cream from somewhere and made butter and cheese in his room. So the picture is complete. Blair amid pamphlets and smoking a rolled Turkish cigarette, stands between churn and samovar holding forth to terrified juniors about the despotism of wealth.

As in any enclosed society of adolescent boys, Eton too had its strangely intense emotional undercurrents. Henry Green wrote of its 'feminine' atmosphere, charged with frustrated sexuality. Connolly recalled and anatomised its complex sub-culture of half-suppressed lust and coded allusions. Even the detached ironist Blair was not entirely immune from the attractions of younger boys. Once he and Connolly found themselves competing for the same object of desire. In a letter to which Connolly added ironic comments from *Eric; or, Little by Little* in the style of *Stalky & Co.*, Blair informed him,

> I am afraid I'm gone on Eastwood (naughty Eric). This may surprise you but it is not imagination, I assure you (with no shame and remorse) . . . I think you are too (to the pure all things are pure), at any rate you were at the end of last half. I am not jealous of you (noble Eric). But you, though you aren't jealous, are apt to be what I might call "proprietary". Don't suspect me of ill intentions either. If I had not written to you until about 3 weeks into the next half you would notice how things stood, your proprietary instincts would have been aroused and having a lot of influence over Eastwood, you would probably have put him against me somehow, perhaps even warned him off me. Please don't do this I implore you. Of course I don't ask you to resign your share in him, only don't say *spiteful things*.

But, wrote Connolly, 'Eastwood . . . is full of suspicion as he hates Blair.'[62]

Away from Eton, girls, whom he regarded as 'something unattainable', were never far from his thoughts. The poet who expressed the feelings of unfulfilled love most perfectly for him was A.E. Housman, whose 'blasphemous, antinomian, "cynical' strain' he approved, and whose *A Shropshire Lad* he knew off by heart at seventeen.[63]

> With rue my heart is laden
> For golden friends I had,
> For many a rose-lipt maiden
> And many a lightfoot man.
>
> By brooks too broad for leaping
> The lightfoot boys are laid;
> The rose-lipt girls are sleeping
> In fields where roses fade.

At Ticklerton Court, where he spent most holidays, Jacintha, who had turned pantheist, was still the centre of his youthful longing. In the autumn of 1918 he dedicated a poem to her, 'The Pagan', with just a hint of lust about it, beginning: 'So here are you, and here am I,/Where we may thank our gods to be;/Above the earth, beneath the sky,/Naked souls alive and free.' But Jacintha was having nothing to do with 'naked souls' and substituted 'unarmoured souls', writing years afterwards, 'It was our minds, our hopes, our dreams, that were confided so freely and so guilelessly; we were not cavorting about in the altogether.'[64] However, for Eric, their friendship was no mere meeting of minds. At Ticklerton at Christmas he wrote her another poem, more in Housman vein, for there in Shropshire, fleetingly at least, he was a Shropshire lad. 'Our minds are married, but we are too young/For wedlock by the customs of this age/When parent homes pen each in separate cage/And only supper-earning songs are sung . . .' From what she said in old age, Jacintha either missed or deliberately ignored the deep feeling which Eric put into these verses.

Eton not only produced men of great power and eminence, but attracted important visitors, too. Monarchs dropped in from Windsor, Francis Bacon had visited the College, as had Milton, Defoe, Boswell, Pepys and Mary Wollstonecraft. In Blair's time visitors included Herbert Asquith (Prime Minister till the end of 1916, next to whom Blair, K. S., would one day find himself in quite other circumstances); M. Coué, inventor of auto-suggestion, and A. E. Housman, friend and sometime lover of A. S. F. Gow, came to talk to the Literary Society. On one occasion a 'living god' paid a visit, young Hirohito of Japan, who the boys (some later incarcerated in Japanese prison camps) greeted in School Yard with cries of 'Banzai!' The end of the war was marked by a visit from seventeen Old Etonian generals, including four of the major commanders on the Western Front under Haig – Rawlinson, Plumer, Cavan and Byng. Rawlinson addressed the assembled College, quoting Kipling's 'If' and announcing that it was the English spirit of 'playing the game' which had brought victory against Germany, and that effectively the war had been won on the playing fields of Eton.[65] The Honour Roll at Eton listed 1,160 dead and 1,467 wounded.

But the buoyant mood of the generals was not shared by the boys. As 'Tubby' Bowling reflects in *Coming Up For Air*, 'a mood of disbelief was moving across England',[66] and it did not bypass Eton. There were minor riots in School Yard, the head of the OTC was booed and forced to resign. The young iconoclasts had come into their own. By the end of the war the most progressive boys at the College would probably have called themselves 'socialists' or 'revolutionaries', or even 'Bolshevists', but mostly as a gesture to upset the 'Vile Old Men'. It was probably his 'socialism' that led

Blair to Jack London's *The People of the Abyss*, first discovered at Eton. Like Gordon Comstock, he was probably already 'against the money-god and all his swinish priesthood'.[67] As to religion, he said that 'the version [of Jesus] that was thrust upon me by my schoolmasters outraged common sense'. Far more impressive was Winwood Reade's *The Martyrdom of Man*, which presented Christ not as 'a Great Moral Teacher' but simply as 'a fallible human being like any other – a noble character on the whole, but with serious faults and, in any case, only one of a long line of Jewish fanatics'. But it was also Reade who warned that communism, once established, could develop into a caste system – 'a penetrating remark to make in 1871', he thought. Even as a young man he had been alerted to a dangerous tendency in the new great Soviet experiment.[68]

Along with other senior Collegers, Blair was now allowed the privilege of taking breakfast with M. R. James, according to Anthony Powell, 'a shrouded but powerful eminence in the wings' of the College. The Provost was a man of great charm and erudition, who very much enjoyed entertaining boys. The highpoint on such occasions was the telling of one of his celebrated ghost stories, remembered by Powell as 'in a class by themselves for a particular brand of eerie horror'.[69] The ones that appealed to Eric most were 'Come to Me and I'll Whistle, my Boy' and 'Casting the Runes'. Considering his fascination with rodents, doubtless he also enjoyed the one called 'Rats', culminating in the horrific image of the creatures swarming under bedclothes over the remains of a dead body. He told Jacintha that James was his hero, and that he admired him greatly as a stylist.[70] One of his least successful ephemeral contributions, however, is an awkward pastiche of a Jamesian ghost story.

Teaming up with King-Farlow to edit *College Days*, gave him a regular outlet for his satire. He inserted a scurrilous personal ad hinting broadly at the Master-in-College's rumoured predilection for pretty boys, and made up a bawdy verse attacking Gow with more than a touch of Limouzin waspishness and sly innuendo.

> Then up waddled Wog and he squeaked in Greek,
> 'I've grown another hair on my cheek.'
> Crace replied in Latin with his toadlike smile
> 'And I hope you've grown a lovely new pile.
> With a loud deep fart from the bottom of my heart!
> How d'you like Venetian art?'[71]

The critic who reviewed *College Days* for the *Chronicle* admired its wit, but deplored its cruelty, and a letter from some Vile Old Man denounced it as 'nauseating nonsense'. Another reviewer was a little kinder, saying, 'The

Editors of *College Days* . . . are undoubtedly humorists; they are equally undoubtedly knaves, and it is impossible for a combination of such excellent characteristics to produce a dull magazine.'[72] On their final issue of June 1922 they made a healthy profit of £128 by aiming at the Eton–Harrow cricket-match crowd, and carrying some prestigious advertising – for Pascall Versailes Chocolates, Aertex Cellular Clothing, Rolls-Royce cars and Sunbeam motorbikes.[73] Gordon Comstock would not have been amused.

In December 1919 Richard was demobilised, and the family moved back to their Henley house, but kept the Mall Chambers flat on as a *pied à terre*. In the following July Marjorie married her old flame Humphrey and settled in London. Shortly afterwards, at Mall Chambers, Eric met the 22-year-old poet Ruth Pitter, who had been invited to dinner. She was very struck by the young Etonian at first sight, 'a tall youth, with hair the colour of hay and a brown tweed suit', with 'formidable blue eyes . . . an exact pair'. He later told her that he had thought to himself, 'I wonder if that girl would be hard to get,' suggesting that he had acquired the habit of fantasising about women sexually.[74] But, whatever he may have been thinking about Ruth and other women, his thoughts were still largely with Jacintha. He became a familiar figure each summer at Shiplake and Ticklerton, hunting and causing explosions with Prosper, and sharing ideas with his sister. One day in August 1920 he went shooting with Jacintha and reportedly shot nothing; all their time together was spent talking.[75] Once, in 1921, when Prosper was ill, he stayed with relatives at Burstall near Ipswich on the River Orwell (again in the footsteps of Defoe), and told Prosper he had spent his Christmas holidays hunting and caging rats. 'This place is overrun with rats. It is rather good sport to catch a rat, and then let it out and shoot at it as it runs.'[76]

The first part of that summer, however, he spent again with his family in Cornwall. En route from OTC camp, he got stranded after leaving the train briefly at Seaton Junction. With almost no money and fearing arrest he bedded down in a field, using his cap for a pillow. After a freezing night he finally got a train to Looe, then walked the last four miles to Polperro in blazing sunshine. He wrote to Runciman about this, his 'first adventure as an amateur tramp'.[77] It would not be his last.

Runciman was growing too fast for his own health and became so ill that he left Eton a year early. Blair had a similar experience, but with not quite such drastic results. Although once at Eton he was struck down with pneumonia, in his fifteenth year he grew a good three inches. By 1921 he weighed 12st 3lbs, giving him the confidence, despite a certain ungainliness, to throw himself more into winter sports, especially the Wall Game. Christopher

Eastwood remembered him coming back into College covered in mud and looking very pleased with himself for 'having achieved something at last'.[78] He played for various College teams both in the peculiar football game played 'in the field' at Eton, and in the Wall Game, that equally peculiarly Etonian sport which required a good deal of brawn. It was in the field that Blair came off badly against his old tormentor Verrall, who had returned to the College on a visit. At short notice, the visitor turned out for a scratch team, giving Blair, on the opposing side, an opportunity to revenge himself. But Verrall was a natural athlete and *his* side made mincemeat of Blair's. As the report says, 'Mr Verrall proved almost invincible behind . . . The best of the behinds was G. J. Verrall Esq., who played extraordinarily well, in spite of his lack of practice . . . Johnson and Blair were very bad.'[79] There would be time enough for him get back at the Verralls of this world.

In the Wall Game, however, some athletic glory still awaited him. Reports of his play were improving, and on one memorable occasion he was party to an event of considerable rarity – the scoring of a goal. In this strange game, played against the long wall separating the College from the Slough Road, a series of scrimmages for possession of the ball give rise to various kicks, passes and throws leading, in theory, to goals. For a goal to be scored the ball has to hit an elm tree with a white line painted on it at one end of the pitch or a door in the wall at the other. On one occasion Blair sent a long pass to Longden who managed to score a goal. John Lehmann, new in College, was thrilled to be present and wrote, 'I had witnessed that extremely rare event, a goal scored in the Wall Game, and what made it more exciting for me it had been scored by my fagmaster Bobbie Longden with the aid of Eric Blair.'[80] When eventually he received his Wall Colours entitling him to wear a long coloured scarf, he was delighted. It was one of the few honours that came his way at Eton, meriting a profile in the *College Chronicle*.[81] Winning his colours, and the St Andrew's Day Wall Game (played annually against the Oppidans) were obviously important to him, and it may be no coincidence that *Keep the Aspidistra Flying*, the novel about his failed poetic self, opens on that saint's day. The long scarf, worn in preference to an overcoat, was for a while his favoured winter dress, once resulting in a severe attack of pneumonia. But recklessness was in style at Eton. One Old Colleger, according to his obituary, went over the top to his death in Flanders proudly wearing his Wall Game colours.[82]

He had his swansong to sing in his final half at Eton. As a Sixth Former, according to tradition, he delivered a public speech, choosing to read a passage from Stevenson's 'The Suicide Club'. The *Chronicle* called his performance 'a fine piece of oratory' and commended 'the even and unmoved coolness with which Blair let the story make its own effect [which] was certainly very successful'.[83] It should be noted, however, that the author of this piece was none other than Blair's old crony King-Farlow.

Although he now loathed Kipling and what he stood for, the idea of colonial service was always somewhere at the back of his mind. Runciman remembered him talking continually about the mysterious East, an enchantment they shared, though for different reasons.[84] Blair's fascination was that of the adventurer, the storyteller, Runciman's that of the scholar curious to retrieve the past. For Blair, missing the war was a serious gap in his life, an adventure denied to him by history. Serving the Empire at least offered a pale imitation of war service in uniform on foreign shores, and he would also be returning to his roots, a powerful attraction in itself. But there was also the tug of university.

To his friends the Buddicoms, Eton and Harrow were the gateways to Oxford or Cambridge, and the idea of throwing away such an opportunity seemed criminal. Eric's feelings for Jacintha were certainly stronger than she imagined, feelings he had tried to convey to her through poems which she had treated merely as subjects for practical criticism. Despite this his feelings persisted, and that she favoured a university career must have weighed with him because of his hopes for their future together. However, as there was no prospect of his father being able to afford the fees, he would need a scholarship.

From what is known, Eric's own views were never recorded, although Gow said later that in discussing his future Blair was intent on Burma, which merely coincided with his own view that he was unsuitable university material.[85] Richard Blair also consulted Gow about his son's chances of a bursary. His hope for him, it seems, was the Indian Civil Service, which required a degree,[86] but Gow told him that Eric was unlikely to gain a scholarship, and would be wasting his time even to try. As far as Richard was concerned that seemed to have settled the matter.[87] Gow later told Bernard Crick that to have recommended Blair for Cambridge would have demeaned Eton. (Curiously enough, Gow's father had taught D. H. Lawrence at Nottingham High School, and had greatly encouraged him. The son, it seems, did not inherit the father's talent to inspire.)[88] He hardly compared with more diligent contemporaries – Runciman, King-Farlow, Yorke and Watkins, or Connolly who had won the Brackenbury Scholarship to Balliol College, Oxford. But Blair's Eton contemporary Hollis thought Gow's advice wrong; Eton Collegers were rarely refused Oxbridge scholarships. Even so, without the support of his tutor it might have been difficult, and Gow considered him a lazy, 'very unattractive' boy, difficult and even insolent. And he may well have had personal reasons for not wanting Blair at the university – his own ambitions centred on Cambridge and the thought of this unpleasant sarcastic atheist dogging his heels might have been too much to bear. Gow was thought by some who knew him at Cambridge later, including Runciman and George Lyttelton, to be an obnoxiously arrogant and high-handed snob. He would have had very little sympathy for a boy who had turned his back on the Classics, taken up Science, and failed to shine even at that. Since university and the Indian Civil Service were ruled out, the Indian Police was probably Eric's own idea.

When he left the College he did not join the Old Etonian Society, but he could never avoid being thereafter an Old Etonian.

Eric did not seem to fight Gow's verdict on his chance of an Oxbridge scholarship. Had Jacintha gone to university – the Buddicom family money was spent on Prosper instead – he might have had a greater incentive to go himself. She seemed oblivious of her own part in this drama and quite unaware of how he felt about her. In what she called the 'glorious, unforgettably, hot summer' of 1921, the Blairs took a house in Rickmansworth, and it was there that he made her a final poetic offering, almost an elegy for what might have been.

> Friendship and love are closely intertwined,
> My heart belongs to your befriending mind:
> But chilling sunlit fields, cloud-shadows fall –
> My love can't reach your heedless heart at all.

Her response in verse was 'By light/Too bright/Are dazzled eyes betrayed:/It's best/To rest/Content in tranquil shade.' As an old woman, still refusing to acknowledge what was being said to her, she commented, 'Typical of both of us, Eric with his straightforward, ten-syllable couplets, and me chopping up the same metre into shorter lines with extra rhymes to them, which I thought more fun to do and more singable.' A year later, Eric proposed marriage, asking her to go with him to Burma, but she refused. She was, of course, two years older than him and did not consider him right for her. Also, being a young highbrow, the fact that he was not going to university probably coloured her decision. She might have embraced the intellectual Eric, but not the passionate adventurer heading off into the heart of darkness. Whatever the case, her rejection affected him deeply, and probably explains much of what happened to him afterwards, as he hinted to her in a letter not long before he died. She had 'abandoned' him to Burma, he told her, 'with all hope denied'.[89]

Soon after Eric left Eton, the Blairs moved from Henley to Southwold on the Suffolk coast. Defoe, passing through the town in 1722, noted the proliferation of migrating swallows in the early summer, the lavish catches of sprats and herrings, the imposing thirteenth-century church and the town's large Dissenter congregations.[90] The Suffolk coast thereabouts had a history of sea battles and bombardments, and many gallant rescues. The light and the sweeping seascapes attracted painters; Wilson Steer and Walter Sickert, Gilbert Spenser and Claude Rogers (founder of the Euston Road group) all spent time there. By the 1920s it had evolved into a somewhat old-fashioned seaside resort, a town much favoured by retired Anglo-Indians. It was also the home of the pottery company for which Ruth Pitter worked, and it was Ruth's partner, Kate O'Hara, who had recommended it to the Blairs.

From 1920, Southwold had been the site of the Duke of York's summer camp, where boys from all classes were encouraged to mingle, and which famously featured community singing around the camp-fire, 'Under the Spreading Chestnut Tree' becoming its symbolic song of shared comradeship. The Blairs lived on Stradbroke Road at South Green, close to the beach and the River Blyth, with its ferry-crossing to Walberswick. They had Anglo-Indian friends there and a golf club, which suited Richard. Eric found the local landscape rather unexciting, as he hints in *A Clergyman's Daughter*: 'Not that there was anything worth looking at – only the low, barely undulating East Anglian landscape, intolerably dull in summer, but redeemed in winter by the recurring pattern of the elms, naked and fan-shaped against leaden skies.'[91] However, in the summer Southwold became something of an artist's colony, and there were literary associations to compensate for the lack of topographical variety. Not only had Johnson and Defoe written about the town in passing, but the East Anglian coast had Dickensian connections and was the setting of some of the most haunting stories of the much-admired 'Monty' James.

In January 1922 he joined a cramming school in Southwold, and three months later applied to join the Indian Imperial Police Force, with a character reference from Crace. No other Etonian, it seems, had ever applied to join the force, and Blair was probably the last. As if to remind him of the orbit of power he was about to abandon for a life of semi-obscurity, the *College Chronicle* proudly announced that the new cabinet included sixteen Old Etonians, with twenty-two others sitting in the House of Commons, while the new owner of *The Times*, the country's most influential daily, was also an Old Etonian. By accident or design he had stepped out of the magic circle into the shadows, not necessarily a bad move for an aspiring writer, but there came a time when he seemed to regret what he had done.

During that year, while he was preparing for Burma, the world was showing signs of change, some ominous. Mussolini led his Fascists in a march on Rome, nationalists murdered the German Foreign Minister in Berlin,

Mahatma Gandhi, the Indian nationalist, was jailed, Lawrence's erotic paintings were banned, Chesterton converted to Catholicism and in Paris James Joyce's *Ulysses* was published. While none of these events may have registered with him at the time, the long-term effects certainly would.

That summer, Steven Runciman, who had already spent two years at Cambridge, was cruising in his grandfather's yacht to Oslo and Copenhagen and through the Kiel Canal to Hamburg, hobnobbing with Danish royalty and German shipping magnates. Meanwhile, two days after his nineteenth birthday in June, Blair was in London sitting through four days of examinations to determine his future career in a remote and little-known corner of the Empire. In August he learned that he had come seventh out of twenty-nine candidates with 8,464 marks out of a possible 12,400, doing best in English and French, and best of all in Greek (1,703 out of a possible 2,000) and Latin (1,782). When his results came through he moved to London to stay with Marjorie and Humphrey at Mall Chambers. He had a medical in September and a riding test in which he scored 104 out of 200. Shortly afterwards his appointment was confirmed. Asked to state a posting preference he put Burma first, giving the reason 'Have relatives there' and United Provinces second, because 'My father was there for some years.' His choice of Burma over India suggests a vote against his father in favour of the Limouzins. But what Nellie and Charlie (and indeed his own mother) thought, having escaped the place as soon as they could, and perhaps remembering skeletons left behind in cupboards, is unknown.

The fact that he achieved higher marks in Classics than in English suggests that, given the right encouragement, he might have obtained that Cambridge scholarship after all, but that opportunity had passed. The *St Cyprian's Chronicle*, always ready to claim achievements for its alumni, carried the note, 'We tender congratulations to E. Blair (Eton) on passing high up on the list into the Indian Police this August.'[92] But here was one Old Boy who would never return, unlike Cyril Connolly, who, as a chastened adult, would dutifully attend Flip's funeral, then choose to live the last years of his life in Eastbourne, a short walk from the site of the old school.*

The newly appointed Probationary Assistant Superintendent Blair was now well over six feet and solidly built like his father. He was about to spend another five years 'within the sound of bugles'. The cost of his kit was £150, a sum that would probably have seen Eric through university for at least a year in those days. But there was no turning back. He had endured the hell of St Cyprian's and in his own way enjoyed the paradise of Eton. Now he was heading for another landscape, another unknown country. It was a

---

* St Cyprian's burnt down in 1939.

pattern he would repeat and which would recur throughout his life and fiction.

As an Assistant Superintendent he would be earning more than his father received in pension, in addition to which, as an incentive to young Britons to serve in those parts, a monthly overseas allowance of 100 rupees would be paid in sterling directly into his English bank account, a nest-egg which would come in useful five years later. But for now it meant abandoning the dream of writing (as Jacintha, his muse, had abandoned *him*), almost as an act of self-mutilation, 'with the consciousness,' he wrote, 'that I was out-raging my true nature'.[95]

What he hoped to get out of Burma is difficult to know – adventure, no doubt, and the sight of mysterious lands like Gulliver, perhaps, or a life of isolated self-sufficiency like Robinson Crusoe, which Runciman thought might have suited him.[96] There was also the guilt felt over the death of Philip Yorke to be expiated. A remote region among strangers offered the chance to begin again with a clear conscience and a clean sheet. Going to Burma was a necessary retreat into the wilderness, where he could come to terms with nightmares, wrestle with his demons. Rather more cynically, Christopher Hollis said the real reason was 'a deep need not to conform',[97] and certainly he seemed always to prefer the poorer option, to occupy the marginal role. However, much later, reviewing E. M. Forster's *A Passage to India*, he implied something quite unintended, saying, 'It is only by some improbable accident that anyone capable of writing a decent novel can be got to stay in India long enough to absorb the atmosphere.'[98] What that 'improbable accident' was in his case we are left to ponder.

Chapter 5

'The Pain of Exile'

'But who that has not suffered it understands the pain of exile?'

Orwell, *Burmese Days*, 1934

Eric Blair, the smartly turned-out new imperial policeman, set sail from Liverpool for Rangoon, a first-class passenger on board the Bibby Line's SS *Herefordshire*, on 27 October 1922. With one other new recruit, his destination was the Police Training School in Mandalay. Ahead lay not just an unfamiliar climate, an alien landscape and a mixture of languages and cultures needing to be understood and mastered, but also the Burmese remnants of the Limouzin family. The passenger list for Rangoon included a fair cross section of Anglo-Indian society, from whom he would have got some idea of what lay ahead.

But no doubt he had taken his own 'false map' of the East with him, absorbed from his family, from novels, and, from shows like *Chu Chin Chow* – the dream of a '"gorgeous East" where, as is well-known, everyone has fifty wives and spends his time lying on a divan, eating pomegranates' with the beguiling prospect of 'droves of women, practically naked and painted to an agreeable walnut-juice tint'. In the nineteen-year-old Blair there was obviously a considerable lack of guile and a great bubble of illusion waiting to be punctured.

The passage to Rangoon took just over four weeks and there was always a faint air of opulence about trans-continental liners such as the *Herefordshire*. Evening dress was de rigueur, and, amid the general *joie de vivre*, sexual escapades were often part of the carnival.[1] Assistant Superintendent Blair readily sampled some of the delights of shipboard life, although he later recalled the mountains of food with an air of mild disapproval.[2] Whether he was tempted into a shipboard romance he never said. He had, of course, little experience with women and was still in mourning for the girl who had abandoned him. However, on such a voyage there was much to observe, many incidents to store away in the memory, to reflect on and later interpret.

As it had been for Conrad, putting into Marseilles was Blair's first chance to set foot on French soil and must have awakened a sense of his French ancestry and an affinity for Gallic culture. Later he would return to the city and choose France as the starting point of his writing career. Back onboard the *Herefordshire*, he witnessed a strangely un-Conradian incident. Strolling on deck, he saw the ship's quartermaster scuttling along 'like a rat' clutching the remains of a custard pudding, obviously a leftover from the passengers' dining room slipped to him by a steward, and he was shocked and astonished that a man so important to the ship should behave in this way. It was a 'revelation': 'that a highly-skilled craftsman, who might literally hold all our lives in his hands, was glad to steal scraps of food from our table – taught me more than I could have learned from half a dozen Socialist pamphlets'. At a glance he was able 'to see the incident in all its bearing', and so take in at once an entire system of privilege and power operating among the passengers and crew. His detachment as a schoolboy had given him a sharp sociological eye, an ability to recognise very quickly how things worked. It was an amalgam of the scientist and the visionary, an attitude picked up from Wells, Shaw and Butler, that of the sardonic observer with ideals – a view of how things are and how things ought to be.

At Port Said he got his first glimpse of the mysterious East, and as the ship passed along the Suez Canal, and he began absorbing the alien landscape, he became aware of a strange change in his outlook.

> In northern Europe, when you see a labourer ploughing a field, you probably give him a second glance . . . Anywhere south of Gibraltar or east of Suez . . . one's eye takes in everything except the human beings. It takes in the dried-up soil, the prickly pear, the palm-tree and the distant mountain, but it always misses the peasant hoeing at his patch. He is the same colour as the earth, and a great deal less interesting to look at.[3]

Doubtless on the ship he had already learned something of the pukka sahib mind-set, and 'tasted the agreeable atmosphere of Clubs, with punkahs flapping and barefooted white-turbaned boys reverently salaaming; and maidans where bronzed English-men with little clipped moustaches galloped to and fro, whacking polo balls'.[4] East of Suez was, of course, Kipling country, and already he would have begun to learn the argot of imperialism and been fed the myth about European skulls needing the topi's protection from the sun unlike oriental skulls,[5] and perhaps, like one of his predecessors, told the proper way to treat natives – 'not to give way to an Indian on the sidewalk, when there was no room to pass, but insist on crowding him into the street'.[6] He had no reason not to swallow all this and the rest of the Anglo-Indian mythology. However, Burma for him would be a process of regurgitating and ridding himself of such beliefs and sentiments, and in the process he would also divest himself of much of his own class ideology.

After Suez came the Red Sea, where Captain Richard Blair had plunged to a watery grave just eleven years earlier, then the long haul across the Indian Ocean before a stopover at Colombo, his first sight of British India, recaptured in *Burmese Days*: 'They sailed into Colombo through green glassy waters, where turtles and black snakes floated basking. A fleet of sampans came racing out to meet the ship, propelled by coal-black men with lips stained redder than blood by betel juice.'[7] If he was still unaware of the true nature of the great Empire, it was brought home to him brutally before ever he stepped ashore. As the ship docked, he was horrified by the sight of a white policeman kicking a coolie without a word of protest from any of the ship's passengers. 'Here were ordinary, decent, middling people,' he wrote, 'people with incomes of about £500 a year, watching the scene with no emotion whatever except a mild approval. They were white, and the coolie was black. In other words he was sub-human, a different kind of animal.'[8] This event must have struck him as ominous, a preview of a far more oppressive system than the English class system onboard ship. Now he was heading in all innocence to become part of such a regime himself. What is more, the oppressor he had observed was a policeman, filling exactly the role he was himself engaged to fill in Burma.

Ashore there were more disturbing sights. Through the colourful crowded streets of Colombo, invisible to most eyes, scurried the rickshaw-men. This 'vile sight of men running between shafts like horses'[9] came to symbolise something deeply offensive to young Blair – one human using another literally as a beast. This memory would resurface later in Paris, triggered by his treatment as a slavish dishwasher.[10] He would be what Somerset Maugham called 'a good traveller', one who observed and compared rather than took things for granted. Maugham, the self-confessed 'bad traveller', merely noted, 'It seems to me just as natural to ride in a rickshaw as in a car.'[11]

The last leg of his voyage brought him to the teeming seaport of Rangoon, the Burmese capital, at the muddy mouth of the Irrawaddy Delta. It was a city with its own ambiguous mystique, its skyline dominated by the great gold-encrusted dome of the Shwe Dagon pagoda, the centre of Burmese religious life, and by the smoking chimneys of the Burmah Oil Company. These two iconic structures, the great glistening symbol of

Buddhism and the murky one of imperial commerce, were the first sight he had of the country which would be his home for the next five years.

On his progress through Burma, Maugham saw Rangoon as a city of other contrasts, memorable but unfocused. On the one hand there were American cars, spacious, shady houses – 'luncheon at this club or that, laughter, pleasant conversation . . . cocktails, a substantial meal, dancing to a gramophone or a game of billiards . . . It was very attractive, easy, comfortable, and gay.' On the other: 'Down by the harbour and along the river were narrow streets, a rabbit warren of intersecting alleys; and here, multitudinous, lived the Chinese, and there the Burmans: I looked with curious eyes as I passed in my motor car and wondered what strange things I should discover and what secrets they had to tell me if I could plunge into that enigmatic life and lose myself in it as a cup of water thrown overboard is lost in the Irrawaddy.'[12] Young Blair would not be content to *wonder*; he would be eager to discover and experience.

On this occasion, however, there was little opportunity for sightseeing. The first full day there was spend meeting the Governor and the Burma police establishment, after which the new recruits entrained for Mandalay and the Police Training School. Now, in crisp new uniforms with a pip on their shoulders they were effectively on duty. The overnight train from Rangoon to Mandalay took around fourteen hours, arriving just after noon the following day. They were met by another recruit, Roger Beadon, and escorted to the Training School mess in time for lunch.

Mandalay, mysteriously relocated beside the sea in Kipling's celebrated poem, was the administrative capital of Upper Burma, annexed and incorporated into British India only in 1886, when the last king, Thebaw, was deposed, and 'beef-fed' English redcoats marched in. It was garrisoned by a brigade of the Indian Army, and linked to Rangoon by both rail and the steamboats of the Irrawaddy Flotilla Company. It was a town of bazaars, pagodas and monasteries, and, while nowhere near as cosmopolitan as Rangoon, was home to many religions and races, predominantly Burmese and Indian. Europeans lived mostly in a cantonment inside the old city fort, Fort Dufferin. The climate was dry, except during the monsoon, which probably suited Blair with his susceptible lungs. It had, according to Maugham, 'a beauty suited to all seasons and all moods . . . beauty which does not carry you off your feet, but which can give you constant delight.'[13] Blair would have different words for it.

The Police Training School stood inside Fort Dufferin – a spacious building with classrooms, offices, a large mess and lounge and billiard room on the ground floor and students' quarters above. There were just three new recruits that year, including Roger Beadon and Eric Blair, but other men followed courses hoping to qualify for extra pay. As Beadon remembered, Blair had brought his Eton aloofness with him, and kept his life and thoughts to himself. He rarely socialised, almost never went to the club, and spent most of his time in his room reading, at times cutting classes to do so.[14] The smartest club in Mandalay favoured by Europeans, the Gymkhana, was very expensive, as was the police mess, and he withdrew, as if recoiling from the situation in which he found himself, deciding not to squander his money or company unnecessarily. He had, in any case, little time for small talk. He did, however, learn local languages, and spent time in Buddhist temples talking with priests and trying to get close to local thought and culture.

There were also occasional forays to Rangoon to haunt the public library and visit Smart & Mookerdum's bookshop. There he first read *War and Peace* and Lawrence's *Women in Love*; the latter struck him as strange. 'I remember reading it . . . in 1924 – the unexpurgated version that time – and how very queer it seemed to me at that age.'[15] That 'very queer' feeling was puzzlement over the absence of obviously 'good' and 'bad' characters. 'Lawrence seemed to sympathize with all of them about equally, and this was so unusual as to give me the feeling of having lost my bearings.'[16] Blair himself was never sufficiently detached easily to adopt a neutral posture in his fiction, which always had its moral centre of gravity firmly fixed. To that extent he was never swept along on a tide of modernism as were many of his generation.

Soon after arriving in Burma he realised that he had made a great mistake.Later he wrote that in the twenties, 'few able men went east of Suez if there was any way of avoiding it'.[17] He wrote telling Jacintha how awful it was, and she wrote back telling him that if it was so bad why didn't he return home? He couldn't, he told her – meaning presumably that he simply could not face the ignominy of crawling back to face his family as a failure. However, now in exile from both home and past, he would slowly begin to reassess his life.

It was during Blair's year at Fort Dufferin that Maugham passed through Mandalay bound for Siam and Indo-China. Quite likely Blair met Maugham at some official reception or at the club. He certainly grew to admire him for his unembellished prose and narrative power, and was more influenced by him than may have been thought. Maugham was more interested in character, but they shared a keen eye for culture and landscape. Doubtless Maugham's early novels were familiar to him, and by now he had probably read his newly published story collection, *On a Chinese Screen*, later quoted from in *The Road to Wigan Pier*. But Maugham was not just a writer in search of character and colour, he also saw through the pretence of British rule in Burma and recognised that the real will to exercise power had all but disappeared under a growing sense of guilt and liberal palliatives. Blair, too, slowly came to see how imperial power in India hung by a thread.

Since deposing the monarch some forty years earlier, the British had ruled more or less without opposition until after the Great War. In 1919 they established a diarchy in India which excluded the Burmese. The unrest that followed led to the system being extended to Burma, but too late to cool nationalist passions. A decade of tensions would lead to a major outbreak of violence in 1930. In the meantime, led by Buddhist monks, mostly students, the population was growing openly contemptuous of British authority, crime was burgeoning and outright opposition increasing. This atmosphere of unrest provides the context for *Burmese Days*, though the novel is centred more on Anglo-Indians trying to cope with the changing times than with nationalist rebellion itself.

No doubt he found his police training tedious. There was much to absorb in addition to basic law and local languages – police practices, duties, routines and procedures, the handling of crime and the training and welfare of native Burmese policemen. Finally the new men would be thrown to the wolves and expected to function almost alone in isolated outposts with responsibility for vast areas of the most inhospitable country, except for a few plum headquarters postings in populated centres such as Rangoon, Mandalay or Moulmein.

There were also the ways of the pukka sahib to be learned and observed or risk ostracism. Through John Flory in *Burmese Days* he indicates the casual manner in which these colonial mores were communicated. 'When his *burra* sahib [boss] (an old Scotch gin-soaker and great breeder of racing ponies, afterwards warned off the turf for some dirty business of running the same horse under two different names) saw him take off his topi to pass a native funeral and said to him reprovingly: "Remember laddie, always remember, we are *sahib-log* and they are dirt!"'[18] As it happened, Blair's own *burra* sahib in Mandalay, the College head, Cline Stewart, was an imposing raw-boned teetotal Scot, and by all accounts this was the sort of thing he might have said. Turning him into an old gin-soaked swindler was very much the sort of thing George Orwell would have done with relish. At that time, Mandalay social life was dominated by Scots,[19] and Eric later said that his anti-Scottish prejudice had been reinforced by the detestable whisky-swilling Scotsmen he had met in Burma.[20]

But, as with the Church of England, he was ambivalent about the Empire. While condemning the bigoted mentality of the *sahib-log*, he still recognised something extraordinary in how the British ran India, as Malcolm Muggeridge observed: 'He continued to cherish a romantic notion of empire builders valiantly bearing the white man's burden. They might be obtuse, but they had qualities of courage and endurance which [he] greatly admired.'[21] It was just another aspect of his contradictory character.

While avoiding the club, the bridge games and the billiards, he still turned out each evening for dinner in the mess, where 'formal dress' included full-dress uniform, spurs and all, and 'casual dress' meant dinner jacket.[22] No doubt such occasions made him value even more the sanctuary of a room to which to retreat with a book and his own thoughts for company. After all, he had escaped the hell of St Cyprian's to find a paradise of sorts at liberal Eton only to find himself now in purgatory, the prisoner of yet another rule-bound system, still within the sound of bugles, imprisoned in an alien world among people with whom he could not easily connect. And although he had tried to shelve the idea of becoming a writer he would compose the occasional verse or attempt a sketch as a gesture against the society in which he found himself – an epitaph to John Flory, reading like a grim projection of himself, some verses in praise of a sinful life, some about lost innocence. He was also still coming to terms with having lost Jacintha. After his first few letters she stopped writing. The only hopeful prospect for him was a posting which would allow more freedom and more time to assess where he stood and where he was heading.

He was not entirely anti-social. With Beadon there were hunting expeditions into the jungle, once after big game, an experience on which he drew for the tiger shoot in *Burmese Days*.[23] The two also bought motorbikes, although the lanky Blair, knees up almost to his ears on his low-slung machine, must have presented a somewhat absurd spectacle. On one occasion, racing through the cantonment towards the great gate to Fort Dufferin, they saw, too late, that it was locked. Beadon managed to brake in time but Blair, unable to stop, merely stood up and allowed the bike to shoot on and crash into the gate. Even so, thereafter in Burma he preferred the motorbike to a horse or even a car.

He also managed to explore Mandalay, its temples, pagodas and what he called its 'stinking labyrinth of . . . bazaars',[24] and almost certainly its opium dens and brothels.[25] 'Mandalay,' he wrote, 'is rather a disagreeable town – it is dusty and intolerably hot, and it is said to have five main products all beginning with P, namely, pagodas, pariahs, pigs, priests and prostitutes.'[26] That is the observation of Maugham's 'good traveller' who looks out for things the guide books don't mention. In the same spirit he began to mingle with those cast out from Anglo-Indian society – British men married to Burmese women, the Eurasian offspring of mixed liaisons, and the strangest Englishman in town, Captain H. R. Robinson, who had left the police service, taken up with a Burmese woman, become a Buddhist priest, and addicted himself to opium. Later, in an opium trance, attempting suicide, he succeeded in blinding himself. Blair was bemused by Robinson, a young, healthy and apparently happy man, addicted to what was then, for a European, 'an unusual vice'.[27] Exploring the dark underside of society became for him a fascination and a new-found role, liberating the romantic and reviving the rebel in him, a role in which he could enter that underworld with a non-judgemental sociological eye and yet partake of it too. In some ways he had discovered his true milieu, the blind side of the moon of respectability. Like Kipling, he was mixing with 'the wrong' people, and, perhaps in some not very conscious way, to the same end.[28]

Opium never appealed to Blair, but there was another illicit habit for which he did develop a keen taste. Discovering the brothels and the beautiful Burmese girls available for so little, was a pleasure he was not long resisting. Over twenty years on, he intimated to his Etonian contemporary Harold Acton something of the fleshly delights he had sampled there. 'His sad earnest eyes lit up with pleasure when he spoke of the sweetness of Burmese women . . . But for his nagging "social conscience" I suspected he might have found happiness there.'[29] To another Etonian he met in Burma he confided that when in Rangoon he frequently visited the waterside brothels there.[30] Like other Anglo-Indians he found the Burmese by no means physically repulsive. The 'natives' might be considered inferior by the pukka sahib, but even the most viciously prejudiced were ready to enjoy physical intimacy with them.[31] Even his socially discriminating sense of smell found something favourable in such contacts. 'Like most other races, the Burmese have a distinctive smell – I cannot describe it: it is a smell that makes one's teeth tingle – but this smell never disgusted me.'[32] And he was perfectly happy to be dressed by Burmese boys whose bodies he also found attractive. But the simple act of handing over money and enjoying a beautiful woman without having to perform the delicate preliminaries, a skill he never did seem to acquire, must have been a revelation to such a sexual innocent. As he wrote in his last notebook, 'It was pressed deep into his consciousness, to remain there till he was abt 20, that sexual intercourse gives pleasure only to the man, not to the woman.'[33] Now, on the brink of his third decade he had learned otherwise. 'When I was young and had no sense,/In far off Mandalay/I lost my heart to a Burmese girl/As lovely as the day.'[34] She might haggle, but once he had paid her he could treat a girl just as he pleased and she would act at being delighted by it.

However, the approach that worked with these girls, did not work everywhere, as he was to discover. Years later, an English woman with whom he had a fling reported, 'He makes love Burma-Sergeant fashion,' afterwards saying, 'Ah, that's better', before he turned over.[35] He could take a perverse pleasure from such indulgences as a gesture against religion, as one of his Burmese poems suggests: 'I thought of all the church bells ringing/In towns that Christian folks were in;/I heard the godly maidens singing;/I turned into the house of sin.'[36] This echoes a favourite story of his, Maugham's 'Rain', in which a pious missionary attempts to lure a prostitute (Sadie Hawkins) from her sinful ways, only to find himself drawn in the opposite direction. Sketching a character in his last notebook he gave another inkling in hinting at why he appeared sometimes to be strongly homophobic – 'Like all men addicted to whoring, he professed to be revolted by homosexuality.'[37] Burma, it seems, would leave him with something of that addiction and in his case also the need to conceal his deviant sexual life. He may have recalled an editorial in the *Eton College Chronicle* declaring that intelligence plus deception was a highly successful combination.[38]

By now he must have known that not only had an uncle and a great-uncle succumbed to the attractions of local women, but had fathered their children. He must have visited Moulmein before ever being posted there in 1926, because he met his Limouzin grandmother who died in 1925. She was, on the face of it, an interesting woman, said to have 'gone native', adopting Burmese dress and having Burmese friends. But she disappointed her clever English grandson, because, although she had lived in the country for forty years, she had not learned to speak Burmese – 'typical of the ordinary Englishwoman's attitude', he wrote sarcastically.[39]

And no doubt he also met Aimée, daughter of William Eugene and Sooma, and Kathleen, Uncle Frank and Mah Hlim's daughter, just four years older than himself. Whether the Flory–Ma Hla May relationship is built on his own association with a Burmese girl or on Francis Limouzin's story is impossible to tell, though the understanding and conviction with which that story unfolds suggest a basis of first-hand experience. Small hints and clues from what he wrote suggest that later, up-country, he followed the practice of many other men posted to lonely outposts and took a Burmese mistress, passing her off as a servant, just as John Flory does with Ma Hla May. In a sketch on which he drew for his novel, Flory, his alter ego, is sternly lectured on the subject by his senior. '"A white man," he said, "is always on his best behaviour before the native. Esprit de Corps! Prestige! Once lower that, & it's all up with you. We white men have to hang together . . . Now this girl you've made friends with, – perfectly respectable girl, I don't doubt, perfectly respectable, – but you've got to realize, my boy, that it won't do. Get entangled with a woman like that, – & where are you? Ruined. Ruined!"'[40]

For a month at the end of 1923, he was sent to the hill station of Maymyo, four thousand feet above sea level, attached to a section of the Staffordshire Regiment, and found the move away from the heat and dust of Mandalay invigorating. 'Suddenly you are breathing cool sweet air that might be that of England,' he wrote, 'and all round you are green grass, bracken, fir-trees, and hill-women with pink cheeks selling baskets of strawberries.' There he was able to put into effect what he had learned in the OTC, drilling and marching and instructing squads of the men. Characteristically, however, his one vivid memory of Maymyo brought on his old phobia about smell. He admired the soldiers and yet, because they were 'common people', they repelled him.

> In the hot mornings when the company marched down the road, myself in the rear with one of the junior subalterns, the steam of those hundred sweating bodies in front made my stomach turn. And this, you observe, was pure prejudice. For a soldier is probably as inoffensive, physically, as it is possible for a male white person to be . . . and a rigorous discipline compels him to be clean. But I could not see it like that. All I knew was that it was *lower-class* sweat that I was smelling, and the thought of it made me sick.[41]

The fact that these young men had fought in the war also rankled, which lends weight to the idea that his Burmese adventure was meant to compensate for that lost experience. As he later said, with the war over, his generation, 'just too young' to have fought, became increasingly conscious of what they had missed. 'I spent the years 1920–1927 mostly among men a little older than myself who had been through the war. They talked about it unceasingly, with horror, of course, but also with a steadily-growing nostalgia.'[42] Some with medals can be seen in the group photograph in which Blair appears. He stands head and shoulders above the others in a slightly creased uniform, clean-shaven and looking mildly amused at being photographed. Half of those pictured have moustaches as Blair did shortly afterwards. Anthony Powell thought his an expression of his French heritage – more likely it was a memento of his time among the police and military men of Empire.[43]

In the mess and at the club there was talk of changing times in Burma. With disaffection growing, and civil disobedience incited by Buddhist monks, policemen became particular targets for hostility. What Blair came to hate most was the mocking insolence of the young monks, and indignities suffered at the hands of locals – red betel juice spat over him in the street, being jostled by crowds of youngsters, and being fouled at soccer while the Burmese referee turned a blind eye. The idea that the British had lost their will to govern was growing. The sentiments of the obnoxious Ellis in *Burmese Days* reflect the frustrations of many Anglo-Indians: 'This country's only rotten with sedition because we've been too soft with them. The only possible policy is to treat 'em like the dirt they are. This is a critical moment, and we want every bit of prestige we can get. We've got to hang together and say, "*We are the masters*, and you beggars—"'.[44] And for himself he wrote, 'With one part of my mind I thought of the British Raj as an unbreakable tyranny, as something clamped down, in saecula saeculorum, upon the will of prostrate peoples; with another part I thought that the greatest joy in the world would be to drive a bayonet into a Buddhist priest's guts'.[45]

His first postings were Myaungmya and Twante, and then, in December 1924, Syriam, where he was in charge of security for a great oil refinery. It was not a healthy place; the air was heavy with chemical fumes, hardly the most salubrious atmosphere for a man with poor lungs. And although occasionally he found congenial company in which books could be discussed and a boozy singsong enjoyed, he was desperately homesick. On one such occasion he was recalled lamenting 'the lack of good bawdy songs these days'.[46] He was missing the music-hall comics, masters of the double entendre, and the vulgar insinuations of Marie Lloyd. The horror of his Burmese existence was slowly dawning on him, as John Flory says to Elizabeth: 'Have you got some picture of the life we live here? The foreignness, the solitude, the melancholy! Foreign trees, foreign flowers, foreign landscape, foreign faces. It's all as alien as a different planet . . . This country's been a kind of solitary hell to me – it's so to most of us – and yet I tell you it could be paradise if one weren't alone'.[47] Flory's words could so easily have been written to the girl he really pined for back in Shiplake.

Syriam, at least, was not far from the delights of the Burmese capital. In *Burmese Days* he offered a glimpse of what a visit to the city could mean: 'Oh, the joy of those Rangoon trips! The rush to Smart and Mookerdum's bookshop for the new novels out from England, the dinner at Anderson's with beefsteaks and butter that had travelled eight thousand miles on ice, the glorious drinking-bout!'[48] And again: 'What debauchery! They swilled whisky which they privately hated, they stood round the piano bawling songs of insane filthiness and silliness, they squandered rupees by the hundred on aged Jewish whores with the faces of crocodiles. That too had been a formative period'.[49]

Reading E. M. Forster's newly published *A Passage to India* might have given him the impulse to start incubating a novel based on his own experiences of Empire. He had tried to keep in touch with cultural life in England, reading the latest novels and literary magazines whenever possible. One for which he later wrote, John Middleton Murry's *Adelphi*, he considered 'a scurrilous rag'. Murry was an early exponent of Marxist literary criticism, which might have been thought would appeal to the one-time Eton College 'socialist', but the magazine so infuriated him at times that he would prop it against a tree and use it for target practice. That could have been simply the reaction of a sometimes Blimpish policeman. It could also have been frustration at seeing in it work by contemporaries with the advantage of a university education, gaining privileged access to the pages of smart magazines – a complaint he put into the mouth of the anti-hero of *Keep the*

Aspidistra Flying. However, his reasons were probably more political than personal. 'What sickens me about left-wing people, especially the intellec-tuals, is their utter ignorance of the way things actually happen. I was always struck by this when I was in Burma and used to read anti-imperialist stuff.'[50] Policing the Empire would set him apart from many writers of his generation who became evermore enthralled by orthodox left-wing ideol-ogy. Orwell, while anti-imperialist himself, saw the Raj from the viewpoint of someone who had participated in it. He would develop his own left-wing position but one based on direct experience rather than textbook theory.

Memories of Eton were stirred when Christopher Hollis passed through Rangoon after an Oxford Union debating tour of Australasia. Discovering Blair's whereabouts he invited him to dinner. Remembering the iconoclastic young Colleger, he was surprised to find Assistant Superintendent Blair a man with 'no trace of liberal opinions'. 'He was at pains to be the imperial police-man, explaining that these theories of no punishment and no beating were all very well at public schools but that they did not work with the Burmese.' Such people were unfit for liberty, especially the Buddhist priests against whom he thought violence was wholly desirable merely 'because of their sniggering insolence'. Here, thought Hollis, was yet another 'common type which has a phase of liberal opinion at school, when life is as yet untouched by reality and responsibility, but relapses easily after into conventional reaction'.[51]

But, as Blair was well aware, it was unwise in Burma to voice disaffection towards the *sahib-log*, especially in public places such as restaurants. Probably what Hollis found was Blair in devil's advocate mood, ironically assuming his old Socratic role. Although he half-admired the British Raj, as an imperial policeman he also found himself in a trap, and was turning strongly against the dirty work his duty required. If Hollis got the wrong impression, that no doubt was the impression he wanted to give him. The more recognisable side of Blair, Hollis was to discover later: 'I afterwards learnt,' he wrote, '[that] he insisted on befriending an Englishman [a near-contemporary Old Etonian called Seeley] who was greatly cold-shouldered by Rangoon society for having married an Indian lady, even though the marriage seemed to [him] a folly.'[52] But he sought out such men as this, as he had Robinson, 'the modern de Quincy', cast aside by Anglo-Indian soci-ety. In his own way he identified with them, felt himself just as guilty – guilty of being 'beastly' and unclean in the eyes of women, guilty of many sins in the eyes of the Ursuline nuns, guilty of breaking unknown rules at St Cyprian's, guilty of Philip Yorke's sudden death, and guilty perhaps of not shining more, as he might have done, at Eton, and guilty now of unspeak-able acts as a policeman of Empire. Perhaps he felt that he had something to learn from men like Seeley and Robinson.

Hollis must have been a reminder of what he had missed by not trying for university, and no doubt he brought news of his contemporaries' onward progress – Connolly at Oxford, the hated Marjoribanks President of the Oxford Union, Harold Acton with a book of poems already published, and Runciman, on a visit to China, inside the Forbidden City teaching the last Chinese Emperor to play the piano.[53] No doubt this visitation from the past further reanimated the writer he had all but suppressed since coming to Burma.

In so far as there was some element of the pukka sahib in Blair's make-up, an incident in November 1924 seems to have sparked the beginning of its elimination. On a Rangoon station platform he became embroiled in a fracas with some schoolboys, which ended with him bringing his stick down on one boy's back. The others surrounded him, following him on to the train, arguing with him until he escaped at his destination.[54] He included a similar incident in *Burmese Days*, in which Ellis strikes a jeering Burmese boy and in effect blinds him. Clearly this most vicious and barbarous character in his novel, represents the dark side of himself, the Mr Hyde evoked in him by his role in Burma. The intense remorse he felt about his actions as a policeman – his abuse and beating of Burmese servants and prisoners to which he later confessed – was what finally worked the transformation. At some moment he stood back and asked, 'What am I doing here?' The role and the uniform had taken him over and he hated what he had become. Once he had taken that step he was quite lost to British imperialism.

This change of mind seems to have come about gradually, but the final step must have been a moment of relief. Probably it began early on, with that first sense of alienation he communicated to Jacintha, and had grown with the feeling that not only was the land alien but also the people with whom he was expected to identify. However, on such matters, he had learned, it was best to remain silent. In *Burmese Days* his alter ego speaks for him:

Each year Flory found himself less at home in the world of the sahibs, more liable to get into trouble when he talked seriously on any subject whatever. So he had learned to live inwardly, secretly, in books and secret thoughts that could not be uttered . . . it is a corrupting thing to live one's real life in secret. One should live with the stream of life, not against it. It would be better to be the thickest-skulled pukka sahib who ever hiccuped over 'Forty years on', than to live silent, alone, consoling oneself in secret, sterile worlds.[55]

The resurrection of his 'true self' (the writer) seems also to have been helped by at least one more meeting which blossomed into friendship and perhaps more. In September 1925, after some nine months in Syriam, he was posted as headquarters' assistant to Insein, where he evolved his own idiosyncratic lifestyle, as Roger Beadon discovered:

> I went there and as far as I can remember he had goats, geese, ducks and all sorts of things floating about downstairs, whereas I'd kept rather a nice house. It rather shattered me, but . . . it didn't worry him what the house looked like and as for female company, I don't honestly think I ever saw him with a woman . . . I had an eye for anything that was going – but I can't say that I think he did.[56]

If Beadon saw no women it was because Blair had turned discretion into an art, and had by now acquired a taste for clandestine affairs. Actions as well as thoughts needed careful concealment if one wished to avoid the wrath of the *sahib-log*.

It was in Insein that he first met Elisa-Maria Langford Rae, wife of a newly arrived fellow police officer. Some forty years later she told an old St Cyprian's contemporary of Blair's: 'I knew Eric Blair when he was stationed in Insein, and later, in Moulmein, Burma. We used to have long talks on every conceivable subject, but the one impression I carried away with me was his profound gratitude to the schools that had trained him. I once remarked to him on the minute care with which he sifted each case, his passion for justice, his dislike of prejudiced remarks about anyone, however lowly, and his sense of utter fairness in his minutest dealings. He replied: "It is the most important part of the education I received at Eton – this and the capacity to think for myself."'[57] Exactly what their relationship was is uncertain, but the claims of knowing him both in Insein and Moulmein and to having 'long talks on every conceivable subject' and her apparently close knowledge of how he worked, suggests something more intimate than mere friendship. She was, it seems, a woman with a strongly independent streak who later gained a reputation as an adventuress, becoming embroiled in Nepalese politics. Whether her adventures with Blair were more than intellectual excursions we can only surmise, but he alludes to adulterous relations with the wives of absent colleagues in his manuscript sketch, 'The Tale of John Flory', and in the epitaph he composed for Flory: 'He spent sweat enough to swim in/Making love to married women.'[58]

Most likely it was at Insein that he attended the execution recalled in his brilliant early essay, 'A Hanging'. It has been suggested that young policemen were routinely sent to witness a hanging as a kind of initiation. More likely he went along out of grim curiosity. His memory of the Eastbourne hanging in 1913 and his familiarity with execution literature from Kipling to Zola, must have made the experience difficult to resist. Also, Maugham's *On*

a Chinese Screen includes a story, 'The Vice-Consul', about an execution carried out in the British concession in Shanghai, which bears a close
resemblance to his own essay. In Maugham's story a British vice-consul, one
of the party escorting a prisoner to his execution, notices how unremark-
able he is, like any other coolie in a blue cotton singlet. He notes his lissom
body, his beautifully formed feet and graceful carriage, and his 'oval, smooth
and unlined face'. He sees that the man is 'green with terror' and is ashamed
of what he is involved in. He finds himself feeling concerned because it
starts to rain and the boy has no protection from it. On the way a poor
coffin stands waiting for him and the vice-consul notices the boy glance at
it. The prisoner is to be shot outside the city wall and is told to kneel down.
His executioner thinks it's a poor spot and asks him to get up and move a
few paces forward, which meekly he does. A bullet is then put into the back
of his head. Suddenly, the group of witnesses – a judge, a journalist and the
vice-consul – smile at one another and say their goodbyes. The vice-consul
repairs to the club for a whisky and soda. 'Everything go off all right?'
someone asks. 'He wriggled a bit,' he replies, and turning to the bartender
says, 'Same as usual, John.' 'A Hanging' bears a close resemblance to this
vignette. It is the same story of official murder carried out in a routine way
by awkward men trying to conceal the horror of what they are doing
beneath a show of brusque insensitivity. Blair's prisoner, 'a puny man, with
a shaven head and vague liquid eyes', is led through the prison courtyard
towards the gallows. The story achieves its most poignant effect when a
stray dog bounds up and tries to lick the prisoner's face, and the nameless
narrator then notices, even just a few paces from death, how fastidiously he
sidesteps a puddle to avoid getting his feet wet. These incidents remind
him of the fact that he is party to the extinction of a conscious human
being. Once the deed is done, the hanging party console themselves with
gruesome gallows humour and go off with the head jailer for a glass of
whisky.[59]

The similarity in tone of these two pieces of writing is remarkable, and
Maugham's story almost certainly inspired Blair's essay, offering a further
clue as to why he attended the hanging in the first place. 'A Hanging' is a far
more powerful and effective piece of writing than 'The Vice-Consul'. The
atmosphere is built up far more skilfully and the detail is more sharply
observed. The hideousness of what is happening is greatly heightened by
being filtered through the mind of a narrator with a conscience. Although
seemingly modelled on Maugham's story, Blair's essay is remarkable for its
freshness, its vividness and the fact that it was composed so early in his writing career. It demonstrates just how retentive and detailed a memory he
had, and although it is somewhat fictionalised, it has the ring of authenticity. There can be no doubt that this event pressed hard on his conscience,

and the man who had talked up the British case to Hollis, even if tongue-in-cheek, had by now shifted firmly into the opposition.

Moving to Moulmein took him to the Burmese home of the Limouzins. It was a large, pleasant town well away from swamps and jungles. His grandmother, Thérèse Catherine, was now dead, and there were only an aunt and perhaps Frank and Mah Hlim and his Eurasian cousins left in the town. But it was at least a salubrious place to live, where his duties were less onerous, he could reassess his past life and, with the prospect of six months' leave little more than a year away, contemplate his future. In the meantime Moulmein again evoked the Kiplingesque fantasy which had drawn him to Burma:

> By the old Moulmein Pagoda, lookin' eastward to the sea,
> There's a Burma girl a-sittin', and I know she thinks o'me . . .

Those Burmese girls certainly held a strange fascination for him, as Elizabeth Lackersteen says: 'They are queer little creatures! . . . I thought they were all boys. They're just like a kind of Dutch doll, aren't they?'[60] Crick even found someone who hinted that Blair might have produced a child with a Burmese women,[61] thus following in the steps of Francis Limouzin, although, unlike Frank, when he left Burma he would never return.

In Moulmein he continued seeing Elisa-Maria Langford Rae, and was even known to frequent the club there. But he was reading more, dreaming more, about Europe – London, English food and the literary reviews; Paris, wine and conversations about Villon, Maupassant, Baudelaire and Proust. All he got at the club were 'Edgar Wallace and whisky'.[62] It could have been Langford Rae who introduced him to Villon. Until he discovered Joyce's *Ulysses*, he said later, this was 'the most important event' in his life.[63] Villon is a presence in more than one of his books, as are Maupassant and Baudelaire. This Frenchness in Blair, often ignored, was a powerful and distinguishing part of the man and his writing.

It was at the club in Moulmein that George Stuart, a railway engineer, remembered Blair, 'a rather ramshackle character', being informed that an elephant had gone 'must', causing great havoc and killing its mahout. Blair, said Stuart, immediately called for a gun and set off in an old Ford car to deal with the matter. In 'Shooting an Elephant' he gave his account of what followed. The event, for him, became symbolic, and, he said, enlightening. 'It was a tiny incident in itself, but it gave me a better glimpse than I had had before of the real nature of imperialism – the real motives for which despotic governments act.'[64]

When he found the beast it had calmed down and was grazing peacefully, but a large crowd had gathered and expected the pukka sahib to take action. He himself was an animal-lover but also a hunter who had killed sitting birds and small hedgehogs, and had once even gone tiger hunting. It must always have been tempting to have something to boast about to women, as Flory does to Elizabeth, finding her 'quite thrilled when he described the murder of an elephant which he had perpetrated some years earlier'.[65] However, in this case, he claimed, it was pressure from the assembled crowd and the need to 'keep face' which egged him on to shoot the great beast. To the devilish glee of the crowd he fired.

> In that instant, in too short a time, one would have thought, even for the bullet to get there, a mysterious, terrible change had come over the elephant. He neither stirred nor fell, but every line of his body had altered. He looked suddenly stricken, shrunken, immensely old, as though the frightful impact of the bullet had paralysed him without knocking him down. At last, after what seemed a long time – it might have been five seconds, I dare say – he sagged flabbily to his knees. His mouth slobbered. An enormous senility seemed to have settled upon him. One could have imagined him thousands of years old. I fired again into the same spot. At the second shot he did not collapse but climbed with desperate slowness to his feet and stood weakly upright, with legs sagging and head drooping. I fired a third time. That was the shot that did for him. You could see the agony of it jolt his whole body and knock the last remnant of strength from his legs. But in falling he seemed for a moment to rise, for as his hind legs collapsed beneath him he seemed to tower upwards like a huge rock toppling, his trunk reaching skyward like a tree. He trumpeted, for the first and only time. And then down he came, his belly towards me, with a crash that seemed to shake the ground even where I lay.

The deed done he was overcome with remorse – much as he had been, according to his story, at the hanging. On this occasion, however, he was not the witness but the executioner. That he altered the story for his own anti-imperialist purposes is evident in the final paragraph. 'Afterwards, of course, there were endless discussions about the shooting of the elephant. The owner was furious, but he was only an Indian and could do nothing.'[66] However, according to Stuart, the elephant belonged to Steel Brothers, the largest timber company in Burma, and something *was* done.

Pressure was brought to punish Blair, and he was duly exiled from 'cushy' Moulmein and sent north to Katha at the furthest end of the Burma railway. Of course, it is possible that Blair was already an embarrassment to authorities in Rangoon, having offended in other ways against the code of the pukka sahib, perhaps talking out of turn or involved in some scandal similar to that between Flory and Ma Hla May. Whatever the case, he was ordered north. Stuart caught sight of him packing, loading his belongings, 'including a lot of farmyard creatures, like hens and ducks and so forth which happened to escape on the platform and caused quite a commotion'.[67]

The journey to Katha took him across vast desert-like wastes, through mountains and deep into jungle – vistas which inspired both love and loathing. 'The landscapes of Burma,' he wrote, 'which, when I was among them, so appalled me as to assume the qualities of a nightmare, afterwards stayed so hauntingly in my mind that I was obliged to write a novel about them to get rid of them . . . In all novels about the East the scenery is the real subject-matter.'[68] In some mysterious way, he claimed, all his beliefs were affected by it.[69] His love of the Burmese countryside and its strange ambience is evinced in his many delicate descriptive passages in *Burmese Days*:

> White egrets stood poised, motionless, like herons, and piles of drying chilis gleamed crimson in the sun. Sometimes a white pagoda rose from the plain like the breast of a supine giantess. The early tropic night settled down, and the train jolted on, slowly, stopping at little stations where barbaric yells sounded from the darkness. Half-naked men with their long hair knotted behind their heads moved to and fro in torchlight, hideous as demons in Elizabeth's eyes. The train plunged into forest, and unseen branches brushed against the windows. It was about nine o'clock when they reached Kyauktada.[70]

What he found loathsome about the country he would exorcise with the same pen.

If discretion were required to conceal an irregular sex life, concealment of unorthodox opinions was even more imperative in a society where 'pukka sahib' meant not just being British but accepting wholesale an elaborate set of ideas. To deviate from the correct line indicated that a fellow was 'unsound' and therefore not 'one of us'. Blair by now was no mere deviant but a fully committed dissident, loathing the system and his own part in it. Only on occasions could he let the mask slip and speak out. In *Burmese Days*, John Flory used the civil surgeon Dr Veraswami as the interlocutor to whom to unburden himself of his cynical hatred of British rule in Burma. The *sahib-log* were mainly decent but dull; their world was suffocating, futile and tedious.

> It is a world in which . . . free speech is unthinkable. All other kinds of freedom are permitted. You are free to be a drunkard, an idler, a coward, a backbiter, a fornicator; but you are not free to think for yourself . . . Your whole life is a life of lies. Year after year you sit in Kipling-haunted little Clubs, whisky to right of you, Pink'un to left of you, listening and eagerly agreeing while Colonel Bodger develops his

theory that these bloody Nationalists should be boiled in oil. You hear
your Oriental friends called 'greasy little babus', and you admit,
dutifully, that they are greasy little babus. You see louts fresh from
school kicking grey-haired servants. The time comes when you burn
with hatred of your own countrymen, when you long for a native rising
to drown their Empire in blood.[71]

Flory's situation had become evermore oppressive. Alienated from
Anglo-Indian society, and always in danger of discovery, he had kept his
own counsel – the silent heretic taking refuge in his secret inner world, or
in books. But he found such a silence corrupting, and such a life sterile and
increasingly intolerable. His mind was enslaved by a repressive system. The
theme would come to dominate his life and work. Flory was the forefather,
to some degree, of all Orwellian protagonists, most notably Winston Smith.

Katha was the model for Kyauktada, the setting of *Burmese Days*, and if
Blair did occasionally speak openly to the civil surgeon there, he encountered other members of the silent brotherhood of unbelievers with whom
he could share his venom:

I remember a night I spent on the train with a man in the Educational
Service, a stranger to myself whose name I never discovered. It was too
hot to sleep and we spent the night in talking. Half an hour's cautious
questioning decided each of us that the other was 'safe'; and then for
hours, while the train jolted slowly through the pitch-black night,
sitting up in our bunks with bottles of beer handy, we damned the
British Empire – damned it from the inside, intelligently and
intimately. It did us both good. But we had been speaking forbidden
things, and in the haggard morning light when the train crawled into
Mandalay, we parted as guiltily as any adulterous couple.[72]

George Stuart again got to know Blair in Katha, where he was often away
for days on horseback patrol. It was during one of his absences that the
other Europeans there became aware of how the police establishment
regarded him. Major Cyril Wellborne, Deputy Inspector-General, on a tour
of inspection, publicly denounced him in the club as 'a disgrace to Eton
College', a remark which roused considerable resentment because Blair was
popular – 'the life and soul of the party', according to Stuart, and not a man
to flaunt his Etonian past. No doubt this uncharacteristic conviviality had
something to do with the looming prospect of a long leave ahead – and the
intoxicating prospect of freedom.

Having become disillusioned with the dirty work of Empire and what it had done to him – hating especially having to arrest men for things he might easily have done himself – this last remote posting, a casting into outer darkness, can only have pushed him towards believing that now was the time to abandon himself to writing completely. He had saved money by living frugally over the years, he had a small nest-egg in the bank in England, and would receive an income over the six months' leave awaiting him. This chance to leap to freedom must have been enormously tempting.

Burma had been a mistake, an adventure that had failed. No doubt he was tormented to think that the verdict of failure he had read in the eyes of Flip Wilkes was now a prophecy fulfilled. Somewhere at the back of his mind, however, was the idea of making failure his *métier*. As he had discovered in Burma, and saw from reading Zola, Dostoevsky, Anatole France and Jack London, poverty, the realm of the outcast and the despised, was a domain he might be well-fitted to explore, one in which he felt oddly at ease. Failure would provide him with a subject with which he was already well familiar.

He might have been popular in Katha but the place was not always good to him. He had bronchial trouble there, and contracted a mosquito-borne tropical disease, dengue fever, probably while on jungle patrol. Because of this he was able to take sick leave and had time to produce sketches for his novel in anticipation of perhaps launching himself as a writer.[73] He knew that he had changed, was well aware of what he called 'the corrupting effect of exile'.[74] Burma had worked on him as Dorian Gray's life had worked on that character's portrait. How he now saw himself can be glimpsed in the sorrowful words of John Flory: 'When he left home he had been a boy, a promising boy and handsome in spite of his birthmark; now, only ten years later, he was yellow, thin, drunken, almost middle-aged in habits and appearance. Still, he was pining for England.'[75]

On 12 July 1927 he began his leave. Two days later he was sailing down the Irrawaddy, out of Rangoon on board the MV *Shropshire*, watching the oil towers of the Burmah Oil Company and the shining dome of the Shwe Dagon pagoda recede on the horizon. The voyage home gave him material for another novel, which never got beyond a few sketched-out scenes, and remained unfinished at his death.

He decided to return to England overland across France, and around mid-August left the boat at Marseilles. After almost five years away, contact with Europe and European culture must have been intoxicating.

> Live among palm trees and mosquitoes in savage sunshine, in the smell
> of garlic and the creaking of bullock-cart wheels, and you pine for
> Europe until the time comes when you would exchange the whole of
> the so-called beauties of the East for the sight of a single snowdrop, or a

frozen pond, or a red pillar-box. Come back to Europe, and all you can remember is the blood-red flowers of the hibiscus and the flying foxes streaming overhead. Yet it seems somehow a pity that the very concept of home-sickness is presently going to be abolished by the machine-civilization which makes one part of the world indistinguishable from another.[76]

But he was returning to a very different Europe from the one he had left. In the Canebière, down by the old harbour, he stood on the steps of an English bank watching a huge demonstration in favour of the condemned anarchists Saccho and Vanzetti, awaiting execution in New York. As he watched with two English clerks, one commented, 'Oh, well, you've got to hang these blasted anarchists.'[77] When he asked whether the condemned men were in fact guilty they regarded him with shocked surprise. But injustice was what had driven him from Burma, something he would never be able to forget. With the war over, the old European tranquillity had not returned, and the times were becoming dangerously out of joint.

He must have travelled to Calais via Paris and spent a little time there, exploring the cafés and absorbing its atmosphere. By now steeped in French literature, he had arrived with a vision of the city, a dream of exile he shared with John Flory of 'sitting in cafés with foreign art students, drinking white wine and talking about Marcel Proust'.[78] What he discovered there would lure him back, a literary ambience which captivated him and evoked the Gallic side of his nature, a romantic side later to be partly suppressed under the weight of events.

The change that Burma wrought on Eric Blair was dramatic, and marked him forever. He had become a political realist rather than a fantasist, a man prepared to embrace the poor rather than flinch from them, a man aware of the violence of which he was capable, a man with an almost anarchistic hatred of authority, a libertine rather than a virgin. He had discovered his own truly dark side – a side to feel even more deeply guilty about, one to conceal, as Flory tries to conceal his birthmark in *Burmese Days*. He went home haunted not only by the beauty of a landscape but also by faces of the men he had beaten or watched hang. He took mementoes, too, notably a collection of Burmese swords with which he would decorate his rooms, as he might have decorated it with tiger heads had he had better luck in the hunt.

Chapter 6

Picking up the Thread

'Exile is probably more damaging to a novelist than to a painter or even a poet, because its effect is to take him out of contact with working life and narrow down his range to the street, the cafe, the church, the brothel and the studio.'

Orwell, 'Inside the Whale', 1940

If he had second thoughts about what he was planning, his nose made up his mind for him. 'I was already half determined to throw up my job, and one sniff of English air decided me. I was not going back to be a part of that evil despotism.' Over the coming months he would continue to wrestle with a sense of disillusionment and remorse towards a clearer idea of what to do with his life. He would not return to Burma but would need to do more than just break free from his job. 'I was conscious of an immense weight of guilt that I had got to expiate.' He pared everything down to a simple idea – 'the oppressed are always right and the oppressors are always wrong'. He had to distance himself from every form of domination and sink into the lower depths, down among the submerged and most trampled-upon, to side with them against their exploiters. To do this he felt he had to reject the idea of 'success in life' as 'spiritually ugly, a species of bullying', and embrace failure. He had become aware of the English working class, the symbolic equivalent to the exploited natives of Burma.[1] Yet he refused to embrace the economic solutions of socialism, seeing the problem as merely the lack of will to end this state of affairs by those with the power to do so.

And his thoughts were less with the socialist's 'proletariat' than with those at the very bottom of the heap – tramps, beggars, criminals and prostitutes. He wanted to leave the respectable world behind and identify with outcasts. It would be difficult for an educated man with a close family, but at least he could try, and, even if temporarily and somehow by reinventing himself, become a part of their twilight existence. The goal was expiation.

'Once I had been among them and accepted by them, I should have touched bottom, and – this is what I felt: I was aware even then that it was irrational – part of my guilt would drop from me.'[2]

His absence from England had been painful, and his return made him acutely aware of what he had missed – the distinctive landscape and natural world, the peculiarly gentle manners of the people, English homes and English cuisine. Absence always affected him deeply, and he would later write about it with touching eloquence.

But during his five lost years in Burma, England had changed and the world context had changed. The growing power of science, the expansion of mass communications and increasing social unrest were now features of everyday life. Those absent years had seen the first rally of the Nazi Party in Munich (February 1923), the death of Lenin (January 1924), the first (minority) Labour Government (February 1924), the rise to prominence of Stalin (May 1924), the murder of Matteotti (July 1924), the Zinoviev letter (November 1924), the expulsion of Trotsky from the Soviet Communist Party (January 1925), rioting in India (April 1926), the General Strike (May 1926), civil war in China (January 1927), the establishment of the British Broadcasting Corporation (February 1927) and the first transatlantic flight (May 1927). He arrived back in Europe just in time for the expulsion of Trotsky from the USSR (December 1927), and the arrival of the talkies in England (*The Jazz Singer*, 1927) – what he later saw as the beginning of the Americanisation of English life.

On his train journey from Dover through London to Southwold, Blair must have been struck by another transformation – the outward sprawl of the city over miles of previously untouched countryside as light industry spread along the major arterial roads, and small market towns changed almost beyond recognition. Soon he would discover how this had blighted some of the loveliest landscape of his youth, out along the Thames Valley. And on the social scene he would discover that the aesthetes who followed him at Eton, including Connolly and Acton, were now leading lights in that high-living, hedonistic, wildly behaved twenties generation, the so-called 'Children of the Sun'.

Blair arrived back in Southwold at the end of August 1927. His family were now renting a house at 3 Queen Street, and although they were probably too polite to comment, they were shocked by his appearance. Five years of tropical sun and a dose of dengue fever had worked a grim metamorphosis. The chubby-cheeked boy who had departed in his smart new uniform in October 1922, was thin, his face drawn and deeply lined. He had grown a moustache and now resembled his father. He had become rather coarse-mannered and threw his cigarette ends down on the floor expecting others to clean up after him.[3] In fact he had become quite a heavy smoker, and chose to smoke the most pungent tobacco.

Richard Blair was now a respected figure in Southwold – spruce-looking, rosy-faced, always sporting a fresh flower in his buttonhole, a prominent member of the Blyth Club and often on the golf links. (He preferred the Blyth Club; Constitutional Club members were mostly tradesmen.)[4] His mother, back on the tea-and-bridge circuit, was much liked in the town. Eric's sister Avril, just twenty-two, had set herself up selling home-made cakes in the nearby village of Walberswick, but had plans for something a little grander – a teashop of her own. Uncle Charlie had also retired to Southwold, drawn there presumably by his sister and the golf club.

Eric quickly renewed his acquaintance with the English countryside. Though he found East Anglia rather flat and unexciting, there were shore-lines and rivers to explore and a heronry at Blythburgh to visit, and, with his descent into the lower depths in mind, there were roads to be tramped and casual wards to visit. He was set upon discovering what he could about the underbelly of English society, and could not get much lower than by iden-tifying with those 'monsters' and 'blackguards', the tramps he had been taught as a boy both to fear and despise.

With the Southwold summer season at an end, still not having men-tioned his decision to resign, he suggested that the family go down to Cornwall for their annual holiday. They spent the whole of September in Polperro, where Eric was laid up for most of the time with a septic foot – the result, perhaps, of tramping in ill-fitting shoes.[5] It was there that finally he declared, first to his mother, that he would not be returning to Burma and planned to make his way as a writer. Avril remembered Ida being 'rather horrified'. Times were hard, post-war inflation had reduced the value of Richard's pension and the family had sunk even further into genteel poverty. Wilfully to throw up a good job and not inconsiderable salary, seemed to her insane. Richard's reaction was even stronger – shock, dismay, outrage. For all the sacrifices he had made to put his son through two of the best schools in England to be thrown away on some hare-brained notion of becoming a writer, was incomprehensible – the worst kind of ingratitude. It caused a deep breach between the two men that never completely healed. Uncle Charlie, who had, it seems, contributed towards his school fees, felt equally aggrieved. Eric's own feelings are reflected through Gordon Comstock in *Keep the Aspidistra Flying*:

> He wanted to burn his boats . . . They thought [he] must have gone
> mad. Over and over again he tried, quite vainly, to explain to them why
> he would not yield himself to the servitude of a 'good' job. 'But what

are you going to live on? What are you going to live on?' was what they all wailed at him.[6]

But, as Avril put it, 'He was quite determined that what he wanted to do was to write, and he wasn't going to be any charge on the family. He was determined to make his way, but he was going to do it in his own way.'[7] He had a few more months' salary and his Burma savings to see him through the first year, at least – or so he felt. He would have to live frugally, but his desire to expiate his guilt overrode any consideration of personal comfort. Indeed, enduring poverty would bring him closer to the oppressed whose suffering he wanted to share.

Perhaps to get away from parental disapproval and the tense atmosphere at Queen Street, he went to stay for a while at Ticklerton Court hoping to see again his old friends the Buddicoms. He saw Prosper and Guinevere, but Jacintha, either by accident or design, was not there to greet the conquering hero. Aunt Lilian was not impressed by the transformed Eric, and wrote to Jacintha telling her that he was 'very different', implying that she wouldn't particularly like what he had become.[8] She made no effort to contact him. And if her earlier rejection had been painful, her continuing silence must have been even more agonising. As he saw it, he had failed at St Cyprian's, failed at Eton, failed in Burma, lost the respect of his father, and quite certainly now had failed with Jacintha. No doubt he saw again that baleful look in the eyes of Mum Wilkes telling him that he would never amount to anything.

Back in Southwold he made a few new friends, including Brenda Salkeld, gym mistress at the local St Felix Girls' Grammar School, whom he met at a dinner party. Others, like Eleanor Jaques, the girl-next-door from Stradbroke Road, and Dennis Collings, the local doctor's son, he had met before going to Burma. Collings had spent time in Africa but, unlike Eric, believed in 'the white man's burden'. He remembered Eric starting out tramping from his home in Queen Street, once staying overnight at the 'spike' at Blythburgh, just a short way upriver from Walberswick. However, he was careful to avoid the White Inn in Southwold, the local tramps' workhouse, for fear of being recognised and embarrassing his parents.

There was already gossip in the town about the boy who had walked out of a good, well-paid job with the wild idea of becoming a writer, and some regarded him as little more than an educated layabout.[9] Ida's friends were rather condescending: 'How terrible for Mrs Blair to have a son like that – he looks as though he never washes.'[10] He loved taking long walks, often with Eleanor or Brenda, walks which became lecture tours on which he would talk about books and astonish them with his encyclopaedic knowledge of flora and fauna. He particularly enjoyed the walk to the heronry at

Blythburgh and the countryside around Walberswick, through which Defoe had passed en route to Southwold.[11] There was also sea-angling from the pier to enjoy, and good freshwater fishing in the River Blyth.

In the autumn he visited Cambridge to stay for a while with Andrew Gow, now tutor and Fellow of Trinity College. He must have been anxious to ask his advice about getting started as a writer, but what Gow must have made of him it is difficult to know. At Eton Blair had been a difficult, rude and rather lazy customer, from his point of view. Now he was looking worn beyond his years and somewhat coarsened in his habits. There was, it appears, no help forthcoming. 'Though he was very kind,' Blair wrote later, 'it seemed to me I had moved out of his orbit & he out of mine.'[12] No doubt Gow, confronted by a man full of resentment at having made a wrong choice and having lost years in which he might have established himself as a writer, felt unable to say very much to him.

To make matters worse, he would, no doubt, have been given more news of his old Eton contemporaries – Runciman and Rylands, now, like Gow, Fellows of Trinity College, and Mynors, Fellow of Balliol – all beginning to publish and acquire reputations. And it must have been galling to hear that, down from Oxford, Connolly was now writing regularly for the *New Statesman* and Acton had three books of poetry in print. Some of the Cambridge group, the self-styled 'aesthetes', including Runciman, Rylands and Cecil Beaton (a near-contemporary at St Cyprian's), had other kinds of reputations. Beaton had arrived in Cambridge in 1923 'wearing an evening jacket, red shoes, black-and-white trousers and a huge blue cravat', and attended 'highly aesthetic lunches' given by Runciman who was described as 'wearing heavy rings, carrying a parakeet on his fingers and having his hair cut in an Italianate fringe'.[13] When Gordon Comstock complains about 'Snooty, refined books on safe painters and safe poets by those moneyed young beasts who glide so gracefully from Eton to Cambridge and from Cambridge to the literary reviews,'[14] these well-heeled, outrageous contemporaries cannot have been far from his mind. Five years later, when Dennis Collings invited him to Cambridge where he was studying anthropology, he made an excuse for not going, but told Eleanor Jaques privately that the real reason was that there were 'two or three people at Cambridge whom I'm not anxious to meet'.[15]

Had he tramped back from Cambridge to Southwold, it would have been a fitting gesture of renunciation of what Gow and all the others stood for.

When he went to Cambridge he had already sent in his letter of resignation from the Indian Imperial Police and knew that, if all went smoothly, from 1 January 1928 he would be a free man. However determined he was to start from scratch, it would not be easy to slough off his past. There were sins to expiate, battles against imperialism and exploitation to be fought.

His thoughts were not yet sufficiently organised to enable him to see quite where he was going. He considered himself some sort of dissident, and was not unsympathetic to the Soviet Union, the great socialist experiment which had already cast its spell over several leading British, French and American writers – Shaw, Wells, Gide, Anatole France, John Dos Passos, and Theodore Dreisler. He had probably not read Marx other than *The Communist Manifesto*, which appealed to him as a powerful and elegant piece of rhetorical prose rather than a call to action. In fact his engagement with radical thought was personal as much as political. He identified with writers such as Zola and Jack London, but had not yet found an ideological peg on which to hang his coat. It was not until 1928, he said, that he became aware of mass unemployment and came to think of himself as a socialist. But even then the commitment was vague and unfocused.

Consumed by the desire to write, and with no real help from Gow, who might at least have suggested some publishing or literary contacts, he knew he was alone with nothing but a few sketches for a novel and a handful of poems in his bag. The logical next step was to follow the footsteps of Dickens, and other literary heroes like Smollett and George Gissing, who had struggled against poverty to achieve literary recognition, and head for London.

Remembering Ruth Pitter, the young poet he had met and fancied when he was seventeen, he wrote asking if she knew of a cheap room he could rent around Notting Hill, where she still lived with her friend Kate in Mall Chambers. The Walberswick Peasant Pottery Company, their employer, had a workshop at 24 Portobello Road, and finding a room vacant at number 22, Ruth recommended Eric, who moved in at the end of the year. It was a small terrace house with a mews behind. The walls were thin, and his room on the top floor was, according to Pitter, 'as cold as charity',[16] but he was not in search of comfort, and the spartan conditions suited his mood.

Working in his unheated attic, he sometimes had to warm his hands over a lighted candle before he could start writing, and wrote a story about it. Unusually for him, he showed the girls his work, but they considered his efforts hilarious. Clearly influenced by Lawrence, he laced his stories with obscene words but to Ruth's amusement he could spell none of them correctly – a fault in his Eton education, she thought.[17] He was teaching himself to write, and would not be discouraged by anything, be it parental anger, scant encouragement from an old tutor or the unappreciative response to his work of two potters. However, Ruth found him always eager to argue, full of anger about the British Raj, and ever ready to challenge her literary judgements. Lawrence, for example, she admired as a gifted writer, but not as a prophet, whereas Eric obviously 'thought the world of him'.[18]

With his regular income about to disappear, and reduced to living on his savings, he became a fully fledged resident of 'Grub Street', that marginal world – 'much inhabited by writers of small histories, dictionaries and temporary poems', according to Dr Johnson – where struggling writers scratch a living from book-reviewing, hoping one day to produce the great work. Without contacts, and knowing no editors, he must have often regretted missing the Oxbridge education which would have opened doors to him. Yet somehow Grub Street seemed more fitting to his purpose. If going down among the tramps satisfied his need for expiation, the sense of failure which clings to the struggling hack accorded more with his mood of self-mortification.

At about this time he began a play that prefigured his later novel, *Keep the Aspidistra Flying*, in attacking fraudulent advertisers – the sort of swindlers he had once taunted mischievously with letters about obesity. The play is coupled with a shadow drama set in the seventeenth or eighteenth century, about the imprisonment and persecution of religious dissenters; that its central character is called Christian suggests a Bunyanesque inspiration. He identified strongly with persecuted heretics of that period, and this spirit of dissidence would powerfully inform his socialism and find fuller expression in two of his finest works, *Homage to Catalonia* and *Nineteen Eighty-Four*.

His landlady, Louisa Craig, had been, according to Eric, 'lady's maid to some woman of title and had a good opinion of herself'. One day she, Eric and her husband John, found themselves locked out of the house. The local builder, George Pipe, had a workshop next door, and Eric suggested they borrow a ladder from him. The idea horrified her. They had lived there for fourteen years, she said, and had always taken care not to know their neighbours. '*It wouldn't do*, not in a neighbourhood like this. If you once begin talking to them they get familiar, you see.' So they had to borrow a ladder from a relative who lived almost a mile away and stagger all the way back with it.[19] It was a stark reminder of the intricate system of snobbery prevailing in England. He was at least reminded where the social distinctions of Empire had their origins.

Aunt Nellie was still living in Ladbroke Grove, and Ruth Pitter remembered them going there for dinner one evening. 'She was living with some old Anarchist, I think . . . She gave us some fearsome dish such as one would have in Paris if one was a native Parisian and dreadfully hard up.'[20] Nellie had been for some years an enthusiastic Esperantist and the 'old anarchist' was probably Eugène Adam, leader of *Sennacica Associo*

Tutmonda (S.A.T. – the World Association of Non-Nationalists), an Esperantist association based in Paris, of whom she was an admirer.

Eric's foot was still causing pain and an elderly woman neighbour kindly bathed and bandaged it for him so that he was soon back to tramping again. This time he set off around the capital's slum districts, directly in Jack London's footsteps, and seemingly taking *The People of the Abyss* as his guidebook. If *Down and Out in Paris and London* is anything to go by, he began exactly as London had by calling at a second-hand clothes shop in Lambeth and exchanging his perfectly good suit for an outfit of rags. Like London he then failed at first to recognise his own reflection in a shop window and was struck by how attitudes of the poor towards him changed – friendly affability replacing silent hostility. But to his friends his height and imposing look made him an improbable tramp. Unable to disguise his accent very well, he passed himself off as a gentleman down on his luck, though the cover story he invented for himself sounds more Kipps than down-at-heel Bertie Wooster. 'The story I always tell . . . [is] . . . that my name was Edward Burton, and my parents kept a cake-shop in Blythburgh, where I had been employed as a clerk in a draper's shop; that I had had the sack for drunkenness, and my parents, finally getting sick of my drunken habits, had turned me adrift.'[21] He had acquired a new identity and constructed a new biography from a variety of elements: Avril's cake shop, H. G. Wells's Windsor draper's shop, and 'Burton', the name of his hated enemy at St Cyprian's – a satisfyingly vengeful touch, no doubt.

And it was not the only vengeance he wreaked while he was at it. As described in *Down and Out in Paris and London*, down in the bowels of a dingy spike, he encountered a drunk and debauched ex-public schoolboy, a chaser of little boys, whom he depicts in this, his first book, as an Old Etonian called M——. Although Blair (as Orwell) writes of him as a fifty-year-old, one can only suppose he is called M—— after the sadistic Marjoribanks, the hated Head of School who beat him in College.[22] He might even have intended it as a form of sympathetic magic to depict an old enemy as an evil hypocrite – the hideous Hyde lurking within the much-garlanded Jekyll. The wretched Marjoribanks, who had had a glittering Oxford career before becoming a Unionist MP in 1929, actually committed suicide in 1932 even as the manuscript of Orwell's book was circulating around the publishers. There are strange echoes here of the Philip Yorke affair, further suggested in his later remark to Richard Rees about the need to conceal his name: 'How can you be sure your enemy won't cut it out and work some sort of magic on you?'[23]

His trudge around the South London spikes was Blair's self-elected descent into hell. Rather like Henry Mayhew, who went round in morning dress and top hat recording the life among the submerged tenth of London's underworld, and Conrad Noel who went as a clergyman intent on saving souls for Christian socialism, Blair went to learn about life at the very bottom of the heap. Unlike them, he did not go as himself. He had shrugged off one role – imperial policeman – and taken on another – that of a man brought down through drink and poverty. As it happened, he had money in the bank and was comparatively abstemious. Nevertheless he endured the misery, the hard beds, the freezing casual wards, the bed bugs, the abysmal food, the harsh rules enforced by grim-faced workhouse Tramp Majors, the unsavoury company, the stench of unwashed humanity, the petty thefts, the spiteful grudges of fellow tramps, the contempt of the wider world and the danger of infection from tuberculous down-and-outs whose coughing kept him awake at nights. He had been taught as a child that tramps were 'monsters' and 'blackguards' and now he knew what it felt like to be treated as such.

Life in London was not all tramping. Maurice Whittome, one of Eric's Election at Eton, remembered a dinner party organised for Blair (perhaps at Gow's instigation) which came to very little.[24] Eric also mentioned having occasionally met another Etonian contemporary, Alan Clutton-Brock, possibly at Whittome's dinner party, or at the British Museum where he obtained a Reading Room ticket at the end of February.[25] This seems a likely meeting place, followed perhaps by a drink in a Museum Street pub. What exactly Blair was studying is not known – literature on poverty perhaps, or seventeenth-century dissidents, or background for *Burmese Days*, the novel simmering away at the back of his mind. He might, of course, have simply been catching up with some serious reading in anticipation of moving soon to Paris properly to launch his writing career.

In Paris he could soak himself in French culture, live out Flory's dream of cafés, wine and good conversation, mingling with the ghosts of Zola, Balzac, Flaubert, Villon, Maupassant and Rimbaud, Anatole France and Proust. The road to Paris had been trodden by so many writers before him – Smollett, Dickens, Leonard Merrick, Arnold Bennett, Ford Madox Ford, Maugham and Joyce. Joyce, he later noted, 'wrote *Ulysses* in the seven years between 1914 and 1921, working away all through the war, to which he probably paid little or no attention, and earning a miserable living as a teacher of languages in Italy and Switzerland. He was quite ready to work seven years in poverty and complete obscurity so as to get his great book on to paper.'[26] That could well have been how he saw himself as he surveyed his own future. The reasons he gave publicly for going to Paris were more mundane – to live cheaply, write a couple of novels, learn French, and, if money ran low, to teach English. There was in that more than an echo of Joyce.

Another factor might have influenced his decision. In March 1928 Somerset Maugham's novel *Ashenden* was published. Since their paths had crossed in Burma, Maugham had offered him a model of the sort he admired, a writer whose stories were rooted in direct experience. However, Maugham's hero, Ashenden, was not just a writer but a secret agent (as Maugham himself had been during the war). This combination doubtless appealed to Eric's secretive side, and he came to identify with this particular Maugham novel in a quite significant way. In Chapter 7 of *Ashenden* the hero is summoned to Paris to join a fictional aunt. To Eric, not without his superstitious side, this could well have seemed like an omen. It so happened that his own aunt, Nellie, had decided to give up her Ladbroke Grove flat and go to Paris to work for Eugène Adam at the headquarters of his Esperanto association. Nellie was now almost fifty-eight, Adam forty-nine. This could well have been for her a twilight love affair, though, more likely, as a devoted Esperantist, she had simply committed herself to work for the man and his movement. She vacated her London apartment on 1 April 1928.[27] In Paris she and Adam bought a top-floor flat together, close to the S.A.T. Headquarters at 14 ave. Corbéra, close to the Gare de Lyon, in the twelfth arrondissement, just across the Seine from the Jardin des Plantes. It was probably there that Eric camped out when he first arrived.

He was twenty-four when he set off for France in the spring of 1928. He was still unpublished, but took with him draft manuscripts and a diary of his tramping. He travelled as 'a student' – at least that's how he later booked into a Paris hospital. Having missed Oxbridge, his Paris years, 1928 to 1929, would be his university years, and in any case it must have made things a little easier at home to say that he was going there to study as well as write. Most importantly, he was now liberated from the unwritten law of silence, free to read and write as he liked, and to debate his opinions openly. Eugéne Adam and Nellie Limouzin, in an informal way, became his political tutors.

Adam was a strange figure. Born in a small Brittany village, he was an anarchist until the Great War in which he served as an ambulance driver. Feeling that anarchism was no answer to world chaos he joined the Communist Party and founded the S.A.T. In 1921 he 'committed suicide', killing off Eugène Adam and adopting the pseudonym 'Lanti' (or L'anti, 'one who is against'). A year later he went to Russia and found the Communist Party there eager to promote Esperanto. But by 1926 there was a Moscow-backed move to take over the association, expel all non-Communists and shackle members to the Stalinist line. Adam refused to co-operate and was threatened with expulsion from the Comintern. When Eric met him in 1928 he had become deeply hostile to Stalin and had just torn up his Party card. Now he was involved in a bitter struggle to save his organisation from

Moscow's clutches. He and Blair had spirited debates about all of this, debates that probably helped define more clearly the kind of socialist he would become. With Adam he returned to his old game of Socratic disputation, precipitating some heated discussions.[28]

After staying briefly with an Esperantist family, he found a room in a cheap hotel at 6 rue du Pot de Fer leading to rue Mouffetarde in the fifth arrondissement, just a short walk from the Panthéon, the Sorbonne, Boulevard St Michael and Luxembourg Gardens, and close to the métro at Place Monge. It was a hotel and street he would make famous as the Hotel des Trois Moineaux in the rue du Coq d'Or in *Down and Out in Paris and London* – the most evocative portrait of the twilight world of the Paris *clochard* by an English writer of that period.

From this new base in the Latin Quarter, he explored the cafés and restaurants of St Germain and Montparnasse – Les Deux Magots, where once he thought he had caught a glimpse of Joyce, and the Cloiserie des Lilas, where Lenin and Trotsky once played chess. The book-browser in him took him to the stalls of the *bouquinistes* along the Seine, the naturalist admired the plane trees along the boulevards and in the city's public gardens, 'so beautiful . . . because the bark isn't blackened by smoke the way it is in London', the sportsman took him fishing in the Seine, and the shade of Edgar Allan Poe perhaps escorted him to the Jardin des Plantes, and haunted his most vivid memory of the place: 'I used to love it, though there was really nothing of interest except the rats, which at one time overran it & were so tame that they would almost eat out of your hand.'[29]

Characteristically he did not spend time in Paris searching out fellow writers or trying to gain entrance to artistic coteries, but mingled instead with anybody and everybody who came his way in the hotel, in the streets, in the cheap cafés and bistros. All the time he kept his sociological eye focused, his notebook ready and his literary instinct honed. The experience provided him material for the first part of *Down and Out in Paris and London*, the story of a life centred on his 'rue du Coq d'Or'.

His stated reason for being in Paris was to write novels, and he seems to have finished at least one before the end of 1928. When that was rejected, he destroyed the manuscript, an impulsive gesture he later regretted. Nevertheless, he did not abandon fiction and turned to writing short stories in the hope of earning some quick money. In the meantime, from Adam he learned a good deal about both French and European politics. In 'Lanti' Eric found someone who had been deeply engaged in the recent history of both anarchism and socialism. However passionately they argued, it was Eric who had most to learn about the left, and in Adam he found an apt and experienced tutor. Nellie, too, helped with this education, and it is evident from her one surviving letter to him that left-wing politics was common currency between them. France he found a good place to learn about such things – 'In France everyone can remember a certain amount of civil disturbance, and even the workmen in the bistros talk of *la révolution* – meaning the next revolution, not the last one.'[30] He visited the Chamber of Deputies to observe French democracy in action, but was not impressed. The Deputies, he said, looked like 'a set of crooks'.[31] Adam had many political connections, introducing him to his close friend Henri Barbusse, author of the powerful war novel, *Le Feu,* and editor of the left-wing periodical *Monde,* and probably also to René Nicole and Henri Dumay who ran the radical *Le Progrès Civique.* However, it was not until October 1928, six months after arriving in the city, that he got any of his Parisian writing into print.

Having had no success with his fiction, he began a series of sketches about tramps and beggars, based on his wanderings round common lodging houses and spikes, and seems to have been quite happy to show his work to others, especially young women who interested him. One of these, Ruth Graves, an American in Paris, wrote to him some twenty years later, reminding him of their times together at her flat just off Boulevard Montparnasse:

> I have always enjoyed recalling those Saturday evenings in Paris, when we took turns about the dinner, and the hours of good talk later in my little cluttered place in rue de la Grande Chaumière. You showed me sketches of your experiences – some of the material I recognized when 'Down and Out in Paris and London' came out. Perhaps I was your first critic? . . . I treasure all the memories of my years there [Paris], including the very good talk of a tall young man in a wide-brimmed pair of Breton hats, who was as kind as he was keen of mind.[32]

Paris at that time, of course, was a place of artistic ferment and pilgrimage for many would-be writers and artists, especially from across the Atlantic. Although the good times were about to end with the Wall Street Crash, Blair at least took in some of that heady atmosphere, even if viewing the period through more jaundiced eyes than those of its celebrated American chroniclers.[33]

> During the boom years, when dollars were plentiful and the exchange-value of the franc was low, Paris was invaded by such a swarm of artists, writers, students, dilettanti, sight-seers, debauchees and plain idlers as the world has probably never seen. In some quarters of the town the so-called artists must actually have outnumbered the working population – indeed, it has been reckoned that in the late twenties there were as many as 30,000 painters in Paris, most of them impostors. The populace had grown so hardened to artists that gruff-voiced Lesbians

in corduroy breeches and young men in Grecian or medieval costume
could walk the streets without attracting a glance, and along the Seine
banks by Notre Dame it was almost impossible to pick one's way
between the sketching-stools. It was the age of dark horses and
neglected genii; the phrase on everybody's lips was '*Quand je serai
lancé*.'[34]

No doubt his friend Ruth was one of those affluent visitors Blair remembered later. 'American tourists were as much a part of the scenery of Paris as
tobacco kiosks and tin urinals . . . [They] spent money like water.'[35] And, of
course, as well as the droves of would-be writers enjoying the low cost and
special ambience of the city, there were significant figures. Henry Miller was
there with his wife June for part of 1928; until March, Hemingway lived in
the rue Férou, and until mid-1929 F. Scott Fitzgerald had an apartment in
nearby rue de Vaugirard. Cyril Connolly, newly married to a rich American
wife, was there in June 1928, haunting the Café Dôme and the Select in
Boulevard Montparnasse, and, in January 1929, interviewing James Joyce
for the *New Statesman* about his *Work in Progress (Finnegans Wake)*, at his
apartment in the rue de Grenelle[36] – 'Now, Mr Connolly, just read this passage and tell me what you think it means.'

By the end of his first year in Paris, Eric, having completed and destroyed
one novel, cannot have felt optimistic about proving to his parents that he
could make a living as a writer. However, Aunt Nellie produced someone
who might have helped, probably one of her Ladbroke Grove contacts. L. I.
Bailey was London agent of the McClure Newspaper Syndicate, which represented Rider Haggard, Mark Twain, Conan Doyle, Kipling, Booth
Tarkington, Ford Madox Ford and Willa Cather. Eric sent Bailey a batch of
stories and mentioned a projected book about 'tramps and tramping'. Bailey
replied that he was prepared to look at what he had but he did not feel very
confident about the book.[37] There was no market, it seems, for tramps.

During 1928 the political atmosphere in France was growing tense. In
January communists were arrested accused of plotting to overthrow the
state. In the same month 'Les Croix de Feu', an extreme right-wing organisation of old soldiers, was formed to combat revolution. And while the two
extremes in France were squaring up to one another, there were street riots
in Berlin and the National Socialists were making great electoral gains in
Bavaria. In Russia Stalin was moving to expel all Trotskyists from the
Communist Party, and in Tokyo, Hirohito was proclaimed Emperor of
Japan. On a less combative note, the French and the Czechs were discussing
the idea of a United States of Europe, while in America Herbert Hoover was
elected President. Meanwhile, in England, the Golden Age of Eric's childhood receded a little more with the deaths of Thomas Hardy, buried in a

country churchyard barely thirty miles from his father's birthplace in Dorset, and Herbert Asquith, buried in a small Oxfordshire churchyard, on the banks of the Thames upstream from Henley.

Europe's growing political ferment deflected Eric from the indulgence of fiction towards the more immediate concerns of the world around him. In doing so he began to see more clearly where his path as a writer might lie, and at last had some success. Barbusse's *Monde*, first to publish him, was a lively, highly respectable and stylish left-wing weekly, whose contributors included Dos Passos, Heinrich Mann, Roger Martin Du Gard, Ortega y Gasset, Diego Rivera and Madame Sun Yat Sen. There was nothing remarkable about the articles he wrote for *Monde* (one on censorship and one on John Galsworthy), nor those he published in *Le Progrès Civique* (on unemployment in England, a day in the life of a tramp, London beggars and British Burma), but the choice of subjects and their treatment are quite revealing. They say something, for example, about the breadth of his reading: Chaucer, Shakespeare, Rabelais, Swift, Smollett, Surtees, Marryat, Dickens, Thackeray, Trollope, Twain, Poe, Charles Reade, Brieux, Ibsen and Shaw, but also Joyce and Radclyffe Hall, whose *The Well of Loneliness* was obtainable in England only in the Reading Room of the British Museum. While these articles appeared between October 1928 and May 1929, he also (no doubt again through Nellie) had an article, 'A Farthing Newspaper', accepted in England by Chesterton's lively review, *G. K's Weekly*. This interesting piece exposed the dishonest motives behind *Ami du Peuple*, a virtually free newspaper masquerading as the people's friend but in fact a pro-capitalist propaganda sheet. It was the kind of swindle which Blair had railed against at Eton and through which his newly focused sociological eye saw immediately.

Behind this early work stands the emerging consciousness of 'George Orwell', a man at this stage mapping a new mental landscape, forming a new creative identity, speaking with a new authorial voice. Here he was at the outset of his adult writing career already rehearsing themes and raising issues that were to become significant features of his later work. His essays on London's underworld of tramps and beggars were clearly taken from early sketches for *Down and Out in Paris and London*, and his pieces on censorship and deceptive newspapers point the way to *Nineteen Eighty-Four*. The focal issue of intentional misuse of language to deceive had already been touched on in the play fragment written in London, and was an issue to which he would return again and again.

His contributions to periodicals such as *Monde*, show him turning to the sociological essay even while flirting, however unsuccessfully, with fiction. That dual engagement would become a feature of his literary oeuvre. If as yet he was not writing overtly political pieces it was probably because at that time his political views still lacked clarity and authority. But what was emerging clearly was that E. A. Blair, as he signed himself, was primarily a literary man with a sociological eye and a sociological imagination.

Life in a cheap unheated hotel room finally caught up with him and his susceptible lungs. In March, struck down with bronchitis, he coughed up blood[38] and took himself to the Hôpital Cochin, a pauper's hospital in the fourteenth arrondissement, which Albert Camus called 'the barracks of poverty and illness . . . its walls drip with the filthy humidity that belongs to misfortune'.[39] This grim institution stood on the Faubourg Saint-Jacques backing on to the mental asylum of St Anne's and La Santé Prison, the Paris home of the guillotine.

The fear of hospitals had haunted him since first being read 'The Children's Hospital', that gory poem of Tennyson's, as a child. Now that hideous vision would recur: 'It is a dark patch not far beneath the surface of our minds. I have said . . . that, when I entered the ward at the Hôpital X [Cochin] I was conscious of a strange feeling of familiarity. What the scene reminded me of, of course, was the reeking, pain-filled hospitals of the nineteenth century, which I had never seen but of which I had a traditional knowledge.'[40] This was a teaching hospital in which the poor were used as subjects for experiment. Blair, the young student admitted to the Salle Lancereaux on 7 March 1929 suffering *une grippe* (influenza), underwent the humiliations to which all poor patients were routinely subjected – a long admission form to fill, a lukewarm bath, a shapeless nightgown and, despite a temperature of 103, a walk through the rain to a crowded ward cram-full of the sick and dying, and permeated by the smell of faeces. He was given a number (3058 – so becoming '*numéro* 58'). The treatment, which included cupping, bleeding and the mustard-poultice torture, was positively medieval. The nurses were slatternly, the doctors coldly impersonal and patients regarded as no more than objects. Blair was found interesting only because of his plentiful 'bronchial rattle' – the old 'Corfe Castle' hacking cough had returned. The inmates were left unwashed and the dead lay uncollected for hours. Like the voice of doom a neighbouring patient would call out the number of each newly deceased and fling up his arms in a cynical gesture of inevitability. In that way he saw the emaciated '*numéro* 57' expire, affording him that uncanny prevision of his own death.

When he came to write his essay 'How the Poor Die', probably drafted in the early thirties, he found literary parallels even with *this* horrible experience – in Tolstoy's *War and Peace*, Zola's *La Débâcle*, Melville's *Whitejacket*, and Axel Munthe's *The Story of San Michele*. His mind was forever relating his experience, however gruesome, to those of other writers, and striving to transform his own suffering into literature. Finally, however, he could only take so much of this, and once he had partly recovered, he escaped, without waiting to be discharged. He had seen the face of death and it terrified him, a nightmare vision which would never leave him. In his somewhat heightened account of Hôpital X, he created a cold, cruel, impersonal world of unremitting misery in which the wretched, numbered victims of an inhuman system are drained of individuality and when no longer living are tossed aside like so much refuse. It was a grim and terrifying prefiguration of the soulless world of *Nineteen Eighty-Four*, especially the little operating-room from which 'dreadful screams were said to issue'.

Before leaving he had a sputum test which proved negative. However, if his picture of the hospital is at all faithful, there is no knowing how accurate it might have been. It could well be that he had already contracted TB, either in the spikes and common lodging-houses of England or in the slums and brothels of Paris.

On the day after leaving hospital, 23 March, the new issue of *Monde* appeared, carrying his article on Galsworthy. It tells us a great deal about the values of the 25-year-old student writer, his taste in literature, his views on English theatre, and his attitude towards didactic fiction and drama. He later changed his opinion of Galsworthy, who he thought turned reactionary in the 1930s,[41] but in 1929 he clearly thought highly of him, comparing him to Zola and much preferring him to Shaw. The following day he was well enough to attend the funeral of Marshall Foch at Les Invalides and there caught sight of another First World War hero, Marshall Pétain, defender of Verdun – 'a tall, lean, very erect figure, though he must have been seventy years old or thereabouts, with great sweeping white moustaches like the wings of a gull'. The crowd whispered his name and Blair, greatly impressed, felt, 'in spite of his considerable age, that he might still have some kind of distinguished future ahead of him'.[42] He had acquired a certain political acumen and a penchant for prediction; however, sometimes his predictions were a little off-target.

Bailey's long-awaited report on his stories, when it came, was disappointing. His reactions were mixed. Some he found immature, some clever, and some beautifully written but too concerned with sex.[43] Nothing came of this contact and the correspondence lapsed. Eventually he came to recognise that he had no gift for short story-writing and, although he continued writing poetry for some years, eventually had to admit that he was no poet either. One of his few Paris stories to survive, called simply 'Short story', gives a clue to the kind of short fiction he was producing – episodic tales, what the French called *contes*, in the style of Maupassant, for which he found no outlet in magazines, but which he was able to incorporate later into *Down and Out in Paris and London*. The violently erotic story told by Charlie in Chapter 2, which hardly seems to belong to the book, for example, stands as a *conte* in its own right, reflecting more than a passing interest in French erotica. He later told T. S. Eliot that he was perfectly au fait with Parisian argot used in the city's brothels – an oblique reference to his having worked in one, or so it is elsewhere hinted. Perhaps his first article in *Monde*, on censorship, indicates how vulnerable he felt, having produced a series of mildly pornographic stories he still hoped to get published.

His apparent fixation with sexual themes was probably no mere fantasy. Paris at the time was a good place to turn such fantasies into reality. Brothels were legal and prostitutes were readily accosted in certain cafés, as Henry Miller described so graphically in *The Tropic of Cancer*. If Blair lacked Miller's capacity for openly guiltless debauchery – he was far too secretive ever to write in quite that candidly confessional manner – he was not, it seems, averse to the pleasures on offer. Later, he told a friend, Mabel Fierz, that he had picked up 'a little trollop' in a café and taken her to live with him at his hotel. 'She was,' he told her, 'beautiful and had a figure like a boy, an Eton crop and in every way desirable,' and he was so enamoured of the girl, he said, that he would even have married her.[44] In *Down and Out* he tells the story of a young Italian robbing his hotel room and leaving him penniless, but he told Fierz that it was his 'trollop' who robbed him and decamped with her boyfriend – some *Apache*, it seems, the sort whose wild and violent dancing he would have enjoyed at the Paris *bal-musettes*.

Left without money and unable to earn enough from English lessons and writing, he was faced with having to borrow from Nellie or survive as best he could alone. He had money in England but, faced with the prospect of imminent poverty, decided to embrace it. In England he had gone tramping, but in an anthropological vein, always aware that he could return to his comfortable life whenever he wished. Now he decided to find out what it was like to be plunged into destitution in a foreign city and deny himself assistance.

Our sole source of what followed is *Down and Out in Paris and London*, bearing in mind that, as he told Brenda Salkeld, some passages were straightforward accounts of what happened, others were based more generally on what occurred, and others fabricated for narrative purposes.[45] As the story goes, he struggled along for a time, pawning his possessions and starving himself to eke out his few remaining francs. At some point he began to feel a strange pleasure in being so impoverished. 'You have talked so often of going to the dogs – and well, here are the dogs, and you have reached them, and you can stand it. It takes off a lot of anxiety.'[46] Sometimes he just lay in bed reading Sherlock Holmes stories; once he borrowed a fishing rod and went down to the Seine hoping to catch dace, using bluebottles as bait. It seems he was unlucky, but how he hoped to cook the fish he did not say.

Finally, he took up with the Russian waiter he called 'Boris', an ex-Czarist officer reduced to menial work but who retained the sardonic worldliness of an aristocrat. Eric found *him* down on his luck, too, out of a job and flat broke. Together they endured starvation while Boris regaled him with unlikely stories and anti-Semitic tirades. But it was finally through Boris that he found work as a *plongeur*, a lowly dishwasher at the Hôtel Lotti, a luxury hotel just off the rue de Rivoli – strangely enough, the very hotel in which Maugham's Ashenden visits his 'sick aunt'.

In Orwell's day the working conditions there were primitive – the *plonguers* worked in a gloomy underworld of grease, grime and foul smells. As usual Eric, with his sociological eye, saw immediately how the system functioned, how the hierarchy worked, and who profited from it. He was able quickly to spot the subtle distinctions in status between management, waiters and scullions and how such distinctions were maintained and enforced through threats, insults and ritual humiliations. Immediately he was considered suspicious by the head waiter for being English, wearing a moustache and being obviously unused to the work. However, he soon became accepted and was even offered a contract.

The *plongeur* was the lowliest form of life at the Lotti, working in filth and slime, bullied by his superiors, treated like a slave and paid the least. For a time he was allowed to stand in as a room service waiter, which brought him into direct contact with some of the Lotti's most prestigious guests. One story in his book features a German waiter (himself in disguise) and 'an English Lord' (another Old Etonian, the immensely wealthy Duke of Westminster, as it happened). The Duke, on a whim, asks for a peach, but no peach can be found in the hotel and the shops are closed. A peach is procured, by the 'German' smashing a shop window and stealing one. In her book, *Grace and Favour*, the Duchess of Westminster writes about meeting a writer at a party, who tells her that he, George Orwell, was the waiter who procured the peach. Sceptics have doubted that Orwell moved in such circles, but, in fact, the Duchess enjoyed the company of writers – Evelyn Waugh was a friend, and so was Connolly. Like Orwell, she attended Connolly's parties, and seemingly also a party thrown for him by Edward Hulton at the Dorchester when he left *Tribune* in 1947.[47]

Boris had persuaded him to work for the proprietor of a soon-to-be-opened Russian restaurant, grandly named the Auberge de Jehan Cottard, so he left the Lotti, only to find the restaurant well behind schedule and was reduced again to starvation. When eventually it opened the conditions were even worse than at the hotel. The *plongeurs* were bullied and the atmosphere in the kitchen was poisonous. The space was cramped, the pots out of reach, the only dustbin soon overflowing, and food was everywhere being trampled underfoot. There was no larder, vegetables were kept in a backyard shed where cats and rats got at them, and there was no hot water for washing up.

All this while he had hung on to his room in the rue du Pot de Fer, sending off manuscripts in the hope of rescuing his fortunes through writing. The London periodical, the *New Adelphi*, previously the *Adelphi*, at which he had once taken pot-shots in Burma, accepted an essay called 'The Spike' (there is a chapter similarly named in Jack London's *The People of the Abyss*), about a day in a casual ward – a sufficiently encouraging response for him to think of returning home.

When he started, he wrote, 'I knew nobody and at first could get no footing.'[48] In his first year of writing he had earned little more than £20, hardly enough to live for a few months at near-starvation level. At least in England, from his point of view, he would be on firmer ground. He left Paris in December 1929, bringing with him not just his surviving manuscripts, but a wealth of experience which would guarantee him his first book. He also returned with a more clearly defined political position.

His time in Paris was an early initiation into the politics of the age. From Eugène Adam, still bearing the scars of his battle with Moscow, he had heard an unequivocal anti-Stalinism, the bitter message of a romantic whose dream of a universal language under socialism had been shattered. He saw the growing divisions and mounting antagonism between extreme right and left in France, and the way in which newspapers were often intent on deluding the reader, selling an underlying message while purporting to inform. He returned to England with a more cynical view of politics and an even more anti-authoritarian outlook, even if that generally anarchic cast of mind was still not fully focused. And, just as interestingly, he had acquired a European perspective. If Europe was the cockpit in which ideologies were increasingly likely to clash, it was also home to the broader tradition on which his own inspiration fed. He saw England as too culturally isolated for its own good, though he knew that isolation could not be long maintained. England drew him back more out of necessity than choice. And although he loved England, from time to time he expressed a strong desire also to return to France.

He later passed harsh judgement on the departing decade, a period in literature, he said, when the emphasis was more on technique than content. It was an age in England when ignorance of politics was considered a virtue.

When one looks back at the twenties, nothing is queerer than the way in which every important event in Europe escaped the notice of the English intelligentsia. The Russian Revolution, for instance, all but vanishes from the English consciousness between the death of Lenin and the Ukraine famine – about ten years. Throughout those years Russia means Tolstoy, Dostoievski and exiled counts driving taxi-cabs. Italy means picture-galleries, ruins, churches and museums – but not Blackshirts. Germany means films, nudism and psycho-analysis – but not Hitler, of whom hardly anyone had heard till 1931. In 'cultured' circles art-for-art's-saking extended practically to a worship of the meaningless. Literature was supposed to consist solely in the manipulation of words. To judge a book by its subject-matter was the unforgivable sin, and even to be aware of its subject-matter was looked on as a lapse of taste.[49]

At the beginning of the next decade Eric Blair would be seen as a minor figure on Grub Street with a talent for forthright criticism and honest reportage. In the course of the change which was about to overcome English letters, he would convert himself into George Orwell and emerge by the end of the thirties with a respectable standing as a novelist and a growing reputation as a fearless socialist critic.

In 1930 Maugham published a book based on his Eastern travels, *The Gentleman in the Parlour,* in which he seemed to foresee the coming of the writer Orwell would evolve into. In his book Maugham envisaged one who would chronicle the decline and fall of the British Empire. He hoped that the great work would be composed 'with sympathy, justice, and magnanimity'. Its author should 'eschew rhetoric . . . write lucidly and yet with dignity'. 'I should like his sentences to ring out as the anvil rings when the hammer strikes it; his style should be stately but not pompous, picturesque without affectation or effort, lapidary, eloquent, and yet sober.' Perhaps George Orwell was not as sympathetic or as magnanimous towards the Empire as Maugham might have wished, but there can be few better descriptions of the style of writer he was to become and the body of work he was to produce.

Chapter 7

Getting a Footing

'We must be thankful for the piece of youthful folly which turned him
aside from a comfortable middle-class career and forced him to become
the chronicler of vulgarity, squalor and failure.'

Orwell, 'George Gissing', 1948

While Eric slaved away in dungeon-like Parisian kitchens, struggling to
live and write on next to nothing, his old Eton chum Steven
Runciman, now a well-established young scholar, was in Heidelberg hobnobbing with André Gide.[1] Connolly, travelling the world in near-luxury,
was at the hub of a new literary generation, including Evelyn Waugh,
Anthony Powell, Elizabeth Bowen, Nancy Mitford, John Betjeman and Peter
Quennell, and could now afford to entertain in grand style at his Chelsea
home. George Rylands had a book in print, Harold Acton now had five. Eric
Blair, it seemed, would have to be patient, like Joyce – or, as his Russian
friend Boris had suggested, 'marry a publisher's daughter'.[2]

He returned to England in time for Christmas, and was struck again by
the beauty of the countryside. Returning from abroad, he said, was the best
way of perceiving and grasping the peculiar ingredients and flavours which
go to make up Englishness. 'There are, indeed, many things in England
that make you glad to get home; bathrooms, armchairs, mint sauce, new
potatoes properly cooked, brown bread, marmalade, beer made with veritable hops – they are all splendid, if you can pay for them, England is a very
good country when you are not poor.'[3] With his savings somewhat depleted
he needed a job, but, with the onset of slump, work was suddenly scarce. On
landing he headed straight to Southwold. It must have been galling to
return home once more an evident failure. In the view of his family, a
writer who failed to make money was not much of a writer.

But the months in Paris had wrought an interesting and significant
change in his literary perspective. He had set out to be the writer of 'enormous naturalistic novels with unhappy endings and arresting similes, and

also full of purple passages in which words were used partly for the sake of their sound';[4] he had returned with a new literary persona – the embryonic writer of stylish reportage, bringing a message from the underground. That message and that style would soon come to match the spirit of the decade and in some way embody it. The fiction writer had up to this point failed, the intrepid and gifted investigator was emerging, even though barely recognisable and certainly as yet unrecognised.

That January, Richard turned seventy. The presence of a son who was such a disappointment was obviously not a very welcome birthday present. Eric's failure and his own failure to rise must have left him resentful and deeply pained. In April he made his will, leaving his entire estate to Ida.

Ignoring local gossip about the prodigal son's return, Eric renewed his local friendships and found a job – looking after what he called 'an imbecile boy' at Walberswick. He found the work disheartening. He enjoyed children, but his frustration can be read behind the description, in *A Clergyman's Daughter*, of a child 'totally impossible to teach' who 'drew nothing but pothooks remaining quiet and apparently happy for hours together', with 'tongue hanging out, amid festoons of pothooks'.[5] Dennis Collings recalled the hopelessness of the boy: 'The poor child was incapable, there was something wrong with his brain. He had to try and teach him something . . . in order to get a bit of money. And that affected him very much – the sight of this poor child, incapable of improvement in any way.'[6] It was hardly stimulating work for a lively intelligence like Eric's, but still an experience to absorb and one day write about.

Walberswick, although a quiet backwater, was reputedly the most haunted village in East Anglia, noted for the phantom hound which prowled the beach at low tide. In the churchyard there Eric himself glimpsed a spectre – a small, silent, stooping man dressed in brown – and wrote about it to Dennis in Cambridge. He had a further uncanny experience, which he wrote about later to Sacheverell Sitwell: a parcel found under a gorse bush, containing a model house complete with furniture and tiny articles of intimate female clothing, and a scrap of paper bearing the words, 'This is not bad is it?'[7] – a bizarre expression of some sexual deviation, he thought. 'Strange events such as ghosts and poltergeists could be genuine psychological occurrences as much as cases of coincidence or human gullibility.[8] That feeling for the occult imbibed from ghost stories as a child, was still very much with him. He was, after all, back in M. R. James's ghost-ridden East Anglia.

With Dennis in Cambridge, he was often seen alone around Southwold, a slightly scruffy figure in ill-fitting clothes, fishing from the pier, standing awkwardly on the sidelines at local dances, walking Hector, the family dog, and occasionally stopping on the beach to take a dip. Apart from walking, swimming was one of the few physical activities he allowed himself. It suited him more to be wrapped in his own thoughts, sitting down to write or simply observing.

In the spring he took up painting seascapes, using a beach chalet belonging to friends. One day he found it had been lent for the summer to a family from London. They, however, had no objection to his painting there and welcomed his company. Francis and Mabel Fierz were from South America. They had a house in Hampstead Garden Suburb, and were both quite cultured. Francis, a steel executive, was a lover of Dickens; Mabel, a vivacious, opinionated woman who enjoyed the company of young artistic people, believed that she had an eye for talent and the drive to bring it on. She met the Blairs, became great friends with Ida, and left Eric with an open invitation to stay whenever he came to London. Faced with this degree of warmth and enthusiasm, he was far more open with the Fierzes than he was able to be at home. He told Mabel that he was under great pressure from his family to make money. As he wrote later, 'A middle-class person goes utterly to pieces under the influence of poverty; and this is generally due to . . . the fact that he has scores of relations nagging and badgering him night and day for failing to "get on".'[9] In particular, he told her, he felt that he had let his father down badly by resigning his job in Burma.

Ida must have been aware of this and told Mabel, 'You know, Eric loves his father far more than he loves me,' to which Mabel replied, 'No, I don't think he does; it's that he wants his father to acknowledge him as a successful son.' But in the old man's eyes, she thought, 'a son who couldn't make money was not the right sort of man'.[10] Like Nellie, Mabel was another strong woman who would feed and encourage Eric's ambitions. If the Blairs were still sceptical of his ability to succeed as a writer, Mabel never doubted it.

Immediately on his return, he had got down to work on his book about tramps and tramping. Meanwhile, Max Plowman, literary editor of the New Adelphi, had sent him Lewis Mumford's biography of Herman Melville to review. The story of Melville's life of struggle and lack of fulfilment, even while writing his masterpiece, Moby Dick, was one with which Blair could identify. 'We see him as an overworked man of genius, living among people to whom he was hardly more than a tiresome, incomprehensible failure.' The book evoked in him not only ideas about the tribulations of the struggling writer, but about the nature of biography itself. He thought the interpretive method the most productive way of approaching the inner life of a writer – to analyse, in Mumford's words, 'his ideas, his feelings, his urges, his vision of life'. He admired Melville as 'a kind of ascetic voluptuary', a man 'superhumanly chaste, and yet amorous of delightful things wherever he found them'. This was 'a man who felt more vividly than common men, just as a kestrel sees more vividly than a mole'.[11] These capacities matched his own aspirations. Certainly he was gifted with the ability to see more vividly than most, though his empathy was directed more towards the human condition than human individuals. The wider context of Melville's life, spanning the years before and after the Civil War, offered him an American topography which accorded with the fictional landscape he had absorbed through his childhood reading. This became his model for comparing what he considered true freedom and democracy with that of a post-industrial America, which he considered a cruel delusion.

The publication of his first *New Adelphi* review coincided with the death of D. H. Lawrence from tuberculosis. The reaction of the press horrified him, and he recognised what he described as 'a grand old English tradition' of flattering the dead unless they happened to be artists. 'Let a politician die, and his worst enemies will stand up on the floor of the House and utter pious lies in his honour, but a writer or artist must be sniffed at, at least if he is any good. The entire British press united to insult D. H. Lawrence ("pornographer" was the usual description) as soon as he was dead.' Ten years later he noted that the same thing had happened to Joyce, *The Times* giving him 'a mean, cagey little obituary', and then refusing to print a letter of protest from Eliot.[12] He can have been under no illusion about the profession he had chosen to join.

The job caring for the boy at Walberswick did not last, but Ida had a friend in Southwold, Georgina Peters, wife of a high-ranking Indian policeman, who was looking for someone to supervise her three boys (Maurice, Richard and Kenneth) during school holidays. Without their father they were running wild, and had once been caught shooting out the lights of the local cinema with their airguns. Eric was proposed for the job and was accepted. The Peters boys, aged between seven and twelve, were all at prep schools and very bright. It was a welcome change to be in charge of children he could hope to teach something. Although not employed as a tutor, in his own friendly, informal fashion he taught them a great deal. For the boys, he was an inspiring presence.

Richard, then eleven, remembered his arriving at their home, Faraday Cottage – 'a tall and spindly character, rather dishevelled, with his hair all over the place and with a nasty hacking cough'. Not particularly promising, but as it turned out he was not only a delightful companion, but also a great authority on boys' magazines. He knew the *Scout* which they all read, as well as the *Gem*, the *Magnet* and the *Boys' Own Paper*, and could talk to them on equal terms about their comic-book heroes.[13] He amazed them by demonstrating how to make bombs by mixing nitrate and sugar, as he had done with Prosper Buddicom. It was as if he were trying to recreate his own childhood, to start where he had left off before leaving for Burma. (To many of his friends he was always a child at heart – 'a child,' said one, 'who loved mechanical gadgets and practical jokes, and rejoiced in his own elementary knowledge of botany, natural history and country lore'.)[14] He once blew up the rose bed at Faraday Cottage, startling the boys' grandmother, who was dozing in a nearby deckchair. As Eric's bombs exploded, the boys all cheered, 'Blairy Boy for bolshie bombs!'[15]

For two summers he supervised them during their school holidays. He took them down onto the beach, dug trenches, fought battles with sand bombs, and led them on long country rambles, always carrying a long forked stick, pointing out birds, showing them where to find toads spawning in remote ponds and birds nesting in undiscovered dells. He told them not to do what he had once seen boys do – blowing up toads with cycle pumps, but said that the best way to catch eels was to blast them with a shotgun. They found him always good-humoured, although, according to Maurice, the closest he came to laughter was a strange crooning chuckle.[16] He took them fishing from the pier and in the river at Walberswick, and, as a special treat, to the heronry in Blythburgh, which meant crossing the old railway bridge over the Blyth. The boys made their way gingerly along the remains of the disused track while Eric walked casually across the iron girders overhead – a feat which both astonished and impressed them. He told them – a piece of old tramp's wisdom this – that the best places to find lost coins were deserted scout campsites, including, presumably, the Duke of York's summer campsite.

Mrs Peters, a very pretty woman, had many admirers, including Eric's father. Richard Peters remembered how 'Mr Blair used to come into the bungalow where we lived and try to have an affair with my mother. Whenever he came my mother always hid from him, wouldn't have anything to do with him. He was a proper old stinker, Eric's father.'[17] Eric's niece, Jane, found this story perfectly credible. Dick, after all, was forbidden his own wife's bed and was probably as keen on women as his son. Eric, however, was more preoccupied with his book than with dangerous liaisons around Southwold which might embarrass his mother.

Still concerned with refining his own philosophical outlook, he told the boys that he distrusted all politicians, and was a Cavalier rather than a Roundhead. Despite his austere image, there was a hedonist trapped inside who broke loose occasionally, not least when it came to women – 'a kind of ascetic voluptuary', like Melville.[18] Although the boys saw him as essentially a realist, his view of the natural world linked him directly to Shelley and the Romantics. As he wrote much later, affirming a sense of awe which Nature inspired, 'Even the pleasure one takes in a flower – and this is true even of a botanist who knows all there is to know about a flower – is dependent partly on the sense of mystery.'[19] His attachment to childhood, his distaste for orthodox politics and his scepticism about hierarchy and scientific utopias further affirm the link. And there was something decidedly romantic about a man prepared to sacrifice so much in order to write. While he had not, up to this point, endured poverty out of necessity, like his Grub Street hero Gissing, he embraced the same destiny – the literary life, come what may. Whatever others thought, his friends and family at least respected his dedication. Dennis Collings, for example, knew that there were certain times when he was simply unavailable:

> Nobody ever saw him writing anything, because he did that in his little back room in the morning. The routine was, he'd have his breakfast, he'd go to his little back room, and he'd sit down at a table with a pen and paper, and he wrote. He didn't mind what he wrote at all; he just wrote. And this he looked upon as his training for writing more serious matters later on. He stopped at twelve, and then he went out and had a pint or something, and then he had his lunch, and then he would roam about the countryside with his friends.[20]

From time to time he would escape to London, staying sometimes with the Fierzes, sometimes in common lodging houses. In London, he met the *New Adelphi* people. Richard Rees had succeeded John Middleton Murry as editor, and would soon be relaunching the magazine as a monthly called the *Adelphi* again. When Blair visited its Bloomsbury Street offices, Rees was much impressed by his strange new contributor, though he thought he 'lacked vitality', failing, as he later confessed, to see beyond this languid exterior to the resolute spirit within. Max Plowman, the literary editor, was someone Eric could admire – a man who, during the war, had, like Siegfried Sassoon, resigned his commission on pacifist grounds and survived without being court-martialled. Afterwards he wrote one of the best first-hand accounts of the fighting, *A Subaltern on the Somme*. He was also a poet, and author of a well-received book on Blake. Although they came to differ over pacifism, Eric admired Plowman his strong moral character and always felt a close affinity for him. Max, in turn, thought Eric both interesting and unusual – an Englishman with a French cast of mind, he told his wife.[21]

Away from home he resumed his forays into the abyss. Dennis recognized that these expeditions were undertaken in an anthropological spirit, to gather material for his writings, although motivated, he thought, by the deep need for self-punishment.[22] This was the motivation to which Eric himself later admitted in *The Road to Wigan Pier*, and through the mind of Gordon Comstock in *Keep the Aspidistra Flying*:

> He wanted to go down, deep down, into some world where decency no

longer mattered; to cut the strings of his self-respect, to submerge himself – to sink . . . It was all bound up in his mind with the thought of being underground. He liked to think about the lost people, the under-ground people, tramps, beggars, criminals, prostitutes. It is a good world that they inhabit, down there in their frowzy kips and spikes. He liked to think that beneath the world of money there is that great sluttish underworld where failure and success have no meaning; a sort of kingdom of ghosts where all are equal. That was where he wished to be, down in the ghost-kingdom, below ambition.[23]

One unwelcome consequence of this decision was that he had made himself dependent on his family for bed and board, and on Aunt Nellie and his mother for an occasional loan. 'Why is it,' asks Gordon, 'that one can't borrow from a rich friend and can from a half-starved relative? But one's family, of course, "don't count".'[24] To escape the pressures of home, in the autumn of 1930 he decamped to Leeds, where Humphrey and Marjorie Dakin lived. He found the atmosphere at the Dakin home so congenial that he stayed on. Times were hard and Marjorie pregnant and far from well, but he was not unwelcome. Humphrey, however, having disliked him as a child, still found him gloomy and pessimistic. He considered his writing ambitions hopeless and kept urging him to find a job.[25] But no one would deter him, least of all Humphrey Dakin. 'I had to struggle desperately at the beginning, and if I had listened to what people said to me I would never have been a writer.'[26] He worked long hours up in his room tapping away on a borrowed typewriter, joining the others for meals and the occasional picnic and getting to know the children, Henry and Jane.

If Humphrey was not particularly close to Eric, Marjorie, his clever sister, was. If there was anyone in the family to whom he felt he could confide, apart from Nellie, it was her. 'Like all the Blairs,' said Humphrey, 'she was undemonstrative . . . she was tolerant, the sort of human being who instinctively invited confidence.'[27] And from her correspondence, she obviously shared her brother's sharp appreciation of English social life as well as his political outlook, which at this time meant a growing conviction that the USSR was no true model for socialism. In fact, he wrote, 'I was struck by clear signs of its transformation into a hierarchical society, in which the rulers have no more reason to give up their power than any other ruling class.'[28] The lessons of Winwood Reade and Eugène Adam had left their mark.

During 1930 he earned next to nothing from writing, contributing just four reviews to the *Adelphi*. Even so, his work showed that he had not lost the facility for turning out informed, assured and polished prose. Nor had he forgotten the lesson so eloquently preached in the *Eton College Chronicle*, about the need for critical honesty and 'being alive to the errors of others'. However, the satirical edge had hardened and his writing sounded distinctly more confident, knowing and ironical. Extra English with George Lyttelton had seemingly provided him with sufficient authority to hold forth as boldly on Edith Sitwell as on Pope and English Classicism, and to be audacious enough to dismiss the then well-regarded J. B. Priestley as 'blatantly second-rate'.[29]

At the *Adelphi* offices he met Jack Common, then 'a circulation-pusher' for the magazine, one of the few working-class men who became a close friend. Common was extremely surprised to find that a man with a growing reputation for having lived among tramps and beggars was in fact an ex-public schoolboy with a languid air and cut-glass accent. To him Blair seemed no more than an upper-middle-class drop-out, a man with ill-defined and suspect political views, pretending to be what he was not. Rather than 'a socialist', as most at the *Adelphi* considered themselves, he declared himself 'a Tory anarchist', an epithet he later applied to Swift. It was a fitting enough label for a man who, as Anthony Powell put it, 'Like most people "in rebellion" . . . was more than half in love with what he was rebelling against.'[30] This was one of the more obviously contradictory features of a man who, as he evolved as a writer and a man, would become evermore multi-faceted and contradictory.

The ability to hold two opposing views simultaneously, used to perverse effect in *Nineteen Eighty-Four*, was a characteristic of his own paradoxical cast of mind. He loved animals and yet was happy to shoot them; he was an atheist yet retained a highly religious sense of morality; he hated the class system but hankered for a time when the English class system seemed immutable; he hated the Scots and yet some of his favourite novelists were Scottish; he sneered at 'pansies' and yet he enjoyed close friendships with homosexual men; he came to call himself a socialist yet wrote witheringly about socialist types; he enjoyed reasoning and argument yet held some highly irrational opinions; he held strong political views and yet remained independent of all political movements and parties. Stephen Spender, who knew him later, saw him as a figure from a different age. 'He was really a radical conservative . . . like Cobbett. What he valued was the old concept of England based on the English countryside, in which to be conservative is to be against changes taking place, especially changes in the direction of producing inequality. He was opposed to the whole hard-faced industrial middle class which arose in the nineteenth century.'[31]

In Southwold, between visits to London and more tramping jaunts, he was pursuing three women simultaneously – Brenda Salkeld, the schoolteacher,

Eleanor Jaques, 'the girl-next-door', and Ruth Pitter, the poet. Ruth saw him as a sceptical pessimist, like Hardy, and although she thought he had a cruel streak, seemingly enjoyed his company, even while thinking him too young for her. She found his behaviour both strange and comic – he had little or no money and felt humiliated to let a woman pay, but for him taking a 'proper job' was bourgeois and contemptible. Knowing he had suffered several bouts of pneumonia she felt sure he was in a 'pre-tubercular condition', yet he still turned out on wintry days with no overcoat, gloves or scarf. 'It wasn't just poverty,' she decided, 'it was suicidal perversity.'[32] Whether or not he grew amorous towards her she was too discreet to say, but as a schoolboy he had wondered whether she would be easy 'to get', and cannot have been oblivious to her attractions. Sometimes she took him to London literary parties; he in turn wrote friendly reviews of her poems, comparing her classical technique to that of Pope.[33]

Eleanor was a lively, spirited young woman with a mind of her own, who shared his interest in literature, nature and gardening. With her he could indulge his prejudices against Scotsmen (especially the gin-swilling Burma Scots) and Roman Catholicism in all its manifestations. To him, 'the poor, unoffending old Church of England' compared well to the 'dogmatic intolerance' of the RCs.[34] The spread of Catholicism and the 'deceptive bluff' of Catholic apologists, were what most provoked his venom. Eleanor was probably too independent for him to want to marry (he preferred his women more pliant), but he found her sexually attractive and was ever hopeful of persuading her to sleep with him. She was just flirtatious enough to encourage him to persist.

Brenda was a different matter. She was tall and athletic, three years older than him, and, like Richard Blair, had been born in a Dorset vicarage. He fell very much under the spell of this clergyman's daughter – the enchantment of unattainability – and would remain so for many years to come. She found him deeply interesting and admired his absolute commitment to literature, but thought that he lacked feeling, especially for women, detecting in him, as others did, a cruel, even sadistic, streak. When someone said that his anti-feminist views were probably due to sadism, he merely remarked that, 'I have never read the Marquis de Sade's novels – they are unfortunately very hard to get hold of.'[35] However, he did get to know Swain's *Pleasures of the Torture Chamber*, a record of horrific cruelties under the Spanish Inquisition – more ammunition for attacking the Catholics. Brenda noticed how he enjoyed trying to shock her with tales of his exploits in Burma and to offend her sense of delicacy with risqué stories and his collection of rude seaside postcards. On one occasion he tramped all the way from Southwold to her home in Bedford, turning up on the doorstep and announcing that he had just come from the casual ward of the local workhouse. Her mother and sisters were predictably horrified and he was immediately packed upstairs for a bath. ('We were all saying, "I hope he doesn't use my loofah."') Brenda was not a little scornful of him acting the vagrant. He knew he could always go home, so could never experience what a real tramp felt, she told him.[36]

Tramping from Southwold along the Roman roads to Bedford through Cambridge, again treading in the footsteps of Defoe, he would have passed through the little Cambridgeshire village of Orwell, a place with close connections to Gow's Trinity College and burial-place of a translator of the *Apocrypha*, which Mr Sillar had read to the boys at St Cyprian's. He knew the Suffolk river called the Orwell, and finding a village of the same name would have struck him as a curious, even significant coincidence.

Whatever he felt about women he was more prepared to open himself to them than to men. He told Brenda how depressed he was by the slow progress of his career, and how at times he lost confidence in himself as a writer. He shared with her his various literary passions, talked about his writing and showed her his work-in-progress.[37] He was still uncertain how to win her round, but that failed to deter him and he became quite jealous on discovering that she was seeing a man called Pat Macnamara, home on leave from the Canadian North West Mounted Police. His letters grew more ardent, moving from 'Dear Brenda' to 'Dearest Brenda', and finally to 'Dearest & Most Belovedest Brenda'.

The Housman-like vision of love inspired by Jacintha had been largely obliterated by the pain of rejection and the compensating pleasures of debauchery among adulterous wives and doll-like prostitutes in Burma and Paris. His correspondence with Eleanor and Brenda carried elements of sexual innuendo, but displayed no level of seductive eloquence. It is evident that with Brenda he spoiled many an evening walk with sudden moves and, to her, shocking proposals. Even in his novels, male characters, such as the importunate Mr Warburton in *A Clergyman's Daughter* and Gordon in *Keep the Aspidistra Flying*, employ the direct approach – the sudden lunge (the farmyard animal technique) or the straightforward proposition – 'Are you going to be nice to me?' (the language of the more businesslike sexual transaction). And the main sexual scene in *Down and Out in Paris and London* takes place in a brothel – the savage rape of a virgin, described with considerable sadistic relish. In November 1930 he wrote woefully to Max Plowman about the unattainability not just of 'spiritual love' but also the objects of 'sinful lust'. 'Attempts to realize the impossible physical desire are even more destructive than attempts on the spiritual side.'[38]

Clandestine sex, such as he enjoyed in Burma and Paris, meant having to play a secretive role, to conceal the beastly Hyde inside the caring Jekyll. It was a dual role from which he did not recoil, and in a way it matched the double life he had already chosen to live between the subterranean world of outcasts and the polite world of home and respectability. 'Oh, what tangled webs we weave . . .' he wrote to Brenda, fearing their relationship would become known to others in Southwold, especially Eleanor.[39] Some who came to recognise this duality in him saw it as an internal conflict, a continuous struggle to suppress the dark side of himself – a secular Pilgrim beset by fleshly temptations. But it was more than sexually deviant thoughts with which he was wrestling; it was, on his own admission, the fearful memories of the diabolical hatred of which he was capable.

In October he sent the 35,000 word manuscript of what he called *A Scullion's Diary*, to Jonathan Cape, intending it, perhaps, for their Travellers' Library series, which included Maugham, Butler, Wells and the tramp-poet W. H. Davies. Feeling, no doubt, a great sense of achievement, he turned next to his Burmese novel. It meant returning to the kind of fiction he went to Paris to write in the first place – naturalistic though colourful, tragic and poetic.[40] However, when Cape rejected his book as 'too short and fragmentary', he quickly set about revising it, this time incorporating material from work already written, including 'The Spike', submitted earlier to the *New Adelphi*, and the pieces on tramps and beggars written for *Le Progrès Civique*. The new revision he called *Days in London and Paris*.

Already in 'The Spike' he had recreated a world of squalor and despair which was a very distinctive literary creation. What he had done, with Jack London and Zola as mentors, was create a style of reportage which had the ring of authenticity about it but was not buried under mountains of facts. At the same time he had somehow captured that quality he admired in Melville – the kestrel view rather than that of the mole. By combining a sense of outrage at the life imposed on English vagrants with another Melville characteristic, 'a passionate sensitivity', he brought a highly humane literary quality to his narrative. He described the squalor of the spikes, the faecal smells, the bugs and lice, the unutterable filth, the foul food, the loathsome habits of the tramps and the heartlessness of the Tramp Majors, with a refined disgust. And to the boredom, the biting cold and gnawing hunger of life in the spike, he brought the occasional flight of imagery – the blossoms on chestnut trees 'like great wax candles' – and the odd touch of literary irony – 'The clock's hands stood at four, and supper was not till six, and there was nothing left remarkable beneath the visiting moon.'[41] Certainly there would be no honey for tea in the spike, just stale bread. The essay revealed the style he was bringing to the revision of his book, turning a short fragmentary journal into an absorbing, buoyant, lightly fictionalised account of his Paris and London adventures. The dark sides of two great cities would be transformed and revealed through a highly literate imagination.

The great slump of the early thirties sharpened political divisions. Orwell's 'golden afternoon of the capitalist age' – the period since 1890 – was ending. Rees joined the Independent Labour Party and began to edge the *Adelphi* leftwards, a move which eventually led to the pacifist Plowman resigning. In February 1931, Oswald Mosley, a one-time Labour Minister, formed his breakaway New Party, and in April a republic was declared in Spain. The *Adelphi* would play its own small part in the changing cultural climate. In April it became the first national magazine to publish poems by the young W. H. Auden, heralding a radical shift in English poetic consciousness and the arrival of a circle of poets Eric found exclusive and phoney, producing work not at all to his decidedly traditional taste. Mosley, of course, heralded something far more sinister. By the end of that year he had already sized him up as a noisy pedlar of 'tripe'.[42]

He spent the New Year with Mabel and Frances Fierz, occasionally leaving in his tramp's costume to gather further material for his book. The Fierzes' son Adrian, like the Peters children, found him quite fascinating. They talked in a grown-up way about politics and literature and laughed over P. G. Wodehouse, and he was always ready to expound on his favourite authors. Invited to do more reviews for the *Adelphi*, he asked for books on India, low-life London, Villon, Swift, Smollett, Poe, Mark Twain, Zola, Anatole France, Conrad, or anything by Maugham or M. P. Shiel, who he seems to have known through Nellie. Rees published 'The Spike' in April, and took Blair to a teashop in New Oxford Street, hoping to learn more about him. He found him pleasant enough[43] and was surprised to discover they were both Old Etonians, although Rees had been an Oppidan. Eric rarely spoke of his education, and, when he did, always denigrated himself, saying that he was not from a social background normally to be found at the Eton.

On his twenty-eighth birthday, on 25 June, reviewing his 'life & achievements', he told Brenda that he had earned £2,000 as an Indian policeman, £220 from tutoring, around £100 from writing, £20 from dishwashing and £20 from other odd jobs. To this he added, sardonically, 'You will notice the only profession I have earned anything appreciable at was the only one I wholeheartedly loathed. Perhaps if I can find a job I loathed more I might become quite rich.'[44] He would find work he loathed, but perhaps not quite enough, because wealth would elude him for many years ahead. The only happy work for him, he said, was writing, but that would never make him rich enough to be able to marry. Even so, he still pursued her with letters beginning, 'Dearest & Belovedest Brenda'.

He was not good at managing his relationships with women. One Sunday in July he invited Brenda for a fishing expedition-cum-picnic. On this occasion she must have permitted a little canoodling, and he must have then gone much too far for her – the abrupt move perhaps or his usual blunt proposition. When she rebuffed him he told her that if she did not want to make love to him it was better they part. Outraged at this, she stormed off back to her lodgings. Next day he wrote, diplomatically avoiding endearments, with a formal 'Dear Brenda', and full of the most abject apologies and heartfelt pleadings.

> Please don't think I am merely heartless. You know I am fond of you, at any rate as I understand fondness, & your friendship means a great deal to me. I am sometimes lonelier than you guess, & it has made a great difference to me to have someone who took an interest in me. [He had only said what he said] because it hurt me to be played with – I did not mean that I merely wanted to discard you because someone else would do as well & be less trouble. But perhaps I conveyed that impression. Don't think that I was merely callous & selfish. It is only that I am fond of you & it hurts me not to have you altogether.[45]

He asked her out again but warned her that he would act in exactly the same way. Obviously expecting the incident would mean an end to their relationship, he signed off simply 'Eric A. Blair'. When years later she said that she thought he did not like women, the heart of the matter probably lay in that Sunday afternoon. As to his attitude towards females, Stephen Spender, a later friend, made no bones about it: 'Orwell was very misogynist. I don't know why. [He] was a strange sort of eccentric man full of strange ideas and strange prejudices. One was that he thought that women were extremely inferior and stupid . . . He really rather despised women.'[46]

His relationship with his father appeared to have improved. Richard had a reserved front-row seat at the local cinema and religiously sat through every film shown. Whenever possible, Eric joined him. Although he did not think it was time well spent, he was anxious to please the man he had so disappointed. He told Brenda an amusing story passed on by Richard, suggesting some thawing of their relationship. 'When my father was a boy he went to Cremorne Gardens & saw a man launched from a balloon in an attempt to fly. He fell straight into Chelsea cemetery, & made such a hole in the ground that all they had to do was to put up a tombstone. Rather a neat ending, I think?'[47] As a writer, he favoured neat endings.

He resubmitted his revised manuscript, *Days in London and Paris*, to Cape while preparing for another tramping jaunt – this time to join East Enders, tramps and gypsies on their annual pilgrimage to Kent for the hop harvest. Rather teasingly, before setting out, he wrote asking the genteel, probably still-outraged Brenda if she would care to join him. She would not, he knew, object to his three-day beard, and he would promise not to have lice. 'What fun if we could both go hopping together. But I suppose your exaggerated fear of dirt would deter you. It is a great mistake to be afraid of dirt.'[48] If she did not rise to the bait, it was because she knew how much Eric loved to shock.

The great expedition began at Ruth Pitter's new workshop in Chelsea, where he now sometimes switched into tramp's outfit. Ruth regarded the whole charade with a jaundiced eye. 'He didn't look in the least like a poor man. God knows he was poor, but the formidable look didn't go with the rags.'[49] His first stopovers were the Lew Levy kips in Westminster Bridge Road. Then he spent two nights in Trafalgar Square among the rough-sleepers, wrapped in newspapers and constantly harassed by police, an experience incorporated into his second novel, *A Clergyman's Daughter*. The accuracy with which he later rendered the talk among the down-and-outs into disconnected dialogue lent it a surreal quality reminiscent of the Nighttown scene in Joyce's *Ulysses*, a book which came to obsess him. His reports from the lower depths show an ear finely tuned in to underworld vernacular – as tuned in as no doubt it was to the Parisian argot he had learned earlier. In Trafalgar Square his disguise almost slipped when he began reading a French edition of Balzac's *Eugénie Grandet* which he happened to have taken along; however, the other tramps merely concluded that it must be a dirty book. Conceal his class origins as he might, he could never shed his literary self, which remained alert, consciously transforming squalid experience into literature.

The diary of his Kentish trek, however, shows that his trampish role by no means fooled everybody. One entry shows how difficult it was for him to 'pass' as a genuine underdog.

> The terrible Tramp Major met us at the door and herded us into the bathroom to be stripped and searched. He was a gruff, soldierly man of forty, who gave the tramps no more ceremony than sheep at a dipping pond, shoving them this way and that and shouting oaths into their faces. But when it came to myself, he looked hard at me and said: 'You are a gentleman?' 'I suppose so,' I said. He gave me another long look. 'Well, that's bad luck, guv'nor,' he said, 'that's bloody bad luck, that is.' And thereafter he took it into his head to treat me with compassion, even with a kind of respect.[50]

Of course, it took an old soldier to recognise an officer and gentleman, but, fortunately for the intrepid observer this was a rare occurrence and on other occasions and in other places he suffered the normal humiliations.

> The food was the same old bread and marg, though the Tramp Major got angry when we asked in good faith whether the stuff they gave us to

drink was tea or cocoa . . . In the morning they told us we must work
till eleven, and set us to scrubbing out one of the dormitories . . . [It]
was a room of fifty beds close together with that warm, faecal stink that
you never seem to get away from in the workhouse . . . The thought of
those grey-faced, ageing men living a very quiet, withdrawn life in a
smell of WCs, and practising homosexuality, makes me feel sick. But it
is not easy to convey what I mean, because it is all bound up with the
smell of the workhouse.[51]

Elsewhere in the diary he implies sympathy for the 'Nancy Boys' his pal
Ginger boasts of having beaten up, and seems to understand the tramps, cut
off from normal female company, who resort occasionally to homosexuality. It was only when the activity observed was combined with the faecal
stink of the workhouse or with artistic privilege that disgust intruded.

On his journey along the Old Kent Road to Sevenoaks, he was retracing
the route taken by David Copperfield to his aunt's house in Dover after his
escape from the clutches of the Murdstones, though, unlike David, Eric
and Ginger covered the first leg of their journey by tram. After that it was a
succession of spikes, nights in roadside hedges, and begging and stealing
along with the light-fingered Ginger, before reaching the hop-fields. His
reports to Dennis included a veritable lexicon of travellers' slang, while his
diary recorded the grinding routine of the casual workers, enlivened only by
colourful descriptions of the hop-pickers, including the gypsies – the closest we got in England to the Noble Savage, he thought.[52]

On his return he found lodgings at a kip in Tooley Street, close to Tower
Bridge, and, despite the bug-ridden beds, 'the best sevenpenny one in
London'. He used Bermondsey Public Library to complete his diary, and
sometimes joined Ginger at Billingsgate fish market earning the odd tup-
pence helping porters push their heavy barrows up the hill into Eastcheap.
But after two weeks at the kip he found he was writing nothing. The noise,
dirt and lack of privacy were depressing. 'The dormitory was also disgusting, with the perpetual din of coughing and spitting – everyone in a lodging
house has a chronic cough, no doubt from the foul air.'[53] If he was not
already, as Ruth Pitter thought, in 'a pre-tubercular state', he was in the
right place to become so.

He wrote home for ten shillings and moved to a room in Windsor Street,
a working-class area off the Harrow Road in Paddington. On a visit to
Mabel, he found a package awaiting him: Cape had rejected his book a
second time. Hoping for some wise advice he handed the manuscript to
Rees, who promised to talk to T. S. Eliot at Faber & Faber, adding that if all
else failed he would include sections of it in the *Adelphi*. Encouraged, he
wrote to Eliot, offering him first a translation of Jacques Roberti's *A la Belle*

de Nuit, about a Paris prostitute ('appallingly indecent'), assuring him that he was quite familiar with the world of Paris prostitutes.[54] Eliot wrote asking to see the book and only decided against it after reading it. Shortly afterwards, Eric sent him his much-revised *Days in London and Paris*.

That autumn, Mabel Fierz, with whom his relationship was to take an amorous turn, decided that Eric needed a good agent. It happened that Leonard Moore, a member of her local tennis club, was one half of the literary agency Christie & Moore, with offices in the Strand. She sent Moore some of Eric's stories and mentioned also the book he had submitted to Eliot.

Even though in need of money, he continued spending time with his vagrant friends around the London spikes. Calling at the *Adelphi* office, he told Jack Common he planned to spend Christmas in prison and asked his advice on how to get arrested. His idea of lighting a bonfire in Trafalgar Square, Common said, would earn Eric nothing but a night in a cell and a friendly caution. He would do better to go in for theft. He opted for neither arson nor theft but still planned to get himself incarcerated. Most of his tramping acquaintances had been 'inside' and he wanted to share their experience. Finally he took to the streets one Saturday just before Christmas, having consumed five pints of beer and more than a half bottle of whisky. The result was 'Clink', an account of a day and two nights in the cells of an East End police station (again as 'Edward Burton'), and his brief appearance before a magistrate before being released. The essay – more low company, more faecal smells, and some persuasively authentic prison dialogue – he never managed to get published, but the experience found its way into *Keep the Aspidistra Flying*, and added the vocabulary of the London jailbird to his lexicon of underworld slang. Now at last he had something truly in common with the other tramps.

Around this time he reported coughing up blood and may have visited the chest clinic at St Mary's Hospital, Paddington, afterwards telling Brenda of a Public Health notice which had amused him, reading 'Consumptives should refrain from kissing' – a good refrain for a ballad, he thought.[55] However, he received no treatment, he said, so the lesion he later lamented having gone unnoticed in his childhood continued to go undetected. At twenty-eight and full of ambition these things were hardly worth worrying about.

Mabel reported that he was thrown out of his lodging in Windsor Street for having women in his room – around Paddington (a red-light district) this no doubt meant street women. To get away from London he went down to Wisborough Green in Sussex to stay with the recently separated Lydia Shiel, an admirer and sharp critic of his work and an old socialist friend of Nellie. He wrote to Brenda saying how idyllic it was to be far from civilisation, miles even from a Post Office, 'in the middle of beechwoods, & the pheasants, squirrels etc. feed almost on the back doorstep . . . The quiet here suits me very well, & my sole disipation [sic] is chess, which I am getting rather good at.'[56] They were now back on 'Dearest Brenda' terms, and he upbraided her for being 'a feminist', acknowledging his male chauvinism when he thanked her for still wanting to see him 'in spite of my hideous prejudice against your sex, my obsession about R.C.s etc.'.[57]

The year 1931 was one of little progress in his career, publishing just three reviews and three essays. However, these included 'A Hanging', one of his most striking and subtly observed prose pieces. In the New Year he moved to another squalid room on Westminster Bridge Road in Lambeth, the slum-ridden stamping ground of Gordon Comstock, before the dreaded aspidistra claimed him for respectability. After two months Eliot returned his *Days in London and Paris*, damning it with faint praise. He found it interesting, he wrote, but 'too loosely constructed, as the French and English episodes fall into two parts with very little to connect them'.[58] He then suggested he write a different book, concentrating just on down-and-outs in England, not surprising advice coming from so intense an Anglophile.

Disappointed after so much effort, rather than rewrite it again he sent the manuscript to Mabel telling her to throw it away but to keep the paper-clips.[59] Unknowingly, this was the best thing he could have done, because she took it upon herself to become his champion. Fired with enthusiasm, she took the book personally to Leonard Moore and insisted he get it published. According to her, Moore was reluctant to take a twice-rejected book by an unknown author, but she was so persistent that finally he agreed at least to read it.

Unaware of this, Eric had left London to stay again with the Dakins in Leeds where he concentrated on *Burmese Days*. It meant reliving the years 1922 to 1927 and attempting to distil from his most exquisite memories of landscape and the remembered extremes of British oppression the sort of narrative he was after, both haunting and stylish. Going over the past in this intense way gave powerful expression to his new *raison d'être* – to confront injustice, and expiate his own sense of guilt. It would not be easy, especially as his situation was discouraging. He had still published very little and had no reputation to speak of. His first book had been turned down, and there was as yet no prospect of earning his living exclusively from writing. What is more, in Leeds he had to endure Humphrey's scathing remarks about a man who hadn't got a proper job, so he took to working in the public library, where he first read Robert Tressell's *The Ragged-Trousered Philanthropists* and Aldous Huxley's newly published *Brave New World*.[60] Tressell's book, a classic piece of proletarian literature, he thought 'wonderful', if 'very clumsily written'.[61] *Brave New World* was the kind of book he had enjoyed since childhood, and this dystopian fantasy clearly struck a chord with him. However, as the thirties unfolded, he came to see Huxley's vision as a 'completely materialistic vulgar civilization based on hedonism' – 'a danger past'. To him, a far more horrific future loomed with the rise of totalitarianism.[62]

One of his stories sent to Moore, 'The Idiot', was about the 'imbecile boy' in Walberswick, which he had considered calling 'The Hairless Ape'. He planned to send it to Rees, he told Brenda, but thought he might be appalled by it and not want to print it. And even if it was published he would not want the boy's mother ever to read it.[63] Mercifully, perhaps, it never saw the light of print. Eric's cruel side, of which he seems to have been only vaguely aware, had obviously revealed itself. Time and again in his writing he made appearance count against people, a sign of their moral condition, an idea arising, it seems, from his considering himself ugly, and from his consuming sense of guilt.

Chapter 8

The Invention of George Orwell

'It seemed a queer thing to have to do, to use a false name; dishonest – criminal, almost.'

Orwell, *A Clergyman's Daughter*, 1935

'Every philosophy is coloured by a secret imaginative background which does not officially form part of its doctrines. Obviously this is even truer of fiction . . . by their subject-matter ye shall know them'.

Orwell, book review, 1940

Finally, no longer wanting to burden anyone and to keep his family happy, Blair took a job at The Hawthorns, a boys' private school at Hayes in Middlesex. This small town, gradually being engulfed by an expanding London, was just a few stops down the line from Henley and Slough (the local station for Eton). Hayes brought home to him the ruination wreaked upon the countryside he loved by post-war urban sprawl and the spread of light industry, symbolised by the grimly intrusive outline of the nearby HMV gramophone factory. (For him the gramophone became an emblem of modern decadence, the mindless reproduction of machine-made ideas and dictated opinions.) But he saw more than just the urban sprawl, he saw such towns as symptomatic of a wider social flux.

In Slough, Dagenham, Barnet, Letchworth, Hayes – everywhere, indeed, on the outskirts of great towns – the old pattern is gradually changing into something new. In those new vast wildernesses of glass and brick the sharp distinctions of the older kind of town, with its slums and mansions, or of the country, with its manor-houses and squalid cottages, no longer exists . . . There are wide gradations of income, but it is the same kind of life that is being lived at various levels, in labour-saving flats or Council houses, along the concrete roads and in the naked democracy of the swimming-pools. It is a rather restless, cultureless life, centring round tinned food, *Picture Post*, the radio and internal combustion engine. It is a civilization in which children grow up with an intimate knowledge of magnetos and in complete ignorance of the Bible.[1]

Hayes, he told Eleanor Jaques, was 'one of the most godforsaken places I have ever struck. The population seems to be entirely made up of clerks who frequent tin-roofed chapels on Sundays & for the rest bolt themselves within doors.'[2]

This depressing backdrop of a changing English landscape and the soulless society it heralded would haunt his work and thoughts throughout the rest of the decade, thoughts expressed most bitterly in *Coming Up For Air* with its diatribe against grim semi-detached, stucco-fronted, privet-hedged suburbia.[3] John Betjeman, contemplating much the same scene in a neighbouring town, was far more brutal.

> Come, friendly bombs, and fall on Slough,
> It isn't fit for humans now . . . [4]

In England it was always difficult for a serious writer to live solely by his craft, as George Gissing had found in the previous century, and teaching as a means of supporting a writing life was not uncommon. Huxley had taught at Eton, Lawrence in a London council school, Christopher Hollis was teaching at Stonyhurst, Evelyn Waugh had taught at a prep school in Wales, and Graham Greene began by tutoring before escaping into journalism. Blair, with no degree, was not attractive teaching material, but being an Old Etonian carried some weight. Even so, the school he did find to employ him was very low down in the educational firmament. The Hawthorns was a converted vicarage, recalled by one of his old pupils as just as dreary as he described Ringwood House in *A Clergyman's Daughter*.[5] With its Dickensian echoes, the school became for him a symbol of vulgar philistinism and greed.

The Hawthorns was owned by a small-time businessman, Derek Eunson, who also worked at the gramophone factory. He ran the school simply as a business and employed others to do the teaching. The dozen or so boys aged between eleven and sixteen were sent there by parents not wanting to educate them at the local council school, and most ended up with a very basic commercial qualification. As the only full-time teacher employed, Blair was in effect headmaster. He lived in and took meals with the family, an arrangement which had distinct drawbacks. Mrs Eunson was the chapel organist and her piano-playing at home and fervent hymn-singing were not exactly conducive to his writing.[6]

He knew the job was well below his capabilities and hated having to teach when he could be writing. The work was boring, and the school, he said, was a 'foul place'[7] and 'a dirty swindle'.[8] Because there were no decent textbooks, he tried being inventive, teaching French St Cyprian's-style, allowing conversation only in French, and producing plays with the boys. However, he was a stickler for English grammar and marked essays with Etonian ruthlessness. One pupil, Geoffrey Stevens, remembered 'Balls!' written at the bottom of one of his efforts. Even so, he was recalled as a stimulating and friendly teacher with a strange sense of humour, best remembered for taking boys on nature rambles and fishing trips, as *he* had been as a schoolboy, showing them how to collect caterpillars, keep a pickle-jar aquarium and how to trap marsh gas. He was amused to find even the sixteen-year-olds still reading the *Gem* and the *Magnet* and he decided, it was at them, the sons of small businessmen and professionals, that the magazines were really aimed.[9]

Amid the general boredom his two consolations were his writing and a friendship with the local curate, Ernest Parker – 'High Anglican but not a creeping Jesus', he told Eleanor.[10] Churchgoing got him away from Mrs Eunson's maddening hymn-singing, and the school's assistant master, Grey – a Roman Catholic! St Mary's, the local Anglican Church, was his refuge from mediocrity, even though it was High Church and reeked of 'popery', with vicar in cope and biretta, processions with candles and images of the Virgin Mary. He often made friends with Anglican clergymen – mostly Oxbridge graduates, and usually among the few educated people in small English towns and villages. As he said of Samuel Butler, despite his atheism, he did not object to Christianity and 'obviously had a sneaking affection for the clergy'.[11] And, as he noted later, some of the best libraries were in country vicarages.[12] To have access to intelligent conversation and a decent library (and perhaps a quiet place to write), he was prepared to conceal his own atheism, attend services, help refurbish church relics, and even take Holy Communion. There was also a garden at the vicarage and a 'Holy Goat', which the Parkers taught him how to milk.

Another advantage of his friendship with Parker was that he could experience Church ritual and vicarage life at first hand – more grist for his fiction mill. It also produced another of his cruel sketches, this time of an elderly communicant, about whom he wrote to Eleanor: 'I [was] sitting behind a moribund hag who stinks of mothballs & gin, & has to be more or less carried to & from the altar at communion.'[13] This poor woman became the model for Miss Mayfill in *A Clergyman's Daughter* after whom Dorothy is revolted to have to drink from the same communion cup. 'A faint scent radiated from her – an ethereal scent, analysable as eau-de-Cologne, moth-balls and a sub-flavour of gin.'[14] As Ruth Pitter noted, he disliked old women who only intensified his misogyny. And as his writing suggests, he seemed to believe that, 'By their stinks ye shall know them.'

Ringwood House, of course, is a caricature, the school's most salient features being exaggerated to expose the mercenary mentality and philistinism of the owners of such schools, and to make the point that the boys and their families were being cheated. However, the story of Dorothy being stopped from teaching *Macbeth* because parents object to the line about him being 'ripped untimely from his mother's womb' carries conviction. *Macbeth* was perhaps his favourite play, Eunson had founded the local Baptist tin-roofed chapel, and The Hawthorns' parents were mostly drawn from his congregation.

Cut off from the women who interested him, Blair invited them to theatres in London or on country walks to Burnham Beeches – well out of sight of curates and sanctimonious school proprietors. These country walks were more than just nature tours, though he always enjoyed displaying his considerable knowledge of wildlife. With women there was also, for him, the prospect of a Laurentian adventure. Like Lady Chatterley's gamekeeper, he saw the countryside as his sexual stamping ground – a place to take women in both senses of the word; indeed, pastoral seduction became a feature of his fiction.

Sometime in June he learned from Moore that Victor Gollancz wanted to publish his book. Unlike Eliot and Cape, Gollancz had spotted Blair as a coming man in tune with the times. His reader, Gerald Gould, wrote of it: 'This is an extraordinarily forceful and socially important document, and I think it most certainly ought to be published.' He found it shocking, but imagined it was intended to shock. Although he thought the author might have 'embroidered a little here and there . . . substantially this is a true picture of conditions which most people ignore and ought not to be allowed to ignore'.[15] Gollancz agreed, with a few reservations, mostly to do with possible libel and obscenity charges. Although he had only been publishing under his own imprint since 1928, libel was a sore point with him, having been sued in 1931 over a book set in an identifiable girls' school in Kensington.[16] Obscenity charges were easily brought in those days simply through a letter of complaint to the Home Secretary, and cases could be prosecuted with great zealotry. Although Eric found such publishing problems irksome, he was happy to co-operate if it meant his dreams of authorship being realised. As requested, he toned down Chapter 2, Charlie's story of sadistic rape, and changed the name of a restaurant to avoid a possible libel. He probably altered the names of some locations, too – there are no English towns called Romton or Lower Binfield. And Gollancz disliked the title *Days in Paris and London*, suggesting instead *Lady Poverty*, from

Alice Meynell's lines 'The Lady Poverty was fair,/But she hath lost her looks of late' – the author's initial epigraph.

Strangely, having appeared often enough in print as E. A. Blair, he suddenly informed Moore that he preferred to publish the book under a pseudonym, explaining that he was rather ashamed of his own name.[17] He told others that he hated 'Eric', and 'Blair' sounded Scottish. He also said that he hid his identity in order not to embarrass his parents and (to Richard Rees) for fear of it being used to work magic against him. After all, his own magic, it seemed, had already claimed two lives –Yorke and Marjoribanks.

While not yet quite 'Eric the FAMOUS AUTHOR', acceptance lent him a certain cachet. He must have sent the news immediately to Mabel together with an invitation to spend a day in the country with him by way of celebration. Her reply suggests that she knew exactly what he had in mind.

> Darling, how splendid! 2.30 then at Hayes Station on Monday. Take me
> then by the quickest route to a punt on the river. I adore a warm sunny
> day in a punt. I will punt you carefully along the prettiest ways and not
> upset your male dignity into the Thames! Take your costume in case we
> find a suitable place. I hate the usual swimming bath. It will be nice.
> Not as you say a decent walk. I prefer the opposite! If it rains. Well, we
> will visit the Pubs in turn. The great thing is to walk as little as possible,
> so try and find out the route . . .[18]

It was not unusual for Mabel to take lovers; her husband, Francis, merely turned a blind eye to her amours.[19] A seductive afternoon on the river or out in the countryside was the sort of idyll of which Eric dreamed. It was sad for him that the girl he really pined for, Brenda, was not so readily seduced.

The magic of success continued to work for him back in Southwold for the holidays. That summer, buoyed up by his contract with Gollancz, his country walks along the Blyth valley finally brought more sexual fulfilment – this time with Eleanor. He was absolutely thrilled by this and could not refrain from telling her so in a letter.

> I cannot remember when I have ever enjoyed any expeditions so much
> as I did those with you. Especially that day in the wood along past
> Blythburgh Lodge – you remember, where the deep beds of moss were.
> I shall always remember that & your nice white body in the dark green
> moss.

The Laurentian fantasy which became reality would remain for him an archetypal experience to be relived again and again. There was, in both these cases, the added frisson of forbidden love which he now found irresistible. He urged Eleanor to get to London whenever she could. 'It would make so much difference having someone like you around the place, even if we could only meet occasionally & then only walk about the streets & picture galleries.'[20] It sounds like the cry of a lonely man suddenly enthralled by unexpected intimacy. Unfortunately, at the time, Eleanor was going seriously with Dennis Collings, something of which Eric was perfectly aware. Dennis, however, had his own rakish reputation, so perhaps Eric felt no guilt at making love to his girlfriend.[21] He confided his double-cross to Mabel, who upbraided him as wicked and unprincipled. Curiously, he defended himself on the grounds that whatever he did his mother would always forgive him.[22] His sins may have been masculine, but his conscience, it seems, was female.

He must have tried to lure Brenda down the same primrose path, but by now she was well aware of his designs and well able to rebuff him. She had also got an inkling of his philandering and told him that she could not take his attentions seriously when he was dallying elsewhere. Again he sought her forgiveness:

I am sorry I worried you the other night. It is necessary that we should come to an understanding sooner or later, but there is no particular hurry. If your answer must finally be no, I don't see why even then we should part, unless a sort of undefined relationship such as we have worries you. I would infinitely rather have you as a friend only than not at all, and I would even, on those terms, undertake to stop pursuing other women if you really wanted me not to. I don't know if you ever quite realised how much you mean to me. Besides, you said that you thought you would finally take a lover, and if so I don't see why it shouldn't be me, unless you have some reason for drawing back from me personally. I don't particularly mind waiting; I should have to wait in any case, as I am not in a position to marry and shan't be for several years probably. So let us continue as we are, unless you have really some reason for wanting to get rid of me. I recognise that there is something in your life which you don't want to sacrifice by tying yourself irrevocably to another person, but surely such a relationship as we have doesn't interfere with that? Only, even if we are only friends, you mustn't mind my making love to you in a small way and occasionally asking you to go further, because it is my nature to do that.[23]

The fact that she allowed their friendship to continue suggests that her feelings for him were strong, even if ambivalent. Obviously his feelings for her were equally intense but his selfish and petulant approach was never going to work with her. His observation in an *Adelphi* review that autumn that Byron had two halves – a 'fundamental decency' seen in his poems, and an 'abominable' attitude towards women – looks remarkably like self-recognition.[24] Despite the strong mutual attraction, neither was able to commit in a way that suited the other. This high-tension relationship was being played out as Eric wrestled with *Burmese Days*, and some of its switchback quality – the feeling of hopes raised and then dashed – seems to infuse the affair between Flory and Elizabeth in the novel. His rival, Pat Macnamara, the Mountie, still appearing occasionally on leave, no doubt stood in for the all-too-attractive cavalryman Verrall.

His sexual appetite was undiminished. He was happy to take satisfaction wherever he could find it. Not only was he having affairs with Mabel and Eleanor, but his accounts of his London perambulations suggest that he was more than a little familiar with the habits and manners of London prostitutes. Dorothy in *A Clergyman's Daughter* finds herself in a house of ill-fame; Gordon, in *Keep the Aspidistra Flying*, is picked up by a predatory streetwalker and taken to a cheap hotel, while, somewhat later, Winston Smith would recall a grisly encounter with an ageing prostitute in *Nineteen Eighty-Four*. And Rayner Heppenstall, with whom he later shared a flat, recalled how he once found it difficult to pry a drunken Eric loose from the clutches of a tart in a Hampstead pub. In his own strange way he may have linked his need for sexual expression to his need to write. He later noted how religious paranoia led Gogol to burn the second part of *Dead Souls*, linking his failed creativity to his sexual impotence. Such a connection, of course, provided a convenient justification for promiscuity.[25]

Despite his sexual successes, he still had the idea that he was unattractive to women. When Moore asked for a picture for an American publisher, he wrote, 'I am not certain whether my photograph would be a very good advert.'[26] This idea went deeper with him than the mirror or the camera. He seemed to believe, as did certain Victorian criminologists, that character is manifest in human physiognomy. Like the picture of Dorian Gray, moral imperfections become engraved upon the human face. When he later wrote that, 'At 50, everyone has the face he deserves,'[27] he was expressing the self-same idea. And when he gave the wretched John Flory a hideous birthmark, his mark of Cain, it signifies not just a flawed complexion but a flawed character, too. He once said memorably that he could not bear to look at the 'corrupt face' of a well-known magazine editor he considered dishonest.[28] This Erewhonian idea may have originated in childhood when he was told that private sins had public manifestations. 'Had I got black rings round my eyes? . . . These were supposed to be a symptom by which masturbators could be detected. But already, without knowing this, I accepted the black rings as a sure sign of depravity, some kind of depravity. And many times, even before I grasped the supposed meaning, I have gazed anxiously into the glass, looking for the first hint of that dreaded stigma, the confession which the secret sinner writes upon his own face.'[29]

In reviews for the *Adelphi* and the recently launched *New English Weekly*, he continued to snipe at the Catholic Church and its 'current drizzle of propaganda',[30] and now turned on H. G. Wells, whose futuristic novels he had begun cynically to question.[31] The idea that science would lead the world towards a new utopia of happy enlightenment had been, to him, exploded in the trenches of the Great War, and the dismal brooding decade of unemployment and suburban ruination then in progress had begun to look more than a little ominous.

In Southwold the Blairs were about to move to a grander home, Montague House, at 36 High Street, which Ida had bought with a bequest – no doubt her share of the Limouzin inheritance. Eric was still working on a draft of *Burmese Days*, and by the beginning of September told Brenda it had reached page 221, with about eighty pages to go. However, he said, he was 'disgusted with it' and was burying his disgust in gardening and rereading Butler's *The Way of All Flesh*. He also amused himself by sending her blasphemous versions of New Testament verses: 'Though I speak with the tongues of men and of angels and have no sex-appeal – I am become as a sounding brass and a tinkling symbol.'[32]

The autumn term at The Hawthorns he found particularly frustrating. He was committed to putting on a Christmas play, which involved writing and directing it and making the costumes. The prospect depressed him and *Burmese Days* sat unfinished on his desk. As an anti-Catholic gesture he began taking the *Church Times* regularly. 'I do like to see that there is life in the old dog yet – I mean in the poor old C of E,' he told Eleanor. He was still writing to her in the most endearing terms, though sometimes with a mixture of pathos and insouciance: 'Dearest Eleanor, it was so nice of you to say you looked back on your days with me with pleasure. I hope you will let me make love to you again some time, but if you don't it doesn't matter, I shall always be grateful to you for your kindness to me.'[33]

For the boys at The Hawthorns, Mr Blair's play about Charles II was a memorable experience; for him it was a grim duty. To Brenda he wrote that producing the play, helping out at the church and correcting proofs of his 'poisonous book' left him quite unable to work on his novel.[34] Again he laid a curse on his old enemy Burton, giving his name to the most cowardly character in the play, and reiterated his sympathy towards the Cavaliers against the narrow-minded Puritans – a dig no doubt at those small-minded parents who attended the local tin-roofed chapel. In the event he was able to salvage something from the experience, giving it to Dorothy in *A Clergyman's Daughter*.

Gollancz was still unhappy about his book title and wanted to know how the author wished to style himself. After some discussion, *Lady Poverty* gave way to *In Praise of Poverty*, then *Confessions of a Down-and-Out*, then *Confessions of a Dishwasher*. Finally, Gollancz came up with *Down and Out in Paris and London*, which satisfied both parties. He then suggested 'X' as a pen name, but Eric thought that if he was going to adopt a pseudonym he might as well have one he could use again. He offered a choice of four names: P. S. Burton (his tramping incognito), Kenneth Miles, George Orwell and H. Lewis Allways. He preferred George Orwell, he said, and Gollancz agreed. *Down and Out in Paris and London* by George Orwell was scheduled for publication in January 1933, a first edition of 1,500 copies. It now carried an epigraph from Chaucer, 'O scathful harm, condition of poverte,' from a passage in 'The Man of Lawe's Tale', on which Gordon Comstock would later dilate angrily in *Keep the Aspidistra Flying*. Eric was delighted with the look of the book; cleverly it gave the impression of being longer than it was.

The origin of 'George Orwell' is uncertain. A novelist he greatly admired and with whom he strongly identified, George Gissing, shared his surname with a Norfolk village just a day's tramping from Southwold. 'Orwell' was the name of both a Cambridgeshire village and a Suffolk river. Adrian Fierz thought 'George' came from his father's habit of applying it to casual acquaintances, and Rayner Happenstall thought it reflected Orwell's predilection for English royalty (Mary, Elizabeth and Jane were his preferred names for girls). But the George Gissing parallel supplies a more satisfyingly literary source.

The taking of a pseudonym raises many questions about Blair, the identity he seems to have wanted to conceal. He had taken a false name as a boy to write joke letters to an advertiser, he had written anonymously for ephemerals at Eton, he chose a false identity when slumming among the down-and-outs, and now chose a literary persona to mask the guilt-stricken Blair. It is evident that in almost every one of his novels the theme of the double life is central. The English writer–teacher Blair in Paris sinks down below his class to work in hotel kitchens as a skivvy, and then lives in London as a tramp; in *A Clergyman's Daughter*, Dorothy, the female alter ego who conceals the male narrator, takes a pseudonym after losing her identity; Gordon, in *Keep the Aspidistra Flying*, sinks out of sight into the slum depths of darkest Lambeth, becoming a wildly different person from the respectable Gordon who works in advertising; George Bowling, in

Coming Up For Air, turns truant husband and attempts to revert to childhood; in *Animal Farm* the pigs live secret lives and Benjamin the Donkey retains his private scepticism; in *Nineteen Eighty-Four*, Winston Smith lives a dangerous double life and is finally obliterated, transformed into a mindless zombie by the Party's torture machine. There was more than one secret self hidden behind the new literary persona.

According to its author, *Down and Out in Paris and London*, which Gollancz published on 9 January and which launched George Orwell, was 'a travel book'. It is a travel book in more than one sense. It is, of course, the story of the journey of an impoverished Englishman along the social margins of Paris and London, but also of a journey into the dark, suppressed side of the bourgeois consciousness, aimed at showing the hidden side of itself to respectable society. Here, Orwell is saying, is what lies beneath the floorboards, behind the wallpaper, down in the sewers beneath your neatly kept houses. Here are the slaves who make your luxury hotels and smart restaurants work; here is the human waste your exploitative society disposes of in slum housing, grim lodging houses and dark alleyways. But this is also a journey of the imagination, which mirrors the inner life of a man in the process of transforming himself into a literary personage. The opening sentence of *Down and Out in Paris and London* bears one of the key characteristics of the author, which recurs throughout his major works:

The rue du Coq d'Or, Paris, seven in the morning.

The clock begins ticking on page one as it ticks throughout all his novels. Time stalks his pages, suggesting a mind urgently aware that time is against him. Here he is down and out, but his pencil is poised and his notebook ready to fill – down and out but also awake and very much alert. Beyond the time-span of unfolding events lies a book and a career to be launched. His descent into the shadow-world of poverty, starvation and vagrancy is a voluntary odyssey, of which he is the grim chronicler.

Because he was a man set on a course of self-mortification, Orwell's book can also be seen as a deliberate plunge into the nether world of indigence and failure, the prospect of which so horrified the bourgeoisie. It is as if he were tasting wilfully the horrors evoked by the high priests of middle-class respectability – the Wilkes, the Vile Old Men of Eton, the Major Wellbornes, the Richard Walmsley Blairs and Tramp Majors of the world. The realm of the social outcast, the skivvies, the beggars, the monstrous tramps and nightwalkers – this was the foreign country he chose to explore; and in exploring that mirror image of bourgeois life he was exploring his own dark side, a dark side already glimpsed in the brothels of Rangoon, the police stations and death cells of Burma. It was a highly conscious experiment by a man hoping to achieve repentance and get a book out of it at the same time.

Down and Out in Paris and London reveals more than one key aspect of Blair's personality. He enjoyed low life and was able to pass as a man without means; he enjoyed taking a false identity and living the double life. It is the story of a man in disguise. But it is also the story of a man with a highly developed sociological imagination, an eye to how systems work, who they benefit and who they are designed to fool – the swindlers who pass themselves off as Russian Bolsheviks; the smart and courteous hotel staff who serve with style the food cooked in squalid kitchens; the hierarchy of waiters and chefs and dishwashers whose system of tyranny and dependence both deludes customers and delivers profits to management. He views these characters and these situations, as Melville might have, from the vantage point of the kestrel.

But his method is not straightforward reportage. The imaginative novelist he was striving to become is always present, working against the sociological eye. Fiction is mixed with actuality in two ways. Some passages are entirely invented, such as the passage taking him from Paris to London – there was no friend fixing up a job for him in England – some, as he told Brenda Salkeld, were worked up from incidents heard about or only vaguely experienced. *Down and Out in Paris and London* is an imaginary journey to the bottom of the heap based on a mixture of experiences, elements from which he produced one of the best pieces of impressionistic autobiography in the literature. And, although he acknowledged the inspiration of Zola, and was following in a tradition reaching back at least to Chaucer, he was feeling his way towards a genre of which he was a pioneer. He explained himself to French readers when the book appeared there a year later: 'I have exaggerated nothing, except in so far as all writers exaggerate by selecting.' While not keeping all events in a strictly chronological order, 'everything I have described did take place at one time or another'. His characters were not portraits of particular individuals, but 'intended more as representative types of the Parisian or Londoner of the class to which they belong'. His portraits of both cities might not be especially favourable, but his theme being poverty he was showing how those places appeared to those without money, and he had not the least animosity towards Paris – 'a city of which I have very happy memories'.[35]

He employed fiction in another way, by including interludes in the form of *contes*, his Maupassant-style short stories, probably first written as discrete pieces – the story of Charlie, a sexual fantasy no doubt, the tale of Henri, a man down on his luck, and of old Roucolle, the miser cheated. There would always be an episodic quality to the prose fiction and prose non-fiction of George Orwell, episodes that slightly disrupt the narrative – though not quite as evidently as here. And in the London half of his book there is more than a hint of Dickens's *Sketches by Boz*, with its scenes of pawnbroker's shops, rough-sleepers on city streets, tatty boarding houses, prostitutes, petty criminals and their cockney banter. This readiness to change register, to switch from reportage or commentary to personal anecdote, would also become a feature of his writing. He had, in fact, what he savoured in Butler, the ability to manufacture 'the perfectly told anecdote'. Butler, he wrote, 'was . . . an ideal observer of life. He was a good listener, and he had a far more genuine appreciation of common speech than most of the novelists who have exploited it.'[36] It was another apt piece of self-description.

The autobiographical element was a means by which he tried always to relate what he wrote to his own life, continually to reveal himself within the mental landscape through which he was passing. It lent his writing a quality of pilgrimage. Here is a man in search of his soul, a man attempting to refine an already refined conscience. The moral voice is not all that evident in *Down and Out in Paris and London*, but the story demands a moral response. George Orwell leaves his signature not just as a 'poet of fact', one who reveals to society its own ugly face, but also as a creative presence with a very distinctive and evolving 'secret imaginative background'. As Ruskin wrote, 'To see clearly is poetry, prophecy and religion all in one.'[37] With Orwell the vision is always clear.

The poetry shows itself in the way he creates, mainly through imagery and caricature. The images are piled up: the rue du Coq d'Or, for example, with its yells, quarrels and 'desolate cries', its rackety hotels with bug-infested wallpaper; the street itself – 'a ravine of tall leprous houses, lurching towards one another in queer attitudes'; the 'dwarfish' Rougiers peddling non-existent pornographic pictures; Henri, the chauffeur reduced to working in the sewers through a crime of passion; and R., the Englishman from Putney, soaking for six months each year on cheap French wine. In similar fashion he builds the atmosphere inside the kitchen of the Hôtel X – the murky, cellar-like *cafeterie*, the filth, the smells, the bedlam at mealtimes, the festering quarrels, the yelling, the running, the swearing, the mountains of litter and waste, the haggard *chef du personnel*, the skull-faced laundress, the foul-mouthed chef, the sweating *plongeurs*, the proud but frenetic waiters. In the London half of the book the atmosphere is conveyed in more leisurely fashion. Here poverty is coupled with hopelessness. Unlike his Parisian paupers there is no struggling for betterment, just resignation. This softer, more measured tone is what proves effective. In a level voice he says, 'This is what is happening here. Aren't you ashamed?' The voice lures with its matter-of-factness; it conveys empathy through imagined shared experience.

The other strand of poetry is seen through the compelling distortion. Orwell's Dickensian tendency leads him towards caricature, to over-gener-alise about places (hotels, restaurants, dingy kitchens, pawnshops) and whole categories of people (waiters, *plongeurs*, chefs, tramps). Like all car-icaturists he exaggerates for a purpose and to make an impact. Sometimes distortion pushes the narrative towards nightmare, that of the author him-self – driven by private grief and tormented by conscience, fearful of poverty, starvation and illness, of violence and arbitrary authority, of the unfulfilled promise and the wasted life. These hobgoblins haunt not just this book; they would haunt his future books too.

Among Orwell's cast of caricatures can be found refracted images of himself. For example, Bozo the screever, a highly intelligent man who had lived in France, read Shakespeare and Swift, and then fallen on hard times, is a projection of what he too might become if ever he became trapped inside a world of destitution. So is the dissolute Old Etonian, M—, slum-ming in search of nancy boys, and the drunken Englishman at the Hôtel des Trois Moineaux, drowning in lethargy and alcohol. These visions, like the vision of the dead man (*numéro* 57) in the Hôpital Cochin, show where the darker side of his life was leading him, reminding him what he had to fight down, repress and transcend. For a man with a weak chest, cursed at times with a hacking cough, and struck down on occasions with bronchitis and pneumonia, the fear of suffocation must have been real. The most mem-orable characters he would create are characters in a trap, unable to breathe freely, and who, despite every effort to escape, are invariably returned to the stifling confines of their wretchedness. They are nightmare images of what failure could bring.

Bozo is another prevision of Winston Smith in *Nineteen Eighty-Four*, a man who clings to the idea that 'whether you've something or nothing' a man is free (tapping his head) 'in here'. After the confining worlds of school and *sahib-log* Burma, the belief in individual freedom was crucial to Blair's thinking. In embracing the vagrant life he was embracing the idea that the vagrant was free – free from bourgeois constraints and even freer if he lived rough and slept in fields or on benches along the embankment. It was an idea expressed in Mark Twain and W. H. Davies, in the gypsy boy glimpsed by Michael Fane in *Sinister Street*, and in Kipling's *Kim*, the white boy who goes native in northern India. What he discovered, of course, was what Jack London revealed in *The People of the Abyss* – the tramp is never free. He is shackled by poverty, hunger, the harassment of the law, the tyranny of Tramp Majors and keepers of common lodging houses. Only in his mind is Bozo free.

Advance copies of *Down and Out* arrived at the end of December and Eric was clearly thrilled. As he wrote later to Jack Common, 'Isn't it a grand feeling when you see your thoughts taking shape at last in a solid lump?'[38] He promptly sent a copy to Brenda, with a series of marginal notes indicating what actually happened, what was exaggerated and what invented. For instance, he indicates that the passage about Boris's wretched attic was somewhat embellished, 'but I have seen people living in just this fashion'. Valenti's story had been reordered but was otherwise as told, and the story of Old Roucolle's death was more or less true. Public records confirm the underlying authenticity of the narrative – the Hôpital Cochin archives register his brief stay there, the residents' list for the district show that lodgers at 6 rue du Pot de Fer were indeed the mixture of nationalities and occupations he describes – Russians, Egyptians, Italians, Palestinian Jews, shoemakers, restaurateurs, booksellers, waiters and tailors. It also points to the likely original of Madame F., owner of the Hôtel des Trois Moineaux, one René Freyemunthe, and Madame Monce, at the hotel opposite, must surely be Madame Mons at the same address.[39] The book grew out of observation and imagination and the voice bears many of the hallmarks of the George Orwell to come.

He may have been nervous about how his book would be received at home, but, according to Avril, although the family was surprised by the outspoken language no one was shocked. 'My parents weren't really easily shockable although my father was a Victorian. There was never any discussion of sex or love affairs or anything of that nature at all, so when all those matters came out in [Eric's] book it almost seemed as if it had been written by a different person.'[40] Mabel and Francis Fierz duly received their copy, bearing the grateful inscription, '. . . many thanks for their great help in getting this book published'.

Down and Out in Paris and London was not exactly acclaimed by the critics, but the reviews were both intelligent and thoughtful. C. Day Lewis in the *Adelphi* thought it a 'tour of the underworld . . . conducted without hysteria or prejudice', which captured 'a simply medieval hell of heat, filth and demonic activity'. He advised the reader that 'if you wish to eat a meal in a hotel without acute nausea, you had better skip pp. 107–108'.[41] In the *New Statesman*, W. H. Davies called it 'the kind of book I like to read – packed with unique and strange information. It is all true to life, from beginning to end.'[42] *The Times Literary Supplement* thought it 'a vivid picture of an apparently mad world',[43] and the reviewer in the *Listener* said that although Orwell had gone out on the streets deliberately to get a story, 'there is nothing fabricated about it . . . he helps us to see things from below instead of from above'.[44] To Orwell's surprise and pleasure it was also well reviewed in the popular press, in the *Evening Standard* and *Daily Mail,* and the *Sunday*

Express named it as a 'best seller of the week'. The first edition of 1,500 and the second impression of 500 sold out within a month, and a subsequent print run of 1,000 also eventually sold out. His schoolboy hero Compton Mackenzie was to declare it a 'clearly genuine human document . . . curiously beautiful with the beauty of an accomplished etching on copper', and J. B. Priestley, whom he had earlier declared 'second-rate', would call it 'an excellent book and a valuable social document.'[45]

The book brought an angry letter to *The Times* from a Monsieur Humbert Possenti of the Hotel Splendide in Piccadilly, 'a *restaurateur* and *hôtelier* of 40 years experience', complaining that 'Orwell' had libelled all the luxury hotels and restaurants of Paris and could do 'infinite harm . . . to the London and Paris restaurant trade'. The disgusting conditions he described were 'inconceivable'.[46] Eric, determined to defend his reputation, wrote a stinging reply. 'The passages objected to in my book did not refer to Paris hotels in general, but to one particular hotel. And as M. Possenti does not know which hotel this was he has no means of testing the truth of my statements. So I am afraid that, in spite of his 40 years' experience, my evidence in this case is worth more than his.'[47] It was the first letter he ever signed 'George Orwell'. And George Orwell, author of *Down and Out in Paris and London*, also began to receive fan letters. The creation of a new persona had been confirmed; and gradually more people would come to know the creation than the creator.

By the time he returned to The Hawthorns in the New Year, he had a hundred polished pages of *Burmese Days* ready for Moore. He had managed to persuade the vicar of St Mary's to rent him a small allotment, but as yet the ground was too frozen to dig. On his way through London he had borrowed a smuggled copy of *Ulysses* from Mabel, and told Brenda that he had been reading it over and over. He called it 'my dear "Ulysses"' and declared it his greatest discovery since Villon.[48] He was particularly taken with its stylistic variations. 'The one thing you have to get used to in *Ulysses* is that great quantities of it are written in parody – some of the styles that I recognize, & some that I don't . . . There is a lot of parody of Homer &, I think, ancient Irish literature, which is sometimes exceedingly funny.'[49] However, when she read it and was less than enthralled, he tried explaining to her why he found it so inspiring and instructive. 'It sums up better than any book I know the fearful despair that is almost normal in modern times. You get the same kind of thing, though only just touched upon, in Eliot's poems.'[50] By contrast, his old literary idols were being discarded – not just Wells for his misguided Utopianism, but now Shaw for his 'windy platitudes'.[51] Shaw, he told Brenda, was nothing but 'Carlyle & water'.[52] Kipling, who had somehow survived his contempt as a schoolboy and a second rejection while in

Burma, was slowly being restored to favour and would stand, with Housman, as the kind of poet he most admired.

Eleanor was living in Roehampton close to London, trying to get started as a fashion model. Eric was still eager to see her, but asked her to keep their affair secret from Dennis. He did not see why a little matter of sharing the same girl should come between friends. 'Dearest Eleanor' was the first person he told that *Down and Out* was to be published in America. Harper Brothers had bought the US rights and planned to publish it in July. However, for the moment, the 'FAMOUS AUTHOR' was concentrating on his vegetable patch. He had finally managed to dig up his plot at the vicarage, and shown himself to be as accident-prone as ever. He had nearly broken his back using a turfing-iron, he told Brenda, and 'yesterday I gave myself one on the shin with a pickaxe'.[53]

At the end of January 1933 Hitler became German Chancellor, and Eric cannot have been entirely unaware of what this implied for the future of Europe. As a letter from Aunt Nellie that summer suggests, few on the left had any illusions that a Nazi Germany meant a distinct possibility of war, and there was a strong move in favour of peace and disarmament. In February Oxford University Debating Society carried the motion that 'this House would not fight for King and Country' – 'a pretty revolutionary situation', thought Nellie.[54] On 23 March Hitler abolished the German parliament, and assumed the role of dictator. By June there was talk of gas masks and air-raid shelters, and in Paris an anti-Fascist congress was convened. What the newly born 'George Orwell' thought of this is not known. Perhaps he had a lot to say about it in lost letters to Nellie; for another two years there is nothing in any of his surviving correspondence which even mentions Hitler or Fascism. However, he does seem to have shared Nellie's forebodings, even if at that stage they were little more than fears of a dark version of *Brave New World*, of a slave state dominated by capitalists and right-wing moralists, something along the lines portrayed in Belloc's *The Servile State*, or Fritz Lang's film *Metropolis*.[55] However, for the most part it seems his attention was directed elsewhere.

The poetry which Ruskin might have detected in the prose of George Orwell, was coming in undiluted form from Eric Blair. Strangely, it reflected facets of his consciousness in partial eclipse as the 'low dishonest decade' gathered momentum, but which would re-emerge in various forms in his later work. His poems in the March, May and October 1933 editions of the *Adelphi* show a man, while still steeped in Georgian poetry, wanting to relate humanity's uncertain state to what is certain in nature. In 'Sometimes in the middle autumn days' he reflects on how the constancy of the seasons

signals the inevitability of death. Against that he places a sad image of a pur-
poseless humanity, unaware and robotic, 'death-marked', 'goalless' and
'rootless'. Time, however, is the tyrant, and death 'the fixed reprieveless
hour,/The crushing stroke, the dark beyond.' The hope is that we will 'Some
thought, some faith, some meaning save,/And speak it once before we go/In
silence to the silent grave.' In one sense this stands as an atheist's prayer –
our souls are ours to shape, and gain significance only if we express some
meaningful thought before the silence descends. Yet there are other ideas
embedded in the verse which persist and recur in his later work. 'The fixed
reprieveless hour', 'the crushing stroke, the dark beyond' betoken terrors to
come – the doom-laden chime of the clock, the place of darkness, the silent
execution, arise out of nightmares of which the origins are long forgotten.

The poem in the May *Adelphi* is strictly a nature poem, more evidently
Georgian, but carrying the same distinctly fatalistic note with 'the bird
unaware, blessing the summer eternal,/Joyfully labouring, proud in his
strength, gay-plumed,/Unaware of the hawk and the snow and the frost-
bound nights,/and of his death foredoomed.' His October poem is another
short sketch with an implied moral. 'A dressed man and naked man/Stood
by the kip-house fire' tells of a tramp ready to sacrifice his clothes for a
meal. When the bargaining is done the two men's positions are reversed,
and once again, 'A dressed man and naked man/Stood by the kip-house
fire.' The poetry of Eric Blair would be absorbed into the prose of George
Orwell, giving it more texture and a deeper sense of humanity.[56]

By Easter he was able to send Moore the second hundred pages of *Burmese
Days*. He was not happy with it, considering it uneven and unpolished.
Moore, however, liked it and urged him to finish it. After the comparative
success of his first book, a well-received novel would underline the arrival
of a new, distinctive and assured literary presence. And the success of *Down
and Out* ensured that he would continue publishing as George Orwell. Eric
Blair would eventually fade from the literary landscape.

In May he learned he would soon be out of a job. The Hawthorns was to
be sold to another businessman who was bringing in his own teachers.
Fortunately he quickly found another post at a much better school, Frays
College, in neighbouring Uxbridge. Frays was a private grammar school
preparing children for School Certificate. There were around 120 boys
between five and sixteen in one house and some 80 girls in another. Some
were boarders, mostly pupils with parents away on colonial service. The
headmaster who appointed him, but who had left before he took up the
post, was a certain Captain Donovan, local commander of Mosley's
Blackshirts.[57]

Meantime, he worked out his time at The Hawthorns, wishing he could 'drop this foul teaching' and spend more time writing – and no doubt more time fishing and gardening.[58] Aunt Nellie wrote saying that Uxbridge was the end of the world, and he might do better working as a travelling salesman for Ruth Pitter's pottery company, or even as an assistant in the new teashop Avril had opened in Southwold, The Copper Kettle. The picture of tall and spindly Eric Blair serving afternoon teas to fat ladies in large hats would have made an excellent *Punch* cartoon, and one can only imagine his chuckles at the very suggestion. As it happened Avril and her mother were working a clever business together. Ida ran a bridge club which met regularly at The Copper Kettle, thus ensuring a healthy turnover. It did so well that Avril was able to buy herself a car, a distinct status symbol in small English towns in the 1930s. She had, in fact, become rather grand; Jack Denny, the local tailor, remembered being made to feel that it was quite an honour to be served cakes by Avril Blair.[59] Things were about to change for Aunt Nellie, too. At the end of 1933 Eugène Adam married her – simply to give her a pension in the event of his death, he told colleagues.[60]

That summer was gloriously hot, and while that meant problems for Eric's garden, it offered the chance of more romantic countryside walks. He invited Eleanor to join him for a stroll along the Uxbridge canal, but added that 'somewhere where there are woods', like Burnham Beeches, would be nicest.[61] To Brenda he wrote about his reading and his progress with *Burmese Days*, which he thought was still 'broken-backed'. 'With me almost any piece of work has to be done over and over again. I wish I were one of those people who could sit down and fling off a novel in about four days.' Although there was no invitation to Burnham Beeches for Brenda, he signed off with an earnest 'wish you were here'.[62] Whether he celebrated his thirtieth birthday alone or with one of his lady-loves is unknown, but he had something to celebrate – the impending US publication of his book.

It might seem a strange book to find a publisher in America. There was of course the tramping theme, long established there by Mark Twain and Jack London, and there was the exile-in-Paris theme, to which Hemingway had given fictional life. Harper Brothers published the book in July, to a perfectly respectable critical reception. The *Nation* said, 'No writer submitting himself for the nonce to a horrible existence, for the sake of material, could possibly convey so powerful a sense of destitution and hopelessness as had Mr Orwell, on whom these sensations were, apparently, forced . . . if this book is not merely a piece of "human nature faking," it is a restrained and all the more damning indictment of a society in which such things are possible.'[63] The *New Republic* took much the same line, complimenting the author for the forceful modesty of his narrative. 'His account is genuine, unexaggerated and intelligent. Possessing a sense of character, Mr Orwell adorns his narrative with portraits and vignettes that give the book interest and concreteness.'[64] Rude remarks in the book about American eating habits, which Aunt Nellie thought might offend American readers, seem to have been swallowed without complaint. Of 1,750 copies that Harpers printed, a little under 400 were eventually remaindered. Orwell got the impression that the book had failed, but it established his presence in America, where he would slowly build up a small but dedicated following. He found fans too in one odd American quarter – Michigan State Prison, where one inmate began a correspondence, and later tried to enlist his support in a parole petition. He also acquired a faithful English readership in Dartmoor Prison, where *Down and Out* was reported to be the most frequently borrowed book at one time.

Shortly before quitting The Hawthorns, he informed Eleanor that he had finished a draft of *Burmese Days*, though, he said, 'there are wads of it that I simply hate, & am going to change'. He now hoped to have a complete manuscript by the end of the year. For one last time he relaxed in the vicarage garden among his beans and potatoes, reading the edited *Letters of D. H. Lawrence*, observing how often Lawrence 'seized on an aspect of things which no one else would have noticed'.[65] It was one of his own defining qualities, but by the end of the decade he had come to see Lawrence's retreat into history as a dangerous escape from reality. 'His exasperation with the present turns once more into idealisation of the past, this time a safely mythical past ... When Lawrence prefers the Etruscans (*his* Etruscans) to ourselves it is difficult not to agree with him, and yet, after all, it is a species of defeatism, because that is not the direction in which the world is moving. The kind of life that he is always pointing to, a life centring round the simple mysteries – sex, earth, fire, water, blood – is merely a lost cause.'[66]

With Brenda at home in Bedford, he spent his few summer weeks in Southwold hammering away at his novel, swimming and spending whatever time he could with Eleanor, before starting at Frays in mid-August, initially supervising holiday boarders. When the term began he became a full-time member of staff, teaching mostly French, but also acting as form master in charge of some twenty boys. His salary was £70 a year plus full board. It was not a demanding job, but required a great deal of preparation, and there was also evening dormitory duty, which left him little time to write during the day. According to Henry Stapley, who taught Maths and Geography, the school in those days was 'one big family', the atmosphere was relaxed and corporal punishment rarely used. When Blair arrived to teach French, Donovan, the Fascist, had left and there was a head in charge called Rathbone.

It soon became known that the new French master had 'some strange left-wing opinions'. But it was not just his views that were considered strange. In the dining hall, at table with the head and other masters, he ignored custom and, once finished, took out his tobacco tin, rolled one of his nauseating cigarettes, and lit up. He got away with this calculated piece of bloody-mindedness because no one was prepared to tackle the school's most imposing master. Stapley and his wife invited him for dinner, and found him surprising in other ways. No one at Frays had any idea that he was a writer, and when he presented them with a copy of *Down and Out in Paris and London*, proudly announcing that this was his new book, Stapley was sceptical. 'But, this book is by George Orwell,' he said, at which Blair smiled and replied, 'That's me.' It was perhaps the first time he had answered directly to the name.[67]

One of his pupils, Tony Hyams, remembered him as a very pleasant, easygoing teacher, who when exasperated would say, 'Oh Lord! You'll drive me to Hanwell!' – the name of the local mental asylum, which the boys thought very funny. On dormitory duty, after lights-out, he would retire to an adjacent room and type until the power was cut at eleven o'clock – hardly calculated to encourage sleep among his long-suffering pupils. But it did ensure that by 26 November he was able to tell Moore that he had completed *Burmese Days*.[68] With his first salary cheque he bought a motorbike, and was able to drive over to Moore's house at Gerrard's Cross and delivery his manuscript in person. Excited by his newfound mobility, he suggested to Brenda that they go off on the bike for a holiday together. After consulting her mother, however, she turned down the idea. Rather annoyed, he wrote telling her that she had been 'indiscreet' to mention it at home. As with Eleanor, he preferred to keep his amours and designs secret. Clandestine relations were obviously more exciting to him than openly respectable ones in the approved bourgeois manner.

But now, as winter encroached, and perhaps to impress Brenda or Eleanor, he drove his bike all the way to Southwold one weekend without an overcoat or any decent protection against the cold except his long Eton College scarf. Refusing advice to wrap up more, he then drove all the way back to Uxbridge. Not surprisingly, he soon collapsed with pneumonia and was taken to the nearby Uxbridge Cottage Hospital, where he coughed up blood and his condition rapidly deteriorated. Brenda, Ida, Avril, Leonard Moore and Ruth Pitter visited him, and Avril recalled a strange scene in which he feverishly raved on about money which he seemed to imagine was tucked under his pillow. In his imagination he was back in the spike terrified of being robbed.[69] He was kept in hospital over Christmas and the New Year and not released until the second week in January.

Chapter 9

Tory Anarchist Meets James Joyce

'The real conflict in Orwell is always between the half Tory, half Socialist good citizen and the Anarchist ever suspicious that the good citizen may be trying to put something over on him.'

George Woodcock, *The Crystal Spirit*

After two days resting at a hotel in Ealing he returned to Southwold to convalesce. He would not return to teaching. He was entitled to six months' unemployment pay, and for the next eight months he would have no need to take a job. By the end of January, however, he felt strong enough to start writing again.[1] For better or worse, he was now working under the inspiration of Joyce and his 'dear *Ulysses*', on which he wrote a long eulogy to Brenda just before Christmas. His Burmese novel had allowed him to relive and reassess his life up to his return to England. *Down and Out in Paris and London* had carried the narrative further. Now he had three more years to mull over, and a fictional style to develop further.

He was still adjusting to life in England, and having spent time observing society's lowest stratum now turned to focus on his own class – the distressed middle class. From his own experience he knew how it was when these two interacted. The lower order of tramps and vagrants was feared and demonised by the middle classes; they in turn were held in contempt by these outcasts. The police, the slumming parsons and the Tramp Majors were agents of the middle class charged with keeping the underclass in its place. He himself was able to cross from one class to the other and find acceptance of sorts in both worlds. Not that he fitted into either comfortably. In middle-class circles he was regarded as 'odd', perhaps 'eccentric'; in the milieu of tramps and prostitutes he was an ill-disguised 'gentleman down on his luck'. These two worlds haunted him and in his new novel he would try to encompass both, thinking to portray them in the manner of Joyce, whose 'new rhythmical scheme' he thought well-suited to his purpose.[2]

But Joyce did not dominate his imagination exclusively. Writing about Dickens in the December *Adelphi*, he demonstrated how the author who had enthralled him since childhood continued to grip him. Unlike Shaw, Wells and Kipling, he never doubted Dickens, and in writing about him gave the uncanny impression of also writing about himself. 'Being a moralist, Dickens did not invent characters merely as characters, but rather as embodiments of human qualities he liked or disliked,' and (quoting Chesterton) he 'saw that under many forms there was one fact, the tyranny of man over man, and he struck at it when he saw it, whether it was old or new'. Another comment gives the same curious impression: 'Dickens had some ugly moods upon which Mr Chesterton does not care to dwell . . . [and] . . . even when one considers him a definitely bad and cheap writer, one cannot help liking him.'[3]

Victor Gollancz, having read *Burmese Days*, was unhappy about it. Clearly it carried a great weight of resentment against the British Raj, which made it timely enough but also very sensitive as the Indian independence movement gained impetus. In August 1933 Gandhi had been much in the headlines having just survived a hunger strike, and Burma was in turmoil. Moreover, to Gollancz the book seemed so personal that he feared that some of the characters were easily identifiable, leaving him open to charges of libel. He therefore rejected it. Heinemann and Cape were then tried without success, and Eric was left feeling rather desperate. To become established, a well-received second book seemed to him essential, and, after all the work he had put in, never to see it in British bookshops would be a crushing disappointment. However, in New York, Harper Brothers took the precaution of submitting it to lawyers who decided that, with a few changes, it would be safe to publish, and a contract was duly agreed.

The novel which had emerged from his long labours during school breaks and odd weeks in Southwold, was the kind of novel he had long intended to write – full of arresting similes, purple passages with an unhappy ending. It demonstrates the range of his powers to evoke both cultural ambience and landscape. Nature in all its manifestations provides the rich backdrop to the book – colours and odours, vivid and subtle, permeate the narrative. And his unerringly accurate sociological eye captures the convoluted system of prejudices and bottomless depth of ignorance which characterised colonial culture at its worst. In *Down and Out in Paris and London* this array of talents was only partially engaged; in *Burmese Days* it is given full rein. Later, however much he narrowed his verbal range in the interests of clarity, there was ever the poet striving to break through to mark and enliven his prose.

Stylistically, again he achieves his effects by piling on the colours and enriching his text with cumulative detail:

At that hour there were beautiful faint colours in everything – tender green of leaves, pinkish-brown of earth and tree-trunks – like aquarelle washes that would vanish in the later glare. Down on the maidan flights of small, low-flying brown doves chased one another to and fro, and bee-eaters, emerald green, curvetted like slow swallows. A file of sweepers, each with his load half hidden beneath his garment, was marching to some dreadful dumping-hole that existed on the edge of the jungle. Starveling wretches, with stick-like limbs and knees too feeble to be straightened, draped in earth-coloured rags, they were like a procession of shrouded skeletons walking.[4]

That last image, a suitably ghoulish one, carries echoes of *The Ingoldsby Legends* and Baudelaire's *Les Fleurs du Mal,* images of horror both English and French.

But other influences are more evidently at work. At times the narrative slides towards the atmospheric realism of Somerset Maugham, and there are distinct suggestions of *A Passage to India* in Elizabeth's story – the young woman journeying from England to find a husband becoming embroiled in an inter-racial scandal. Traces of 'Orwell's' Etonian past can also be found in fragments from Dante, Milton, Blake, Gray, Surtees, Tennyson, Dickens and Arnold, and phrases from Cicero and Horace.[5]

Burmese Days is, of course, an attack on the moral decadence and injustice of the British Raj, with Flory as its vehicle. The method is in part Dickensian, with characters representing human qualities the author finds deplorable – U Po Kyin typifying cunning and greed, Mrs Lackersteen the worst kind of English snobbery, Ellis unrestrained race hatred, Verrall public-school arrogance, and Elizabeth middle-class mindlessness. Flory represents the corrupted innocence of the author, a sinful pilgrim in a quest for salvation, a subject throughout for searching self-analysis. The narrative can therefore be read as a confession of misdeeds, which George Orwell would make more personal and political in *The Road to Wigan Pier*. It is also an essay on the meaninglessness of isolation, the cry of a man who feels sundered from human, especially female, companionship. And so, beyond the confession of public misdeeds, stands the confession of personal sins and suffering, the dark side of a man who could never quite escape the moral landscape of a Christian upbringing.

Gollancz was right in thinking he might be paying off old scores through his depiction of character; the drunken Scottish *burra* sahib, the intemperate racist Ellis, the attractive but shallow Elizabeth, the effortlessly arrogant Verrall are all recognisable types with recognisable persons behind them. Ma Hla May no doubt existed somewhere in his Burmese past and needed to be exorcised. Revealingly perhaps, in the girl's case, it is she who wreaks revenge on Flory, the benighted doppelgänger, and the hoped-for Paradise with Elizabeth is suddenly and dramatically lost.

Curiously enough, a year which started so badly for him was to become his first year of self-sufficiency. 'It was only from 1934 onwards,' he wrote, 'that I was able to live on what I earned from my writing.'[6] If so, it was not from reviews, of which he published only six that year. Income from writing would only have been moderately substantial from the French translation of *Down and Out* (*La Vache Enragée*) and the US edition of *Burmese Days*, scheduled for publication in October.

But now, as both novelist and critic, he felt able to pronounce on the state of English letters. In the March *Adelphi* he wrote, 'Most English critics, apart from the publishers' touts who review novels in the Sunday papers, are much keener to prevent one from enjoying the books they disapprove of than add to one's enjoyment.' The leading 'publishers' touts' he was getting at were Sir John Squires of the *Sunday Times* and Gerald Gould of the *Observer*. Unknown to him Gould was the reader who recommended *Down and Out* to Gollancz and would strongly recommend *A Clergyman's Daughter* in due course. The more serious critics caught in his sights were obviously F. R. Leavis and T. S. Eliot. 'The prevailing type of critic is the young gentleman who wants to cut off our supply of Milton, Wordsworth, Shelley and Keats, and deliver us over, bound hand and foot, to Mr. Eliot's frigid and snooty Muse.' The poetry Eliot had produced since *The Waste Land,* work reflecting his move from unbelief towards Anglo-Catholicism, failed to enthuse him. He himself was moving in exactly the opposite direction.

'Some people,' he wrote, 'think chiefly by a series of visible symbols, others almost entirely abstractly.'[7] In the April *Adelphi* his own cast of mind was revealed in one of his better poems, 'On a Ruined Farm near the His Master's Voice Gramophone Factory'. Its mood is Wordsworthian, and employs both visual symbols and abstractions. It is also very personal. The poet is trapped in decaying suburbia, at the point where old and new worlds collide, where industrialisation has eaten into the countryside. Surveying the desolate scene and the factory towers, he reflects back to the Golden Age which forms a key part of his imaginative world. 'Yet when the trees were young, men still/Could choose their path – the wingèd soul,/Not cursed with double doubts, could fly,/Arrow-like to a foreseen goal;/And they who planned those soaring towers,/They too have set their spirit free;/To them their glittering world can bring/Faith, and accepted destiny;/But none to me as I stand here/Between two countries, both-ways torn ... Between the water and the corn.' This torn-apart world represents the moral and spiritual dilemma facing the poet. Material progress is no progress; the past is irretrievable. An Erewhonian hatred of machine-made civilisation, a feeling that the past is where he truly belongs, and that the essential freedom of the self is now imperilled – these images, thoughts and deeply personal feelings run throughout his work.

Unlike many of his intellectual contemporaries, Orwell did not look towards the Soviet Union for the way out of his dilemma; he had been sceptical of the Soviet model since 1928, and in any case his idiosyncratic temperament made him difficult to conscript into any movement or party. However, the Marxist perspective could help expose the sources of social corruption, and cast a new light on literature. Writing about Mallarmé that summer, he revealed a first hint of Marxism in his critical writing. Mallarmé, he argued, moved towards greater and greater obscurity in an attempt to achieve the abstractness of the Platonic ideal but it took enormous scholarly research to make his poems comprehensible. 'Artistic obscurity, so common this last seventy years, is only one of the morbid growths of our decaying civilization, and is traceable directly to economic causes.' He was making a connection between art and the economy, which would become a feature of his increasingly political treatment of culture. However, on Baudelaire he seems to take a quite different, idealistic, tack. Not unlike Butler, he argued, Baudelaire, the atheist, 'clung to the ethical and the imaginative background of Christianity, because he had been brought up in the Christian tradition and because he perceived that such notions as sin, damnation, etc., were in a sense truer and more real than anything he could get from sloppy humanitarian atheism.' This duality – identifying the causes of social ills as economic while continuing to embrace Christian ethics – defined his philosophical outlook. His comments on Mallarmé and his interpretation of Baudelaire, illuminate key features of his own understanding, imagination and morality.[8]

But his peculiar attachment to Christianity did not include the Catholic Church, whose Inquisition he regarded as the historical expression of its bigotry and ruthlessness. Writing to Brenda, he harked back to Poe. 'It appears . . . that the pendulum in Poe's story was actually used, though not at such a late date as Poe makes out.'[9] The terrifying vision in 'The Pit and the Pendulum' of the tortured victim overrun by rats in a dark cellar, which had haunted him as a boy, would resurface in another form in his own Inquisitional horror, *Nineteen Eighty-Four*.

In July 1934 Dennis Collings married Eleanor Jaques, robbing him of a lover and friend simultaneously. Shortly afterward they left for Singapore where Dennis had been appointed Assistant Curator of the Raffles Museum. Orwell now felt more isolated than ever, and wrote to Brenda, on holiday in Ireland, 'How I wish you were here! I am so miserable, struggling in the entrails of that dreadful book and never getting any further, and loathing the sight of what I have done.' He hoped to have it finished by October, when he had plans to go to London to find a flat – Islington or Camden Town, he thought, both districts with strong Dickensian associations.[10] A month later he sounded even more despairing. Everything about his work was going badly, he told her. *Burmese Days* had made him sick when he saw it in print. 'I would have rewritten large chunks of it, only that costs money and means delay as well.' *A Clergyman's Daughter*, despite some good passages, made him throw up even more. 'I don't know how it is, I can write decent passages but I can't put them together.'[11]

What depressed him most was that, having finally obtained his own smuggled copy of his 'beloved' *Ulysses* and reread it, his mind was suddenly unreceptive to it. 'I wish I had never read it. It gives me an inferiority complex.' And it was not only his work that weighed him down. 'This age makes me so sick that sometimes I am impelled to stop at a corner and start calling down curses from Heaven like Jeremiah or Ezra or somebody – "Woe upon thee, O Israel, for thy adulteries with the Egyptians," etc.'[12] His hatred of the times did not prevent him taking to one form of modernity. He acquired a driving licence and occasionally got the use of Avril's car (once, it seems, to take Brenda to Eton to watch the Wall Game).[13] It made a change from the old motorbike with its accompanying health hazards.

Brenda was now the woman friend to whom he felt best able to unburden himself. When *Burmese Days* came out in America, he told her he was hoping for a sale of 'not less than 4,000 copies', and asked her to pray for its success. 'I understand that the prayers of clergyman's [sic] daughters get special attention in Heaven, at any rate in the Protestant quarter.'[14] By October *A Clergyman's Daughter* was finished and ready to dispatch. But he already anticipated problems with Gollancz, and told Moore that, although the school depicted was imaginary, it was based on his general knowledge of such establishments.[15] Now he was preparing to move to London, thinking about another novel and hoping that *Burmese Days* would find a British publisher.

In *A Clergyman's Daughter* time again precipitates the action – an alarm clock 'explodes' at half-past five, on a 'coldish . . . August morning'. The idea for the novel might have been sparked by James Stephens's newly republished *The Charwoman's Daughter*, the story of Mary Makebelieve, enslaved to a routine of toil (*her* day begins at six o'clock) who escapes to a new future after eluding the rough intentions of a predatory lover. The influence of Gissing's *The Odd Women*, a depressing tale of middle-class spinsterhood, should not be ignored either. Another possible source was Lawrence's 'Daughters of the Vicar', a tale of unlikely liaisons, which he described as the story of 'the underfed, downtrodden, organ-playing daughter of a clergyman wearing out her youth, and suddenly a vision of her escaping into the warmer world of the working-class'.[16] His own clergy-man's daughter in search of herself, Dorothy Hare, represents the unobtainable, enigmatic woman, locked into a meaningless ritual yet unconsciously striving to realise herself. Like all of his characters, she escapes from her prison to a new dawn, only to find herself back finally in the soul-destroying routine from which she thought she had freed herself. It is the same reversed Miltonian design of *Paradise Gained* and *Paradise Lost*, also the formal story of his own life, of illusion and failure. Dorothy remains an enigma to men and perhaps also to herself. Brenda, and his rela-tionship with her, was certainly there in some form, as was his life on the road. The novel drew him back to Trafalgar Square and the hopping excur-sion to Kent, and returned him to the vicarage, the mouldering congregation and the demoralising Hawthorns. Knype Hill, where Dorothy lives, is a thinly disguised Southwold, providing him an opportunity to satirise the town in which for so long he had felt imprisoned among dull, respectable provincials.

He readily acknowledged the novel's weaknesses. The passages drawn from his time on the road and his time teaching fit together awkwardly. Dorothy, the only female protagonist in his work, is unconvincing, and there are exaggerations and caricatures which render the narrative unwieldy and the characterisation unbelievable. And although some of his critics thought it showed a courageous willingness to experiment, the effect of the various changes of register – the Stephens/Lawrence passages about Dorothy's search for her soul, the Orwellian trek to the hop fields and the disconnected Joycean dialogue of his Trafalgar Square chapter – is less a seamless web than an unsightly patchwork. And, apart from that sometimes highly comic play of voices, there is insufficient satirical power to give the book as a whole the force of a good parody, although in Mr Tallboys, the unfrocked clergyman, who inverts the Lord's Prayer and cites obscure Latin texts, there lurks a touch of self-mockery. (Solicited for a comment on the book by Gollancz, Sean O'Casey wrote, 'Orwell has as much chance of reaching the stature of Joyce as a tit has of reaching that of an eagle.')[17] Even so, he manages, in passing, to take swipes at the Anglican and Catholic Churches, domineering fathers, small-town scandalmongers, casual wards, workhouses, exploitative hop farmers, tenth-rate private schools and the gutter press. Unsurprisingly, perhaps, he conceived of his next book as a loosely connected set of essays.

Escaping from Southwold was his own bid for freedom from the provincial world of his just-completed novel. At least in London he would be free from the sort of gossips who made Dorothy's life hell in Knype Hill. On 11 October he moved to the capital, staying initially with the Fierzes. Then, through Aunt Nellie, he met Francis and Myfanwy Westrope, a couple who owned Booklovers' Corner bookshop in South End Road, Hampstead, and was taken on as an assistant in return for a small wage and free board. The Westropes were Esperantists, pacifists, vegetarians and members of the Independent Labour Party. His living quarters were in Warwick Mansions, above the shop, where he had a bedroom and use of the Westropes' sitting room. It was a typical bookshop of the period – a second-hand side of mostly classics, and a tuppenny lending library of lowbrow popular fiction (Ethel M. Dell and Warwick Deeping became prime targets of his scorn), said to be the only part of the shop not exaggerated in *Keep the Aspidistra Flying*. Initially he shared the job with another young writer, Jon Kimche, who remembered Blair's conversation as little more than diatribes against Roman Catholicism. He refused to discuss his work, as if fearful that some-one might steal it.[18] When Mrs Westrope asked him what he wanted most, he replied, 'Freedom,' to which she replied, 'Do you want to have women up here all night?' When he said, 'No,' she replied, 'I only meant that I didn't mind whether you do or not.' He was delighted, and immediately wrote to Brenda urging her to come to London to stay with him – a strange letter laced with smutty jokes.[19] Again she resisted the bait.

He found Hampstead congenial enough and soon settled down to work, quickly completing an introduction to the French edition of *Down and Out in Paris and London* (*La Vache Enragée*). Two weeks later came the US publication of *Burmese Days*. He was disappointed with the first review he saw, from the *New York Herald Tribune*, which said that his axe-grinding had destroyed all interest in the situation he wished to expose. However, he was now cynically aware of how newspaper criticism worked, telling Moore, 'Rather a bad one . . . however, big headlines, which I suppose is what counts.'[20] More favourable notices in the *New York Times Book Review* and the *Boston Evening Transcript*, applauding the book's 'faithful realism', retrieved the book's fortunes somewhat.[21] Harpers' first edition of 2,000 sold out, and the second impression of 500 followed. However, the 4,000 he hoped to sell with the aid of Brenda's prayers, were never sold. He knew, he said, that 'that sort of book had no interest in the USA'.

Nor, it seems, was there much interest in England. 'I am very depressed . . . Had my novel about Burma been published in England and had as it ought a moderate success, I should have been "lancé".' Worse still, he felt that no one would want his future work either, because it was now regarded as 'experimental'. He would have to get that out of his system, he thought, before he could again write a saleable novel. Curiously, in view of what he wrote later about bookselling, he thought it might offer him a future. 'I wish I had £700, or even £500, and I could start a bookshop of my own.'[22]

Apart from the Fierzes, his friend Ruth Pitter was one of his few close contacts in the capital. She invited him to a soirée at her Chelsea flat and to a cocktail party thrown for her by her publishers. *His* publishers never gave cocktail parties for *him*, he complained. Still considering himself a poet, he told Ruth rather proudly that his poem about the gramophone factory had been chosen for *The Best Poems of 1934*; she told him that there were dozens of such anthologies and she had a poem in one called 'Twenty Deathless Poems'.[23] That seems to have quite shaken his self-confidence, and he published almost no poetry thereafter.

However, he was already at work on his next novel – about the vicissitudes of a poet working in a bookshop trying to escape the stultifying embrace of respectability. For books he favoured the ironic title. *Burmese Days* suggests the biography of a staunch old district commissioner rather than a suicidal cynic; *A Clergyman's Daughter* has a smack of the ribald quip – 'She was only a clergyman's daughter but . . .', and *Keep the Aspidistra Flying* evokes the 1928 hit song 'The Biggest Aspidistra in the World'. Later, the northern comedian, George Formby Senior, who made a running joke out of the non-existent Wigan Pier, would provide him with yet another ironic title. These playful allusions point towards that still favourite haunt of his, the music hall, a place to savour popular culture, the world of the seaside postcard brought to life, as it were. And much music-hall humour was laced with the irony of poverty. The down-and-out sleeping 'Underneath the Arches' was always ready to lampoon toffs like 'Burlington Bertie'.

Gollancz was having the same misgivings about *A Clergyman's Daughter* that he had had over *Burmese Days*. Norman Collins, one of the readers, wrote to Gollancz: 'I know nothing of Orwell, but it is perfectly clear that he has been through hell, and that he is probably still there. He would certainly be a plum for a practising psycho-analyst. There is in his work, either latent or fully revealed, almost every one of the major aberrations. Indeed the chaotic structure of the book would suggest some kind of mental instability.'[24] Gerald Gould, his other reader, recommended it as 'an extraordinary book . . . very original', but saw that it might create 'snags and difficulties'. As it turned out he owed its publication to one man he despised, Gould, and one he would come to despise, Collins. The threat of libel was Gollancz's main concern, and this was conveyed to the author.

While expecting trouble over the book, he was anxious to get it published, asking Gollancz to specify which passages worried him. His description of Ringwood House he knew might test the reader's credulity, and said he would be happy to discuss all this, including concerns expressed about his use of swearwords. On 19 November he met Gollancz in his Covent Garden office and agreed to rewrite the end of the book. A month later he returned the amended manuscript. He had omitted a reference to

Mr Warburton trying to rape Dorothy, an offensive reference to a Catholic priest, a mention of Bertrand Russell and the *Sunday Express*, and toned down his account of Ringwood House. He had also tried to make the loutish and concupiscent Warburton's friendship with the genteel and virginal Dorothy more credible, inserting 'a line or two . . . remarking on the fact that pious and immoral people appear to have a mysterious attraction for one another',[25] another revealing reference to his relationship with Brenda.

If she was nervous about visiting him in his Hampstead den, other young females were not. One girl he met at the bookshop, Sally Jerome, who worked for an advertising agency, broke up with him when she found out about his other girlfriends, but left a trace of herself in Gordon's girlfriend Rosemary in *Keep the Aspidistra Flying*.[26] A second girl, Kay Welton, was different. She and Eric also met in the shop and soon began dating. Kay was twenty-two and ran her own typing bureau. She typed authors' manuscripts, belonged to the PEN Club, and attended 'at homes' given by Edwin and Willa Muir, which Eric refused to attend believing the Muirs to be Scots. Kay was small and slim and wore her hair cropped short – the kind of boy-like young woman he fancied. And, though not a beauty, she was an attractive, lively personality. She thought Eric nice enough, even though his pale dry skin gave him an unhealthy appearance. There was never any thought of marriage on either side, and they agreed to part if someone else came along; nevertheless they became lovers and Kay grew quite fond of him. Eric hated using a contraceptive – 'the sleek, estranging shield' which came 'between the lover and his bride'[27] – and Kay was expected to take the necessary precautions.[28] He told her that in any case he was incapable of having children, and when she asked him how he knew said: 'Well, I've never had any.' They shared a love of Dickens, talked a good deal about poetry and he told her he was writing a Chaucerian epic on the history of English character.

He took her to restaurants and theatres, and for walks over Hampstead Heath, where he again paraded his exhaustive knowledge of wildlife. What astonished her was that a man who happily talked about his hunting exploits could also be so fond of the creatures he was prepared to shoot. He was forever complaining of poverty, which she thought absurd. More surprising to Kay was the extent of his prejudices, not just against Catholics and Scots but against writers such as Shaw, Wells, Barbusse, Walpole and especially Arnold Bennett. However, he continued to admire Chesterton, despite his conversion to Catholicism. She interpreted his refusal to go Dutch in restaurants as simply an expression of his 'ultra-masculine' opinion that women were 'secondary'. On one occasion, after receiving his American advance for *Burmese Days*, he took Kay, Rees, Mabel Fierz and a couple of others to Bertorelli's Restaurant in Charlotte Street, at the heart of London's 'Fitzrovia', and blew the best part of £50. Afterwards, very drunk, he knocked off a policeman's helmet and Rees had to smooth things over and take him home. This splurge seemed nothing more than financial reck-lessness, but the incident found its way into *Keep the Aspidistra Flying*, suggesting that he acted like this (as in sleeping in Trafalgar Square) simply to obtain copy for his novels.

Nineteen thirty-five would bring great changes to his life. In January Rees invited him to dine at Bertorelli's to meet a young poet called Dylan Thomas. Thomas brought along another young writer, a Yorkshireman called Rayner Heppenstall, who wrote about ballet for the *New English Weekly* and *Time and Tide*. He thought Blair 'a nice chap though a bit dotty', and they became friends. The evening ended in a pub crawl with Eric staggering back to Warwick Mansions well after midnight, and having to rouse the Westropes to get inside – a hint, perhaps, of the new novel then incubating.

As if to contradict his general air of pessimism, his run of luck contin-ued. Gollancz now asked for a copy of the US edition of *Burmese Days* with a view to publishing it himself. If it had been launched without trou-ble in America it might after all be safe in England. On rereading it he expressed enthusiasm but insisted it be thoroughly sifted through by his lawyer.[29] Lack of money and the long interval since his last English novel had appeared, made Eric anxious to get this book out. He wanted his new one to be 'a work of art', something requiring 'much bloody sweat'.[30] To that end, he told Brenda, he had set himself a strict regime. '7 a.m. get up, dress etc, cook & eat breakfast. 8.45 go down & open the shop, & I am usually kept there till about 9.45. Then come home, do out my room, light the fire, etc. 10.30 a.m.–1 p.m. I do some writing. I get lunch & eat it. 2 p.m.–6.30 p.m. I am at the shop. Then I come home, get supper, do the washing up & after that sometimes do about an hour's work.'[31] This was the book he described to Moore as written in the form of a series of essays, though what sort of essays he did not specify.

When in February the Westropes required his room for someone else, Mabel found him a room at the top of Parliament Hill, with a fine view across Hampstead Heath, a more salubrious location, she thought, for a man with poor lungs. According to Kay, unknown to Eric, Mabel paid half the rent.[32] His new landlady, Rosalind Obermeyer, a South African, was studying for an MA in psychology at University College. Eric had his own room plus a pleasant sitting room in which to work and entertain. He acquired a Bachelor Griller and invited friends to dinner; Kay, Rees and Heppenstall all savoured his basic cuisine – 'a very good steak, and . . . beer out of tree-pattern mugs', recalled Heppenstall,[33] who on another occasion brought Michael Sayers, a young red-headed Dublin Jew who reviewed plays for Eliot's *Criterion*, and books for the *New English Weekly*. He was described by Eric as 'a very out-at-elbow young Irish poet' – an affected bohemian image, according to Sayers.

For Eric, still under the influence of Joyce, Sayers, ten years younger than him, must have seemed like a young Leopold Bloom. He was educated at Cheltenham College and, like Joyce, at Trinity College, Dublin, where his French tutor was Samuel Beckett. As a student he wrote poetry and worked as production assistant at the Gate Theatre, mingling with the actors, including Orson Welles and Mícheál Mac Liammóir. His father, owner of the Albion Greetings Card Company, was separated from his mother who lived in a large house in Hampstead. He was then conducting a torrid love affair with his cousin, Edna and, anxious to keep well clear of his father, shared a small flat in Camden Town with Heppenstall.

Meanwhile, Gollancz, now keen to publish *Burmese Days*, again asked for changes. Katha, the setting, was disguised more; names were altered, including that of Dr Veraswami and Mrs Lackersteen. Eric's meeting with Collins, who sat in on this meeting, left him with an intense dislike of the man – 'a squirt', he said later. In March a deal for the novel was concluded on what he considered 'very good terms'. His faith in the book and his efforts to get it published in England had been vindicated, but he would always look on Gollancz's edition as 'a garbled version'.[34]

A Clergyman's Daughter, which appeared on 11 March, was undoubtedly his least satisfactory novel. In view of his often hostile attitude to women, it seems odd that he chose a woman as its central character, and his fixation on Brenda probably lies at the heart of this. Unable to penetrate his object of desire, it was as if he wished to penetrate her mind, whisk her off on that hopping expedition on which she had declined to accompany him two years earlier, and, knowing her fastidious nature, put her through the degradation of the down-and-out life which so horrified her family. To what extent Dorothy's relation with her clergyman father reflected Brenda's relation with her mother is difficult to tell, but Brenda had escaped from her home through teaching and seems to have settled for a life of celibacy. He, no doubt, was represented by the bohemian Mr Warburton, who so disconcerted and mesmerised the virginal Dorothy. In an enigmatic passage in a letter to Brenda he wrote, 'You will see if you read *A Clergyman's Daughter* that I have employed you as a collaborator in two places.'[35] Dorothy's expression of distaste for sex as 'all that sort of thing' sounds the very thing Brenda, in her dedication to spinsterhood, might have said. But if he failed to possess his clergyman's daughter, he failed to possess Dorothy, too.

However poor he thought his novel, he was gratified by the positive critical response, especially in the popular *Daily Herald* and *Daily Mail*, the left
and right of the political spectrum. From the serious papers it received
more guarded praise. In the *Observer*, L. P. Hartley wrote that 'its merits lie
in the treatment, which is sure and bold, in the dialogue, which is always
appropriate and often brilliant', but he also referred to exaggeration and
strains on the reader's credulity.[36] V. S. Pritchett, the *Spectator* reviewer,
was unimpressed by the Trafalgar Square scene – 'written in a "stunt" Joyce
fashion which utterly ruins the effect'. 'Mr Orwell's satirical facility,' he concluded shrewdly, 'has lured him away from his best manner to the glib
cruelties of caricature.'[37] It was left to Peter Quennell in the *New Statesman*
to spot the novel's central weakness – that, despite the forceful writing,
Dorothy remained little more than a cipher.[38] However, to receive so much
coverage was encouraging from the author's point of view, and he was
delighted when Moore reported that Gollancz had said of him, 'In my opinion, he is likely to be in years to come one of the half dozen most important
authors on our list.'[39] Despite this, the book was far from a success.
Although Gollancz printed 2,000 copies the type was quickly distributed. In
America, where it was published in August, one reviewer found it 'pessimistic' and 'morbid'.[40] Harpers sold only a few hundred.

The six months he spent at the Parliament Hill flat would change his
life out of all recognition. In March Rosalind threw a party for some
fellow students from University College (just over their Part I examinations), to which he and Rees were invited. One of Rosalind's friends,
Lydia Jackson, a Russian, found them unimpressive, looking to her, 'in
Chekhov's immortal phrase, rather "moth-eaten".'[41] Another friend, Eileen
O'Shaughnessy, Eric found completely captivating, and that evening he
insisted on escorting her to the bus stop. Afterwards he told Rosalind,
'That's the sort of girl I'd like to marry.' (Eileen, in turn, told a friend that
she had been more than a little drunk and outrageous that evening, and
perhaps that was what excited his initial interest.) He was not the only one
who found her attractive. She was tall, slim, animated and independent,
with dark hair, 'dancing' pale blue eyes and an infectious sense of humour.
Kay, also at the party, thought her 'gay, lively and interesting'.[42]
Heppenstall thought Eric really loved her, after treating his previous girlfriends rather sadistically. Lettice Cooper, who worked with her during
the war, recalled Eileen's relaxed intelligence:

> She moved slowly, she always looked as if she was drifting into a room
> with no particular purpose there. She had small, very shapely hands
> and feet. I never saw her hurry, but her work was always finished on
> time . . . Eileen's mind was a mill that ground all the time slowly but

independently. Diffident and unassuming in manner she had a quiet integrity that I never saw shaken.[43]

Eileen was twenty-nine and came originally from South Shields, where her father was a Collector of Customs. At Sunderland Church High School for Girls she had excelled at debating, written poetry, and ended up as head girl. She won a scholarship to St Hugh's College, Oxford, to read English under Ernest de Selincourt, editor of Spenser and Wordsworth, Frank Wilson, the Shakespearan scholar, and J. R. R. Tolkien, who taught Anglo-Saxon, wrote books on Chaucer and Beowulf, articles on fairy stories, and, in 1937, would publish his first fantasy novel, *The Hobbit*. Among her Oxford contemporaries were the poet Geoffrey Grigson, Geoffrey and Kathleen Tillotson, both future professors of English at London, and Harman Grisewood, later Controller of the BBC Third Programme. Up at Oxford at the same time were Auden, Spender and MacNeice, soon to make their collective presence felt. Sadly for her, she failed to get the First essential for the academic career she dreamed of. This, according to friends, crushed all her ambition and she became a dilettante, losing her taste for scholarship. However, she retained her links with Oxford, and often escaped there to read poetry and haunt the Bodleian Library.[44] Since Oxford she had been a teacher, reading companion to Dame Elizabeth Cadbury, supervisor in a secretarial school and briefly a freelance journalist. She lived with her widowed mother in Greenwich, and when Eric met her, was studying for the same Psychology MA as Rosalind and Lydia. On the side she gave occasional lectures for the Workers' Educational Association.

They met for dinner and found they had a great deal in common, not least a shared passion for the countryside and for literature. He still considered himself a poet (still working as he was on that Chaucerian epic), and talked about his novels and his determination to write at all costs, even if it meant living in near penury. For Eileen there must have been a strong romantic attraction in this. She loved Chaucer and the Lake Poets, and here was a poet and novelist, dedicated fully, as they had been, to his art. To him she was perhaps what Jacintha might have become, the bluestocking steeped in literature, but in no way intellectually pretentious or exclusive in her tastes and passions. She had largely sublimated her own creative drive by helping her brother Laurence, a brilliant thoracic surgeon, edit and revise his medical papers. She and Laurence, married to Gwen, a GP, were very close, and she spent a great deal of her time at his home in Blackheath. But now she had found a man as devoted to literature as herself. It was not long before he raised the question of marriage, telling her, as he had told Kay, that he was infertile and therefore might be considered 'ineligible'. She did not reject him (not knowing if he had actually proposed), but had her own ideas on the subject, and did not exactly discourage him.

Her friends became aware of a mutual interest between them when she was seen reading *Burmese Days*. She had told Lydia that she had decided that if she were still unmarried at thirty she would marry the first man who asked her. She may well have told Eric this, because he timed his proposal accordingly. On the day before her birthday, 25 September, he told Heppenstall, 'She is the nicest person I have met for a long time. However, at present, alas! I can't afford a ring, except perhaps a Woolworth's one.'[45] Just over a week later he reported that 'Eileen says she won't marry me as yet . . . as she is not earning any money at present and doesn't want to be a drag on me. However, that will arrange itself later when she has finished her course at London University.'[46] That meant waiting till at least the following June when she would have completed her dissertation. He asked Heppenstall to keep all this to himself. He certainly kept it from Brenda, whom in May he was still addressing as 'Dearest Brenda' and signing off 'With much love and many kisses'. Meantime, Lydia was horrified by unfolding events. To her, Eric Blair did not seem good enough for Eileen – rather seedy and unattractive, she thought, hardly the man her delightful friend deserved. Kay, too, thought she would be sacrificing a great deal: 'She'd been to university, and had very much an intellectual standing in her own right. I thought it was rather tragic that she should give it all up, you know. I don't think I would have.'[47] But Eileen was perfectly prepared to devote herself to a writer, even though she could well have made her own literary career, as Eric himself admitted.[48]

With *Burmese Days* accepted for publication in England, and with *A Clergyman's Daughter* about to appear, he now felt himself at last *lancé*. In the March *Adelphi* for the first time he had signed a review 'George Orwell', and from then on always signed his work pseudonymously. The birth of Orwell was pretty well achieved, and, although his family, friends, agent and publisher still knew him as Eric Blair, he received more and more letters addressed to Orwell and replied to them in that persona. The curious transitional stage through which he was passing is nicely illustrated by Michael Sayers who referred to him invariably as 'Eric Orwell'.

He had, on his own admission, always had a secret fictional inner life, and Orwell was no doubt the public expression of that subjective narrator. So there, in between the lines, can be glimpsed the evolving consciousness of both the man and the man of letters. There were other personae, of course, in his complex make-up – ex-policeman, man among down-and-outs, importunate lover, patron of brothels, friend of curates, rectors and clergymen's daughters, drunken writer on a congenial pub-crawl, naturalist, gardener, and failed son of Richard Blair. All of these are to be found in the works and letters of George Orwell. Different personae, different worlds. But at the core of this many-faceted personality stood the conscious life of its author.

In more ways than one he was at a crossroads. The way to marriage would involve him adopting yet another albeit shared identity. At the same time he was caught between following the experimental route indicated by the Trafalgar Square chapter of *A Clergyman's Daughter* or that of natural-ism. Perhaps the fact that he was coming to recognise that he was, after all, not a poet had some influence on where he next went. But that experience – the experience of having to decide which way to turn – would be dealt with in his next novel.

That novel, once intended to take the form of a book of essays, in fact became something less fragmentary. *Keep the Aspidistra Flying* would be his most autobiographical work to date, and signal the abandonment of an old unfulfilled poetic part of himself. He knew his novels were based heavily on his own life. 'One difficulty I have never solved,' he wrote later, 'is that one has masses of experience which one passionately wants to write about . . . and no way of using them up except by disguising them as a novel.'[49] In this barely disguised form, he would again review his life. Gordon Comstock's prep school and public school are less prestigious than Orwell's, his family enjoy a lower social status, and he is a far less successful writer than his cre-ator, but the autobiographical voice is still recognisable, revealing sides of Orwell not always picked up elsewhere. Gordon is a sardonic dropped-out copywriter, determined to live the poetic life in a world that devalues poets, and desperate to bed Rosemary, his sexually reluctant girlfriend. That much chimes with the revealed Orwell. But Gordon emerges as a wild Rabelaisian, a suburban Baudelaire who hates the society dedicated to 'the money-god' and denounces it with all the vehemence of a Bunyan denouncing sin. Orwell's own image of Baudelaire comes close to describing Gordon – 'a poet of squalor, or perversity, of self-disgust, and of ennui'.[50] Through him is revealed, all too briefly, an amusing, wickedly comic, rumbustious, pro-fane and dissolute Orwell, not normally on display. There are caricatures (Mrs Wisbeach, the nosy, censorious landlady; Ravelston, the wealthy socialist editor – based on Rees, it seems; Flaxman, the fat jovial commer-cial traveller – younger brother of George Bowling perhaps) and outrageous generalisations, but in Gordon he created a character through whose words and thoughts these exaggerations flow as easily as platitudes flow from a copywriter.

The dreary daily round at Booklovers' Corner is recreated (even though a caricature of the real shop), the idyllic rural seduction scene with Eleanor is replayed with Rosemary, complete with her 'beautiful white body', so admired and lusted after. Here, too, is his distaste for contraception, his spendthrift dinner with Kay and Rees, his days of squalor in Lambeth, and some entanglement with a prostitute – far too convincing to be mere invention. His modus operandi is evident. He sought out-of-the-ordinary experiences, digested them and later regurgitated them as fiction. It had worked for other writers he admired; to a degree it worked for him. If his personal odyssey into the social underworld had given him *Down and Out in Paris and London* and *A Clergyman's Daughter*, his journey through bookselling and the frustrations of authorship now yielded *Keep the Aspidistra Flying*.

This story was particularly personal. He scorned those who took the easy Eton–Oxbridge road to success, and had chosen instead the thorny path of poverty and struggle (within the Stygian world of the hack writer so familiar to his much-admired Gissing). It was suitably self-punitive and would, after much labour, result in a rather better novel than his previous one. Through Gordon he could rant eloquently against swindling advertisers, corrupt critics and the third-rate novelists they boosted, philistine customers of tuppenny libraries, snobbish waiters, narrow-minded landladies, Rackhamesque Peter Pan sentimentality and suburban pretension symbolised by the indestructible aspidistra. But it is the power of advertising, the handmaiden of capitalist greed, which is his prime target here – 'the money-god' 'who marks with jealous, watchful care,/Our thoughts, our dreams, our secret ways,/Who picks our words and cuts our clothes/And maps the pattern of our days' – the power of the distorted word to reach into the mind and steal away individual autonomy. The epigraph he chose for the book makes the point more succinctly and perhaps more subtly. For Brenda he had altered St Paul's oft-quoted words from Corinthians, substituting the phrase 'sex appeal' for 'love'; here it reads, 'And now abideth faith, hope, money, these three; but the greatest of these is money.' This game of subverting sacred texts would be replayed, notably in his last two novels.

Once again a striking clock sets the narrative running. Time, like a death-watch beetle, ticks away for another sad soul enslaved by dull routine and stifled ambition. But time is also ticking away for Europe and sleepy old England. A theme appearing for the first time in Orwell's work is the threat of war, and especially the bombing of open cities, something which now was very much on his mind. 'I was down at Greenwich the other day,' he told Heppenstall, 'and looking at the river I thought what wonders a few bombs would work among the shipping.'[51] His private nightmares were now being given an external focus.

Again, the narrative follows the familiar design – the Hell of bourgeois life, the Paradise of impoverished freedom, and the Paradise lost to

aspidistra-ruled respectability. And again a life is wasted. As he had written in the *Adelphi* earlier that year, 'It is curious, but the cult of
disillusionment . . . has a certain resemblance to the old Christian cult of
self-mortification.' The failure to attain Christian sainthood had been
replaced by the failure to achieve 'a life fully lived'.[52]

Playfully, he stole a few things from real life which went undisclosed to
his publishers – the name of Michael Sayers' father's firm for his New
Albion Publicity Company, for example – and he neatly hoodwinked the
censor by including a couplet from a poem in medieval French (attributed
to Villon) that can be read as an invitation to fellatio:

> Veillez le dire donc selon
> Que vous estes benigne et doulche,
> Car ce doulx mot n'est pas si long
> Qu'il vous face en la bouche.
>
> See what is being said,
> That you are kind and sweet,
> The word is not so long
> That it should hurt your mouth.[53]

It was a little more subtle than the usual direct proposition, but not much.
Another of Orwell's jokes is the name of his anti-hero, Comstock, the name
of a notoriously draconian American censor, and the irony of having him
utter these words. Gordon, of course, is rabidly hostile to all forms of
imposed bourgeois morality. Inside an Orwell novel, however, he was
bound to be returned to the hell from which he had laboured so hard to
escape. *Keep the Aspidistra Flying* embodies better than any other of his
novels a quality that E. M. Forster recognised in Orwell – his air of grimness
and gaiety.[54] Sour and savage though it is at times, it is certainly more of a
heedless romp than any other of his novels.

Hard on the heels of *A Clergyman's Daughter*, came British publication of
Burmese Days. *The Times*'s anonymous reviewer called it 'a bitter book', yet
admitted that 'The local colour is good, much of the incident is true to type,
and the book has power.' His main reservation was a quaintly ethnocentric
one. The novel, he said, was 'marred by overemphasis . . . not uncommon in
French writers on colonial life'.[55] The perceptive reviewer had spotted the
French cast of mind in Orwell's novel. The other highly insightful review
came from his old school chum Connolly, in the *New Statesman*, who called
it 'a crisp, fierce, and almost boisterous attack on the Anglo-Indian'. He
quoted a passage from Flory's anti-imperial diatribe to Veraswami to give an

idea of 'the vigour and rapidity if this extremely biased book'. It lacked the depth of a Forster and the detachment of a Maugham, he said, and its 'ferocious partiality', in the mode of D. H. Lawrence or Richard Aldington, could have been toned down, but, 'personally I liked it and recommend it to anyone who enjoys a spate of efficient indignation, graphic description, excellent narrative, excitement, and irony tempered by vitriol'.[56]

Orwell was delighted with Connolly's review and invited him to dinner at Parliament Hill – one of his special recipes rustled up on the Bachelor Griller, no doubt. Connolly recalled 'an excellent meal cooked by himself'. It was their first meeting for almost fourteen years, and it took a while for each man to take in the other.

> His greeting [wrote Connolly] was typical, a long but not unfriendly stare and his characteristic wheezy laugh, 'Well, Connolly. I can see that you've worn a good deal better than I have': I could say nothing for I was appalled by the ravaged grooves that ran down from cheek to chin. My fat cigar-smoking persona must have been a surprise to him.[57]

Their literary interests, they found, had diverged. Connolly was interested in young poets such as Dylan Thomas and David Gascoyne, and attracted to the Surrealists. None of these appealed to his old Colleger friend. 'Orwell was not on my beat at all,' he said,[58] but even so, they re-cemented a friendship that would last for the rest of their lives.

Fan letters came from Geoffrey Gorer, the social anthropologist, and two old Burma hands – G. E. Harvey, an ex-Assistant Commissioner in the Indian Civil Service in Burma, and Beaven Rake, who had been one of Orwell's superiors in the Burma Police, Deputy Inspector General, senior even to the hostile Wellborne. He had been prematurely retired and, he said, was now a socialist, and invited Orwell to visit him in Norfolk. As to old police colleagues who read it, Roger Beadon reported that Cline Stewart, the pugnacious head of the Mandalay Police Training School, had said that if ever he saw Blair again he would horsewhip him. That was probably the critical response he would have most appreciated. Clearly he had scored a bull's eye.

Gorer, a friend of the Sitwells, was linked to Bloomsbury, and to the homosexual circle of William Plomer, E. M. Forster and J. R. Ackerley. Also a traveller in colonial parts, he had just published his first book, *Africa Dance*, and, as he lived nearby, he and Orwell agreed to meet. In his letter he had written, 'I wonder if you intend your stricture on the Burmese sahib-log who are "living a lie the whole time" to apply to their domestic counterparts.' Shrewdly he had seen just where Orwell's work could lead. When they met Orwell struck him as a rather awkward figure, gangling, uncoordinated and very lonely. 'He was fairly well convinced that nobody would like him, which made him prickly . . . He was happy to talk about anything, but I would have said he was an unhappy man.'[59] Their discussions about anthropology probably led Orwell towards becoming one of the first serious writers about English popular culture. After reading an article by Gorer in *Time and Tide* the following year, Orwell told him, 'What you say about studying our own customs from an anthropological point of view opens up a lot of fields of thought . . . I have often thought it would be very interesting to study the conventions etc. of *books* from an anthropological point of view.'[60]

Lydia Shiel also wrote, having received a copy of *Burmese Days*, passing on the comment that he was as a writer what Hogarth was as a painter.[61] And his new friend Sayers, never greatly impressed by Orwell's fiction, still found good words to say for both *A Clergyman's Daughter* and *Burmese Days* in the August *Adelphi*. 'George Orwell is a popular novelist sensitive to values that most other novelists are popular for ignoring. One feels he has ideas about the art of the novel, and that his future work is going to be unusually interesting.' He noted especially 'the lucidity' and 'transparence' of *Burmese Days,* applauding 'its clarity of style, which presents the scene with the vivacity of hallucination'. Orwell's career, he concluded, had only begun.[62]

Increasingly he used his clarity of style to attack the state of English letters. In the *Adelphi* he assailed newspapers that corruptly boosted books in return for advertising and lamented the severance of the English from European literature, even though as a connoisseur of the banned book and the dirty joke, he acknowledged the changing 'sense of decency'. Finally he took a blast at 'those slimy Low Church scoutmasters, Charles Kingsley and Tom Hughes', which poses the question, 'What had happened to him as a boy that he so detested the humble scoutmaster?' Years later, he told Michael Meyer that 'various attempts had been made on him at some time or another', and scoutmasters were mentioned, as they were also to Michael Sayers.[63] In the Orwellian dictionary of over-generalisations, 'All scoutmasters are homosexual.' Only certain cliques of poets and intellectuals merited the same epithet.

In July he found another flat, and asked Heppenstall and Sayers to share with him. The three-room flat Orwell found was in Kentish Town, at 50 Lawford Road ('a road with an air of decay about it', recalled Sayers). Orwell took the largest room at the back, also used as a sitting room; Heppenstall, the poorest of them, had the smallest, 'a mere boxroom', and Sayers had the other – for him just a pied-à-terre where he could continue his affair with Edna. According to Heppenstall Orwell was always up first, shaving religiously before making breakfast. He disapproved of the others' more slovenly habits, saying that unshaven in a dressing gown he felt 'unworthy to write'. The two younger men considered him a kindly old eccentric, and thought his literary tastes antiquated, even bizarre. Heppenstall concluded that behind his fascination with forgotten writers like Butler and Gissing, and cultural trivia such as boys' comics and seaside postcards, stood something darkly obsessive. 'There underlay it all some unsolved equation of love and hate, some memory of childhood nursed through Eton, through Burma, taken out and viewed secretly in Paris kitchens or upon the thresholds of doss-houses. The fondness for country parsonages, comic postcards, the *Magnet* and the *Gem*, anecdotes about Queen Victoria and bishops, all betrayed something quite inaccessible to us.'[64] Meanwhile, Orwell continued to sleep with Kay during the week, reserving weekends for Eileen, who came to lunch before setting off with him on long country walks. Occasionally she would bring along Lydia, who was not impressed – a dingy, depressing street and an uneatable meal, were her lasting impressions.[65] Orwell's flatmates were not always there. Heppenstall sometimes stayed with Mabel Fierz or went to visit Middleton Murry. Sayers would spend time with his mother when not pursuing his romance with Edna.

To Sayers, Orwell was a lowbrow author of popular fiction wishing to reach a wide readership. He and Heppenstall, on the other hand, were dedicated to a higher form of literature. Sayers himself was in thrall to Joyce, Pound and Yeats but becoming increasingly interested in Marx. They shared an enthusiasm for Joyce, but Orwell dismissed Pound as 'a ferocious pedant', and Dylan Thomas as 'too rhetorical'. Nor was he at all keen on Yeats. 'My poetry,' he said, 'is Housman's "Shropshire Lad" and Kipling.' According to Sayers, he would rattle off Kipling 'like a barrel-organ', but with great feeling, and hold forth at length on the *Gem*, the *Magnet* and *Boys' Own Paper*, which the younger man thought odd in one particular way. 'I was struck by the fact that in these stories of Harry Wharton and the Famous Five, Bob Cherry and the Terrible Three, there was a conspicuous absence of women.' More seriously, they discussed Ireland, of which Orwell knew little, and he talked passionately about Swift – 'the savage irony, the clarity and the power'. They talked about *The Communist Manifesto*, and agreed 'that it was one of the most powerful and beautifully written political documents imaginable . . . an epic poem in the magnificence of its vocabulary and passion'. Orwell, however, still referred to himself as a Tory Anarchist. 'He was sympathetic to the idea of a change but didn't think it was possible to retain the values that make life worth living. He said the leadership of such movements could not be trusted and pointed to the outcome of the French Revolution.' They read poetry together and Sayers believed he persuaded Orwell to soften his antipathy to Yeats. But his attitude to other poets had not softened, and he warned Sayers to steer well clear of the 'nancy poets' Auden and Spender.

He and Orwell developed, he thought, a very close, very tender, even homoerotic relationship. The older man would bring him a cup of tea in bed in the morning and sit and talk with him. They discussed their parents, and Orwell sympathised with the fact that Sayers did not get on with his father, saying, 'Neither do I.' He was thrilled about his affair with Edna, and grew quite excited when Sayers brought her to the flat to make love. In allowing Sayers close to him, he appears to have revealed aspects of himself not disclosed to others. One morning, for example, he brought Sayers his usual cup of tea but remained standing, looming over him, cigarette in mouth and coughing horribly. 'He looked down at me and said, "Spite and malice, Michael. Spite and malice! Don't let me write today!"' Sayers got the overwhelming impression that Orwell was aware of 'something inside himself that was repellent and dangerous to him', which he was constantly wrestling to keep repressed. To him, this was Flory trying to conceal his birthmark, the poet revealing that his 'clothed man and naked man' were in fact his own two selves.

He thought he had glimpsed Orwell's hidden face one day when he turned up toting a rucksack and produced from it a blue-covered book which he flung across to him, saying, 'You want social significance, Michael? Then read that.' It was Henry Miller's *Tropic of Cancer*, then unobtainable in England. Sayers thought he must have just returned from France and had brought the book back with him. Having read it, he was puzzled – 'I couldn't understand what Orwell saw in his jerk-off book.' Shortly afterwards, when he saw Orwell's review of it in the *New English Weekly*, he realised what an impact it had had on him.[66]

It was an important review, probably the most significant he had so far written, and took him to Swift, Wells and the *Book of Common Prayer*. He began with the image of a sadistic act – the wasp cut in half – recalled from his childhood: 'Modern man is rather like a bisected wasp which goes on sucking jam and pretends that the loss of its abdomen does not matter.' Miller seemed to have caught man in this act with his repeated descriptions of casual sexual encounters, capturing 'sexual life from the point of view of the man in the street – but, it must be admitted, rather a debased version of the man in the street . . . Taken as whole, the book might even be called a vilification of human nature.' The breakdown of religion had produced 'a sloppy idealization of the physical side of life', 'the monstrous soppification' of sex, and the comforting optimism of 'H. G. Wells and his Utopiae infested by nude schoolmarms'. Miller brutally insists on the facts. 'Man is not a Yahoo, but is rather like a Yahoo and needs to be reminded of it from time to time.' If what Miller described was ugly, he nonetheless showed a 'Whitmanesque enthusiasm for the process of life' which left one feeling that 'life is not less but more worth living'. As to his prose style (always important to Orwell) it had 'a fine rhythm' and although the American language was 'less flexible and refined' than English, it had more vigour. *Tropic of Cancer* was, he thought, not the great novel of the century, but a remarkable book, which he strongly advised everybody to read.[67] The review brought him the friendship of Miller, and Miller's publisher, Jack Kahane, had copies printed to publicise the book.

Sayers came across Orwell one day writing in his room and discovered another unexpected side of him. 'He was sitting at the table with two books propped up in front of him – Swift's *A Modest Proposal* and Maugham's *Ashenden*, and he was reading passages from them, closing them and copying them out from memory.' Questioned about this he said, 'I'm trying to find a style which eliminates the adjective.' He was striving to develop the window-pane-clear prose which would later become the most characteristic feature of his writing. In retrospect, Sayers was astonished that Orwell went to so much trouble to turn himself into the writer he became. 'I did not know one could teach oneself how to write; I thought one wrote or one did not. *He* actually worked at it.'[68] The results of that effort to produce a purer, more effective style, he thought, could be seen in 'Shooting an Elephant', which appeared the following year. As the thirties progressed, the change of style became more evident. His use of Latinisms and classical reference all but vanished, the colourful language dissolved into plain and lucid prose. What Connolly called 'excursions into Mandarin' gave way to something direct and colloquial.[69] In 1940 he wrote, 'I believe the modern writer who has influenced me most is Somerset Maugham, whom I admire immensely for his power of telling a story straightforwardly and without frills.'[70]

When Heppenstall returned to Lawford Road after spending time with Middleton Murry in Norfolk, he was half way to embracing Catholicism. He knew he had to keep this from Orwell, who, he said, thought 'Vatican spies were everywhere', and would not have taken kindly to living with a Papist convert. What he called 'Orwell's winter cough' had returned, but even so, he and Eileen would set off together on their country walks, Eric carrying his rucksack and a recently acquired shooting-stick. If not yet engaged they certainly had 'an understanding'. Whatever their relationship, Kay must have been hurt to discover how serious he was about Eileen. According to Heppenstall, one evening in November she came to the flat and 'from Orwell's room the two voices seemed to be raised in continuous argument until after midnight'.[71]

Late one Sunday night Heppenstall returned drunk, and Orwell complained loud and long at being disturbed. Heppenstall told him to shut up and, when he failed to do so, threatened to hit him. Finally he tottered over and took a swing at Orwell. The next thing he knew he was on the floor, his nose pouring blood. He crawled into Sayers' room and Orwell then locked him in. Drunk and battered, he began banging and kicking at the door, which was finally yanked open. 'There stood Orwell, armed with his shooting-stick. With this he pushed me back, poking the aluminium point into my stomach. I pushed it aside, and sprang at him. He fetched me a dreadful crack across the legs and then raised the shooting-stick over his head. I looked at his face. Through my private mist I saw in it a curious blend of fear and sadistic exaltation.' Now barely able to stand, Heppenstall saved himself from a final crack across the head by parrying it with a chair before passing out.[72] Next morning Orwell told him he must go. When he reported this to Mabel, she simply commented, 'I think it's disappointed homosexuality.'

When Sayers came back he found Orwell still in an angry mood.

> Eric was very upset, pale and anxious – rigid, like an angry
> schoolteacher with a pupil, you know – and he said, 'Well, I'm not
> going to have Rayner here. He's out of the house. He's not going to
> come in.' And I didn't say, 'Why?', 'because he was the older man and
> that was the ruling. But I didn't know what was going on, and he said,
> 'We had a great quarrel,' and 'He and Murry belong with the
> Blackshirts; they don't belong with us. When he's drunk he's a lout and
> he's anti-Semitic and I think you should avoid him, too.' I was
> absolutely astonished, 'cos there was no hint of this before, but I
> accepted it completely. I never spoke to Rayner Heppenstall after that,
> and I'd been very friendly with him, and I know that Heppenstall felt
> very cut and hurt by my silence.[73]

When, at the end of that year Sayers left for the USA to become play-editor to the Broadway theatre designer Norman Bel Geddes, it was without wishing Heppenstall goodbye. In fact, according to Sayers, they never met again, and Heppenstall remained perplexed at what had come between them. However, Orwell later made it up with Heppenstall and they remained friends throughout Orwell's lifetime.

Taking out more than one woman must have impoverished him some-what and with Heppenstall no longer paying rent, he asked for a further advance from Gollancz. 'I am very hard up,' he told Moore.[74] Gollancz replied with a proposal. He wanted a book about unemployment in the industrial north on which he was prepared to offer a small advance – prob-ably around £100.[75] A hardback edition only was commissioned but in May 1936 Gollancz planned to launch the Left Book Club (left-wing and anti-Fascist), and the possibility of a Club edition was indicated, with an additional payment. It did little to make him financially secure but it pro-vided him with the initiative to propose to Eileen, despite his near poverty-level income – 'Three pounds a week from all sources,' he wrote later.[76] In the event it also offered him an opportunity to focus his own political thoughts and put into practice the clarity of prose he had been working on with his exercises from Swift and Maugham.

The New Year would be a watershed in Orwell's life. It was in 1936, he said, that he dedicated himself always to write in favour of democratic socialism and to turn political writing into an art. And to Arthur Koestler he said that for him nothing was ever the same after 1936. By mid-January he had delivered the manuscript of *Keep the Aspidistra Flying* to Gollancz and begun making plans to travel north. Those arrangements were delayed by the firm's requiring, as usual, changes to possibly libellous passages. Again he had to deal with Collins, and grew to dislike him even more. Again he agreed to changes – the names of well-known products were changed, known advertising slogans altered, some locations disguised. Since the book was an attack on commercialism and advertising, having to make these particular cuts was particularly galling.[77]

The focus of much intellectual thought, in the mid-1930s, was the condition of the working class. Documentary films from John Grierson, Basil Wright and Humphrey Jennings were beginning to reveal the nature and extent of industrial poverty. In 1937 Mass Observation would take social anthropology in the same direction. Now Gollancz asked Orwell to report on mass unemployment, the most evident mark of the failure of capitalism, the problem which most stirred educated middle-class opinion. Committed to fiction, he might have refused the invitation had there not been the possibility of a Left Book Club edition and so good money in prospect. Stephen Spender would receive a £300 advance for his *Forward from Liberalism*, and Clement Attlee, the new Labour Party leader, £600 for *Labour Party in Perspective*. Orwell, although by no means as well known, might expect to receive £150.

As he was contemplating his expedition to the north, on 18 January, the death of Kipling was announced, and the *New English Weekly* asked for an obituary. Writing it took Orwell back to his childhood and back to Burma. 'For my own part I worshipped Kipling at thirteen, loathed him at seventeen, enjoyed him at twenty, despised him at twenty-five and now again rather admire him.' He was, he said, 'the only popular English writer of this century who was not at the same time a thoroughly bad writer' – an accolade he might not himself have disdained – and, if poems like 'The Road to Mandalay' were 'something worse than a jingle', they did 'stay with one'. More distasteful was his imperialism which, though once acceptable, was now seen as 'sentimental, ignorant and dangerous', the product of even 'a man of alien and perverted genius', who would have been 'a better and more lovable writer' as a composer of music-hall songs. However, he admired Kipling's undoubted 'personal decency', and his essential modesty in spite of his wide popularity, and now that he was dead, he offered 'a salute of guns' to 'the story-teller who was so important to my childhood'.[78]

All Orwell's writing reflects some part of his inner being, and in this short obituary can be seen certain definitive images of disposition and presumption – an admitted readiness to change his mind, a strong awareness of himself in relation to other authors, a taste for good-bad writing, a deep concern with literary texture, a sympathy for the victims of imperialism, a love of music hall, and, above all, a valuing of human decency – a key feature of his secular morality. Previously, he had written about 'decency' mostly in relation to matters of taste; now more and more he would use it as a central value in the judging of moral conduct.

Three days before setting off for the north, he got a snapshot of the state of the English people when caught in crowds in Trafalgar Square watching the funeral of George V. He was struck by the obvious physical degeneracy of the mostly middle-class people. 'Hardly a well-built man or a decent-looking woman, and not a fresh complexion anywhere,' he wrote. When the men took of their hats as the king's coffin passed by, a friend remarked, 'The only touch of colour anywhere was the bald heads.' Nor were the escorting guardsmen what they once were – 'pale-faced boys', some 'like hop-poles in overcoats'. The Great War had culled a million of the best men before they had a chance to breed, but this obvious degeneracy was mostly due, he thought, to industrial processes providing cheap substitutes for real things. 'We may find in the long run,' he concluded, 'that tinned food is a deadlier weapon than the machine gun.'[79] In that one image of dowdy, emaciated crowds he saw a whole system, a historical process and a diminished way of life. In the north he would see the same picture but drawn in even starker lines.

Chapter 10

Journeys of Discovery

'Don't you ever feel lonely about being the only man in step?'

(Fan letter about *The Road to Wigan Pier*)

The road to socialism for George Orwell went via Wigan Pier and would involve further journeys towards self-realisation. The northern excursion also provided him with the wherewithal, however minimal, to get married. He said later that he undertook this commission from Gollancz for the money and he was rather ashamed of the book he produced. He even asked before his death that it should be suppressed, along with a few others. However, *The Road to Wigan Pier* would establish him as a major socialist writer.

It had been agreed that once Eileen completed her MA in June 1936, they would get married. They also agreed for the time being to keep it secret even from their families for fear of any opposition – probably Orwell's paranoia rather than Eileen's. He was, after all, a man who never expected things to go well, and even though he was now just managing to live by his writing and had a publisher who believed in him, not to mention a small but growing readership, he still seemed haunted by the prospect of failure.

There were also the guilt and the nightmares – the nightmare of sins committed in childhood, the nightmare of having participated in a cruel colonial system, the nightmare of poverty and now the looming nightmare of war, foreseen in that vision of bombs falling on London docks. This journey into the industrial north would expose him to the worse kind of squalor and enable him to define where he stood politically. Faced with lives destroyed by exploitation, he directed his sociological eye not just outwards on the grim landscape, but inwards, too, on his own inner turmoil. *The Road to Wigan Pier* would be both a factual account of a social enquiry and a personal record of conversion, tracing his social consciousness back to childhood and forward into the bowels of a Lancashire coalmine. It provides a windowpane into the soul of 'George Orwell', an insight into the source of the daemon which drove him to write as he did. That confessional half of the book could well have discredited him as an impartial observer. It certainly made him enemies on the left but also won him friends. He was moving, together with most young intellectuals of his generation, towards revolutionary socialism, but at his own rate and in his own distinctive manner, and in the process turned a sociological document into something like a work of art.

He set off for the north a somewhat reluctant pilgrim, telling Cyril Connolly that he hated to leave Eileen for any length of time. At the end of January, in freezing cold weather, he travelled to Coventry by train, then the rest of the way to Wigan by bus and on foot, staying in rooming houses, youth hostels, small hotels and (once) a common lodging-house. He kept a meticulous diary, recording not only poor food, unpleasant smells, degrees of frowsiness, discomfort and lack of warmth, but also encounters with oddities and the occasional nature note. It took Orwell just two months to gather the material for *The Road to Wigan Pier*. As he set out, Hitler had already reoccupied the Saarland and moved to exclude Jews from public life in Germany, Mussolini's troops had invaded Abyssinia and there had been a left-wing takeover in Spain.

Wigan was at the heart of the coalmining industry, then employing over a million workers, and had always been at the centre of class struggle – it was, after all, the miners who had led the 1926 General Strike. Orwell had gone armed with introductions to various *Adelphi* contacts of Rees and Middleton Murry. In Wigan, after a few days staying with an unemployed miner and ILP worker, he spent four nights at a house in Warrington Street, experiencing the unemployed working class at close quarters, noting living conditions and incomes of fellow lodgers, some of them impoverished birds of passage – casual workers and itinerants. Meantime he attended meetings of the National Unemployed Workers Union, and talked to workless men on street corners. Again he moved, this time to a room over the tripe shop described so memorably in his book.

Orwell portrays the Brookers' household at 22 Darlington Street as a truly abysmal slum – crowed, filthy, malodorous and sickeningly squalid. He was cramped with three others into an old drawing-room-cum-bedroom:

> . . . and a beastly place it was, with that defiled impermanent look of rooms that are not serving their rightful purpose . . . Hanging from the ceiling was a heavy glass chandelier on which the dust was as thick as fur. And covering most of one wall there was a huge hideous piece of junk, something between a sideboard and a hall-stand, with lots of

carving and little drawers and strips of looking-glass, and there was a once-gaudy carpet ringed by the slop-pails of years, and two gilt chairs with burst seats, and one of those old-fashioned horsehair armchairs which you slide off when you try to sit on them. The room had been turned into a bedroom by thrusting four squalid beds in among this other wreckage.[1]

Most other lodgers were commercial travellers, newspaper canvassers and hire-purchase touts passing through. The windows were jammed shut and in the morning the room stank 'like a ferret's cage'. On a sofa under grimy blankets in the over-heated, beetle-infested, subterranean kitchen lay the permanently ill Mrs Brooker. 'She had a big, pale yellow, anxious face. No one knew for certain what was the matter with her; I suspect that her only real trouble was over-eating.'[2]

The dining table was covered in newspaper stained with Worcester Sauce and strewn with crumbs from past meals. Mr Brooker, who prepared the meals and sold tripe in the shop at the front, was 'a dark, small-boned, sour, Irish-looking man, and astonishingly dirty', and 'like all people with permanently dirty hands he had a peculiarly intimate, lingering manner of handling things'.[3] In the morning when he brought out the tripe his hands were already black; neither the couple nor the residents ever ate tripe themselves, Orwell noted. What was more, one was likely at any time to meet Brooker on the stairs, 'carrying a full chamber-pot which he gripped with his thumb well over the rim'. He was also a very bitter man – 'one of those people who can chew their grievances like a cud'.[4] The sight of the squalid kitchen supplied Orwell with a Hogarthian picture he could do justice to, complete with the resentful Brooker and his slothful wife: 'She had a habit of constantly wiping her mouth on one of her blankets. Towards the end of my stay she took to tearing off strips of newspaper for this purpose, and in the morning the floor was often littered with crumpled-up balls of slimy paper which lay there for hours. The smell of the kitchen was dreadful, but, as with that of the bedroom, you ceased to notice it after a while.' What struck Orwell was that nobody complained. Only one, a sharp-nosed Cockney traveller, after enduring the place for one night, spoke his mind: '"The filthy bloody bastards!" he said feelingly.'[5]

Even Orwell finally gave up. 'On the day when there was a full chamber-pot under the breakfast table I decided to leave. The place was beginning to depress me. It was not only the dirt, the smells and the vile food, but the feeling of stagnant meaningless decay, of having got down into some sub-terranean place where people go creeping round and round, just like black beetles, in an endless muddle of slovened jobs and mean grievances.' What he thought most dreadful about the Brookers was the way they repeated the same things endlessly. 'It gives you the feeling that they are not real people at all, but a kind of ghost for ever rehearsing the same futile rigmarole.'[6] Orwell, the social historian, added his own gloss on the sad Brookers and their dingy household, who, thanks to him, now occupy their own place in literary history.

> They exist in tens and hundreds of thousands; they are one of the characteristic by-products of the modern world. You cannot disregard them if you accept the civilisation that produced them. For this is part at least of what industrialism has done for us. Columbus sailed the Atlantic, the first steam engines tottered into motion, the British squares stood firm under the French guns at Waterloo, the one-eyed scoundrels of the nineteenth century praised God and filled their pockets; and this is where it all led – to labyrinthine slums and dark back kitchens with sickly, ageing people creeping round and round them like black beetles. It is a kind of duty to see and smell such places now and again, especially smell them, lest you should forget that they exist; though perhaps it is better not to stay there too long.[7]

In fact he remained at the tripe shop for almost two weeks, during which he attended large gatherings of 'sheeplike' miners, concluding, 'There is no *turbulence* left in England.'[8] He watched unemployed miners scrambling for coal over slag heaps, and went underground at Crippen's mine, down a shaft 900 feet deep. The journey to the coal face, which meant bending double for three-quarters of a mile, was completely exhausting for the six-foot three Orwell with his weak chest. On one occasion his helmet hit an overhead metal girder and knocked him out cold.[9] The experience so drained him that he took a day off to recover.

He had time to reflect on what he had seen and relate it to his own life. 'If I live to be sixty I shall probably have produced thirty novels, or enough to fill two medium-sized library shelves. In the same period the average miner produces 8,400 tons of coal; enough coal to pave Trafalgar Square nearly two feet deep or to supply seven large families with fuel for over a hundred years.'[10] And again his sociological imagination supplied the appropriate lesson:

> It brought home to you, at least while you are watching, that it is only because miners sweat their guts out that superior persons can remain superior. You and I and the Editor of the *Times Lit. Supp.* and the nancy poets and the Archbishop of Canterbury and Comrade X, author of *Marxism for Infants*, all of us owe the comparative decency of our lives to the poor drudges underground, blackened to the eyes with their

throats full of coal dust, driving their shovels forward with arms and belly muscles of steel.[11]

Towards the end of February he went to Liverpool and met dockers, some communists, observing the unjust system of hiring stevedores at dock gates. However, he found the city's new housing estates and slum-clearance efforts impressive. From there he went to Sheffield, 'one of the most appalling places I have ever seen – monstrous chimneys belching black smoke, the all pervasive smell of sulphur, blackened buildings, huge jets of flames shooting up from the steel foundries [and] no decent architecture,' and noted with satisfaction that 'The town is being torn down and rebuilt at enormous speed.'[12] Yet even in these grim surroundings he had time to jot down nature notes, delighted to record that for the first time ever he had observed rooks copulating. In Leeds there were more communists to meet, including an *Adelphi* contributor who told him it was absolutely necessary to hate the bourgeoisie and that he (Orwell) was obviously a bourgeois from his 'public school twang'. However, he was ready to treat him as 'an honorary proletarian'.

Needing a break, in early March he went to Leeds and stayed for a week with the Dakins. There he wrote up his diary and drafted passages for his book, despite a houseful of adults, three noisy children and several animals. In Barnsley, his next stopover, the radio announced the news that Hitler had reoccupied the Rhineland. That evening in a pub, he said casually, 'The German army has crossed the Rhine.' The response surprised him. 'With a vague air of remembering something, someone murmured "Parley-voo". No more response than that . . . So also at every moment of crisis from 1931 onwards. You have all the time the sensation of kicking against an impenetrable wall of stupidity.'[13] The impression that England was asleep was a strong one and became for him an abiding image of the 1930s. He later attended a Mosley rally in the town. To his dismay he found the audience of some seven hundred mostly supporting him. Mosley, he thought, although a very good orator, spoke 'the usual tripe' and tried to bamboozle the audience by seeming to speak from a socialist point of view. He was struck by how gullible the poorly educated audience seemed, and wrote to the *Manchester Guardian* about it, a letter which was never printed. He went down two further pits again surviving crouching walks to the coalface, making notes and drawings about the use of the coal cutters, blasting charges and 'skip wagons' carrying the coal to back to the shaft.

One evening, this time at a Communist meeting, he watched 'the usual crowd of men of all ages gaping with entirely expressionless faces and the usual handful of women a little more animated than the men'. His attempt afterwards at Socratic dialogue with Party members was not successful. All the while he recorded details of squalid living conditions and patterns of working-class behaviour. He noted the great burning slag heaps ringing Barnsley and also sighted a great tit, which he had only previously noticed in Suffolk.[14]

At the end of March, his researches complete, he returned to London. He realised that his pilgrimage to the north had moved him deeply and altered him profoundly, and others agreed. Rees noted a distinct change in Orwell's outlook and in his writing. 'It was almost as if there'd been a kind of fire smouldering in him all his life which suddenly sort of broke into flame at that time. But I can't understand it or explain what happened.'[15] There were several letters awaiting him from Gollancz requesting changes to *Keep the Aspidistra Flying*. They did not, however, complain about the Villon poem, either unable to understand medieval French or hoping that others wouldn't – a victory of sorts for the put-upon author.

Shortly afterwards he moved into a sixteenth-century cottage in the tiny Hertfordshire village of Wallington, some three miles from Baldock and thirty-five miles from London. It was the sort of quiet country place Orwell had long hoped to find, away from the stresses and distractions of the capital. It had a twelfth-century church, and a population of around a hundred. There, according to legend, 'people live as long as they please', and wild hops grew in the hedgerows. A bus into Baldock ran twice a week but Orwell acquired his own transport – a pushbike. The cottage had, until a year earlier, housed a village store (hence its name, 'The Stores'), but the business had failed through lack of custom, most villagers preferring to shop from vans which visited the village regularly.

The cottage had two bedrooms and two downstairs rooms, plus a kitchen with a door to the back garden. There was a tap outside but no internal water supply, lighting was by oil lamp, and heating and cooking by oil stove. There was a hob at the fireplace but the chimney was blocked and any fire was likely to fill the house with smoke. In winter the bedrooms were like ice. The old thatched roof had been replaced with unsightly corrugated iron and there were noises from it at night which, to Orwell's delight, people thought sounded like rats. It was, he told Connolly, 'quite a nice little cottage but with absolutely no conveniences', and the garden was 'a pigsty'. Getting his own vegetable patch started was important to him and he began work on it right away. 'The garden is still Augean,' he told Jack Common; 'I have dug up twelve boots in two days.'[16] To Brenda he wrote, 'This is a tiny cottage, quite primitive but at this time of year quite comfortable. My landlords are "going to" put in running water and proper sanitation, but they are the kind of people who can go on "going to" do a thing for two or three years at a stretch.'[17]

Others were less kind about 'The Stores'. Lettice Cooper, who stayed there during the war, remembered, 'Nothing in it worked. The sink would be blocked. The primus stove wouldn't work. The lavatory plug wouldn't pull. The stairs were very dark, because there were never any bulbs in the lights, and they'd put piles of books on the staircase at odd places, so there were lots of traps, and the place was rather dusty. But it was a nice cottage, in a lovely part of the country.'[18] Directly opposite was a piece of common land, and immediately next door the Plough Inn, which served beer by the jug. The old church was just a short walk away, and there were two farms in the village – Bury Farm where John Wilson was the farmer, and Manor Farm, owned and run by John Innes. It was not just an ancient village, but ancient in its ways too, and Orwell never ceased to wonder at the narrowness of the world and the impoverished conditions in which many villagers lived.

The garden wasteland was gradually replaced by carefully cultivated rows of vegetables and neatly tended fruit trees. At the front of the cottage he planted an Abertine rose which cost him sixpence at Woolworths and which he was proud to report continued to flourish seven years later.[19] As the place took on a more civilised aspect, he planned to entertain friends there, telling Richard Rees, 'it is a good place to be quiet if you don't mind the primitiveness'.[20] This was to be his first home with Eileen. The willingness of a woman to share his poverty was an important indication of her worth to Orwell, who, like Gissing, knew how difficult it was to find a wife of refinement and sensibility ready to make that sacrifice. There would be no social pressure from her to get on for respectability's sake, and she would show qualities which, again like Gissing, he preferred in a woman – a readiness to be self-effacing and to keep a home for him.

He decided there was a small income to be made from reviving the shop, selling 'mainly groceries, no perishables at first, and stamps and sweets'. It would, he calculated, bring in enough at least to cover the 7/6d weekly rent, and the garden would provide enough vegetables to live on. As he told Jack Common, 'I suppose it isn't more complicated than a bookshop. If I do open it will be only for certain stated hours so as not to interfere with my work.'[21] Work, of course, meant his book about the north, but he was also finding a wider market for his reviews, not just the *Adelphi* and *New English Weekly* but now, through an introduction from Gorer, *Time and Tide* – his '*bête noire*', he told Brenda: 'You see to what depths one has to sink in the literary life.'[22]

By mid-April he reported to his agent Leonard Moore that he had started *The Road to Wigan Pier*. On the 20th, *Keep the Aspidistra Flying* appeared – a print run of 3,000, of which 2,256 were sold and 422 went as a cheap edition. Moore could not find an American publisher for so English a book. However, even in England its reception was tepid. William Plomer, in the

Spectator, called it 'bitter throughout and often crude'.[23] In the *New Statesman* Connolly compared it unfavourably with *Burmese Days*, clearly hating its all-pervasive air of squalor. 'The realism of one book was redeemed by an operating sense of beauty, that of the other is not.' The book, he thought, suffered from 'an irony which the author would appreciate . . . that the obsession with money about which the book is written, is one which must prevent it from achieving the proportion of a work of art'.[24] Reviewing it in the *Adelphi*, even Rees criticised 'the loose violence of style' and commented 'one only has to compare the conversations in *Keep the Aspidistra Flying* with those of Huxley's novels to see what a lot Mr Orwell still has to learn'. Both Rees and Connolly, like Orwell, were adhering strictly to Etonian tradition, refusing to trim their critical sails for a friend. The book's reception left him feeling rather detached. He told Brenda that it had received 'the most awful slating', adding that 'even Cyril Connolly has deserted me'. But, with the gladdening prospect of his marriage looming, he insisted on seeing something good in it. 'I am not certain that kind of thing does a book much harm . . . Also, because of the abuse I had received elsewhere the *Daily Worker* for the first time deigned to notice me.'[25] Unlike some writers, he read all his reviews, religiously pasting them into a scrapbook. It stood, as it were, as his passport to authorship.

Gorer wrote expressing admiration for the novel, comparing him to Swift.[26] He had sent a copy to Edith Sitwell, who declared, 'He is gloomy and often displeasing, but really rather good.'[27] And if Connolly had deserted him, he caught the attention of at least one other Old Etonian. The young novelist Anthony Powell wrote saying how much he had enjoyed the book, and commiserating with him over the reviews. Orwell's belated reply, polite and friendly though it was, seemed to Powell to cast 'a faint chill, making me feel . . . that Orwell was not for me'.[28] He did not pursue the correspondence, and it took them another five years to meet and become friends.

In late May he informed Gorer of his impending marriage. The banns were to be called in the parish church, and the date was fixed for 9 June. 'This is as it were in confidence,' he wrote, 'because we are telling as few people as possible till the deed is done, lest our relatives combine against us in some way & prevent it. This is very rash of course but we talked it over & decided I should never be economically justified in marrying so might as well be unjustified now as later. I expect we shall rub along all right – as to money I mean – but it will always be hand to mouth as I don't see myself ever writing a best-seller.'[29] Like all marriages it was a leap into the unknown, but both had a streak of adventurousness in their make-up which sometimes bordered on recklessness.

They revealed their marriage plans only shortly before the date set, but Eric had broken the news to Brenda earlier, giving her his new address and inviting her to stay. It took several weeks for her to reply, suggesting that she had not taken the news well. In his reply he described how the cottage had been slowly made habitable and he was getting the store in shape, adding, as always with her, his latest nature notes – birds spotted and wildflowers noted. He had, he told her, had an amusing communication from Rees. '[He] conceived that I had put a caricature of him in "Keep the A" and sent me an unspeakably vulgar postcard . . . of a man looking under the bed, and his wife says, "What are you looking for?" and he says, "An aspidistra."'[30]

As he neared his wedding day his book was pushed aside, but he was not too distracted to respond to a letter from John Lehmann inviting a contribution for his projected 'anti-Fascist' literary magazine, New Writing. Orwell offered him a sketch he had thought to write about shooting an elephant, saying that he was not very sure if there was anything anti-Fascist in that. Kipling's death, probably, and mulling over what he had seen in the north had stirred memories of his time in Burma. 'It all came back to me very vividly the other day,' he told Lehmann, '& I would like to write it, but it may be that it is quite out of your line.'[31] It was not, and Lehmann was delighted eventually to find himself publishing one of the finest essays to come from anyone of that generation.

On the morning of the great day, yet another old Etonian contemporary surfaced. Denys King-Farlow, back after many years in the American oil business, wrote inviting him to a celebration dinner for his Election on 11 June. He had the perfect excuse not to attend. 'I am getting married this very morning – in fact I am writing this with one eye on the clock & the other on the Prayer Book, which I have been studying for some days past in hopes of steeling myself against the obscenities of the wedding service.' Whatever had changed since the pair co-edited College Days, Blair the Cynic was still alive and well and living in rural Hertfordshire. 'I have had a bloody life a good deal of the time,' he told his friend, 'but in some ways an interesting one.'[32]

Perhaps to placate her mother, Eileen had invited the parson who had christened and prepared her for confirmation in South Shields (John Woods, who by 1936 had become Vicar of Glaston in Rutland) to conduct the wedding ceremony. Eileen was probably no more religious than her husband-to-be but came from a strong Anglican background and had, after all, been head girl of an Anglican girls' school. Orwell, too, despite his proclaimed atheism, retained a fond attachment to the Anglican Church, an attachment closely bound up with what Connolly called his 'love of 1910'. All the family turned out for the great occasion – Richard, Ida, Marjorie and Avril, Mrs O'Shaughnessy, Eileen's brother Laurence and his wife Gwen.

Eric was remembered for vaulting over the side-gate of the churchyard and sprinting round to the lych-gate to greet his bride – thus breaking with the convention of the groom nervously awaiting the bride's arrival at the altar rail. But if that was a surprise to Eileen there was also a surprise awaiting the groom. When the vows came to be read, Eileen, it seems, had arranged with John Woods to omit at least one of the promises. Orwell wrote to his old love Brenda the following day: 'We were married yesterday in correct style at the parish church here but not with the correct marriage service, as the clergyman left out the "obey" clause among other things.'[33] What 'other things' were omitted he did not say. Richard Blair and Eileen's mother signed the marriage certificate.

Afterwards there was lunch at a country inn with a choice of Fillet of Sole with Tartar sauce, Roast Aylesbury Duck with Sage and Onions, new potatoes and garden peas followed by Sherry Cream trifle, biscuits and cheese and Coffee. According to Lydia Jackson, 'Eileen gave me a comic account of the wedding lunch . . . during which old Mrs Blair talked without stopping, while Avril said not a word the whole day.'[34] Another report had it that after the ceremony Mrs Blair and Avril took Eileen aside and commiserated with her for what she had taken on;[35] and according to a Blair family friend, 'Avril did not like Eileen – they didn't "cog". There was something about Eileen that Avril and Ida Blair didn't cotton to. They suspected something.'[36] As a wedding present, Eric was bequeathed the family silver. He also inherited, temporarily at least, Hector, the family dog. Eileen brought to the marriage not just an intimate female presence into his life, so ending his sense of loneliness, but also an intellectual companionship that he rarely found with other women. From home she also brought her library, mostly the Elizabethan and Lake poets she loved to read on those return trips to Oxford. Brenda cabled her congratulations followed by a friendly letter wishing the happy couple well. One small problem for Eileen was that Laurence was also known as 'Eric'. The solution was to call her husband 'George', in this way symbolically confirming the new literary persona.

With the wedding behind him, George returned to his book. He also returned to his garden, and decided to keep a goat on the common land opposite the cottage. The 'wilderness of tin cans, boots and nettles' had been tamed, he told Brenda. 'Now I have got parts of it under cultivation and am going to open up the shop on Monday week . . . This is a tiny village and I can't make very much out of it, but I doubt whether I can lose and I am happy it will at least pay my rent for me.'[37] To keep Hector company they acquired a little sandy cat, some chickens and finally that goat, which was christened Muriel after one of George's Limouzin aunts.

Whatever her intentions, on agreeing to marry Eileen seems to have stopped work on her thesis. She had settled on a title, 'The use of imagination in school essays', but whereas her friends Lydia and Rosalind completed theirs and obtained their degrees, Eileen did not. Some have thought that marrying Orwell ruined her career, but though she had a year in which to complete the work, two months of which George was away in the north, she appears to have abandoned it. She could have obtained a year's extension and submitted her work later, gathering material at a school in Baldock or Greenwich, where she often stayed with Laurence and Gwen. But in fact she had chosen to live a life which, in many ways, was far more to her taste than that of professional psychologist – married to a writer with a fellow-feeling for literature, whom she would have liked to help more than he allowed, but with whom, through her sharp wit and ready sense of humour, soon established a highly relaxed and stimulating rapport. (Friends noticed how she caught his manner and would echo and satirise some of his more outrageous remarks, a playful game he seemed thoroughly to enjoy.) She could have pursued an independent career but chose to partner a man whose strange brilliance deeply attracted her. It is likely that the transformation in Orwell's work from *Wigan Pier* onwards owes a great deal to the intellectual stimulus his marriage brought him. Gorer said he had never known Orwell so happy as he was during the first year of his marriage to Eileen.

He soon wrote to Brenda again inviting her to visit them. He could still not get her out of his mind. His unfulfilled passion for her would continue to haunt him, and must also have haunted Brenda, who lived to be ninety-eight and never married. Nor did she ever reveal his most intimate love-letters, which came to light only after her death in 2001. Eileen also had her admirers. One was Karl Schnetzler, a German friend of Laurence's, who Lydia Jackson was sure was in love with her, though there is some doubt as to whether she reciprocated.[38]

The shop proved its modest worth and by June had a turnover of between thirty and thirty-five shillings a week, yet they still found it hard to get by, even though the vegetable garden helped. As George told Jack Common, 'When Eileen and I were first married, when I was writing "Wigan Pier", we had so little money that sometimes we hardly knew where the next meal was coming from, but we found we could rub along in a remarkable manner with spuds and so forth.'[39] However, they still managed to serve a decent meal when friends turned up. King-Farlow, the Commons and Humphrey Dakin were among their early guests, Humphrey casting a typically jaundiced eye on the new homestead – 'That comic place where the post office was and what he called his farm, with a few moth-eaten hens wandering about on it', he called it.[40]

Now seemingly contented, Orwell resumed his writing with renewed zest. The elephant sketch mentioned to Lehmann was finished and dispatched within sixteen days, demonstrating not only a great advance in his power as a writer, but also just how memories of Burma still preyed on him. Thinking about and writing this essay seems to have fed into *The Road to Wigan Pier*, and in the second half of that book he would link the two places in tracing his own political progress from oppressor to champion of the oppressed.

Connolly had warned him that his review of *Keep the Aspidistra Flying* would be a poor one but told him that when his novel, *The Rock Pool*, came out he could then 'have his innings'. Orwell 'had his innings' with Connolly's novel in the *New English Weekly* in late July, and in the course of it revealed their deep philosophical difference. It is a mark of their friendship that this never came between them. The novel was set on the French Riviera among a group of well-heeled drop-outs. While admiring the treatment, said Orwell, he found the subject-matter 'tiresome'. And although he considered that bothering to study these drinking, cadging, lecherous 'so-called artists who spend on sodomy what they have gained by sponging' betrayed 'a spiritual inadequacy', he still found the novel both interesting and amusing.[41] Rejection of the money-god and the god of cultural snobbery, were not just themes in *Keep the Aspidistra Flying*, but central to his whole being.

Slowly composing *The Road to Wigan Pier*, he was edging towards admitting for the first time that he was a socialist. His suspicion of Communism surfaced that summer, in reviewing *News From Tartary* by Peter Fleming. Travelling through Asia, Fleming had observed the growing influence of Soviet Russia in part of China. Orwell commented, 'It is a queer tribute to the moral prestige of Communism that we are always rather shocked when we find that the Communists are no better than anybody else.' This was one of his first written pronouncements on a power that would largely overshadow the rest of his life. Not long before he died he wrote, 'I have never fundamentally altered my attitude towards the Soviet regime since I first began to pay attention to it some time in the nineteen-twenties,'[42] an acknowledgement, perhaps, of the important influence of Eugène Adam on his thinking.

On 19 July the Civil War erupted in Spain, when part of the army attempted to seize power from the Popular Front Republican government and succeeded in taking over most of western Spain. Parts of the army and Civil Guard loyal to the government, together with armed militias formed by the trade unions and left-wing parties, almost succeeded in overthrowing the coup. But Hitler sided with the rebels and flew General Francisco Franco from Morocco with soldiers of his Army of Africa, mostly Moors, saving the rebellion and leading to stalemate. For the Republicans, Madrid was the prize to be defended at all costs, and in Catalonia the local militias, dominated by Anarchists, had precipitated a revolution, dispossessing landlords, appropriating land, despoiling churches and shooting priests. Anti-Fascist volunteers hurried to join the government side and International Brigades were hurriedly formed (mostly Communist-dominated). The war was seen by many on the left as the first great fight against Fascism – a war for revolution and democracy. If Franco could be defeated, it was thought, the looming war against Hitler could be stopped. When the Russians sided with the Republicans it became a major Communist cause, too.

From the outset, according to George, he and Eileen felt they ought to go to Spain to help the Republican cause. He followed the war closely from the very start. After all, he was about to declare himself finally a socialist, and here was a great drama being played out between socialists and their enemies. He was a writer, but also a man with a military bent, who had 'lived within the sound of bugles' for much of his early life. He had missed the Great War and felt somehow diminished by the fact. Spain would at least give him the one experience he had envied in his old Burma colleagues. At this point, however, he still had a book to finish.

Eager to become politically involved, in August he attended the *Adelphi* Summer School at Langham near Colchester, and gave a talk, 'An Outsider Sees the Distressed Areas', sharing a platform with John Middleton Murry (now turned pacifist), Richard Rees and John Strachey, an old Labour Party comrade of Mosley. Rees remembered Orwell in discussions producing 'breathtaking Marxist paradoxes and epigrams' – not an impossibility, since he had certainly read *The Communist Manifesto* and probably other Marxist literature, and his fascination with paradox dates from first reading Chesterton, a playful connoisseur of the form. At Langham he ran into Rayner Heppenstall again. Their quarrel was forgotten and they went for a drink to the nearby pub as if nothing had happened eight months earlier in Lawford Road.

At much the same time he attended the annual ILP Summer School at Letchworth, a short journey from Wallington. It was in that Garden City, renowned for its 'progressives', that he encountered the absurd figures he lampooned so savagely in *The Road to Wigan Pier*:

> They were both about sixty, both very short, pink and chubby, and both hatless. One of them was obscenely bald, the other had long grey hair bobbed in Lloyd George style. They were dressed in pistachio-coloured shirts and khaki shorts into which their huge bottoms were crammed to tightly that you could study every dimple. Their appearance created a mild stir of horror on the top of the bus. The man next to me, a commercial traveller I should say, glanced at me, and then, back at them again, and murmured, 'Socialists'.[43]

It is reported that at one of the Summer School discussions he berated the mostly middle-class gathering saying, 'You wouldn't even recognise a miner or a docker if they came into the room.' The middle-class socialist – of whom he was one, of course – now became a favourite target of his derision. The difference between them and himself, one supposes, was that he *would* have recognised a miner and a docker when he saw one and *he* was 'lower-*upper*-middle class'.

Henry Miller, having finally acquired a copy of *Down and Out*, wrote a letter of appreciation, but told Orwell that his sufferings as a *plongeur* were due to his own failings – his 'false respectability' or his 'bloody English education'. He also expounded his own philosophy of quietism: 'I think that human society is founded on injustice absolutely, and any attempt to alter that fundamental aspect must be tentative and transitory and doomed to failure.'[44] Orwell replied telling Miller what he had liked about *Tropic of Cancer* – the rhythmic quality of his English, his candour and his ability to 'wander off into a kind of reverie where the laws of ordinary reality were slipped just a little but not too much'. However, in his new novel, *Black Spring*, he had moved 'into a sort of Mickey Mouse universe where things and people don't have to obey the rules of space and time'. His own attitude was 'belly-to-earth' and getting away from green grass and hard surfaces made him uneasy. He commiserated over his having to follow one unusual book with another, but told him as diplomatically as he could, that he thought he had failed.[45] Reviewing the book later in the *New English Weekly*, he went on to compare Miller to Whitman – 'Whitman but without Whitman's American puritanism . . . or his American bumptiousness'.[46]

With Miller indifferent to world affairs, the Moscow Show Trials of that year no doubt failed to register in the way they did with Orwell. On 25 August the old Bolsheviks Zinoviev and Kamenev were executed in the Lubyanka prison after 'confessing' to involvement in the assassination of another Party man, Sergei Kirov. Fourteen others were shot at the same time. Stalin's paranoid war on suspected Trostkyists was gaining momentum. The ILP newspaper *New Leader* condemned these trials as a fraud, and was in its turn damned by the Communist press.

Now happily married, Orwell at least had a well-regulated sex life. The couple's physical intimacy was evident and they seemed happy enough in their rural idyll. Eileen certainly seemed to enjoy helping George with the shop and the animals, and even helped clean out the foul garden latrine. But the idyllic picture taken away by his friends concealed a problem that had arisen between the couple. Eileen is said to have complained that her new husband had had too much sex before marriage, hinting perhaps at his less than delicate performance in bed. He seemed to suggest (in his last notebook) that it was his wife's 'devouring sexuality' which became problematic. Wives, he suggested, use sex as a means of controlling their husbands.

> And he suspected that in every marriage the struggle was always the
> same – the man trying to escape from sexual intercourse, to do it only
> when he felt like it (or with other women), the woman demanding it
> more & more, & more & more consciously despising her husband for
> his lack of virility.[47]

Referring later to a notorious Edwardian murderer, he wrote of 'the sympathy everyone feels for a man who murders his wife'[48] – clearly Orwell in misogynist mood (even if ironically so), a mood he normally made an effort to muffle or suppress. Lydia Jackson, who felt Eileen's marriage had been a mistake, certainly saw *him* as the problem. 'My impression was that he was taking her very much for granted. Any man, I thought, ought to treasure such a wife – most attractive to look at, highly intelligent, an amusing and witty talker, an excellent cook. Yet I did not detect any fond glances, or small gestures of attention from him to her. Eileen did all the work, prepared the meals and served them, and answered the shop bell when it rang.' Eileen, she claimed, expressed disappointment that George seemed not to need her help with his work, or want to discuss it with her, as her brother did.[49] But other friends – the Commons, Gorer and Rees – found them an amorous and perfectly happy couple.

Perhaps the flush of sexual fulfilment in his first months of marriage made him more attractive to women. Connolly recalled a cocktail party that he and his American wife gave in Chelsea:

> We had quite a lot of Right-wing friends, rather nice, jolly girls with
> lots of money who were unpolitical, and then there were one or two
> Left-wing political people, and poets. It was the watershed between the
> unconscious political generation and the people who were beginning to
> get engaged in the 30s struggle. And he [Orwell] came along, looking
> gaunt and shaggy, shabby, aloof, and he had this extraordinary magical
> effect on these women. They all wanted to meet him and started talking
> to him, and their fur coats shook with pleasure. They were totally
> unprepared for anyone like that and they responded to something –
> this sort of John the Baptist figure coming in from the wilderness – and
> suddenly the women feel it doesn't matter what his political views are,
> he's a wonderful man. And that was rather the effect he had
> everywhere, I think.[50]

One of Connolly's rich lady friends was the Duchess of Westminster, and this may well have been the occasion on which she discovered who it was who got her husband a peach at the Hôtel Lotti in 1929.

The Road to Wigan Pier would confirm him in a new role on the left, but what Connolly had noticed, and Stephen Spender would also observe, was the socialist with the aura, the secular saint – even though there was a comic element to the performance. He may have found the saintly role to his taste, coming to see himself in a tradition of Christian socialism, identifying personally with martyred Anglican dissenters. But his old book-selling colleague Jon Kimche, himself a member of the ILP and later an editor of the left-wing paper *Tribune*, was not particularly comfortable with the new political Orwell.

> Orwell was always pontificating. He wasn't a phony, but he was affected. It was natural for him to play a role, I think. He played it almost semiconsciously, but it was a role all the time. He created [it] early on. It wasn't created by a public, because he had no public when he created the role. In some way it was imposed on him by this duality of having been to Eton and then the Burma Police and then down-and-out and then suddenly coming upon an entirely new world, with Victor Gollancz and the politicos and the literary people. They were something quite different, and I think he realized that if he was to make his way in this world he would have to play the part of 'Orwell'.[51]

However, if Orwell himself is to be believed, he took on this role somewhat reluctantly. Almost his last, highly confessional, poem appeared in that December's *Adelphi*, just as he was preparing for Spain. It provides insight into the mind of a man undergoing the painful transition from free-floating artist to committed writer. The religious image and its renunciation links him in its way to the dissidents prepared to die for their denial of orthodoxy.

> A happy vicar I might have been
> Two hundred years ago,
> To preach upon eternal doom
> And watch my walnuts grow;
>
> But born, alas, in an evil time,
> I missed that pleasant haven,
> For the hair has grown on my upper lip
> And the clergy are all clean-shaven.

This once-upon-a-time dreamworld had given way to a world of wakefulness, a world of dictators, secret police and concentration camps.

I am the worm who never turned,
The eunuch without a harem;
Between the priest and the commissar
I walk like Eugene Aram;

And the commissar is telling my fortune
While the radio plays,
But the priest has promised an Austin Seven,
For Duggie always pays.

I dreamed I dwelt in marble halls,
And woke to find it true;
I wasn't born for an age like this;
Was Smith? Was Jones? Were you?[52]

As the Wigan Pier book came close to completion, on 10 December Orwell told Moore that he had got his passport and would soon be ready to leave for Spain. Eileen would handle the proofs, and any contractual matters after his departure. Four days later he sent in the finished manuscript.

The two parts of *The Road to Wigan Pier* represent both a physical journey and a parallel journey of the soul. In the first part he reports on the living conditions of the unemployed in three northern towns. In the second he charts his own path to socialism, from the lower-upper-middle class through Eton and Burma to dosshouses and finally through the depths of working-class poverty. In doing so, he offers his personal insights into the subtleties and complexities of the English class system, the means by which class hatred is generated and fostered, the need for a revolution, the illusory Utopianism of some on the left, and the need to defend socialism not only against capitalism and Fascism but also against enemies within. Most threatening to the movement he saw were the middle-class fake-socialist and the authoritarian communist.

'Socialism' calls up, on the one hand, a picture of aeroplanes, tractors and huge glittering factories of glass and concrete; on the other, a picture of vegetarians with wilting beards, of Bolshevik commissars (half gangster, half gramophone), of earnest ladies in sandals, shock-headed Marxists chewing polysyllables, escaped Quakers, birth-control fanatics and Labour Party backstairs-crawlers. Socialism, at least in this island, does not smell any longer of revolution and the overthrow of tyrants; it smells of crankishness, machine-worship and the stupid cult of Russia. Unless you can remove that smell, and very rapidly, Fascism may win.[53]

There is a strange opposition between these two halves of what Fredric Warburg called 'one of the most contradictory books ever written'[54] – a mirror of the man, of course. Despite his readiness to generalise to the point of caricature – as he does in this book about cranky socialists and vegetarians – he was essentially honest about himself. If he was guilty of contradictions he was prepared to let them show.

It begins characteristically with a sudden awareness of time, marked on this occasion not by a screaming alarm or an hourly chime but by the sound of the mill-girls' clogs on the cobbles outside his bedroom window in Wigan. Again it is an awakening to wretchedness. The first chapter stands as an essay in its own right, and draws the reader into the fetid hell of the Brookers' tripe shop. He retraces his steps to meetings with the unemployed and miners underground, down squalid streets into the most appalling slums, to slag heaps to observe people scrabbling for coal, to the Liverpool docks and the Mosley meeting; finally, on his way out of Wigan, the poignant sight of a poor woman on her knees attempting to unblock a waste pipe.

Then in the second half comes Orwell's own personal testimony, culminating in an attack on middle-class socialists who, he thought, brought socialism into contempt, and who in time would have to settle down to where they truly belonged, among the working class: 'Probably when we get there it will not be so dreadful as we feared, for, after all, we have nothing to lose but our aitches.'[55] What offended many on the left who failed to read the book carefully was his mentioning the fact that as a child he had been taught that the working class smelt. And although he went to some pains to say that he had divested himself of the belief, he exposed himself to attack by remaining ambivalent on the subject – denying the middle-class prejudice but saying that as an observation there was truth in it. If there was a subtle distinction to be made, there were those who chose to ignore it. The Bolshevik commissars (half gangster, half gramophone) depicted by him as mere figures of fun would soon become a more threatening reality, and adherents of 'the stupid cult of Russia' would soon have George Orwell in their sights, thanks, in part, to this book.

From his Wigan Pier diary the image of the young woman trying to unblock the drain with a stick was one which struck him forcefully. 'I thought how dreadful a destiny it was to be kneeling in the gutter in a back-alley in Wigan, in the bitter cold, prodding a stick up a blocked drain. At that moment she looked up and caught my eye, and her expression was as desolate as I have ever seen; it struck me that she was thinking just the same thing as I was.'[56] In his book this scene, observed from a departing train, becomes strangely emblematic. (The same image would recur some thirteen years later in a somewhat different context, in *Nineteen Eighty-Four*.) Orwell's obsession with dirt and foul smells is, of course, an identifiable feature of his writing. Stinks, stenches, reeks and odours of unimaginable repugnance swirl and permeate throughout his wretched worlds – faecal smells, the smell of the drain, the workhouse, the prison cell, the squalid hospital ward, the smell of incense, of decayed religion and false doctrines.[57] Orwell was repelled by filth and evil odours, but sought them out as if to rub his own nose in them to exorcise his demons through self-inflicted suffering.

The Road to Wigan Pier fits a form of which Orwell was himself a pioneer, what he called 'the "political book" – part reportage and part political criticism, usually with a little autobiography thrown in'. It was, he said, a product of the anxious years from 1933 onwards, a genre that 'depended a good deal upon the orthodoxy of the moment', which made trying to write a truthful book difficult.[58] In fact his writing was never dispassionate; he is always ready to insert a comment or personal anecdote. But in this book he made every effort to separate reportage from the personal and anecdotal, the exception being his account of the tripe shop and its sad inhabitants. In this, and in the second half of the book, the power and force of Orwell's style can be seen to derive in part from his tendency to exaggerate to make a polemical point. 'This is an untrue picture,' he commented on someone else's polemic, 'but remember that it is only untrue in the way in which a caricature is untrue.'[59] In this he was an apt pupil of his master, Dickens.

The book's main weakness lies in Orwell's inability to portray working-class life from the inside. He later admitted that only a proletarian writer could get beyond the surface of proletarian life, but in an age where the bourgeoisie was the dominant class, proletarian writers had yet to find their own voice.[60]

As usual, he could also see some of its shortcomings – it was 'too fragmentary and, on the surface, not very left-wing'. He thought it unlikely to be considered suitable for the Left Book Club, and in any case he was due to leave around Christmas Day which left very little time for it to be considered. However, after only four days he had a telegram from Gollancz asking to meet him. Afterwards he told Moore that it seemed highly likely that it would be a Left Book Club Choice for March. In the meantime, a contract was issued, offering a £100 advance and the prospect of more in the event of the book being chosen.

The Left Book Club was to become a highly influential enterprise, and has been credited with turning many middle-class people into socialists and even communists. Gollancz was seen as a major mouthpiece for the communist cause, and John Strachey, also on the Club committee, had close ties to Harry Pollitt, Secretary of the British Communist Party, and was himself either a member of the Party or at least a fellow traveller. Despite his own antipathy towards communism, and perhaps touched by the spirit of the

United Front against Fascism, Orwell thought that Pollitt might help him to get to Spain.

> Just before I started someone told me I should not be able to cross the frontier unless I had papers from some left-wing organisation (this was untrue at that time although party cards etc. undoubtedly made it easier). I applied to John Strachey who took me to see Pollitt. P. after questioning me evidently decided that I was politically unreliable and refused to help me, also tried to frighten me out of going by talking a lot about Anarchist terrorism. Finally he asked whether I would undertake to join the International Brigade. I said I could not undertake to join anything until I had seen what was happening. He then refused to help me but advised me to get a safe-conduct from the Spanish Embassy in Paris, which I did.[61]

Still without the balance of his advance from Gollancz, Orwell was so broke that to make his journey possible he asked his bank for a £50 overdraft. He also asked Moore to try getting him war-reporting work with the Labour *Daily Herald*. Probably the bank was slow responding, because finally, and without reference to his parents, he pawned the family silver. (When Ida and Avril came to Wallington shortly afterwards and asked what had happened to it, Eileen said that Eric being away seemed a good opportunity to have it engraved with the Blair family crest.)[62] Visiting Greenwich, he broke the news of his leaving to the O'Shaughnessys with the wry remark to Eileen, 'Shan't be kissing you under the mistletoe this Christmas.' Her friend Lydia was shocked and appalled that he would think of leaving his new wife alone in what she considered a ramshackle isolated old cottage. She was further shocked when Eileen's brother Laurence approved the idea, remarking that 'George has a warrior cast of mind.'[63] All of them, it seems – George, Eileen, Laurence and Gwen – now saw eye-to-eye on the threat of war.

After Pollitt's refusal to help, Orwell turned elsewhere. 'Just before leaving England I also rang up the ILP, with which I had some slight connections, mainly personal, and asked them to give me some kind of recommendation. They [Fenner Brockway and Noel Brailsford] sent me to Paris [with] a letter addressed to John McNair at Barcelona.'[64] His course was now set. If Wigan had turned him into a socialist, Spain would harden his socialism and give it a particular edge and temper.

When Orwell left for Spain just before Christmas, *Wigan Pier* was still under consideration by Gollancz. It was this second section of the book that concerned him. He knew it would offend many of the readers he hoped to attract to his Left Book Club. The matter would finally be settled by a committee of three – Gollancz, Strachey and Harold Laski. However, first

Gollancz tried to persuade Leonard Moore to agree to Part One of the book appearing as a Club edition with the second part appearing separately in hardback. Eileen, on George's behalf, rejected this; the committee would have to decide. A Club Edition would bring a guaranteed readership of over 40,000, which would mean being *lancé* on a grand scale by anyone's measure. Orwell himself was never satisfied with *Wigan Pier* and, just before he died, suggested that only the first chapter be salvaged for a collection of sketches.[65]

The past year had been a year of journeys for Orwell – the journey to Wigan, the journey of self-discovery which accompanied it, and the journey into marriage. It was ending with yet another journey. This time the lesson to be learned was a hard one, and he would never recover from it.

Now, the only problem he had before leaving was to find a suitably comfortable pair of size twelve boots.

Chapter 11

The Spanish Betrayal

'A law of the Suspected, which struck away all security for liberty or life . . .
delivered over any good and innocent person to any bad and guilty one;
prisons gorged with people who had committed no offence, and could
obtain no hearing; these things became the established order and nature of
appointed things, and seemed to be ancient usage before they were many
weeks old.'

Charles Dickens, *A Tale of Two Cities*

O rwell was about to plunge into the Spanish labyrinth in which many
were lost and many devoured. 'I had intended going to Spain to gather
materials for newspaper articles etc.,' he wrote, 'and had also some vague
idea of fighting if it seemed worthwhile, but was doubtful about this owing
to my poor health and comparatively small military experience.'[1] Armed
with Fenner Brockway's letter, he travelled to Paris to obtain the necessary
travel documents for Barcelona.

Once in Paris he decided to visit Miller in Montparnasse, a quarter familiar to him from his down-and-out days. He found the city 'decayed and
gloomy' and much changed since 1929. 'Half the cafés I used to know were
shut for lack of custom, and everyone was obsessed with the high cost of
living and the fear of war.'[2] En route to Miller's studio, he had a violent alter-
cation with a taxi driver, and ended up threatening to smash his face in. Later
he felt ashamed of how he had behaved and could hardly bring himself to
write about it. Again what others saw as his sadism had broken through and
again he felt guilt-stricken. He saw later how the cab-man regarded him – as
just another wealthy bourgeois – and the man's aggression as an expression of
the revolutionary spirit which was now taking on Fascism in Spain.[3]

Miller was pleased to meet the man who thought so highly of his *Tropic
of Cancer*, but despite having the 'down-and-out life' in common the two
men could not have been more at odds philosophically. Miller had adopted
the other-worldly detachment of a Buddah. To him the search for happiness

lay within the human soul rather than in the external world. Orwell was more sceptical and socially engaged, suspicious of metaphysics and what he called 'the lure of profundity'. Unlike Miller he believed that human conditions could be improved through political action, and now by fighting Fascism in Spain. As Orwell remembered it, Miller did not try to dissuade him from going – that was his own affair, he said, but it was 'the act of an idiot'. Western civilisation was doomed and it did not worry him one bit.[4]

Although he was shocked by Miller's irresponsibility, Orwell explained how his experiences in Burma had left him with a heavy weight of guilt to expiate. It was for that reason he had suffered the deprivation and humiliations of the down-and-out life in Paris. Miller's attitude was that, having already punished himself in Paris why flagellate himself further? Orwell said that in Spain a momentous struggle for human rights was taking place and he could not shirk his responsibilities. Although he disagreed, Miller was impressed by his earnestness and humility and offered him a corduroy jacket, more practical in a fight, he said, than the smart blue suit he was wearing. On this, Miller's friend Alfred Perlès commented, 'Henry discreetly refrained from adding that Orwell would have been welcome to the jacket even had he chosen to fight for the opposite side.'[5]

Paris was a brief, surrealistic interlude. Next day Orwell took the train to Perpignan and on to Cerbère, trying to learn Spanish from a dictionary en route. As the train crossed Southern France, he was deeply moved by the sight of peasants in the fields giving the anti-Fascist clenched-fist salute, 'like a guard of honour, greeting the train mile after mile'. He felt a great sense of solidarity with the working class, even with the angry Paris taxi driver he had crossed the day before. On the last leg of his journey, still in his smart London suit, a commercial traveller in his compartment told him, 'You mustn't go into Spain looking like that. Take off that collar and tie.' Anarchist frontier guards had been known to turn back people who looked too bourgeois. It was a first taste of what was to come.[6]

He arrived in Barcelona on Boxing Day. The effect on him was overwhelming. Catalonia was largely under Anarchist rule and his first sight of the city produced one of the most memorable descriptions of the whole war:

> It was the first time I had ever been in a town where the working class was in the saddle. Practically every building of any size had been seized by the workers . . . every wall was scrawled with the hammer and sickle and with the initials of the revolutionary parties . . . Churches here and there were being systematically demolished by gangs of workmen. Every shop and café had an inscription saying it had been collectivized even the bootblacks had been collectivized and their boxes painted red

and black . . . Tipping was forbidden by law . . . There were no private motor-cars . . . The revolutionary posters were everywhere . . . Down the Ramblas, the wide central artery of the town where the crowds of people streamed constantly to and fro, the loudspeakers were bellowing revolutionary songs all day . . . Practically everyone wore rough working-class clothes, or blue overalls, or some variant of the militia uniform. All this was queer and moving. There was much in it that I did not understand, in some ways I did not even like it, but I recognized it immediately as a state of affairs worth fighting for . . .[7]

The Tory Anarchist, having lived so long in a Tory-dominated world, now found himself in one dominated by Anarchists. It was for him a living embodiment of what revolution offered.

He reported to McNair at the ILP office at the top of the Ramblas. In Spain the ILP was affiliated to a largely Catalan revolutionary socialist party, the POUM (Partido Obrero de Unificación Marxista, or United Marxist Workers' Party). Although Marxist, it was anti-Stalinist, and loosely allied to the FAI (Federation of Iberian Anarchists), the dominant revolutionary party in Catalonia and Aragón. Its leader, Andrés Nin, had once been a close ally of Trotsky. The party had moved away from Trotsky politically, except on the question of land collectivisation and workers' control. Nin had been a minister in the Catalan government until December when he was forced out by Communists whose influence had grown in Spain after the first Russian supply ships arrived in October. The Spanish Communists, once a small party in Catalonia, had aligned themselves with the PSCU, the Socialist Party, and were a growing force throughout Republican Spain.

McNair, a tough, self-educated Tynesider in his forties, had run a business in France for twenty-five years, having been blacklisted for his politics in England. His first impression of Orwell was poor. The accent, the suit, the rather languid manner betrayed him not only as a bourgeois but a public-school man. It was only when he read Brockway's letter and learned that he was George Orwell, author of *Down and Out in Paris and London* and *Burmese Days*, that he warmed to him. As Orwell was there to report the war, McNair sent him along to the POUM newspaper, *La Batalla*, and a twenty-year-old journalist, Victor Alba, was asked to show him the scenes of the July street fighting, and give him the story of what had happened in Barcelona.

After a day or so absorbing the atmosphere, Orwell told McNair that he had decided to enlist. At the time he did not know that the POUM was quite separate from the Communist-dominated International Brigade, and McNair did not trouble to enlighten him. Orwell said later that had he known anything about Spanish politics he would probably have joined the militia of the CNT, the Anarchist trade union organisation. However, McNair took him straight to the Lenin Barracks, where POUM forces were based, to see him properly enrolled. There he signed on as 'Eric Blair, grocer', hoping perhaps to disguise his bourgeois origins. But the ILP leaders were not going to allow an author like Orwell to go unnoticed, and, much to his annoyance, would use his presence for propaganda purposes in their paper, the *New Leader*. This gave him a prominence that later would become positively dangerous.

While waiting to sign on at the Barracks, he saw an Italian militiaman at the officers' table poring over a map. Orwell was immediately struck by this man – 'a tough-looking youth of twenty-five or six, with reddish-yellow hair and powerful shoulders'. But it was his face that moved Orwell, 'the face of a man who would commit murder and throw away his life for a friend . . . There were both candour and ferocity in it; also the pathetic reverence that illiterate people have for their supposed superiors.' They exchanged a few words, shook hands and parted. 'Queer,' wrote Orwell, 'the affection you can feel for a stranger! . . . With his shabby uniform and fierce pathetic face he typifies for me the special atmosphere of that time.'[8] It was a momentous encounter for Orwell who later immortalised the youth in a striking poetic image:

> Your name and your deeds were forgotten
> Before your bones were dry,
> And the lie that slew you is buried
> Under a deeper lie;
>
> But the thing that I saw in your face
> No power can disinherit:
> No bomb that ever burst
> Shatters the crystal spirit.[9]

Unknown to Orwell, long before he had left for Spain the fate of the POUM had been decided. In July in secret messages to Moscow (intercepted by British Intelligence), the Spanish Communists were already complaining about the Anarchists and Trotskyists.[10] That same month the POUM paper, *La Batalla*, condemned the Moscow Show Trials. On 7 August the Spaniards again complained to Moscow: 'The anarchists, having taken large quantities of arms, are making use of them, not to fight at the front but to pillage in the rearguard . . . Our militias are applying capital punishment against the authors of acts of pillage . . . in Catalonia, and especially in Barcelona, anarchists are perpetrating deeds of vandalism. They shoot and pillage everything they find.'[11] More attacks in *La Bataille* and complaints from the Spanish Communists against 'Trotskyists' now made the POUM a prime Soviet target.[12] In September General Alexander Orlov of the NKVD arrived in Madrid and a month later supplies for the Republic began arriving from Russia. Communist influence and Orlov's power now began to extend itself throughout Republican Spain.

Over the next couple of months, Hitler and Mussolini would recognise Franco's provisional government, German troops would arrive in Spain to aid the rebels, and Communist pressure forced Andrés Nin out of the Catalan government. In January 1937 more angry messages reached Moscow from the Spanish Communists. The Anarchists and Trotskyists, they complained, were not only attacking them, but were also 'benefiting from the prestige of the international brigades'.[13]

In Barcelona Orwell seems to have picked up no hint of these machinations. A few months later they would be all too evident. But, for the time being, to him the Communists were fellow anti-Fascists fighting the same war against Franco, and, in the cafés along the Ramblas, he was happy to talk with anyone in that spirit. Dr Kenneth Sinclair-Loutit, leading a medical unit with the International Brigade, who met him there, remembered thinking that Orwell had got the picture of the war completely wrong in supporting the POUM line. Like the Anarchists, while they believed in fighting the Nationalists, they were also committed to making a revolution. The Communist position, linked to their Popular Front policy, was that winning came first and the revolution would have to wait.[14]

Orwell found the so-called 'instruction' at the Barracks comical and the teenage Catalan volunteers little more than a chaotic rabble. They seemed unable to stand in line, argued about orders and recognised no authority whatever. Even the lieutenant-instructor refused to be addressed as '*Señor*'. The drill was antiquated and there was no instruction in the practical arts of warfare. 'This mob of eager children, who were going to be thrown into the front line in a few days' time,' he wrote, 'were not even taught how to fire a rifle or pull the pin out of a bomb.'[15]

Despite not understanding Catalan and having to use a dictionary most of the time, he was utterly seduced by the camaraderie and warmth of the other POUMists. 'I defy anyone to be thrown as I was amongst . . . the Catalan working class . . . and not be struck by their essential decency . . . a real largeness of spirit, which I have met with again and again in the most unpromising circumstances.'[16] And, while he found them exasperating, especially their inefficiency and *mañana* mentality, he admired the fact that they did not share his own 'Northern time-neurosis'.

He was one of only two Englishmen in a section of thirty, but because he could drink the local boys under the table, he found himself extremely popular. After a few days McNair found him in khaki trousers and sweater drilling the young recruits (mostly sixteen- or seventeen-year-olds from the backstreets of Barcelona) on the barrack square. The POUM commander, José Rovira, told him that with a hundred men like Orwell they would certainly win the war.[17] Still in a comparatively raggle-taggle state, wearing an odd assortment of military clothing – not 'uniform', said Orwell, but 'multiform' – they paraded through the city to cheering crowds, but never learned how to handle a rifle or grenade let alone a machine gun, a weapon he had never used and was desperate to learn about.

Ordered to the front, they were given just two hours to prepare. After a torchlight procession past cheering crowds along the Ramblas with red and black flags flying, and after a harangue from a commissar, they marched, still only pitifully equipped, to the station, bound for the Aragón front and the sound of guns.[18] They were now a *centura*, part of the Lenin Division under Rovira's overall command. Their destination was Alcubierre, 1,500 feet above sea level – a mountainous region, freezing cold and often engulfed in swirling mists. He was to spend the next few weeks in trenches full of mud and excrement, old bones, dead rats and jagged tin cans, with young Catalan boys who knew no discipline, and whose idea of fighting was to stand up and fire in full view of the enemy.[19] They had no tin helmets, bayonets, maps, range-finders, telescopes or periscopes. They had no artillery, their weapons were antiquated German Mausers, and most casualties were self-inflicted.[20] He had imagined Great War barrages under screaming shells and shards of flying metal, and he found the lack of action disappointing.

The captain in charge was a twenty-year-old Pole, Benjamin Levinsky, a one-time Paris fur trader; the commander of the *centuria* ('eighty men and several dogs') was a strange Belgian adventurer, George Kopp – a tall, stout, colourful, charming character, immensely intelligent, resourceful and almost recklessly brave.[21] He was born in Russia, his mother from Odessa, his father a St Petersburg doctor, but had grown up and was educated in Belgium. In Brussels and Switzerland he studied civil engineering, married a Belgian wife, had five children, and divorced in 1934. In Spain Kopp gave a different version of his life, saying that he was Belgian-born, had fled abroad after being discovered smuggling arms to the Spanish Republic, was a widower and a Belgian reserve officer.[22] But, rather like Orwell, he enjoyed the clandestine life and delighted in living dangerously. He was a ladies' man, with his own seductive charm, in which his penchant for exaggeration obviously played its part.

The first shot fired was a dud. A bad omen, thought Orwell. He was made *capo* (or corporal), and although the men would not obey orders without a discussion, and were so incapable as to be positively dangerous, he grew to admire their peculiar indiscipline and youthful bravado, even while wondering how the war could be won with such a disorganised rabble. 'I had British Army ideas, and certainly the Spanish militias were very unlike the British Army. But considering the circumstances they were better troops than one had any right to expect.'[23]

The front was static. Neither side had heavy artillery so would not attack. There were occasional exchanges of fire and Orwell was annoyed to find himself ducking the first time a bullet flew past his ear – something he had vowed never to do. But the lack of action was deeply frustrating, and Kopp, on one of his periodic tours of inspection, said, 'This is not a war, it is a comic opera with an occasional death.'[24] Behind inaction and lack of decent weapons lay not just tactics but also politics and the efforts of the Communists to marginalise the Anarchists and POUM. But, as yet, Orwell was ignorant of such things, and in good British fashion learned to live with the boredom and the wretched conditions.

The cold was as much an enemy to him as were the Fascists – perhaps more so – and he felt he could never have enough warm clothing. To pass the time, one icy night he indulged his passion for making lists. 'I was wearing a thick vest and pants, a flannel shirt, two pullovers, a woollen jacket, a pigskin jacket, corduroy breeches, puttees, thick socks, boots, a stout trench-coat, a muffler, lined leather gloves, and a woollen cap. Nevertheless I was shivering like a jelly. But I admit I am unusually sensitive to cold . . . It was pneumonia that we were fighting against, not against men.'[25] He told doctors later that he had no trouble with his lungs in Spain, but others remember his wheezing chest and permanently streaming cold, and he frequently risked being shot to bring in the meagre supplies of fuel still to be found in no man's land. On top of the cold, and the filth underfoot, the trenches were overrun by rats and mice. There was little water for washing, and Orwell resorted to shaving in wine. But they could always smoke the foul-tasting Spanish tobacco, and were issued with tinder-lighters and several yards of yellow wick, which stayed alight in the fiercest of winds.

After three weeks Orwell and Williams, the other Englishman, were transferred to an ILP section of about thirty men just out from England. They were based several miles west at Alcubiere defending a position within sight of Fascist-held Saragossa. Bob Edwards, their leader, remembered Orwell's arrival:

He wore corduroy riding breeches, khaki puttees and huge boots, I've never seen boots that were so large, clogged in mud. He had a yellow pigskin jerkin, a coffee coloured balaclava hat and he wore the longest scarf I've ever seen, khaki scarf wound round and round his neck right up to his ears, on his shoulder he carried an old-fashioned German rifle, I think it must have been fifty years old; and hanging to his belt were two hand grenades. Running beside him, trying to keep pace, were two youths of the Militia, similarly equipped; but what amused me most was that behind Orwell was a shaggy mongrel dog with the word POUM painted on its side.[26]

He had brought the dog simply to save it from the Catalan boys who were, he thought, unkind to their animals.

Edwards, a member of the ILP National Executive, later became a Labour MP and strong European. He took a sceptical and disparaging view of Orwell, suspecting his motives for being in Spain, once calling him 'a bloody scribbler'. Eighteen-year-old Stafford Cottman was also struck by his incongruous dress, and 'Oxford accent', but to him he was 'a natural leader' with 'the common touch', and, like most of the other men, he came to admire Orwell enormously.[27]

Among the ILP militiamen there was a little more respect for rank than among the Catalans, and at least one of them, Paddy Donovan, was a Great War veteran. The group included staunch ILP members like Douglas Moyle and Jack Branthwaite, and Trotskyists like New Yorker Harry Milton. Cottman, the youngest, had belonged to the League of Communist Youth and had joined the POUM in the innocent spirit of all being anti-Fascists together. Some, like Orwell, had enlisted thinking they were joining the International Brigade, having been persuaded by McNair that there was no difference between them.[28] Jon Kimche, Orwell's old book-selling companion who visited Barcelona as an observer, thought that a separate ILP unit existed mainly to bring prestige to Brockway and McNair, and to give the ILP influence with the POUM.[29] Interestingly, this was also the line taken in secret Communist reports on the contingent.

Not all the men were ready to succumb to Orwell's charisma. Frank Frankford, an East Ender, took a strong dislike to him, resenting his class background, accent and public-school manner. Milton, while liking him, considered him politically naïve, quite unaware of the political tensions existing within the Republican side, and not appreciating the part the Communists were playing in the International Brigade. To Orwell, the most impressive member of the contingent was Bob Smillie, grandson of Robert Smillie, a famous miners' leader prominent during the General Strike.[30] Smillie had come to Barcelona to work with McNair at the ILP office, but, like Orwell, had been swept up in the spirit of revolution and joined the militia instead.

The squalor and filth of trench life were bearable to him after his down-and-out experiences, but rats were another thing. 'If there is one thing I hate more than another,' he wrote, 'it is a rat running over me in the darkness.'[31] It was an image straight from Poe's 'The Pit and the Pendulum'. On one occasion, Edwards recalled Orwell finding a rat gnawing his boots and promptly shooting it. The shot echoed so widely it brought Fascist fire down on them. 'The whole front and both sides went into action. The artillery started, we threw patrols out, machine-gun nests set going and after it all our valuable cookhouse had been destroyed and two buses that had brought up our reserves.'[32] The detail of the boots is important. Orwell always had difficulty obtaining the size twelves he needed. Any rat that dared chew on them risked instant liquidation.

There was one brief abortive attack from the Fascists who were celebrating the fall of Malaga, captured by Italian Fascists without a shot being fired and ending with a massacre of civilians. For the first time Orwell heard talk of treachery and began to have doubts about the cause for which he was fighting. A week later they were sent to reinforce the siege of Huesca. His naturalist's eye took in the clipped vines and 'the blades of the winter barley . . . just poking through the lumpy soil', and his painter's eye observed how 'four kilometres from our trenches Huesca glittered small and clear like a city of dolls' houses'. From the earlier conquest of nearby Siétamo, the victorious general's boast had now become a standing joke – 'Coffee in Huesca mañana.'[33] The town was just twelve hundred metres away, but sadly for Orwell and the others, that day and that coffee never came.

In February Eileen heard from Gollancz that *The Road to Wigan Pier* had been chosen for the Left Book Club. What might have swung the committee in Orwell's favour was the suspicion in some influential left-wing quarters that the Club was intended as a vehicle for Communist propaganda. G. D. H. Cole, the distinguished social historian, who had a book turned down for the Club, had already accused Gollancz of wanting only Communist or near-Communist authors on his list. Anxious to dispel this impression he assured Cole that he had commissioned a book from Clement Attlee, the Labour leader, and another, which he had just accepted – Orwell's book – was 'quite violently anti-Communist'.[34] However, it was agreed that Gollancz should write a preface dissociating the Book Club committee from Part 2, explaining that this was the author's own highly personal view of socialism. No such preface was included in the hardback edition. (Left Book Club members were clearly thought to be in need of guidance with their reading.) *The Road to Wigan Pier* was finally published on 7 March. In the Book Club edition 44,000 copies were sold. Not only was Orwell for a second time *lancé*, but now had a previously undreamt of stature. The book attracted many admirers, but created many enemies, too, not least among Communists who took every opportunity to denounce it, usually by wilfully misrepresenting what it said. It also had the effect of making him even more prominent among the ILP contingent and bringing him directly into the sights of the Russian Communists, too.

With the book's future settled, Eileen set out for Barcelona. McNair had advertised for a secretary in the *New Leader* and she was taken on. She left Aunt Nellie Adam (alone since Eugène had embarked on a world tour, never to return) in charge of the store. She took along the things she knew George missed most – Typhoo tea, chocolates and some cigars as well as the tobacco he liked. Charles Orr, at the ILP office editing the English edition of the POUM paper, *The Spanish Revolution*, for whom she also worked, found the Blairs an impressive if incongruous couple. 'Eileen was a round-faced Irish girl, prim and pretty, with black hair and dark eyes. Eric was tall, lean and gangling, to the point of being awkward . . . He was tongue-tied, stammered and seemed to be afraid of people. Eileen was friendly, gregarious and unpretentious.' Among those working for the POUM her superiority was evident. '[She] just could not resist talking about Eric – her hero husband, whom she obviously loved and admired . . . He was still just an unknown writer . . . [but] . . . as I came to know Eric better – through Eileen – my respect grew . . . A man who could win a woman of such quality must have some value.'[35] Jack Branthwaite also saw George and Eileen as soul-mates: 'She worshipped the ground he walked on. She'd do anything for him. Anything Eric did, he was the greatest.'[36] And Paddy Donovan remembered how she had caught certain of his mannerisms and habits – including smoking the same unsavoury black tobacco.

All through March, with the front still quiet, the ILP men continued to endure mud, rain and piercing winds and periodic snowfalls. Now *everyone* was saying that the war was 'pantomime', although there were occasional casualties from stray bullets. Orwell made several forays into no man's land to collect unharvested potatoes. He had a great belief in the potato as a staple food; it appealed to the Robinson Crusoe in him. He also discovered that at the front the humble 'spud' was a valuable means of exchange. At the cookhouse you could swap a sackful for a water-bottleful of coffee. But for every comfort there was a discomfort. As the weather got warm the battalions of rats were reinforced with mosquitoes and lice.

Orwell made careful notes throughout his time at the front. Cottman found him writing at five a.m. before going on guard duty, and by candlelight in the evenings. Even while fighting, his commitment to writing was overriding, his literary instinct never lulled. On cold nights in the trenches he would recite Gerard Manley Hopkins' elegy to 'Felix Randal', the blacksmith. As he wrote elsewhere, in exile his thoughts were always with England, and perhaps thoughts of the blacksmith's forge helped keep him warm. On one occasion, to relieve the boredom, he asked Cottman to sing 'The Eton Boating Song'.[37] Being tone-deaf and unable to sing the tune, he was delighted that his young friend remembered it. No doubt he helped out with the words.

Eileen had been sending tea and tobacco from Barcelona and shipping in other goodies, such as biscuits, from the Army and Navy Stores. In mid-March she persuaded Kopp to take her in his staff car to visit George at the front. She was an immediate hit with the men, who all thought her wonderful. They appreciated the fact that she took a motherly interest in them, made sure they got their mail, looked after their money and even spent her own money on them when their pay was delayed. She was quite thrilled when there was a brief exchange of fire across the lines, mentioning it in her next letter to Moore: 'The Fascists threw in a small bombardment and quite a lot of machine gun-fire, which was then comparatively rare on the Huesca front, so it was quite an interesting visit – indeed I have never enjoyed anything more.'[38]

It was Orwell's openly talking of joining the International Brigade that made Edwards suspicious of him. He tried to convince Orwell that the civil war was 'a war of ideas', and without the support of the majority of Spanish people and the promise of social change the war against Franco could not be won.[39] He warned him that in Madrid there was a ferocious commissar, André Marty, who would not tolerate even the mildest criticism of the Party line and would have him taken out and shot. But Orwell did not understand or chose not to listen. Characteristically, he argued against the prevailing orthodoxy. While he agreed with 'revolution first', he also wanted to get closer to the action and get his hands on decent weapons; going to Madrid with the International Brigade (equipped with Soviet weapons) seemed the only answer. Harry Milton also tried to persuade him to no avail.[40] He was determined to get to Madrid.

When Edwards returned to England to attend the ILP Annual Conference at the end of March, Orwell took his place as section leader. Edwards left behind a growing sense of dissatisfaction. The men were unhappy about McNair continually postponing their leave, the lack of tobacco, poor food, censorship of their letters and being restricted to one paper – the *New Leader*, in which exaggerated stories about them and their exploits continually appeared. Above all, they were fed up with the lack of action. That, at least, is what a Communist agent who met them later reported to his masters.[41]

Finally they did see some action in early April when the POUM forces staged an incursion to divert the Fascists from a planned Anarchist assault on Jaca. There was an attack across no man's land. Wires were cut, bombs thrown and the enemy driven back. Orwell found himself chasing along trenches trying to bayonet a man. There was a counterattack and Orwell flung a grenade. 'There was the roar of the explosion,' he wrote, 'and then, instantly, a diabolical outcry of screams and groans. We had got one of them, anyway; I don't know whether he was killed, but certainly he was badly hurt. Poor wretch, poor wretch! I felt a vague sorrow as I heard him screaming.'[42] Paddy Donovan remembered it slightly differently. 'The patrol got up close to the barbed wire and Orwell got way in front. Grenades were bursting right, left and centre. He stood up, very tall, and shouted: "Come on, move up here you bastards" and I yelled, "For Christ's sake, Eric, get down."' When the grenade was thrown, 'a scream was heard and Orwell said: "That's got one bastard."'[43] Finally came the order to retreat. No ground had been taken, though Fascist troops had been drawn away from the Anarchists' attack. Nothing was brought back except a few boxes of ammunition, and two men were wounded. Orwell comforted himself with one of the cigars Eileen had brought from England.

Occasionally the boredom was relieved by moments of fleeting action, even bathos. Once, Orwell found himself in much the position he had in Burma faced with a peaceful elephant to shoot. This time it was a Fascist soldier, no threat because, as he ran across his sights he was holding up his trousers. Unlike Burma, there was no crowd to urge him to shoot and he resisted pulling the trigger. 'I did not shoot partly because of that detail about the trousers,' he wrote. 'I had come here to shoot at "Fascists"; but a man who is holding up his trousers isn't a "Fascist", he is visibly a fellow creature, similar to yourself, and you don't feel like shooting at him.'[44] Like the elephant incident this was clearly a moment of self-discovery, of self-definition.

The men were now quite exhausted after four months in the line and finally McNair granted them leave for the end of April. One reason he delayed allowing them back to Barcelona was Orwell's declared intention of joining the IB, and his suspicion that others would follow him. Having boosted the contingent so proudly in the *New Leader*, it would be devastating to ILP prestige to lose a whole swathe of men in one go to the Communists who were already agitating against them and the POUM.

The great Spanish drama which had begun to unfold ahead of Orwell's arrival would soon engulf him in events far beyond his control. The suppression of the Spanish Trotskyists had been decreed in Moscow, and the British Communist Party had already sent its spy to Barcelona to report back personally to Harry Pollitt. Hugh O'Donnell, a Londoner, had attached himself to Dr Sinclair-Loutit's medical aid unit, much to the disgust of the doctor who disliked him on sight, and remembered him as 'a slightly greyed washed-out blond, of medium height speaking colourless middle English – a model copper's nark'.[45] He wanted him removed, but the medical unit was O'Donnell's cover for sniffing out heretics within the Party and spying on the dissident left, which meant, among other things, mixing with ILP people in their favourite cafés. Charles Orr soon realised that certain so-called 'friendly Communists' were in fact Comintern agents. Orlov, the NKVD man, now in Valencia where the Republican government had relocated, already had men infiltrating the non-Stalinist left, spreading rumours and trying to disparage groups opposed to the Communists. Anarchists and Trotskyists were his special targets, and the men he controlled were ready to use imprisonment, torture and even murder to achieve their ends. So, even before Orwell arrived in Barcelona, the machinery was in place to discredit the POUM as 'Fascist traitors'. Ironically, on the very day the British ILP contingent left for the Aragón front in January, the order had come from Moscow: 'Launch a campaign among the masses and in the press against Trotsky and Trotskyists as terrorist and saboteurs . . . spies liaising with the German Gestapo.'[46]

A few days after Orwell arrived in Barcelona, a young Londoner, David Crook, just arrived from England, passed through the city and, like him, found the revolutionary air intoxicating.[47] Crook, the son of Jewish immigrants, was born in London's East End in 1910 and emigrated to America in 1928, intending, he said, 'to become a millionaire'. He enrolled at Columbia University where he became involved in radical politics. In 1936 he returned to London, and, under instruction from the Communist Party, joined the North Kensington branch of the Labour Party, subsequently becoming personal secretary to Labour MP John Parker.

At the outbreak of the Spanish war he volunteered for the International Brigade, and, unlike Orwell, seems to have received Pollitt's blessing. Before long he was in the firing line near Madrid and on 12 February was badly wounded at the battle of the Jarama Valley. While recovering, he was approached by George Soria, a Comintern agent working for the Soviet magazine *Imprecorr*, and invited to do 'special work for the international movement' rather than returning to the front. Fired with ideological enthusiasm, he agreed, and on 9 April was transferred to Albacete, ostensibly for officer training. However, after brief instruction as a political commissar, he was switched to the 'special work' for which he had been recruited. He received a crash course in Spanish from a Catalan comrade, Ramon Mercader, was taught the techniques of surveillance and briefed for his first assignment. Mercader was later sent on his own special mission, to Mexico, where he ingratiated himself with Leon Trotsky before murdering him with an ice pick. Crook, in fact, had been recruited to play a part in the wider Stalinist conspiracy to eliminate not just Trotsky but his followers wherever they might be, and his first mission took him to Barcelona. As he put it in old age, 'I was assigned to play a small part, of which I am not proud, in the crushing of the POUM.'[48]

On 26 April Orwell and his ILP comrades returned to Barcelona on their long-delayed leave. They were shocked to see how things had changed. The revolutionary atmosphere of four months earlier had all but evaporated, previous inequalities were returning as the bourgeoisie emerged from the shadows to reassert old class divisions. Smartly dressed men and elegant women paraded around the town, tipping was back, sleek cars had reappeared. They had only an inkling of what lay behind this, but the Communists' efforts to undermine the revolutionary left were taking effect.

Orwell felt drained. He joined Eileen at the Hotel Continental, where she was staying, and spent his first two days in Barcelona in bed recovering from general exhaustion. After that it was time to enjoy again the taste of good food and wine. It was said that on reaching the hotel, he found Kopp, also staying at the Continental, being over-solicitous towards Eileen, but that she was careful to keep him at arm's length.[49] Certainly she had been caught up in the war atmosphere and the whirl of café life in Barcelona. As she told her mother, 'I have coffee about three times a day & drinks oftener, & although theoretically I eat in a rather grim pension at least six times a week I get headed off into one of about four places where the food is really quite good by any standards though limited of course. Every night I mean to go home early & write letters or something & every night I get home the next morning.'[50] Some of Orwell's comrades thought Kopp was definitely working his charms on Eileen and had probably seduced her into an affair. When Richard Rees had passed through Barcelona in April, he found her seemingly scared, telling him it would be dangerous for him to be seen with her in public. Rees interpreted this as the reaction of someone living under terror.[51] It could equally have been the fear of an amorous Kopp appearing suddenly and embarrassing her in front of an old friend of George's. (Rosalind Obermeyer later remarked how Eileen's eyes lit up at the mention of Kopp, suggesting to her that there probably had been an amour.)[52] It is conceivable, of course, that one of those mysterious omissions from her marriage vows left affairs open to both her and George. In any event, whatever Orwell saw on his return or whatever he thought did not come between him and Kopp, whom he continued to hold in the highest regard.

Two copies of *The Road to Wigan Pier* had arrived for Orwell, and it was not long before members of the ILP contingent had read it or knew about it. The book further inflamed Frankford, who resented the kudos authorship brought to Orwell among the other men. As he saw it, here was a man who claimed that the working class smelt, and must therefore look upon the rest of them, Frankford included, as personally offensive imbeciles. He was even ready to attribute pro-Fascist sympathies to him and any who considered him important. Orwell was probably oblivious to Frankford's antipathy, but soon became aware of the antagonism the book had created for him on the left.

In his preface, Gollancz stressed that the book did not accord with the Club's 'policy' – 'that of equipping people to fight against war and Fascism'. He applauded the book's 'burning indignation against poverty and oppression', at least in Part 1. It was 'the kind of thing that makes converts'. The second part was another matter – 'an autobiographical study . . . to explain the class feelings and prejudices of a member of "the lower-upper-middle class" . . . and then goes on to declare his adherence to Socialism'. However, he went on, Orwell had also played devil's advocate, explaining why, in his view, 'so many of the best people detest Socialism', and concluding that this lay with 'the "personal inferiority" of so many Socialists and their mistaken methods of propaganda'. These should be ditched, and 'the elemental appeal of "Liberty and Justice"' should stand at the heart of socialism. There were well over a hundred minor passages with which he would like to have taken issue with Orwell, he said, but he hadn't the space, nor did he wish to tire his readers. The claim that the middle classes were all taught that the working classes smelt was an over-exaggeration, although it threw 'a most interesting light on the reality of class distinctions'. However, he was puzzled by Orwell's 'devil's advocate's case' expressing hostility to minorities such as feminists, vegetarians and especially birth controllers, having described in the first part of the book the degrading housing conditions associated with overcrowding. While declaring himself a socialist, Orwell still seemed to cling to his middle-class prejudices, revealing attitudes to war, women and human happiness that could themselves be regarded as cranky. Revealingly, he regarded Orwell's attack on Russian commissars as an 'indiscretion', and saw a vague socialism upholding freedom as too ill-defined to have much meaning.[53]

Gollancz's self-righteous, hand-washing preface may have deflected Communist hostility from himself and his Book Club, but it won him little admiration from the author. Diplomatically he told Gollancz, 'I like the introduction very much, though of course I could have answered the criticisms you made. It was the kind of discussion of what one is really talking about that one always wants & never seems to get from professional reviewers.'[54]

Those reviewers revealed something of the ambiguity with which the book was received on the left. Harold Laski, went out of his way in *Left News* (the Left Book Club's own publication), to praise Gollancz's preface as 'admirable'.[55] Curiously enough the Communist Arthur Calder-Marshall produced a review for *Time and Tide* beginning, 'Of Mr Orwell's book, there is little to say except praise.' He did, however, detect a certain lack of humanity, especially in his description of the Brooker household.[56] The *New Statesman* thought Orwell's arguments had 'considerable force', and the *Fortnightly* called the book 'brilliant [and] disturbing'.[57] Connolly wrote separately to say it was much his best book so far.[58] The most vitriolic review came from Pollitt in the *Daily Worker*, a review that most Communists seem to have swallowed whole.

Here is George Orwell, a disillusioned little middle-class boy who, seeing through imperialism, decided to discover what Socialism has to offer . . . a late imperialist policeman . . . If ever snobbery had its hallmark placed upon it, it is by Mr Orwell . . . I gather that the chief thing that worries Mr Orwell is the 'smell' of the working-class, for smells seem to occupy the major portion of the book . . . One thing I am certain of, and it is this – if Mr Orwell could only hear what the Left Book Club circles will say about this book, then he would make a resolution never to write again on any subject that he does not understand.[59]

If Communists like Pollitt thought they could eliminate Orwell by character assassination, they had underestimated their man.

The day after Orwell's return to Barcelona, David Crook arrived there with the mission to spy on the ILP allies of the POUM. He told his American biographer, 'My ultimate KGB [NKVD] orders were to spy on one of the opposing sides in the impending conflict: the POUM and their allies. These included the Spanish anarchists and, of special interest to me, the British Independent Labour Party, with whom George Orwell was aligned.' In particular he was to spy and report on McNair, Kopp and the Blairs. These, he was told, were the major ILP figures working with the POUM, Eric Blair being the author of books on working-class life and the most popular member of the British contingent. He was instructed to pass his reports through a contact to NKVD Headquarters in Albacete.

Initial information about his target quartet had already been provided by George Tioli, an ex-International Brigade member then passing as a journalist, known to the Blairs as 'a good friend of ours'.[60] In fact, Charles Orr noted that the handsome Italian was frequently in Eileen's company during George's absence at the front and later concluded that he must have been spying on both himself and on the Blairs.

Orwell had told McNair that he intended switching to the International Brigade once he signed his discharge. But McNair was anxious not to lose someone as prestigious as Orwell, or any others also considering the move. At a meeting on 28 April, at which the men aired their grievances, he got them to promise to wait until after the May Day celebrations. But he was not alone in contending for the souls of his men. Comintern agents were thronging the cafés. Walter Tapsell, a prominent British Communist, had been sent from Albacete to mingle with the ILP volunteers to judge their mood. He reported considerable dissatisfaction, and listed the names of those he thought ready to defect, including Orwell. This report was sent both to Albacete and to Pollitt in London. Although he did not think much of the Communists, Orwell was still ready to treat them as friends and allies. That would soon change. In his report to Albacete, Tapsell wrote:

The leading personality and most respected man in the contingent at present is Eric Blair. This man is a Novelist who has written some books on proletarian life in England. He has little political understanding. He is not interested in party politics, and came to Spain as an Anti-Fascist to fight Fascism. As a result of his experience on the front however, he has grown to dislike the POUM and is now waiting his discharge from the POUM militia. In a conversation with the writer on 30th Blair enquired whether his association with the POUM would be likely to prejudice his chances of enlisting with the International Brigade. He wishes to fight on the Madrid front and states that in a few days he will formally apply to us for enlistment when his discharge from the POUM has been regularised.[61]

Clearly the Communists regarded Orwell as a potentially significant recruit.

On 3 May he was passing through the lounge of the Continental when someone said, 'There's been some kind of trouble at the Telephone Exchange, I hear.' He barely took it in at the time but later, walking down the Ramblas, he heard shots, and saw Anarchist youths exchanging fire with someone in a tall tower. Immediately he knew that the trouble which had been brewing between the Communists and Anarchists had at last erupted. The Catalan Communist Commissioner of Public Order, Roderiguez Salas, had ordered assault troops to take the Telephone Exchange in the Plaza Cataluña, then under Anarchist control. When they resisted, a firefight ensued in which Communist machine guns commanding the Plaza from their headquarters, the Hotel Colón, caused heavy Anarchist casualties.

Orwell hurried to the Falcon Hotel lower down the Ramblas, a hotel used exclusively by the POUM, and there acquired a rifle and some grenades before retracing his steps towards the Continental. When he, Kopp and a few others arrived at the POUM headquarters the party executive was in emergency session. With their allies, the Anarchists, under attack, the party leaders could do nothing but side with them against the Communists. It was a fateful decision but they were trapped by circumstances, and, quite inadvertently, walked into a Soviet ambush.

The ILP group was sent across the Ramblas to cover the front of the headquarters, which had come under attack from Assault Guards holed up in the Café Moka, a few doors down. Kopp, who had very bravely approached the Guards unarmed and assured them that no one wanted any killing, managed to establish a truce. For the next three or four days Orwell and a small band, including Branthwaite and Moyle, sat perched on the roof of the Poliorama Cinema which had a commanding view of the café and the whole of the Ramblas below. They spent their time alternately assuring the Assault Guards opposite that they had no intention of firing and, in

Orwell's case, reading Penguin books. But it was all very depressing. He and his comrades had wanted a fight, but not to fight other Republicans.

Although little happened along that sector of the Ramblas, some five hundred died in the street fighting – mostly Anarchists who had the habit of charging recklessly against machine guns and were mown down in large numbers in the Plaza Colón. When finally a cease fire was agreed, the Communists had a pretext openly to denounce the POUM as a Francoist Fifth Column acting against the Republic from the rear. A particularly nasty poster appeared, showing a head with a POUM mask being ripped off to reveal a Swastika-covered face beneath. (The Communist line was that the POUM were 'objectively' Fascist, that is, they might as well be Fascists because of the way they were hindering the Republican cause.)

By the time the May fighting ended on the 7th little of Orwell's leave remained. He was again approached by Tapsell and asked whether he would join the International Brigade, but now he said that, having fought with the POUM in the streets, he would be considered politically suspect. His attitude towards the Communists had altered and hardened, and the result of the previous three or four days had been to strengthen his ties with the POUM. He saw that by joining the Communists he could be used against the working class.

Disillusionment had set in. Orwell recalled the cynical words of a journalist when he first arrived in Barcelona the previous December: 'This war is a racket, the same as any other.'[62] He still did not believe that entirely, but it seemed to make more sense now than it had then. In fact, he was undergoing a profound change. A month later he wrote to Cyril Connolly: 'I have seen wonderful things & at last really believe in Socialism, which I never did before.'[63] He also complained that the war was being misreported in the English press which was repeating the Communist line uncritically. Connolly himself had been in Spain, but, like many other writers – including Auden, Spender, Malraux, Dos Passos and Hemingway – more as a journalistic spectator than a participant. Some had even attended a congress of 'Anti-Fascist Writers' in Madrid – 'against a background of starvation', wrote Orwell, horrified when he heard about it.[64]

One who would readily succumb to Communist blandishments was Frankford, who, together with a South African called Tanky, was later lured away, reputedly by the wife of the author Ralph Bates. They were imprisoned on some trumped-up charge and then induced by the *Daily Worker* correspondent Sam Lesser to sign a document confirming that the POUM were dealing with the Fascists, and that Kopp in particular was conferring with them regularly across no man's land. This would be duly reported in the *Daily Worker* and used to justify much that followed. As a reward for their 'co-operation' Frankford and Tanky would not only be freed but provided with first-class tickets back to England.[65]

In the aftermath of the street fighting the Valencia Government sent some twenty thousand Assault Guards to Barcelona and effectively brought an end to Catalan autonomy. Suddenly the police were going after foreign dissidents and Orwell felt vulnerable. 'I had got to the point when every time a door banged I grabbed for my pistol. No one who was in Barcelona then, or for months later, will forget the horrible atmosphere produced by fear, suspicion, hatred, censored newspapers, crammed jails, enormous food queues and prowling gangs of armed men.'[66] To McNair he reportedly said, 'This is bloody awful . . . these buggers [the police] are shooting our chaps in the back.'[67] The Anarchist-controlled city that he had found so exhilarating in December was now, less than five months later, nothing but a ghostly memory. The politically naive revolutionaries had lost to their more ruthlessly cynical opponents.

Even before the May events began unfolding, Crook had moved into the Hotel Continental, passing as a war reporter probably for the *News Chronicle*. Tioli introduced him to Eileen Blair and through her he insinuated himself into the ILP office and into the confidence of McNair and his staff. (His credentials as a Labour Party member and secretary to John Parker MP no doubt helped.) George Kopp, under observation in the Continental, would call into the office from time to time and Crook came to the conclusion, duly reported to Albacete, that it was 90 per cent certain that Kopp and Eileen were on intimate terms. He had been instructed to look for such things – information giving Party agents the power of blackmail over vulnerable targets.[68] His masquerade seemed to have worked, and he soon had the run of the ILP offices, so much so that during lunch breaks, when McNair and the others repaired to the nearby Café Moka, he slipped into the empty office, stole files, took them to the Russian Embassy, had them photographed and returned before anyone got back. It was a point of pride for him that, in the course of not many days, copies of everything on the ILP Barcelona files were in the hands of his Russian handlers.[69]

Crook's reports on the Blairs, Kopp and McNair were normally passed to Pollitt's man, Hugh O'Donnell, who was also working directly for Moscow. O'Donnell's code name – amazingly – was 'O'Brien'! It seems unlikely that Orwell ever knew that Crook was spying on him, or that his contact worked under that name, but the fact that the character in *Nineteen Eighty-Four* who first wins the confidence of Winston Smith and then betrays him is given the name 'O'Brien' must be one of the strangest coincidences in literature.

O'Donnell and Crook ('gangster-gramophone' in Orwell's political lexicon) was seemingly part of the espionage arm which kidnapped Andrés Nin, the POUM leader, and the abduction of the Austrian socialist Kurt Landau. Both these Englishmen were characters straight from the Ingsoc world of spying, intrigue, dissemblance and cold elimination. Both were convinced and dedicated Communists ready to give their all for the Party, feeling that they were acting in accordance with the Party 'line' and for the glory of the cause. It is ironic that two fanatical Englishmen unwittingly played a crucial role in transforming the mildly socialist Orwell into an equally fanatical *anti*-communist, whose books would play a not inconsiderable part in the final destruction of the God they served.

After Orwell and his comrades had returned to the front, Gwen O'Shaughnessy, Eileen's sister-in-law, arrived in Barcelona from London in Laurence's big American car packed with medical supplies for the POUM. With her she brought another English recruit to the Republican cause. David Wickes, a language teacher who had spent many years in France, appeared to have followed the same path as Orwell. Rejected as unsuitable for the International Brigade by Pollitt, he approached Brockway who told him that Gwen was about to leave for Spain and would take him along. In Barcelona he met McNair and Eileen and at first attached himself to the ILP office as an interpreter. But he was in fact all the time under Communist Party control, and was soon instructed to switch to the International Brigade as an example to ILP waverers. However, to them, in the wake of the May events, switching to a Communist-backed outfit was nothing less than moral dereliction. Wickes later wrote a plaintive letter to Eileen hoping that she would not think badly of him, and hinting that he was deeply attracted to her. Even so, in Albacete, he seemingly briefed Soviet intelligence against both the Blairs and John McNair and was cited as a major source of information in an indictment for treason brought against them. Shortly afterwards he was denounced for moral cowardice by the British Communist Bill Rust for being part of an execution squad and refusing to fire when ordered and was sent to fight in the front line. Ironically, on his International Brigade discharge papers, of the Spanish Government he commented: 'Too much talk of leniency to traitors. Spanish history shows one must be ruthless with them.'[70]

At the Huesca front Orwell and his comrades found themselves part of the newly formed rank-conscious People's Army, the 29th Division. Benjamin was now a captain, Kopp a major, and Orwell a second lieutenant. There they heard the bad news that Bob Smillie, on his way home on leave, had been arrested at the border, found in possession of a bomb – in fact a dud taken as a souvenir. It only went to confirm their growing fear that the Communists were now working actively against the POUM.

Just five days after returning to the trenches, at dawn on 20 May, Orwell was hit. Jack Branthwaite remembered warning him about not crouching down at the parapet. 'I said to him, "Eric, you know, one of these days you're going to get shot." (You see, Eric was six foot four, and we were building parapets for Spaniards. He was head and shoulders above them.) Well, he just said, "They couldn't hit a bull in a passage.'"[71] He was, or so Frankford implied, standing talking about his experiences in a Paris brothel[72] when suddenly he fell to the ground, shot in the throat. He was conscious enough at the time to register the experience. 'Roughly speaking, it was the sensation of being *at the centre* of an explosion. There seemed to be a loud bang and a blinding flash of light all round me, and I felt a tremendous shock – no pain, only a violent shock, such as you get from an electrical terminal; with it a feeling of utter weakness, a feeling of being stricken and shrivelling up to nothing.'[73] Strangely, the last few phrases echo his description of the death of the elephant he shot in Burma. Assuming that he was about to die he uttered what he probably thought would be his last words: 'Tell Eileen that I love her.'

Harry Milton was nearby when he fell. 'He had bitten his lips, so I thought he was a goner. The speed of the bullet had seared the entrance of the wound. I put his head in my arms, and when I put my hand under his neck there was a puddle of blood.'[74] He was rushed to the field hospital, seemingly a lost cause. Not only was he weak from shock and loss of blood, but the bullet had narrowly missed his carotid artery, leaving his right arm and one of his vocal cords paralysed so that he had lost his voice. He was moved to Lérida where he remained for about a week and there began to show signs of recovery. Within a few days, he was able to get up and walk about. Finally he was transferred to the Sanatorium Maurin in Barcelona, the main POUM hospital, where a few others from the 29th Division were patients, including Stafford Cottman, suspected of having TB. Fernandez Jurado, a wounded POUM militiaman who met him there, found him barely able to talk but also profoundly depressed.

The cause of his depression was evident. In Barcelona the aftermath of the May fighting, he wrote, had left 'a peculiar evil feeling in the air – an atmosphere of suspicion, uncertainty and veiled hatred'.[75] Furthermore: 'It was as though some huge evil intelligence were brooding over the town. Everyone noticed it and . . . expressed it in almost the same words . . . "like being in a lunatic asylum."'[76] In this unpleasant climate of fear he and Eileen passed their first wedding anniversary.

Kopp managed to see the doctor in charge of Orwell's case and got a report from him, which he sent in a detailed letter to Laurence O'Shaughnessy in England. The first version of this letter seems to have been 'lost',[77] turning up later in Orwell's KGB file, so was presumably lifted by Moscow's own man about the ILP office, Crook. Orwell had been shot with a high-velocity 7mm bullet from a Mauser rifle from around 175 yards, the shot having passed between his trachea and carotid artery.

Surprisingly, in view of his general health, his improvement was steady. The doctor had told him cheerfully that he would never recover his voice, but gradually even that came back, progressing from a whispering falsetto to an audible rasp. Some friends said that his voice never recovered completely, remaining high-pitched and reedy. Others, like his old Eton tutor Gow, for example, thought it had always been a discordant croak.[78] It would take him some weeks, however, to recover full use of his arm.

Orwell felt that he could be of little more use in Spain and he and Eileen decided to return home once he had been given his discharge. He spent five days on trains and lorries trailing around the forward areas, obtaining the signatures he needed. Meanwhile, on 16 June, the order was given to move against the POUM. Its offices in the Ramblas and the Falcon Hotel were raided and its newspaper, *La Batalla*, suppressed. The left-wing Republican Government of Largo Caballero had been replaced by a more centrist one under Juan Negrin, a government more amenable to the Communists. As Orwell wrote, 'The "Stalinists" were in the saddle, and therefore it was a matter of course that every "Trotskyist" was in danger.'[79] Two days later, at dawn, the Spanish secret police, the SIM (infiltrated and controlled by the NKVD), raided the Hotel Continental with the Blairs among its targets.

Crook later claimed to have known about the raid in advance and tipped off the Blairs. He also claimed, as did Tioli, to have helped Eileen and McNair by passing sensitive notebooks and other documents from balcony to balcony, so that each room would be clean when the police burst in. According to Orwell, Eileen got into bed and managed to hide their passports and chequebooks under the bedclothes, which fortunately the Spanish secret policemen were too chivalrous to remove. He did, however, lose all his diaries and press cuttings, his letters to Eileen (including his notes made at the front), fan letters about *Wigan Pier*, Kopp's letter to Eileen about his wound, war souvenirs, photographs, and even some dirty linen – all now presumably mouldering in some dusty file in the old KGB archives in Moscow. Interestingly, one item taken was Orwell's copy of Hitler's Mein Kampf; when Crook was later arrested on a trumped-up charge to facilitate his spying activities, in his possession was found a copy of the same book.[80]

Orwell's taste for the clandestine made him highly sensitive to this poisonous atmosphere of betrayal and police raids, in which no one could be trusted. He had been spied on since early May and by someone he and Eileen took to be a friend – perhaps by more than one. Ironically, writing about that time, he said, 'You had all the while a hateful feeling that someone hitherto your friend might be denouncing you to the secret police.'[81] Once he had thought that Vatican spies were everywhere; now it was Comintern spies, the agents of the new Inquisition.

*

Having finally obtained his discharge and returned to Barcelona, he headed for the Continental. Eileen met him in the lounge, embraced him and hissed in his ear, '*Get out!*' Outside she told him, 'The POUM's been suppressed.' She told him about arrests and rumours of shootings. POUM people were being thrown into jail, some dragged from hospital beds and taken away, no one knew where. The Communist press was denouncing POUMists as 'Fascist plotters', and even some foreigners from the International Brigade were being arrested. Eileen had been left alone, they concluded, to lure George into the Communist net. Because of press censorship, sinister rumours were circulating. Andrés Nin, the POUM leader, was said to have been shot and his body dumped in the street. Kurt Landau, the Austrian socialist, was in hiding. (Crook, most likely connected to the espionage arm responsible for the kidnap of Nin, himself claimed to have fingered Landau.)

Kopp had been arrested earlier that same day en route to the front, which made Orwell particularly angry because he was a close friend whose bravery he greatly admired. Now, to have served with the POUM militia was enough to be deemed guilty of 'Trotskyism' and jailed. 'This,' Orwell noted, 'was not a round-up of criminals; it was merely a reign of terror'.[82] Eileen made him destroy his POUM militia card and some incriminating photographs. He hung on to his discharge papers, even though, bearing the seal of the 29th Division, they could still endanger him.

Now they had to get out of Spain. With McNair, Cottman and a few others, they met at the British Consulate and learned it would take three days to get their passports ready. Eileen returned to the Continental while George wandered the streets, reverting to his tramping role, and slept the night in a ruined church. Next morning, back at the Consulate, they heard that Bob Smillie was dead. No one could say how he died but they assumed he had been shot. It was later announced that he had died of appendicitis. Orwell was naturally sceptical. Smillie was only twenty-two, very tough and had been three months in the trenches without illness. 'People so tough as that do not usually die of appendicitis if they are properly looked after.'[83] He had, they decided, died of neglect.

This was a crucial event in Orwell's life, more disturbing to him even than Kopp's arrest. 'Smillie's death is not a thing I can easily forgive. Here was this brave and gifted boy, who had thrown up his career at Glasgow University in order to come and fight against Fascism, and who, as I saw for myself, had done his job at the front with faultless courage and willingness; and all they could find to do with him was to fling him into jail and let him die like a neglected animal . . . what angers one about a death like this is its utter pointlessness.'[84] Kopp later claimed that, while in a slackly run prison, he had managed to get hold of Smillie's file and saw it recorded that he had died from heavy kicks to the stomach.[85] If anything tipped Orwell finally from a simple hostility to Stalinist Communism into a deep-dyed loathing of it, it was the death of Smillie. John Dos Passos who also had a friend killed in custody by the SIM in Spain, reacted by deserting the Communists and shifting decidedly to the right.[86] Orwell never did abandon his socialism; if anything, his Spanish experience strengthened it.

After Kopp was imprisoned, Crook's Party handlers arranged for him also to be arrested and put into the same cell as Kopp, with the mission to pump him for potentially incriminating information. When Orwell and Eileen risked visiting him in prison, they found Crook there, too. Conditions were bad – cells overcrowded, filthy and foul smelling – but Kopp was in good spirits, saying cheerfully, 'Well, I suppose we shall all be shot.' The rumour of Nin's death had just reached them and a massacre of 'Trotskysts' was expected. At some risk to himself, Orwell managed to retrieve a letter from the Chief of Police, which might have helped Kopp's case. Sadly it did not and Kopp would spend many months in jail, being interrogated and severely tortured.

While George tried to help Kopp, Eileen offered to assist Crook, with money and smuggling letters out. When Crook was later released on some pretext, he promised Kopp to smuggle out what he confidently thought would be the man's last letter. But the astute Kopp took the precaution of smuggling out a separate copy addressed to Eileen in Greenwich. Crook duly reported their conversations and handed his letter to one of his controllers, code-named 'Gertrude'.[87] 'His next job was to cultivate an American Anarchist called Abe Bluestein hoping to locate the Austrian socialist, Kurt Landau.

After another night on the run and another visit to see Kopp, they were able to collect their passports from the British Consul, and after another day hiding out finally caught the train to Port Bou. As they headed for the border with McNair and Cottman, Orwell noticed another symptom of the change since his arrival. The train on which classes had been abolished now had both first-class compartments and a dining car. En route, detectives came through the carriages, checking papers looking for deserters, but they all managed to pass as respectable tourists and finally they crossed the border into France. Orwell mused that coming into Spain the previous year, bourgeois-looking people would be turned back at the border by Anarchist guards; now looking bourgeois gave one easy passage. He took out few souvenirs – a goatskin water bottle and a tiny olive-oil-burning lamp – but his prize memento was his tinder-lighter, with its long wick and elaborate mechanism. He used it for years afterwards, a badge of his having fought in Spain.

The experience of being on the run, fearing arrest and even worse, left a deep mark on Orwell. On his return, he told Heppenstall, 'Though we our-selves got out all right nearly all our friends and acquaintances are in jail and likely to be there indefinitely, not exactly charged with anything but suspected of "Trotskyism". The most terrible things were happening even when I left, wholesale arrests, wounded men dragged out of hospitals and thrown into jail, people crammed together in filthy dens where they have hardly room to lie down, prisoners beaten and half starved etc., etc. Meanwhile it is impossible to get a word of this mentioned in the English press.' The person who had survived the experience best was Eileen, who 'was wonderful, in fact actually seemed to enjoy it'.[88] In his own way Orwell also benefited from what happened. Above all, it had given him a vision of what libertarian socialism was like in practice. Barcelona under the Anarchists would remain with him for long afterwards. 'No one who was in Spain during the months when people still believed in the revolution will ever forget that strange and moving experience. It has left something behind that no dictatorship, not even Franco's, will be able to efface.'[89] The people who had effaced that *reality*, the Soviet Communists, now had an implac-able enemy they would come to regret having made.

It was 23 June, two days short of Orwell's thirty-fourth birthday. In Perpignan, they met Fenner Brockway, on his way to Spain to try to obtain the release of the arrested POUM leaders. They talked all night about the situation in Barcelona and how to alert the men on the Huesca front to the danger they were in. Orwell mentioned the book he intended writing but said that Gollancz, after his reservations about *The Road to Wigan Pier*, was unlikely to want to publish it. Brockway suggested Secker and Warburg, who were sympathetic to the ILP. Next day, George and Eileen decided to spend a few days at the fishing port of Banyuls, while Cottman and McNair headed home. Brockway travelled on to Barcelona with names of people McNair suggested might be useful to him, one of them David Crook. He met Crook at the Continental, and was clearly taken in by him. The Londoner undertook to help Brockway find out all he could about the imprisoned POUM leaders, no doubt reporting everything to either 'Gertrude' or 'O'Brien'. It was possibly through Brockway, and later Bluestein, that Crook discovered the whereabouts of Kurt Landau before betraying him to the SIM, and thus sending him on his way to torture and death in Moscow.)

In Banyuls Orwell wired the *New Statesman* proposing an article about his Spanish experiences, and they cabled back, 'Yes'. He then began writing 'Eye-Witness in Barcelona', which tells concisely and vividly the story he would subsequently elaborate in *Homage to Catalonia*. McNair had managed to rescue Eileen's typescript of his diary notes copied from his letters, telling police who raided his room that it was a call to arms to British workers to join in the heroic anti-Franco struggle, and seemingly they had swallowed his story.[90] It was probably from these notes that Orwell was able to work.

The sentiment in Banyuls was pro-Franco and the town itself disappointing. A choppy sea, a chilly sea-wind and debris-polluted harbour, meant there was little chance of any swimming or fishing. And Spain still possessed him. 'Curiously enough,' he wrote, 'the whole experience has left me with not less but more belief in the decency of human beings.'[91] However, despite this note of optimism he was left with persistent nightmares – the haunting fear of assassination (the later fate of some anti-Stalinist leftists in exile), of the concentration camp and the torture chamber (the fate that overtook Kopp). Evidently, in the home of the Spanish Inquisition, even amid the desecrated ruins of churches, the ghost of Torquemada had arisen, and the cruel and tyrannical methods of medieval Catholicism had been revived –imprisonment without trial, confessions extracted under torture with summary executions to follow. Orwell, like those early Protestant dissenters with whom he so identified, torch-bearers of freedom of thought and conscience, was now a target of the oppressors. The gangster-gramophones, the O'Donnell/O'Briens of this world, were not just caricatures, figures of fun like the Letchworth socialists, but real and extremely dangerous enemies.

He wrote in 1940, 'I served four months on the Aragon front with the POUM militia and was rather badly wounded, but luckily with no serious after-effects.'[92] This was just not true. The after-effects on him would be long lasting and profound.

They returned to England via Paris, which, by contrast with Spain, looked gay and prosperous. Briefly they visited Miller – to return that corduroy jacket presumably – before heading back home. From Spain he brought back a vision of the New Jerusalem. That vision had been snatched away – 'But it lasted long enough to have its effect upon anyone who experienced it . . . One had breathed the air of equality.'[93] He had learned a hard lesson, especially about the new political Europe. Totalitarianism, the new creed of 'the streamlined men' of Fascism and Communism, was a new manifestation of his old Catholic enemy, the doctrine of Absolutism: 'The essential fact about a totalitarian regime is that it has no laws. People are not punished for specific offences, but because they are considered to be politically or intellectually undesirable. What they have done or not done is irrelevant.'[94] More fearfully still, as he later pointed out, the Inquisition failed only because it did not have at its disposal the resources of the modern state. 'The radio, press-censorship, standardized education and the secret police have altered everything. Mass-suggestion is a science of the last twenty years, and we do not yet know how successful it will be.'[95] The

Trotskyist and Anarchist dissenters from the Soviet line were the new heretics.[96] The seeds of his last two great novels had been sown.

Even as they left Spain an indictment for treason was being prepared against Orwell, Eileen and McNair. Ironically, two 'friends' were behind the resulting document – David Crook and David Wickes. If Charles Orr is correct, George Tioli also fed information about them through to Albacete. Tioli later disappeared and Orr thought that he had probably met the end that often comes to those who play a double game. The charge of Trostkyism read as follows:

13 July 1937: 'Tribunal of Espionage & High Treason, Barcelona 13 July 1937./ERIC BLAIR and his wife EILEEN BLAIR/Their correspondence reveals that they are rabid Trotskyites./They belong to the I.R.P. [sic] in England./Liaison with ILP in England (Correspondence with D. Moyle and John McNair)./In Charles Dolan's [Doran's] material there is a letter addressed to Eric B. from John MacNair [sic] asking him to write with news from the ILP./One has to consider them as ILP liaison agents of POUM./They used to live in the Falcon Hotel supported by the POUM executive committee./Credential of the POUM executive committee signed by Jorge [sic] Kopp (its nature leads one to suppose that it is a credential which was valid during the events that took place in May) and made out in favour of Eileen B./Eric B. Took part in the events of May./Liaison with Albacete [H.Q. of the International Brigade] through David Wickes./Liaison with Moscow./Eileen B. was at the Huesca front on 13.3.37 (the date written on the photograph). She has a credential issued in Barcelona on 17.3.37./Her husband has a permit to leave from the front to go to Barcelona issued on 14.3.37.[97]

What depressed Orwell about Spain, apart from the betrayal of the POUMists, the terror and the murder of Nin and Smillie, was the behaviour of the British press. 'In Spain,' he wrote, 'for the first time, I saw newspaper reports which did not bear any relation to the facts, not even the relationship which is implied in an ordinary lie ... I saw, in fact, history being written not in terms of what happened but of what ought to have happened according to various "party lines".'[98]

Chapter 12

The Road to Morocco

Rick: 'I came to Casablanca for the waters.'
Captain Renault: 'The waters? What waters? We're in the desert.'
Rick: 'I was misinformed.'

Casablanca

A s ever on returning home, Orwell was overcome by the beauty of the countryside and the civilised quality of English life. But, after the events of the past six months, the paradise of Southern England, 'the sleekest landscape in the world', had taken on a new significance. It now seemed to him a country of sleepers unaware of the impending nightmare. Earthquakes, famines and revolutions happened elsewhere, the smoke and misery of industrial towns were out of sight and far away.

> Down here it was still the England I had known in my childhood: the railway-cuttings smothered in wild flowers, the deep meadows where the great shining horses browse and meditate, the slow-moving streams bordered by willows, the green bosoms of the elms, the larkspurs in the cottage gardens; and then the huge peaceful wilderness of outer London, the barges on the miry river, the familiar streets, the posters telling of cricket matches and Royal weddings, the men in bowler hats, the pigeons in Trafalgar Square, the red buses, the blue policemen – all sleeping the deep, deep sleep of England, from which I sometimes fear that we shall never wake till we are jerked out of it by the roar of bombs.[1]

After a short rest, convalescing with the O'Shaughnessys in Greenwich, he heard from Kingsley Martin, editor of the *New Statesman*, that his 'Eye-Witness in Barcelona' was unacceptable. Orwell's conclusion that in Spain 'the present Government has more points of resemblance to Fascism than points of difference'[2] 'could cause trouble'.[3] As a sop he was offered Franz

Borkenau's *The Spanish Cockpit* to review, and in doing so, with character-
istic bloody-mindedness, took the same line. This, too, was rejected with a
letter from Martin stating that it controverted 'the political policy of the
paper', but assuring him that he would be paid – 'practically hush-money',
Orwell called it. He never forgave Martin, referring to him later as a
'Decayed liberal. Very dishonest', no more than a supine fellow-traveller.[4]
The review was finally taken by *Time and Tide*, and 'Eye-Witness in
Barcelona' appeared in *Controversy*, a magazine with mostly ILP readers.
Whether Orwell took Martin's 'hush-money' is unclear. He was now taking
the ILP line that war against Germany would be a capitalist war that would
reduce Britain to Fascism, as the war in Spain threatened to do there.

'Eye-Witness in Barcelona' refuted the Communist version of the May
events, explaining the intricacies of Spanish politics and the various
Catalan factions. The story of an Anarchist and POUM uprising was
false, the Government's response revealing it as more anti-revolution
than anti-Nationalist. The move to crush the POUM appeared well-
prepared and involved decidedly Fascist methods. The arrest and killing
of POUM leaders had been kept out of the papers and from the troops at
the front. The same could soon happen to the Anarchists, now the only
hope for revolution and victory against Franco. It is evident why the
New Statesman, wedded to the Soviet idea of the Popular Front, found
this unacceptable – it was brilliantly argued and carried the conviction of
first-hand experience.[5]

A second piece, 'Spilling the Spanish Beans', followed in the *New English
Weekly*, beginning with the telling sentence, 'The Spanish war has probably
produced a richer crop of lies than any event since the Great War of
1914–18.' From the outset he attacked the left-wing press for suppressing
the truth about Spain, indicting the Communists for instigating a 'reign of
terror'. In effect a 'Liberal-Communist bloc' was robbing the Catalan
worker-revolutionaries of what they had won in 1936. This anti-revolu-
tionary coalition of Communists and right-wing Socialists known as the
Popular Front, was like 'a pig with two heads or some other Barnum &
Bailey monstrosity'. Fascism and bourgeois 'democracy' were 'Tweedledum
and Tweedledee'. He defended the POUM as 'an opposition Communist
Party roughly corresponding to the English ILP'. Communism, on the other
hand, was now 'a counter-revolutionary force'.[6]

The feeling of being silenced was only intensified when he contacted
Gollancz. From Spain, Orwell had written to him, saying, 'I hope I shall get
a chance to write the truth about what I have seen. The stuff appearing in
the English papers is largely the most appalling lies.'[7] Now, arm in sling and
with his voice still hoarse, he visited Gollancz's office and outlined the book
he had in mind to his old enemy Norman Collins who undertook to pass on

the proposal. Within a week he received Gollancz's reply, in effect a rejection. His book, he was told, might 'harm the fight against Fascism'. Gollancz then went on to remind him that he still had an option on his next three novels.[8] 'Ten years ago,' wrote Orwell bitterly, 'it was almost impossible to get anything printed in favour of Communism; today it is almost impossible to get anything printed in favour of Anarchism or "Trotskyism".'[9] The following day he received an unexpected invitation to meet Fredric Warburg, Brockway's publisher, saying that it had been suggested to him by certain ILP people that, 'a book from you would not only be of great interest but of considerable political importance'.[10]

When he and Eileen arrived back in Wallington, they found that Aunt Nellie, unable to cope, had left The Stores in a complete mess and overrun by mice, but Orwell enjoyed getting things back to normal, tending his garden and livestock. With Hector back in Southwold, they acquired a black poodle which they christened Marx, though whether after Karl or Groucho visitors were left to ponder. They also acquired another goat, which they called Kate, this time after Aunt Nellie (Kate being her middle name).

Letters arrived from Kopp, describing his perilous situation in jail in Barcelona. These were sent, significantly perhaps, to Eileen, care of Laurence. 'I agreed with your sister,' he wrote, 'to communicate with her through you. Tell her I am intensely thinking of her and give her my love. Shake hands to Eric.' It was she in turn who took up his case with McNair, urging that it receive maximum publicity in the *New Leader*. Since he had not been charged, he wrote, he had gone on hunger strike and written to the chief of police asking for a chance to defend himself. He was being held in squalid conditions with common criminals, denied exercise and been poorly fed. A second letter ended in characteristically positive mood: 'I am not at all downhearted but feel my patience has definitely gone; in one or another way I shall fight to freedom for my comrades and myself.' He also mentioned in passing that 'David' had sent him a book of French poetry inscribed, 'from an almost subterranean swine', which sounds like a cryptically ironic confession from the man who had spied on him.[11]

Not all letters from fans about *The Road to Wigan Pier* had fallen into the hands of the Spanish secret police. One, from a young trainee midwife, Amy Charlesworth, led to a correspondence which appeared to animate Orwell. Signing himself 'Eric Blair ("George Orwell")', he told her he would quite like to meet her sometime,[12] later confessing to Heppenstall that he had concealed from her the fact that he was married, imagining that she was young and single. When it transpired that she was a 35-year-old divorced mother of two, Eileen was gleeful, which suggests that the occasional dalliance was tolerated on both sides. *He* turned a blind eye to Kopp, *Eileen* indulged his fantasies over an impressionable admirer. Some stresses and strains in the relationship did eventually surface, mostly because of George's philandering. However, in his mind at least, the marriage seems to have been declared open and he was at liberty to cast his eyes elsewhere whenever the mood took him.

It soon became apparent that English POUMists were not altogether beyond the long arm of the Stalinists. When Stafford Cottman arrived back in Bristol his home was picketed by a group of Young Communists with banners denouncing him as 'an enemy of the working class', and people going in and out were questioned. When Orwell heard about this he got Laurence to drive him to Bristol where they organised a protest in defence of the young rebel. 'What a show!' he wrote. 'To think that we started off as heroic defenders of democracy and only six months later were Trotsky-Fascists sneaking over the border with the police at our heels.'[13] He was clearly shocked that Communist attacks on people with POUM connections had been taken up back in England. After all, he even more than Cottman was a prime target of Communist spite.

Following Pollitt's hostile review of *Wigan Pier*, attacks on him continued in the *Daily Worker*. Finally he complained to Gollancz, hinting at possible libel action.[14] Gollancz passed on the complaint to Pollitt, and for the time being the attacks ceased. It confirmed to Orwell just how closely his publisher was embroiled with the extreme left. He told friends that obviously he was 'part of the Communism-racket',[15] and 'not too bright intellectually'.[16] Since he now saw Gollancz as little more than a Soviet propagandist, he arranged to meet Warburg at his office just off the Strand, to discuss his proposed book. Warburg had taken over the business from Martin Secker a year earlier in partnership with Roger Senhouse, Lytton Strachey's quondam lover and another Eton contemporary of Orwell's. The firm had an impressive list including Kafka, Mann and Lawrence, but was then financially weak and lacked prominence. Unlike Gollancz, however, Warburg warmed to the eccentric Orwell and became a personal friend and confidant.

Orwell's angry state of mind is evident from his reply to Nancy Cunard who sent him a questionnaire soliciting his views for a book to be called *Authors Take Sides on the Spanish Civil War*. 'Will you please stop sending me this bloody rubbish ... I am not one of your fashionable pansies like Auden and Spender, I was six months in Spain, most of the time fighting, I have a bullet-hole in me at present and I am not going to write blah about defending democracy or gallant little anybody.' She had obviously knowingly 'joined in the defence of "democracy" (i.e. Capitalism) racket in order to aid in crushing the Spanish working class and thus indirectly defend your dirty little dividends'. He concluded with a dig at one of his *bêtes noires*: 'By the way, tell your pansy friend Spender that I am preserving specimens of his war-heroics and that when the time comes when he squirms for shame at having written it, as the people who wrote the war propaganda in the Great War are squirming now, I shall rub it in good and hard.'[17] However, he was perfectly happy to answer Amy Charlesworth's questions at length, adding, 'I must apologize for lecturing you about Spain, but what I saw there has upset me so badly that I talk and write about it to everybody.'[18]

His feeling of solidarity with the POUM, drew him to the ILP Summer School at Letchworth – well-attended, no doubt, by a goodly crowd of fruit-juice-drinking, nut-eating, sandal-wearing vegetarians. He shared a platform with Douglas Moyle, Stafford Cottman, Jack Branthwaite, Paddy Donovan and John McNair, although his contribution was brief and hindered by the lingering effects of his throat wound. 'My voice is practically normal,' he told Heppenstall, 'but I can't shout to any extent. I also can't sing, but people tell me this doesn't matter.'[19]

Moyle, Donovan and Branthwaite were invited to Wallington, and were amused to find that, after working in his garden and tending his livestock all day looking like a tramp, Orwell insisted on dressing for dinner. Noting the number of animals around the place, Branthwaite remembered saying, 'I wonder if we handed over the reins of government to the animals, if they'd do any better?' He was thinking about the horrors of Spain, but Orwell, he felt, had been taken by the idea, and after dinner disappeared upstairs. 'It may or may not have started a train of thought which ended up as *Animal Farm*, an idea that he thought might come in handy.'[20] Orwell certainly placed the book's origins as 1937, but his story of its origins is slightly different:

> On my return from Spain I thought of exposing the Soviet myth in a story that could be easily understood by almost anyone and which could be easily translated into other languages. However, the actual details of the story did not come to me for some time until one day (I was then living in a small village) I saw a little boy, perhaps ten years old, driving a huge carthorse along a narrow path, whipping it whenever it tried to turn. It struck me that if only such animals became aware of their strength we should have no power over them, and that men exploit animals in much the same way as the rich exploit the proletariat./I proceeded to analyse Marx's theory from the animals' point of view. To them it was clear that the concept of a class struggle between humans was pure illusion, since whenever it was necessary to exploit animals, all humans united against them: the true struggle is between animals and humans.[21]

What he did not mention was that directly opposite The Stores stood the entrance to John Innes's[22] Manor Farm, which in those days boasted a fine herd of Berkshire pigs. Farmer Innes must be a strong candidate for the original Farmer Jones, and Manor Farm, Wallington for Manor Farm, Willingdon. But if the idea of *Animal Farm* was conceived in the summer of 1937, in the six or seven years of gestation leading to its being written, there would have been proddings and promptings and encouragements from various directions, not least from Eileen, whose help with it he later acknowledged.

The couple's Spanish experience seemed to have brought them closer. When Heppenstall came visiting he noted how fondly they acted towards one another. 'He and Eileen behaved with conspicuous affection, fondling each other and sitting, if not on each other's knees, at any rate in the same armchair.'[23] Cyril Connolly, who had been to Spain as a journalist, wrote saying he was also keen to see him. He shared Orwell's concern about censorship used against anyone expressing sympathy for the Spanish Anarchists or Trotskyists. To Connolly, Orwell was one of the few people able to articulate a clear non-Communist anti-Fascist line, and slowly he would emerge as the spokesman of his generation (its 'wintry conscience', according to V. S. Pritchett), to whom others would look to clarify their own political ideas. Geoffrey Gorer was also eager to talk to him about Spain, and soon even the 'nancy poet' Spender would be asking to meet him.

The Blairs had lived in the village for only six months before George left for Spain and were still considered outsiders, and rather odd ones at that. Some villagers thought that a man who could be heard tapping a typewriter late at night must be up to no good, could even be a spy.[24] On his parish rounds, the vicar was concerned to learn that he had fought for the Republicans in Spain, revolutionaries who, according to the newspapers, destroyed churches and executed priests. However, when they told him they were only Catholic churches he seemed happier.[25] Eileen later reported that the vicar's wife had told her in confidence that her ladies' prayer circle had included George in their weekly prayers.

That summer, invited to contribute to the Soviet magazine *International Literature*, he first informed them that he had served with the POUM militia in Spain. The reply was stern. 'Our magazine, indeed, has nothing to do with POUM-members; this organisation, as the long experience of the Spanish people's struggle against insurgents and fascist interventionists has shown, is a part of Franco's "fifth column" which is acting in the rear of the heroic army of Republican Spain.'[26] With Moscow as well as Pollitt ready to denounce him and Gollancz refusing to publish him, he felt like a marked man with his name on some hit-list. He told Gorer that 'the *Daily Worker* has been following me personally with the most filthy libels, calling me pro-Fascist etc.,'[27] and to the Editor of the *Manchester Guardian* he wrote, 'As I was serving in the POUM militia, my name is probably on the list of political suspects.'[28]

The Frankford allegations denouncing the POUM as a fifth column had surfaced in the *Daily Worker*. Kopp was named as a traitorous go-between, and the charges were clearly being used as a pretext to hold and interrogate him. Brockway later reported Frankford turning up at McNair's London office and apologising on his knees for what he had done, saying that he was in prison for stealing paintings and signing the statement had been the price of his release. The Communists, he said, had distorted the story he had given them.[29] But the damage was done, and Orwell was outraged. It was bad enough being lied about by Communists but to be lied about by one of your own men was too much to bear. He wrote a letter, signed by fourteen other old comrades, to the *New Leader* denouncing Frankford as a poor, undisciplined soldier and a troublemaker, and refuting all his charges in detail. 'He was arrested as a deserter,' he wrote, '[and] in the circumstances was lucky not to be shot.'[30] No doubt this sad case only heightened his sense of not knowing quite who could be trusted.

By the end of August his book was making good progress, thanks no doubt to the notes McNair had salvaged. On 1st September he signed Warburg's contract for *Homage to Catalonia*, for an advance of £150.[31] Orwell was embarking on a new writing career. His transformation into a writer 'against totalitarianism and for democratic Socialism' would be completed with this book. In *The Road to Wigan Pier* he had still not grasped who were his enemies and where he wanted to go. Now he was a wiser man and a more surely directed writer, also more aware of his own prejudices and tendency to caricature. 'Everyone writes of [politics] in one guise or another . . . And the more one is conscious of one's political bias, the more chance one has of acting politically without sacrificing one's aesthetic and intellectual integrity.'[32] To him honesty was the prime virtue, even though one might be honestly wrong. At the same time he saw himself not as simply a crude propagandist, but as also a man of letters, a man who believed he could turn political writing into an art.

Still not fully recovered from his wound and the exhaustion of trench life, the effort of writing this book had taken a great deal out of him. Again he had produced the kind of work he admired, 'part reportage and part political criticism . . . with a little autobiography thrown in', responding to the prevailing orthodoxy of a time 'when fierce controversies were raging and nobody was telling the whole of the truth'. In it the voice and vision are clear, the eye to detail precise, the quiet narrative tone perfectly pitched for conveying the experience of idealism betrayed, of high hopes brutally crushed. Here again are Paradise Gained and Paradise Lost. It was, he said, a difficult book to write even when one knew the facts.[33]

Homage to Catalonia is not just a work of shining integrity, but the clearest expression of Orwell's own version of socialism, one inspired more by

Christianity than Marx. T. R. Fyvel considered it 'The starting-point for the ideas of a new humanist English Left movement which he [Orwell] tried to express later.'[34] Stephen Schwartz, the distinguished American political journalist, has cast the book in a Dantesque light – the Paradisal vision of Barcelona and the saintly image of the Italian militiaman giving way to the Purgatory of trench life mitigated by a sense of comradely solidarity, and finally the dream destroyed in the Hell of Communist terror after the May events. It was this religious dimension of the story (embodying compassion) that Schwartz believed so angered the pagan Stalinists (embodying revenge). On this view, *Homage to Catalonia* stands as the quintessential expression of Christian Socialism (and the highest virtues of Judaism and Islam).[35] No doubt this book went a long way towards confirming the image drawn by both Cyril Connolly and Stephen Spender, of Orwell 'the secular saint'.[36]

The Communist position was that Orwell was largely ignorant of the big picture and of Spain.[37] But *most* British volunteers who went to the war were ignorant of it – the International Brigaders had little or no contact with Spaniards in the fighting line and could not, or would not, learn the language, nor were many of them aware of the cruel methods used against other left-wing parties by their own side or how they were used as tools of Russian foreign policy. Orwell admitted that he knew little about Spanish politics until the May events, but at least he learned to communicate with Spaniards, fought beside them in Aragón, and saw through unclouded eyes what happened to the POUM in Barcelona. Only at that point, it seems, did his sociological imagination wake up and take notice. The Communists condemned his 'ignorance' because he did not buy their version of events. *They* were required to swallow a 'correct' line – dissenters risked either excommunication or something worse. To fight Fascism in company with those who would themselves impose totalitarianism was horrific to Orwell, who set about trying to inform the world of the sort of people they were up against.

Although he thought it necessary to include two chapters on the labyrinthine nature of Catalan politics, such matters made the man of literature uneasy. He told Stephen Spender, 'I hate writing that kind of stuff and I am much more interested in my own experiences, but unfortunately in this bloody period we are living in one's only experiences *are* being mixed up in controversies, intrigues etc. I sometimes feel as if I hadn't been properly alive since the beginning of 1937.'[38] Apart from Spain there was good reason for him to hate Stalinism; it had brought about what he saw as a vile confusion of argumentation of such boring mindlessness as to deflect him from his main literary purpose. He damned 'all the political controversies that have made life hideous for two years past'.[39] The 'happy vicar' would never forgive those who had frustrated his creative ambitions, and he was outraged by their blatant injustice and readiness to lie.

The Spanish Civil War had a mesmeric effect on many of Orwell's contemporaries, who felt that stopping Fascism in Spain might prevent a European-wide war. The left poets – Auden, Spender and Day Lewis – wrote with biting lyricism about the fate that had overtaken their generation in having to face up to Fascism. Some, like Ralph Fox and John Cornford, paid with their lives; others, like Dylan Thomas, George Barker and Malcolm Lowry, never went but could not avoid writing about it. Most were sympathetic to the Communists of the International Brigade, Auden even referring to the 'necessary murder', something to which Orwell took great exception, having himself seen the bodies of murdered men. In *The Road to Wigan Pier* he had sneered at Auden as 'a sort of gutless Kipling', a remark he later withdrew as 'unworthy', but his contempt for the Oxbridge clique never entirely vanished.

It was evident to Orwell, as to many others, that war with Germany was now brewing. After Spain he saw that a war against Fascism would be followed inevitably by a war against Soviet Communism, which he also regarded as Fascistic. Desmond Young, who got to know him around this time, remembered Orwell saying to him that this was 'only the first act of a tragedy that would be played not in two acts but in three'.[40] Already he saw clearly the enemy beyond Hitler, the enemy he would depict with such savage irony in *Animal Farm* and *Nineteen Eighty-Four*.

By December he had completed a draft of *Homage to Catalonia* and had time to spare to meet friends. Connolly asked if he would like to meet Spender for lunch, and he responded eagerly, though he wondered how the poet would regard him after the rude things he had said of him.[41] Spender remembered how well they got on and was surprised when afterwards Orwell took him aside, apologising for having attacked him.[42] Later Orwell told Connolly, 'Funny, I always used him & the rest of that gang as symbols of the pansy Left . . . but when I met him in person I liked him so much & was sorry for the things I had said about him.'[43] After meeting Spender, Orwell almost never again referred to 'nancy' or 'pansy' poets.

He took every opportunity to speak and write about Spain. Not long after he delivered the manuscript of his book to Warburg, who planned to bring it out in the spring, he reviewed Arthur Koestler's *Spanish Testament*. From very different backgrounds and political experiences, Orwell and Koestler had arrived at very much the same position at the same time and would eventually become close friends. Koestler, a Hungarian Jew, had been a staunch Communist, but had fallen foul of the Party. At the outbreak of the Civil War he went to Spain as a war correspondent for the *News Chronicle*. Hoping to get a good story, at the fall of Malaga he remained behind and was captured, put into a Fascist jail, condemned to death and threatened with execution. Orwell found the book 'of the greatest psychological interest –

probably one of the most honest and unusual documents to be produced by the Spanish war'. It laid bare, he said, 'the central evil of modern war – the fact that, as Nietzsche puts it, "he who fights against dragons becomes a dragon himself"'. Koestler had written that, faced with the bestiality he had suffered at the hands of the Fascists, he could no longer pretend to be objective. Orwell agreed: 'You cannot be objective about an aerial torpedo. And the horror we feel of these things has led to this conclusion: if someone drops a bomb on your mother, go and drop two bombs on his mother.'[44] He may have thought that a war with Germany would be nothing short of a capitalist war, but his warrior spirit had been by no means diminished by his time in Spain.

Homage to Catalonia was published at the end of April 1938.[45] Orwell was hoping for a good sale and wide coverage. In the event, Warburg printed 1,500 copies but sold only 800. The remainder was not finally sold until after Orwell's death. There were reviews, some eulogistic. The *Observer* called Orwell 'a great writer',[46] and the *Manchester Guardian* noted the author's 'fine air of classical detachment' in describing the horrors of war.[47] There were highly appreciative notices from Geoffrey Gorer in *Time and Tide*, John McNair in *New Leader*, Philip Mairet in the *New English Weekly* and Max Plowman in *Peace News*. Mairet observed shrewdly, 'It shows us the heart of innocence that lies in revolution; also the miasma of lying that, far more than the cruelty, takes the heart out of it,'[48] and Gorer concluded, 'Politically and as literature it is a work of first-class importance . . . George Orwell occupies a unique position among the younger English prose writers, a position which so far has prevented him getting his due recognition.'[49] Gorer had reason to stress this. Orwell had told him that he was convinced Gollancz was using every means to prevent his book being mentioned. He was even frightened, he said, that he might have him eliminated.[50] If this is what he told Gorer, it reveals how paranoid he now was about the Communists. After all, in Spain there were English commissars prepared to excuse 'the necessary murder' and sanction executions. 'An education in Marxism and similar creeds,' he wrote, 'consists largely in destroying your moral sense.'[51] Herbert Read wrote to say that his book was 'as good as anything that came out of the so-called Great War'. His referring to the Stalinists as 'the new Jesuits' would have struck a resounding chord with Orwell.[52] He hoped that Connolly would review the book, promising in turn to write up his *Enemies of Promise* when it appeared ('You scratch my back and I'll scratch yours') but, in the event, neither review was ever written.

There were hostile notices in the *Tablet*, however, from a Catholic critic who wondered why he had not troubled to get to know Fascist fighters and enquire about their motivations, in the *TLS*, from a Party-liner misrepresenting what Orwell had said (prompting an indignant letter from the author), and in the *Listener*, also from an obvious Communist, attacking the POUM but never mentioning the book – producing another angry response from Orwell. The *Listener's* literary editor, J. R. Ackerley, sided with Orwell, but the chance of a fair notice there was lost.[53] A somewhat ambivalent review in the *New Statesman* by V. S. Pritchett, appeased the editor no doubt by declaring Orwell politically naïve about Spain, but adding, 'No one excels him in bringing to the eyes, ears and nostrils the nasty ingredients of fevered situations; and I would recommend him warmly to all who are concerned about the realities of personal experience in a muddled cause.' When he heard how few copies Warburg had sold in three months Orwell was horrified, and wrote asking Moore to confirm the figures, fearing he had misread them. Gollancz and his friends, he now felt sure, were pressurising papers not to review it.

In what had come as a complete yet intriguing surprise, the previous November he had been invited by Desmond Young, editor of the *Lucknow Pioneer* in India, and later a distinguished war reporter, to work for him as a leader writer. The idea of returning to the land of his birth as a journalist, and to work for the *Pioneer*, as Kipling had, must have appealed greatly to the romantic in Orwell, and the chance to write against British imperialism was obviously a great temptation. But when Young approached the India Office in February he was discouraged from pursuing Orwell, who, because of his honesty and strength of character, was thought likely to cause trouble to the authorities.[54]

In fact he was in no condition to travel to India, or anywhere for that matter. Just before *Homage to Catalonia* appeared, after a week in bed with bronchitis, he began coughing up blood. It was extremely frightening for Eileen, who told Jack Common, 'The bleeding seemed prepared to go on for ever & on Sunday everyone agreed that Eric must be taken somewhere where really active steps could be taken if necessary – artificial pneumothorax to stop the blood or transfusion to replace it . . .'[55] Laurence O'Shaughnessy saw him and had him transferred immediately by ambulance to Preston Hall Village, a British Legion sanatorium, near Maidstone in Kent, where he was consultant thoracic surgeon. He was admitted on 17 March. Since childhood, hospitals had held a peculiar dread for him and he grumbled to Eileen about being sent to 'an institution devised for murder'.[56] But the fact that he was in the care of a doctor he knew clearly helped. Not only that, but he was put in a private room paid for by Laurence.

Hard work and neglect had taken their toll. Since returning from Spain, in addition to writing his book he had produced four articles, twelve reviews and several letters for publication. He was clearly exhausted, but still refusing to admit his wretched condition. Although no tubercle bacilli were found in his sputum, further tests told a rather different story, as his medical record reveals. The doctors found 'heavy mottling over the lower lobe of the left lung'. He was treated initially for pulmonary tuberculosis, but tests suggested 'bronchiectasis of the Left lung, with nonspecific fibrosis of the Right lung', and he was treated with injections of vitamin D. However, at the conclusion of their tests the doctors drew a darker conclusion, and a postscript to his report reads 'T. B. confirmed'.[57]

Even though, finally, he had to face up to the bad news, he still tried to play it down, telling Stephen Spender, 'I am afraid from what they say it is TB all right but evidently a very old lesion and not serious.'[58] Two weeks later, writing to Gorer, the old complacent Orwell had returned, denying the cruel reality of his broken health. 'I am much better,' he wrote, 'in fact I really doubt whether there is anything wrong with me.'[59] (Years later, clearly diagnosed as having full-blown tuberculosis, he blamed it on the freezing Spanish winter he had spent shivering and coughing in the trenches on the Aragón front. But he could have acquired it at any time in his life – as a child, out in Burma, among tramps, even in a Paris hospital.)

He was ordered to rest and refrain even from 'literary research' for three months. It was particularly galling for Orwell, who already had another novel in mind. In December he had outlined the idea to Moore: 'It will be about a man who is having a holiday and trying to make a temporary escape from his responsibilities, public and private. The title I thought of is "Coming Up For Air".'[60] Escaping from reality, of course, is just what he found so unacceptable and difficult to understand in Henry Miller, the fatalist who himself advocated living like Jonah, 'inside the whale'. Orwell clearly wanted to explore this tendency in himself, a tendency already explored in a less political context in the 'escapes' of Dorothy Hare and Gordon Comstock. But the man who most needed air was George Orwell, the man whose lungs were refusing to work for him.

Two and half months after his admission he was still unable to get the novel started. Eileen told Leonard Moore that 'the book seethes in his head and he is very anxious to get on with it', but surrounded by movement and noise it was not easy to work.[61] She told Lydia Jackson it was a novel 'about a man with a couple of impossible children and a nagging wife'.[62] His hope was to escape from the shadowland of European politics into sunlit uplands of literature, but he knew that was not possible. As he told Jack Common in May, 'The rest . . . has made me keen to get started . . . though when I came here I had been thinking that what with Hitler, Stalin & the rest of them the day of novel-writing was over. As it is if I start it in August I daresay I'll have to finish it in the concentration camp.'[63] The novel he was writing was somehow different, a first-person narrative with past, present and future ponderings mimicking the mind's reflective movements and Orwell's own attempt to see a way through the chaos of the times providing a political commentary. But he could not hope to do any serious work until the summer and would not be able to let Gollancz have the book until Christmas at the earliest. Meanwhile he killed time doing crossword puzzles and worrying about the state of his garden.

He felt a bit isolated in a private room, but was able to mix a little with other patients and receive visitors. Once a fortnight Eileen took the tortuous journey from Wallington to Maidstone (two buses to London, a trip across the city and a train down to Kent and back), once accompanied by her admirer Karl Schnetzler. There were also visits from Douglas Moyle, Reginald Reynolds and his wife Ethel Mannin, Stephen Spender and Lydia Jackson. Denys King-Farlow came more than once, and Max and Dorothy Plowman brought the novelist L. H. Myers, another Old Etonian, who had long admired Orwell's work and was keen to meet him. Eileen, in fact, had written to all of his friends with news of his illness and this produced a spate of sympathetic letters and promises to visit. Richard Rees, still in Spain, wrote as soon as he heard of his illness. But Orwell was less worried about his health than his literary future. He continued to express anger with the dictators for interrupting his career now it was in its own rocky way at last launched. 'I . . . see a lot of things that I want to do and to continue doing for another thirty years or so, and the idea that I've got to abandon them and either be bumped off or depart to some filthy concentration camp just infuriates me.'[64]

Spender found him endearingly phoney. He thought that the deliberate descent into tramping had been an act, turning himself into a make-believe member of the working class. However, he did not find this annoying. 'Even his phoniness was perfectly acceptable, I think. Orwell had something about him like a character in a Charlie Chaplin movie, if not like Charlie Chaplin himself. He was a person who was always playing a role, but with great pathos and great sincerity. He probably impressed us more than he impressed the working class; in fact, I'm sure he did. I always found him a very nice and rather amusing kind of man to be with.'[65] Jon Kimche had observed this role-playing element in Orwell previously; Anthony Powell and Michael Foot would notice it later, and Ruth Pitter noted his 'dual nature'. Most intriguing to Spender was Orwell's telling him that, although he had attacked him, he had changed his mind on meeting him. 'It is partly for this reason that I don't mix much in literary circles,' he said, 'because I know from experience that once I have met & spoken to anyone I shall never again be able to show any intellectual brutality towards him, even when I feel that I ought to, like the Labour MPs who get patted on the back by dukes & are lost forever more.'[66]

One visitor who intrigued him was John Sceats, a contributor to

Ida Limouzin and Eric at his baptism in Motihari, 1903

Marjorie, Avril and Eric at home in Henley, *c.* 1909

Eric (in the back row, second from right), one of the bugle boys of St Cyprian's School Corps

Eric, Ida, Avril and Richard in his lieutenant's uniform, probably at home on leave, in 1918

Eric, aged fourteen, with Prosper and Guinever Buddicom

Jacintha Buddicom

Eric (third from left) and Cyril Connolly (second from right, drinking from a water bottle), at the Eton Field Day in 1920

Eric (back row, first from left) at Eton, in the 1921 college Wall Game team. He was extremely proud to win his Wall Game colours, his only significant sporting achievement at Eton

Eric the delinquent, smoking on his way back from swimming at 'Athens' on the Thames near Eton

Philip Yorke, whom Eric and his friend Runciman thought they had killed through sympathetic magic

The Mandalay Police Training School, *c.* 1923. Orwell is in the back row, third from left, an aloof and solitary figure in the ranks of the *sahib-log*

Henri Barbusse, editor of *Monde*, friend of Eugène Adam and the first to publish the adult work of Eric Blair

Orwell in his tramp's uniform, on his return to England

The Hôpital Cochin, the Parisian hospital for the poor where Orwell spent just over two weeks in March 1929 with 'une grippe'. It was here that he seems to have had a vision of his own death

Eric's father Richard, on his daily stroll through Southwold, perhaps on his way to the Blyth Club

Ida Blair in the 1930s. She ran a bridge club in Southwold which met at the Copper Kettle, Avril's teashop

Eric before (or after) a swim on the beach with the family dog, Hector

The three Peters boys (right to left, Maurice, Richard and Kenneth), whom Eric supervised during their school holidays, and taught to make home-made bombs

Brenda Salkeld, gym mistress at St Felix Girls' Grammar School, Southwold. She was the object of Eric's unrequited passion, and he suggested a *ménage à trois* to her with his first wife, Eileen O'Shaughnessy

Kay Welton, whom Eric met at the Hampstead bookshop in which he worked, and with whom he carried on an affair even after he had proposed to Eileen

Sally Jerome, another bookshop girlfriend, who rebuffed Eric's sexual advances. She probably gave him the character of Rosemary in *Keep the Aspidistra Flying*

Mabel Fierz, Eric's lover, who found an agent for *Down and Out in Paris and London*, in her garden with Eric and a neighbour's daughter

Michael Sayers, Irish poet and critic. He shared a flat with Eric and Rayner Heppenstall in 1935 and described their relationship as 'homerotic'. He discovered 'Eric Orwell' copying passages from Swift and Maugham, in an attempt to produce a prose devoid of adjectives

Rayner Heppenstall. Orwell terminated their friendship in a fight and threw him out of their shared flat in Kentish Town. They later made up and were friends thereafter

Laurence O'Shaughnessy, a brilliant young surgeon and Orwell's brother-in-law, who applauded his 'warrior cast of mind'. He was killed at Dunkirk

Eileen O'Shaughnessy, who abandoned her career as a psychologist for a literary life as Orwell's wife

The Stores, Wallington. In Orwell's day it was a dilapidated cottage with a corrugated iron roof. The rose in the front garden is the Woolworth's rose he planted there in 1936

Orwell feeding Muriel, the goat he named after one of his Limouzin aunts

Bob Smillie, whose death in a Spanish jail converted Orwell into a lifelong and deadly adversary of the Stalinist Communists

Frank Frankford, who first deserted the POUM ranks, then signed a statement for the Communists testifying to collaboration between the POUM and the Fascists

David Crook. A photograph from the KGB files of the man sent to spy on the ILP contingent in Barcelona – on John McNair, George Kopp and the Blairs in particular

Orwell and Eileen in the POUM lines in Catalonia. Orwell is the tallest figure at the back; Eileen is kneeling in front of him

Orwell among members of the International Brigade at the beginning of May 1937. He was planning to join their ranks, but the events of the following days turned him against the Communists

George Kopp, Orwell's commander, imprisoned and tortured by the Communists on trumped-up charges. Winston Smith's torture by rats in *Nineteen Eighty-Four* owes something to Kopp's prison experiences

The Communist poster Orwell saw in Barcelona, urging that the Fifth Column be crushed ruthlessly. It gave him the terrifying line in his final novel: 'If you want a picture of the future, imagine a boot stamping on a human face – for ever'

Orwell at the ILP summer school in 1937. Left to right: John McNair, Douglas Moyle, Stafford Cottman, Orwell, John Branthwaite

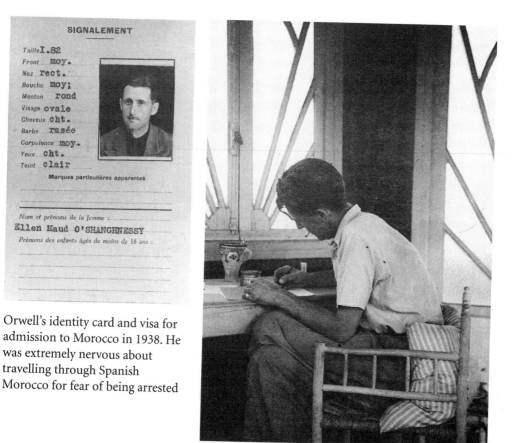

SIGNALEMENT

Taille 1.82
Front moy.
Nez rect.
Bouche moy;
Menton rond
Visage ovale
Cheveux cht.
Barbe rasée
Corpulence moy.
Yeux cht.
Teint clair

Marques particulières apparentes

Nom et prénoms de la femme :
Ellen Maud O'SHANGHNESSY

Prénoms des enfants âgés de moins de 18 ans :

Orwell's identity card and visa for admission to Morocco in 1938. He was extremely nervous about travelling through Spanish Morocco for fear of being arrested

Orwell at work in the Villa Simont just outside Marrakech, where he completed *Coming Up For Air*

Victor Gollancz, Orwell's first publisher. He published *The Road to Wigan Pier*, despite greatly disliking the second half, but later refused *Homage to Catalonia* and thereby lost the author of *Animal Farm* and *Nineteen Eighty-Four*

Fredric Warburg, who had the courage to publish *Homage to Catalonia*, and won Orwell's loyalty and friendship

David Astor, *Observer* editor, staunch friend and best man at Orwell's second marriage

Cyril Connolly, Orwell's old school friend, who praised *Burmese Days*, slated *Keep the Aspidistra Flying*, but published some of Orwell's best essays in *Horizon*

Orwell at the BBC, recording one of his 'Voice' magazine programmes. Left to right, standing: Orwell, Nancy Parratt (secretary), William Empson. Sitting: Venu Chitale, J. M. Tambimuttu, T. S. Eliot, Una Marson, Mulk Raj Anand, Christopher Pemberton, Narayan Menon

Stevie Smith. Two characters in her novel *The Holiday* represented what she saw as two halves of the schizophrenic Orwell, one a homosexual Spanish Civil War veteran, the other a 'lanky melancholic murderous mad sadist'

Inez Holden, with whom Orwell had a 'fling' during the war and who hoped to marry him after Eileen's death

Arthur Koestler. In 1941 he bet five bottles of burgundy that within five years Orwell would be a great best-seller. His *Darkness at Noon* was a strong influence on *Nineteen Eighty-Four*

Tosco Fyvel, who first saw Orwell as 'a seedy sahib' but came to admire him greatly, although they disagreed strongly about Zionism

Julian Symons. Orwell first called him 'vaguely Fascist', but later apologised – both directly and in print – and earned himself another lifelong friend and admirer

Jon Kimche, who worked with Orwell at Booklovers' Corner in Hampstead in the mid-thirties and later at *Tribune*. He thought 'George Orwell' was an act, a carefully cultivated literary alter ego

George with Richard. Orwell had long wanted a child and he became a devoted father to Richard, who was adopted just before Eileen died, caring for the boy as well as any mother

Avril digging for peat

Eileen's grave. Orwell planted a polyantha rose on it, the rose that was later planted on his own grave

Barnhill, with its tent for harvest workers. In the top-floor attic room Orwell completed and typed *Nineteen Eighty-Four*

Sonia Brownell, Orwell's second wife, who may have seen him as a 'cause' through whom she could expiate guilt feelings about a death she felt responsible for in her youth. According to friends, Orwell was 'nuts' about her

The resting place of Eric Blair in the churchyard at Sutton Courtenay. As an unbeliever he did not properly qualify for burial in sacred ground, but David Astor persuaded the local vicar, who in turn had to persuade his church wardens. One only agreed after seeing a copy of *Animal Farm*

HERE LIES
ERIC ARTHUR BLAIR
BORN JUNE 25TH 1903
DIED JANUARY 21ST 1950

Sonia en route to Hollywood for the premier of *Animal Farm*, 1954. When she saw the film she hated its doctored ending, and felt she had betrayed Orwell in some way. Thereafter she refused to allow it to be shown in schools

Controversy, whose articles Orwell admired. They spent a day together discussing *Homage to Catalonia*, and the prospect of war with Germany. To Sceats Orwell seemed defeatist on the question of war, feeling that Fascism within would be the main problem, and the need to oppose it through secret political activity and the use of clandestine presses. The fact that his visitor had once worked as an insurance salesman gave Orwell the occupation of the central character in his new novel. Even though he was unable to get down to serious work, the character of 'Tubby' George Bowling was obviously evolving.

It was spring when Lydia visited him. The time of year and his improved health probably led to a situation which, according to her, left her profoundly embarrassed. Orwell took her for a stroll through the sanatorium grounds and, to her embarrassment made a sudden pass to which she responded. She did so, she said, out of pity for the man but in truth found contact with him distasteful, and felt guilty because of Eileen. Unfortunately for her she failed to make her feelings clear enough to Orwell and he was encouraged to think she welcomed his attentions. Perhaps it was Bowling (the fat man struggling to get out of the emaciated Orwell) whose wayward lusts were being rehearsed in this moment of dalliance.[67]

In June he joined the Independent Labour Party. That warrior cast of mind which had urged him to fight in Spain had been supplanted by a pacifism based on opposition to the Popular Front policy of the Communists, which he saw as yet another racket – to lure the democracies into a war against Fascism, a war that he thought would not defeat Fascism but simply bring it to Britain. The ILP served no moneyed interest and he found its vision of socialism closer to his own than that of any other party.[68] But he was in no mood or condition to accept an invitation to attend the Eton Collegers Dinner held on 7 July at the Park Lane Hotel. King-Farlow and members of his Election, saluted their sick schoolfellow afterwards, sending him the menu, signed by all present, bearing the slogan, 'Homage to Blair'. It was a kind recognition of his latest work by erstwhile readers of *College Days*.

When finally allowed to do a little writing he reviewed *Assignment in Utopia* by Eugene Lyons who had spent several years in the USSR, witnessing starvation in the Ukraine, the Five-Year Plan and the all-pervading power of the secret police. 'The system that Mr Lyons describes,' he wrote, 'does not seem to be very different from Fascism.' All real power was in the hands of the few, the proletariat 'reduced to a status resembling serfdom'. 'The GPU are everywhere, everyone lives in constant terror of denunciation, freedom of speech and of the press are obliterated to an extent we can hardly imagine.' There were periodic waves of terror, 'liquidations' of whole peoples, idiotic show trials, betrayals of parents by their children, while the invisible Stalin was worshipped like a Roman Emperor. Here too one was expected to accept unquestioningly all pronouncements by the omniscient and omnipotent ruler. If 2+2=5 (the slogan for the Soviet Five-Year Plan) so be it. Lyons had interviewed the dictator and, like Wells, found him 'human, simple and likeable'. But, observed the old College cynic, Al Capone was a good husband and father, and the Brides in the Bath murderer was deeply loved by his first wife.[69] Lyons's description of a totalitarian state was a foreshadow of the fictional state Orwell himself created out of the nightmare of Spain which would consume him until the end of his life. It was one that would be glimpsed also in his next novel. By the end of June he was able to report to Leonard Moore that he had complete a sketch of it, and also a pamphlet on pacifism.

He was to remain at the sanatorium for five and a half months, by which time he had gained nine pounds. That summer it was decided that he needed to go abroad, 'somewhere south' to convalesce for the coming winter. He asked Yvonne Davet, a French woman who was translating *Homage to Catalonia*, to help find him a place beside the Mediterranean, and suggested to Common that he might like to have the Wallington cottage rent-free in return for looking after the animals – thirty chickens and two goats – and George's lovingly tended garden.

The idea of the south of France was dropped when Laurence suggested Morocco which, according to a French colleague, would be both equable and dry, the perfect place for a man in his condition. The only snag was that their money had again run out. Their plight came to the ears of L. H. Myers who arranged with Max Plowman to send them an anonymous gift of £300 to cover their expenses. Myers was a wealthy Marxist who readily gave away his money (from a sense of guilt, according to Orwell). He never knew the source of this money but happily accepted it on the understanding that it be regarded as a loan.

They planned to travel to Marrakech via Gibraltar, Tangier and Casablanca, while Common and his wife moved into The Stores. Marx was evacuated temporarily to the Dakins' new home in Bristol, after accompanying Eileen on a brief visit to Windermere, probably to commune with the Lake poets. Later, together, they visited Southwold, where Richard Blair was in failing health. Now eighty-one, he had still not been persuaded that his son could make anything of his life from writing. What this old Tory thought of having fathered a boy who was a socialist and had fought with Communists in Spain, can only be surmised.

Just before leaving for Morocco Orwell began a Domestic Diary, mostly nature notes following the tradition of Gilbert White and W. H. Hudson, which he kept up throughout his time in Africa and on his return to

Wallington. They reveal his love of lists, of detail, of how things work and his encyclopaedic knowledge of flora and fauna. His old teacher Mr Sillar's enthusiasm had produced a more-than-enthusiastic disciple.

When Orwell left England, there was always the hope of escaping to a better future. On 3 September he and Eileen sailed from Tilbury tourist class on the SS *Stratheden*. It was Orwell's second voyage out through the Bay of Biscay and he must have looked with some amusement on the colonials and their memsahibs heading East to take up the white man's burden. On the passenger list he had designated himself 'Profession – Novelist', while Eileen had written 'Profession – Nil'. He had taken a patent seasickness remedy which he was pleased to find worked, and, according to Eileen, 'walked around the boat with a seraphic smile watching people being sick & insisted on my going to the "Ladies' Cabin" to report on disasters there'.[70]

On board the *Stratheden* he had a strange reunion. Tony Hyams, his old pupil from Frays College, was also a passenger, travelling with his mother to the Sudan where his father was in government service. He spotted Mr Blair standing alone on the deck one day and went up to say hello. Orwell was quite pleased to see him but seemed preoccupied. He told Hyams that, having fought in Spain, he was now terrified that, passing through Spanish Morocco to reach Marrakech he might be arrested and end up in a concentration camp.[71] The terror inspired in Catalonia obviously lingered.

From Gibraltar they went by boat to Tangier, and next day ran the Spanish gauntlet into French Morocco without incident. The following day they arrived in Marrakech where they chose the highly recommended Hotel Continental. However, as Eileen told Ida Blair, it might have been quite good once, but 'lately it has changed hands & is obviously a brothel', something she noticed immediately but George did not. They quickly moved to the cheaper, more respectable Majestic, where Eileen took to her bed with a fever while George made plans for them to move into a villa of their own.[72]

Although surrounded by luxuriant groves and gardens and set on the Blad el Hamra plain with spectacular views of the Atlas Mountains, Marrakech was in a state of some decay. Apart from the impressive palace of the sultan and its imperial parks, and the dominant presence of the Katubia Mosque, many areas were crime-ridden slums. They found a villa outside the town but were unable to move in for a month, so were stuck meantime in a city they found uncongenial. The countryside around was practically all desert; in Marrakech itself the native quarter was, according to Eileen, picturesque, but with smells which were only rivalled by the noise.[73]

The day after they arrived, Neville Chamberlain flew to Munich to discuss Hitler's demand to incorporate the Sudetenland into his Third Reich. Orwell noted the lack of interest in the local papers and the refusal to believe that a war was likely. 'The whole thing seems to me so utterly mean-ingless,' he told Common, 'that I think I shall just concentrate on remaining alive.'[74] At that moment his lungs must have seemed a greater threat to his health than the Wehrmacht or the menacing prospect of a Fascist Britain. However, letters from England spoke of war fever – air-raid shelters being built, gas masks being issued, and pro- and anti-war demonstrations in London. Both he and Eileen were firmly in the anti-war camp. Eileen thought that had they been at home George would probably have landed in jail, but they were strangely supportive of the Conservative Prime Minister. Eileen wrote to her sister-in-law Marjorie, 'It's very odd to feel that Chamberlain is our only hope, but I do believe he doesn't want war either at the moment & certainly the man has courage.' They decided that the English people, given a voice, would not want a war either, but would fight if a war was declared.[75]

They were finding Marrakech not much to their liking – interesting but dreadful to live in. 'There are beautiful arches with vile smells coming out of them & adorable children covered in ringworm and flies,' wrote Eileen, and an open space which they thought a lovely spot for observing the sunset turned out to be a graveyard.[76] It was, Orwell told Connolly, 'a beastly dull country' – no forests, no wild animals and the people near the big towns 'utterly debauched by the tourist racket' which had turned them into 'a race of beggars and curio-sellers'.[77] The place seemed so unhealthy, that they wondered how a leading doctor could recommend it as a place to convalesce.

Arab funerals both fascinated and horrified them. Eileen described one to Gorer: 'The Arabs favour bright green [shrouds] & don't have coffins which is nice on funeral days for the flies who leave even a restaurant for a few minutes to sample a passing corpse.'[78] This memorable and revolting image would form the opening to an Orwell essay on Marrakech, and sug-gests that key ideas in his later work may have emerged from mutual observations and discussion with the poetic Eileen.

In their temporary villa, Orwell worked on his novel, kept up his diary and wrote regularly to his parents and friends. In his diary he monitored the daily press, observed the strange ethnic composition of the French colonial forces, noted the effect of a two-year drought, the prevalence of female labour on French estates, the large numbers of homeless, beggars and street children, the blackmailing tourist guides and the poverty and squalor of the Jewish quarter. As in Burma he hoped to visit a place of worship to talk to Muslim priests but found the mosques closed to foreigners. He was fasci-nated by the veiled Arab women, by the Touareg tribesmen and the French Foreign Legionnaires, who seemed to him surprisingly puny. He was hoping vaguely to write a book about Morocco on his return to England, where his future looked a little insecure. With the sales of *Homage to Catalonia* so poor, he faced the prospect of returning with little more than £50 to his name and a debt of £300.[79]

War to him was a nightmare prospect, not only because he had a vision of Fascism and the concentration camp descending on England, but also saw his writing plans for the coming thirty years under threat. A sense of isolation and defeatism threatened to overwhelm him. He and Eileen planned to survive if possible if only to 'add to the number of sane people'.[80] He signed several ILP anti-war manifestos, one asserting 'the need for resisting political censorship and the suppression of truth'. In this frame of his mind his new novel was taking shape – 'Tubby' Bowling was articulating his pacifist sentiments and seeking comfort in memories of the England of his childhood.

When Chamberlain returned from Munich at the end of September clutching his 'piece of paper' signed by Hitler, guaranteeing peace, Orwell recorded his relief. 'Thank goodness the war danger seems to be over, at any rate for the time being, so we can breathe again.'[81] They were in one mind over this. Eileen told Geoffrey Gorer, 'I am determined to be pleased with Chamberlain because I want a rest.'[82]

With the weather growing hot and intolerable, in October they moved to their new home, the Villa Simont, which stood in an orange grove at the foot of the Atlas mountains. They furnished it cheaply from the bazaars and attempted to recreate their Wallington life by keeping chickens and goats and even growing a few vegetables. Orwell soon buckled down to work, reviewing two books on Spain for the *New English Weekly*, producing an article, 'Political Reflections on the Crisis' for the *Adelphi*, attacking 'gangster and pansy' warmongers, and continuing with his novel.

The fate of the POUM leaders on trial in Spain began to concern him, and he wrote to various people seeking their support. But Moscow's attempt to mount a show trial against the Spanish 'Trotskyists' failed when their confessions, extracted under threat, were retracted in court, and the charges were shown to be preposterous. As yet, Republican Spain was not a Soviet dictatorship, but Orwell was suitably horrified when British papers such as the *News Chronicle* and *Observer* and pro-Franco French papers reported that they had been found guilty. 'It gives one the feeling that our civilization is going down into a sort of mist of lies where it will be impossible ever to find out the truth about anything.'[83] Another dimension of his nightmare – the end of truth – seemed to be getting that much closer.

Much to his disgust, in November he became ill and was confined to bed for three weeks. 'What with all this illness,' he told John Sceats, 'I've decided to count 1938 as a blank year and sort of cross it off the calendar.'[84] In that frame of mind he was cheered by a request from Penguin Books for permission to republish one of his novels in paperback. He offered *Burmese Days, Down and Out in Paris and London,* and *Keep the Aspidistra Flying* (which later he would want suppressed, along with *A Clergyman's Daughter,* written, he said, simply for money).[85] As the weather improved and there were signs of things growing, his health showed some improvement, he coughed less and began putting on a little weight. Their hens were laying, their two goats kept them well-supplied with milk, and they acquired bicycles for shopping excursions to the town bazaars.[86]

In his essay, 'Marrakech', Orwell captured the drift of his thoughts about the place. It begins with that disturbingly gruesome image Eileen had conjured up for Gorer: 'As the corpse went past the flies left the restaurant table in a cloud and rushed after it, but they came back a few minutes later.' It developed into a methodical attack on European imperialism. Somehow the hurried funerals, the shallow burial ground, 'merely a huge waste of hummocky earth', symbolised for him the degradation to which imperialism condemned whole populations, in Morocco as much as in Burma. In a few vivid images he captured the wretchedness of the people's lives: the neglected graveyard, the wolfish hunger of the poor, their windowless homes, crowds of sore-eyed children clustered like flies, the swarming Jewish ghetto, the back-breaking misery of peasant life, shrunken old women 'mummified by age and the sun', invisible under heavy bundles of firewood. But finally he wondered how long it would be before the black colonial soldiers he saw would turn their guns on their French masters.[87]

Writing *Coming Up For Air* focused his mind on his childhood, and he discovered how very retentive a memory he had. He told Jack Common, 'It's suddenly revealed to me a big subject which I'd never really touched before and haven't time to work out now.' Reflecting a fortnight later on his family and idyllic days in Henley and Shiplake, he had conceived the idea for a further novel, in fact a trilogy. 'I have been bitten with the desire to write a Saga. I don't know that in a novelist this is not the sign of premature senile decay, but I have the idea for an enormous novel in three parts which would take about five years to write.'[88] Since he thought himself incapable of perpetuating the Blair line, at least he could leave some trace behind by enshrining his family history in a novel – yet another reason not to want a European war.

　　Doubtless in that same mood of nostalgia he and Eileen passed their spare time reading Dickens, Thackeray, Trollope and Henry James to one another. Connolly may have helped prompt this plunge into literary nostalgia. His *Enemies of Promise,* of which Orwell had now seen reviews, dwelt on his Eton and prep school years, reliving memories with which he had long wrestled and which he would deal with head-on in his own later reminiscence of St Cyprian's. His passion for Dickens and other nineteenth-century novelists stemmed from his schooldays, and rereading them was another way of returning there in imagination. In that world an England threatened by war would have been unthinkable.

However, with the left baying for a Popular Front war 'in defence of democracy', and Chamberlain, having bought time at Munich, now slowly gearing up to confront Hitler, the outlook for peace looked uncertain. In the New Year he wrote, in some secrecy, to Herbert Read, the anarchist, suggesting that, in anticipation of this, they should organise a clandestine press to ensure that a dissenting voice could continue to be heard once the totalitarian darkness descended.[89]

George Kopp, in Paris and free at last, got a letter to them which can only have intensified Orwell's nightmares. Kopp described in detail his eighteen months in prison, how he had been isolated, beaten and left in a dark room overrun by rats. When he refused to sign papers admitting collaboration with Franco and implicating others, his Communist gaolers had attempted to poison him, and then to work him to death. He was released finally when Belgian trade unions put pressure on the Republican Government through the Belgian embassy, but his health was shattered and he had lost seven stone. By now, however, the Francoists were winning the Spanish war, the power of the Communists and NKVD was reduced, and Barcelona was a shambles. The 'war for democracy' in Spain was about to be lost.

In the New Year a draft of Coming Up For Air was completed, and he and Eileen left for a week's break at Taddert in the Atlas Mountains. He was very struck by the Berbers who lived there, especially the women. '[They] are fascinating people,' he told Gorer, ' . . . & the women have the most wonderful eyes. But what fascinates me about them is that they are so dirty. You will see exquisitely beautiful women walking about with their necks almost invisible under dirt.'[90] He later told the wife of a friend that 'he found himself increasingly attracted to the young Arab girls and the moment came when he told Eileen that he had to have one of these girls . . . Eileen agreed and so he had his Arab girl.'[91] In his diary he only hinted at the attraction they held for him. 'All the women have tattooing on their chins and sometimes down each cheek. Their manner is less timid than most Arab women.'[92] Harold Acton, the Old Etonian aesthete, reported him enthusing not only about the 'sweetness' of Burmese women but also about the beauties of Morocco. 'This cadaverous ascetic whom one scarcely connected with fleshly gratification admitted that he had seldom tasted such bliss as with certain Moroccan girls, whose complete naturalness and grace and candid sensuality he described in language so simple and direct that one could visualise their slender flanks and pointed breasts, and almost sniff the odour of spices that clung to their satiny skins.'[93] Eileen's friend Lettice Cooper neatly summed up this aspect of Orwell. 'I don't think George was the kind of person who likes being married all the time,' she said.[94]

His encounter with the Berber women and the mood of secrecy he had shared with Herbert Read perhaps inspired him to write to Lydia Jackson, in the hope of pursuing further their amorous encounter at Preston Hall. As with Read, he asked her to keep his letters secret. 'So looking forward to seeing you!' he wrote. 'I have thought of you so often – have you thought about me, I wonder? I know it's indiscreet to write such things in letters, but you'll be clever and burn this, will you? . . . Take care of yourself. Hoping to see you early in April. With love. Eric.'[95] He wrote to her again but neither letter appears to have brought a reply.

Their plan was to return directly to England by boat from Casablanca at the end of March (thereby avoiding Spanish territory), then find a house somewhere a little warmer and further south than Wallington. Dorset was the preferred choice, no doubt reflecting his prevailing mood of nostalgia and urge to write a family saga. With his father's life approaching its end, how better to get back to his Blair roots than to live in the county of his paternal ancestors? His novel was almost finished, and as usual he thought it good only in parts. Now his mind turned homewards – to the flowers, the rhubarb, Muriel and Kate. He wrote asking Common if he would mind putting up Kopp, presently convalescing in Greenwich with the O'Shaughnessys. Kopp, however, declined the invitation. Perhaps the primitive cottage sounded too much like the grim conditions he had just escaped in Spain.

On 28 March 1939 they sailed from Casablanca on board the SS *Yasukunimaru*, a Japanese liner bound for London from Yokohama. The weather was good and he hardly needed his seasickness pills. Arriving in London, the first thing he did was deliver to Moore the manuscript of *Coming Up For Air*, which Eileen had typed just before they left. One thing about it made him rather proud – there was not a single semi-colon in it. It was an unnecessary stop, he had decided, and had to be banished. He was still unhappy about Gollancz. 'If he tries to bugger me abt I think I shall leave him,' he had told Common.[96] He then hurried to Lydia's flat in Woburn Place, and was disappointed to find her out, even though he had cabled ahead to be sure she was there.

Unable to linger, he travelled on to Southwold, where his father's condition continued to deteriorate and his mother was also ill with phlebitis. From there he rang Lydia three times, without success, so wrote to her complaining that she had let him down. When Eileen arrived at Montague House he had gone down with flu and taken to his bed. But his mind was still on Lydia. As if she had not ignored his letters and avoided him, he wrote to her again, apologising for not turning up and promising to meet her when next in London.[97] However, she was not, she claimed, at all flattered by his attentions. 'I was annoyed by his assuming that I would conceal our meetings from Eileen, revolted by deception creeping in against my wishes. I wanted to avoid meeting him when I was in that hostile mood, capable of pushing him away if he tried to embrace me.'[98] At this stage, it was a strange, one-sided affair, conducted by an apparently self-deluded Casanova. However, she did reply to him later, and even agreed to see him, though, according to her, only on a platonic basis.

After his bout of flu, his brother-in-law Laurence referred him to the Miller Chest Hospital to see Herbert Morlock, a Harley Street consultant, inventor of the bronchoscope. Orwell was duly tested, and confirmed as having bronchiectatis, an enlargement and distention of the bronchial tubes leaving the lungs prone to infection – a condition possibly caused by childhood pneumonia and explaining that 'chronic cough' to which he was still susceptible. Morlock was a breezy extrovert who wore morning dress, stiff shirts and cuffs, a cravat with a pearl pin and (when out) a silk top hat. Blithely he told Orwell not to worry about coughing up blood; it might even be good for him.[99] Orwell was impressed with the up-beat manner of this colourful character, and years later, when he was very much worse, he expressed a repeated wish to see him again. After his tests Orwell spent a week with the O'Shaughnessys in Greenwich.

The novel he had left with Moore reflected the state of mind in which Orwell faced the prospect of war. Many of the acute fears he felt at this time permeate *Coming Up For Air* – a repetition of 1914 and the abolition of truth, the bombing of towns and the threat of the concentration camp. Isolation in Morocco had distanced him from the daily ebb and flow of news and the prevailing air of crisis which would have engulfed him in England. Apart from events and yet part of them, he was able to achieve a novel that was both highly personal and yet politically and socially perceptive at the same time. Its first person narrator is his self-reflective alter ego and social commentator rolled into one. As he himself said of fiction-writers, 'By their subject-matter ye shall know them.'

He hoped it would offend Gollancz, with its sneers at young Communists and its guying of Left Book Club meetings, even if it meant losing the £100 advance on acceptance specified in his contract. But neither the sneers nor the satirical jibes put off the publisher who paid up promptly and put the novel on his list for publication in June. If *A Clergyman's Daughter* was the Orwell novel most influenced by Joyce, *Coming Up For Air* is more suggestive of Proust. But whereas it is a subtle taste that triggers the memory of the author of *A La Recherche du Temps Perdu*, here it is sparked by a veritable spectrum of smells. This was no mere device, and can only be an honest account of how memory worked for the author attempting consciously to recapture a forgotten past. More obviously it is a novel in Wellsian vein, the tale of a 'little man' trying to make sense of the modern world – 'Wells watered down', Orwell called it.

George Bowling (a surname borrowed from the old folk song about Tom Bowling or perhaps from Smollett's *Roderick Random*) is, like all Orwell's protagonists, trapped in a soul-destroying routine and champing to get free. The action begins with Orwell's usual chronological precision. 'I remember the morning well. At about a quarter to eight I'd nipped out of bed and got into the bathroom just in time to shut the kids out.' He has been fitted with his first set of false teeth and feels that his life is already more than half over. A newspaper headline and a whiff of horse dung arouse memories and stir longings, and soon George is set upon rediscovering the Golden Age of his past. A win at the races tempts him into truancy – a lie to his wife, an illicit trip to the small town where he grew up, with its memories of boyhood adventures in a bygone age. He is also in search of Katie Simmons, the love of his youth and the idyllic countryside where he played, but above all the hidden pool where he dreamed one day of fishing for a massive and elusive pike. There again is the Laurentian reverie, recalling his first taste of sex with Katie out in the open fields. Here, in Orwell's memorable phrase, is his 'thin man struggling to get out' of the fat insurance salesman. Not only is Bowling fat but unattractive in many other ways – worn down by a loveless marriage, the expense of a family, children who despise him, a man henpecked by a colourless money-obsessed wife and her carping mother. Of course, his journey is doomed – the small town had been engulfed by suburbia and his woodland paradise infested with fruit juice-drinking, sandal-wearing, nudist vegetarians, and Garden City cranks. The Golden Age is done for, Katie, his childhood sweetheart, is now a worn out middle-aged drab and the secret pool with its giant pike, the symbolic centre of his childhood fantasy, turned into a rubbish dump. The horrors of mass society have overwhelmed the holy places and Doomsday threatens in the form of Hitler, Stalin and their streamlined battalions, dedicated to ruling through terror, the distortion of the truth and the elimination of the past. George returns to his bourgeois prison to face again his nagging wife and unlovable children. The Paradise Gained was no more than a sad illusion.

Coming Up For Air was published on 12 June. Gollancz ('that Stalinist publisher', Orwell now called him) is said to have disapproved of it politically, but published it nevertheless – perhaps to deflect accusations of prejudice against a dissident leftist, and perhaps because he saw in its singularly oracular quality a book that would strike a chord with readers. If so, his judgement was sound. It proved to be a novel of the moment, catching the mood of nervous tension widespread during that uncertain summer of 1939, and the feeling that an old world, already fading over the past two decades, was about to pass away for ever. The *TLS* made it a Recommended Novel of the Week, highlighting a passage that had clearly touched the imagination of its anonymous critic:

> And yet I've enough sense to see that the old life we're used to is being sawn off at the roots. I can feel it happening. I can see the war that's coming and I can see the after-war, the food-queues and the secret police and the loud-speakers telling you what to think . . . There are millions of others like me . . . They can feel things cracking and collapsing under their feet.[100]

The reviewer noted that the book's indirect, 'conversational and slangy' style, which made it so readable, carried not just a narrative but a running commentary on the state of the world. The author seemed to be saying that the old way of story-telling was over and readers must nerve themselves for the bad times ahead.[101] There was also applause from *The Times*, heralding it as the answer to 'one of the age's puzzles' – 'the cult of the "little man"'.[102]

Kate O'Brien in the *Spectator*, thought it 'above average' but not as sharp as *Keep the Aspidistra Flying*, and detected signs of haste and weariness. She did, however, note that Orwell 'manages to make his novels easily distinguishable from those of other people', perhaps the first public recognition of the authentically 'Orwellian' voice.[103] There was recognition, too, in the national press, where James Agate featured it prominently in his book column for the *Daily Express*. Most interesting, and perhaps significant, was a letter from Max Plowman who wrote, 'My Golly! What a book! I could write another about it . . . It's done to the life and your little man lives all right & so gets his immortality,' adding the strangely portentous after-thought, 'Imagining I know you, I rather hope you've started on a Fairy Tale by way of reaction!'[104] Plowman was right, and, if Orwell is to be believed, that fairy tale was already ticking away in his mind and had been doing so for the past two years.

Two weeks after his book appeared his father's condition worsened, and Orwell went home to Southwold to be with him. On 25 June, George's thirty-sixth birthday, Richard was close to death. That day, the *Sunday Times* carried a review of his novel. At the very last it must have seemed that an erring son had somehow redeemed himself. In a letter to Moore he gave a touching account of the old man's end:

> I was with the poor old man for the last week of his life, and then there was the funeral etc., etc., all terribly upsetting and depressing. However,

he was 82 and had been very active till he was over 80, so he had
had a good life, and I am very glad that latterly he had not been so
disappointed in me as before. Curiously enough his last moment of
consciousness was hearing that review I had in the *Sunday Times*. He
heard about it and wanted to see it, and my sister took it in and read it
to him, and a little later he lost consciousness for the last time.[105]

He told Rees that, in accordance with tradition, he had placed pennies on
the old man's eyes, and had then thrown the pennies into the sea. 'Do you
think some people would have put them back in their pockets?' he asked.[106]
He now inherited the Blair family Bible to stand beside Great Uncle
Horatio's books, and a portrait of Lady Mary Blair to hang in the cottage
beside his Burmese swords, all perhaps to act as totemic inspirations in the
writing of his family saga. The death of a parent is often the occasion for an
increased sense of one's own mortality. No doubt he found some consolation in contriving to meet his old flame Brenda Salkeld and taking her for
a nostalgic walk, across the old bridge to Blythburgh. George Bowling
would have done no less. He tried to broach the subject of an affair, inti-
mating that he and Eileen enjoyed an open marriage and neither was at all
jealous and possessive of the other. But Brenda, the clergyman's daughter,
no doubt scandalised, had simply changed the subject. She had read all
about Mr Warburton and knew just how to handle his real-life alter ego.[107]

After attending his father's funeral, he returned to Wallington and again
opened a diary. He wanted to plot the slow but inevitable approach of war
from a careful reading of the press and weekly reviews. Ruminating later on
diary keeping, he wrote how it helped to put the immediate present into
wider perspective and keep track of one's opinions. 'Otherwise, when some
particularly absurd belief is exploded by events, one may forget that one
ever held it. Political predictions are usually wrong, but even when one
makes a correct one, to discover *why* one was right can be very illumin-
ating.'[108] In July he recorded the build up to the Danzig crisis, fighting in
Manchuria, agitation for Churchill to be allowed into the Cabinet, British
and German overtures to Russia and the call up of reservists. In passing he
noted the annual Eton versus Harrow cricket match at Lord's had ended in
fighting, for the first time since 1919. It was strangely symbolic of the times.

Chapter 13

One Character in Search of a War

'War is simply a reversal of civilized life, its motto is "Evil be thou my good".'

Orwell, War-time Diary, 14 June 1940

The psychological effects of his illness had made him a man in a hurry, but he was also a man with deep resentments, even though these could be said to be mostly of his own making. His career had been blighted, as he saw it, by a variety of accidents and poor judgements – the misguided choice of Burma, rather than the Royal Road to literary success by way of Oxbridge, his adventure to Spain where evil men would have eliminated him, a press determined to gag him, and the curse of a potentially fatal illness which had robbed him of a whole year of writing. Now war threatened to stifle him at the moment he had conceived his great family opus. On the one hand he had time to make up and on the other he was intent on surveying his whole life back through his ancestry. In April he had told Moore that he had ideas for two books he thought of writing simultaneously. As he wrote just before he died, throughout his writing life there had never been a day when he did not think that he was idling and that his output was negligible. 'Even at the periods when I was working 10 hours a day on a book, or turning out 4 or 5 articles a week, I have never been able to get away from this neurotic feeling that I was wasting time . . . as soon as a book is finished, I begin, actually from the next day, worrying because the next one is not begun, & am haunted with the fear that there never will be a next one.'[1] Now, it seemed, he was a man writing against the looming prospect of death, either in war or through a silent enemy within.

The two books in question were his projected novel and a collection of essays, one of them a close examination of the work and significance of Henry Miller of whom he was growing increasingly critical. In this case his 'intellectual brutality' would not desert him, and would even intensify as

Miller's work became, in his view, evermore degenerate. He ordered Miller's novels from the Obelisk Press, and discovered that in face of the threat of war, their author had escaped back to America. The other essays were to be on Dickens and boys' weekly comics for which he had never entirely lost his appetite and which had sparked his sociological curiosity. By mid-July he had finished his Dickens essay and was on to 'Boys' Weeklies'.

Reviewing was not well paid. There was some income from *Coming Up For Air*, but over the period taken writing it, that amounted to little more than £1 a week. The shop, however, continued to pay for itself – just. He had a few eggs and vegetables to sell and managed to supply himself with certain essentials, including goat's milk. The sooner he finished his essay collection the better. At least he had a supportive wife. Connolly, who came to dinner in Wallington, found Eileen very impressive: 'She was a very charming person. Very nice. She was intelligent . . . and she loved him, and she was independent, and although she did not wear make-up or anything like that, she was very pretty, and totally worthy of him as a wife; he was very proud of her, I think.'[2]

As war threatened, the question of whether to stand by or even protest if hostilities broke out began to weigh on his mind. All his reasoning since Spain had told him that war with Hitler would produce the backlash he had seen against the libertarian left in Spain and England, too, would go Fascist. There were voices on the Tory right and among the aristocracy favouring Mussolini, or who spoke of Hitler as the man to destroy Russian Communism. For the time being the 'martial spirit' which had taken him to Spain and urged him to fight was in check, and the anti-war pessimist was uppermost.

Because he had been ill, Lydia's feeling of irritation at Orwell's advances had, she said, melted into compassion. 'When we met at last, I could not be unpleasant to him. He, no doubt, chose to think that I let him kiss me because I liked it. I did not. He was not merely failing to attract me as a man, but the fact of his being a sick man vaguely repelled me.' He told her had almost 'slipped up' by mentioning to Eileen a letter from her which would have revealed an on-going correspondence, but had managed to pass it off as just a friendly note.[3] She hated being made part of his deception, she said, and wondered why on earth he wanted to make love to her. Even so, although she claimed that it never developed into an affair, she continued to meet him and collude with him by not telling Eileen.

Apart from his readiness to indulge his lust, given the opportunity, he clearly derived pleasure from acting secretively. That summer he was also back in touch with Brenda and contrived to meet her in Wallington, some distance from the cottage. But he had not reckoned with village gossip and Eileen soon got wind of it. She was angry enough to travel to London to unburden herself to Lydia, unwittingly confiding in one of her husband's loves that he was seeing another. 'It's that woman!' she said. 'He knew her before he married me . . . This affair goes on because she wouldn't sleep with him. If she had, it would have been finished long ago.'[4] Lydia was just relieved that her own rendezvous with George had not been discovered. For him, however, the double life had become part of his nature. 'He was,' said Fredric Warburg later, 'as secretive about his private life as any man I ever knew.'[5]

On 12 August one part of that private life was taken from him. His letter to the Obelisk Press ordering Miller's novels had been intercepted, and in a police raid all his smuggled books were seized. He was also served with a warning by the Director of Public Prosecutions not to import such material again on pain of prosecution. Powers of censorship had been stepped up and it would not be the last time he would fall foul of them.

Events were moving fast, not only in Europe but for Orwell himself, and finally it was not reason that decided him on the issue of war. The night before the Russo-German Pact was signed, on 24 August, he dreamt that the war had started. The effect on him was dramatic. Whatever its Freudian meaning, he wrote, it revealed to him 'the real state' of his feelings, and taught him that he would actually be relieved once 'the long-dreaded war' had begun, and that he would support it and fight in it if he could. 'What I knew in my dream that night was that the long drilling in patriotism which the middle classes go through had done its work, and that once England was in a serious jam it would be impossible for me to sabotage.' For him the revolution had started and could happen quickly if Hitler could be kept out. 'I dare say the London gutters will have to run with blood. All right, let them, if it is necessary. But when the red militias are billeted in the Ritz I shall still feel that the England I was taught to love so long ago and for such different reasons is somehow persisting.'[6]

In Malcolm Muggeridge's pessimistic book, *The Thirties*, he caught his own reflection – 'the middle-class man, brought up in the military tradition, who finds in the moment of crisis that he is a patriot after all'.[7] With him, extreme hostility to Stalin probably counted for as much as reawakened patriotism. Whatever he felt about Fascism, the men who killed Bob Smillie would never be forgiven. For him, this would not be a war 'For King and Country', but, as in Spain, a war against reaction, and so in fact a civil war in which he was perfectly ready to risk death or injury. 'If I was biologically a good specimen and capable of founding a new dynasty,' he told Jack Common, 'I would devote all my energies during the war to keeping alive and keeping out of sight.'[8] As it was, he considered himself expendable. The idea that he could not have children still haunted him.

Ironically, shortly after Orwell had undergone his conversion from pacifism, Ethel Mannin wrote to him, clearly impressed with *Coming Up For*

Air, and saying how glad she was that he had written it 'whilst there is still time'. She was urging everyone to read it.[9] She was amused at the discomfort of the Communists having to adjust to their leadership's about-face on Nazi Germany, unaware that Orwell had made his own U-turn and was now ready to fight. When he wrote and told her so, adding that he wished he were fit enough to get into uniform to help smash Hitler, she reacted with astonishment. 'Is it because you like fighting for its own sake? Or what? After all you wrote in *Coming Up For Air*. I don't understand it. It leaves me bitched buggered and bewildered . . . I thought you went off the boil in 1916! I thought you thought it all crazy, this smashing in of Nazi faces. For the luv of Mike write a few lines to enlighten our darkness.'[10] His reply has not survived.

In late September, with the war just a few weeks old, he and Eileen stayed for a while in Greenwich. Laurence, a pre-war Territorial now in the uniform of a Royal Army Medical Corps Major, asked Eileen to keep Gwen company whenever possible if he was posted abroad. George duly registered for war service, and in October Eileen obtained work with the Censorship Department of the War Office in London, commuting to and from Greenwich each day, and to Wallington at weekends. However, no one seemed to want Orwell, despite his efforts to enlist. Not only did he fear he would be found unfit for service but, with Russia now in the enemy camp, that his having fought in Spain would also count against him. It must have been exasperating to hear that Kopp was now on active service in France with the Foreign Legion. He remained in Wallington, tending his garden and completing his essay collection, to be called *Inside the Whale* after his main essay on Miller. Just before Christmas he sent it to Gollancz, half-hoping it would be rejected so that he could take it to Warburg, who he knew better and trusted more. Meanwhile, Connolly and Spender, with the backing of Peter Watson, were about to launch a new literary magazine, *Horizon*, and were anxious to see the book, hoping to publish an extract. They chose the essay 'Boys' Weeklies'.

To his surprise, Gollancz quickly accepted *Inside the Whale*, saying he thought it first-rate, and that he was completely in sympathy with its general political viewpoint. Obviously the Russo-German Pact had finally shaken his faith in the Communist line and suddenly he had swung over to Orwell's point of view. 'Isn't the only thing worth doing,' he asked, 'to try to find some way of reconciling the inevitable totalitarian economics with individual freedom?'[11] He then asked to borrow his copy of *Tropic of Cancer*, which Orwell had to tell him sadly was now in police custody. Whether a totalitarian economic system could accommodate individual liberty could not be judged, he told Gollancz, 'until a collectivized economy has been tried out in a western country'. In the present circumstances he was optimistic, hoping that 'when the pinch comes the common people will turn out to be more intelligent than the clever ones' and want to defend their liberties.[12] The irony, which Orwell was too polite to point out, was that certain barbed passages in the book were aimed specifically in Gollancz's direction. When they met shortly afterwards, the publisher had grown a beard and turned openly anti-Russian, even asking Orwell if it was true, after all, that the Soviet secret police had been active in Spain. Orwell was cynically amused, telling Gorer, 'He is furious with his Communist late-friends, owing to their lies, etc., so perhaps the Left Book Club will become a power for good again, if it manages to survive.'[13] It survived another seven years, but was never the force it had been, membership dwindling ultimately to around seven thousand.[14] The £20 advance for his book hardly eased his financial difficulties. A return to Grub Street seemed imminent.

He had reached a natural hiatus in his career. He felt written out and needing to lie fallow. 'I am sort of incubating an enormous novel,' he told Gorer, '. . . only I don't want to begin it before I'm all set. It's frightfully bad for one, this feeling of the publisher's wingèd chariot hurrying near all the time.'[15] The title he had in mind for his trilogy was either *The Lion and the Unicorn* or *The Quick and the Dead* – Englishness and the passing of the old order were clearly to be its major themes.

Early in the New Year, through Warburg he met Tosco Fyvel, a Swiss-educated Jewish writer and keen Zionist, who produced a snapshot of the 1940 Orwell, expressing surprise at what he saw. The haggard look, the deep lines of suffering etched on his face, his shabby sports jacket and frayed trousers, failed to disguise his social background. 'He looked,' wrote Fyvel, 'like a seedy sahib.'[16] But he was struck also by his Gallic aspect – French workman's blue shirt, and the foul-smelling cigarettes he continually rolled, giving off an air of back-street Paris. This, he thought, was Orwell's way of identifying with a proletariat to which he very obviously did not belong. Although they disagreed over the desirability of an independent Jewish state in Palestine, they got along very well, and from time to time met at Warburg's home in Reading. During the Battle of Britain, they would sit on the lawn watching the vapour trails of the dog fights overhead. From these meetings came the idea for a series of short books on war themes, to be called Searchlights Books. Orwell was reluctant to undertake anything of the kind himself; he was a writer not a propagandist, he said.[17] Nevertheless, he was finally persuaded to write a short book on English socialism, taking for it one of the proposed titles for his saga, *The Lion and the Unicorn*.

Much to his disgust, he spent the winter of 1940 on the sidelines of the war, but at least he would soon have another book published. *Inside the Whale* appeared on 11 March, just 1,000 copies, shortly preceded by an edited version of 'Boys' Weeklies' in *Horizon*. In this collection Orwell's sociological eye is at its most sharply focused. He had long wanted to indulge in this kind of cultural analysis, and unknowingly all but invented an academic genre. His earlier essays on a farthing newspaper and the tuppenny lending libraries were forays in that direction. There were literary precursors, of course – Hazlitt on newspapers, Stevenson on picture postcards, for example – and there were the Leavises in Cambridge adopting a more academic approach to similar material. But Orwell's ability to stand aside and look askance at aspects of popular culture had much in common with the social anthropological approach to so-called 'savage societies'. As usual he was looking for social meaning, a reading that would say something about authors, the contexts in which they wrote and the messages implied in their work. What Orwell brought to this kind of study, however, as he had to his Wigan Pier book, was literary style. He told Gorer, 'I find this kind of semi-sociological literary criticism very interesting & I'd like to do a lot of other writers, but unfortunately there's no money in it.'[18]

Orwell's essay on Dickens is eminently rereadable. It is a fond and familiar meditation on a writer who had been important to him since childhood. It tells us as much about Orwell as about Dickens, and shows how closely he identified with his great predecessor. And yet he seemed strangely unconscious of how much of himself he was revealing. He located Dickens, like Wells, in the lower-middle commercial class, showing how this limited his understanding of aristocrats and proletarian characters and shaped his belief that spiritual revolution rather than social revolution was the way to creating the good society. Unlike Dickens, Orwell, with his aristocratic strain and Eton education, was by birth and experience a man familiar with all social classes who believed that change of heart (misers becoming charitable) was no answer to the evils of capitalism. However, his criticism of Dickens's uncomprehending caricatures of toffs and proletarians ignores his own caricatures of British colonials in *Burmese Days* for example, and of women in *Coming Up For Air*. His main focus, he admitted, was Dickens's 'message', but he also saw that the great author's genius lay in the durability and familiarity of his characters – the immortality of Scrooge, Micawber, Pickwick, Mrs Gamp, Oliver Twist, Fagin, and the host of associations his novels evoke. And yet these characters were somehow fixed, giving no sense of their 'struggling to make their souls'. He was always preaching a message though he was only vaguely a radical. His morality was a Christian morality but never expressed in a devotional sense, and he was always on the side of the underdog.

Perhaps the secret of Orwell's affection for Dickens lay in what he saw as his 'common decency'. 'The common man is still living in the world of Dickens,' he wrote, 'but nearly every modern intellectual had gone over to some or other form of totalitarianism.'[19] With a few reservations, he regarded Dickens as very much a man in his own image. Orwell's Dickens emerges as 'a face behind the page . . . the face of a man about forty . . . He is laughing, with a touch of anger in his laughter, but no triumph, no malignity. It is the face of a man who is always fighting against something, but who fights in the open and is not frightened, the face of a man who is generously angry – in other words, of a nineteenth-century liberal, a free intelligence, a type hated with equal hatred by all the smelly little orthodoxies which are now contending for our souls.'[20] There is more than a semblance of Orwell in this fond portrait.

Orwell was one of a few writers who could demonstrate that a Marxist critique, if it was well-argued, not pontifical, and carried wide enough reference, was not entirely unfruitful. He had once written, 'I am not a Marxist', but nevertheless retained a Marxist perspective on the world, recognising history and economics as major forces for change and accepting the imminent death of capitalism. And, while he was scornfully hostile to the gramophone Marxism of the 1930s, he also thought that the period 'did a great service to literary criticism, because it destroyed the illusion of pure aestheticism. It reminded us that propaganda in some form or other lurks in every book, that every work of art has a meaning and a purpose – a political, social and religious purpose – and that our aesthetic judgements are always coloured by our prejudices and beliefs.'[21] He modified that position a little later, arguing that while Marxist criticism demonstrated that 'the subject-matter and imagery of a book can be explained in sociological terms . . . its texture seemingly cannot'.[22] It was style to him that made the writer, and judging books by their content alone he thought philistine.

His essay on 'Boys' Weeklies' is also born of affection. Here he is back in a Mr Pollyish world of small newsagents, with their newspapers, sweets, cigarettes and 'vilely printed twopenny papers'.[23] Among the boys' comics on sale, he focused mainly on his old favourites, the *Gem* and the *Magnet*, with a sidelong glance at the newer adventure comics (*Wizard*, *Rover*, *Hotspur* etc.) which embodied the same conservative values. Their main feature and attraction were the stories of so-called public-school life – schools such as Greyfriars and St Jim's, ancient institutions similar to Eton and Winchester. They were little fantasy worlds within themselves, peopled by caricatures – Billy Bunter, 'the Owl of the Remove', Harry Wharton & Co., 'the Famous Five', Vernon-Smith, 'the bounder of Greyfriars'. Typical stories involved japes, raggings, practical jokes, sporting clashes, and often stories of decent boys falsely accused of misdeeds. Sex was strictly taboo, as was religion. The chief feature of these schools was an order of snobbery, from the aristocratic Gussy, 'the swell of St Jim's', down to Tom Redwing, 'the scholarship boy'. Working-class characters were always comic or adventurers. The politics, observed Orwell, were pre-1914 Conservative, and all foreigners were presented as comic stereotypes – the French were 'Froggies', Italians 'Dagoes', Americans all old-style stage Yankees and Chinese all wore pigtails and spoke pidgin English. The papers were 'cheerfully patriotic', but entirely unpolitical until 1939 when Hitler was finally mentioned. Since the Great War there had been some growth in 'bully-worship and the cult of violence', though not so much as in 'the Yank Mags' which gave the reader 'blood-lust' and 'gory descriptions of the all-in jump-on-his-testicles style of fighting'. In the British papers, patriotism was the main theme. 'The clock has stopped in 1910. Britannia rules the waves, and no one has heard of slumps, booms, unemployment, dictatorships, purges or concentration camps.' He thought people were more influenced by these papers than was generally thought, that youngsters were being pumped full of out-dated Conservative ideals, and it was about time an up-to-date left-wing paper was established aimed at twelve- to fourteen-year-olds.

Orwell was clearly torn when it came to childhood friends like the *Gem* and the *Magnet*. They conveyed a reactionary philosophy which he considered harmful to children, yet through them he could also relive his idyllic childhood years. At the beginning of 1941, on a country walk, Warburg recalled him running down a railway cutting, placing a penny on the line, and, after a train had passed over it, bringing back the flattened penny, beaming with delight.[24] That was the Blair who still enjoyed the company of Bob Cherry and the Famous Five. The adult Orwell wrote cultural criticism and hoped to explode bombshells under the comfortable prejudices of Blimpish schoolmasters.

To excite controversy, when this essay appeared in *Horizon*, Connolly sent a copy to Frank Richards, author of the *Gem* and *Magnet* school stories. On hearing that Richards intended to reply, Orwell admitted to 'some uneasiness', sure that he had made many mistakes.[25] According to Richards he certainly had. In a witty though decidedly Blimpish reply, he refuted Orwell's charges. There was no sex in his stories, he wrote, because it played less part in the lives of his readers than in those of 'realists' like Orwell. He was no snob, but in point of fact 'noblemen generally are better than commoners' and, as it happened, foreigners *were* funny. However, working-class boys were neither absent from Greyfriars nor treated disrespectfully. As to bringing strikes, slumps, unemployment or sex into his stories, why destroy childhood innocence? 'Let youth be happy, or as happy as possible. Happiness is the best preparation for misery.' The writer's duty was to entertain. 'Boys' minds ought not to be disturbed and worried by politics.'[26] Orwell did not think much of this reply and told Geoffrey Trease, who also advocated a left-wing comic for boys, 'It's well-nigh incredible that such people are still walking about, let alone editing boy's papers.'[27]

'Inside the Whale' is probably the most important of the three essays. It came only five years after he had reviewed Miller's *Tropic of Cancer* with such enthusiasm and just three years after their meeting in Paris. The book had clearly made a lasting impression on Orwell. At one level it reminded him vividly of 'down-and-out' Paris, but it was also unique for its time, and whole passages were firmly lodged in his memory. 'Now and again there appears a novel which opens up a new world not by revealing what is strange, but by revealing what is familiar.' Joyce's *Ulysses* and Céline's *Voyage au Bout de la Nuit* were other such cases. *Tropic of Cancer* was inferior to *Ulysses* and different. Joyce was an artist in a way that Miller was not. And whereas Céline protested, Miller accepted the encroaching horrors of the modern world – a sort of modern Whitman, apostle of early America's wide 'democratic vista'. But Miller lived in a quite different world from Whitman. 'To say "accept" in an age like our own is to say that you accept concentration-camps, rubber truncheons, Hitler, Stalin, bombs, aeroplanes, tinned food, machine-guns, putsches, purges, slogans, gas-masks, sub-marines, spies, provocateurs, press-censorship, secret prisons, aspirins, Hollywood films and political murders.'[28] Yet curiously enough, with this passive attitude Miller got closer to the common man than did writers with a 'purpose'. The literature of the Great War was not written by propagandists but by victims. Miller was closer to them than the fashionable writer claiming omniscience.

This led him to examine how the present literary situation had been reached, and, in doing so, charted his own journey through that 'low dishonest decade'. He began his literary history in the years just before and after the Great War, when Housman captured the new urban middle-class nostalgia for a romanticised country life. His antinomianism also chimed with the post-war revolutionary spirit and the intense hostility of the young towards the old. The literary generation following – Joyce, Eliot, Pound, Lawrence, Wyndham Lewis, Huxley and Lytton Strachey – were pessimistic and opposed to the idea of 'progress'; Lawrence, like Dickens, was a 'change of heart' man who found sanctuary in ancient Etrusca, while Eliot escaped into Anglo-Catholicism, and Pound into Fascism.

The early thirties saw the arrival of Auden, Spender, Day Lewis and MacNeice and like minds – largely public school and university men, embracing 'purpose' and ultimately Communism. They accepted a left-wing orthodoxy decreeing that 'a writer must be actively "left" or write badly'. Communism became a substitute for a discredited religion – the new monolithic doctrine to replace Catholicism. 'Joining the Party' became as fashionable as 'being received into the Church' had been for an earlier generation. But submission to the Party meant becoming a slave of Moscow and its shifting foreign policy. Underlying this was the widespread feeling after 1930 that laissez-faire capitalism and Western civilisation were

finished. The soft, secure life in England, far removed from purges, secret
police, arbitrary arrests, torture, concentration camps, enabled this new
Russophile intelligentsia to swallow totalitarianism without understanding
it. This was the generation that believed 'that there is something noble in
telling lies and degrading your aesthetic standards for a political cause'.[29]

But the conclusion should not be that the writer must eschew politics –
his freedom to write depended on liberty of thought, which could be
defended only by political action. Again he drew the religious analogy, linking the twentieth century to the seventeenth, Catholicism versus
Protestantism, dogmatic collectivism versus liberty of conscience. 'The
novel is practically a Protestant form of art; it is a product of the free mind,
of the autonomous individual.' Political orthodoxy, like religious orthodoxy, was deadly for fiction. 'Good novels are not written by
orthodoxy-sniffers, nor by people who are conscience-stricken about their
own unorthodoxy. Good novels are written by people who are *not frightened.*' This brought him back to Miller.

Miller's position was 'individualistic but completely passive'. World
events were beyond his control and he had no desire to control them. He
was fiddling while Rome burnt, but fiddling with his face to the flames, representing a present in which many, recognising that both reaction and
progress were swindles, had retreated 'inside the whale', comfortably deaf to
and uncaring about what happened in the world at large. Perhaps for the
time being that was the best place to be, passive though conscious, able to
endure and record what could not be controlled. He ended by acclaiming
Miller 'a writer out of the ordinary, worth more than a single glance. He was
also a completely negative, unconstructive, amoral writer, a mere Jonah, a
passive acceptor of evil, a sort of Whitman among the corpses.' But as an
author he was a significant symptom of the time.[30]

Reviews were all complimentary, some even encomiastic, with only the
occasional barb. Arthur Calder-Marshall in *Time and Tide* began with an
unsolicited blurb. 'Must read . . . Brilliant writer. Super,' but also wondered
what the 'accepting' Henry Miller would do if he found himself dragged
from inside the whale to the concentration camp? Orwell, it seems, was not
the only one haunted by that particular nightmare.[31] Philip Mairet, in the
New English Weekly, applauded Orwell's clarity of mind and ability to translate thought to word. 'He is really a sociological writer . . . one of the
contemporary writers best worth having: he lives to learn, he knows something about the society he lives in, he has courage and, as this book shows,
a progressive faculty for criticism.'[32] Only slightly less admiringly, the *TLS*
reviewer, while suggesting that Orwell had treated Miller's work with 'an
excess of seriousness', was nevertheless impressed by his 'blunt and tena-
cious honesty of mind'.[33] A quirky review from Q. D. Leavis in *Scrutiny*,

concluded, 'If he would give up trying to be a novelist Mr Orwell might find his *métier* in literary criticism, in a special line of it peculiar to himself and which is particularly needed now.'[34] Although the book did not appear in America at the time, Dwight Macdonald later hailed it as a pioneering work in 'cultural studies'.

A not altogether surprising response came from Gollancz who attempted to acquire an option on Orwell's next three *non*-fiction works. He still had first choice of his next two novels, but Orwell was determined not to be pinned down further by the man who had rejected and, as he saw it, helped sabotage his book about Spain, so refused to agree.

His obvious love of Dickens led to an invitation to address the Thirty-Fourth Annual Conference of the Dickens Fellowship, presided over by Compton Mackenzie at the Comedy Restaurant on 25 May. According to a report of the occasion, Orwell told the meeting that 'Dickens was in our inner consciousness putting our innermost thoughts into words and action.'[35] It proved a fateful occasion. Mackenzie, an admirer of Orwell, was known in the literary world for one overriding eccentricity – his islomania, once owning a whole island group in the Outer Hebrides. He was the target of a satirical story by Lawrence, 'The Man Who Loved Islands', which he had found offensive and tried to have suppressed. However, there was no doubting his passion for Hebridean life, as his celebrated novel *Whisky Galore* testifies. It was Mackenzie who excited Orwell – always fascinated by Robinson Crusoe – with the prospect of one day living the self-reliant island life, remote from the horrors of the modern world, its streamlined falsity and genocidal wars. On 20 June, in his diary, he wrote, 'Thinking always of my island in the Hebrides, which I suppose I shall never possess nor even see. Compton Mackenzie says even now most of the islands are uninhabited . . . and most have water and a little cultivable land, and goats will live on them.'[36] The dream would one day come true, but only when it was rather too late for him fully to savour the idyll.

In the spring of 1940 he wrote a short retrospect of his life for an American writers' directory, listing his tastes and predilections:

> Outside my work the thing I care most about is gardening, especially vegetable gardening. I like English cookery and English beer, French red wines, Spanish white wines, Indian tea, strong tobacco, coal fires, candlelight and comfortable chairs. I dislike big towns, noise, motor cars, the radio, tinned food, central heating and 'modern' furniture. My wife's tastes fit in almost perfectly with my own. My health is wretched, but it has never prevented me from doing anything that I wanted to, except, so far, fight in the present war. I ought perhaps to mention that

though this account that I have given of myself is true, George Orwell is not my real name.[37]

Later he was less candid about his identity, but as yet Orwell was more of a pen name than a fully evolved persona.

The war, he still thought, was an occasion for revolution. Asked to sign a war manifesto he commented, 'I would have . . . emphasized both ends of the programme (defeat Hitler – equalize incomes) more plainly.' He went further, extending his idea of a rational morality based on common human decency, adding that 'My chief hope for the future is that the common people have never parted company with their moral code.'[38] This anticipates: 'If there is hope . . . it lies with the proles.'[39] And, before the year was out, he was reiterating the sentiment and foreshadowing another work to come: 'The common man is wiser than intellectuals, just as animals are wiser than men.'[40] Certainly there was one 'wise man' he felt had got things dangerously wrong – his fallen idol Wells. That summer, in a review, he attacked him for 'his confusion of mechanical progress with justice, liberty and common decency'. Wells's 'greatest gift . . . was his power to convey the atmosphere of the golden years between 1890 and 1914', but 'now that we are almost in earshot of Hitler's guns, the Wellsian Utopia, a super-Welwyn [Garden City] constructed by benevolent scientists is somehow unconvincing'.[41]

Probably at this point he would have done anything to get into uniform. He applied for a job with Field Security, which would have meant going to France on intelligence work. But, with France threatened with collapse the unit's future was uncertain, and his application got nowhere. Yet he felt angry that people who were sympathetic to the enemy – both on the fellow-travelling right and the Communist-loving left – still occupied positions of influence. (Communists, he told George Woodcock later, had probably tipped off the Vice Squad about his Obelisk Press books.) It was outrageous to him that Gollancz – a political ignoramus, he thought – should exercise so much power through his press. His old paranoia was now directed not at the Catholics so much as against Stalinists.

Unable to accept an invitation to speak at the ILP Annual Conference at Langham, he sent a talk to be read for him, attacking pacifism. He never heard back, and shortly afterward left the ILP. 'I considered that they were talking nonsense and proposing a line of policy that could only make things easier for Hitler,' he wrote. It was obviously a relief for him. Spain had given him 'a horror of politics', and he wished to be free of any political organisation that dictated a 'line' to its members. 'In sentiment I am definitely "left", but I believe that a writer can only remain honest if he feels free from party labels.'[42]

Unexpectedly he was offered steady work reviewing plays and films for

Time and Tide. To be nearer theatres and cinemas, he moved to London. He and Eileen found a cramped flat in Dorset Chambers, a small apartment block in a quiet backwater in Marylebone close to Regent's Park. There he brought his family mementoes, the Blair Bible, his leather-bound books, and Lady Mary's portrait. The cottage they would keep for weekends. The chickens were put down, and friendly villagers agreed to look after Marx, Muriel and Kate.

Throughout that summer he attended the theatre regularly, covering one Shakespeare play (*The Tempest*), a Noël Coward (*I'll Leave it to You*), and a Shaw (*The Devil's Disciple* – 'the best play Shaw ever wrote'). He was able to indulge his nostalgia further, seeing *Chu Chin Chow* again after twenty-four years. With writers disappearing off to war, he was also more in demand as a book reviewer – by the *Listener*, *Tribune*, the *Adelphi*, and *Life and Letters* – together giving him a more comfortable Grub Street income than he had ever had.

The war news was grave. The end of May brought the fall of France and the debacle of Dunkirk. There had been no news of Eileen's brother Laurence, over there with the Army Medical Corps. On the night of 1 June Orwell went to Waterloo and Victoria stations, where the evacuated troops were disembarking, hoping to get news, but they were under orders not to talk. Finally, after several days, they heard that Laurence had been killed at Dunkirk tending the wounded. The effect on Eileen was profound. Lydia Jackson thought that from that moment she lost all interest in life. George was simply no substitute and failed to look after her as he should have. 'If I were at the opposite end of the world and I sent [Laurence] a telegram saying "come at once"', she said, 'he would come, George would not do that. For him his work comes first.'[43] Mary Fyvel, Tosco's wife, found her sitting 'sunk in unmoving silence',[44] and Margaret Branch, a friend of the O'Shaughnessys, told Tosco that for about eighteen months, severely depressed, 'she was facing her dark night of the soul. Nobody could get through to her.'[45] A year later her mother died, which can only have added to the weight of her despair. In the wake of Laurence's death, Gwen decided to evacuate their young son to Canada, and Marjorie Dakin was toying with the same idea.

An invasion seemed imminent. Orwell was not just despondent but angry. Like others, he blamed the Establishment for the mess, and imagined that the Blimp class would now lead the country towards Fascism, and even further disaster, as in France. Depressingly he saw the old 1914–18 gang coming back in force – 'a necklace of corpses', he called them.[46] The intelligentsia, with its contempt for patriotism, also had to bear its share of responsibility. He was depressed at noticing how most people seemed unable to grasp the danger they were in. Newspapers were still mostly advertising frivolities and unnecessary luxuries, and advertisers were cashing in on war neurosis. The war, he hoped, would sweep such things away, but he was unsure it would. 'War is simply a reversal of civilized life, its motto is "Evil be thou my good", and so much of the good of modern life is evil that it is questionable whether on balance war does harm.'[47]

Had there been any worthy leadership on the left, he said later, the return of the troops from Dunkirk was the moment for revolution. But at this point the British working class had revealed their innate patriotism, something the left had not foreseen. He adopted the old POUM-Trotskyist slogan: 'The war and revolution are inseparable,'[48] and drew parallels with the position of French Revolutionaries in 1793 and Paris Communards of 1871. As in Barcelona, it was a hope that could be so easily dashed.

Astonishingly in the circumstance of his wife's bereavement, Orwell was openly hankering after Brenda. Finally, on 25 June, his birthday, presumably in the hope of shutting him up, Eileen agreed that he should write to her. It was perhaps the most personally revealing letter he had so far ever written, and the fact that Brenda kept the letter secret until her death speaks volumes about her relationship with Orwell:

Dearest Brenda, I've tried so often to forget you but somehow didn't succeed. I wonder where you are & what doing . . . I wonder if you are happy. If things just break up & go to pieces as I fear they may, I must try & see you once again. You are such a big piece of my life. Do you remember our walks to Blythburgh, & the time we found the nightingale's nest? And that beautiful walk we had last summer just before the war began. How long is it since I last saw you? I think it was at Christmas, wasn't it? I couldn't explain then abt you & me & Eileen, you didn't want me to, & of course such relationship [as] was between us was unfair and impossible for you. Eileen said she wished I could sleep with you abt twice a year, just to keep me happy, but of course we can't arrange things like that. It's a pity though we never made love properly. We could have been so happy. If things are really collapsing I shall try & see you. Or perhaps you wouldn't want to? I've no rights over you, & I dare say you've found somebody else long since, but we have been friends so long that you are part of me in a way. I've been longing for months to write to you & compelling myself not to. But today is my birthday & Eileen said I was to give myself a birthday treat. Write, if you feel like it, to the above address, & tell me what you're doing & what your plans are, & whether you are happy. Take care of yourself, dear love, take cover when the air raids start, & try & be happy./With love/Eric.[49]

This rather clumsy attempt to establish a *ménage à trois* seemingly failed, and they lost touch for the next five years. In the meantime, with the social flux of war and consequent loosening of morals, Orwell would have other opportunities to satisfy his wayward lust.

Almost the first thing he had done in the aftermath of Dunkirk was join the Local Defence Volunteers, created to back up the army in the event of a German invasion. He attended an inaugural LDV meeting at Lord's Cricket Ground, noting ironically that one poster on display, showing a foot treading on a swastika, was cribbed from one he had seen in Spain. That crushing boot had made a particular impression on Orwell and would provide him with probably the most memorable single image of totalitarian power ever captured in literature.

Because of his OTC and Spanish war experience he was made sergeant in the Volunteers' St John's Wood Section. From the start he was a keen part-time soldier, but not too engrossed at Lord's to miss a kestrel killing a sparrow in the middle of the sacred turf, and later, in the midst of an air-raid, to notice a heron flying over Baker Street. He had fun with the new words that were appearing in the language, predicting one week that 'Blitz' would soon be used as a verb, and two weeks later triumphantly recording that the *Daily Express* had duly obliged. He also worried that over time morale would crack under a ceaseless bombardment. When a group of East Enders marched to the Savoy and occupied the air-raid shelter there, he saw it as a sign that the revolution was at hand.[50] Next, no doubt, it would be those red militias at the Ritz.

During the September Blitz, images and sounds of destruction evoked grim memories. A pile of plaster dummies outside the bomb-damaged John Lewis's Oxford Street store recalled a pile of plaster saints from desecrated Barcelona churches, the whine of bombers brought back the sound of mosquitoes inside his mosquito net in Burma.[51] Later in Greenwich, taking cover during a raid in a church crypt, he was horrified to see children playing among vaults full of corpses.[52] And in May 1941, sheltering in a London Tube station, it was again the children who caught his eye – 'the large families one sees here and there, father, mother and several children all laid out in a row like rabbits on the slab'.[53] The sight had clearly moved the man who thought himself destined to be childless. Other memories were less fleeting – 'sitting in Connolly's top-floor flat [in Piccadilly] and watching the enormous fires beyond St. Paul's, and the great plume of smoke from an oil drum somewhere down the river, and Hugh Slater sitting in the window and saying, "It's just like Madrid – quite nostalgic." The only person suitably impressed was Connolly, who took us up to the roof and, after gazing for some time at the fires, said, "It's the end of capitalism. It's a judgement on us".[54] Slater, whose real name was Humphrey and called himself 'Hugh' to sound more proletarian, was a novelist, an ex-International Brigade commissar, and later editor of *Polemic*, an intellectual version of *Horizon*, which would publish some of Orwell's best essays.

He hoped that when the inevitable move towards Fascism occurred in England, the LDV would provide the core of a workers' militia. Slater and Tom Wintringham, another ex-commissar, tried to push this line in lectures at Osterly Park, the training camp financed by Edward Hulton, owner of *Picture Post*. 'At present the whole organization is in an anomalous and confused state, which has many different possibilities,' wrote Orwell. 'Already people are forming local defence squads, and hand-grenades are probably being manufactured by amateurs. The higher-ups are no doubt thoroughly frightened by these tendencies.'[55] What he feared was the force being taken over by Blimps who would impose a class structure on it and crush any chance of his hoped-for socialist revolution.

His suspicions were heightened when, in June 1940, LDV members were ordered to hand in all revolvers for use by the army. But when the first sixty men turned out for drill parade he thought them 'really admirable'.[56] His company commander was a grocer, his second in command a garage owner. Many of his comrades-in-arms were Jews, including later Fredric Warburg, who Orwell was instrumental in recruiting. Warburg, an officer in the Great War, was, in this amateur army, a mere corporal, serving under Sergeant Blair. This sense of belonging to a civilian force with an egalitarian air, fed his belief that here was a genuine people's militia. He attempted to master the intricacies of the Spigot mortar, but, using the wrong ammunition, almost decapitated a fellow soldier. He brought various weapons home with him, something which made Eileen nervous. 'I can put up with bombs on the mantelpiece,' she told a friend, 'but I will not have a machine gun under the bed.'[57] However, he was most concerned to pass on what he had learned in Spain, especially the rudiments of street fighting, and wrote a letter to *Time and Tide* calling on the government to 'Arm The People'.[58] For him the Barcelona parallel was a close one, and his fighting spirit was aroused. Warburg called him positively 'Cromwellian' in his zeal.

The 'sadistic' side of his nature had reasserted itself. At the news of the death of Italo Balbo, Mussolini's air force chief responsible for bombing Ethiopia, he wrote that he was 'thoroughly pleased . . . E[ileen]also delighted.' And when Jean Chiappe, Fascist head of the Paris police, perished when his plane was shot down, he positively cheered. 'That bastard Chiappe is cold meat. Everyone is delighted . . . This war is at any rate killing off a few Fascists.'[59] He later confided to Koestler, 'How lovely it was to be in a hot bath and dream of the tortures one is inflicting (in fantasy) on one's enemies.'[60]

Reviewing plays and films he felt was somehow demeaning, and, rather than treating cinema as an art, he wrote about the sociology of the film industry, deploring Hollywood escapism and glorification of sadistic violence, and the 'intellectual contempt which American film producers seem to feel for their audience'.[61] American films, he wrote, showed an 'utter lack of any decent, intelligent vision of life'.[62] His great exception was Chaplin, a one-time performer on the London music halls, for which he retained a minor passion, especially for the bawdy patter of performers such as Max Miller – and which elsewhere he compared to seaside postcards as a harmless celebration of saturnalia, the Sancho Panza side of human life. He admired the fact that, even at the height of the Blitz, audiences were still prepared to enjoy a hearty laugh and stayed on even after the sirens had sounded and the bombs were falling.[63] All this showed an appreciation of the peculiar flavour of English character, which he celebrated later in *The Lion and the Unicorn*.

The pressure of the times and the increase in the amount of work he was doing led to a change in his working practices:

> Nowadays, when I write a review, I sit down at the typewriter and type it straight out. Till recently, indeed till six months ago, I never did this and would have said that I could not do it. Virtually all that I wrote was written at least twice, and my books as a whole three times – individual passages as many as five or ten times. It is not really that I have gained in facility, merely that I have ceased to care, so long as the work will pass inspection and bring in a little money. It is a deterioration directly due to the war.[64]

He found film and theatre reviews hardly fulfilling. So eager was he to get close to the action that he was prepared to consider anything. He found occasional work for the Ministry of Information (Britain's answer to Goebbels' Ministry of Propaganda), which had its headquarters at the University of London's Senate House – one source for his Ministry of Truth in *Nineteen Eighty-Four*.[65] On 28 June he was finally seen by a medical board and given a grade 'C'. There was to be no romantic role for Orwell in this war. 'Horribly depressed by the way things are turning out,' he wrote.[66] Had he chosen to use his Eton contacts he would probably have found some active role with ease, but to do so would have been to ally himself with the very people obstructing the revolution he was hoping to see.

From discussions with leading Labour figures at the *New Statesman*, he learned about the Nazis' lists of British left-wing intellectuals destined for the concentration camp and felt the nightmare of Spain about to re-engulf him. Eileen suggested he consider evacuating to Canada, but he felt strongly that he must stay and endure whatever befell England and hope to live to tell the tale. 'Better to die if necessary, and maybe even as propaganda one's death might achieve more than going abroad and living more or less unwanted on other people's charity. Not that I want to die; I have so much to live for, in spite of poor health and having no children.'[67]

There can be no doubt the dread with which he contemplated a possible Nazi-occupied Britain. His writing at this time is shot through with images of brainwashing, incarceration and torture. Reviewing Clifford Odets' play *Till the Day I Die*, he pictured the central character, a young Jewish Communist, so terrorised that he says he will never know any sort of peace 'till the day I die'. This becomes clear when he is arrested. 'Under the influence of torture, loneliness, fear and drugs he can feel his mind giving way. Sooner or later the Gestapo will break him down and he will become an informer.' It was this and similar images that would threaten Orwell's peace of mind until the end of *his* life, too.[68] In his diary of 22 August he noted briefly the murder of Trotsky the day before, a gruesome demonstration of the long arm of the NKVD, which only deepened his paranoia and brought the fear of imprisonment, torture and 'the bullet in the back of the neck' even closer. He wondered how the Russians would get along without such a hate figure. 'Probably they'll have to invent a substitute,' he wrote.[69]

Not long after Churchill had become Prime Minister in July the LDV was transformed into the Home Guard which Orwell took to mean that either the Government were taking the force seriously or that they feared it.[70] His section was now incorporated in the 5th County of London Battalion, a pale imitation of the absorption of the Spanish militias into the Popular Army in 1937 – resulting, as Orwell feared, in Blimps taking over. Again he felt anger against certain people in positions of influence. 'It is a terrible thing to feel oneself useless and at the same time on every side to see halfwits and profascists filling important jobs.'[71]

All this activity – reviewing, Home Guard duties, journeying to and from the cottage at weekends – had put a full stop to his creative writing. The novel was on hold, and he had to apologise to John Lehmann for not having written a promised essay for his magazine *New Writing*. However, a month later he offered him 'My Country Right or Left', capturing his retrospective mood in a comparison of how he felt in 1940 with how he felt as a boy in the First World War. It was also his justification for having turned against pacifism, arguing 'the spiritual need for patriotism and the military virtues for which . . . no substitute has yet been found'.[72] A number of the ideas in this short essay he developed further in *The Lion and the Unicorn*, the book he had now almost finished for Warburg. But as to a novel, only an insensitive person, he thought, could write a piece of large-scale fiction under such circumstances.[73] To him emotion was important in driving a creative work, but the times were inimical to the creative emotions. When the moment came he would wreak his own kind of revenge on the barbarians who were stifling his literary daemon.

Through Warburg he was able finally to meet Wells, who had greatly admired *Homage to Catalonia*. Orwell's criticisms of him cannot have been ventilated because they seem to have enjoyed each other's company and not come to blows. Wells, who had Establishment contacts, confirmed his suspicions that Blimps were consciously acting to forestall a revolution by imprisoning anti-Fascist refugees. When J. B. Priestley's popular broadcasts from a mildly socialist point of view were stopped at the insistence of the Conservative Party, it only underlined to him the resurgence of the extreme right, the ruling class reasserting its grip. He began to feel that the revolutionary moment had passed, the chance of change had been missed. The right were more likely to betray Britain than defend her. What to expect from a right-wing, pro-Nazi government continued to dominate his thoughts. Reading a novel about the Gestapo he commented, 'In such a society the practice of lying becomes so habitual that it is almost impossible to believe that anyone else can ever be speaking the truth.'[74]

A letter came from Kopp, who had survived the German invasion of France, after being wounded and taken prisoner when the Germans attacked. He had managed to escape from hospital and, after many adventures, ended up living in the Vichy-administered south of the country. There he was working as an engineer, a cover under which he was spying for British Intelligence. He would escape back to England in 1943, and eventually marry Gwen O'Shaughnessy's step-sister Doreen. The letter, addressed to Eileen, and signed 'with love', included the postscript, 'How *you* must have suffered in this war, Eileen dear!' What Orwell thought of these endearments was never recorded, but nor were Eileen's true feelings about him and Brenda.

As the air raids on London intensified in the late summer, he was stuck by how quickly they both adapted to it. Woken one night by the tremendous crash of a nearby bomb, they merely remarked on the loudness and went back to sleep. He recorded the havoc the raids were causing in the East End, the comments of people in the streets and the grim speeches from Churchill warning of imminent invasion. But beneath his casual manner old fears had been rekindled, and he dreamt, as in Spain, of being bombed without cover and waking up 'frightened out of my wits'.[75]

He had never thought much of the radio, associating it with the noisily intrusive chromium-steel milk-bar civilisation he despised. However, in October he was invited to take part in a radio discussion on 'The Proletarian Writer' by Desmond Hawkins who until it folded in 1939 had reviewed novels for *Criterion*, and had been literary editor of the *New English*

Weekly.[76] Orwell's case was characteristically succinct: 'So long as the bourgeoisie are the dominant class, literature must be bourgeois . . . I believe we
are passing into a classless period, and what we call proletarian literature is
one of the signs of the change.'[77]

In December Penguin Books republished *Down and Out in Paris and
London*, an edition of 55,000 copies, which earned him something like
£120, a good basis on which to enjoy Christmas. One curious result of the
book's reappearance was that Andrew Gow, his old Eton tutor, rediscovered
him. In a circular letter to certain of his Cambridge students serving overseas, he listed having read *Down and Out*, and a year later, among his
recommendations, included '*Inside the Whale*, leftish literary criticism by G.
Orwell, an ex-pupil who I have mentioned before.'[78] The fact of his tutor's
recommendation was, one supposes, worth at least a grudging B-plus.

The New Year brought two significant events. Hawkins asked him if he
would take over the writing of a regular London Letter for the American
left-wing periodical *Partisan Review*, which Orwell was happy to do for
$11 a letter (around £2.75 at that time). He wrote the feature for the next
five years, including some of his best wartime writing – wide-ranging
pieces, covering the current political situation, wartime conditions in
England, literary gossip, attitudes towards American soldiers in Britain,
and, of course, strongly expressed personal opinions about everything.
Then, in January, he published a review of Koestler's *Darkness at Noon*, a
novel that would influence him profoundly and make him eager to meet its
author. It made the 'bullet in the back of the neck' that much more real to
him. Koestler's entanglements with Soviet Communists and his time in a
Franco prison in Spain had given him unique insight into the methods of
psychological torture and brainwashing employed by the modern police
state. In this story of Rubashov, the old Bolshevik, arrested, interrogated and
forced to confess to crimes of which he is innocent, stood the indictment of
Stalinist Russia. Here could be found all the paraphernalia of that totalitarian society – secret police, human gramophones, denunciations, Stalinist
paranoia, cold interrogators, the abolition of history. These were features of
organised terror he already knew about; Koestler had given them an added
force by personalising them through his fiction.[79]

Shortly afterwards Warburg arranged for Orwell to meet Koestler, just
released from Pentonville Prison where he had been held since escaping to
England from a French concentration camp. Having both barely escaped
execution in Spain, they had much in common, especially their strong hostility to Stalin, their facility to write powerful prose and an urge to translate
political realities into fiction. But they were quite different in temperament.
Koestler was highly combative, volatile and hedonistic; Orwell was ironic,
more controlled and ascetic. Like Warburg and Fyvel, Koestler and Orwell

agreed to disagree over Palestine. Even so, Koestler recognised Orwell immediately as the most important English writer he had met so far. At a PEN dinner in 1941 he bet five bottles of burgundy that within five years Orwell would be a great bestseller.[80]

The Lion and the Unicorn (despite its title) was not quite the 'fairy tale' Max Plowman had hinted he might write; it was a distillation of Orwell's thinking over the previous quarter of a century, since when in 1916 he turned against 'the swindle' of King, Country and Empire. His image of Englishness drew heavily on memories of his Edwardian childhood; his attack on the English class system reflected a hatred of a structure of snobbery he was once deceived into upholding; his disillusionment with left-wing intellectuals arose from his Spanish experience, and his vision of the future embodied a socialism based on a Christian moral code rather than an ideological blueprint. Here was the voice of a dissident Englishman who saw himself in a tradition of protest dating at least from the sixteenth century. Historically his *bêtes noires* were Catholic Inquisitionists, his present and future archfiends were totalitarian Inquisitionists of both left and right. Ever the caricaturist, he exaggerated to give force to his arguments, and somehow brought to the book the prophetic tones of the secular high priest. One can't help feeling that this book is the social and historical background to the planned family saga that was never written, hence the title, which he had originally intended for his trilogy.

It began memorably enough: 'As I write, highly civilized human beings are flying overhead, trying to kill me.' It went on to argue that patriotism is a far more potently cohesive force than the supposed class solidarity of international socialism. He then tried to isolate what was distinctive about England and the English, something best experienced when returning from abroad:

> The beer is bitterer, the coins are heavier, the grass is greener, the advertisements are more blatant. The crowds in big towns, with their knobby faces, their bad teeth and gentle manners, are different from a European crowd. One of the most endearing characteristics of the English was that they did not go around killing one another. Then the vastness of England swallows you up, and you lose for a while your feeling that the whole nation has a single identifiable character.

He cited what he called 'the diversity of it, the chaos!' 'The clatter of the clogs in the Lancashire mill towns, the to-and-fro of the lorries on the Great North Road, the queues outside the Labour Exchanges, the rattle of pin-tables in Soho pubs, the old maids biking to Holy Communion through the mists of the autumn morning . . . only fragments, but *characteristic* fragments, of the English scene.'[81] He discussed and accepted certain English stereotypes – love of flowers, addiction to hobbies, not very musical, no Party rallies or Jew-baiting, a genuine popular culture, no great religious beliefs but 'a deep tinge of Christian feeling', the anti-militarism, the good temper and gentleness of its people and the respect for law. In contrast to this stood England's criminal, barbaric side – the hanging judge, bad cheap public schools, treacherous rich businessmen, working-class xenophobia and artistic insularity. Nevertheless, England's strength was that it was something like a family – 'a family with the wrong members in control'.[82]

Having declared them unworthy, he grudgingly allowed that the English ruling class, unlike the French, were 'morally sound' – prepared to fight and die for their country, as many had in Flanders. The apparent weakening of British morale during the 1930s was largely the work of 'the left-wing intelligentsia', people marginalised within a philistine country, who had embraced the 'anti-Fascist' cause then turned pacifist when war broke out. 'Underlying this is the really important fact about so many of [them] – their severance from the common culture of the country.'[83] They had renounced England, looking to Paris or Moscow for their opinions. He noted the rise of middle-class England, the diminution of overt class differences and the changes brought in its wake – the soul-destroying spread of suburbia, the growth of a new world of glass and brick, 'the naked democracy of the swimming-pools'. The war would wipe out all remaining class differences, the Eton and Harrow match would be forgotten, but England would still be England.

As to 'The English Revolution' he reiterated the line that 'The war and the revolution are inseparable.' Not only must class differences be abolished but attitudes to Empire radically altered. The prospect of revolution would give people something to fight for. The war gave socialism a chance. Some obstacles, however, needed removing – private enterprise, greatly unequal incomes, and those 'festering centres of snobbery', the many private schools run simply for money. A benign version of English socialism would be neither doctrinaire, nor quite logical. 'It will abolish the House of Lords, but quite probably will not abolish the Monarchy . . . It will not set up any explicit class dictatorship. It will group itself round the old Labour Party and its mass following will be the Trades Unions, but it will draw into it most of the middle class and many of the younger sons of the bourgeoisie.' Its directing brains would be mostly meritocrats. The tradition of compromise would prevail, traitors would be executed only after 'a solemn trial' and sometimes acquitted. The Church would be disestablished but the country would 'retain a vague reverence for the Christian moral code', and, although open revolt would be crushed, freedom of speech would be tolerated.

Finally, he put the argument against pacifism. Toughness was the price of survival. 'A nation trained to think hedonistically cannot survive amid peoples who work like slaves and breed like rabbits, and whose chief national industry is war.' English left-wing intellectuals, from a sense of inferiority, grew to believe that the English were finished as a martial race and incapable of enduring. But it was necessary to stand up to Hitler, who was out to destroy Judaeo-Christian civilisation. Those not prepared to fight would have to be prepared to submit to Hitler's rule. 'A few rich men and their hired liars' would welcome a compromise peace with Hitler, which is why a revolution was necessary before victory could be achieved.[84]

The book was hailed in the *Listener* as 'exciting and important'. 'Mr Orwell is a socialist and a patriot – a rare combination among our intellectuals.' The idea of a peculiarly English socialist state based on common ideals of equality was 'an idea upon which many who do not call themselves socialists can unite, first to win the war, and then to create a new society'.[85] A longer, more disputatious notice appeared in the *New Statesman*, from V. S. Pritchett, who saw him as a pamphleteer in the best tradition of Cobbett and Defoe. He saw how deceptively and effectively Orwell's prose worked: 'He writes in a lucid conversational style which wakens one up suddenly like cold water dashed in the face.' In the name of commonsense he sometimes exaggerated, 'with the simplicity and ignorance of a savage', but that was the way with pamphleteers. He agreed with Orwell's identifying the rising middle class of Slough and Dagenham as the face of the future. 'They are as new to their age as that terrible man Robinson Crusoe was to his.'[86]

He did not escape a gentle whipping from the Catholic press. Christopher Hollis, writing in the *Tablet,* saw Orwell as a proponent of bureaucratic state socialism. His argument strangely foreshadowed Eliot's later criticism of *Animal Farm*. 'All Governments, whatever they are called, are in point of fact oligarchies. The only question is whether you get good oligarchs or bad oligarchs.' If Britain went socialist after the war, he preferred Orwell as dictator to other potential candidates. But Germany got Hitler that way. He then wondered how people could reverence what Orwell advocated, 'a Christian moral code', when, according to him, Christianity was untrue.[87]

At the start of his review, Hollis raised a question that must have mystified many of Orwell's friends. 'Many things interest me about Mr Orwell, and not the least among them the question why he prefers to confront the world with that peculiar name rather than with the very respectable one under which I have had the honour of knowing him for the last quarter of a century.' Orwell had answered this question in several ways: to protect his family, hating his birth name, fear of sympathetic magic. However, it is unsurprising that some thought there might be complex psychological reasons behind the assumed mask. Was Blair the dark 'sadistic' self that the noble Orwell was wrestling to suppress? Was he the libertine who visited brothels, seduced married women, betrayed his wife, while the saintly Orwell remained morally aloof? Or was he the homoerotic-inclined guilt-ridden individual glimpsed by Michael Sayers? That he had one or more dark sides is fairly obvious; that he was anxious to present Orwell as a very specific kind of person is also evident, and that he built up and defended his reputation vigorously is also clear.

One person his book seems to have stirred up was Wells, also a Secker and Warburg author, whose tetchy comments were recorded by Roger Senhouse: 'H. G. W . . . A propos of Orwell – to whom he's written on various points in his analysis of English character. Fondness for flowers, unmusical, shocked him . . . Bad teeth? He hadn't noticed it . . . "What can you expect? All public schoolboys in the 6th learn [is] sodomy & side." "What does Orwell mean by saying the English are not intellectual?" "Too sweeping in his general arguments," I said, "but that is controversy in embryo." "He's not a deep thinker."'[88] Wells's mild irritations over *The Lion and the Unicorn* were nothing compared to what was to come.

He kept revising his opinions about the future. By March 1941, with the war just eighteen months old, he had concluded that the British ruling class was incapable after all of developing its own brand of Fascism, and that the chance of a successful Hitler invasion had passed. However, such moments of optimism did not remain long. Two months later he wrote, 'Within two years we shall either be conquered or we shall be a Socialist republic fighting for its life.'[89] When Gollancz published *The Betrayal of the Left* in March, finally acknowledging the Stalinist deception, Orwell contributed two essays. In one, 'Democracy and Fascism', he denounced Western Communist parties as 'mere publicity agents for the Russian regime'.[90]

By early April he and Eileen had moved from Dorset Chambers to another small flat in Abbey Road, St John's Wood, on the fifth floor of Langford Court, a large, modern eight-storey block. It is said to have shared many of the features of Victory Mansions, where Winston Smith lived in *Nineteen Eighty-Four*. Most of the residents were foreigners and a friend recalled, 'I remember Eileen Orwell ringing me up one day to tell me the "sensational news" that she had actually met *another* Englishwoman in the lift and they had fallen on each other's necks.'[91] But they were still close to Regent's Park, close to Orwell's Home Guard base. There Orwell heard that he had been rejected for a public relations job with the Air Ministry. He was now a celebrated author but could still find only casual employment around Grub Street.

Living in London had plunged him back into the literary society he had always been keen to avoid. Through the *New Statesman* and *Tribune* he met left-wing writer-politicians – Richard Crossman, Aneurin Bevan, Michael Foot and George Strauss. Through Warburg he had met Fyvel, Koestler and Wells, and through other acquaintances would meet Anthony Powell, Malcolm Muggeridge, Hugh Kingsmill and Graham Greene. He began to frequent certain Soho pubs and cafés, and rub shoulders with the shifting population of aspiring poets, writers, artists and their hangers-on. The Barcelona in Beak Street was his favourite restaurant, the Wheatsheaf his favourite pub. He was now a widely read Penguin author and, through *The Lion and the Unicorn*, well-known among the intelligentsia of both left and right. For a man of his reputed modesty, he never shied away from publicity, readily supplying author profiles and photographs, writing pieces about himself and often representing himself in his books and essays. This focus on the self, according to Muggeridge and Powell, reflected a curious kind of egotism, a careful crafting of his literary self.

The reputation he found himself enjoying by 1940 was no sudden thing. As a friend wrote of him: 'It's strange the way a writer's fame begins slowly creeping up on him and then racing so that after a while he seems to be a poor relation of his own fame. People of taste and sensitiveness, writers, political workers and actors (who now show signs of being extremely left wing), socialist doctors, factory workers and technical instructors in touch with their labour organisations are all well aware of Orwell.'[92] Literary success was a powerful, all-consuming obsession, and the fame he had dreamed of as a schoolboy must have seemed almost within his grasp. Among other things this growing reputation made him more attractive to women, even though he was not always particularly successful. At *Horizon* there was Connolly's entourage of handsome female editorial assistants to meet, including on occasions the beautiful Sonia Brownell. John Craxton, the painter, remembered the strangely solitary Orwell hanging around the *Horizon* office, hoping, he thought, to chance upon the luscious, Rubenesque Sonia.[93]

As the war atmosphere thickened, the easing of sexual morals saw the lustful Orwell drawn into various liaisons and dalliances as the opportunity arose. That April, at dinner with Wells, he met the writer and journalist Inez Holden. Holden was Orwell's age, her parents were Warwickshire gentry, an ill-matched pair who drank heavily and quarrelled ferociously. She had left home at fifteen, living first in Paris then London. Anthony Powell, who knew her in the 1920s, recalled her 'fragility of feature' and 'consumptive charm'. By the time she met Orwell, due to a bungled operation she had lost her youthful figure, but even so, she was a highly entertaining woman, a clever mimic and amusing raconteur. She had published three novels in her twenties, and was an accomplished short-story writer and journalist. In the previous year, bombed out of her Albany Street flat, Wells had lent her the mews flat behind his grand house in Hanover Terrace. Orwell began meeting her regularly in early 1941, taking her to lunch and back to the flat while Eileen was at work. He talked a great deal about himself – about Burma, Paris and Spain. On one occasion, after a visit to the zoo, he took her back to Langford Court for tea. There, after changing into his Home Guard uniform he suddenly 'pounced' on her, and she recorded in her diary that she was astonished by his 'intensity and urgency'.

Next day he took her out and explained to her about his marriage. What he said was not recorded, but doubtless he spun the same story he had spun earlier to Brenda – as long as what he did made him happy, Eileen did not mind. Inez found his explanation 'helpful and clarifying', seeming to confirm that by now he and Eileen had worked out some form of open relationship – at least Orwell thought they had. That evening he and Eileen took Inez out to dinner. 'There was rather an atmosphere of submerged strain,' she wrote. 'Might be worth writing a short story about this sort of thing. Also almost subconsciously [Orwell] seemed to have disappeared as if to disassociate himself from the whole story.'[94] It might have been a story he was already composing in his head, so that George the 'pouncer' was just 'a character' from whom he could readily distance himself. Inez and he became very close. As she told Ian Angus, 'I saw him several times a week for about ten years. I also knew his first wife Eileen reasonably well and saw her often.'[95] Whatever Eileen knew about their relationship she was obviously prepared to tolerate, but whether she suffered because of it is unknown and Orwell himself never hinted at knowing or even caring.

Escaping to Wallington in the spring, out of earshot of the bombs, he gained some sense of renewal, tending his garden and writing up his diary. 'When this autumn comes those potatoes [may] seem a more important achievement than all the articles, broadcasts etc. I shall have done this year,' he wrote.[96] In Hertfordshire, at least, Robinson Crusoe was alive and well. But he could not escape the bombs for long. On 11 May Langford Court was hit. The first thing he and Eileen did, after being woken by the crash, was to retreat to the roof to watch the flames. Soon they were forced to evacuate the building. 'I noticed afterwards,' he wrote, 'that what I had taken out was not my typewriter or any documents but my firearms and a haversack containing food, etc. which was always kept ready.'[97] It seems at this point he decided that Eileen was overworking at the Censorship Department and urged her to resign. By June she was again a free woman.

He visited Oxford twice during the war, in May speaking to the Oxford University Democratic Socialist Club on 'Literature and Totalitarianism', warning that the age of the autonomous individual was coming to an end, but that totalitarianism and literature were incompatible. 'The totalitarian state,' he argued, 'tries . . . to control the thoughts and emotions of its subjects . . . as completely as it controls their actions.' However, unlike previous orthodoxies, it did not fix thought. 'It sets up unquestionable dogmas, and it alters them from day to day . . . it attacks the very concept of objective truth.'[98] He was already rehearsing the argument that would lie at the heart of *Nineteen Eighty-Four*. The student magazine *Cherwell* gave him a lukewarm notice: 'He talked in vague generalizations, which to students of logic are perhaps upsetting, but in answering questions . . . he showed that his position as a leading Left Wing critic is clearly justified.'[99]

Orwell's power of prophecy faltered that summer. On 14 June he wrote that a German attack on the USSR was now unlikely. Eight days later the Wehrmacht crossed the Soviet border and he had to eat his words. The following day he grudgingly approved Churchill's speech welcoming this new ally against Hitler. He found his Home Guard comrades completely pro-Russian, and by the beginning of July had come to see this swing of opinion as characteristic of the age. 'One could not have a better example of the moral and emotional shallowness of our time, than the fact that we are now more or less pro-Stalin. This disgusting murderer is temporarily on our side, and so the purges, etc. are suddenly forgotten.'[100] They had not been forgotten by George Orwell, nor would they ever be. England might have been forced into temporary alliance with one evil to defend herself from a more immediate one, but should never think that this new friend was anything other than an oppressive tyrant. He noted sardonically, 'The Communists will no doubt be super-patriotic within ten days – the slogan will probably be "All power to Churchill" – and completely disregarded.'[101] On 3 July he recorded Stalin's latest volte-face – 'a direct return to the Popular Front, defence of democracy line, in effect a complete contradiction of all that he and his followers have been saying for the past two years.'[102] These cynical Communist line-changes both amused him and confirmed how the western gramophones simply played Stalin's conflicting tunes on request. It would be another key theme in *Nineteen Eighty-Four*.

There were limits to even his hostility to the Soviets. He refused to ally himself to others with whom he fundamentally disagreed. '[Catholic] hatred of Russia is so venomous, enough even to disgust an anti-Stalinist like myself.'[103] Nor would he align himself with laissez-faire capitalists. He opposed Stalin as a socialist, not as an anti-socialist. But for now he was prepared to live with the situation. 'I never thought I should live to say, "Good luck to Comrade Stalin," but so I do.'[104] However, it was with heavy irony that he noted in the New Year that 'An enormous hammer and sickle flag flies daily over Selfridge's, the biggest shop in London.'[105]

Orwell cannot have known how amusingly eccentric some of his friends and acquaintances regarded him. In August, Roger Senhouse listed some of his peculiarities in his diary agreed in a conversation with Peter Watson:

Things ceased to be good for the future if they ceased to interest him, or again he only thinks good those things which he liked at a very early age. The 'Gem' he enjoyed reading when he was very young & that must be the best of boys' papers. He has no use for women of 40 who can afford to dress well & make up. So all became ugly or useless in the future if they have not the heart to work. Something stopped short [he said] when he went to Eton. Yet, I pointed out, he owes his classical education to Eton & without that he would not be able to write as he does – well & truly earn his living. 'Once you are established you may be asked to write many things' (a propos T[ime] & T[ide] film criticism).[106]

Despite Eton, he was saying, he was still down in Grub Street at the beck and call of literary editors.

It was Inez who introduced him finally to Anthony Powell, who had so admired *Keep the Aspidistra Flying*. They met at the Café Royal, where Powell was dining with his wife. He was worried that Orwell would disapprove of this show of militaristic style – he was dressed in his Brigade of Guards 'blues', with brass buttons and high collar – but his fears were quickly allayed. Orwell was fascinated to find that Powell's trousers were strapped down. 'I used to wear ones that strapped under the boot myself,' he said, nostalgically, recalling Burma. 'These straps under the foot give you a feeling like nothing else in life.'[107] The meeting reassured and impressed Powell. He found Orwell unspoiled by an Oxbridge education, and still very much the Etonian, however much he disowned the place. Even so, he thought, the slight rasp in his voice was less Etonian than Kiplingesque, and he had cut himself adrift from his own social class without having found another one to join. With his tall bony frame, grooved cheeks and narrow clipped moustache he reminded Powell of Gustave Doré's Don Quixote. The moustache he thought perhaps a gesture towards dandyism, a Wodehousean affectation from his youth, or a vestigial sign of his part-French ancestry. The tatty outfit worn as part of his made-up proletarian persona could not disguise his distinguished appearance. At the same time, despite his readiness to embrace austerity, he obviously enjoyed the good life, especially good food and wine, though, Powell thought, he was left feeling guilt-stricken whenever he did indulge.

Chapter 14

War of Words

'Among the calamities of war may be jointly numbered the diminution of the love of truth, by the falsehoods which interest dictates and credulity encourages.'

Dr Johnson, *The Idler*

Events had forced him willy-nilly into the role of mere spectator of great and momentous happenings. The sense of frustration was acute. He needed the oxygen of action. As Arthur Koestler said of him, he was pitted as much against the enemy of his wretched physical condition as against the forces of totalitarianism which threatened to crush him in other ways.[1]

Like many of his literary contemporaries, he had found work on the fringes of the BBC – occasional reviews for the *Listener*, a discussion for the Home Service and a few talks on literary criticism for the Empire Service. In June 1941 Z. A. Bokhari, the Indian Section's programme organiser, who produced his talks, recommended him for a new post as English language producer in his department, and he was invited to apply. Just prior to this he had written that the BBC was 'very truthful' and more reliable than the press, 'in spite of the stupidity of its foreign propaganda and the unbearable voices of its announcers'.[2] The job on offer, as he must have known, involved producing the very 'foreign propaganda' he had already judged 'stupid'. The fact that he agreed to apply says a good deal about his state of his mind at the time. There was, of course, the encouraging thought that he might contribute, however marginally, towards the freeing of India from imperial rule.

He was not first choice for the post. Stephen Spender had been canvassed, as had the author L. A. G. Strong, and Edward Thompson, biographer of Rabindranath Tagore. All had been discounted for one reason or another. On 25 June 1941 – Orwell's thirty-eighth birthday – R. A. Rendall, Assistant Controller of the BBC Overseas Service, having interviewed Orwell, advised the Director General and the Head of the Empire

Service that he considered Orwell a far more suitable candidate. Apart from his Anglo-Indian background and his time in Burma,

> He is a distinguished writer – one of the same group of Left Wing writers as Spender . . . I was much impressed by him. He is shy in manner but was extremely frank and honest in his interview. He has held strong Left Wing opinions and actually fought for the Republican Government in Spain. He is of the opinion that that may be held against him, though when I questioned him closely about his loyalties and the danger of finding himself at odds with policy, his answers were impressive. He accepts absolutely the need for propaganda to be directed by the Government and stressed his view that in war-time discipline in the execution of Government policy is essential. His past experience and his interest in India and Burma, his literary abilities and contacts, and his [attractive] personality . . . all mark him out as a very suitable person to work on English talks, etc., intended for Indian listeners, particularly Indian students.[3]

That brief was tailor-made for Orwell, and although not everyone thought him a good broadcaster, he would come to be regarded as a highly innovative one. He was duly appointed, 'subject to approval by "The College"', the powerful BBC committee overseen by the Secret Service. Although appointed as E. A. Blair, his suggestion that his pen name 'George Orwell' be used whenever any publicity was involved, was accepted. If he was to be lost inside the air-waves for the rest of the war there was no point in allowing George Orwell to be drowned along with Eric Blair. At last he seemed to have found a part to play in the war against Fascism. It would bring him into contact with a wide range of his literary contemporaries, as well as historians, scientists and politicians, not to mention attractive young women. It would also bring about his final transformation from Blair to Orwell.

As a probationary assistant talks producer, his starting salary was £640 rising by yearly increments of £40. Suddenly his ever-pressing money problems were a thing of the past, and Grub Street just a bad memory. His father would have been proud of him as no doubt was his mother. She had moved to London and was working as an assistant at Selfridges (under that hammer and sickle presumably), living not far from George and Eileen in a small flat in Hampstead with Avril, who was now doing factory work, a far cry from the genteel world of the small-town tea shop.

There was an element of farce in the obtaining of references for Orwell. Sir Arthur Keith, the distinguished surgeon and palaeontologist and Laurence O'Shaughnessy's old mentor, wrote to say he did not know an Eric Arthur Blair and had to be reminded that Blair was also Orwell. Leonard

Moore, his agent, sent a reference for an entirely different person, a sergeant he had known in the Artists' Rifles in the First World War.[4] Keith, once aware of who he was being asked to recommend, and having just read *The Lion and the Unicorn*, gave Orwell a suitably glowing reference.[5] No one seems to have checked Moore's improbable story of the artist-sergeant. The real Blair had already reported for duty and begun training. Obviously the references were immaterial to his appointment, though they may have caused some amusement at the BBC.

Among those on his induction course on 'General Broadcast Technique' were the poet William Empson (author of *Seven Types of Ambiguity*) and his future wife, Henrietta (Hetta) Crouse. Hetta, a beautiful, high-spirited South African and committed Communist, not only caught Empson's eye, but Orwell's, too. He was so smitten by her, she claimed, that he said he would even leave Eileen for her, and refused to attend her wedding.[6] Empson referred to the course, held at Bedford College in Regent's Park, as 'the Liar's School', meaning that there they were taught to recognise some of the Nazi's baser propaganda techniques. He recalled Orwell bemoaning the fact that he was unfit to fight. "'I hold what half the men in this country would give their balls to have," he said, ". . . a yellow ticket [giving exemption from call-up], but I don't want it.'"[7] Another new recruit, Henry Swanzy, was sent with Orwell to record a short eyewitness report from Hyde Park Corner. Swanzy found the BBC's informal atmosphere very agreeable, despite some snobbery, which Orwell simply ignored.[8] According to Martin Esslin, then with the German Service, the influx of brilliant young new people, which also included Louis MacNeice, Roy Campbell and Dylan Thomas, brought a touch of Soho's artistic Bohemia to the place. The secretaries, however, he remembered as 'elderly women, looking like members of the anti-sex league' (though Orwell's all seemed young enough).[9]

While at the Corporation, working from a poky partitioned cubicle (next door to Empson's equally poky cubicle) in what used to be the menswear department of the Peter Robinson store at 200 Oxford Street, he produced a wide range of programmes – talks on science, the arts, politics and current affairs, cooking and various aspects of the war. Many of the lecture courses aimed at Indian students foreshadowed the Open University. He wrote and read weekly news reviews and war commentaries, produced and presented arts magazine programmes and drama documentaries.

By the time he started at the BBC he had reached the conclusion that the 'quasi-revolutionary' phase of the war has passed.[10] This probably made it easier for him to swallow his feeling that the BBC was not exactly a force for change (exemplified by the gagging of J. B. Priestley). But he attempted to broadcast a line which, while not exactly subversive, did not advance the imperialist case. He came closest to subversion with talks on such subjects as 'The Meaning of Scorched Earth' and 'The Meaning of Sabotage'. The news reviews, for which he had access to the BBC's monitoring service, gave him a daily overview of the worldwide struggle between contending power blocs engaged in total war. He could also follow the shifting nuances of Nazi propaganda accompanying the ebb and flow of battle. This kestrel-eye vantage-point gave him a clear view of how wider power struggles worked and so provided him also with the dramatic background against which his last great novel would be set.

Apart from Hetta Crouse, and his continuing friendship with Inez Holden, during his time at the BBC he had liaisons with other women. He was close to Stevie Smith (a friend of Inez) who may have been a victim of the Orwell 'pounce' – she is said to have hinted at 'a fling'. They were on close enough terms for him to accuse her of 'grizzling' and she to accuse him of lying, when a broadcasting engagement he had arranged for her broke down, and for him to end up being satirised in her 1949 novel, *The Holiday*. There he appears as two characters, representing what she saw as two halves of the schizophrenic Orwell – Basil Tate, the Spanish Civil War survivor, and Tom Fox, the object of Basil's lust, 'lanky melancholic murderous [and] mad'.[11] The homosexual Tate 'thinks that women are biologically necessary and resents the necessity, he is like a twelve-year-old boy, he thinks that "girls are no good"'.[12] Tom is icy and homicidal. Here we see in only slight different form the two characters Sayers glimpsed six years earlier – the dangerous Orwell full of 'spite and malice' and the homoerotic Orwell.

An affair with a young BBC secretary is said to have become quite serious, and he may also have had a close relationship with the Jamaican poet, Una Marson, 'a dear creature', according to Henry Swanzy. One of the first things Orwell did at the BBC was take part in a radio play with Marson, acting the part of her West Indian slave-owner. For a man still pondering a family saga this must have evoked strong echoes of the plantation-owning Charles Blair and perhaps a deep sense of guilt to be shared with her. In 1949 she wrote about what had been happening to her, saying, 'I know you have some interest in me & must be wondering a bit . . .'.[13] He was honest enough to admit that he had not always been faithful to Eileen, and she, according to Orwell, had strayed, too. Kopp, of course, is the most likely of her paramours, and her brother's friend Karl Schnetzler another. She was also rumoured to have had an affair with a 'famous' BBC man called Grisewood, meaning either the prominent broadcaster Freddie Grisewood or his brother Harman, later head of the Third Programme, who had been at Oxford with her.[14] Orwell claimed that he was never physically jealous and spiritual loyalty was what mattered.[15] Eileen may not have shared this casual attitude completely and may have suffered more than he imagined, as Lydia Jackson suggested.

Stevie Smith was not alone in including him in a novel. Orwell wrote the first instalment of a 'Story by Five Authors', an idea he cooked up for the Indian Service. Four other writers, including Inez, were to pick up the baton and write following chapters. When Inez wrote her instalment she turned the rich upper-class villain into an Orwell doppelgänger. She made him the survivor of an awful prep school where the boys were all 'snob-brats', using a tinder-lighter acquired while fighting in Spain, recovering from a wound in a squalid Paris hospital where patients call out the number of the newly dead ('numero neuf' etc.), and working in filthy hotel kitchens. Orwell was not amused. In Smith's characterising him as a split personality and Holden turning him into the hate-figure in his own story, unfamiliar images of him appear – Orwell through the eyes of keenly perceptive but put-upon women. He was not the only writer who could use writing to get his own back.

One clause in Orwell's BBC contract, a source of irritation to him from the start, required him to seek permission before undertaking outside work, such as writing. Martin Esslin got round this by writing under a pseudonym; Blair's pseudonym was too well-known for that. To begin with, he simply ignored what he'd signed up to. One or two articles were in the pipeline when he started at the Corporation, including his important essay on seaside postcards, 'The Art of Donald McGill' for *Horizon*. This was another example of the cultural studies essay at which he had become so adept. It stressed the similarity between this mildly obscene art form and the music hall he so much enjoyed, an expression of shared culture and an escape from the pressures and tensions of wartime London. After that he wrote and simply 'forgot' to ask permission.

Orwell was at a watershed in his career, unable to begin the long, contemplative family trilogy he had conceived while working on *Coming Up For Air*. He could have withdrawn to some remote part of the country and ignored the war to pursue his calling, but that was not in his nature. The happy vicar was not to be, but the chaotic events through which he was now passing would make him an author no one could possibly ignore.

The Spanish Civil War had turned his attention back to Europe and the upheaval of this new war had forced him to think about Europe's future. It was this turn of mind that would eventually put paid to any remaining friendship with Wells.

All BBC employees working close to Portland Place used the BBC canteen, where Orwell was often to be found. Mary Treadgold, who had a cubical close to Orwell's, remembered him being in there most days and sometimes at night.[16] According to Martin Esslin, the bleak atmosphere of this gloomy eating-place – 'the drabbest and dreariest environment', with chipped cups and foul food, tables covered with unwashed dishes – was perfectly captured in *Nineteen Eighty-Four*. 'At two or three o'clock in the morning the badly cleaned, stuffy, blacked-out, windowless building was at its most depressing: an atmosphere of hopelessness and futility oozed from the dimly lit corridors and the empty, echoing canteen. Anyone who has experienced these night shifts instantly recognizes their mood in the pages of Orwell's novel.'[17]

Surprisingly, perhaps, it was an atmosphere in which Orwell seemed to thrive. The oppressive buildings, the grim canteen, the rundown, half-blitzed city, made a not unfamiliar environment. It was the world of wretched common lodging houses, filthy hotel kitchens, sordid hospital wards and rat-infested dug-outs – a purgatory in which he was strangely happy to suffer. The blackout, the threat from air raids, the reduced standard of life, and, above all, the inedible food, were all welcomed as generally improving, the prelude to something momentous and uplifting. It was Pilgrim readily shouldering his burden of sin to face dangers lurking along the road to the Holy City. 'Most of us,' he wrote cheerfully in a London Letter to the *Partisan Review*, 'are rapidly going native,'[18] and in one broadcast to India he positively celebrated the end of large incomes through high taxation, the return to home-made amusements and more time spent on the simple pleasures – walking, swimming, playing football and working on allotments – than on cheap commercial entertainment. More people were reading better books, thanks largely to cheap Penguin paperbacks, and 'women who in peacetime might have been sitting in the cinematograph are now sitting at home knitting socks and helmets for Russian soldiers'.[19] In London he had found himself a barber who would give him a short-back-and-sides proletarian haircut to emphasise his sense of belonging among 'the people'.

A notable feature of Orwell's BBC career was his readiness to help friends and acquaintances. At various times he commissioned Cyril Connolly, Stephen Spender, John Lehmann, Rayner Heppenstall, Ethel Mannin, her husband Reg Reynolds, Inez Holden, Stevie Smith, Lydia Jackson, Herbert Read, V. S. Pritchett, and his kind friend Desmond Hawkins. He got on well with his Indian contributors. One, Mulk Raj Anand, became a personal friend, cooking Indian meals for him and Eileen at Langford Court. And, perhaps remembering the plight of his mixed-race relatives in Burma, he was particularly generous to the young Eurasian writer Cedric Dover, not only using him in the Indian Section but recommending him to publishers and editors, and supporting him for a grant from the Royal Literary Fund – although later he concluded that he was 'dishonest' and too pro-Russian.[20] Talks programmes enabled him to meet T. S. Eliot quite frequently and get to know many other distinguished literary figures, including E. M. Forster, Edmund Blunden and (briefly by correspondence) George Bernard Shaw.

Just two months after his appointment, his superiors judged his work 'extremely good – indeed, out of the ordinary' – and his continued employment was duly confirmed.[21] His innovations included a literary competition and a radio literary magazine called 'Voice', which ran for six editions and consisted of poetry and prose readings interspersed with discussions by a studio panel of writers and critics. The chosen themes reflected his immediate concerns. One on war took him back to the sound of bugles. One on American poetry allowed him to make his peace with Eliot after writing an essay for *Poetry (London)* dismissing his recent work as 'gloomy mumblings'. (Eliot appeared in the last three of the six programmes.) In one on 'Christmas' he focused on childbirth, and in one on 'Childhood' declared himself in favour of enlightened libertarian forms of upbringing. He had long wanted children, felt himself unable to have any and was deeply envious of friends who became fathers. 'Thousands of congratulations on the kid,' he had written to Heppenstall. 'What a wonderful thing to have a kid of one's own, I've always wanted one so.'[22]

He worried that he was expected to broadcast an imperialist line to his Indian listeners, but was able to avoid this mostly by producing programmes specifically for Indian university students. He told one contributor, 'We are addressing in the Indian students a difficult and hostile audience and one can probably best approach them by keeping up what one might call an atmosphere of intellectual decency.'[23] The one persuasive line he did use was that the Japanese were not, as some Indian Nationalists assumed, a better alternative to the British; they would not free Indians but enslave them. He favoured independence but (with some reservations) despised Gandhi, whose pacifist tactics he thought played into British hands and illustrated the worthlessness of non-violence in the face of ruthless oppression. And independence he thought would be problematic: 'India is very unlikely to be independent in the sense in which Britain or Germany is now independent . . . In a world in which national sovereignty exists, India cannot be a sovereign state, because she is unable to defend herself . . . it is clear that India has little chance in a world of power politics.'[24]

However carefully he trod the line between propaganda and his conscience, he was still subject to censorship, both within the department and from higher up in the BBC. A particular source of irritation, was that one of these higher-ups, who occasionally censored his programmes and insisted on correct procedures, was his old enemy at Gollancz, Norman Collins, which further alienated him from the intrusive bureaucracy. There were, he complained, too many people at the Corporation churning out enormous numbers of reports and memoranda while publishers were being starved of paper to print books.

One person Orwell was unable to get to the microphone was Wells, partly because he was then suspect at the BBC (and had been kept off the air, along with Shaw, since the outbreak of war), and partly because Orwell's friendly relationship with him had soured dramatically. Wells was by no means party to the Eton tradition of ruthless criticism within a continuing friendship. In fact he was hypersensitive to any adverse opinion. Orwell, of course, believed that brutal honesty was the critic's duty and he could never understand those who thought otherwise. If Orwell, as Pritchett said, enjoyed dashing cold water in your face, he was also the boy to explode a bomb in your garden. His essay 'Wells, Hitler and the World State', which appeared in *Horizon* in August 1941, pulled no punches, made no concessions to friendship. In effect he accused Wells of naivety in failing to understand what kind of enemy Britain was facing. Recently he had depicted the German army as overstretched, poorly equipped and incapable of continuing the war much longer, when in fact it had just invaded the Balkans and gone into Russia. His alternative to the Nazis, said Orwell, was his old scientific utopia of steel and concrete, vegetarianism and reason together with a vision of a society of human rights under a liberal world government. Unfortunately, however, this was a vision for which no one would fight. It was the atavistic emotion of patriotism which mostly shaped the world, and liberals like Wells had always failed to grasp the point. Denigrating and underestimating a dangerous enemy was the same error Wells had made in 1901 and 1914. He came from 'the non-military middle class ... [with] ... an invincible hatred of the fighting, hunting, swashbuckling side of life'. He was 'too sane to understand the modern world'.[25]

A few weeks after the essay appeared Wells had been invited to dine with the Orwells at Langford Court with Inez joining them later, because only three could fit around their small dining table. Wells had not read the article but asked Inez to get him a copy. 'I felt the storm about to brew up like a wave of heat and mist,' she wrote in her diary. 'I sent it round . . .' When Wells saw it, he was incensed that anyone – let alone an upstart youngster of thirty-eight, who had dined at his home – should dare to attack him in such a forthright and derisive fashion.

Inez went on to record what happened after her arrival. Wells, she wrote, sat 'looking half good half pettish', while Orwell 'had the look of an embarrassed prefect'. Empson had shown up, slightly drunk as the expected row was beginning to simmer. 'Thank you for that document,' said Wells ominously. The two men sat opposite one another, with Orwell's essay in front of them, squaring up for a showdown. Wells (in his high-pitched squeaky voice) started quoting, punctuating his reading with 'So says Orwell' and 'this is Orwell'. When Wells called him a defeatist, Inez went to protest, but Wells said, 'No, I want to have this out with Orwell.' The Germans, he said, were *not* all over the Balkans. 'Of course they are,' said Orwell. 'Look at the map.' When Wells said sarcastically, 'Soon we shall be told about Orwell's world, the Orwell Utopia,' Orwell (in his high-pitched grating voice) began to tell him, but was interrupted, at which he said, 'Every time I try to tell you how you ask me what and every time I try to tell you what you ask me how.' Finally they agreed that they both wanted much the same future, Wells being more concerned with what it should be and Orwell with how to achieve it. Empson told Wells that he should retract the charge of defeatism, since Orwell had fought in the worst of conditions in Spain, but Wells was deeply upset by Orwell's dismissing him as 'old fashioned' and his ideas for world government as 'the usual rigmarole'. 'Orwell,' recalled Inez, 'had put some whiskey and snuff between them, and tried to keep it on as friendly as possible a footing. He never got rude or impertinent although it was agreed that his manners were not so good on paper.' Empson went out of his way to defend his BBC colleague, saying, 'Great man Orwell . . . There is an old Etonian and his honesty and fight against his upbringing compels him to say anything he wants to say in a rude manner.' To this Wells replied that it was not Orwell's rudeness that had angered him, but his wrongheaded values. He then declared that it had been an amusing evening, and went home, with the drunken Empson in tow.[26] Wells appeared to have been placated, but, according to Inez, he never forgave Orwell and it would take just one more gaffe for him to be excommunicated irrevocably from the great man's circle.[27]

Orwell was always keen to entertain, as, it seemed, was Eileen who, by the end of the year, was working at the Ministry of Food, and could experiment with the dishes she was recommending to the nation on the BBC's 'Kitchen Front' programmes. He asked Henry Swanzy to dinner saying he wanted him to meet his wife. 'She's not a bad old stick,' he said, a remark which Swanzy thought most peculiar, since it implied that she supported him even when she might have had good reason not to. Lettice Cooper, a friend from the Ministry, thought Eileen handled him brilliantly, mocking him and teasing him about his sweeping generalisations – 'All tobacconists are Fascists,' or 'All scoutmasters are homosexual.' He seemed to enjoy this bantering and chuckled with amusement at her mimicry. But she was finding her new job together with their social life extremely demanding. Cooper, portraying her as Ann in her novel *Black Bethlehem*, wrote, '[She] finds it hard to get through the day. She does her work very well, but she almost always stays late to finish it. She goes home at night without meat or vegetables which she meant to buy in her lunch hour, but had not bought because she had not finished what she was saying at lunch. In the flat when she cooks and cleans for her brilliant erratic husband and their friends, she is generally washing up at midnight.'[28] Curiously, Eileen asked to be known at the Ministry as 'Emily', though no one knew quite why.

Physically they both felt the strain of the times. Eileen took her turn fire-watching at the Ministry, as George did nights on Home Guard duty. The long hours took their toll. Just two months after joining the BBC Orwell suffered an acute attack of bronchitis, and was off ill for a week. In December he was again struck down, this time for two weeks, recuperating at Hinton Martell, close to his father's birthplace in Dorset – both Hardy country and Blair country. A year later he was off sick twice more. One attack occurred on a day when he should have attended a committee meeting of the Eastern Service, but, being ill, had to leave and report to the doctor. That day, 22 October 1941, the committee met in Room 101, 55 Portland Place. Since he chose 'Room 101' for his *Nineteen Eighty-Four* torture chamber, the association of that room with an acute bronchial attack would explain a lot.[29]

By this time, over the years since 1937, he had acquired many of the basic ingredients for *Nineteen Eighty-Four* and *Animal Farm*. Many were incorporated into a talk to the Fabian Society in 1941, 'Culture and Democracy', which gave a clear Orwellian picture of the totalitarian state: 'The totalitarian state exists for the glorification of the ruling clique, which means that the ruling clique are the prisoners of their own power and are obliged to follow any policy, no matter how self-contradictory, which will keep them in power. And having followed their policy they are obliged to justify it, so that all thought becomes a rationalization of the shifts of power politics.' Conformity in a writer achieved at the end of a loaded pistol damaged the emotional source of the creative process. 'Six months ago, Stalin was Bad with a big B. Now he is Good with a big G. A year ago the Finns were Good. Now they are Bad. Mussolini is Bad at this moment, but it would not particularly surprise me to see him Good within a year . . . Literature as we know it is inseparable from the sanctity of the individual, and therefore it is absolutely incompatible with the totalitarian way of life.' Here we have, in outline, the world of *Nineteen Eighty-Four* and the plight of the sensitive individualist Winston Smith.[30]

An important meeting and step forward in Orwell's career occurred at the end of 1941 when he met David Astor, the youngest son of Lord Astor, owner of the *Observer*, and Nancy Astor, the first woman MP to sit in Parliament. David, an Old Etonian, was a captain in the Royal Marines, but his father had given him a column to edit in the *Observer*, and he was looking for likely contributors. Connolly, then the paper's acting literary editor, recommended Orwell. Astor, who knew and had admired *The Lion and the Unicorn*, met him for lunch at a hotel near the BBC, and was immediately struck by the open honesty of the strange tall character who turned up.

'Are you David Astor?' he asked, and, without preliminaries, began to talk as if they'd known one another all their lives.[31] The two became firm and lasting friends, Orwell contributed to Astor's page, and became in due course a celebrated *Observer* contributor.

He had good reason to value his friendship with Connolly. He had introduced Orwell to the *New Statesman* in the mid-thirties, given *Burmese Days* an enthusiastic review, published him in *Horizon* and now put him in touch with the future editor of the *Observer*. The aesthetic Connolly always had a high regard for Orwell as a literary man but felt that, with *Homage to Catalonia*, for example, he lost his touch by becoming entangled with party politics. Orwell in turn regarded Connolly as a man lost to hedonism, but a man whose work gave him pleasure – especially *Enemies of Promise*, which he also found moving. In David Astor he had a great admirer who considered Orwell a writer on whom, as an editor, he could always rely.

Orwell remained angry that people with obvious Fascist sympathies continued in positions of influence. Reflecting on collaborators of Vichy France, he wrote, 'If the Germans got to England, similar things would happen, and I think I could make out at least a preliminary list of the people who would go over.'[32] From his other writings it can be seen who was on his list, not all of them British: Pound 'seems to have plumped definitely for Fascism';[33] Wyndham Lewis spent years 'witch-smelling after "Bolshevists"'; Osbert Sitwell had 'connections with Mosley's movement'; Liddell-Hart was 'inclined to go German'; Hugh Ross Williamson was 'mixed up in the Fascist movement for some time'; the Duke of Bedford was a member of 'a fresh Fascist party' before the war. As to the wider world,

> When one thinks of all the people who support or have supported
> Fascism, one stands amazed at their diversity. What a crew! Think of a
> programme which at any rate for a while could bring Hitler, Pétain,
> Montagu Norman, Pavelitch, William Randolph Hearst, Streicher,
> Buchman, Ezra Pound, Juan March, Cocteau, Thyssen, Father
> Coughlin, the Mufti of Jerusalem, Arnold Lunn, Antonescu, Spengler,
> Beverley Nichols, Lady Houston, and Marinetti all into the same boat![34]

Sometimes he went too far, accusing the pacifist Alex Comfort of being 'objectively Fascist' and falsely naming the Jewish writer Julian Symons as 'pro-Fascist'. He had become all too ready to label and pigeonhole people according to their supposed political affiliations. This listing of enemies or assumed enemies would continue; only their political complexion would change.

Although Orwell claimed that his two years at the BBC were 'wasted years', he did produce some of his most significant essays during that period, including 'Gandhi in Mayfair', 'Rudyard Kipling', and 'Looking Back on the Spanish War'. He wrote articles for *Tribune* on Hardy, Miller and Gissing, essays on Yeats and on the Detective Story, several anonymous contributions for Astor at the *Observer*, and a vigorous exchange of poetic insults with Alex Comfort. There were reviews for *Horizon, Time and Tide, Spectator, New Statesman, Observer* and the *Listener*, several radio dramatisations, a radio talk on Jack London, and a conversation with Swift in good Lord Lyttelton style. He also edited a book of talks from the Indian Service. His conversation with Swift is noteworthy in again comparing his own age to an age of religious dissent and persecution through satirical eyes – both a Swiftian and an Orwellian vision. His essay on the Detective Story foreshadowed his longer lament over the decline of the English murder, already touched on in passing in *Coming Up For Air*.

Writing about Kipling in *Horizon*, he began in uncompromising mood, attacking Eliot for using the wrong arguments to prove that Kipling was not a Fascist. The question needed to be faced, but was more complex than Eliot implied. Kipling was a jingo, 'morally insensitive and aesthetically disgusting'. Once that was admitted, the question was why he had survived the sniggering of refined people who wore so much more badly. He was not 'enlightened', but 'tawdry', 'shallow' and a 'vulgar flag-waver'. He patronised the working class, glorified war and had a hunger for cruelty. But he was 'the only English writer of our time who has added phrases to the language'. His verse was vulgar and sentimental but vital and shamefully pleasurable – he was in fact 'a good bad poet'. In a world of platitudes, Kipling's platitudes stuck and were 'less shallow and less irritating than the "enlightened" utterances of the same period, such as Wilde's epigrams or the collection of cracker-mottoes at the end of *Man and Superman*.' Here was the Tory side of the Tory Anarchist responding to a fellow Tory and recalling the Orwell who wrote *Burmese Days*, who thought the Empire an evil swindle, but some of the people who ran it admirable.[35]

If he expressed an attachment to Kipling, one that was broken and then restored, in another essay he pronounced 'The End of Henry Miller'. 'No more that is of any value,' he predicted, 'will come out of Henry Miller.' Since the power and virility of *Tropic of Cancer* and *Black Spring* his work had petered out. His most recent book, *The Colossus of Maroussi*, about a brief sojourn in Greece, was little more than a pedestrian travel book. One reason why Orwell turned on Miller was that, after stating clearly his hatred of both England and America, once war threatened he quickly escaped to New York. If war came to America, said Orwell, Miller would be in Argentina. And yet, although he thought the American was finished, he pronounced him a true chronicler of his time and place in the thirties, and such men were not common.[36] The Miller he admired – the guiltless hedonist – closely resembled his own mirror image, his looking-glass self, or at least one distinctive facet of it.

Familiarity with Nazi propaganda methods probably coloured his essay 'Looking Back on the Spanish War', published only in extracts at the time. It showed how the experience of six years earlier still haunted him, and how it was still contributing to his ever more refined ideas about a threatening future. 'Nazi theory . . . specifically denies that such a thing as "the truth" exists . . . The implied objective of this line of thought is a nightmare world in which the Leader, or some other ruling clique, controls not only the future but the past. If the Leader says of such and such event, "It never happened" – well it never happened. If he says that two and two are five – well, two and two are five. This prospect frightens me more than bombs . . .'[37] And in his diary that April he wrote, 'We are all drowning in filth . . . I feel that intellectual honesty and balanced judgement have simply disappeared from the face of the earth.'[38] The distinctive ideology of Ingsoc was taking shape.

In the spring of 1942, seemingly having patched up his relationship with Wells, Orwell broadcast a talk, 'The Re-discovery of Europe', later published in the *Listener*, yet again accusing him and his contemporaries of insularity and ill-founded Utopianism. A furious Wells promptly forbade Orwell to set foot on his property ever again, and sent him an angry letter, saying, 'Read my early works, you shit!'[39] Thereafter he always referred to Orwell as 'that Trotskyite with big feet'. To be fair to Wells, he was an insulin-dependent diabetic in declining health. Explosions of rage and Jekyll-to-Hyde personality changes are not uncommon in advanced diabetics. 'The Re-discovery of Europe' could be said to mark the re-awakening of Orwell's Europeanism. Britain's economic vulnerability and isolation at the outbreak of war, made him realise that self-sufficiency was no longer possible, not just in terms of trade but for purposes of defence against a ruthless modern enemy. The choice, as he saw it, was between the Soviet Union, America or a socialist Europe. His preference was for the latter.[40]

The gloomy old Orwell, at home amid blitz and blackout, relishing powdered milk and wartime rations, working late at the BBC, damning hedonism, was by no means oblivious to the comic side of what he called 'this bloodstained harlequinade in which we are living'. Sometimes John Craxton found himself travelling on the underground with Orwell to St John's Wood, and they became friends, occasionally repairing to Langford Court for a late-night coffee. Orwell was fascinated by Craxton's stories of funny incidents involving him and his friends around wartime London – John almost arrested for spying while admiring the architecture of a particular building and wearing a woollen tie (echoed later by the men in *Nineteen*

Eighty-Four arrested for wearing the wrong shoes), and a policeman solemnly and idiotically accusing his friend Lucian Freud, suspiciously contemplating a statue in a London square, of flashing. They both agreed that since the war had broken out England had gone mad.

Craxton in turn considered Orwell a bizarre figure, with his military bearing and strange moustache, something no respectable Bohemian would have been seen dead wearing. But he found him immensely friendly. 'I suppose I was a bit of a wild student, a painter, and he had a nice kind of school-mastery feeling about him, you know, comfortable; and I really enjoyed the way that he was so nice to me. I was terribly flattered.' There was the Etonian manner, but his mind and sense of the absurd gave him an attractive aspect, and his writing on seaside postcards impressed both Craxton and Freud. To Craxton Orwell was the man who discovered pop art. 'To us it was absolutely breath-taking coming from this rather staid school-mastery man with a little officer-class moustache.'[41] He was, for Craxton, 'a visionary realist', a great thinker and multi-faceted personality.

Not so appreciative was John Morris, another old India hand turned broadcaster. Morris was ex-Cambridge, homosexual and a friend of E. M. Forster. He was senior to Orwell at the BBC, but Orwell, it seems, treated him with some disdain, and Morris resented it. Sunday Wilshin, another BBC colleague, claimed that Orwell and Morris had a bantering relationship, one always seeking to score off the other,[42] but Henry Swanzy said Morris grovelled in front of Orwell, felt greatly inferior to him, and envied him deeply.[43]

At the end of June, just after his thirty-ninth birthday, Orwell took a two-week fishing trip to Worcestershire, staying at Beauchamp Court Farm at Callow End, where the rivers Severn and Stour converge, an excellent spot for a keen angler. The land belonged to Lord Beauchamp, an Eton contemporary and childhood friend of Phillip Yorke, whose ancestral home, Madresfield, was close by. (Connolly knew the place and had visited it in the thirties.) The ghost of Yorke might well have drawn him there, July 1942 being the twenty-fifth anniversary of his untimely death. His Lordship's tenant farmers, William and Florence Phillips, grew hops and kept pigs, hens, geese and turkeys. According to Rachel Clapton who worked there during the war, 'Mrs Phillips cooked marvellous meals and all the workers ate together in the farm kitchen.'[44] In view of the novel about an animal revolution Orwell was still gestating, it is worth noting that at Callow End there was not only a Manor Farm, but a farmer called Jones and a family called Pilkington.

Shortly after his return, the Head of the Eastern Service wrote in his yearly report of him: 'Good, sensitive, loyal work. He has strong convictions but is never too proud to accept guidance.' He recommended his promotion to talks producer with a £40 increment on his salary.[45] But, despite his good performance, he was feeling far less happy at the BBC than he had hoped. Policy was vague and the place disorganised – 'halfway between a girls' school and a lunatic asylum,' he called it.[46] Then, barely a month after his promotion, a BBC Intelligence Officer, Laurence Brander, returned from India with the bad news that hardly anyone there listened to the Indian Service programmes, and a despairing Orwell wrote in his diary, 'Our broadcasts are utterly useless . . . This is what I have been saying for some time past.'[47] The demand for 'high-brow' talks he had been assured was there in India was now exposed as a myth, and he began hoping there might be an audience among British troops in the Middle East who could also pick up his broadcasts.

Brander recommended that Orwell broadcast his own news reviews, capitalising on his popularity among Indians. He was ready to do this but stressed that, as 'Orwell', he would be selling his literary reputation – that of an independent commentator roughly 'agin the government' – and thought it best if he took an anti-Fascist line rather than an imperialist one and kept off subjects on which he disagreed with official policy.[48] But the move was not an unqualified success. In a listener research survey a year later, Orwell's popularity rating was low, only 16 per cent voting for him against 52 per cent for E. M. Forster and 68 per cent for J. B. Priestley, while J. B. Clark, Controller of Overseas Services, who listened to one of his broadcasts, reported that he found Orwell's voice unattractive and unsuited to the microphone. It might actually repel some of Orwell's admirers and provide easy grounds to those who might want to get Orwell off the air, he said. Using him would only attract hostile criticism to the BBC.[49] No action followed. Orwell had powerful defenders, not least the people who had appointed him, including his immediate boss, Bokhari.

By now the Orwells had moved to a ground-floor-and-basement flat in Mortimer Crescent, a tree-lined backwater of mid-Victorian semi-detached houses a few streets north towards Kilburn High Road. They had the run of the garden in which Orwell kept chickens, and the basement became a carpentry workshop, where they kept a spare bed for visitors. Henry Dakin, Marjorie's boy, stayed for a week, and remembered 'Uncle Eric' taking him to see Chaplin's *The Gold Rush* which he thought hilarious but Henry found thoroughly boring. His lasting memory of Eileen was of a woman, cigarette permanently dangling from her lips, spilling ash down the black overcoat she wore constantly against the cold in the poorly heated flat.[50] Chain-smoking was now a permanent feature of their lives together.

Anthony Powell, who also slept one night beside the carpenter's bench, recalled being kept awake by a thunderous barrage from the neighbourhood anti-aircraft battery. Orwell said the noise suited him; it ensured that he was up early enough to restoke the boiler for the morning's hot water.

Powell had a glimpse of the martial spirit of the unfulfilled romantic when he told him that Evelyn Waugh was now a commando and got the reply, 'Why can't someone on the Left do that sort of thing?' It was just the role Orwell himself coveted.[51] When David Astor stayed over at Mortimer Crescent, what he remembered was being woken by the clang of buckets as George fed his chickens at sunrise.[52] One person who resisted invitations to dinner and the bed in the workshop was Eliot who suggested lunch in town instead. Ruth Pitter, who came to dinner, found him looking ill and ghost-like and even thought he must be dying, and Eileen, too, she thought seemed to be going through a bad time.

With the British victory at El Alamein, the feeling that the balance of power in the war had shifted was widespread. On 15 November church bells rang throughout the country and Orwell marked the occasion by closing his Wartime Diary. He suggested it might be worth publishing as a joint diary with Inez – his rather news-based factual record, full of political reflections, complementing her more personal anecdotal journal. However, it soon became evident that they did not sit well together. Orwell's diary remained unpublished during his lifetime; Inez's was published separately in 1943.[53]

He found personal antagonisms difficult to sustain, especially when he got to know people, as he found with Spender. George Woodcock, the Anarchist writer, had appeared on one of his programmes, then attacked Orwell as an ex-colonial policeman who sided with his old imperialist friends, an anti-war writer who now criticised pacifists.[54] Orwell responded angrily, accusing Woodcock of not knowing what he was talking about and of compromising his own principles by broadcasting to India himself. Woodcock then replied that he had simply been trying to find out what the Indian Service was up to and had refused the BBC's fee. Later, recognising him on a London bus, Orwell beckoned Woodcock to join him, saying he thought it wrong to allow arguments in print to carry over into personal relationships. The two men became friends thereafter. There was a side of Orwell very sympathetic to the Anarchists, even though he thought their wartime pacifism was wrong and only aided Hitler. They disagreed on various issues, but to Woodcock Orwell was always 'the Crystal Spirit' after his poem about the Italian militiaman briefly encountered in Barcelona.

The romantic wartime role he hankered after was never to be. At the beginning of 1943 a proposal to employ him as a war correspondent for the *Observer* fell through when he failed the medical, and at the end of January he again went down with bronchitis, an attack serious enough to have kept him off work for three weeks. He had barely recovered when his mother fell ill and was taken to New End Hospital in Hampstead, ironically once a workhouse, a short walk from Booklovers' Corner. She, too, had contracted bronchitis, in her case complicated by emphysema – another victim of those vulnerable Limouzin lungs. Even so, it failed to make her son think twice about smoking; the rolled cigarette and pungent shag tobacco were now an integral part of the Orwell persona, as much as Tolkien's pipe or Churchill's cigar. On 19 March, with George at her bedside, Ida died of heart failure. She was sixty-seven. There would be something for him when her will was made probate later that year – a share from the sale of the family home at Southwold, but little more. In the New Year he, Avril and Marjorie returned for the last time to Montague House to sort out and divide up what was left of their inheritance.[55]

As is clear in his essay on Dickens, there was often a strongly egotistical focus to Orwell's writing. One of his 'undeclared' articles while at the BBC was a rather self-revealing sketch about Gissing for *Tribune*. He was, thought Orwell, the best and purest novelist England had produced. Dickens, Fielding, Smollett and Joyce were all superior in 'natural talent', perhaps, but never satisfied just to be 'like life' and always wanting 'to get a laugh as often as possible'. Gissing gave in to no such temptation, and was 'genuinely interested in character and telling a story'. The central theme of his major novels was 'not enough money', the poverty, not of the working-class poor whom he truly despised, but of the respectable middle class. This class, Gissing thought, suffered more under poverty than did the working class. Orwell tended to agree, and considered books like *New Grub Street* too horrible for the professional journalist to read and *The Odd Women* too distressing for spinsters. Obliquely he was referring to himself, *Keep the Aspidistra Flying* and *A Clergyman's Daughter*. Gissing, however, was anti-socialist and anti-democratic. Hating a society ruled by money he had no desire to change it, hoping only to escape it in order to live 'a civilized, aesthetically decent life' lost in classical learning. Orwell had enough in common with Gissing and also differed from him enough to find his fear and hatred of the poor fascinating. Studying him, he believed, one could learn something about the origins of Fascism. However, to understand it, he thought, one needed to have a streak of Fascism in oneself, thereby hinting at the dark side he kept mostly concealed behind his saintly socialist reputation.[56]

Towards Yeats, who also hated equality and democracy, he was less forgiving. At first he disliked his work, then Michael Sayers seemed to have persuaded him otherwise. By the late thirties he had come to regard him as a Fascist, too, though by 1943 he had softened towards him somewhat. Now, he concluded, 'Yeats may have held some absurd and undesirable beliefs, but he would never in any circumstances have committed what he would have regarded as an aesthetic sin.'[57] Writers whose ideas were shrouded in mystical language and rooted in a belief in magic were at far remove from Orwell's own commitment to clear, perspicuous prose, but he could not quite bring himself to ignore Yeats's poetic achievements.

Orwell greatly enjoyed the company of young writers. Through J. M. Tambimuttu, who edited *Poetry (London)*, he met a 21-year-old Oxford undergraduate and poet, Michael Meyer. Meyer, a university contemporary of Keith Douglas and Philip Larkin, already knew Graham Greene, and wrote to Orwell hoping they could meet. They met for lunch at the Hungarian Czarda restaurant in Soho's Dean Street. Meyer was greatly surprised by his appearance – 'his great height and thinness, his staring pale-blue eyes and his high-pitched drawl with its markedly Etonian accent, so out of keeping with most (not all) of what he wrote'. Meyer had been at Wellington when Orwell's old Eton contemporary Bobby Longden was head and was wearing the Wellington tie, which Orwell recognised. He was invited to dinner at Mortimer Crescent and met Eileen, 'a pretty brown-haired Irish girl . . . only two years Orwell's junior, though she looked much younger'. One outstanding feature of any visit to the Orwells, he remembered, was the tea – 'always black and strong, with large leaves floating on top, poured by George from a huge metal pot which must have held the best part of a gallon'.[58] Six heaped teaspoons to the quart was his preferred measure – the Eton samovar tradition lived on. There, over the teacups, he heard the story of the disastrous evening with Wells. Later he would be one of the privileged few ever to be told about an Orwell work-in-progress.

By now, almost invariably in writing to literary people he signed himself 'George Orwell', even to those such as John Lehmann, who had known him at Eton. However, some letters he signed 'E. A. B. (George Orwell)', some simply 'E. A. Blair', and a few 'Eric Blair'. Old friends and family still referred to him as Eric (Avril positively insisted on it), but Meyer found that Eileen had long got used to calling him George. The literary persona had still not completely taken over, was not quite set in its mould, but was there to deploy when the occasion afforded itself, a mask to adopt or dispense with at will. Later he said that the two names sometimes caused confusion and he considered changing it by deed poll, but, as a lawyer would have to be involved, he recoiled from doing so.

With his BBC colleague John Morris he could switch to fake proletarian when occasion demanded. Morris wrote a hostile memoir of Orwell portraying him as a boorish inverted snob who sneered at his middle-class manners, slurped his tea from his saucer deliberately to discomfort him, and ridiculed his bourgeois drinking habits. That Orwell was probably playing with him was seemingly unnoticed. Morris also claimed that he was once unforgivably rude to L. H. Myers who, unknown to him, had funded his convalescence in Marrakech. But Orwell and Myers had their own robust relationship: Orwell often teased him because he was wealthy and pro-Russian (a way of coping with his liberal guilt, Orwell thought), and Myers defended himself and provoked Orwell with statements such as, 'I don't believe in freedom'.[59] The origins of 'Freedom is slavery', perhaps.

He was in good polemical mood in the late summer, broadcasting a straightforward attack on simplistic Marxist literary criticism for confusing art with politics (socialist art good; non-socialist art bad), criticising social- ist antipathy towards intellectuals, and engaging in a lively exchange of poetic insults with Alex Comfort who, in Woodcock's magazine *Now*, had condemned the war and poets and writers engaged in it.[60] His earlier attack on Comfort had been brutal; in verse he was rather more polite. Although Orwell used his reply to Comfort to justify his own participation in BBC propaganda (he had come to distinguish between 'honest and dishonest propaganda'), there was a sense of his wanting to liberate himself from that treadmill, to free his own voice to speak out for itself, away from the blue-pencilling bureaucrats.

As 1943 wore on, Orwell was finding life with the bureaucrats increas- ingly irksome, and having to submit to censorship more and more distasteful. Although he hoped that by broadcasting during that 'blood- stained harlequinade' he was somehow 'keeping a tiny lamp alight somewhere', he had also grown contemptuous of the means by which he was doing so. By the summer he was referring to the BBC as 'a mixture of whoreshop and lunatic asylum'.[61] Perhaps the fact that he began a 'log of earnings' on 12 July indicated that he was already considering resigning and was calculating his likely income as a freelance writer.[62]

His superiors must have realised that the restrictions under which BBC staff were required to work were vexatious to Orwell, but they held him in very high regard. Rushbrook Williams, Head of the Eastern Service, was a particular champion of his brilliantly eccentric colleague and again recom- mended him for an annual increment in the most sympathetic and glowing terms, recognising the unique qualities and deep integrity which distin- guished his writing. But:

Conscientiously as he endeavours to achieve objectivity, he finds it difficult to realise the shock which certain sentiments, to him plain matters of fact, may cause to the conservatively minded. For which reasons, his scripts require close scrutiny: and he is himself a poor judge of 'political expediency'. He supports uncomplainingly a considerable burden of poor health. This never affects his work, although it occasionally strains his nerves. I have the highest opinion of his moral, as well as his intellectual capacity. He is transparently honest, incapable of subterfuge, and, in earlier days, would have been either canonised – or burnt at the stake! Either fate he would have sustained with stoical courage. An unusual colleague: but a mind, and a spirit, of real and distinguished worth.[63]

Despite his £40 rise and his growing prestige as a producer, Orwell was by now deeply unhappy at the BBC. In mid-August his departmental head, Bokhari, challenged him over articles published in the *Observer* and *New Statesman*, asking whether he had obtained permission to write them. Orwell replied: 'No; I did it in the beginning but I can't be bothered with it any more. In any case, I intend to leave the Corporation as soon as possible.' Bokhari was clearly annoyed by this and wrote to Rushbrook Williams: 'We simply must maintain a certain amount of discipline in the office. Blair, or anybody else, can't have the best of both worlds: he cannot be working for an organisation whose policy is well known and also try to please the Leftists.'[64] But having to clear what he wrote with bureaucrats, including Collins, he now found just too intolerable. When Rushbrook Williams saw him about this, he said he intended to resign and revert to full-time journalism. But he was in no immediate hurry, and planned to take two weeks' leave on full pay before resigning formally. On 1 September his annual salary rose to £720, and he immediately went on leave, giving in his notice on his return.

Orwell had been particularly frustrated at seeing two years pass without publishing a book. Now, however, came the prospect of Penguin reprinting *Burmese Days* (it appeared the following May with certain corrections – 'Chinese' for 'Chinaman', 'Burmese' for 'Burman', 'Oriental' for 'native'), and a book on *The English People* was commissioned by the British Council. He also published his anthology of radio talks. Since none of Orwell's many recordings has survived, this collection, *Talking to India,* stands as the single wartime epitaph to his broadcasting career.

Having indicated his intention of resigning, he continued reviewing at full stretch. In deference to Bokhari and Rushbrook Williams he asked permission in each case with heavily ironic notes beginning, 'I am instructed to inform you of articles etc. in the press which I contemplate publishing.' In signalling his permission Rushbrook Williams pencilled, 'These articles are not to be written under Mr. Blair's own name but under his pen name (and personality) as George Orwell. I recommend permission.'[65] His boss, it is worth noting, recognised Orwell as a personality quite distinct from Blair.

That summer he wrote to Heppenstall: 'Re. cynicism, you'd be cynical yourself if you were in this job. However I am definitely leaving it probably in 3 months. Then by some time in 1944 I might be near-human again & able to write something serious. At present I'm just an orange that's been trodden on by a very dirty boot.'[66] But, perhaps anticipating freedom and wanting to try something different, he dramatised four short stories – Anatole France's 'Crainqueville', Ignazio Silone's, 'The Fox', Wells's 'A Slip Under The Microscope' and Hans Andersen's 'The Emperor's New Clothes' – all stories with a moral. The Andersen story reflected a lively new interest in the fairy story, a vein Max Plowman had once suggested he explore, and which probably he shared with Eileen, the one-time student of Tolkien. Like Andersen's little boy, Orwell, too, had a readiness to point to naked truths which others were reluctant to acknowledge.

In his resignation letter to Rushbrook Williams on 25 September, Orwell was anxious not to give the impression that it was on a matter of policy or because of a grievance. 'I feel that throughout my association with the BBC I have been treated with the greatest generosity and allowed great latitude. On no occasion have I been compelled to say on air anything that I would not have said as a private individual. And I should like to thank you personally for the very understanding and generous attitude you have always shown towards my work.' But he felt that broadcasting propaganda to India in the political circumstances was an impossible task, and said he preferred to go back to journalism which did, he thought, produce a verifiable effect.[67] Of him Rushbrook Williams wrote: 'I cannot speak too highly of his character or his attainments. He is of a rare moral dignity: his literary and artistic taste is unerring. He leaves at his own request to the regret of the whole Department.' Asked about his suitability for re-employment at the Corporation, he wrote, 'Without reservation: Without reservation.'[68] On the day he left the India Section gave him a surprise farewell party, organised by his secretary.[69]

A year after leaving the BBC, Orwell wrote his post-mortem on the experience, implying that writers like him came out of it 'with nothing to show for their labours and with not even the stored-up experience that the soldier gets in return for his physical suffering'.[70] He clearly underestimated what as a broadcaster he gained as material for future work. The war years at the BBC (plus occasional work for the Ministry of Information – telegraphic address: 'Miniform') gave him much that he would use for *Nineteen Eighty-Four*: the Ministry of Truth – Minitrue (the BBC censorial bureacracy), Newspeak (Nazi and Soviet propaganda), Winston's cubicle (his BBC 'office'), the telescreen (the BBC's rudimentary television service), and Room 101. His experience of Communist propaganda and Nazi propaganda picked up via the BBC Monitoring Service must have strongly suggested Doublethink and Newspeak, although Esperanto, Lance Hogben's 'interglossa', and the Basic English scheme developed by C. K. Ogden (both of which greatly interested him) also made their contributions.

When he was preparing to leave the BBC the *Observer*'s editor again wondered if he might go for them as a war correspondent to North Africa. The job would have brought him close to the military action, a prospect that excited him greatly. But again he failed his medical (he had been given a grade 'D' at his previous medical), and judged 'Unfit for Service Overseas owing to the condition of his chest.' Unfortunately for Orwell, the examination took place just a week after he returned from yet another sick leave, and three days before bronchitis struck him again. From the doctor's report it is evident that he was quite ill – probably identified again as tuberculous. If he was prepared to submit to a programme of treatment and responded well enough, said his report, he might be reconsidered at a later date.[71] He told Empson, 'The impudence of it, when they know perfectly well I'm too ill to stay here. Probably save my life going to North Africa. But if it didn't, they might have to give the widow something, d'you see.'[72] Even so, there was some talk of him joining the *Observer* full-time, but to David Astor's relief, this idea came to nothing. After the war Astor became the paper's editor and the worst thing he could have imagined, he said, was having to reject anything written by Orwell.[73]

The main reason Orwell turned down the *Observer* job was an invitation from *Tribune* to become its literary editor. The job paid only £500 a year compared to the £720 he left at the BBC, but involved only three days' work a week, which meant free time for writing – far more valuable to him than money. And at *Tribune* he could write articles without having to ask permission from some office-bound bureaucrat. He also had a new book to write.

On leaving the BBC he also left the Home Guard, resigning he said 'on medical grounds'. Of course, those medical grounds were there when he joined, so there were probably other reasons – Orwell was now forty-one, so no longer required for National Service, the threat of invasion – and hope of revolution – had passed, and now he needed every spare moment to make up time lost as a creative writer, to accelerate towards that long-held goal of becoming Eric (now George) THE FAMOUS AUTHOR. That long-projected family saga was still aching to be written, but the idea of an animal revolution had come to grip him more powerfully, an idea that would give him a novel to make him more famous than he had ever dreamt.

Orwell's penchant for role-playing was noted once in a rather vivid way by Anthony Powell. Orwell came to visit one day when Powell's young son was asleep in a cot by the window. Powell went out to get a book, and on his return saw Orwell engrossed by a picture at the far end of the room. When he went to the cot to adjust the covers, he felt something hard. It was a huge clasp knife. 'How on earth did that get there?' he asked. Orwell seemed embarrassed, and then said, 'Oh, I gave it him to play with. I forgot I'd left it there.' This incident, thought Powell, illustrated aspects of Orwell normally difficult to describe – 'his attitude to childhood; his shyness, part genuine, part assumed; his schoolboy leanings; above all, his taste for sentimental vignettes'.

> Why, in the first place, should he want to burden himself, in London, with a knife that looked like an adjunct of a fur-trapper's equipment? Echoes perhaps of Dangerous Dan McGrew? Why take such pains to avoid being found playing with a child, a perfectly natural instinct, flattering to a parent? If some authentic masculine sheepishness made him hesitate at being caught in such an act, why leave the knife behind as evidence? It was much too big to be forgotten.

It also, he thought, revealed the romantic side of Orwell, the man who liked to see himself coping alone with a young baby. In fact he had a 'mixture of down-to-earth scepticism with a dash of self-dramatization . . . a contradictory element in Orwell's character. With all his honesty, ability to face disagreeable facts, refusal to be hoodwinked, there was always also about him a touch of make-believe, the air of acting a part.'[74]

Chapter 15

Tribune of the People

'The driving force, the dynamo as you might say, of any artist is his emotions, and his emotions do not necessarily correspond to the political necessity of the moment.'

Orwell, 'Culture and Democracy', 1941

On 26 November 1943, the day after he left the BBC, *Tribune* announced, 'George Orwell, the well-known writer and critic, is joining the staff of *Tribune* as Literary Editor.'[1] He had gone to the BBC as Blair, he went to *Tribune* as Orwell.

He already had a considerable pool of literary contacts on which to draw, but, oddly enough, his first letters from *Tribune* were to poets – Eliot, Comfort, Henry Treece – a sign perhaps that the poet in him had not expired completely. He also alerted friends and acquaintances to his new position, hoping that they would be able to write for him. Before long, in his columns, their names duly began to appear: Koestler, Fyvel, Empson, Powell, Spender, Heppenstall, Inez Holden, Stevie Smith and Elisaveta Fen (Lydia Jackson). Showing again that he could not easily sustain personal hostilities over a long period, he even reprinted an article on Kipling by Auden (whose wartime absence in America he deplored).

The job gave him the chance to make new friends among a new generation of young writers, notably Julian Symons, David Sylvester, Peter Vansittart, Paul Potts and Margaret Crosland. Orwell the literary editor was recalled by Vansittart as 'too enigmatic and teasing to like too much',[2] Margaret Crosland remembered being almost drowned in his extraordinary sea-blue eyes,[3] Sylvester thought he suffered fools too gladly,[4] and Potts, the rangy Irish-Canadian poet (Catholic-educated, Whitmanesque libertarian, notorious sponger and haunter of London's Bohemia), recalled him paying starving poets for poems he never intended publishing.[5]

To Potts he was more than kind, taking him to lunch with other writers in Soho and even recommending him to Ivor Brown, the editor of the

Observer. He was not as kind to everyone, and when he asked John Morris to contribute and Morris, after writing four or five reviews, complained of not been paid, Orwell simply replied, 'Oh, we don't pay for reviews, you know. It's all for the Cause!' It was probably his last chance to score off his old BBC adversary.[6]

Orwell was popular with his contributors and gained a considerable following among readers but he had a poor opinion of himself in the job.

> The fact is that I am no good at editing. I hate planning ahead, and I have a psychical or even physical inability to answer letters. My most essential memory of that time is of pulling out a drawer here and a drawer there, finding it in each case to be stuffed with letters and manuscripts which ought to have been dealt with weeks earlier, and hurriedly shutting it up again. Also, I have a fatal tendency to accept manuscripts which I know very well are too bad to be printed. It is questionable whether anyone who has had long experience as a freelance journalist ought to become an editor. It is too like taking a convict out of his cell and making him governor of the prison. Still it is 'all experience', as they say, and I have friendly memories of my cramped little office looking out on a back yard, and the three of us who shared it huddling in the corner as the doodle-bugs came zooming over, and the peaceful click-click of the typewriters starting up again as soon as the bomb had crashed.[7]

The tall, dark, bearded Symons, who, in his *Partisan Review* column, Orwell once implied was a 'Fascist' then characteristically befriended, found him deeply impressive. 'You couldn't meet him without being aware that you were in the presence of a kind of "original", a character,' he wrote.[8] What he found especially remarkable when they first met was his readiness to admit past errors. 'After about half an hour or so, he said in a gruff, apologetic tone, "Very sorry I called you a Fascist or pretty well called you a Fascist. I shouldn't have said that." And he actually in a later letter to *Partisan Review* apologised for this. This is a rare thing for a journalist.' He could also be amusingly naive. Once he appeared in an army greatcoat which had been dyed dark brown. 'This is an army greatcoat,' he announced proudly. 'You wouldn't know that, would you?' 'Well, I would, as a matter of fact, George,' said Symons. And once, in a restaurant he recalled Orwell tucking into the inedible Victory Pie and saying with great gusto, 'You won't find anything better in London than this.' But beneath this apparently guileless innocence stood the heroic Orwell, happy to endure the hardships and discomfort of wartime life, who told Symons, 'I hate London. I really would like to get out of it, but of course you can't leave while people are being bombed to bits all around you.'[9] Orwell never introduced him to Eileen, because, Symons thought, he liked to keep his various friends in compartments.

George Strauss and Stafford Cripps had founded *Tribune*, a paper of the non-Stalinist left, in 1937. It was a platform for many Labour Party and other left-wing radicals. As literary editor (and fully paid-up member of the National Union of Journalists), Orwell worked there under Aneurin Bevan, the paper's managing editor, and his deputies Jon Kimche (Orwell's fellow assistant at Booklover's Corner in the thirties) and Evelyn Anderson, with Sally McEwan as his secretary. At the weekly press conferences the separation between the political front section and the literary back pages was dramatised by Bevan holding forth uninterrupted at the beginning and then Orwell holding forth uninterrupted at the end.[10]

Orwell was given his own column, called 'As I Please', enabling him to range across a wide spectrum of topics – from racism and neo-Fascism to the solar topi and the Woolworth's rose. Although these were often controversial, Bevan always defended him. The kind of short essay he produced followed in the long tradition of Hazlitt, Lamb, Stevenson, Belloc and Chesterton. It was a form of good-humoured prose rumination practised in Orwell's day at Eton in the *College Chronicle* and in Butler's 'Written Sketches', which he so enjoyed. Kimche claimed credit for the title (although Wells had used 'As I See It' for his pre-war BBC broadcasts, and 'I Write As I Please' was the title for a 1935 American bestseller). It captured Orwell's new mood of liberation from the grip of censorial bureaucrats. In that same spirit of independence he threw himself into his writing with great élan, and his output duly accelerated. On top of his weekly column and occasional reviews to *Tribune*, he continued his London Letter for *Partisan Review* and began reviewing regularly for both the *Observer* and the *Manchester Evening News*. He also got down at last to writing a novel (*Animal Farm*) and preparing a collection of essays for Warburg.

One issue he took up in his *Tribune* column was racism and anti-Semitism, and he was especially critical of the anti-black racism of American soldiers in Britain. It was something he had noticed among Americans in Paris in the late twenties, rather tarnishing his fond image of the US as a Whitmanesque democracy. He would later imply that through the GIs, violent and sadistic crime had been imported into England from America, which he also saw as a strangely female-dominated culture. Of the cover of a New York fashion magazine showing a woman with a man at her feet apparently kissing the hem of her dress, he commented, 'not a bad symbolic picture of American civilization, or at least one important side of it'.[11]

But it was more state-sponsored violence that preoccupied him at that time. In the *Manchester Evening News* he reviewed Koestler's *Arrival and Departure*, a novel set in an imaginary country. This exploration of the motivation of revolution Orwell called 'a sort of fable of our times', a genre then very much on his own mind. It was, he argued, to foreigners like Koestler that English people, ignorant of totalitarianism, largely owed their political education, especially in the menacing atmosphere of the thirties, for which here he coined the phrase 'cold war', a 'first usage' which even the *Oxford English Dictionary* failed to pick up. The book might not work as a novel, but as an allegory it did – 'a story of temptations', of the World, the Flesh and the Devil. Only Heaven was absent. It was full of horrific stories of Nazi terrorism, stories which needed to be told as a warning.[12] It was the same rationale he would employ later in writing his own political horror story.

He was well aware that his long-term reputation as a writer could hardly rest on his novels alone, and that his essays had a very distinctive even pioneering style, works of cultural as much as literary criticism. As contributions to periodicals they were ephemeral; only between hard covers could they hope to survive. In January he listed for Leonard Moore the essays he hoped to have published as a collection, including 'Charles Dickens', 'Wells, Hitler and the World State', 'Rudyard Kipling', 'W. B. Yeats' and 'Gandhi in Mayfair'. This would not appear until 1946 under the title *Critical Essays*, and would by then also include 'Boys' Weeklies', 'The Art of Donald McGill', and essays on Salvador Dali ('Benefit of Clergy'), detective stories ('Raffles and Miss Blandish'), Koestler, and P. G. Wodehouse. More importantly he announced the new novel on which he was working. 'It is a fairy story but also a political allegory, and I think we may have some difficulties about finding a publisher. It won't be any use trying it on Gollancz nor probably Warburg, but it might be worth dropping a hint elsewhere that I have a book coming along. I suppose you know which publishers have paper and which haven't?'[13]

For Orwell the year 1944 would bring dramatic changes, not least a new book completed. On a visit to George and Eileen that winter, Michael Meyer was let into the secret of the work-in-progress. It was, he was told, 'a "kind of parable" to remind people of the realities of Stalinist Communism, which he [George] felt were in danger of being forgotten because of sympathy for Russian resistance to the Germans. His summary went something like this. "There's a farm, and the animals get fed up with the way the farmer runs it, so they chuck him out and try to run it themselves. But they run it just as badly as the farmer and become tyrants like him, and they invite the humans back and gang up with them to bully the other animals . . . It's a kind of parable, you see."' Meyer thought it most unpromising. When he finally came to read it he was astonished. 'Never can a book have been so much better than its author's account of it.'[14] Another who was let into the secret by Eileen, was Lettice Cooper at the Ministry. 'He read it aloud to her every night he was writing it . . . And she saw at once that it was a winner, the most attractive thing he'd done yet. And she used to tell us about it every morning when we were having our coffee. It was very exciting.'[15]

The evolution of *Animal Farm* is complex, but one event looms over all others. The idea of an animal revolution had come to him on his return from Spain in 1937, and the urge to warn against the totalitarian evil in some simple and dramatic way had never left him. The sights and smells of the farmyard were of course familiar to him since childhood around Henley and in Cornwall. Not far from St Cyprian's School was a village called Willingdon with a Red Lion pub and a stone quarry nearby, which he could hardly have avoided on his schoolboy rambles across the Sussex Downs. Callow End had its Manor Farm, its Farmer Jones and Mr Pilkington, while Wallington had its Farmer John Innes and a Manor Farm, which reared pigs. All of these in their way must have furnished Orwell with the setting and landscape for his novel.

Although he called the book 'A Fairy Story', Eileen's old teacher, J. R. R. Tolkien (whose own 1937 fairy tale, *The Hobbit*, is itself a political allegory), would have classed it as a 'beast fable', 'in which the animals are the heroes and heroines, and men and women, if they appear, are mere adjuncts'.[16] Orwell acknowledged Eileen's influence on the book, 'her fondness for it and her help with the planning of it'.[17] They were no doubt familiar with the long tradition of 'beast fable' stretching back to Chaucer and Aesop through Kafka and Kipling, and Orwell, of course, had read Beatrice Potter, Kipling and Swift as a child, and studied Aristophanes ('The Frogs' and 'The Birds') with Gow at Eton. Another likely source of inspiration was Thurber, with whose political fables he was familiar. The one closest in tone to *Animal Farm* is 'The Very Proper Gander', the tale of a gander expelled from the farm by malign rumour-mongers, a case of the slippery nature of language and the turning of it to cruel political ends. Then, in Kenneth Grahame's *The Golden Age*, children ponder the overbearing power of adults in a passage that smacks of Old Major's peroration against humans in *Animal Farm*. Orwell's book also turns another Grahame book, *The Wind in the Willows*, on its head. Grahame's bourgeois animal heroes are at war with a dangerous underclass of stoats and weasels. Orwell's heroes are proletarians, working animals; the pigs are leisured villains, manipulating through twisted intelligence. Nor should be forgotten Orwell's schoolboy penchant for fables, or his comment that Swift, 'when he wanted to describe good instead of evil, had to turn from men to horses'.[18] In *Animal Farm* Orwell's horses perform that same symbolic role. There are echoes, too, of Wells's

The Island of Dr Moreau in which pig-men walk on their hind legs and where there are rules about walking on four legs.

It was, once again, a story of Paradise Gained and Paradise Lost, but now concentrated into a political parable of considerable power. The book brought into play a wide range of his reflections on the nature of totalitarianism. The emergence of a class devoted entirely to the pursuit of power and its retention at all costs (the pigs), the use of language to deceive and manipulate through sudden switches of line and their justification (the principle of Animalism cunningly inverted), the use of arbitrary and lethal terror (the dogs), and rewriting of history in the interests of the powerful (the story of the Battle of the Cowsheds rewritten). 'The really frightening thing about totalitarianism,' wrote Orwell, 'is not that it commits "atrocities" but that it attacks the concept of objective truth: it claims to control the past as well as the future.'[19]

Even as he was completing his 'fairy story', a 'horror story' was beginning to intrude itself, hinged upon this fear (of the large-scale falsification of history), but also drawing on a succession of nightmares, some of which had plagued him since childhood. He wrote to Gleb Struve, a Russian lecturer at London University, referring to *Animal Farm* as 'a little squib which might amuse you', and enquiring about a book called *We* by Yevgeny Zamyatin, which would add a further dimension to the horror story he was now contemplating.[20]

That city winter was a grim time for bronchitis sufferers. It was, he said, 'foul . . . not at all cold, but with endless fogs, almost like the famous "London fogs" of my childhood'. There were air-raid alarms and rumours of German rocket guns directed at London, and giant bombs to be towed across the Channel in gliders by fleets of aircraft. There was an air of *The War of the Worlds* about it. It was this gloom-ridden, shabby and broken-down London, threatened by flying bombs and later that year by V2 rockets, which would supply the immediate backdrop to his last and most terrifying novel.

Michael Meyer discovered that Orwell had never met Graham Greene, so invited them both to lunch at the Czarda on 11 June, his twenty-third birthday. He was delighted how well they got on but disappointed that they talked more about politics than literature. They were still talking when the restaurant closed, so carried on at the pub across the road. The following week they met at one of Orwell's favourite restaurants, the Elysée in Percy Street. It was directly opposite the Akropolis, a restaurant from which Orwell had been ejected for removing his jacket. He now patronised the Elysée so that the Akropolis proprietor could see him dining in shirt sleeves. Next, Greene played host at Rules in Maiden Lane, just off the Strand, a favourite restaurant of Dickens.[21] This friendship did not, however, prevent Orwell from later attacking Greene's novel *The Heart of the Matter* for religious pretension. If the protagonist genuinely believed in Hell, he said, 'he would not risk going there merely to spare the feelings of a couple of neurotic women'.[22] Orwell, it could be confidently said, certainly would not! Almost immediately he felt remorse at what he had written, telling Anthony Powell: 'If you happen to see Graham Greene, could you break the news to him that I have written a very bad review of his novel for the *New Yorker*.'[23]

On 19 March he wrote simultaneously to Moore and Gollancz announcing the completion of his new novel. It was around 30,000 words and being typed. Somewhat uncertain into which category it fell, he said, 'it is a sort of fairy story, really a fable with political meaning'. While Gollancz had first refusal of his next two novels, he thought it unlikely he would want to publish this one because of its strong anti-Stalinist bias. 'Nor,' he added, 'is it any use wasting time on Warburg, who probably wouldn't touch anything of this tendency and to my knowledge is very short of paper.' He proposed that, to save time, Gollancz be told that it probably would not suit him, and be sent it only if he asked to see it. He also mentioned an interested contact at Nicholson and Watson (André Deutsch), and an interest also at Hutchinson. 'This book,' he added, 'is murder from the Communist point of view', an observation that would come back to haunt him, if it did not already fill him with apprehension.[24] He later included Cape and Faber on his list, and in America the Dial Press, but he definitely excluded Eyre and Spottiswoode, for whom Greene was then working, and Hollis and Carter, run by two old Etonian contemporaries, because they were Catholic.

To Gollancz he described the book briefly, adding, 'I must tell you that it is, I think, completely unacceptable politically from your point of view (it is anti-Stalin).'[25] Gollancz's reply was somewhat indignant. He had no idea what 'anti-Stalin' meant. Communists regarded him as 'violently anti-Stalinist' because of his opposition to the Nazi–Soviet pact and criticism of 'illiberal trends in Soviet internal policy'. But there was a big distinction to be made between a criticism of the USSR from a socialist and the anti-Stalinism of the Nazis and 'the more reactionary Tories' which he utterly rejected. 'Certainly,' he told Orwell, 'I should like to see the manuscript.'[26] Orwell replied saying, 'Naturally I am not criticizing the Soviet regime from the Right, but in my experience the other kind of criticism gets one into even worse trouble.'[27] By the 29th Gollancz had the book. It took him just four days to reply, and his letter was short and to the point: 'You were right and I was wrong. I am so sorry. I am returning the manuscript to Moore.'[28] Michael Meyer, who had been unimpressed by Orwell's summary of the story, was not surprised when George told him, 'That damned fool Victor

Gollancz has turned my book down. He doesn't want to publish anything anti-Russian.'[29]

The book that had so alarmed Gollancz was superb in its lucidity and economy. The well-known story of the animals of Manor Farm over-throwing the tyrannical Farmer Jones, was, of course, a parable of its times with the power, like a stone dropped into a pond, to produce ever-widening ripples of meaning extending well beyond the simple narrative itself. In the event, the dropped stone was more of a high-explosive bomb intended not simply to shake and excite bourgeois intellectuals like Gollancz but to undermine a powerful myth propping up a huge totalitarian empire. The force and the beauty of his 'beast fable' lay in its very simplicity. Old Major (Marx) preaches the philosophy of liberation through revolution. When the moment comes, Jones is run off the property which is renamed 'Animal Farm'. The pigs make the running, led by Napoleon (Stalin), the fierce Berkshire boar, and the more vivacious Snowball (Trotsky), with the fat porker Squealer as their lieutenant. The great draft-horse Boxer is the model worker (Stakhanov), industrious and obedient; Molly the white mare is the frivolous hedonist who never accepts the frugal post-revolutionary life; the sheep are the masses who repeat (gramophone-like) the slogans of Animalism; Moses the raven speaks for religion and Benjamin the donkey is the voice of scepticism, and perhaps, too, of the author. The principles of Animalism are posted up: 'All animals are equal,' 'Four legs good, two legs bad' . . . There is a counter-revolutionary intervention from Jones and his friends, which is beaten back at the Battle of the Cowsheds. Then things begin to go wrong. It is ordained that pigs need extra apples and milk. Snowball is expelled, anyone who speaks out against the regime is branded a supporter of his, and a band of savage dogs (KGB) bred up in secret by Napoleon is used to eliminate them. The history of the Battle of the Cowsheds is revised to exclude Snowball's part in it. The personality cult of Napoleon is inaugurated. The animals then see that the principles of the revolution have been altered. 'All animals are equal' has become 'All animals are equal, but some animals are more equal than others,' and the others follow. At the end of the book the animals discover the pigs carousing with Jones and his friends. 'The creatures outside looked from pig to man, and from man to pig, and from pig to man again: but already it was impossible to say which was which.'[30]

It is, of course, yet another Orwellian tale of a failed adventure, of attain-ment and loss, the very configuration of his own life. The book came from a deep sense of bitter anger. It stemmed from the vision of anarchist Barcelona destroyed by power-hungry villains. 'Like the anarchists,' wrote V. S. Pritchett, 'he would like to believe that men are born good; but he finds that the formative things in the world are power, passion and interest . . . Mr

Orwell cannot forgive the fact that there is always a ruling class; that virtue is not an individual's vision, but the devious collective mind of the tribal leaders.'[31] The emotional dynamic behind *Animal Farm* and the novel to follow was what to Michael Sayers he had called his 'spite and malice', and what Sayers himself saw as 'Swift's "savage indignation" – 'cruelty, hatred that he must have had steaming inside him for a long, long time, and which comes out in his work'.[32]

Even in England the same pattern was in danger of repeating itself. He had begun to be troubled by the idea that laissez-faire capitalism could make a comeback after the war. He saw signs of it everywhere. The rich seemed somehow to get around the supposedly egalitarian rationing system; they could afford expensive restaurants and hotels that were exempt from state control; voices were being raised again in favour of the old free-market system; first-class compartments were back on the railways; the wearing of evening dress had returned and in *The Times* advertisements for servants had reappeared. Fear of a capitalist resurgence led some socialists to refrain from criticising the USSR. If one attacked the Soviet secret police or 'Soviet millionaires' one was likely to be accused of defending capitalism. When he attacked Laski's book, *Faith, Reason and Civilization*, on exactly these grounds,[33] his review was rejected by the *Manchester Evening News*. This, he thought, was a prime example of the fear of offending the Russians and undermining the reputation of the 'heroic' Red Army. In his 17 April London Letter to *Partisan Review*, he grumbled, 'Russophile feeling is on the surface stronger than ever. It is now next door to impossible to get anything overtly anti-Soviet printed.'[34]

Gollancz was not alone in not wanting to upset the Russians. Nicholson and Watson took the same line, Jonathan Cape, although initially keen, took the precaution of consulting 'an important official' at the Ministry of Information who advised him that publishing Orwell's book would not be in the national interest. Unknown to either Cape or Orwell at that time, this 'important official', Peter Smollett, a Czech by birth, was a Soviet agent. Cape chose the easy path, rejecting the book on the grounds that it was aimed specifically at the Soviets and representing them as pigs gave partic-ular offence.[35] Orwell was amused at the idea of Stalin reading the book and announcing that he was offended, but was in no mood to give up trying. It was the seventh anniversary of the May fighting in Barcelona and his old urge for revenge was no doubt driving him on. He told Moore, 'I particu-larly want this book published on political grounds.'[36] The spite and malice he endeavoured always to suppress was now being unleashed against those who had terrorised him and had murdered young Bob Smillie. He also got in a blow against pigs, animals he strongly disliked; the rats' turn would come later.

Hoping for a better response from Eliot, he offered the book to Faber, asking for an early decision. Eliot's response was disappointing. He considered the work 'distinguished' and compared it favourably to Swift's Gulliver. But his reading was a conservative one, identifying the book's point of view as 'Trotskyite' and consequently, he said, finding it unconvincing. The pigs, he argued, were obviously the most intelligent of the animals, they had created Animal Farm and were best able to run it. 'What was needed,' he concluded, 'was not more communism but more public-spirited pigs.'[37] He had, however, missed the point. Orwell was saying something about the nature of revolutions, not about the predisposition of a particular ruling faction. The book was not Trotskyite. Snowball, the Trotsky figure, was little better than the other pigs, having supported Napoleon's first moves against egalitarianism on the farm. It was not selfish pigs who had wrecked the dream, it was something beyond that.

He regarded Cape's suggestion that his pigs should be changed to another animal as 'imbecilic'. At the time he made no direct comment on Eliot's verdict, but did so indirectly, in writing about Koestler's *The Gladiators*: 'Revolutions,' he wrote, 'always go wrong.'[38] It was never a matter of individual character; the Russian Revolution would have gone the same way even if Lenin had lived. A year later he wrote, 'The trouble with Eliot is that though of course he is anti-Stalinist he is at heart simply a conservative and doesn't like fighting against public opinion for the sake of some left faction he feels no sympathy for.'[39] However, he remained on good terms with Eliot, frequently defending him for his ready use of demotic English in his verse, and continuing to see him occasionally for lunch. He would even come round to writing favourably of *The Four Quartets* (which earlier he had dismissed), even while regretting that he was no longer doing what he did best, 'chronicling the decay of a civilization which he frankly dislikes'.[40]

Others did consider the book, but to no avail. William Collins is said to have rejected it because of the political climate, and André Deutsch, Orwell's contact at Nicholson and Watson, was tempted to launch his own imprint with the book, but felt the timing was not quite right for him.[41] In America the Dial Press would eventually turn it down not just because of the pigs but because 'it was impossible to sell animal stories in the USA'.[42] Having exhausted his preferred publishers, he toyed with the idea of producing the book as a pamphlet and discussed this possibility with George Woodcock and Paul Potts who each ran small presses. A proposal to serialise it in *Tide and Tide* he rejected on political grounds. He knew exactly how its readers would interpret the book.

During this period of frustration he began an essay on Salvador Dali and wrote a particularly scathing review of Wells's latest book on the war for the

Observer. If Wells had written him off there seemed no reason not to take off the gloves and hit him where it hurt. Essentially it was his earlier argument restated.

> Hitler is dismissed as simply a lunatic: that settles Hitler. He does not seriously enquire why millions of people are ready to lay down their lives for a lunatic, and what this probably betokens for human society. And in between his threats that homo sapiens must mend his ways or be destroyed he continues to repeat the slogans of 1900 as though they were self-evident truths. For instance, it is startling to be told in 1944 that 'the world is now one'. One might as well say that the world is now flat.'[43]

This produced a furious letter from Wells to Ivor Brown at the *Observer*. Brown showed it to David Astor, who was so shocked by the language that he destroyed it.[44]

Orwell's essay on Dali is significant in that it is one of the few things he wrote about art, and offers his reflections on biography and artistic judgement. He considered Dali's autobiography, *The Secret Life of Salvador Dali*, to be dishonest and incredible, a 'narcissistic . . . strip-tease act conducted in pink limelight'. Dali's confessed catalogue of childhood perversions included kicking his three-year-old sister in the head, biting a wounded bat in half, masturbating in front of a mirror and coming close to murdering his wife Gala. His illustrations were characterised by sexual perversity and necrophilia. Skulls, corpses and putrefaction featured prominently. The moral atmosphere clearly disturbed Orwell, and his own imagery reflected this. 'It is a book that stinks,' he wrote. 'If it were possible for a book to give a physical stink off its pages, this one would . . . He is as antisocial as a flea. Clearly, such people are undesirable, and a society in which they can flourish has something wrong with it.' Where 'Art for Art's sake' is the creed and where the artist is regarded as an exceptional person whose irresponsibility must be tolerated, the line between art and morality becomes blurred and the role of artist and citizen becomes confused. 'It should be possible to say, "This is a good book or a good picture, and it ought to be burned by the public hangman." Unless one can say that, at least in one's imagination, one is shirking the implications of the fact that an artist is also a citizen and a human being.' He regarded Dali and his work as pathological cases requiring investigation. 'They are diseased and disgusting, and any investigation ought to start out from that fact.'[45]

Orwell may have missed the point, that the book was no more than a publicity-seeking Daliesque joke, not to be taken seriously. But his attitude is revealing, in that Orwell himself had confessed on numerous occasions to childhood cruelties – wasps cut in half, toads inflated with bicycle pumps – and some adult ones – beating his Burmese servants – and was capable of making art out of sadistic cruelty as he would demonstrate in *Nineteen Eighty-Four*. He may not have been as narcissistic as Dali, but some thought him egotistical. And while no one could accuse Orwell of stunt-writing, his violent reaction to Dali's excesses is intriguing in itself.

With the fate of *Animal Farm* still undecided, he produced two more important essays, one on Koestler, and one expanding further his thoughts on the evolution of the detective story. In 'Raffles and Miss Blandish', which appeared in both *Horizon* and the American periodical *Politics*, he looked at two British authors, E. W. Hornung and James Hadley Chase, creators of the English gentleman cracksman, Raffles, and the violently sadistic American-style *No Orchids for Miss Blandish*. Each portrayed criminality, in one case that of the roguish public-schoolboy Raffles for whom crime is a game not unlike cricket, in the other, that of both crooks and policemen for whom the unrestrained use of gratuitous violence is the norm. Raffles embodied essentially English values – the gentleman crook does not kill but most often steals for the thrill of it, and finally takes the gentlemanly way out, a bullet in the Boer War; the other embodies the essentially American value of money-greed and unfettered cruelty.[46] It was a theme he would take up again in a later essay on the decline of the English murder, prompted by a killing-spree involving an American deserter. Underlying his thinking was the idea that this was a sign of things to come. The war, in brutalising millions, made this kind of violence a more likely feature of any post-war world – the violence of the concentration camp, a product of tyranny, or the violence of the freelance killer, a symptom of social instability.[47]

Koestler had long been for him a looking-glass self. Writing about him enabled him to write about himself. He bracketed him with Ignazio Silone, André Malraux, Franz Borkenau and Victor Serge, all continental Europeans who had been trying to write the unofficial history of totalitarianism, against the lies published in newspapers, the Left Book Club and in standard textbooks. In his essay on him (published later in *Critical Essays*) Orwell's summary of Koestler's central thesis is characteristically succinct: 'His main theme is the decadence of revolutions owing to the corrupting effects of power, but the special nature of Stalin's dictatorship has driven him back into a position not far removed from pessimistic Conservatism.'[48] That could almost stand as a self-portrait, except that Orwell kept his conservatism separate from his politics. Koestler's principal argument matched that of *Animal Farm* – 'Revolutions always go wrong' – but he failed to explain why because he was at heart a hedonist. Revolutions fail not because of psychological factors – hence Eliot's point about 'public-spirited pigs' is discounted – but because they carry with them the seeds of their own destruction. No matter who is in power, revolutions are destined to fail; it is built into their structure and nothing to do with individuals. As he wrote later, with reference to Koestler's 'The Yogi and the Commissar', where he thought Koestler tended to blame Stalin for what went wrong with the Russian Revolution, 'One ought, I believe, to admit that all the seeds of evil were there from the start and that things would not have been substantially different if Lenin or Trotsky had remained in control.'[49] Two years later he put a slightly different slant on this, suggesting that the terroristic methods employed by the Bolsheviks meant that after that 'the Russian Communist party developed in a direction of which Lenin would probably have disapproved if he had lived longer'.[50]

In the meantime he seems to have embarked on yet another affair, this time with Sally McEwan, his secretary at *Tribune*. Again he succumbed to the compulsion to enjoy a clandestine encounter, no doubt accompanied by the story that his wife understood. He had always had a penchant for pastoral seductions; in the city the nearest he could get to this were the parks. 'Have you ever had a woman in the park?' he once asked Anthony Powell. 'No – never.' 'I have.' 'How did you find it?' 'I was forced to.' 'Why?' 'Nowhere else to go.'[51] Crick tells of a party at the Empsons' Hampstead flat that summer, at which Orwell, who had been drinking heavily, met a young woman he had known vaguely at the BBC. Afterwards he offered to walk her home across the Heath and there attempted to make violent love to her. She fended him off by promising to meet him next day, and when she failed to show up, received an angrily reproachful letter about the iniquity of breaking promises.[52] Eileen is said to have found out about Sally McEwan, was much distressed about it, and threatened to leave him.[53]

Whatever the state of Orwell's marriage, with animals having been given their say, his mind turned, as it often did, towards children again. The feeling that time was not on his side was accompanied by a powerful desire for fatherhood. Just before leaving the BBC he was asked to complete a form to ascertain his entitlement to Family Allowance. To one of the questions he could only answer 'No children', which must have hurt. He greatly envied friends who had children, and by 1944 the desire for a son seems to have become irresistible. Certain that he was unable to have children, the question of adoption came up. Eileen, it seems, was uncertain, not knowing whether she could come to love someone else's child, but George was so keen she did not have the heart to disappoint him.[54]

That summer he fulfilled his dream, and lost his home. In June, with the help of Gwen O'Shaughnessy, he and Eileen took possession of a three-week-old boy. They called him Richard Horatio – two traditional Blair names. Clearly he was meant to continue the family line, to add a further chapter to the still-incubating saga. Then, on the night of the 28th, three days after Orwell's forty-first birthday, and three weeks after D-Day, 10 Mortimer Crescent was hit by a 'doodlebug' (nickname for Hitler's V-1 flying bomb). Luckily, that night George and Eileen were in Greenwich with the new baby, but returned next morning to find their home in ruins. Eileen, who to her surprise had taken well to motherhood and given up her job at the Ministry, took Richard first to stay with Marjorie and Humphrey in Bristol, then up to family friends in Stockton-on-Tees. Inez (involved in an unhappy affair with Humphrey Slater) had gone to the country to convalesce from a recent illness, and lent the Orwells her flat in George Street until they could find a place of their own. It was bad timing for Orwell. After three years in London, he had finally got round to moving his library up to town from Wallington. As he told Inez, he went rummaging every day in the rubble, retrieving as many books as he could and carting them off in a wheelbarrow, making the eight-mile round trip to his office during his lunch-hour.[55] Most of his books and papers had to be put into storage. The grim atmosphere of routine terror which the coming of the flying bomb brought to war-torn London would go straight into *Nineteen Eighty-Four*.

Warburg had heard about Orwell's new novel, and was anxious to read it. Now, at last, in late July, it was sent to him. It seems strange that Orwell did not offer *Animal Farm* directly to Warburg once Gollancz had rejected it. His excuse was that he thought he was short of paper, and would probably be as inhibited as the others by the book's anti-Soviet message. Also he wanted it published quickly, which he might have thought Warburg, whose office had just been blitzed, might be unable to do.

Hopes of an early end to the war rose with the fall of Paris on 25 August. By this time, with the help of the Kopps, now living in Canonbury Square, Islington, the Orwells found a new flat nearby, at number 27b. Islington, with its Dickensian associations and where Gissing-like hacks had scratched out their Grub Street livings, was in those days rather down-at-heel, even 'slummy'. Canonbury Square, a somewhat gloomy enclave of rundown, 'leprous', three-storey tenements, lying between Upper Street and Essex Road and bisected by the busy Canonbury Road, was mainly a working-class district, close to shops and pubs. The house at number 27 was owned by the Marquis of Northampton and the rents were modest (around £200 a year), but the Orwells' flat was on the top floor, reached by a brick staircase at the rear, a climb which always left George wheezing and breathless. In September they moved in.

The new flat had five rooms, one of which was a long sitting room with a fireplace at the far end. On the mantelpiece was placed a photograph of Eileen holding Richard, and on the walls were hung his Burmese swords and the portrait of Lady Mary Blair. His furniture was heavy and old and Victorian, inherited from Montague House, and there was a divan for use as a guest bed. Behind a heavy basket chair stood a Victorian scrap screen (pasted with Christmas cards, pictures from art magazines, advertisements etc.), salvaged by Orwell from a junk shop – 'the scrap book's big brother', he called it, and later wrote somewhat affectionately about it, in his *Evening Standard* column. (He loved junk shops and what he called 'scraps of useless information'.)[56] At one end of the room was a dining table where the solemn ritual of high tea was observed at five o'clock every afternoon. The district suited Orwell's plebeian persona, and the mean streets between the square and King's Cross Station, through which he would often walk on his way to and from work, became the proletarian quarter where Winston Smith seeks sanctuary above Mr Charrington's antique junk shop in *Nineteen Eighty-Four*.

Once settled in, Eileen fetched Richard from Stockton-on-Tees. Being a father brought out Orwell's gentle, caring side. He was absolutely delighted with his new son, carefully burned the name of his real parents (Robertson) from his birth certificate with a cigarette, and, according to Lettice Cooper, announced two immediate ambitions –to acquire a white perambulator with a gold trim, and to put young Richard down for Eton. The white pram never materialised, and the public school was later changed to Westminster (Warburg's old school) when he heard that boys there were no longer required to wear top hats. And to show that the old fascination with mysticism still lingered, when Heppenstall offered to read Richard's horoscope, he accepted with alacrity.

Although Tosco Fyvel found the Canonbury Square flat cheerless, badly built and draughty, Orwell, it seems, immediately felt at home there.[57] It was at least spacious, so he had plenty of room to entertain friends, as he had done at Wallington, sometimes in great Pickwickian style. In a fond memoir Paul Potts captured the Dickensian scene:

> Nothing could be more pleasant than the sight of his living-room in Canonbury Square early on a winter's evening at high tea-time. A huge fire, the table crowded with marvellous things, Gentleman's Relish and various jams, kippers, crumpets and toast. And always the Gentleman's Relish, with its peculiar unique flat jar and the Latin inscription on the label. Next to it usually stood the Cooper's Oxford marmalade pot. He thought in terms of vintage tea and had the same attitude to bubble and squeak as a Frenchman has to Camembert. I'll swear he valued tea and roast beef above the OM and the Nobel Prize. Then there was the conversation and the company, his wife, some members of his family or hers, a refugee radical or an English writer. There was something very innocent and terribly simple about him. He wasn't a very good judge of character. He was of roast beef, however. He loved being a host, as only

civilized men can, who have been very poor. There was nothing bohemian about him at all. However poor he had been it did not make him precarious. But he tolerated in others faults he did not possess himself.[58]

Orwell, in fact, despite the wartime penchant for Victory Pie and mashed potatoes, and despite scorning the patrons of expensive restaurants, was a greater lover of English cuisine and was commissioned to write a book on it at the end of the year. He wrote with great gusto about Welsh rarebit, English puddings, treacle tart and crumpets – in fact his gastronomic tastes were distinctly bourgeois. The dishes he disliked, the working class favoured – fish and chips and boiled cabbage. The smell of boiled cabbage almost always featured in Orwell's descriptions of low-life squalor. As to his reputation for austere living, he defended with great relish the Christmas blow-out, arguing that 'The whole point of Christmas is that it is debauch.'[59]

The move to Islington coincided with Warburg's acceptance of *Animal Farm* (against the wishes of his wife, he claimed), and therefore the opening of a completely new chapter in Orwell's life. Warburg wrote later that as soon as he read the book he realised that he had a major work on his hands. Orwell was less certain, and quite apprehensive about how his old enemies the Stalinists would react to it.

After the efforts expended on journalism, trying to get his book published and picking up after being bombed out, he felt in need of a break. He learned from David Astor that his family owned a property on Jura, a mountainous, sparsely populated island just off the west coast of Argyllshire, and his dream of living in the Hebrides was revived. Hearing his friend talk about the beauty of the place, and about fishing in the sea and lochs, he arranged to spend a couple of weeks there in late September, staying with people known to the Astors. On his return he spoke of renting a cottage on the island the following summer. The journey was complicated and arduous, involving two sea-ferry trips on which he was invariably seasick. But he was captivated. Jura would be a refuge, well away from the city he hated so much, and well away from the alarums of war and the danger of being rained on by bombs and rockets from nowhere. The V2 rocket only increased his fear that the next war would be something indescribable and universal – 'just war in the abstract'.[60] Each time he heard a rocket explode, he wrote later, 'I find myself thinking, "Is it possible that human beings can continue with this lunacy very much longer?" You know the answer, of course.'[61] It was a lunatic situation to be avoided, especially now with a young son to care for.

In his *Tribune* column he had used the occasion of the Russians' failure to aid the Home Army's uprising in Warsaw in August of that year openly to attack the Soviets, who he believed were deliberately allowing the Germans to annihilate them. He then went on to attack left-wing intellectuals for not daring to raise the matter, and concluded with 'a message to English left-wing journalists and intellectuals generally': 'Do remember that dishonesty and cowardice always have to be paid for. Don't imagine that for years on end you can make yourself the boot-licking propagandist of the Soviet regime, and then suddenly return to mental decency. Once a whore, always a whore'.[62] This brought, predictably enough, some quite violent responses from Stalinists and their fellow-travellers who labelled him a Trotskyist and blamed his hostility on his Catalonian adventures. One letter, typical of this, from the journalist Douglas Goldring, read, 'George Orwell's experiences in the Spanish war, in which he served in a "Trotskyite" formation, seem to have aroused in him a pathological hatred of not only the USSR but of all left-wing intellectuals who do not share his opinions . . . I consider his article a disgrace to the profession he has so recently condescended to join and an insult to readers of *Tribune*'.[63] Goldring earned himself a place on an Orwell list of crypto-Communists, compiled later. Another correspondent condemned his 'pro-Fascist, neo-Jesuit posturings'.[64] It reminded him, if he needed reminding, that some on the left had a pathological hatred for him. But he was lucky in his friends. Both Koestler and Symons mounted a vigorous defence of him in the ensuing correspondence.

As the Allies advanced into Europe the question of how to treat Nazis and their collaborators arose. Orwell was horrified by news photographs of shaven-headed French women being abused in the streets of Paris, likening them to pictures of Jews being humiliated in German streets ten years earlier. Seeing more recent ones of public hangings by the Russians in Kharkov, he quoted Nietzsche: 'He who fights too long against dragons becomes a dragon himself: and if thou gaze too long into the abyss, the abyss will gaze into thee'.[65] This was Orwell's stand. Once an enemy has been beaten, humiliating and punishing him further only demeaned and diminished the victor. But the tide in favour of retribution grew as the first news of Hitler's death camps began to filter through. Orwell was aware of a public thirst for vengeance, but did not change his position. 'If . . . it were announced that the leading war criminals were to be eaten by lions or trampled to death by elephants in the Wembley Stadium, I fancy that the spectacle would be quite well-attended'.[66]

That autumn, six months after their having taken on Richard, it was necessary to attend court to have the adoption approved. All went well and Lettice Cooper remembered Eileen just afterwards. 'She came round to the Ministry with Richard – frightfully proud and pleased. And for the first time in her life she was wearing a hat. She had a neat coat and skirt on – she wasn't generally very neat, and she had bought a yellow felt hat so that the judge should think she was an entirely suitable person to look after Richard, and Richard was fine, very cheerful.'[67] But one child did not seem to satisfy Orwell, and he and Eileen agreed that before long Richard should be joined by a sister.[68] When Michael Meyer visited their new home, he found that Orwell, the family man, had installed a workbench and was practising his rough-and-ready carpentry – a bookshelf, a wooden toy for Richard, a rudimentary stool. But in the bad winter of 1944–45, the flat was not exactly the most comfortable home in London – melting snow penetrated the roof and brought down the ceilings.[69]

His love affair with popular culture produced another essay at the end of the year. 'Funny, But Not Vulgar' takes an Orwellian look at English humour from Chaucer to Wodehouse, with a passing glance, significantly enough, at Thurber. Not surprising, in view of Orwell's belief that all art is propaganda, he took the line that 'A thing is funny when . . . it upsets the established order. Every joke is a tiny revolution . . . Whatever destroys dignity, and brings down the mighty from their seats, preferably with a bump, is funny.' Even more revealingly from the author of *Animal Farm*, and seeming to defend his own satirical bent, comes the observation that 'Animals . . . are only funny because they are caricatures of ourselves.'[70] His conclusion that 'It would seem that you *cannot* be funny without being vulgar,' rather confirms his own taste for low comedy.

Orwell was a natural pamphleteer – like Swift, a man dedicated to challenging and subverting the status quo at every opportunity, whether through humour or through his many satirical blasts against received opinion or established authority. He was a long-time collector of pamphlets of all descriptions, linking him to the dissident tradition with which he so closely identified. At the close of 1944 he noted the viciousness and dishonesty of current political controversy. No one was in search of the truth; they were all putting a 'case' without regard to fairness or accuracy, and ignoring facts that did not suit them. He was especially scathing of those who disregarded human motives and argued that actions alone were what counted, for example the argument that 'pacifists, by obstructing the war effort, are "objectively" aiding the Nazis: and therefore the fact that they may be personally hostile to Fascism is irrelevant'. He admitted taking the same line himself in the past, and having been made the target of it by Communists in Spain. The dishonesty lay in the claim that pacifists or Trotskyists were consciously treacherous. The important thing was to discover who was honest and who was not.[71] The logic of this, it seems, was that a list needed to be drawn up, much like the list of crypto-Fascists he held in his head.

Now, with *Animal Farm* on the way to being published, and with the sound of V2 rockets still echoing in his ears, he was absorbing further ideas that would become part of the world of *Nineteen Eighty-Four*. The idea of permanent war, of a world dominated by two or three super-states, first advanced by James Burnham in his book, *The Managerial Revolution*, seemed closer than ever. These imagined super-states would be separate, and, even though technically at peace, in a state of permanent war with one another.[72] The vision taking shape in his mind was the landscape of his own political nightmare-novel, a story with a moral, and a warning to mankind at large. As Stephen Spender remarked, 'Always you felt with Orwell the presence of some kind of idea, a rather noble idea.'[73]

Chapter 16

The Dark Side of Solitude

'People are imprisoned for years without trial, or shot in the back of the neck or sent to die of scurvy in Arctic lumber camps: this is called *elimination of unreliable elements.*'

Orwell, 'Politics and the English Language', 1946

Some of those opposed to totalitarianism Orwell found uncomfortable bedfellows. One was Cyril Connolly, who, he thought, opposed it as a threat to his self-indulgent life style rather than to freedom of thought.[1] Even less attractive allies were the anti-Communist Tories. Invited to address the so-called League for European Freedom, dominated as Orwell saw it, by 'the anti-Russian wing of the Tory Party', he wrote making it clear where he stood ('I belong to the Left and must work inside it'), and indicating that he had no intention of allying himself with such people as them.[2]

With the European war drawing to an end, Orwell was keen to see the effects not just of the fighting but also of years under totalitarian rule. He was again proposed as an *Observer* war correspondent, this time to cover the fighting in Europe. He could not have passed a serious medical examination so David Astor probably pulled strings to get him accepted. He was scheduled to go in the middle of February for two months, accredited to both the *Observer* and *Manchester Evening News*, while Eileen would take Richard to her family home in Stockton-on-Tees. Meanwhile he slaved away at his journalism, and prepared his essay collection for Warburg.

However cosy Paul Potts had found the flat in Canonbury Square, in the winter it was cold, the ceilings leaked, and that year frozen pipes left him with no water for three days.[3] Luckily, before Eileen departed north, both she and George had read and corrected the proofs of *Animal Farm*. When she did leave, neither could have guessed that they would never see the other alive again. Orwell did seem to consider the possibility that he would not return alive and while in Germany would draft 'Notes for My Literary

Executor' listing which of his works he wished to see republished, which suppressed, including *A Clergyman's Daughter*, *Keep the Aspidistra Flying* and *The Lion and the Unicorn*.[4]

In mid-February, as he set off for Paris in the captain's uniform of an official war correspondent, the Big Three were at Yalta deciding the fate of post-war Europe, several great German cities had been razed, including Dresden, and Allied troops on both fronts had gained footholds in Germany itself. At the Hotel Scribe, where he was billeted with other Allied correspondents, he met the suave and cynical Malcolm Muggeridge (working for British Intelligence), whose book, *The Thirties*, he had reviewed five years earlier, the Oxford philosopher A. J. Ayer (also an Intelligence Officer), and Harold Acton (employed as a press censor with SHAEF), who had known him vaguely at Eton, and with whom he dined most evenings in Paris.

To Acton he cut a strange figure among the other correspondents. He noted his 'dry frustrated manner' but found his 'mournful dignity' impressive. He talked about his new son and about his lung trouble 'as if it were something to be ashamed of'. 'There was,' he concluded, 'ample cause for the gloom that was deeply engraved on his features.' But when he spoke about 'the sweetness of Burmese women' and the satiny skins of Moroccan girls, 'gradually the gloom dissolved'. Acton was touched by his 'spontaneous bursts of confidence', and saw something of a Kipling hero about him, but knew that his politics prevented anything more than a temporary companionship between them.[5] To Ayer, yet another Old Etonian and ex-pupil of Gow, Orwell gave no impression of caring much for philosophy – a deceptive impression, as became evident in *Nineteen Eighty-Four*, where a key philosophical argument lies at the heart of the novel. Ayer met both Camus and Orwell in Paris and was struck by the similarity of their outlook, but also how hard Orwell was on himself.[6]

Muggeridge took Orwell to meet P. G. Wodehouse, then under some kind of house arrest in Paris having been accused of treachery for broadcasting for the Nazis. Orwell took the Wodehouses to dinner, and was convinced that the creator of Jeeves was no Nazi but an innocent abroad who had been bamboozled by the Germans into making the broadcasts. Shortly afterwards he wrote his essay 'In Defence of P. G. Wodehouse', for which the author duly thanked him, 'most pathetically', according to Orwell.[7] However, the socio-cultural treatment of his work was not to 'Plum's' taste, and shortly after Orwell's death, he wrote, somewhat ungraciously, about it being 'one long roast', falsifying the facts to make a point.[8]

Rather more curious was his encounter with Ernest Hemingway, which revealed a greater anxiety than his health, women or Wodehouse then preying on his mind. According to Hemingway, Orwell came looking for him at his room at the Ritz, and told him that he was afraid he was going to be assassinated by the Communists. He was, recalled Hemingway, 'fairly nervous and worried', looking 'very gaunt and . . . in bad shape'. He asked for the loan of a pistol he could easily conceal, and borrowed a snub-nosed .32 calibre colt – not a very effective weapon, Hemingway thought, but it might have made him feel better to have it. Friends whom the American sent to shadow Orwell later reported that he was quite safe and happily 'amusing himself' in Paris.[9] The summary justice handed out by Communists immediately after the Liberation must have been on his mind as well as assassinations carried out in Paris by Comintern agents during the Spanish Civil War. His paranoia would only intensify after the publication of *Animal Farm*, the more so because Hemingway had asked him to return the pistol to its original owner when he left France.

He found Paris depressing and 'a bit ghostlike'[10] compared with how it had been. Beside the Seine the booksellers still plied their trade and fisher-men still fished for the same fish. But in the Latin Quarter he found things very changed – no cosmopolitan artists in the cafés, the Panthéon scarred by machine-gun bullets and, in the rue du Pot de Fer, everything closed except an undertaker's and one little bistro. However, 'across the street the tiny hotel where I used once to live was boarded up and partly ruinous. It appeared empty. But as I came away, from behind the broken window pane of what used to be my own room, I saw two hungry-looking children.'[11]

Unlike Acton and Ayer, he seems to have met few of the French writers he might have been expected to meet. He did meet André Malraux and gave him a copy of *Homage to Catalonia*, finding him 'very friendly, and . . . far from being pro-Communist in his views'.[12] He arranged a rendezvous with Camus at the Café des Deux Magots which illness prevented the Frenchman keeping. Had they met they might have compared medical notes, suffering as they did from the same condition. Camus was also the French writer with whom Orwell had most in common for their anti-Stalinism and shared attitude to the art of political writing. He certainly thought *Combat*, which Camus edited, 'the best of the Resistance newspapers'.[13] Camus was also an admirer of Orwell's work, especially *Burmese Days*, perhaps his most Gallic novel, a passage from which found its way into his *Notebooks*.[14] He may have met others, and when a French translation of *Animal Farm* appeared in 1947, he asked for copies to be sent to André Gide, Jean-Paul Sartre, Simone de Beauvoir, Paul Mounier, Julian Green and Jules Romains as well as Malraux and Camus.[15]

His articles from Europe (some nineteen in all) were not considered among his best work. David Astor thought his true *métier* was the essay rather than journalism. His dispatches as a whole reflected his major inter-ests – the prevailing social conditions, the state of the French press, the emerging post-war politics of France and Germany, and the looming con-frontation between East and West. Orwell had gone to Europe hoping to get a feel of life under a totalitarian regime, but, as Astor pointed out, immediately the Allies moved in there was no more Nazi Germany to experience. For him, Cologne, the first German town he entered, proved to be a bad trip because there he suffered one of his bronchitis attacks and ended up in a military hospital.

Three weeks after Orwell left London, Eileen had become seriously ill with uterine tumors causing great pain and heavy bleeding. She had been unwell for some time and knew she required a hysterectomy, but, agonising over the cost, had kept the bad news from George, not wanting to trouble him or jeopardise the adoption of Richard. She had almost passed out just before he left; now, on a visit to London, she did collapse. Knowing that George disapproved of hysterectomies, in writing to tell him about it, she played the whole thing down, saying, 'I really don't think I'm worth the money.' But the relief of at last owning up about it released a torrent of unhappiness she had bottled up throughout the war.

> I don't think you understand what a nightmare the London life is to me. I know it is to you, but you often talk as though I liked it. I don't like even the things that you do. I can't stand having people all over the place, every meal makes me feel sick because every food has been handled by twenty dirty hands and I practically can't bear to eat anything that hasn't been boiled to clean it. I can't breathe the air, I can't think any more clearly than one would expect to in the moment of being smothered, everything that bores me happens all the time in London and the things that interest me most don't happen at all and I can't read poetry . . . But all these years I have felt as though I were in a mild kind of concentration camp. The place has its points of course and I could enjoy it for a week. I like going to theatres for instance. But . . . in London . . . as you know I never go to a theatre. As for eating in restaurants, it's the most barbarous habit and only tolerable very occasionally when one drinks enough to enjoy barbarity. And I can't drink enough beer . . . I like the Canonbury flat but I am suicidal every time I walk as far as the bread shop.[16]

This outpouring suggests that there was a silence between them over matters quite central to their lives.

In Newcastle she had found a surgeon-friend of her brother, who agreed to operate within days. George, just back in Paris, had finally been contacted and given his consent, probably still unaware how seriously ill she was. The day before the operation she wrote him a rather sad, almost apologetic letter.

Harvey Evers has a very high reputation . . . and I am sure that he will finish me off as quickly as anyone in England as well as doing the job properly –so he may well come cheaper in the end. I rather wish I'd talked it over with you before you went. I knew I had a 'growth'. But I wanted you to go away peacefully anyway, and I did not want to see Harvey Evers before the adoption was through in case it was cancer. I thought it just possible that the judge might make some enquiry about our health as we're old for parenthood and anyway it would have been an uneasy sort of thing to be producing oneself as an ideal parent a fortnight after being told that one couldn't live more than six months or something.[17]

In the circumstances she was rather glad he was away. As she told Lettice Cooper, 'George visiting the sick is a sight infinitely sadder than any diseased wretch in the world.'[18]

She seemed well aware that she might not survive the operation, and wrote long letters to friends. She also made her will leaving all her worldly goods to George, including a house inherited from her mother. Although generally she played down her illness, in a letter to Leonard Moore she admitted, 'I suppose I shall be out of all running for a week . . . it's rather a big job.'[19] On 29 March, awaiting her operation she wrote a last letter to George beginning, 'Dearest . . . already enema'd, injected (with morphia in the right arm which is a nuisance), cleaned & packed up like a precious image in cotton wool & bandages.' She closed on an image which she knew would speak to him. 'This is a nice room – ground floor so one can see the garden. Not much in it except daffodils & I think arabis but a nice little lawn. My bed isn't next to the window but it faces the right way. I also see a fire & the clock . . .' At that point, it seems, she was taken to the operating theatre, so curiously enough, the last word she communicated to George was 'the clock', with which so many of his novels began. Next day he received news that she had died under the anaesthetic. It was two days before he could get a flight back. Ayer remembered him being very buttoned-up about the whole thing. 'He just said, "Oh, I have got things to do at home. I shall be away for a fortnight. See you then."'[20] Back in England he went straight to see Inez who recorded his visit in her diary. She had only just received the news about Eileen herself.

The bell rang and George Orwell was outside. I did not recognize him at first. He wore a long Guardsman-like coat. He was in the uniform of a war correspondent. A Captain. He had taken eight M and B tablets and left the hospital and flown over. At first I thought that perhaps he did not know. But he had received a telegram. He thought that it was especially sad for Eileen because things were getting better, the war ending, Richard adopted and she believed that her health would be all right after this operation. George was terribly sad.[21]

She took him to the station for his journey to Stockton and suggested he stay with her on his return to London, but he was intent on returning to Germany in the hope of taking his mind off things.

There must have been guilt mixed in with his grief. He was aware that, although he had not been faithful to her, she had loved him deeply. According to Paul Potts, 'He told me that the last time he saw her he wanted to tell her that he loved her much more now since they'd had Richard, and he didn't tell her, and he regretted it immensely.'[22] Later he told his housekeeper, 'It wasn't an ideal marriage. I don't think I treated her very well sometimes.'[23] Within his family, he unburdened himself to Aunt Nellie and no one else. She told Marjorie, 'Eric wrote to me at some length of Eileen's death and appeared to me to be very grieved about it.'[24] When Stephen Spender expressed his condolences he said simply, 'Yes, she was a good old stick,' which Spender took to be Orwell acting out his proletarian role, saying what he thought a working-class man would say in the circumstances.[25] Underneath that performance, however, he felt sure that Orwell was deeply fond of Eileen and would miss her greatly.

Others were less charitable, feeling that Eileen's death was not unconnected with his neglect of her, and to his somewhat chequered sexual history. Ironically, Connolly had written in The Unquiet Grave, 'The true index of a man's character is the health of his wife,' and some would have said that described Orwell's case perfectly. Lydia Jackson always thought him not good enough for her, and blind to her suffering, and another friend, Edna Bussey, linked her early death to his failure to look after her properly.[26] Her more forgiving friend Lettice Cooper agreed that George rather neglected her, but then, she said, 'He couldn't even look after himself.'[27] And to be fair to Orwell, neither was the type to complain, especially to the other, which is almost certainly why their health deteriorated together. Eileen's love for Orwell was highly sacrificial, putting her own career aside and devoting herself to caring for him. She believed in his great gifts and great potential and was prepared to suffer with him and, to an extent, to live with his neglect of her. She found him brilliant and comic at the same time, and, in adopting Richard, was prepared to sublimate her own feelings to please him. She had survived the loss of her brother, but by the end of her life had come to share George's fear of poverty and, fatally, his casual attitude to his health. He was probably unaware of the depth of her devotion to him until after her death. 'It was,' he wrote, 'a real marriage in the sense that we had been through awful struggles together and she understood all about my work.'[28] What he did not mention was how her intellectual stimulus contributed to his work, especially his last two novels. More than one friend noticed how his writing was transformed after he married Eileen.

There was an inquest into the death, but immediately after the funeral Orwell returned to London with Richard, telling Powell that he did not want to know the official verdict, as it would not bring Eileen back. His own belief was that the anaesthetic had killed her. (Later he attributed her death to overwork during the war.)[29] In the event, the coroner entered the cause of death as 'Cardiac failure whilst under anaesthetic of ether and chloroform skilfully and properly administered for operation for removal of uterus,'[30] thus exonerating the doctors concerned. The general belief was that she had succumbed immediately the anaesthetic was administered. The cheaper operation seems to have been a bad choice and her sad state of mind cannot have helped. Behind all that, of course, was grief over the loss of her brother, the death of her mother and the privations of wartime London, all of which weighed more heavily on her than even Orwell realised. She was just six months short of her fortieth birthday.

With Eileen's death a deep sense of loneliness overwhelmed Orwell. Almost a year later he told Dorothy Plowman that the memory of being with Eileen at Wallington upset him so much that he had put off returning there. In a sadly ironic sense this mood probably served its purpose. It may be no more than a coincidence, but the day following Eileen's funeral, 4 April, was the date on which Winston Smith began his fatal diary in *Nineteen Eighty-Four*.

Eileen had not got along with Avril and hoped that, in the event of her death, Richard would be brought up not by her but by George and Doreen Kopp. So, after the funeral, Orwell asked the Kopps to look after the baby at their flat in Canonbury Square, while he returned to Europe. However, as he told Powell, he did not wish to bring up his son in the city. 'As soon as I can get a nurse and a house I shall remove him to the country, as I don't want him to learn to walk in London.'[31] Back in Paris a letter of condolence from Warburg also confirmed to him that *Animal Farm* was on target for summer publication.[32]

His tour of defeated Germany took him to Nuremburg and Stuttgart where he was just one day behind the advancing French army.[33] Observing freshly dead Germans and captured SS men he realised that for him any feelings of revenge were quite meaningless. Just as he hated the retribution meted out to collaborators in the streets of Paris, so he opposed the repatriation to Soviet Russia of the Ukrainian and Baltic soldiers who had fought for the Nazis. By 19 May, just nineteen days after Hitler's suicide, he crossed into Austria, where he observed the manoeuvring that would, he thought, probably lead to separate Soviet and Allied Zones of Occupation.

The feeling that there would be an inevitable showdown with the Russians was already gaining ground. The collapse of Hitler's Reich led him to ponder the sources of nationalism and racism which had so obviously given rise to the war, and in Paris he wrote 'Notes on Nationalism' (later published in *Polemic*). This cannot have been entirely unconnected with the revival of the European Movement and its meetings in Paris attended by Camus, with whom he was at least in touch even if they never met.[34] He spent VE Day in Paris, celebrating with the crowds in the Place de la Concorde, not far from where he had once slaved in a subterranean hotel kitchen.

On 24 May he returned to London where the forthcoming General Election was concentrating minds. Orwell was keen to get involved and threw himself into canvassing for his local Labour Party. As he had when he returned from abroad before, he marvelled at those qualities that made the English distinct from others – 'the pacifist habits of mind, respect for freedom of speech and belief in legality [that] have managed to survive here while seemingly disappearing on the other side of the Channel'. And there again was the old impression of a slumbering England. 'I don't know whether this semi-anaesthesia . . . is a sign of decadence, as many observers believe, or whether on the other hand it is a kind of instinctive wisdom.'[35]

With *Animal Farm* due to appear in August, he raised with Warburg the question of his future novels. Gollancz still had an option on the next two, and even argued that *Animal Farm*, being short, did not count. Warburg suggested he try to break all contractual links with Gollancz and switch to him. When they discussed this over lunch in Soho on 25 June, Orwell announced that he had already written the first twelve pages of his new novel (he had begun sketching it as far back as 1943), but, because of the need to make a living from journalism, thought it unlikely to be completed before 1947.

Polemic, launched with the backing of a rich Australian, Rodney Phillips, and with Humphrey Slater as editor, was, in some ways, tailor-made for writers like Orwell – independent and unorthodox. Contributors would also include Koestler, Ayer and Bertrand Russell. Orwell's 'Notes on Nationalism' was accepted for the first edition in October and he was given a contract for four more at a fee of £25 each. His essays for *Polemic* are among his most important shorter works – 'The Prevention of Literature', 'Second Thoughts on James Burnham', 'Politics vs. Literature', and 'Lear, Tolstoy and the Fool'. He also wrote the editorial to the third number – an attack on J. D. Bernal, the Communist mathematician and propagandist. Orwell warmed to Phillips, confiding to him one day over a meal that he feared that he could be a target of a Communist assassination. The Australian, who had brought a German Lugar home from the war, sold it to

Orwell for £5. It was a far more effective weapon than the one Hemingway had lent him in Paris. The only problem was, it had no ammunition. Now his paranoia about Communists was not just fear of spies and eavesdroppers, but of assassins, too, the sort who had found and murdered Trotsky in Mexico, and had murdered others in Paris and even in America. He told George Woodcock that Randall Swingler, a Communist writer who had attacked him in *Polemic* had then tried to shake his hand (a gesture Orwell refused): 'What a smelly little hypocrite Swingler is! Just like the rest of them! If he could do it without risking his cowardly little hide, he'd take the greatest delight in pushing me under a bus.'

Needing someone to keep house and take care of Richard for him, in July he hired a housekeeper. Susan Watson was the daughter of Wyn Henderson, a Communist and an editor at Lawrence and Wishart. Susan was twenty-seven, divorced with a small daughter of her own. After a brief interview at the Empsons' place he hired her at £1 a week plus keep. When her mother heard the news she was none too pleased. 'Don't work for him,' she told her. 'He's on the wrong side.' But Susan liked him and found him a kind, considerate employer. And although he looked cadaverous and ill, she was taken by his blue eyes, good humour and directness. She had a sweet, innocent nature, which Orwell clearly found endearing, and, despite a limp and a slight lack of co-ordination due to childhood polio, she was a willing and conscientious worker.

She soon got to know his habits, the foul tobacco he liked, the food he enjoyed – kippers for breakfast, Gentleman's Relish, Oxford Marmalade, and chocolate cake for high tea. He in turn developed a close relationship with her – protective, she thought, in a Dickensian way – and felt able to share certain confidences with her. However, he could not resist the opportunity to tease her, once telling her that his anthropologist friend Geoffrey Gorer was coming to look at Richard to compare his development with that of his chimps. Afterwards, he solemnly informed her that there was no problem: Richard was well in advance of Gorer's apes. The joke was that Gorer, being a *social* anthropologist, did not keep chimps, but Susan swallowed the story and was duly impressed. He was very strongly against the restrictive upbringing to which had been subjected, wanting Richard brought up in a permissive atmosphere, telling Susan, 'You will let him play with himself, won't you.' She was instructed not to smack him. If necessary, he would do that. When Mary Fyvel admired the way he handled Richard he said, 'Yes. You see, I've always been good with animals.'

A natural routine developed. George worked from eight-thirty or nine in the morning before lunching at the local pub or meeting friends. He always returned for high tea, the most important meal of his day, after which he worked, sometimes until three in the morning. At ten o'clock Susan took him a mug of chocolate in a Queen Victoria mug. Occasionally he would take a break to put in a spot of carpentry, Richard acting as his 'mate' and handing him the nails.[36]

Orwell was planning a new will appointing Rees as his literary executor, and was thinking seriously about his and his child's future. When the *Observer* asked him to return to Europe he declined. The separation from Richard would be too great a distraction from the book he had just started. He recommended Inez as a substitute. In June, on assignment for the *Observer*, he took her on the election trail with him. Out in the street after one meeting someone shouted, 'Look at those Trotskyists,' which Orwell thought highly amusing, but he must have been a little worried to be so easily recognised by his political enemies.[37]

His eccentricity was becoming rather more evident. On General Election Day, 24 July, he appeared unexpectedly after lunch in the office of Roger Senhouse, bringing along the corrected proofs of his *Critical Essays*, as Senhouse recorded in his diary:

> He said, 'Oh hello Roger I've brought back the proofs corrected not many mistakes but I've had to make some alterations and there isn't anything libellous left in . . .' All one sentence and one tone, no punctuation, and while he was speaking he threw off a mass of accoutrements in White Knight disarray onto my sofa. First a fishing rod in a good cover, just bought 2nd hand, then a mac and a parcel, probably rations of some sort & then a portfolio; then he plopped down himself, looking thoroughly exhausted & remarking as much. A thick coat of buoyant blue tweed – yellow green tie – and his eyes being noticeably the truest colour of all. Steel blue and seeming more deep-set in his haggard state, and I looked closer into his piercing glance than usual, for I wanted to be sure that the extraordinary wheezing sound was synchronized with his breathing. It was pretty bad so I was not surprised when he sat down. He'd been after the rod for some time (about £8 I guessed) and wanted to be off with [it] at once . . . It was exciting to hear him talk even. But instead he waded into the cost of living in Islington and the time taken up in buying food . . . It is obvious the rod is the equivalent of a week's living cost to him, for he entered into detail . . . he . . . told me that Dicky Rees was back in this country . . . 'I've made him my literary executor. Much the best, don't you think?' 'Scrupulously painstaking and much more than that, of course; astonishing integrity and devotion.' 'Yes, he'll be able to sort out my papers all right & know what to do with all the scraps and there may well be quite good things among them – don't really know how much I've got written . . . I want to go up to Scotland – right up in the

north. You know I've got some sort of cottage up there & I don't know what state I'll find it in and then I'll come back & look after the kid . . . By the way I've started my new novel, but I shan't finish it until 1947 & I'll put it aside now. I've only just come to see that I can always make more money out of my best articles in book form and you'll always be ready to publish them, won't you?' . . . We were all waiting for the Election Results on Thursday. 'Everyone is saying that [there] is a big swing over and I believe it will be so . . .'[38]

Labour won the election with an overwhelming majority, and set the country on a socialist course to nationalisation and a planned economy, which Orwell thought heralded an irreversible change. The age of laissez-faire seemed dead and done for. It highlighted the question which had long fascinated him – in a collectivised world how could individual freedom be preserved? He had already given his answer in reviewing Hayek's *The Road to Serfdom*. It could only happen, he wrote, 'if the concept of right and wrong is restored to politics'. It was to be the central theme of his new novel.

Since his return from Europe, he had kept in touch with Malcolm Muggeridge, now writing for the conservative *Daily Telegraph*, and lunches with Anthony Powell became regular events for the three of them. Orwell was a source of some amusement to these right-wing gossips and the subject of much ironic comment. Muggeridge's diary entries about him always had a caustic edge to them: 'Lunched with Tony Powell and George Orwell, the latter exactly like Don Quixote, very lean and egotistic and honest and foolish; a veritable Knight of the Woeful Countenance. A kind of dry egotism has burnt him out. Hughie Kingsmill and Hugh Trevor-Roper joined us afterwards, and Hugh Trevor-Roper said that Orwell wrote like Johnson. Hughie would not have this at all, and shouted out "Cobbett!"'[39] Orwell attracted many such comparisons. Some who knew him, like Michael Foot and Jon Kimche, saw George Orwell as a consciously cultivated alter ego. Julian Symons thought 'Orwell' was a new skin intended to cover up 'Blair', the failure. George Woodcock saw him concealing his deeper truer self behind these various masks. Powell also believed that his whole puritanical persona was a calculated act. Perhaps what Muggeridge and Powell and Kingsmill saw as egotism was Orwell continually rehearsing and exploring his own personal creation, his literary persona, in the presence of his literary contemporaries. Powell would include a caricature Orwell (Alf Erridge, the eccentric revolutionary Lord Warminster, a duke turned make-believe prole), in his novel-cycle, *A Dance to the Music of Time*. But Orwell's artist friend, John Craxton, knew a different Orwell – quite out of the ordinary, but 'certainly no imitation Cockney'.[40]

At the beginning of August the war in the Far East was brought to a sudden and dramatic end when atomic bombs were dropped on Hiroshima and Nagasaki. This introduced a new horrific dimension to the incubating nightmare. It also reminded him that Wells had predicted nuclear weapons years before in *The World Set Free*.[47]

The sight of an obliterated Europe with its total breakdown of civilisation, refugees on the march, public humiliations and executions – an Hieronymus Bosch landscape of horror – only cast him into deeper gloom. Over Europe hung a morbid cloud of oppression, poverty and uncertainty, like one vast dilapidated workhouse. The wartime London to which he returned still lay under its own mist of gloom, and he had been robbed of the bright, lively partner who actually cared about him and his newly adopted son. On top of all this came the Bomb. In these circumstances Jura would become his new Golden Country, unspoilt by time, unaffected by modernity, distant from the wreckage of war and the machinations of obsessed politicians. Jura was also a chance to renew himself, to start afresh, to return, as it were, to the primitive simplicities he had enjoyed as a boy at large.

Just three days after the Japanese surrender, on 17 August, *Animal Farm* was published, and Orwell's reputation took a great leap forward. Now his name would become known to a vaster readership than he could have ever imagined. The first edition was of a modest 4,500 copies, but even before publication interest in the book was so wide that Warburg, his opinion of Orwell seemingly confirmed, had arranged to rush out a second impression of 10,000. Many more would follow.

This story of an animal revolution is widely considered Orwell's finest achievement, although Eileen's influence, which he admitted, needs also to be acknowledged. In *Animal Farm* Orwell was, as usual, strangely off-centre, subjecting the political dynamics of the time to his own brand of lateral thinking, yet the result was a singularly well-directed missile. The form may have been fairy story (or Tolkienian 'beast fable'), but its style is satirical, Swiftian and savage. Much from the novel was to become part of the common cultural currency of many countries, not just Britain – 'Four legs good, two legs bad', 'All animals are equal but some animals are more equal than others' – and Orwell's Napoleon, Snowball, Squealer and Boxer are instantly recognisable literary figures. Benjamin the Donkey, the Farm cynic, was recognised by some as none other that the lugubrious author himself.

Most reviewers greeted the book as a minor masterpiece. Fyvel, in *Tribune*, referred to it as 'a gentle satire on a certain State', inviting a broadside from Symons saying that he should at least have the courage to say what the book really was – a political satire on the Soviet Union, that Napoleon was Stalin and Snowball Trotsky – and he should also say whether he agreed with the author or not. The *Spectator* reviewer, W. J. Turner, called Orwell 'brilliant'. His book had exposed 'a colossal deception', and was 'calculated to drive the amateur Bolsheviks of Battersea, East Aldgate and Mayfair into a frenzy of rage'. Not surprisingly, in *Horizon*, Connolly pinpointed Orwell precisely: '[He] is a revolutionary who is in love with 1910. Never before has a progressive political thinker been so handicapped by nostalgia for the Edwardian shabby-genteel or the under-dog. Nevertheless, *Animal Farm* is one of the most enjoyable books since the war, it is deliciously written, with something of the feeling, the penetration and the verbal economy of Orwell's master, Swift.'[42] His *bête noire* at the *New Statesman*, Kingsley Martin, like Eliot, misread his message as meaning that all would have been well with Russia's revolution, 'if the wicked Stalin had not driven the brave and good Trotsky out of Eden'. This reading made it easy for Martin to dismiss the book as little more than a passing amusement – historically false and simplistic but good for a laugh.[43] Graham Greene in the London *Evening Standard* recommended it to Walt Disney, adding, 'But is it perhaps a little too real for him?'[44]

Individual reactions varied. Reg Reynolds wrote from his hospital bed, 'It is GREAT – positively the first ANIMAL CLASSIC.'[45] Julian Symons said how much he admired it and how much he disagreed with Martin's review. E. M. Forster sent word to say that he'd mentioned it in a radio broadcast, and Dwight Macdonald thought he had brought out 'the pathos of the Russian degeneration' better than anyone in a long time. 'The ending . . . is one more triumph of inventiveness. Congratulations on a beautifully done piece of writing.'[46] Not everyone in America agreed with MacDonald about the ending, as became evident later. Muggeridge had tried it out on his young son and found 'his enjoyment . . . was quite authentic . . . It's the supreme test of all good allegory that it appeals to children.'[47]

After all the difficulty he had had getting it published, Orwell was surprised and delighted at its reception. As he told MacDonald later, 'The comic thing is that after all this fuss the book got almost no hostile reception when it came out. The fact is that people are fed up with this Russian nonsense and it's just a question of who is first to say, "The Emperor has no clothes".'[48]

But a note of warning came from Empson, by no means blind to the perils of ambiguity, anxious to applaud the book, but also to reflect his and his wife's strong Communist sympathies. It was, he said, 'a most impressive object, with a range of feeling and the economy of method, and the beautiful limpid prose style. I read it with great excitement.' However, on reflection and showing it to others, he realised 'the danger of this kind of

perfection is that it means very different things to different readers'. One
Conservative friend who had read it greeted it as 'very strong Tory propaganda'. He was not altogether persuaded that the parallel with the Soviet
Union held nor that the story was altogether consistent in its own terms,
and he did not wish to fault the allegory – 'But I thought it worth warning
you (while thanking you very heartily) that you must expect to be "misunderstood" on a large scale about this book; it is a form that inherently
means more than the author means, when it is handled sufficiently well.'[49]
This friendly warning left open the question of how far Empson himself
had 'misunderstood' Orwell's book.

Empson's prediction, however, was not wrong. The right-wing Evelyn
Waugh, who learned of it, oddly enough, from the *Daily Worker*'s chief anti-
POUM propagandist, his 'Communist cousin' Claud Cockburn,[50] wrote to
Orwell, congratulating him on his 'ingenious & delightful allegory'.[51]
Through Waugh, Churchill's son Randolph heard of the book and wrote
asking Orwell for a copy, later giving it an encomiastic review when it was
published in America. Even the Queen is said to have sent out for a copy. Six
months later Churchill made his 'Iron Curtain' speech, and there was talk of
a Cold War with Russia, anti-Russian sentiment gathered momentum, and
yet again Orwell had written a book that caught the moment. Soon
American opinion would swing violently against its wartime ally, making it
suddenly highly receptive to Orwell's 'little squib'. Within two years it was
being quoted widely on the right, and used specifically against the Labour
Government which Orwell broadly supported. It would be published in
German translation by the American-funded *Der Monat* magazine in Berlin
and presented as an anti-Stalinist novel (as later would *Nineteen Eighty-
Four*). And when in the following year the book appeared in the US, the
publisher sent a copy to J. Edgar Hoover for his endorsement.

Orwell was labouring on with his new novel. By September he told
Humphrey Slater he had completed only fifty pages, so progress was slow.
Shortly afterwards, in a *Tribune* article on the atomic bomb, he hinted at the
thoughts now preoccupying him. In the wake of Hiroshima and Nagasaki,
he argued, the prospect of a world divided into three great power-blocks in
a mutual state of undeclared war (as predicted by James Burnham) seemed
close to reality, 'but few people have yet considered its ideological implications – that is, the kind of world-view, the kind of beliefs, and the social
structure that would probably prevail in a State which was at once *unconquerable* and in a permanent state of "cold war" with its neighbours.'[52]
Other hints were dropped in 'The Prevention of Literature', written for
Polemic, where he drew parallels between Catholic and Communist persecution of free thinkers, with a passing reference to the Inquisition. 'A society

becomes totalitarian when its structure becomes flagrantly artificial: that is, when its ruling class has lost its function but succeeds in clinging to power by force or fraud. Such a society, no matter how long it persists, can never afford to become either tolerant or intellectually stable. It can never permit either the truthful recording of facts, or the emotional sincerity, that literary creation demands.' In fact, 'Totalitarianism demands . . . the continuous alteration of the past, and in the long run probably demands a disbelief in the very existence of objective truth.'[53] Here are the major themes of *Nineteen Eighty-Four* and the implied sense of horror – the emotional dynamo driving him to write it.

Eileen had urged him not to return to *Tribune* but to get on with another book and clearly he had taken her advice. For the immediate future he would earn his basic income by reviewing for the *Observer* and *Manchester Evening News*, freeing himself from the shackles of an office desk. However, he was to find the tyranny of journalism just as crushing as the tyranny of literary editorship. Eventually the city and the pressures of journalism became intolerable. In September he left for two weeks holiday on Jura, this time to stay in the deserted crofter's cottage he hoped would become a permanent summer home. There, close to the beach, armed with his big jack-knife (and no doubt his Lugar) and with his youthful sense of adventure intact, he could perform his Robinson Crusoe role in complete isolation, exploring the local flora and fauna, catching the odd rabbit and fishing for his supper.

On Jura he had ample opportunity to reflect and mourn and, of course, to use his new fishing rod. There were mackerel to be caught offshore, and an abundance of trout in a lacework of lochs and tarns. Suddenly he was back to how he had been before his marriage, a solitary, unhappy-looking figure. Now he had cast himself in another role – the hermitic widower in mourning for a lost past, the romantic adventurer subsisting alone.

It was on this visit that he came across a large deserted farmhouse, Barnhill, set in an idyllic if barren landscape on the northern tip of the island, with the mountains as a backdrop and the ocean lapping at the foot of the garden. It held more promise than the crofter's cottage, a far roomier place, with five bedrooms, to which he could invite family and friends to alleviate the isolation. He applied to the Laird, Robin Fletcher, for permission to lease it. Fletcher was an Old Etonian, which probably eased negotiations, and by the time he left the deal was done. However, the long-abandoned farm had no electricity and required several hundred pounds' worth of repairs to make it habitable.

There was something hauntingly remote about Jura and especially Barnhill. In winter the old greystone farm building, shrouded in mist, swept by gales and darkened by louring skies, stood like some Bleak House, eerie and inhospitable. At other times, bathed in sunlight and lapped by blue water, it offered a more welcoming prospect. Although it was poor farming land the island was rich in wildlife – red deer, wild goats, rabbits, rats and snakes in abundance, and teeming with birds – just the place for the solitary naturalist to ramble and observe while being close to the heath-like, boggy surface of the earth and the unpredictable elements. Barnhill, he hoped, would make the ideal summer retreat. The fact that there was no daily postal service, no electricity, no telephone and it was twenty-five miles from the nearest doctor or store along a road that ended in eight miles of pot-holed moorland track, counted for nothing in his calculations. Jura offered him a way of escape into the solitude he sought as a writer, a way to take on the romantic role of castaway. There were other reasons, too, but for the time being, to the hated city he had to return.

On his way back, close to Eileen's fortieth birthday, he visited her grave in Newcastle where he had had a shining white headstone erected bearing the simple inscription: 'Here Lies Eileen Maud Blair wife of Eric Arthur Blair Born Sept 25th 1905 Died March 29th 1945.' It lay (and still lies) in the St Andrew's and Jesmond Cemetery – a fitting enough place, but an urban setting, never far from the muted roar of city traffic. Appropriately enough, next to her lies an eminent surgeon, and Fellow of the Royal College of Surgeons. George planted a Polyantha rose on her plot.

The visit to Eileen's grave must have made him ever more conscious of his own mortality, and, in his poor state of health, aware that he might only have a short time to live, he soon began to cast around seriously for a wife.

At least five American publishers turned down *Animal Farm* before Frank Morley of Harcourt Brace read it on a visit to England in December 1945, and bought the US rights on the spot for £250.[54] A month later, *Time* magazine approached Orwell for an interview. Reluctantly he agreed, telling Moore, 'I suppose it's possible they may do something very unfriendly, but I don't think it matters, because I suppose any kind of publicity is helpful.'[55] But the encouraging news from America was balanced by depressing news from France. His French publisher, Nagel, worried about left-wing opinion, had got cold feet about bringing out *Animal Farm*. Orwell was shocked, and told Gorer, 'I think it's a sad thing to think of a thing like this happening, in France of all countries.'[56] Yvonne Davet, his translator friend, wrote, 'I am afraid that no French publisher will agree to compromise himself by publishing a book which speaks ill of the Communists!'[57] Finally he found a firm in Monaco sufficiently courageous to bring it out. He also had the consolation of learning that the book was being translated into nine foreign languages simultaneously.

Michael Sayers, fresh from a journalistic assignment in Europe, was passing through London late in the year and looked him up. They met for a long supper at the Elysée in Percy Street, catching up on their lives since their Kentish Town days. Sayers had spent the past nine years in the American theatre and had become quite wealthy. He was very much on the left and had written books exposing American Nazis. At that time he was elated at the German defeat, full of admiration for the Russian victories, and thinking there would be great opportunities for friendship and trade between the USA and USSR. He found Orwell looking very ill and deeply depressed. He remembered talking with him at length about the end of the war, his wasted years at the BBC, nationalism, the Bomb and the bleak future. He also spoke touchingly about the death of Eileen. The advent of the Bomb had cast Orwell down and he feared for the future of his young son. To Sayers it all seemed very sad. 'He was so despairing. He said "I almost wish they'd exploded that goddamned atom bomb over all of us. We've gone too far down the wrong alley."' He talked about Communist duplicity in Spain and ridiculed Stalin's show trials, on which the Irishman took the Orthodox Communist line. Over Sayers' Communist sympathies all that Orwell would say was that they were on the same side but had taken different paths. 'I remember him saying to me, "You over in America and me here . . . we both started from the same place but you went along the Stalin road and I went the opposite. But if the Tories were in power I'd be just as much against them."'[58] Sayers felt again some of the warmth they had shared together ten years earlier. 'We had a very long and loving talk – there was an intimacy between us that was quite extraordinary.' They didn't leave the Elysée till two in the morning, well after closing time, with the waiters hovering to lock up.

His antipathy to the Soviet Union was more intense than ever, and he feared assassination. Throughout the war he had been highly critical of American capitalism. Sayers must have seemed to him its embodiment, and yet their friendship continued, and four years later he was prepared to do his old friend a favour in writing to Ruth Fischer, a woman seemingly hunting for communists for the CIA, who had mentioned Sayers as the co-author of a book in praise of Stalin. He told Fischer that when he had met Sayers in London, 'He was very pro-USSR, but in what struck me as a curious way, ie from the angle of a businessman who saw Russia as a powerful and potentially rich country with which America could do a profitable deal. One could not possibly have credited him with any proletarian sympathies.'(59) No doubt he hoped to put Fischer off her interest in the young Irishman. In fact their conversation had had an effect on Sayers, and by the time Orwell wrote that, he had withdrawn from Communist circles and adopted what he called a politically 'neutral' position. Even so, he was later subjected to McCarthyite persecution and forced to live abroad.'

Rayner Heppenstall remembered Sayers, Orwell and himself dining together, and afterwards Sayers telling him that their old friend was 'killing himself with hate' against the Soviet Union. Sayers could recall no such meeting. He did, however, meet H. G. Wells (He had recently published the deeply pessimistic *Mind at the End of Its Tetner*) and found him in much the same dejected state. Over dinner Orwell had talked about Zamyatin's *We* (just available in London in French translation), saying that he was taking it as the model for his next novel.[60] Sayers bought it in the Charing Cross Road to read on the trip home, but found it so boring he left it on the plane in New York.

Before leaving, at a *Horizon* party, Sayers met Sonia Brownell, telling her that Orwell was extremely depressed and suggesting she go along and try to cheer him up. (Koestler claimed that it was he who made the suggestion.) She did visit him, and for the occasion he asked Susan to get in a bottle of sherry; strong tea did not have quite the effect he was hoping for. Sonia, who was of a generous disposition and inclined to plunge into affairs, took pity on him and surrendered to his advances, although she reported to friends that 'it was not much'. Whether he pounced or simply propositioned her is not known. According to Koestler, Sonia was 'a very primitive animal in her sexual demands', and Orwell no doubt found her sexually extremely exciting. (Asked by an interviewer if Orwell was a puritan, she replied, 'He wouldn't have married me if he had been.')[61] But she discontinued the affair because as a lover George himself was too animalistic and crude – that 'Burma-Sergeant fashion' performance, no doubt.[62] But more than that, Sonia found it difficult to sustain an intimate relationship for long, feeling hemmed in by a man's possessiveness, preferring herself to be the dominant partner. She could, it was said, end a relationship very violently when she tired of it.[63] (She later told the novelist and playwright Nigel Dennis, with whom she had an affair, that she hated all men.) Even so, this apparently ill-assorted pair found things in common which established a bond between them.

Sonia was born in India, and rebelled against a strict convent upbringing, always spitting when a nun passed her in the street. She had a deep sense of guilt, partly the result of a boating accident in Switzerland when she was seventeen in which her three companions were lost, and, to save herself, she had to leave one boy to drown, pushing him under to free herself from his frantic clutches. She had a series of unsatisfactory affairs throughout her twenties, found some degree of fulfilment first as an artist's model (the celebrated 'Euston Road Venus') and as literary secretary at *Horizon*, and had a passion for France and French culture, imbibed mostly from Cyril Connolly who she considered the supreme arbiter in all matters of taste. Orwell, Indian-born, too, had had his own taste of convent education, and as a youth at Eton was also stricken by guilt over the death of another boy.

Like Sonia he felt intellectual outrage over the convoluted thinking by which totalitarians (Catholic or Communist) held contradictory ideas simultaneously. Sonia called it 'Double Vision'; he, in a more elaborated form called it 'Doublethink'. Her lack of sexual inhibition and hard-headed, matter-of-fact approach to the world is well-captured by Orwell in Julia, the girl from the fiction department in *Nineteen Eighty-Four*.[64] Michael Meyer, who met her years later, said of her, 'Sonia was smart and hard-drinking, and amusing and dangerous and quick tempered – all the things Eileen was not.'[65] She was the centre of a good deal of sexual speculation and gossip, a voluptuous mystery after whom not a few men lusted. (At some point she is said to have had an abortion after being made pregnant by Koestler.) But she was also down-to-earth and practical, someone on whom Connolly came to depend at *Horizon*, whose hard exterior hid a vulnerable, uncertain and emotionally damaged woman. When Orwell proposed to her she retreated rapidly, though they never lost touch. Occasionally, when Susan had her day off, she would babysit for him, but without much enthusiasm, it seems. 'Oh the smell of cabbage and unwashed nappies,' she once commented.[66] Orwell was not the only one with a highly refined sense of smell.

Now that he had made a new will naming Rees his literary executor, and wrote a series of important articles which amounted to a last will and testament to his readers. These essays – 'The Prevention of Literature', 'Politics and the English Language' and 'Why I Write' – contained his warnings against political dangers ahead, and a statement of his own commitment to decency, open politics, literature and individual freedom of thought. This summing up would culminate in the explosive *Nineteen Eighty-Four*, the bomb intended finally to wake up sleeping England.

Having been ill and now heavily overworked, Orwell was happy to accept an invitation from Koestler to spend Christmas at his farmhouse in Wales. Koestler was now married to the beautiful ex-debutante, Mamaine Paget, whose recently divorced twin, Celia Kirwan, was editorial assistant to Humphrey Slater at *Polemic*. As Celia was also invited, she arranged to meet Orwell and Richard at Paddington to travel together down to Wales. For her it was a momentous meeting, and for Orwell an unexpected delight to find himself in the company of such a beautiful young woman. She was immediately struck by this tall, shaggy figure carrying a child under one arm and a suitcase under the other, and by something highly attractive about him ('not charisma, just this terrific quality'). Instinctively she felt that she wanted them to become friends. During the four-hour journey, she took charge of Richard while George looked on with pleasure at her obvious love of small children.

Over Christmas he told Koestler of his great sense of loneliness. This became evident when they all told each other the quality they would like to have if they could choose. Orwell said, 'I should like to be irresistible to women.' But he did not always know how to please either sex. Shortly before Christmas, in *Tribune*, reviewing a play by Koestler he began, 'The drama is not Arthur Koestler's line,' and ended, 'The dialogue is mediocre, and . . . the play demonstrates the gap that lies between having an idea and working it up into dramatic shape.'[67] Koestler was pained, but discovered that friendship with Orwell did not guarantee favourable reviews. 'Why did you give such a stinking review?' he asked. 'Well, it was a stinking play,' replied Orwell.[68] However, as Tosco Fyvel said, 'In his writing he was a fierce critic, yet in person a gentle and considerate friend and acquaintance.'[69]

The death of Eileen had hit him harder than he first realised. His reaction seems to have been a sort of emotional double-take. He wrote later that he had hoped to come to terms with her loss but on returning to the cottage in Wallington had found some of her letters there and his loneliness for her became suddenly unbearable.[70] And, after meeting John Middleton Murry for dinner, the old *Adelphi* editor recorded, 'Essentially his attitude is based on the irrelevance of material amelioration to the experience of death – not one's own death so much as the deaths of those we love.' He had some close women friends, such as Inez Holden, Brenda Salked and Sally McEwan, but what he wanted was an impossible dream – a young woman who could share his ideas and make him feel attractive, as Sonia had done briefly, and would also take on Richard. Seemingly, Sonia's readiness to sleep with him had encouraged him, and from then on young women were apt to find themselves singular objects of his interest and desire.

Now he turned his attentions to Celia. On their return to London, he asked her round for high tea – sardines and sausages followed by toast and marmalade. She saw him bath Richard and was very impressed by how he handled and cared for the little boy. He told her that he had bronchiectasis, which she knew about because she and her sister both suffered from asthma. As she reported to Mamaine, 'Sometimes he has bad haemorrhages and he easily runs a temperature, which he can only keep down when he is ill by not eating anything but bread . . . He says the doctor [Morlock] says that his haemorrhages are not dangerous really.' But she was sceptical about this tale of woe. 'I think he only says it in order to belittle his own advantages as a husband for me. For instance he says "I am fifteen years older than you, and if I die in ten years' time you will be 37 which is not too good a time to be left a widow," and all that sort of thing, which I say is rather phoney logic, because we might easily all be liquidated in five years' time, or on the other hand I'm not all that strong myself, and he might live to be 90.' Five days later, she reported having had him to lunch at her Chelsea flat: 'He . . . asked me again whether I would consider marrying him, or at any rate having an affair with him. I am awfully worried about this last, as he makes it somehow awfully difficult to refuse. I told him the only reason I had for refusing was that I was not in love with him, but I can see that it is going to be more and more difficult to cope with him if I continue to see him, which of course I shall do.'[71]

He felt very sexually attracted to Celia and wrote her a letter so explicit in his desires for her that she could not bear either to show it to anyone or even talk about it. She preferred rather to think of him as a friend and a brilliant mind and ignore the animal side of his nature. This left her feeling even more confused.

> When I got this letter I didn't know quite what to do. I didn't want to marry George, because I didn't quite think that it would be the right thing for me. For one thing he was quite a lot older than me, and I didn't want to have an affair with him either, not because I didn't think George was attractive, but because he was such a serious person that you couldn't have an affair with him without getting involved with him, and if you were going to get involved with him you might as well marry him, and I didn't want to marry him! You see. So, I was in a real dilemma about the whole thing. So, I wrote back to George some rather ambiguous letter. Anyway, it got sorted out.[72]

Her boss at *Polemic*, Humphrey Slater, had taken to referring to Orwell as 'Grisly George' or, after his anthropomorphic alter ego in *Animal Farm*, 'Donkey George', a nickname which Koestler and the twins quickly picked up. It was, after all, his own choice of animal.

Winters always brought him flu or bronchitis. In early 1946 he wrote an article on 'Bad Weather', declaring February, in particular, 'a detestable month with no virtue except shortness'. He then promptly fell ill. One Monday night, shortly after his return, Susan heard a commotion in the passage and found George having a haemorrhage. She sent him to bed with an ice pack. It was the first she knew about his lung problem, having put his 'short barking cough' down to his throat wound from Spain. 'He was,' she said, 'a very concealing person.' He told her he had once been diagnosed with TB, but would not see a doctor saying he did not trust them. Two weeks later he seemed to have recovered. As usual after one of these haemorrhages, he began to wonder how long he had left, and now he had Richard the question tormented him more than a little. He told Susan that he hoped to live until Richard was thirteen, and asked if she would stay with him until then at least. The need for a wife must have seemed ever more imperative.

He was ill again in March and it may have been these bouts of illness and his recent haemorrhage, which prompted him to dig out and revise his brilliantly recalled essay about his stint in the Hôpital Cochin, 'How the Poor Die' (rejected earlier by *Horizon*). It certainly carried with it intimations of mortality, and reflected the depressed state of his mind at this time. What gives it more immediacy is its dating: Orwell entered the dreaded Paris hospital in March; in his essay he makes it 'detestable' February.

Having had no luck with Celia he decided to renew contact with Brenda, to whom he had not written since he proposed a *ménage à trois* with Eileen. He invited her to high tea, again using the lure of Richard, hoping to appeal to her maternal instinct. 'I am generally at the above, as I don't go to an office nowadays. I would like you to see my little boy, now aged 21 months.'[73] She did go to tea and would eventually also visit him on Jura.

Occasionally one short piece of writing led to something more serious. 'Decline of the English Murder' perhaps owes something to de Quincey's 'On Murder Considered as a Fine Art'. With his nervousness about possible assassination, a murder case that gave him more than usual pause for thought was the so-called 'Cleft Chin Murder', involving a crime spree by a young Welsh waitress and a US Army deserter (the man with the cleft chin). He had reviewed a book about it for the *Manchester Evening News* in November and now wrote a more ruminative article on the subject for *Tribune*. It was a bitingly ironic piece of nostalgia, comparing the predominantly domestic, almost genteel, English murders of the past with the more anonymous, random, brutal homicide imported from America. (It was an extension of his thoughts about 'Raffles and Miss Blandish', applied now not to fiction but to a social reality which he obviously found chilling.) He feared that this crime provided a vision of a heartless and more casually violent future. If that kind of thing could come to England from the West, he no doubt thought, what was to prevent political assassination coming from the East? At least with the latter he knew who his enemy was and was prepared for him.

When his *Critical Essays* appeared in February, he received £100 advance on signature and £100 on publication. In April Reynal and Hitchcock, one of the publishers who had rejected *Animal Farm*, published it as *Dickens, Dali and Others* in America. Not only did he get the good opinion of Edmund Wilson in the *New Yorker*, but a personal letter of appreciation from Randall Jarrell inviting him to contribute to the *Nation*. The first print run of 3000 copies sold out quickly following what Senhouse called 'a blaze of reviews', and a further run of 5600 copies went within a year. Orwell's name could now sell books, and Warburg became aware of his importance as a potentially profitable author. 'It was clear to me his publisher,' he wrote, 'that we must take over his books from the Gollancz list and reissue them. I waited eagerly for news that he had embarked on a new novel.'[74] The pressure from Warburg would slowly replace the pressure to meet journalistic deadlines.

Curiously enough, Orwell's *Critical Essays* probably aroused more interest in literary circles than did *Animal Farm*. It was widely reviewed by many leading thinkers of the day, including some of Orwell's friends. The main focus of interest was on Orwell's sociological perspective on literature. Middleton Murry distinguished Orwell the moralist from Connolly the aesthete and sided with Orwell. Evelyn Waugh saw his work as an expression of 'the new humanism', a 'habit of mind' exploring the psychology, world-view and values of an author and his readership. But his work lacked 'neutrality' and a 'religious sense'. His schoolmasterly conclusion was: 'There is nothing in his writing that is inconsistent with high moral principles.'[75] V. S. Pritchett, always appreciative of Orwell, thought the essays 'brilliant examples of political anthropology applied to literature by a nonconforming mind'. 'His traditions . . . are those of the Right, and he cannot quite forgive the world for driving him to the Left.' He 'spoils for trouble, dislikes his own side more than the enemy, [and] is closer to continental writers'. He was 'a kind of Kipling turned upside down', seeing that it was in the Empire that the truly violent English political drama was being played out.[76]

Without close female company he continued feeling depressed. Like Flory he wanted a woman who would take an interest in his work and his well-being, as Eileen had. Two young women lived below him at Canonbury Square, and one of them, Ruth Beresford, invited him to dinner one evening with V. S. Pritchett as the other main guest. Ruth's flat-mate, Anne Popham, home on leave from Germany where she worked for the Allied Control Commission, made up the party. Orwell was clearly taken with Anne whose fiancé had recently died. When she was again home on leave, he slipped a note under her door asking her to drop by. When she arrived he promptly dismissed Susan with Richard to the kitchen, and asked her to sit beside him. As she did so he made a pass and she was so startled that she fled.

Having clearly embarrassed her, he wrote to smooth things over. In his somewhat insensitive fashion he seems to have been taken aback at being rebuffed (as he had with the girl on Hampstead Heath). He agreed that he was unsuitable for her and hoped she had not been shocked by his behaviour. All he had left in life, he said, was his work and Richard, and it was just that sometimes he felt 'so desperately alone'.[77] When she wrote back asking him what on earth had attracted him to her, his reply gave a rare insight into his then rather desperate state of mind and his sense that time was running out for him. It was, he said, scandalous that he should make advances to her, but she had seemed lonely and he had thought she might find it interesting to share her life with an older man. Of course, if she wanted a handsome fertile man he was no use to her, but perhaps she liked the idea of being the widow of a literary man. He did not know how long he had to live, he said.

'I have a disease called bronchiectasis which is always liable to develop into pneumonia, and also an old "non-progressive" tuberculous lesion in one lung, and several times in the past I have been supposed to be about to die, but I always lived on just to spite them, and I have actually been better in health since [taking] M and B [tablets]: He would not mind her sleeping with other men – intellectual and emotional faithfulness was what mattered. 'I was sometimes unfaithful to Eileen, and I also treated her very badly, and I think she treated me badly too at times,' but they had gone through a lot together and she understood his work. Being young and healthy, he said, she deserved someone better than him, but if she thought of herself as 'essentially a widow' she could do worse, 'supposing I am not actually disgusting to you'. He thought he might live another ten years and have 'three worthwhile books' inside him. 'But I want peace and quiet and someone to be fond of me.' He also needed someone to look after Richard. He invited her to Jura, promising not to rape her. It sounded rather like a line he may have used before, to Sonia perhaps and perhaps to Celia.

Finally he dangled the prospect of money in front of her. In America *Animal Farm* had been chosen by the Book-of-the-Month Club, and even after tax he would have money to keep him in idleness for some months.[78] In fact it would mean far more sales – and the first taste of the huge success awaiting him. Anne saw him only once after that, when he asked her to his flat to witness his signature on a document – probably his new will. She was surprised to find Sonia there to supply the second signature. They seemed to be in the middle of a noisy argument about Mallarmé, so after signing she left them to it.

According to Rayner Heppenstall around this time he also tried his wife-catching tactics on a friend of his called Audrey Jones, who he had met at one of Empson's parties. On only their second meeting he proposed to her, but she thought it a bit of a joke and laughed off both him and his proposal. This relentless pursuit of pretty young women reflected the view he shared with Gissing – 'that intelligent women are very rare animals; and if one wants to marry a woman who is intelligent and pretty, then the choice is still further restricted, according to a well-known arithmetical rule'.[79] To get such a woman one needed good looks and money. He considered himself too ugly to qualify on the first count, but on the second, he could at least now hint at a probably secure widowhood for any willing candidate.

Since Spain he had remained sympathetic to the Anarchists, despite attacking their wartime pacifism. Now he became involved in helping defend three Anarchists jailed for selling literature inciting disaffection among members of the armed services. Later he joined the Freedom Defence Committee organised by George Woodcock, and contributed occasionally to *Freedom*, a magazine edited by one of the three, Vernon Richards (born Vero Ricchioni), son of a leading Italian Anarchist, then married to Marie Louise Berneri, the daughter of an Anarchist leader murdered by the Communists in Spain.

In the New Year he would also become involved with Koestler, Bertrand Russell and Michael Foot in trying to revive the pre-war League of the Rights of Man. More meetings, more petitions to sign. In his meetings with Russell, who was greatly interested in his writing, it is very likely that he was able to engage him in the kind of debate Winston Smith has in *Nineteen Eighty-Four* with his tormentor, O'Brien, on the question of solipsism. It was a question on which Russell had written at length and the opportunity to rehearse this projected Inquisitorial encounter with one of the greatest philosophers of the age must have been irresistible. One attempt to inaugurate the League in conjunction with *Polemic* was stymied by Humphrey Slater, who suspected that Koestler was bringing in an American anti-Communist who planned to use the organisation to serve American Cold War aims and bias *Polemic* in the same direction. Slater was being strangely prescient, foreseeing exactly what happened later to *Polemic's* successor, *Encounter*. To Koestler's fury, he sabotaged the meeting by cancelling all bookings.

Chapter 17

The Man Who Loved Islands

'Let not the man who is beast or who thinks he is God come near me.'

Louis MacNeice, 'Prayer Before Birth'

There was something undoubtedly romantic both in Orwell's life and his work, standing as he did in the same revolutionary tradition as Shelley and Byron. He was a born adventurer, a man of action, drawn often by the romantic dream – drawn to Burma, drawn down into the lower depths, drawn to Spain, drawn to London to suffer its Blitz, drawn to the dream of a socialist utopia. And, as his friends have pointed out, he enjoyed acting out roles, putting himself into dramatic situations – even in his relations with children. And in his work there is always a part for him – the down-and-out, the alienated Anglo-Indian, the *poète maudit* haunting the London slums, the married man in mid-life crisis, the cynical donkey, the last free man battling against Big Brother's Inquisition, always the only one in step, battling against a world of injustice. Always, too, was the man who revered the natural world and drew inspiration from it. There stands the romantic Orwell.

As the harsh winter of 1945–46 wore on, Orwell was pining for Jura. He thought that away from London he might concentrate on his novel, telling Leonard Moore that when he returned he hoped to have a wad of it completed.[1] However, preparing to move was a heavy task for him. He was ill again in March, and arranging for his furniture to be moved up to Scotland proved more arduous than anticipated, 'almost like stocking up a ship for an arctic voyage', he told Koestler. However, the prospect of escaping London, the telephone and the journalistic grind buoyed him. During 1945 he had written over one hundred thousand words and his income was for the first time in excess of anything he had earned previously – some £967 before tax. By the beginning of 1946 he was clearly suffering from overwork. He told

Dorothy Plowman that he was 'smothered under journalism'; to Andrew Gow, he wrote, 'I have become more and more like a sucked orange,' and to his old POUM comrade Stafford Cottman, he wrote, 'For two months I mean to do nothing at all, then maybe I shall start another book, but anyway, no journalism until next autumn . . . I have given up the cottage in Hertfordshire and taken another in the island of Jura in the Hebrides . . . I think I can make it quite comfortable with a little trouble, and then I shall have a nice place to retire to occasionally at almost no rent.'[2]

In January, in an office memorandum, Warburg had written, 'George Orwell plans to throw up his journalism from the beginning of May until November for six months to write a novel, which he has clearly in mind.'[3] He asked for an advance of £300 to cover his expenses on Jura. As if bidding his old life farewell, in one of his last pieces for *Tribune* before leaving, 'Confessions of a Book Reviewer', he painted a grim picture of life on sordid Grub Street where the hungry hack scribbles for his supper. 'In a cold but stuffy bed-sitting room littered with cigarette ends and half-empty cups of tea, a man in a moth-eaten dressing gown sits at a rickety table trying to find room for his typewriter among the piles of dusty papers that surround it.' The routine grinds the poor scribbler down, leaving him crushed, and leads him to invent lies and grind out 'the stale old phrases' which characterise newspaper reviews.[4] He had once written that he enjoyed reviewing; but after his recent heavy stint for at least three papers, his view of it could not have been more jaundiced.

When the winter, which had been so cruel to Orwell, finally showed signs of departing he celebrated with one of his best-ever short pieces for *Tribune*. 'Some Thoughts on the Common Toad' was a lyrical and sensitive appreciation of the mating habits of one of nature's least appreciated creatures. 'A toad has about the most beautiful eye of any living creature,' he wrote. 'It is like gold, or more exactly it is like the gold-coloured semi-precious stone which one sometimes sees in signet rings, and which I think is called a chrysoberyl.' Spring came to even the gloomiest London streets around the Bank of England, seeping everywhere, a gas heralding a miracle. While some wartime winters had appeared to be permanent, spring, like the common toad, always stirred eventually.[5] Anticipating the usual complaints about any *Tribune* article celebrating pleasure, he wrote:

> At any rate, spring is here, even in London N1, and they can't stop you enjoying it. This is a satisfying reflection. How many a time have I stood watching the toads mating, or a pair of hares having a boxing match in the young corn, and thought of all the important persons who would stop me enjoying this if they could. But luckily they can't. So long as you are not actually ill, hungry, frightened or immured in a

prison or a holiday camp, spring is still spring. The atom bombs are
piling up in the factories, the police are prowling through the cities, the
lies are streaming from the loudspeakers, but the earth is still going
round the sun, and neither the dictators nor the bureaucrats, deeply as
they disapprove of the process, are able to prevent it.[6]

The article brought a brief letter of praise from the poet John Betjeman,
who told him he was 'one of the best living writers of prose', and that he had
'enjoyed & echoed every sentiment'.[7] On one last visit to the cottage at
Wallington to pack for the removal men, he had gone to the pool where he
and Eileen used to watch the toads spawn. The place was obviously haunted
by memories of their life together and the garden was full of the plants they
had planted ten years earlier when they first moved in, including the
Woolworth's rose which continued to flourish.

With the Book of the Month Club deal for *Animal Farm*, Orwell was at
last faced with the prospect of high taxes. He had approved of increased
income taxes during the war as a step towards abolishing high incomes;
now he was anxious to find ways of minimising what he himself had to
hand over. Previously he had never bothered to open letters from the
Inland Revenue. They couldn't get blood from a stone, he once told Mary
Fyvel. And in 1940 he had written, 'I feel no scruples and would dodge tax
if I could . . . No one is patriotic about taxes.'[8] Jon Kimche recommended
the London accounting firm of Harrison, Son, Hill and Co., and they
advised him that by establishing a corporation in his name he could
spread his earnings over two years for tax purposes. It took from him the
worry of dealing with complicated money matters, but it turned out to be
a move not without its subsequent complications. However, now he could
afford it, he sent a cheque for £150 to Dorothy Plowman to repay the
anonymous loan received through her for his Morocco trip in 1938. Sadly,
L. H. Myers, the secret benefactor, had died two years earlier, and the
courageous pacifist, Max Plowman, who had been the go-between, had
died back in 1941.

Not long before he set off for Scotland, news came that his sister Marjorie
Dakin was ill with pernicious anaemia. On 3 May 1946 she died of uraemia
and hypertension in the Nottingham General Hospital. She was forty-eight.
Within three years Orwell had lost his mother, his wife and sister. With his
father also having died just before the war, three members of his immediate family and a massive part of his past had suddenly gone – the Golden
Age that bit further removed from him. He was now quite familiar with personal grief. On his return from the funeral he wrote to Humphrey Dakin,
'One can't really say anything about Marjorie's death. I know what it is like
and how it sinks in afterwards.'[9] Unknown to him, however, Humphrey had

been having an affair for some years and shortly afterwards married his mistress.[10]

On his way to Jura he again visited Eileen's grave in Newcastle. He noted that the rose he had planted there was blooming, and planted more flowers before leaving. He then stayed briefly with the Kopps, now farming in a small way thirty miles south of Glasgow. George (roguish as ever) had promised him 'some rabbit shooting . . . and any amount of poaching'.[11] Before Orwell left, his old commander offered to sell him a small 10-horse-power Ford van, which that he would return to pick up in early June. In his diary he detailed his journey from Glasgow to Jura. It took almost six hours and involved eight changes of transport.

Why he went to Jura is no mystery. He had grown to hate London, and certainly thought it an unfit place for Richard to grow up. On Jura the boy would be free to 'roam about with no traffic to be afraid of', as he told Celia Kirwan.[12] What is more, he had longed to live on a Hebridean island since 1940 when Compton Mackenzie ('The Man Who Loved Islands') put the idea into his head. The prospect of an island home, as deserted as possible, appealed to the castaway spirit in him. Its remoteness offered the hope of escape from the nuclear war he had told Michael Sayers he now felt was imminent. It was to this sanctuary, well away from that nightmare, the feared bullet in the back of the neck, and the totalitarian terror of *Nineteen Eighty-Four*, that he was taking the child he loved. There he could also escape the suffocating weight of journalism and concentrate on his novel. 'Serious prose,' he had written, 'has to be composed in solitude.'[13] Emotionally this island was where he wanted to be, and where he could give full vent to his creative dynamic. The nightmare could be bottled up, like some evil genie, inside his novel.

Something of his state of mind can be found in the 'As I Please' column he wrote for *Tribune* on his return to London later that year, reflecting on the impending collapse of world order as well as the impending collapse of his health. Beyond that he saw the horrific future he would try to portray in his new novel.

When one considers how things have gone since 1930 or thereabouts, it is not easy to believe in the survival of civilization. I do not argue from this that the only thing to do is to abjure practical politics, retire to some remote place and concentrate either on individual salvation or on building up self-supporting communities against the day when the atom bombs have done their work. I think one must continue the political struggle, just as a doctor must try to save the life of a patient who is probably going to die. But I do suggest that we shall get nowhere unless we start by recognizing that political behaviour is largely non-rational, that the world is suffering from some kind of mental disease which must be diagnosed before it can be cured . . . Exactly at [this] moment . . . half the world is ruled by secret police forces . . . The desire for pure power seems to be much more dominant than the desire for wealth . . . it is no more natural, in the sense of being biologically necessary, than drunkenness or gambling. And if it has reached new levels of lunacy in our own age, as I think it has, then the question becomes: what is the special quality in modern life that makes a major human motive out of the impulse to bully others?[14]

He once hated Scots and the idea of Scotland that had been dished out at St Cyprian's, but once he got to know Jura and some of its poor crofters, he began to develop a close feeling for what he saw as the fundamentally working-class Scots, the exploited victims of an essentially English aristocracy. In such a remote spot, often rain-swept, gale-blasted and freezing, he was putting his precarious health at ever-greater risk, but he had always put his work before his well-being, and from his time in Burma he knew about living in remote country – no doubt it aroused the schoolboy adventurer in him. Perhaps the anarchist in him also felt more at ease remote from state authority. Not surprisingly, his friend Woodcock also emigrated to an island off Vancouver in 1949, no doubt with the same idea in mind. With its five bedrooms, Barnhill, of course, gave him space to have friends to stay, to mitigate the solitude. It was to become his final home, a place of some permanence, as the Wallington Stores had been.

Much of Jura, especially the west side, is deserted, virtually uninhabitable and unsuitable for cultivation. From north to south runs a chain of hills, the highest point being the Paps of Jura; the Tarbert Loch almost bisects the island from east to west. The port of Craighouse, the main settlement, stands at the southern end of the island looking south-east across the Sound of Jura to Kintyre. Ironically perhaps, Jura was once regarded as a particularly healthy place. An early eighteenth-century visitor, Martin Martin, whose book Dr Johnson took on his *Journey to the Western Isles of Scotland*, wrote of it:

This isle is perhaps the wholesomest plot of ground either in the isles or continent of Scotland, as appears by the long life of the natives and their state of health, to which the height of the hills is believed to contribute in a large measure, by the fresh breezes of wind that come from them to purify the air . . . There is no epidemical disease that prevails here . . . Convulsions, vapours, palsies, surfeits, lethargies, megrims, consumptions, rickets, pains of the stomach, or coughs, are not frequent here, and none of them are at any time observed to become mad . . . If any contract a cough, they use brochan only to remove it.[15]

There were dangers, however, in the surrounding waters, often treacherous and storm-tossed. In particular, in the straits between Jura and the neighbouring island of Scarba was the Corryvrekan whirlpool, which, at the tide's turning, caused the seas to erupt and boil in most spectacular fashion. Had Orwell lived there just in the summer it might not have been a problem for him, but during the winter the island was an alien place, harsh and insalubrious for anyone in delicate health. Also it is unlikely that he knew the true nature of his condition, how advanced it was and how very vulnerable he was.

At Ardlussa, a tiny hamlet seventeen miles north-east of Craighouse, Orwell was remembered for turning up that spring of 1946 with little more than a suitcase, a kettle, a saucepan and a typewriter. When asked by the laird's wife if he needed help with food supplies he said he preferred to manage alone. To her he seemed 'a sad and lonely man' who 'looked as if he'd been through a great deal'.[16]

Despite all his good intentions to work on Jura, little more than those already completed pages were written by the time he returned to London six months later. The dynamo was, it seems, not quite up to speed. In May he wrote to Michael Meyer in Oxford asking him if he could procure some black powder and percussion caps for his gun. But he had no licence and had to do without.[17] Whether he needed these for a shotgun or for his Lugar is not clear, but probably the latter because he was soon out shooting small game. He was also practising his various practical skills – curing rabbit skins, cultivating a vegetable patch, fishing for lobsters, hauling in pollock and coalfish – and noting with fascination the primitive methods of cultivation employed on the island.

> Everything is done here in an incredibly primitive way. Even when the field is ploughed with a tractor the corn is still sown broadcast, then scythed and bound up into sheaves by hand . . . Owing to the wet they don't get the hay in till about the end of September or even later, sometimes as late as November, and they can't leave it in the open but have to store it all in lofts . . . In the 18th century the population here was 10,000 – now less than 300.[18]

For the purpose of retrieving the past and getting close to the surface of the earth, he could hardly have found a better place.

Avril joined him a week after he arrived and together they began to make Barnhill habitable. She had planned just a brief stay, but quickly decided to remain. Now that her mother was dead, she was in need of a new home, and running Barnhill for her brother was not an opportunity to be lost. As it happened Orwell was quite pleased to share his new northern paradise. He wrote to his friends extolling the unspoiled beauty of the island, but then explaining in such complicated detail how to get there that many were put off going. In late June he sent the following instructions to Brenda Salkeld who had said she would be able to come:

> It is actually easier than it sounds./Boats leave for Jura on Mondays, Wednesdays and Fridays. The times and places are as follows:/8am leave Glasgow Central for Gourock/Join the boat at Gourock/12 Noon arrive at East Tarbert/Take bus to West Tarbert (bus runs in conjunction with boat)/Join boat at West Tarbert/3pm (about) arrive Jura/Hire car to Ardlussa where we will meet you./You can book through from Glasgow to Jura or you can get your tickets on the boat. I think you can book right the way through from London . . . You might have to walk the last seven miles, in which case it would be better for you to make do with a rucksack and haversack. (I'd carry part of it for you, of course!)[19]

When, much later, Inez Holden visited the island, she noted in her diary, 'It took me almost forty-eight hours to get here from London. Mulk Raj Anand came over from India in twenty-four hours.'[20] Celia never went, nor did Sonia to whom he held out the alluring prospect of a room with a sea view, boat rides around the island and vistas of 'white sand and clear water with seals swimming about in it', romantic caves to shelter in from the rain and deserted shepherd's huts in which to picnic.[21] Despite his somewhat ambiguous plea, 'I do so want to have you here,' it's clear that the daunting travel itinerary – and the prospect of more smells of 'boiled cabbage and nappies' – kept her decidedly away. Humphrey Slater and Warburg also declined the invitation.

The conditions were fairly primitive. Without electricity he used Calor gas for heating water and cooking. The Valor stove and storm lanterns burned paraffin and he burned coal and peat to heat the house in the evenings. The sole means of communication with the outside world was a battery radio. But the weather was surprisingly good. June was glorious, and August, though it turned briefly foul, ended marvellously. By September it had become variable again and at times cold and wretched. Even so, Orwell was left feeling that it was not exactly an unfavourable place for a man in his poor state of health. 'It is not a cold climate here,' he wrote, 'actually the mean temperature is probably warmer than in England, but there is not much sun and a great deal of rain.'[22]

He was especially keen to invite his women friends. As well as Brenda and Sonia, he invited Lydia Jackson, Inez Holden and Sally McEwan. One early visitor who did brave the long journey was Paul Potts, and Karl Schnetzler, already on the island staying with the Astors, also came briefly. Another guest was Viscount Astor, David's father, who visited Barnhill and stayed overnight, apparently taking to Orwell straight away. It is an intriguing meeting to contemplate – the Conservative peer often associated with the appeasement of Hitler, and the radical revolutionary who considered his class to be finished. They were, of course, both old Etonians.

To begin with Barnhill had no hot water and no decent transport. In June he went to Glasgow to pick up Kopp's van, but no sooner did he get it to Jura than it broke down on the quayside. Kopp, it appears, had sold him a dud, but somehow their friendship survived this hiccough, and that year Orwell bought a goose from him for Christmas and Michel, Kopp's eldest son, visited Barnhill that summer.[23] However, without the van, he was reduced to using an ancient motorbike, on which he became a familiar sight – usually trying to get it started after it had broken down on the pot-holed track leading north to Barnhill. He is remembered locally as suddenly appearing through the rain, a tall, gaunt figure in oilskins, sometimes, even more sinisterly, carrying a scythe (for the clearing of reeds from the track, apparently). It was a scene straight from an M. R. James ghost story or a ghastly verse from the *Ingoldsby Legends*.

He entertained a lot and, though rations were tight, most of the time he was able to supplement them with food supplies from his garden, from fishing, from shooting rabbits, or from the few ducks he kept for the table. Celia sent him a bottle of brandy; Woodcock sent him an extra supply of tea; from Craighouse he bought gin and wine. By July food was in good supply at Barnhill. As Avril told Humphrey, 'Eric has bought a little boat & we go fishing in the evening which is the time the fish rise. They are simply delicious fresh from the sea. In fact, on the whole we live on the fat of the land. Plenty of eggs & milk & ½lb butter extra weekly on to our rations. Our landlord gave us a large hunk of venison a short while ago which was extremely good. Then there are local lobsters & crabs. Also the ubiquitous rabbit.'[24] She did not mention the snakes, but her brother took a certain amount of pleasure in killing any he came across, and that large jackknife he carried was just right for the purpose.

Visitors were expected to lend a hand. The eccentric Potts proved to be worse than useless, but Orwell went out of his way to treat him well. 'I once went out to collect some wood,' he recalled, 'and I chopped down the only nut tree on the place. Orwell took great care at dinner that night to be kind to me. I had extra roast beef.'[25] Originally, Rayner Heppenstall (now a BBC producer) was due to travel up with Susan Watson, but when he heard that Potts was there he made his excuses and stayed in London. When Susan arrived, bringing her eight-year-old daughter with her, she found she had walked into a drama. Like Eileen before her, she simply failed to connect with Avril, but on Jura there was no escape. When Avril began sniping at her because of the way she handled Richard and about her disability, Susan complained to Orwell who managed to smooth things over temporarily.

Avril, like her mother, had an acid tongue. She told Humphrey Dakin in July, 'Paul Potts takes all my shafts of scintillating wit quite seriously & suffers from fits of temperament, but I think I am melding [sic] him into a more human shape.'[26] Susan was even less thick-skinned. She found Avril's abrasive manner upsetting. After she inadvertently kindled the fire with a manuscript of Potts', he departed in high dudgeon, leaving her even more the target of Avril's 'shafts of scintillating wit'. She wrote home saying how miserable she was, and her mother suggested to the young David Holbrook, Susan's lover at the time, that he should visit Jura to cheer her up. Holbrook, twenty-three and a member of the Communist Party, was just out of the army, and finishing an English degree at Downing College, Cambridge. He was anxious to meet the controversial author of *The Road to Wigan Pier* and *Animal Farm*, and was quite expecting to enjoy long conversations with him about literature and politics. He was to be disappointed. After struggling with his luggage over the last eight miles of track to Barnhill, menaced by rutting deer, he was greeted by the sight of Orwell shooting a duck with a shotgun. Inside the house the mood was sombre, the conversation gloomy and the atmosphere tense. He thought that having been told that he was a Communist, Orwell suspected he had come to spy on him. He was not to know that he feared something even worse, which was precisely why he had bought that Lugar (Susan remembered him with a loaded handgun always at the ready on Jura).[27] After all, Trotsky had been eliminated by a Communist agent who had insinuated himself into his household. Like Susan, Holbrook had walked on to the set of a Kafkaesque drama being played out in Orwell's own mind.

To the young student the place seemed a kind of Cold Comfort Farm, with all means of escape – the van and the motorbike – broken down, seemingly a deliberate act of self-isolation. He was warned grimly against the cliffs one could topple over in the dark – leaving him more than a little nervous. When, to his relief, Susan showed up, to lighten the gloom they developed what he called 'a jokey apart-ness', making up funny stories about their joyless hosts. At supper that first day, Avril had burnt the goose, and Orwell droned on interminably about an arctic tern he had spotted that day. 'I wanted to talk to him about life, about politics, Spain and that sort of thing, but he was wheezing away about an arctic tern.' The two youngsters laughed and giggled behind their hands, but it was all a strain, and they disappeared for long walks to escape the hostile atmosphere. Apart from feeling under suspicion, Hobrook also thought that Orwell disapproved of his carrying on his affair with Susan under his roof at Barnhill.

He did, however, manage to get a rare sight of Orwell's unfinished work. 'I was prowling around the house one day, when he was out, you know. I went up to the attic and there was a big attic room, and there was a desk, all untidy, and this typewriter where he was working. And it was obviously *Nineteen Eighty-Four*.' On another occasion, Robin Fletcher, the laird, came visiting, and he and Susan were asked to stay out of the way. It added another comic touch to the occasion. 'It was so funny to be put below stairs,' said Holbrook – a touch of *Burmese Days*, he thought. 'We coped with it by giggling. A great sense of class descended on the house, and it was so funny, because I thought I was going to stay with this left-wing writer, and it would all be very matey. But it wasn't.' He left after what he recalled as 'a very unpleasant two weeks', with the impression of Orwell as an obviously ill, 'pretty cadaverous-looking fellow', and 'a miserable bugger really', who never laughed or smiled the whole time he was there. 'It was,' he recalled, 'a great relief to get back to civilisation.'[28]

At the time of Holbrook's departure, Orwell had barely touched what he now called 'my novel about the future'. He told Woodcock on 12 August that he had done no work on it for three months. But he was entertaining visitors rather more than he had planned. At the end of August he expected there to be between seven and eight people at the house.[29] The atmosphere at Barnhill can't have helped the creative process much either. The tension between the women of the house was now approaching breaking point. According to Susan, Avril was constantly criticising her work, taunting her that as a cripple she was unfitted for life on Jura, that she ought not to call her brother George when his name was Eric, and that she was treating Richard in entirely the wrong way and should smack him more. It could have been a simple clash of personalities, or Avril staking her claim to be mistress of Barnhill and 'mother' to her adoptive nephew. If she had discovered that Eileen had not wanted her to bring up Richard, that could have made her doubly determined to do so. Whatever the reason for their mutual hostility, George finally stepped in. Regretfully he suggested to Susan that she should leave, and paid her a month's wages in lieu of notice.

Avril was, of course, right about one thing. On Jura George Orwell could be left behind and he could revert to his old familial role of Eric Blair, the naturalist and prodigious walker who slept under the stars when he could – the amateur carpenter and awkward motorcyclist who kept chickens, grew vegetables in his garden, and went off on lonely fishing excursions. To be George Orwell he would retreat to his attic and incarcerate himself alone with his books and typewriter.

Celia's brandy arrived in time for him to celebrate the American publication of *Animal Farm* on 26 August. A hardback edition of 50,000 copies was printed followed up shortly with a Book of the Month edition of

400,000. The book was to rank second on the US best-seller list for 1946, beaten only by Dr Spock's *Pocket Book of Baby and Child Care*, a book that Avril might have found useful now that she was effectively mothering young Richard. (Had he remembered the bet, it was time for Koestler to collect his five bottles of burgundy.) A short portrait based on an interview he had given earlier at Canonbury Square appeared in *Vogue*. In *Animal Farm*, it said, Orwell's farmyard animals are led into revolution and so to 'a circle of subjection by some mighty smart pigs'. The author was 'fairly much a left-ist' and 'a defender of freedom, even though most of the time he violently disagrees with the people beside whom he is fighting'.[30] There were plenty of 'smart pigs' in England who would have agreed with that. He told Gleb Struve that this huge success in America was just 'a bit of luck'.[31]

But first American reactions were mixed. Edmund Wilson was delighted that *Animal Farm* would bring Orwell to the wider attention of American readers. He much preferred it to Kipling's animal fables. 'Mr Orwell has worked out his theme with a simplicity, a wit, and a dryness that are closer to La Fontaine and Gay, and has written in a prose so plain and spare, so admirably proportioned to his purpose, that *Animal Farm* even seems very creditable if we compare it with Voltaire and Swift.'[32] In the *Nation* Isaac Rosenfeld found it 'a disappointing piece of work'. Orwell seemed to have fallen for the bad-man theory of history. The fault seemed to lie with the pigs and their piggishness rather than elsewhere.[33] (Eliot's misreading again.) Much the same line came from Orville Prescott in the *Yale Review*. 'As a satire of Russian totalitarianism *Animal Farm* is . . . completely inconclusive . . . As far as his story goes, the only error on the farm, or in Russia, was in letting the smart and wicked leaders seize control. He has no suggestions to make as to how such a disaster could be prevented.'[34] Only Edward Weeks, in the *Atlantic*, pointed to a wider context, noting that Orwell had fought against Franco and detested all tyranny, whether of the right or left. 'It has the double meaning, the sharp edge, and the lucidity of Swift; it also has a clever hostility if one applies the analogy to Soviet Russia.'[35]

As Empson had predicted, even some on his own side in America mis-understood the book. Dwight Macdonald reported that certain anti-Stalinist intellectuals claimed that the parable of *Animal Farm* meant that revolution always ended badly for the underdog, 'hence to hell with it and hail the status quo'. He himself read the book as applying solely to Russia and not making any larger statement about the philosophy of revo-lution. Which of these views, he asked, came closer to Orwell's intentions? Orwell replied, 'Of course I intended it primarily as a satire on the Russian revolution. But I did mean it to have a wider application in so much that I meant that that kind of revolution (violent conspiratorial revolution, led by unconsciously power-hungry people) can only lead to a change of masters.

I meant the moral to be that revolutions only effect a radical improvement when the masses are alert and know how to chuck out their leaders as soon as the latter have done their job.' Had the animals stood up to the pigs when they kept the apples for themselves it would have been all right. In the Russian case, 'I think the whole process was foreseeable – and was foreseen by a few people, eg. Bertrand Russell – from the very nature of the Bolshevik party. What I was trying to say was, "You can't have a revolution unless you make it for yourself; there is no such thing as a benevolent dictat(or)ship."'[36]

Orwell had now begun to realise that he could come to be regarded as an important literary figure who might even attract a potential biographer. The matter neither frightened nor repelled him but he felt he should make appropriate provisions for such an eventuality. He wrote to Richard Rees, his new literary executor:

> I don't know if I would, as it were, get up to the point of having anything biographical written about me, but I suppose it could happen and it's ghastly to think of some people doing it. All I can say is, use your discretion and if someone seems a B.F., don't let him see any papers. I am going to include among my personal papers, in case of this happening, some short notes about the main events in my life, chiefly dates and places, because I notice that when people write about you, even people who know you well, they always get that kind of thing wrong.[37]

In this same frame of mind, reviewing his writing career to date he had, a little earlier, written an important, if premature literary testament, 'Why I Write', which was published that autumn. And in that same self-reflective mood, and with a future biographer in mind perhaps, he spent time on Jura revising his reminiscences of his prep-school days, 'Such, Such Were The Joys'. As he put it in 'Why I Write':

> I give all this background information because I do not think one can assess a writer's motives without knowing something of his early development. His subject-matter will be determined by the age he lives in – at least this is true in tumultuous, revolutionary ages like our own – but before he ever begins to write he will have acquired an emotional attitude from which he will never completely escape. It is his job, no doubt, to discipline his temperament and avoid getting stuck at some immature stage, or in some perverse mood: but if he escapes from his early influences altogether, he will have killed his impulse to write.[38]

Those early influences of which he wrote were still very much with him, bearing down upon him, impelling him towards his last, all-consuming novel. Into that he would pour the distillation of the many terrors, anger and bitter frustrations that had accrued in his life. It would bring to the surface much of the spite and malice and 'sadistic' urges he had for so long wrestled to keep in check.

That autumn everyone pitched in to help the local tenant farmer with his harvest. George busied himself with his garden, tried his hand at his primitive carpentry and took the others on fishing trips. He had been all along keeping a meticulous domestic diary, recording changes in the weather, the fluctuating mood of the sea, the progress on his garden, the flora and fauna observed, and the state of his fuel supplies.[39] He described in almost loving detail how to set, sharpen and maintain the scythe he now carried around on the back of his motorbike, and also recorded how he lost his tobacco pouch and replaced it from a rabbit skin. He was where he most loved to be – in touch with the raw texture of life.

In early October he returned to London, taking time again to visit Eileen's grave on the way south. Obviously the grief still lingered. He rejoined the staff of *Tribune*, where Jon Kimche was now managing editor. There he would contribute the occasional review and take up again the 'As I Please' column to attack anti-Semitism, deplore the growing commercial adulation of cosmetic beauty, and reflect sombrely on the atomic threat, censorship and hanging. The wholesale public executions of war criminals after 1945 (sometimes shown on newsreels) depressed him a great deal, and, asked for an essay by the magazine *New Savoy*, he offered them 'A Hanging', one of his first contributions to the *Adelphi* in 1931. He also declared war on the cliché, and this became a running feature of his column.

Probably as a result of Avril's taunting, Susan Watson had undergone an operation which had left her more lame than ever. Back in Islington, Orwell invited her to collect the things she had left there, but when she arrived and he came to the door with Richard it was to see Avril glowering in the background. When Richard greeted her and wanted to play with her Avril commented, 'There you are, he's forgotten you already.' Susan declined to stay for lunch. But others came visiting, including Humphrey Slater and Heppenstall and the anarchist Vernon Richards who, with his wife, Marie Louise Berneri, had earlier that year taken a series of photographs of him and Richard, photographs revealing the domestic Orwell, tending his son, wheeling him in a pushchair, working at his carpentry bench, rolling the inevitable cigarette – enduring images which seem to capture not just the man but his whole singular being.

On his return from Jura he had been commissioned to dramatise *Animal Farm* for the BBC, with Heppenstall as producer, and two important Orwell essays had appeared – 'Politics vs Literature: An Examination of *Gulliver's Travels*', written on Jura, and published in the Autumn *Polemic*, and 'How the Poor Die' included in George Woodcock's new review *Now*.[40] He still showed himself by no means averse to the idea of a biography, and when he heard that Woodcock was planning to write an article about his life and work he wrote 'I am very flattered'.[41]

Anthony Powell has shrewdly observed that 'Orwell's gift was curiously poised . . . between politics and literature. The former both attracted and repelled him; the latter, close to his heart, was at the same time tainted with the odour of escape.'[42] In 'Politics vs. Literature' he looked at one of his great literary heroes, Swift, a writer who also performed that same balancing act. So closely does Orwell identify with Swift that he pronounce him a 'Tory Anarchist' ('anarchistic outlook covering an authoritarian cast of mind'), the title he often used for himself. Yet again, in dilating on what he saw as Swift's virtues and less admirable qualities – his hatred of authority but his distaste for humanity, for example – he was seemingly conducting us around the landscape of his own mind as much as that of his subject.

The imagery reflects the imagery of his own circumstances. He reflected that in Book IV of *Gulliver's Travels*, Gulliver, stricken by a horror of the human race, became 'a sort of unreligious anchorite whose one desire is to live in some desolate spot where he can devote himself to meditating on the goodness of the Houyhnhnms'. And he saw 'his resourcefulness and his observation of physical detail' as 'a sort of continuity in his character'. The observant Orwell, hoping to survive by his resourcefulness, had withdrawn to his own desolate spot to meditate on the imperfection of mankind. As to his politics, 'Swift was one of those people who are driven into a sort of perverse Toryism by the follies of the progressive party of the moment.' For Swift read Orwell. The state of mind perceived in the pages of *Gulliver* – rancour and pessimism, and hatred of the human body as well as inexplicably contradictory views – are all parts of Swift reflecting back to us key aspects of Orwell's own image of himself.

Most remarkably, perhaps, he identifies 'Swift's greatest contribution to political thought, in the narrowest sense of the words . . . his attack . . . on what would now be called totalitarianism'. This turns out to be the very nightmare that had been plaguing Orwell since those grim days on the run in Barcelona, the nightmare that was to pervade the 'novel of the future'.

He has an extraordinarily clear prevision of the spy-haunted 'police State,' with its endless heresy-hunts and treason trials, all really designed to neutralise popular discontent by changing it into war hysteria . . . For example, there is the professor at the School of Political Projectors who 'shewed me a large Paper of Instructions for discovering

Plots and Conspiracies', and who claimed that one can find people's secret thoughts by examining their excrement.

In Swift's masterpiece Orwell perceived the very vision of totalitarianism he had himself built up painfully over the preceding decade.

There was something close to the bone in his reading of Swift's novel and his reading of its author. 'Swift is a diseased writer. He remains permanently in a depressed mood which in most people is only intermittent, rather as though someone suffering from jaundice or the after-effects of influenza should have the energy to write books.' We have an inner self, he argued, which had a horror of existence. 'In the queerest way, pleasure and disgust are linked together. The human body is beautiful: it is also repulsive and ridiculous, a fact which can be verified at any swimming pool. The sexual organs are objects of desire and also of loathing, so much so that in many languages, if not in all languages, their names are used as words of abuse . . . [Swift's] attitude is in effect the Christian attitude, minus the bribe of a "next world".'[43] That last was key to Orwell's own system of ethics – in a godless world we should still act like the children of God.

Although 'How the Poor Die' harked back to pre-war Paris, it carried many disturbing images for a sick man. The images of anonymous wretchedness, of callous and impersonal treatment inside a cold, inhospitable institution and the images of men at the point of death (and that operating room from which issued occasional screams – an early glimpse of Room 101), were to haunt the novel which was dragging itself out of him, however slowly and intermittently between bouts of journalism. Despite the delays and diversions, he still hoped to finish it by the end of 1947.

That November, since they had not been reprinted, all rights of his early work reverted to him. He was determined to break all contractual ties with Gollancz and in future publish exclusively with Warburg. The books he listed at Warburg's request as suitable for inclusion in a uniform edition were *Homage to Catalonia, Animal Farm, Critical Essays, Down and Out in Paris and London, Burmese Days* and *Coming Up For Air.* The running order is significant and probably indicate where these six works stood in his own estimation.[44] The dream he had once shared with Jacintha Buddicom of becoming 'Eric the FAMOUS AUTHOR' with his own uniform edition was now closer than ever to fulfilment. Only his health and loneliness seemed to threaten the pleasure of that achievement, as he must have reminded himself every time he wheezed up the steep brick steps to his flat at the rear of 27 Canonbury Square.

It seems that clumping about on Jura had worn out the shoes which had lasted him for five years. He wrote to Dwight Macdonald in New York asking whether he could get him a pair of size twelves, as boots of that size were unobtainable in England. Cost was immaterial, he said, as he now had dollars in the US to pay him.

On New Year's Day he was travelling up to Jura. The crossing from the mainland was rough and he was seasick. But the weather on the island that day was beautifully sunny. He surveyed his garden, repaired some of damage done to it by rabbits, planted some fruit tress, checked his fuel supplies and after a week returned to London. There he had an excuse to throw a small party when the BBC broadcast his dramatisation of *Animal Farm*. Celia, Sonia, Fyvel, Inez and Humphrey Slater came along to listen, and Orwell was said to have been delighted with Heppenstall's production.

There was a further cause for celebration when he received his American royalties – this time £3433 14s 11d. As Warburg noted, 'When *Animal Farm* was published in New York in August 1946 and became a selection of the Book-of-the-Month Club, Orwell became really well-off for the first time in his life. This period can be seen as a high-water mark in his career.'[45] That American money worried him, because bringing it to Britain meant having to pay both US and UK tax. His new accountant, Jack Harrison, suggested he form himself into a limited liability company in both countries, so enabling him to spread his annual earnings across two years for tax purposes, and to a degree avoid double taxation. Consequently on 3 October 1947 George Orwell Productions was constituted with himself as major shareholder. In August the following year he recorded the remarkable sum of £7826 8s 7d, though whether this was received in one lump or was a total for the year, and whether it was kept abroad or in the UK was not clear. Having that sort of money was quite new to him, but what probably excited him more was the uniform edition Warburg was preparing.

His continuing opposition to Communism was sharpened by a belated response in the *Partisan Review* to an earlier London Letter in which he had named Communists as the main danger facing the new Labour government. 'The USSR,' he had written, 'is and must be implacably hostile to a social-democratic government of the British type.' Many Communists and fellow-travellers, he argued, had seized control of important unions and several Labour MPs were 'underground' Party members. He named Konni Zilliacus as a crypto-Communist and the author J. B. Priestley as a Communist sympathiser. They were both defenders of Soviet foreign policy and, as such, could be very dangerous. Zilliacus replied indignantly that he was never a member of the CP and the views he expressed were consistent with the line on which the Labour Party was elected. Orwell's reply was along the lines, 'Well, he would say that, wouldn't he?' and went on to reiterate the charge, pointing out that in the past he had attacked politicians on the right just as vigorously. However, he certainly highlighted what had become a right–left split over attitudes to Russia within the governing party.[46]

The English winter of 1947 was turning into the worst for many years. There was a national fuel crisis, London was often fog-bound, Orwell had water coming through the roof of his flat in twelve places, and at one point he was reduced to burning Richard's toys to help heat the place. By March he was completely out of fuel. The experience, he told Brenda, had become unbearable. He must have thought he would have been better back in Jura, where, on his last visit, it was at least sunny for a time and there was plenty of peat to burn. He now planned to return there in April, and the following winter he would decide to remain on the island – just one of the many ill-judged decisions in a life littered with misjudgements.

Orwell's important essay, 'Lear, Tolstoy and the Fool', which appeared in *Polemic* in March, barely conceals the main theme uppermost in his mind at the time. He shows how, in attacking Shakespeare, Tolstoy was attacking a Shakespeare of his own invention. He saw Tolstoy, despite his self-denial and his pacifism, as essentially coercive, wanting to get into the mind of Shakespeare lovers to change their opinions of him. He was warning the reader against Tolstoy, just as he wanted to warn against others who would steal into minds in order to control them.[47] Sadly for Orwell, *Polemic*, which ran some of his best essays, was destined to go the way of many high-minded journals, and after the March edition ceased publication. It was failing to increase its circulation and Rodney Phillips was not prepared to keep pouring money into it, especially when Humphrey Slater continued to run up such excessive lunch bills.[48]

The elegant polemical essay of which he was so much the modern master was the blood-brother of another literary form whose demise he lamented that spring in his introduction to a collection of *British Pamphleteers*, which he edited with Reginald Reynolds. There he compared the sixteenth-, seventeenth- and eighteenth-century pamphlet with the poorer efforts of the twentieth to illustrate how the language of politics had decayed over that period. Individual expression had been replaced by expressions of some party 'line'. The earlier tradition of arguing the unpopular cause from an individual point of view was threatened by a capitalist press and by party tyranny. These latter propagandist pamphlets, he wrote, were not produced by writers, 'because no one who feels deeply about literature, or even prefers good English to bad, can accept the discipline of a political party'.[49] The age of Swift and Defoe, he was saying, had gone; now there was no one to take their places. Some might consider Orwell himself had more than amply filled their shoes. If so, it was only under protest. 'In a peaceful age,' he wrote, 'I might have written ornate or merely descriptive books, and might have remained almost unaware of my political loyalties. As it is I have been forced into becoming a sort of pamphleteer.'[50]

That appalling winter had taken its toll on him. At the beginning of April he suffered his usual annual bout of flu and was confined to bed for a week. Once recovered he prepared to escape London and the intolerable pressures of journalism, and finally even to give up his *Tribune* job, which had allowed him to write so freely as he pleased. From then on he wrote mostly for the *Observer*, the *TLS*, where Anthony Powell now worked, and occasionally the *New Yorker*. He became highly critical of the way *Tribune* developed after he left it, particularly for its inconsistent support for the Labour Government and its perpetual anti-Americanism.[51] Just before leaving London he finally managed to sever all connections with Gollancz. The memory of his rejecting two of his books – *Homage to Catalonia* and *Animal Farm* – had remained a source of resentment, and, despite Gollancz's having been first to publish him, he wanted to put their association behind him. Gollancz was reluctant to release this now bestselling author, who was still contracted to supply him with two more novels, but Orwell insisted, explaining that he wished to be with a publisher he could trust would publish his work come what may. That man, he said, was Warburg. Faced with this unreserved withdrawal of confidence, Gollancz finally agreed to Orwell's release.[52]

He made arrangements with a woman friend of Powell's, Miranda Christen, to have the Islington flat at a reduced rent in return for some typing work, and prepared to move out. Over the coming months she would type up the first complete draft of his novel-in-progress and the manuscript of his St Cyprian's memoir. This time, rather than take the tedious journey from Glasgow – the trains, buses and ferries – he took to the air and flew the short hop from the Scottish capital to Islay. By the 11th he was back at Barnhill.

Chapter 18

The Nightmare and the Novel

'Either power politics must yield to common decency, or the world must go spiralling down into a nightmare of which we can already catch some dim glimpses.'

Orwell, 'Gandhi in Mayfair', 1943

The first person he wrote to on arriving back on Jura was Sonia Brownell. He still retained a passion for her, only heightened by their brief if lustful affair. Sonia, however, suffered from what Koestler referred to sneeringly as 'French 'flu'. Like her mentor Connolly, she was more than a little scornful of English culture, regarding France as the gravitational centre of all things artistic. According to her friend John Russell, 'she was so profoundly Frenchified that for many years she really had trouble reading English authors',[1] and so may have found Orwell's Englishness less than appealing, and, apart from his *Horizon* contributions, been relatively ignorant of his work. However, they had not argued over Mallarmé for nothing. Orwell was well-read in French literature and had his own French cast of mind, and must have seen the volatile but intelligent Sonia as the almost perfect, even if sadly unobtainable, intellectual partner. All he lacked, he thought, was the power to attract the women who attracted *him*. He also lacked the subtle art of seduction. She was sent the usual train-bus-ferry-taxi itinerary and advised to bring stout gumboots and a week's rations. She could come whenever she liked for as long as she liked, he told her.[2] The sophisticated Sonia did not, it seems, find the invitation difficult to resist, and did not make the trip to Jura until after Orwell's death.

If he had hoped to escape the cold by coming north he was disappointed. However, there were compensations. 'The weather here is as disgusting as in England,' he wrote, 'but it isn't quite so cold and a little easier to get fuel.' He had originally thought of Barnhill as a holiday home for just the summer months, but Jura had by now cast its spell over him. 'These islands are one of the most beautiful parts of the British Isles and largely uninhabited. This island, which is as large as a small county, only has 300 people on it. Of course it rains all the time, but if one takes that for granted it doesn't seem to matter.'[3] In his mind it had become his new spiritual home, close to the natural world and the bare surface of the earth. There he could cultivate his bit of soil, take off on fishing or hunting expeditions and record his day-to-day existence in his domestic diary. Above all he had the almost complete seclusion in which to create the private world of his novel, to turn his nightmares into literature.

At Barnhill Avril did the cooking and they rationed themselves to one luxury – a single glass of brandy after dinner. Avril's attachment to the island was strengthened when a young ex-soldier working at a croft at nearby Kinauchdrach, began helping out at Barnhill. Bill Dunn had lost a leg fighting in Italy with the Argyll and Sutherland Highlanders, and was hoping to get started as a farmer. Despite his handicap, Dunn was a handsome, rugged, outdoor type and Avril quickly became attracted to him. Later that year he and Orwell would form a partnership, with the financial backing of Richard Rees, to farm the land around Barnhill, and Dunn moved into the house.

The path for Orwell never ran quite as smoothly as intended. On the third day after they arrived on the island, Richard fell and gashed his head badly, which meant a twenty-five mile trip to the doctor to have the wound stitched. No sooner had the boy recovered from that than he went down with measles. A week later Orwell collapsed and took to his bed, dosing himself with M & B tablets. He had thrown himself into work from the moment he reached Barnhill, digging his garden, tearing down corrugated iron sheeting from the side of the house and building a heavy wooden-framed hen-house for his chickens. His own frame, weakened by that last cruel London winter and attacks of influenza, could not take so much hard labour, and the still-cold weather on the exposed northern tip of the island did little to help. However, spring lightened his mood, and when he finally got up and out into his garden, he found his cherry trees blossoming, violets and a few tulips blooming, and gladioli just peeping through. Even one of the roses planted in memory of Eileen was showing a bud. 'Beautiful day,' he wrote in his diary. 'Vegetation all jumping.'[4] It did not take much to encourage him back, not just to his garden but to the island landscape beyond. Within a week he was out on the moors with Avril, cutting peat. On one day in two hours they cut two hundred blocks and planned to cut at least a thousand over the next few days.[5]

Whatever the state of his health, Orwell found it difficult to resist the lure of the primitive Jura countryside. Out across the peat marshes, a ghostly, emaciated figure with scythe, jackknife and shotgun, he could take pot-shots at rabbits, keep an eye out for deer and on occasions bag a wild goose.

His hunting instinct had more than a trace of cruelty about it – a compensation, perhaps, for strongly suppressed 'sadistic' feelings towards humans, those tortures dreamt up in the bathtub. Bill Dunn remembered their once visiting a neighbouring island:

> He, Avril, young Richard, and I went for a picnic to Scarba . . . Well, the first live thing we met on stepping ashore was an adder. Eric put his foot on it, just behind its head. I expected him to bash it with the other foot or a stone or stick or something, but surprisingly he deliberately took out his penknife and opened it and slit the snake from top to bottom. He degutted it, filleted it.[6]

*

An idea which had long possessed Orwell was the effect on western civilisation of the lost belief in personal immortality. 'There is little doubt,' he wrote, 'that the modern cult of power-worship is bound up with the modern man's feeling that life here and now is the only life there is.'[7] If so, why bother what happens after we are dead? In 1947, alone with a child and the feeling that his own time was short, this idea was plaguing him, and he groped for alternatives to the Christian hereafter and the totalitarian abyss. 'So long as human beings stay human,' says Winston Smith, 'death and life are the same thing.'[8]

Intimations of mortality, the pressure of ideas and persisting nightmares had for a long time been drawing Orwell with some urgency towards his new novel. So many strands of what was to become *Nineteen Eighty-Four* are to be found already in his writing. The fearful future is hinted at in *Homage to Catalonia* and *Coming Up For Air*; his writing about totalitarianism in the late thirties and his deep concerns about language and propaganda became focused during his years at the BBC. Orwell rarely talked about his work, but often his pen spoke for him. In 1944, reflecting on Koestler, he wrote, 'Nowadays the present and the future are too terrible to escape from, and if one bothers with history it is in order to find modern meanings there . . . Nothing is in sight except a welter of lies, hatred, cruelty and ignorance, and beyond our present troubles loom vaster ones which are only now entering into the European consciousness.'[9] He himself was conscious of having made powerful enemies and that his health was failing. The sense of impending disaster was only exaggerated by his personal feelings of threat, even as he planned to escape to his remote island.

And yet another key idea behind his grim message was that in his nightmare world there was no escape. This passage, written in 1944, encapsulates the thesis at the heart of his novel:

> The fallacy is to believe that under a dictatorial government you can be free *inside*. Quite a number of people console themselves with this

thought, now that totalitarianism in one form or another is visibly on the up-grade in every part of the world. Out in the street the loudspeakers bellow, the flags flutter from the rooftops, the police with their tommy-guns prowl to and fro, the face of the Leader, four feet wide, glares from every hoarding; but up in the attics the secret enemies of the regime can record their thoughts in perfect freedom – that is the idea, more or less.

This was a delusion, he said, because the human being is not an autonomous individual. Under a despotic government your thoughts were never your own. Philosophy, art and science progressed only through the 'constant stimulation from other people. It is almost impossible to think without talking. If Defoe had really lived on a desert island he could not have written Robinson Crusoe, nor would he have wanted to. Take away freedom of speech, and the creative faculties dry up.' When the truth about Europe was unveiled it would be found that little worthwhile writing, even in diaries, had been produced under dictatorships.[10] The secret diary delusion, of course, was to be the fatal delusion of Winston Smith.

By the first part of 1947, in an article for *Partisan Review*, absorbed by newly woken fears of a nuclear war, he envisioned the terrifying world he was in the process of creating:

The worst possibility of all . . . would mean the division of the world among two or three vast super-states, unable to conquer one another and unable to be overthrown by any internal rebellion. In all probability their structure would be hierarchic, with a semidivine caste at the top and outright slavery at the bottom, and the crushing out of liberty would exceed anything that the world has yet seen. Within each state the necessary psychological atmosphere would be kept up by complete severance from the outer world, and by a continuous phoney war against rival states. Civilizations of this type might remain static for thousands of years.[11]

To him now an atomic war was not simply a fear but a fearful certainty, he told Fyvel. 'This stupid war is coming off in abt 10–20 years, & this country will be blown off the map whatever else happens. The only hope is to have a home with a few animals in some place not worth a bomb.'[12] To Orwell this was not the stuff of fiction, but a very real sense of approaching apocalypse. 'If the show does start and is as bad as one fears, it would be fairly easy to be self-supporting on these islands provided one wasn't looted.'[13]

The idea of there being no escape in a totalitarian world was also very real to him in another way. Since the end of the war, and especially since *Animal Farm* was published, he had felt the need to arm himself against the fate of Koestler's Rubashov – the bullet in the back of the neck. Trotsky's fate could just as well be his. His paranoia led him to confide to Geoffrey Gorer that he thought Gollancz might have him bumped off, to go around London armed with a large hunting knife, to obtain a pistol from Hemingway in Paris and a Lugar from Rodney Phillips in London. Just before leaving for Jura in 1946, writing to Warburg about a biography of Stalin by Trotsky, he suggested that 'it might be worth trying to get a little more information about the circumstances of Trotsky's assassination, which may have been partly decided upon because of the knowledge that he was writing this very book'.[14] He, too, of course, was writing a book which could make *him* a quarry, just as Winston Smith, in keeping a diary, made himself a target. Clearly, in his own mind he was living the drama of Winston Smith, so that when he came to write the horror story of *Nineteen Eighty-Four* it was his own horror story that he was setting down. The book, he told Warburg, was 'a novel about the future – that is, it is in a sense a fantasy, but in the form of a naturalistic novel', which made it especially difficult to write.[15] His publisher was not impressed – such books tended to sell badly.

Undoubtedly the novel was written in the shadow of death. He guessed that he might not have long to live and his writing was not untouched by that fact. He recognised how the expectation of an early death must show itself in a writer's work – Katherine Mansfield, for example, dead of TB at thirty-four.[16] Since his sojourn in the Hôpital Cochin the idea of dying was never far from his thoughts, and Eileen's early death had only intensified it. Even when writing about socialism, in theory a philosophy of hope, pessimistic thoughts of approaching mortality intruded: 'A socialist today is in the position of a doctor treating an all but hopeless case. As a doctor, it is his duty to keep the patient alive, and therefore to assume that the patient has at least a chance of recovery. As a scientist, it is his duty to face the facts, and therefore to admit that the patient will probably die.'[17] The idea of the fragility of life and the imminence of death was to be the haunting motif of *Nineteen Eighty-Four*.

By the end of May he reported to Warburg that a third of his novel was complete, though his poor health and the complex conception on which he was working made progress slow and difficult. However, he hoped to have it finished by the spring of 1948. At the same time he sent him his memoir of St Cyprian's. 'Such, Such Were The Joys', originally intended as 'a sort of pendant to Cyril Connolly's "Enemies of Promise"'. It was far too libellous to appear while Flip and Sambo were still alive, but he hoped it would fit eventually into a collection of his essays. The connection between this story of an enclosed authoritarian school society and the stifling dictatorship of Airstrip One in *Nineteen Eighty-Four* – especially the idea advanced by Anthony West[18] that Orwell was trying to make the reader share his childhood suffering by applying the same horrors to an adult world – has been rather dismissed by critics, but that there are associations and reverberations cannot be denied.

If he had not already begun to develop the individual consciousness to pit against unreasonable authority while with the Ursuline nuns, he certainly developed it at St Cyprian's. The small boy waiting outside Sambo's study for a beating is only the youthful version of Winston Smith waiting to be summoned to Room 101. The deceitfulness of authority, the feeling that spies are everywhere, the harsh cross-examinations, the rote learning in an atmosphere of threat – these are all present in both essay and novel. It is easy enough to see the boy who emerged from St Cyprian's to become the College cynic at Eton, evolving into the secretly subversive Winston Smith. Orwell himself drew a tenuous parallel to his schooldays. Whereas most English people found it impossible to understand what life under a totalitarian regime might be like, boys who went to boarding schools were better prepared. 'The brutal side of public-school life, which intellectuals always deprecate,' he wrote, 'is not a bad training for the real world.'[19] Under close surveillance Winston expresses what amounts to the Eton code: 'His face completely inscrutable. Never show dismay! Never show resentment. A single flicker of the eye could give you away.' And when Tosco Fyvel put it to him that aspects of his novel resembled horror stories told in school dormitories, he laughed and agreed there was perhaps something in it.[20] Of course, one may just as well say he was trying to convey the feeling of being trapped inside a wracked and suffocating body. And obviously to press the school analogy too far, would be absurd. St Cyprian's was not exactly a totalitarian institution; but the parallels where they exist are worth noting.

A short diary entry for 12 June 1947 shows that not even all the horrors of Big Brother's torture chamber were entirely imagined, though they do retain that strong element of Inquisitorial myth. Recording that five rats, two of them enormous, had been trapped in his barn, he added, 'I hear that recently two children at Ardlussa were bitten by rats (in the face, as usual).'[21] The mind of the diarist, one feels, was now more than half-buried in his book. 'I am getting on fairly well with the novel,' he told Moore at the end of July, 'and expect to finish the rough draft by October. I dare say it will need another six months [*sic*] work on it after that.' He had plans to spend October in London then retreat to his island again; he did not want to sit shivering in Islington without fuel. On Jura at least there was peat for the taking. Away from London and the temptations of journalism, he felt more confident of finishing his book by the spring.[22]

It was a good July and a blazing August. Shortly after his forty-fourth birthday, Henry, Jane and Lucy Dakin, Humphrey's children, joined the Barnhill household. Henry was now with the British Army in Germany, Jane was in the Land Army, a conscripted agricultural worker, and Lucy was on her school holidays. They had not gone to Jura to spend time with gloomy Uncle Eric, but with Avril whom they liked a great deal and found extremely funny and entertaining.[23] It meant there were plenty of eyes to watch over Richard who was growing evermore sturdy and adventurous and evermore accident-prone. Although Orwell was busily working on his book, he was obviously very pleased to see this gathering of the Blair/Dakin clan at Barnhill. He took them on excursions around the island, wheezing along, determined to keep up with the youngsters.

One day in August he took them by boat to camp at Glengarrisdale on the wild uninhabited west coast. It meant navigating the sometimes hazardous waters between Jura and Scarba and the notorious Corryvrekan whirlpool. The boat was a small dinghy with an outboard motor, and with George, Richard, Avril and the three Dakin youngsters on board it lay quite low in the water. Despite this they managed the journey and enjoyed an idyllic two-night camp at a deserted croft. When it came time to return, Avril and Jane decided to walk back overland. The others – George, Richard, Lucy and Henry – set off back the way they had come. George, however, had miscalculated the tides, and as they approached the straits they found themselves on the edge of the churning waters of the great whirlpool. The outboard motor was washed away and Henry had to grab the oars and row as best he could. Just managing to stay afloat, they made for a small uninhabited island (Eilean Mór) but, attempting to land, the boat overturned and all four were pitched into the sea. Richard went under and George had to dive down to rescue him before scrambling ashore with the others. They salvaged the boat but the oars and outboard motor had gone, and George's precious size-twelve boots were well nigh ruined.

It was the stuff of youthful adventure, and George seemed almost enthused by the experience. Like a castaway in Ballantyne's *Coral Island*, he said they must build a fire. He produced a lighter, which strangely enough worked, and kindled a grass and peat fire. Then he went off to explore the tiny island looking for food, but all he found were nesting seabirds. 'You know,' he said on his return, 'these puffins . . .' and launched into one of his interminable lectures. To him, it seemed to the others, it was just an opportunity for some unscheduled bird-watching. Finally, after three hours, they attracted the attention of a passing fishing boat and were ferried back to the mainland – a three-mile barefoot trek back to Barnhill where they found the others busily haymaking. It was yet another Orwell adventure that came to grief. Shortly afterwards Henry returned to Germany with strict instructions from George to find him some size-twelve boots. (Warburg, about to leave for America, received a similar request, as did Muggeridge.) The day after this near-disaster, Orwell calmly set off on a fishing trip to a distant loch and returned with twelve trout in his basket.

The summer activities had taken a lot out of him. He soon got back to his work, but even the effort of writing had become fatiguing. In September he told Anthony Powell, 'I know that if I return to London and get caught up in weekly articles I shall never get on with anything longer. One just seems to have a limited capacity for work nowadays and one has to husband it.'[24] As a man of only forty-four such feelings of frailty must have been exceptionally painful.

Apart from the Dakins there were other visitors that summer, including Gwen and her family. All that entertaining and work on his new book meant that in 1947 his output of occasional writing plummeted. The great journalistic effort of the previous year had been meant to buy time to finish his novel. The sense of that wingèd chariot at his heels hung over his work. Death had been a close companion since childhood. Since Spain, the cruel fate of Winston Smith had seemed to stalk him in one guise or another. Now what energy he had left would be poured almost exclusively into finishing his book.

As autumn turned to winter and the weather deteriorated, his health again began to fail. Had he moved back to a less strenuous life in London, where this time the winter was clement, he might have avoided this relapse. But the outdoor life and near-drowning, plus the intensive effort going into his book and the conditions under which he was working (an overheated room with an atmosphere thick with oil fumes from the Valor stove and tobacco fumes from his chain-smoking), all played their part in bringing him to the point of collapse. The usual minor calamities only added to the increasing sense of wretchedness. There was a drought, the gas ran out, his typewriter broke down, he was without a decent pair of boots.

Astonishingly, Orwell had continued working outdoors and even made a list of jobs to do before leaving for London, including dragging up the boat from the beach, weighing down his hen house, greasing his tools and mapping his property. He had intended going south in November but began to feel ill in early September. On 30 October he was struck down with what he called 'an inflammation of the lungs' and was confined to bed. He had lost almost two stone and was suffering discomforting night sweats. Now he realised that he was very ill and there would be no trips to London for the foreseeable future.

However, he continued to work in bed, and by the end of November he had a complete draft of Nineteen Eighty-Four, although he admitted it was very rough and two-thirds of it would have to be rewritten. He certainly was not ready to show it to anyone. 'I always say a book doesn't exist until it's finished,' he told Symons.[25] Despite knowing it to be impossible, he talked of getting to London to see his specialist – the eccentric Morlock, no doubt, who had told him his haemorrhages might be good for him. Ironically, shortly after becoming ill, he was invited by the *Observer* to go to East Africa. But he was not even fit enough to leave his bed, and in December was visited by a specialist from Glasgow who pronounced the diagnosis he feared – tuberculosis of the left lung. He would need to spend three or four months in a sanatorium. It was, he finally admitted, 'a disease I've had hanging over my head all my life',[26] and 'the disease which was bound to claim me sooner or later'.[27] From now on there could be no more denial, no more closing of the mind. To Humphrey Dakin he was even more forthright. 'Of course, I've had this coming to me for years,' he wrote,[28] hinting that it was a punishment he deserved.

The day after receiving this deadly news, he informed Moore, 'It's TB, as I suspected. They think they can cure it all right, but I am bound to be hors de combat for a good while.'[29] Curiously enough, the same day he wrote to Celia Kirwan (now working in Paris) with not a mention of the dread disease, merely saying that he was unwell, had to go to a sanatorium, and what a bore it all was.[30] Now, he also feared that he might pass the disease on to young Richard and arranged for him to be x-rayed. All milk would have to be boiled and a TB-tested cow bought for the farm. He was feeling so wretched that, when a bed was found for him at Hairmyres Hospital at East Kilbride, near Glasgow, he said he was pleased to be gone so that the others could enjoy Christmas without him being there 'as a deaths-head'. He would simply have to be the ghost at the feast and miss out on a plateful of Kopp's goose.

He was under the care of Bruce Dick, the consultant thoracic surgeon, a giant of a man with a strong and forceful personality. He was placed in a side room which offered some degree of privacy, but was forbidden a typewriter, and discouraged from writing altogether. The regime was strict bed rest and a nutritious diet. Only then did he inform Fred Tomlinson, at the *Observer*, that his going to Africa was not possible. 'It was TB as I feared,' he wrote. 'I've had it before, but not so badly. This time it's what they call "extensive" but they seem confident they can patch me up in a few months.'[31] The whole thing, he implied, was just a passing irritation. He was already feeling better, and asked for some books to review. However, on Boxing Day, in a letter to Symons, he admitted feeling ill since the beginning of the year but foolishly had put off doing anything about it in order to finish his book. That book, he told Warburg, 'is just a ghastly mess as it stands, but the idea is so good that I could not possibly abandon it. If anything should happen to me I've instructed Richard Rees, my literary executor, to destroy the MS. without showing it to anybody.'[32] He blamed the previous arctic winter in London for his wretched condition, but again managed to strike a hopeful note. 'With luck I'll be all right by the summer. They seem confident of being able to patch me up . . . I think all the same I'll spend next winter in a warm climate if possible.'[33] However, that winter at Barnhill had been deceptively mild with sunshine and 'sea as blue and smooth as the Mediterranean'.[34] The 'warm climate' he chose the following winter was Jura!

The medical reality was far worse than Orwell's letters suggest. It was not classic tuberculosis – galloping, toxic and fevered, the sort that put paid to Keats and the Brontës – but it was both chronic and infectious. According to James Wilkinson, one of the doctors who attended him, he had what was called 'fibrotic tuberculosis'. 'There wasn't much "cavitation". His lung would have been tough, like leather. With chronic fibrotic TB you could live for quite a long while, although at a lower level of health and fitness and comfort, as he did.' The treatment he received was a routine treatment but quite drastic:

> It was a fairly trivial operation: you could do it in five minutes. You just pull the muscle aside, expose the nerve, and tweak it with a pair of forceps. The patient would get one sudden pain, and the diaphragm would jump, and that was the diaphragm paralysed for three to six months, until the nerve recovered again. Then we pumped air into his abdomen. The diaphragm was pushed up by this, and the lungs were collapsed. You put anything from four hundred to seven hundred cc of air in, under low pressure, with a special machine, through a needle which was a fairly elephantine-looking thing, a hollow needle about three inches long, actually. The first time you did it, you used a local anaesthetic, because you had to go very cautiously and advance it very slowly. But after that you just stuck it in, because patients agreed that if it was done expertly, one sharp jab was better than all this fiddling about with anaesthetics and things.

Both lungs were affected but it was the left one that was subjected to collapse. While extremely unpleasant for the patient, this weekly treatment brought out the stoic in Orwell. 'I remember he used to dread each "refill" and couldn't relax at all when he was on the table. But he never complained. In fact we all noticed how much self-control he had. There was never a gasp, or any kind of noise from him when we did this.'[35] 'They pump me so full of air,' he told David Astor, 'that I feel like a balloon for two days afterwards.'[36] The treatment left him feeling 'pulled down and weak'. But, despite his suspicion of such places, he liked the hospital and thought everyone very kind to him.[37] The excruciating experience of having his lung collapsed may well have been translated into Winston's cruel sufferings in Room 101 – a brutal reminder too perhaps of the attack which seemingly had once felled him in that very room at the BBC. Despite the drastic treatment, and now on his back in bed, he was trying to write with a newly acquired Biro pen (only recently available in England), but was limited to just two hours' work a day.

In the New Year Astor visited him with Karl Schnetzler, bringing extra food, obviously anxious to see him build himself up again, and finally he confessed to Celia that he had TB. However, for her benefit he continued to play the matter down, saying, 'I don't think it's very serious, & I seem to be getting better slowly.' Certainly after a month's rest he reported feeling less 'death-like',[38] but because of his condition and a problem with his right arm he was reduced to writing his *Observer* reviews in a shaky hand in Biro. However, although he felt mentally alert, he had put on very little weight and still felt weak.

Then Bruce Dick mentioned streptomycin, an anti-tuberculosis 'wonder drug' recently available in America, and Orwell wrote to Astor, who had important American connections as well as contacts at the highest levels of government, asking if he could help acquire some of the stuff. Through him, not only was a supply of streptomycin (70 grammes) procured, but authority to import it was obtained from Aneurin Bevan, now the Minister of Health. Astor, who had the greatest possible regard for Orwell, refused payment, and by the 15th the treatment of three injections daily had commenced. Astor told Dick that if more of the drug was required he should not hesitate to ask.[39]

Once past his 'most detestable' month of February, he was feeling much better and looking forward to being discharged in the summer. The drug, he was delighted to find, appeared to have no side effects,[40] and he began to look forward to his release. Once out of hospital he planned to stay in Glasgow in order to attend as an outpatient until fully cured. There might also be the occasional trip to London, and he planned to keep the Canonbury Square flat as a pied à terre for that purpose.

With Warburg, who visited him in March to discuss his forthcoming uniform edition, he had agreed to a volume a year for six years. But would it be a 10/6d edition in pale green, as Warburg wished, or the five-shilling one in blue buckram with the words 'Uniform Edition' printed on the cover, which the author demanded?[41] As Warburg's prize author he got what he wanted. When the proofs of *Burmese Days*, number two in the series, arrived, he found it somehow distant and queer, 'almost like reading a book by somebody else'.[42] It was yet another opportunity to look back over his creative life. It showed how far the Eric Blair of the 1920s had been overtaken by his literary doppelgänger. Orwell must have told Warburg more about his novel-in-progress, because suddenly he became extremely anxious to see it finished and submitted.

Even from his sick-bed he was able to do *some* writing, and managed to produce two essays, including 'Writers and Leviathan', a serious reflection on the role of the writer in the twentieth century, his need to be involved with politics yet apart from it, his need to defend the democracy that alone guaranteed his creative freedom, while not allowing himself to become a party hack.[43] However, the steady improvement in his condition was marred when he began to suffer an extreme allergic reaction to streptomycin. In his diary he listed discoloration at the base of finger- and toenails, reddening of the skin which tended to peel off, a severe sore throat, for which he had to suck penicillin lozenges; ulcers appeared in his throat and blisters in his mouth which bled, his nails began to disintegrate at the roots, his hair started falling out, and patches of it turned white.[44] The doctors admired the way he bore his torment. 'He was very stoical about it,' said one. 'Most people would have been round the bend with that.'[45]

In this condition his dystopian vision must have seemed even grimmer, compounded by the news that, following the Communist takeovers in Hungary and Czechoslovakia, on 1 April the Berlin Blockade began and war became a real threat. Even the pacifist Middleton Murry conceded the danger. Where once he had called the USSR 'the only inherently peaceful country', now he had written a book calling for a preventive war against it.[46]

As he was no longer testing positive for TB he was taken off the streptomycin (after a fifty-day course) and the symptoms disappeared. It had been an ordeal but he was temporarily through it. 'It's all over now & evidently the drug has done its stuff,' he told Senhouse. 'It's rather like sinking the ship to get rid of the rats, but worth it if it works.'[47] He wrote sadly to Symons: 'I'm afraid that even when completely cured I shall be not much good physically for the rest of my life – I never was strong or athletic, but I don't like an altogether sedentary life, & I shall have to readjust my habits so that I can get about without making too much muscular effort, no more digging or chopping wood, for instance.'[48]

Feeling slightly better and able to get up for two hours he wrote to Lydia inviting her to stay nearby at his expense. 'I would love to see you again,' he wrote. 'The other night I was wishing very much that you were with me.'[49] The tone is that of ten years earlier and suggests a relationship rather more intimate than was ever admitted. If his thoughts were straying to earlier encounters with Lydia, they were also straying further back to the twenties. When Celia wrote from Paris he replied sadly recalling the trees there in springtime and the Jardin des Plantes which he must have known he would never see again. Nostalgia was very much on his mind, as opposed to its antithesis embodied in America and modernity – and when Celia sent news that the Koestlers had gone to America and thought of remaining there, he told her: 'I can't help feeling that it's a bit treacherous on Arthur's part if he does settle down in the USA.'[50]

By now he was out of bed for two hours a day, sitting out and going for short walks, but he was still very frail and unable to walk far. He had acquired a typewriter and was able to do a little work, not just on his novel, but the occasional journalism. In the spring he began a long essay on George Gissing. As with Dickens, when writing about Gissing he is also writing about himself, however indirectly. When he wrote that one of his reasons for liking Gissing was that his novels 'are a protest against the form of self-torture that goes by the name of respectability',[51] we know to whom he is also alluding. He identified closely with Gissing's total commitment to literature, his life of poverty, his love of the countryside and hatred of the city, and perhaps also his dim view of most women. The women of sensibility and intelligence whom Gissing admired but feared for their love of respectability, were the sort he had been both propositioning and proposing to since Eileen's death. He noted how Gissing had failed in his ambition for a quiet life of scholarship and writing because of missing Oxford after getting himself into prison, and having to spend his life in poverty existing on hack work writing against the clock. At the moment of his genuine success, when he might have lived more comfortably, he died of tuberculosis at the age of forty-six. Orwell reached forty-five while writing the essay. Substitute 'Burma' for 'prison' and you have the case of George Orwell. His final thought on Gissing might have served as his own epitaph: 'We must be thankful for the piece of youthful folly which turned him aside from a comfortable middle-class career and forced him to become the chronicler of vulgarity, squalor and failure.'[52]

The feeling that he was not attractive must have intensified greatly during his illness. The sight of himself in the mirror is echoed in both 'How the Poor Die' and in *Nineteen Eighty-Four*. On his forty-fifth birthday he told Anthony Powell that his hair was turning grey and he had acquired some false teeth – to Orwell always a symbol of genteel decay in seaside residential hotels, and a childhood image associated with his ageing father. At the same time he had to come to terms with a future as an invalid, spending time in bed or in wheelchairs, able perhaps to write the novels he had in mind, but unlikely to catch the sort of woman he would dearly have loved to marry.

The impending republication of *Coming Up For Air*, his current wrestling with *Nineteen Eighty-Four*, and his intense sense of his own fragile mortality, prompted increasing forays into nostalgia, a mental disposition valuable to any author, he thought. The idea that one must live in 'a continuous present, a minute-to-minute cancellation of memory', he regarded as 'a sort of intellectual face-lifting', 'a snobbish terror of growing old'.

> One ought to realise that a human being cannot continue developing indefinitely, and that a writer, in particular, is throwing away his heritage if he repudiates the experience of his early life. In many ways it is a grave handicap to remember that lost paradise 'before the war' – that is, before the other war. In other ways it is an advantage . . . one is likelier to make a good book by sticking to one's early-acquired vision than by a futile effort to 'keep up'. The great thing is to be your age, which includes being honest about your social origins.[53]

Whether the secretive Orwell had always been honest about his social origins is doubtful. His Limouzin and slave-owning ancestry, and even his Etonian education, were largely unknown.

Lydia finally visited him in July, staying overnight at a nearby hotel before travelling on for a brief holiday on Jura. It seems she agreed to do some typing for him while at Barnhill, which must have lifted his spirits, as did a visit from Avril bringing along the boisterous young Richard, beginning to talk at last. Suddenly, rather than stay close to the hospital he was eager to return to Barnhill and, within limits, take up where he had left off. By mid-July he was allowed up for six hours at a stretch and ventured out on ever-longer walks. He told George Woodcock, 'I am leaving here on the 25th & my address will be Barnhill as before. Of course I've got to go on living an invalid life, only getting up for half the day, for some months, perhaps for as long as a year, but they seem to think I am pretty well cured & will end up perfectly O.K. so long as I don't relapse during the next few months. It will be rather a bore not being able to go fishing etc., but it's worth it & I don't mind being in bed as I have got used to writing there.'[54]

When he left hospital on 28 July he did so with every intention of nursing his health and staying alive. However, just before leaving, he received a letter from Warburg which seemed designed to undermine that good intention:

> I was of course specially pleased to know that you have done quite a substantial amount of revision on the new novel. From our point of view, and I should say also from your point of view, a revision of this is far and away the most important single undertaking to which you could apply yourself when the vitality is there. It should not be put aside for reviews or miscellaneous work, however tempting, and will I am certain sooner rather than later bring in more money than you

could expect from any other activity. If you do succeed in finishing the revision by the end of the year this would be pretty satisfactory, and we should publish in the autumn of 1949, but it really is rather important from the point of view of your literary career to get it done by the end of the year, and indeed earlier if at all possible.[55]

Although he may have known little about *Nineteen Eighty-Four*, he felt certain that a new novel by the author of *Animal Farm* would be highly profitable. When he again fell ill, Orwell told Woodcock that one of the reasons he had not gone for treatment was that Warburg was chasing him for the book.[56] If he still felt like a squeezed orange he would be squeezed even more both before and after his death. Under such pressure, the prospect of a gentle convalescence was rendered impossible.

According to Avril, it was a mistake for him to return to Barnhill. 'If he'd gone into a convalescent home then, he probably would have been cured, but as it was he came back and insisted on living a quite ordinary life. It really was extremely stupid. Several times I had to go out and take the mowing-machine out of his hands and stop him from digging the garden and things like that, but somehow one doesn't have an awful lot of authority over one's own family, and he never really was one much to listen to other people.'[57] Warburg agreed. He thought that what Orwell needed was a wife, or even just a competent nurse – someone who would not take no for an answer.

Other factors precluded a restful recovery for Orwell. He found staying indoors difficult. The day after returning to Barnhill he was out inspecting his acres as if nothing had happened. More than a dozen visitors arrived for the summer and a tent was pitched in the garden to take the overflow. For a couple of weeks he entertained Richard Rees, Inez Holden and her cat. Inez was in 'a despairing state of mind' having recently split with Humphrey Slater who had returned to his wife. She later told her friend Cecily Mackworth that she rather hoped Orwell would ask her to marry him. The evening talk was about Evelyn Waugh's *Brideshead Revisited*, which Inez was reading, André Malraux, who Rees praised as a man of action, and Slater who had recently sent Orwell a dud cheque. Inez had brought along the newly published *I Chose Freedom* by Victor Kravchenko, which Orwell had been wanting to read for the past year. This exposé of Stalinism by a man who had served the Comintern in Spain must have given Rees and Orwell much to talk about – especially the feeling they had shared of living under terror in an atmosphere of suspicion in which nobody was to be trusted. It was probably at this time that they began to compile a list of people they suspected of being crypto-Communists or fellow-travellers, something which reviewing a new book by James Burnham (highlighting Communist subversion tactics) had also prompted in Orwell's mind. Rees claimed they did this as a game, but for Orwell it would be the left-wing equivalent of the list of crypto-Fascists and Nazi-sympathisers he had kept in his head in the early 1940s, people he thought should be kept from positions of power and influence when social democracy was at risk.

He was careful to avoid hard work around the farm, not even milking the cows, but did other small chores in the garden he should probably have avoided. He felt his health was improving, was able to walk a little further each day, and began to talk about being back to normal by the next year. The rest of the time he spent in bed working on his novel, which he told the eager Warburg he hoped to be able to send him at the beginning of December.

In September he returned to Hairmyres for a check-up. The trip was a disaster. He failed to book a hotel in advance and found himself trekking all over town to find a room. When finally he got to the hospital he was in poor condition. 'Very unwell, temperature about 101 (degrees) each evening,' he noted. But Bruce Dick recalled that 'When we saw him in September we thought he was as good as when he left us.'[58] Almost immediately he left the hospital, however, he felt ill, but instead of returning there, went straight home to Jura.

There he was soon back into his old routine – when not resting or working gently at his book, he was up and about for six hours or so, sailing his boat one day, collecting firewood the next. Not surprisingly, on 24 September he was back in bed again, getting up only briefly the following morning. Shortly afterwards, after picking apples, he was laid up in pain for two days. He told Astor that Bruce Dick was well pleased with his progress and he would probably be all right if he lived 'a senile sort of life'. But having continually to retreat to his bed only got in the way of the work which meant most to him. 'I am still struggling with the last stages of this bloody book, which is supposed to have been done by early December, and will be if I don't get ill again.' Neither author nor work excited optimism exactly. It was, he told Astor, about a possible state of affairs where an atomic war proved inconclusive.[59]

Completing his work on time was a point of pride with him, but on this occasion it was not entirely an unforced conclusion. On 22 October he told Warburg that the book would be finished in early November and, Mrs Christen having gone abroad, he raised the question of having it typed. The prospect of doing it himself was too disheartening to contemplate. It was, he said, very long – between 100,000 and 125,000 words – and too messy to send away. He needed someone to type it under his supervision. He would cover all expenses and provide a comfortable place in which to work. 'I am not pleased with the book,' he said, 'but I am not absolutely dissatisfied . . .

I think it is a good idea but the execution would have been better if I had not written it under the influence of TB.' As to titles, he was hesitating between 'Nineteen Eighty-Four' and 'The Last Man in Europe'.[60] Warburg favoured *1984*, but Orwell insisted on *Nineteen Eighty-Four*. From the draft manuscript it seems that initially he projected the date of the novel as 1980, thirty-six years ahead of 1944 (both Winston Smith's and Richard Blair's year of birth) when he first began it. So *1984* was seemingly derived from the year he finished it, 1948+36. The idea that he simply reversed the last two digits of *1948* to make *1984* (Warburg's supposition) is intriguing but lacks corroboration.[61]

There is another explanation – a poem composed by Eileen to mark the fiftieth anniversary of her school in 1934 which looked ahead to the next fifty years. It was called 'End of the Century, 1984' and was a clever poetic reflection on a future that suggests a recent reading of Huxley's *Brave New World*. It foresaw a time when 'Shakespeare's bones are quiet at last,' and 'No book disturbs the lucid line,/For sun-bronzed scholars tune their thought/To Telepathic Station 9/From which they know just what they ought,' and refers to 'mental cremation that should banish/Relics, philosophies and colds.'[62] Whether she showed it to Orwell or not, it strongly suggests a shared attachment to the old world and a nervousness about a Wellsian future. The date 1984 might have lingered in Orwell's mind from Eileen's poem. That title and the first date of Winston's diary (4 April) could well have been his silent homage to the wife with whom he must have discussed the terrible book he was planning at least eighteen months before her death.

He was still without a typist at the end of October. Warburg had promised to find him someone but gave the job to Senhouse who merely passed on the request to his niece in Scotland, 'an efficient girl who knows half the people in Edinburgh', indicating that the matter was not particularly urgent. Feeling desperate, Orwell asked Moore for help, but no London typist seemed willing to make the long trip to Jura in cold weather. He shared his frustration with Symons, bringing him up to date with his failing state of health:

> I can work, but that is about all I can do. Even to walk half a mile upsets me. I was going to come down to London in January, but I am consulting with my doctor and if he thinks it best I shall go into a private sanatorium, if I can find one, for the worst of the winter, i.e. Jan–Feb. I could go abroad perhaps, but the journey might be the death of me, so perhaps a sanatorium would be best.[63]

When he expressed disappointment to Senhouse over the typist, telling him of the stress and uncertainty under which he had been working, he was merely told to be patient and congratulated on completing his book. 'The astonishing feat of putting "finis" to the work is surely a triumph,' Senhouse replied,[64] seemingly oblivious to his author's plight.

Orwell's eagerness to get his book to Warburg now led him to make a fatal error. Tired of waiting for a stenographer, and able to get out of bed for only a short period each day, and with only his own 'very decrepit type-writer' to hand, he began what he called 'the grisly job' of typing the manuscript himself. Even so, he was feeling somewhat better and told David Astor, 'I seem to be all right so long as I stay in bed till lunch time and then spend the rest of the day on a sofa, but if I walk even a few hundred yards or pull up a few weeds in the garden I promptly get a temperature.'[65] The thought of the coming winter, especially February, 'the most detestable of months', was daunting. Had he been able to escape abroad from it he would have done so.

But he also wanted to escape from his book, and within a couple of weeks of starting he was able to tell Warburg that the typing was nearly half-complete. Suddenly consumed with guilt, Warburg replied saying how 'bitterly disappointed' he felt at having let him down over a stenographer. However, his enthusiasm was evident: 'There is no book in preparation . . . which arouses the interest of Roger and myself to a greater extent than "1984".'[66] On 4 December Orwell sent him the final typescript. The completion of his novel, a truly heroic achievement, was a moment to savour and celebrate. The last pig at Barnhill was slaughtered and he, Avril and Bill Dunn consumed the last bottle of wine in the house.[67] It is ironic to note that *Nineteen Eighty-Four* was completed in the hundredth anniversary year of the publication of *The Communist Manifesto*. (Had Orwell finished it the previous February, as originally intended, it would have been the hundredth anniversary month!)

Now it was necessary to start putting certain affairs in order. Avril was dispatched to London to dispose of the Canonbury Square flat and transport his remaining furniture and effects to Barnhill. She wrote to Humphrey blaming her brother's decline on the doctors at Hairmyres for discharging him too soon, and saying that he would now have to be going for more treatment in the New Year. In London she spent a day with Aunt Nellie who had grown evermore eccentric, complaining about her rent, and saying that she did not pay her landlord enough and was saving up to pay him more.[68]

It did not take Warburg long to recognise that he now had a very great and unusual novel in his hands. Within ten days of receiving it he had produced a strictly confidential 1400-word report on it. 'This is amongst the most terrifying books I have read,' he began. 'The savagery of Swift has passed to a successor who looks upon life and finds it becoming evermore intolerable.' He recognised Orwell's debt to Jack London's *The Iron Heel* but, he said, he had surpassed 'that not inconsiderable author'. It was a study in unrelieved pessimism. The only weakness he could see was his failure to show how his imagined society robbed its inhabitants of their humanity. It was '*Animal Farm* writ large'. 'Here is the Soviet Union to the nth degree, a Stalin who never dies, a secret police with every device of modern technology.' However, he then seemed to misread Orwell's message (apparently lending it his own ideological slant): 'The political system which prevails is Ingsoc – English Socialism. This I take to be a deliberate and sadistic attack on Socialism and socialist parties generally. It seems to indicate a final breach between Orwell and Socialism, not the socialism of equality and human brotherhood which clearly Orwell no longer expects from socialist parties, but the socialism of Marxism and the managerial revolution.' It was, he declared, 'worth a cool million votes to the conservative party; it might well be the choice of "Daily Mail" and "Evening Standard"; it is imaginable that it might have a preface by Winston after whom its hero is named.' The book, he said, should be published as soon as possible.

Warburg's more detailed comments reveal his unvarnished opinion of Orwell. In the second part of the book, he wrote, when Winston reads passages from Goldstein's book, *The Principles of Oligarchical Collectivism*, 'it is a typical Orwellism that Julia falls asleep . . . (Women aren't intelligent, in Orwell's world.)'. In Part Three, 'Orwell gives full rein to his sadism and its attendant masochism, rising (or falling) to the limits of expression in the scene where Winston, threatened by hungry rats which will eat into his face . . .' The contrast between the light of logic (the place where there is no darkness) leading to destruction, and the darkness of the womb and vital life processes (the darkness of safe, anonymous individuality), was the central symbolism of Part Three, which he also saw as symbolic of Orwell's condition. Here hope and rebellion were crushed by Pain and the Party, leaving behind 'smells of death, decay, dirt, diabolism and despair'. 'I cannot but think,' he concluded, 'that this book could have been written only by a man who himself, however temporarily, had lost hope, and for physical reasons which are sufficiently apparent.'

Warburg saw that he had a potential best-seller on his hands, and could not resist the temptation to speculate on other ways in which it might make money. With a sales-enhancing propaganda movie in mind, he added, '"1984" by the way might well be described as a horror novel, and would make a horror film which, if licensed, might secure all countries threatened by communism for 1000 years to come.' This revealing aside throws light on the subsequent treatment of Orwell's work, in which Warburg seems to have had a guiding hand.[69] What Orwell probably never knew was that his publisher would be promoting the book as an attack on Labour.

Orwell's novel was informed by his past reading as much as by his political experiences. From Burnham he took the vision of the world divided into three great, mutually hostile power blocs. From Zamyatin came the general shape of the novel and the idea of a total surveillance state, from Koestler the terrifying interrogation involving brainwashing through fear. The whole tone and thrust of Goldstein's book suggests Trotsky's *The Revolution Betrayed* (Crick also suggests pamphlets by Andrés Nin were influential here). There are, too, as Warburg had noticed, strong echoes of Jack London's *The Iron Heel* (most notably in O'Brien's grim speech about the crushing use of power), as well as Belloc's *The Servile State*, Poe's 'The Pit and the Pendulum' and M. R. James's 'Rats'. His horror of the Inquisition, his experience of terror in Barcelona, of propaganda machinations at the Ministry of Information and the BBC, of being subjected to censorship, of wretched wartime London and the mysteries of city junk shops are all there. Newspeak arose out of an awareness of how language was distorted by propagandists and advertisers and how artificial languages, such as Esperanto and Basic English, intended to make human communication easier, gave power to those who would manipulate minds through the limitation of thought. The conundrum 2+2=5 was taken from Eugene Lyons writing about the Soviet Five-Year Plan (it also crops up in *Tristram Shandy*).[70] His fascination with Chestertonian paradox is there in the form of 'Doublethink' ('The power of holding two contradictory beliefs in one's mind simultaneously, and accepting both of them', e.g. 'War is Peace', 'Freedom is Slavery' etc.), as is his identification with Protestant dissenters and martyrs, his penchant for nursery rhymes, his fascination with fiction factories (offering formulae for novel-writing), and the paranoia that led him to arm himself against possible assassination. As ever, there is the Laurentian fantasy of unrestrained sexuality with a willing and available woman. And there, too, is Winston's remarkably revealing sado-sexual fantasy about Julia: 'He would flog her to death with a rubber truncheon . . . tie her naked to a stake and shoot her full of arrows like Saint Sebastian. He would ravish her and cut her throat at the moment of climax.'[71] As he wrote, 'The imaginative writer . . . cannot misrepresent the scenery of his own mind.'

The torture scenes in *Nineteen Eighty-Four* are (as Symons suggested) common schoolboy horror stories, but they also have historical roots – rats in a heated pot forced to escape by eating through the victim's stomach was a method employed by Torquemada. That Orwell was aware of medieval forms of torture is evident in references to *The Pleasures of the Torture Chamber*, a book graphically illustrating the gruesome means employed by religious inquisitors. Torquemada's method was to pinion the victim, show him the instruments of torture and then strap him on to them, the very method O'Brien uses on Winston Smith. His strong identification with the Protestant martyrs is evident, reflected elsewhere in Spender's depiction of him as 'a secular saint', and Rushbrook Williams's description of him as a man who might once have been canonised or burnt at the stake.[72]

Rees highlighted the religious subtext of *Nineteen Eighty-Four*, suggesting that in Winston's betrayal of Julia, Orwell was making a philosophical pronouncement on human nature – Man is a Fallen creature, and human nature fundamentally egoistic. This, thought Rees, made the book as much a profound religious meditation on the human condition as 'a pessimistic political prophesy'. The moral state of man had been 'his true and permanent preoccupation' and at heart he was not so much a political prophet as a 'pious atheist', for whom morality meant common decency without transcendental belief.[73] The novel was, on this view, Orwell's contribution to a religious tradition – the 'happy vicar' turned secular socialist. Faced with totalitarianism, Orwell constantly drew the religious parallel. In early 1940 he wrote: 'What we are now moving towards at this moment is something more like the Spanish Inquisition, and probably far worse, thanks to the radio and the secret police.' Freedom of thought and individual self-expression were the products of Protestantism, of which the novel was the great cultural achievement.[74] The same analogy is there in his novel. Many of the names of the characters in *Nineteen Eighty-Four* are those of persecuted religious and political dissenters – Rutherford, Scottish dissident condemned to be burned, saved himself by confessing under torture; Jones, Chartist leader, persecuted and imprisoned for sedition; Tillotson, seventeenth-century preacher against popery; Wither and Ogilvy, Civil War turncoats. And the nursery rhyme 'Oranges and Lemons' evokes a past age of religious persecution and public decapitations. On this understanding, the story becomes more than just a warning based on the rundown England of 1948; it also offers a comparison with a barbaric past, underlining the disconnection between scientific advance and moral progress. During his cross-examination of Winston, O'Brien even reiterates the parallel:

> In the Middle Ages there was the Inquisition. It was a failure. It set out to eradicate heresy, and ended by perpetuating it. For every heretic it burned at the stake, thousands of others rose up. Why was that? Because the Inquisition killed its enemies in the open, and killed them while they were still unrepentant: in fact, it killed them because they were unrepentant. Men were dying because they would not abandon their true beliefs. Naturally all the glory belonged to the victim and all the shame to the Inquisitor who burned him. Later, in the twentieth century, there were the totalitarians, as they were called. There were the

German Nazis and the Russian Communists. The Russians persecuted heresy more cruelly than the Inquisition had done. And they imagined that they had learned from the mistakes of the past; they knew, at any rate, that one must not make martyrs. Before they exposed their victims to public trial, they deliberately set themselves to destroy their dignity. They wore them down by torture and solitude until they were despicable, cringing wretches, confessing whatever was put into their mouths, covering themselves with abuse, accusing and sheltering behind one another, whimpering for mercy. And yet after only a few years the same thing had happened over again. The dead men had become martyrs and their degradation was forgotten. Once again, why was it? In the first place, because the confessions that they had made were obviously extorted and untrue. We do not make mistakes of that kind. All the confessions that are uttered here are true. We make them true. And above all we do not allow the dead to rise up against us. You must stop imagining that posterity will vindicate you, Winston. Posterity will never hear of you. You will be lifted clean out from the stream of history. We shall turn you into gas and pour you into the stratosphere. Nothing will remain of you; not a name in a register, not a memory in a living brain. You will be annihilated in the past as well as in the future. You will never have existed.[75]

There again the great Miltonian thematic structure is reversed. Living in Hell, Winston dreams of Paradise. Through Julia Paradise is gained, through O'Brien it is lost. It is Orwell's pessimistic nightmare. The socialist Paradise glimpsed in Barcelona is always destined to fail because there will always be O'Briens, as there will always be Hitlers and Stalins. All good things are echoed by evil. In the same way he inverted the Lord Prayer, through the mouth of Mr Tallboys the unfrocked priest, in *A Clergyman's Daughter*, and mocked the words of St Paul in *Keep the Aspidistra Flying*, he takes the bland, uplifting words of 'Under The Spreading Chestnut Tree', sung in celebration of brotherhood at the Duke of York's Southwold Summer Camps, and twists it into the cynical

> Under the spreading chestnut tree
> I sold you and you sold me:
> There lie they, and here lie we
> Under the spreading chestnut tree.[76]

Equally cynically, the café where doomed men play chess until the bullet in the back of the neck arrives is called The Chestnut Café.

Nineteen Eighty-Four contains many of the characteristic features of an

Orwell novel. It is full of clocks and chimes and strikings of the hour, time-markers ever full of menace. As the book opens the clocks strike thirteen, beginning the countdown to the destruction of the soul of Winston Smith; and the title of the book itself sets the clock ticking – the countdown to apocalypse. In 1948 a time thirty-six years ahead must have seemed a likely date for a new post-atomic dark age. And even after its passing, 1984 became a symbol, a writing on the wall, a hideous warning of other threats to freedom of thought ever-present in an age increasingly dominated by science and amoral politics.

Behind the novel stands a long continuity of thought. There is a very strange relationship, for example, between *Nineteen Eighty-Four* and *Keep the Aspidistra Flying*. *Nineteen Eighty-Four* can be seen as a grotesque parody of his earlier novel – as if Orwell thought 'I can tell this story better second time around.' Gordon Comstock is in advertising, sickened by the fact that he is paid to mislead and swindle the public; Winston Smith is in the business of misleading and swindling through deliberate falsification. *Keep the Aspidistra Flying* attacks the money-god, *Nineteen Eighty-Four* attacks the power-god. Gordon wallows in poverty; Winston lives in a world of semi-squalor, inedible food and lies. Gordon is spied upon in his wretched flat by Mrs Wisbeach; Winston is spied on in his by the Parsons children and the Thought Police. Gordon's Rosemary is sexually inhibited, defensive and wants marriage – an upholder of the bourgeois life; Winston's Julia is her antithesis, abandoned and promiscuous – seemingly committed to subverting the Ingsoc anti-sex code. Both novels reveal a similar mental topography and many continuities. Only the nature of the threat to human freedom differs. Symons demonstrated equally strong parallels between *Nineteen Eighty-Four* and *Burmese Days*, suggesting that the familiar Orwellian landscape was established very early on. There is always a powerful urge towards freedom, always a suffocating system to fight against. And there was also, for him, the important subtext: 'Literature is doomed if liberty of thought perishes.'[77]

More than any other Orwell novel, *Nineteen Eighty-Four* is concerned with role-playing and deception. Winston's world is a labyrinth of deception. The Party is deceiving everyone; Winston is deceiving the Party; Julia is deceiving the Anti-Sex League; Charrington and O'Brien are deceiving Winston; Winston is deceiving himself. 'Truth' is also a deception because the Party controls the present, past and future. Once this 'shifting reality' is established, no one can be taken at face value. Julia seems to be a secret hater of the Party and Big Brother, seems to be a candidate for the dissident Brotherhood, seems to go off to be tortured after her arrest and finally seems to have been purged of her thought-crime. But in the world of the book she could, like O'Brien and Charrington, also be a dissembler leading

Winston straight into the arms of the Thought Police. On Airstrip One truth rests on ever-shifting sands, only pain and Room 101 are real. Such a reading gives the book a strangely modern character, making it a novel about the slippery, unstable nature of meaning.

What gave *Nineteen Eighty-Four* such power when it was published was that, unlike dystopian novels such as Huxley's *Brave New World* and Zamyatin's *We*, it is set in a familiar wartime London, not in some ill-defined and unrecognisable future. That lent greater force and conviction to the message: 'It could happen here!' The things he feared most were loss of the past and future uncertainty, the distortion of reality at the behest of a Party, the eradication of the individual self, the power of streamlined men who lack all known human emotions. All are manifest in this world of Airstrip One. More decidedly than either Huxley or Zamyatin, Orwell killed off the Wellsian Utopia.

When Warburg wrote saying how excited he was about the novel, Orwell replied, 'It isn't a book I would gamble on for a big sale, but I suppose one could be sure of 10,000 anyway.'[78] He became worried about how it might be publicised when Senhouse sent a draft blurb he had concocted. 'It makes the book sound as though it were a thriller mixed up with a love story, & I didn't intend it to be primarily that. What it is really meant to do is to discuss the implications of dividing the world up into "Zones of influence" (I thought of it in 1944 as a result of the Teheran Conference), & in addition to indicate by parodying them the intellectual implications of totalitarianism.' He thought quotations from certain eminences, such as Bertrand Russell or Lancelot Hogben, would make better blurbs.[79]

Once his book was finished his health soon deteriorated.[80] 'During that autumn of 1948,' wrote Avril, 'it was obvious that he was getting ill again. On one occasion he said to me, rather despairingly: "Whatever I do, it seems my temperature rises: if I take the slightest kind of action or motion." We both decided that he'd better be under hospital treatment as soon as possible.'[81]

Although Bruce Dick found him a place in a reputable Scottish sanatorium (interestingly enough, one in which Somerset Maugham had once been treated), Orwell had set his mind on going south and booked into one at Cranham near Stroud in Gloucestershire. It meant bidding farewell to the Robinson Crusoe life, admitting that another adventure had failed, and adjusting himself to a future of infirmity. He knew that his poor condition was due to time spent trying to finish his novel, but he was determined not to give in easily. 'I must try to stay alive for a while,' he told Astor, 'because apart from other considerations I have a good idea for a novel.'[82] He hung on for one last Christmas at home.

The progress of Orwell's illness is difficult to map. He seemed to have inherited bronchiectasis, a condition that would have made him susceptible to lung infection from birth. His recurrent influenza and bronchitis, his persistent cough, and his several bouts of pneumonia would be symptoms of that susceptibility. But the condition also made him especially vulnerable to tuberculosis, and he might well have been infected since childhood. By the time he was finally diagnosed with TB at the age of thirty-five, he had exposed himself to risk on several occasions – in Burma, in the poor ward at the Hôpital Cochin, in casual wards, in squalid lodgings in Wigan, and in the Huesca trenches during a bitter Spanish winter. When Laurence O'Shaughnessy was killed he lost a friend who might have kept him under closer supervision, and the flamboyant Morlock hardly helped by dismissing his haemorrhages as somehow benign. From childhood he had a phobia about doctors and hospitals, only confirmed by his experience in Paris, and he almost certainly neglected his health during the war, ignoring a medical officer's advice to get treatment in 1943. If Jura was inimical to his health, it was not so much because of the climate as the physical effort of living there. The tuberculosis weakened him but the more direct threat to his life came from his tendency to haemorrhage. With a left lung as sclerotic and pitted as his, the danger was that a worn artery would rupture and his lungs would flood, which meant that violent coughing or sudden jolting could do for him. Whenever he could he tried to carry on as before, under the delusion that he was on the mend or could simply continue at a gentler pace.

Perhaps he was anticipating the many travails he endured with *Nineteen Eighty-Four* when he wrote in 1946, 'Writing a book is a horrible, exhausting struggle, like a long bout of some painful illness. One would never undertake such a thing if one were not driven on by some demon whom one can neither resist or [*sic*] understand. For all one knows that demon is simply the same instinct that makes a baby squall for attention. And yet it is also true that one can write nothing readable unless one constantly struggles to efface one's own personality. Good prose is like a window-pane.'[83] The goal was certainly noble, and he came as close as any to achieving a window-pane prose, but one thing he could never achieve in his writing was the effacement of his own personality. *Nineteen Eighty-Four* had been written against death. Now he had to face that prospect head-on.

Chapter 19

The End of the Beginning

'To hang on from day to day and from week to week spinning out a present that had no future, seemed an unconquerable instinct, just as one's lungs will always draw the next breath so long as there is air available.'

Orwell, *Nineteen Eighty-Four*, 1949

The loyal Rees accompanied him on the four hundred miles south to The Cotswold Sanatorium, set in beech woods at Cranham, nine hundred feet above sea level, a few miles south-east of Gloucester. Close by were the villages of Painswick and Birdlap and the Benedictine Abbey of Prinknash, overlooking the spectacular Vale of Gloucestershire. He arrived, he said, feeling rather sorry for himself,[1] but still under the impression that he would be there for just the worst winter months. Bruce Dick, disappointed to lose his patient, told David Astor that he might respond to another course of streptomycin wherever it was administered. 'It's all bad luck for such a fine character & gifted man,' he wrote. 'I know he gets great heart from your continued comradeship and kindness.'[2]

The Cotswold Sanatorium director was Dr Geoffrey Hoffman, whose father, a pioneer of the Sanatorium Movement, had established it before the First World War. Hitherto, its most distinguished literary patient had been the Georgian poet, James Elroy Flecker, who was there in 1910, and wrote about it, as Orwell might have done, reflecting on past Laurentian idylls: 'Have I not chased the fluting Pan/Through Cranham's sober trees?/Have I not sat on Painswick Hill/With nymph upon my knees,/And she as rosy as the dawn,/And naked as the breeze?'

But there would be no chasing Pan through Cranham woods for Orwell. He was put in a small wooden chalet, which at first he found 'rather grim'. Part of the cure (other than rest and good food) was to be left for periods in the 'fresh air', even though in the winter this left patients shivering. However, the huts had central heating and hot and cold water, so there was a degree of comfort. He was also lucky to arrive when the weather was mild, even spring-like, and although he could not see the landscape for trees, he was in fact in the heart of some of the prettiest countryside in England. The fee was twelve guineas a week, plus extra for special medicines and doctors' services. 'This disease,' he told Herbert Read, 'is an expensive hobby.'[3]

After two weeks at Cranham he wrote to Warburg. He was, he said, 'trying to do no work whatever', was being treated with PAS (Para-amino-salicylic acid), was feeling better and eating more.[4] He was also now at last a little more alert to the serious state of his health and told Rees that, if he was well by the summer, he must arrange to spend every winter in the south, close to doctors. Ironically, he was considering Brighton, in Sussex, the very county he had sworn never to revisit after leaving the hated St Cyprian's.[5]

Yet the pull of Jura was still very strong and Barnhill still the emotional focus of his existence. That was where his books and papers were now located, where his family were, and where, thanks to him, the tip of a remote part of Britain had been brought back under cultivation. Even as he lay in his chalet bed, he was contemplating the state of his vegetable patch and flower beds. But now he realised that his determination to farm the land had caused him to remain at Barnhill when he would have been better off in a warmer climate.

Anxious to keep tabs on his hottest author, Warburg and his wife, Pamela, visited him towards the end of January. It was not just a social call; for Warburg this was a business trip. 'I was keen to tell him,' he wrote, 'of the high hopes we had for the sale of 1984, which might produce a boost to his morale, helpful to a man in so perilous a situation . . . I had already written him on January 19th "Your future is important to more people than yourself . . . you are a much loved writer and your public wants you to get well and wants you to do everything that you can to this end." Third, there were a number of minor points to discuss in connexion with the publishing details of 1984.'[6]

Now that he realised that Orwell's life was in the balance, he was also anxious to see that his most promisingly profitable author was receiving the best possible treatment. The Warburgs had in mind a friend of theirs, Dr Andrew Morland, consultant physician at University College Hospital and, like Laurence O'Shaughnessy, a leading authority on pulmonary tuberculosis. More than some, he was alive to the psychological effects of TB having been tuberculous himself as a child. After recovering in a Swiss sanatorium, he was convinced of the restorative properties of fresh air at high altitude. He was a Quaker, self-assured but reticent, a member of the Savile Club, with a penchant for literary society. He counted a number of writers among his friends and patients, including Graham Greene, and was well-known as one of the last doctors to see D. H. Lawrence. What was not so well-known was that Lawrence considered his advice poor and grumbled to friends about it. However, there were non-medical reasons why Morland might have been a good choice for Orwell. He shared his enthusiasm for farming and fishing, and the Warburgs felt that his experience with writers like Lawrence and Greene would make him acutely sensitive to the mind of such a writer.

The Warburgs' first impression of the sanatorium was not propitious. The weather was icy, the hutment looked squalid. Pamela quickly formed a low opinion of the place and began to quiz Orwell. Yes, he said, it was cold but he had been promised an electric blanket. No, he had not seen Hoffman, but a woman doctor, Dr Margaret Kirkman, saw him every morning. No, he had not been thoroughly examined yet, but the place was somewhat understaffed. Pamela was outraged and said he must ask to see Hoffman right away. But Orwell was in no mood to make a fuss. 'I expect he'll come and see me fairly soon,' he said. 'The place is really very comfortable, they look after me quite well. I expect the doctors know what they are doing.' It was all too vague for Pamela, who urged him to see Morland in the hope that he would take him into University College Hospital, close to his friends – and close to Warburg, too, of course. Orwell was reluctant, but promised to consider the suggestion. On the way back to London, Pamela told Fred, 'I don't think he'll live for more than a year.'[7]

No doubt the coming of the Warburgs made Orwell more conscious of how ill he was, and there was a slight air of alarm in the letter he wrote to Rees a week later. He was being well looked after, he said, but had only been weighed and x-rayed once since admission. He now saw death looming and was worried about his uncertain future. He was having dreams about being lost in large buildings or wandering in sunlight, which he interpreted as dreams of death. 'They can't do anything for you,' he wrote, 'but I want an expert opinion on how long I am likely to live, because I must make my plans accordingly.' However, Warburg's man, Morland, was not his first choice. 'When I am about again, I suppose in the summer, I shall see a London specialist, if possible the man I saw just before the war.' That man was the over-optimistic Morlock, a last link to the medical man he had most trusted, Laurence O'Shaughnessy.[8] A few days later his feeling of dissatisfaction had increased. 'The doctors,' he told Symons, 'don't strike me as very brilliant.'[9]

In February he heard from Celia, now back from Paris and working for a new agency of the Foreign Office, the Information Research Department, set up by the Attlee government to counter Soviet propaganda efforts to undermine the west. He was quite keen to see her, as he was some of the other women he had known. In the following months a long procession of friends trekked to Cranham, including Brenda, Inez, Lydia, Celia and, most significantly, Sonia. Humphrey and Jane Dakin, Orwell's brother-in-law and niece, drove down from Yorkshire on a motorbike and found him comparatively cheerful, producing a bottle of brandy from his cupboard and entertaining them in grand style. Even Jacintha, whose Aunt Lilian had discovered that Orwell was her childhood friend Eric, made contact, having just read *Animal Farm*. It seemed as if that moon-faced, witty, cheerful boy-next-door with vaulting literary ambitions had finally achieved his goal of becoming the FAMOUS AUTHOR, with at least the first volume of a uniform edition in print.

He was clearly delighted to hear from the love of his lost youth, and she received two replies in one envelope. Her letter had caught his mood of sad reminiscence, and in his letters he returned to their Shiplake childhood, then brought her up to date with his life. He was a widower, he told her, with a small adopted son. 'I have been having this dreary disease (TB) in an acute way since the autumn of 1947, but of course it has been hanging over me all my life, and actually I think I had my first go of it in early childhood.' 'All I do,' he wrote sadly, 'is read and do crossword puzzles.'[10] His second letter struck a rather more fateful note, echoing their youthful greeting: 'Hail and Fare Well, my dear Jacintha.' He told her how difficult it had been for him to get started as a writer and said they must meet when he got well.

> Are you fond of children? You were such a tender-hearted girl, always full of pity for the creatures we others shot & killed. But you were not so tender-hearted to me when you abandoned me to Burma with all hope denied. We are older now, & with this wretched illness the years will have taken more toll of me than of you. But I am well cared-for here & feel much better than I did when I got here last month. As soon as I can get back to London I do so want us to meet again. As we always ended so that there should be no ending. Farewell and Hail, Eric.[11]

Muggeridge and Powell arrived at Cranham, having walked the ten miles from Stroud station. According to Muggeridge, they found him 'the same old trusty, lovable egotist', looking wretched but seeming cheerful. He told them he hoped to live another ten years until Richard was fifteen, but Muggeridge doubted whether he would make it. 'He spoke a lot about Gissing, for whom he has a particular fondness, I think because he sees himself in Gissing's position; also about Kipling, whom he greatly admires. Though he has TB he goes on smoking cigarettes, and was able to produce a bottle of rum from under his bed, which we consumed.'[12] Muggeridge's insight into Orwell's close identification with Gissing was shrewd. Gissing, like him, was a man against the world, who had fought poverty as a disgruntled hack writer, had to endure the hated city so damaging to his health, had retreated finally to the countryside and come to enjoy some degree of success only when his life was fatally blighted by tuberculosis.

Two days after his visit, Muggeridge lunched with Warburg and reported, somewhat uncomfortably, that 'a characteristic remark of Warburg's was, in a rather plaintive voice, that what George should do was to use his little remaining span of life and energy to write at least two more books'.[13] *Nineteen Eighty-Four*, he told him shortly afterwards, 'had a very good chance of having a large sale'.[14] The implication was that Warburg now saw his ailing author only as the source of more books and, presumably, more profit to Warburg. If so, it is not surprising that he wanted him to have the best care and, if possible, to have him under his eye somewhere in London.

The rest and lack of pressure seemed to be working, and he had begun to feel better. And even if his hands were often too cold for him to write a firm hand, David Astor had sent a bed jacket and an electric blanket which at least meant he was warm in bed. The PAS seemed to help, his temperature steadily came down, his appetite continued to improve, and he was cheered to see *Burmese Days* republished, the second volume in his cherished uniform edition. More than ever he was convinced that because he had been ill and under pressure from Warburg, *Nineteen Eighty-Four* had been 'mucked up'. His concerns about the book, he told Fyvel, were primarily literary – the characters were too flat and there were verbal infelicities which would have been ironed out had he been feeling better.[15] Even so, he felt that finishing the book had been a great achievement. As he wrote to Powell, 'It's a god-awful job getting back to writing books again after years of time-wasting, but I feel now I've broken the spell & could go on writing if I were well again.'[16]

But even as he reflected on his work in remotest Gloucestershire, he could never entirely escape the deadly wider world. Gleb Struve, the expatriate Russian writer, had sent him a translation of two articles from *Soviet Literature* attacking first him then Koestler as slanderers of the Soviet Union. Orwell was intrigued to be the subject of such hostility, and told Rees, 'Doesn't it strike you that there is something queer about the *language* of totalitarian literature – a curious mouthing sort of quality, as of someone who is choking with rage & can never quite hit on the words he wants?'[17] If Orwell had long suspected that his name was on a Moscow hit list, that suspicion was now confirmed.

By the beginning of March the proofs of the US edition of *Nineteen Eighty-Four* had arrived as had some early British reactions to the book. Bertrand Russell had greeted it as 'a major work of fiction' and the conservative London *Evening Standard* had made it their 'Book of the Month' for

June.[18] Meantime, he was strictly confined to bed for at least another two months – more likely to be four, he told Rees. His main concerns, however, were the expense and not being able to see young Richard.

In America *Nineteen Eighty-Four* was being considered by the Book-of-the-Month Club, so offering again the possibility of huge sales and large royalties. However, he was told that the committee wished to cut the extracts from Goldstein's book and the Appendix on Newspeak. Despite the likely financial sacrifice, he rejected these proposals outright. 'A book is built up as a balanced structure and one cannot simply remove large chunks here and there unless one is ready to recast the whole thing.' It would also mean a great deal of rewriting, which was beyond him in his present condition.[19] In April news came that the Club had agreed to bring it out in full, the chairman writing that it was probably the most important book they had published in twenty-three years.[20] To Orwell it was a small but comforting victory. 'That shows that virtue is its own reward,' he told Rees. He was not sure how much he would end up in pocket, but he thought that at least he would be able to pay off his tax arrears.[21] In fact it was the first clear sign that his financial future (and that of his heirs) was assured. A meeting of George Orwell Productions was arranged at his bedside and it was agreed that all his income should become the property of the company and that he be employed at an annual salary of £2000 per annum, plus such bonuses as the board (Orwell himself in this case) decided.

As before, his health proved unpredictable and fragile. Towards the end of March he became suddenly quite ill, spitting blood again and barely able to write. It was decided to put him back on streptomycin but, now being allergic to it, he reacted so badly to the first dose that it was stopped immediately. It later transpired that his 'relapse' was due to pleurisy, but, as he wrote later, 'I thought I was a goner.'[22] Once over that he began to feel well again, so much so that he ordered himself some new clothes, and even renewed his passport, just to keep up his morale.[23] He was keen to make a new will and confirm Rees as his literary executor. He told Gwen O'Shaughnessy, his executrix, 'If I should die in the near future there are considerable income tax claims to be met, but there is also a good deal of money coming in and I think the "estate" would be easily cleared without encroaching on my savings.' There would be 'a small income from royalties for some years to come'. He also asked her to decide Richard's future upbringing with Avril, who he wanted to care for the boy. Eileen's wish to the contrary seems to have been long forgotten.[24]

The English sense of class continued to haunt him. On Easter Sunday he was struck by 'the large number of upper-class English voices' to be heard among visitors. After the working-class and lower-middle-class Scottish accents to which he had grown accustomed, he became newly aware of the 'over-fedness', the 'fatuous self-confidence' of these intrusive voices – 'a constant bah-bahing of laughter about nothing, above all a sort of heaviness & richness combined with a fundamental ill-will – people who, one instinctively feels, without even being able to see them, are the enemies of anything intelligent or sensitive or beautiful. No wonder everyone hates us so.' He and his class, he thought, still had nothing to lose but their aitches.[25]

When Celia came visiting, she found him under strict instructions to remain in bed. In confidence she told him about her work for the IRD and said she hoped he could write something for them. That, he told her, was impossible because of his illness, but he did suggest other writers he considered had serious anti-Communist credentials. A week later he wrote suggesting more names, adding, 'I could also, if it is of any value, give you a list of journalists & writers who in my opinion are crypto-Communists, fellow-travellers or inclined that way & should not be trusted as propagandists.' The list, which he had compiled with Rees, was in a notebook at Barnhill and would have to be sent for. 'If I do give you such a list,' he added, 'it is strictly in confidence, as I imagine it is libellous to describe somebody as a fellow-traveller.'[26]

For him it was an opportunity he would love to have had early in the war, to help keep potential quislings out of positions of influence in the event of an enemy invasion. (He prided himself that he had a better idea than most of the cruel fanaticism such people represented.) 'It isn't a bad idea to have people who are probably unreliable listed. If it had been done earlier it would have stopped people like Peter Smollett worming their way into important propaganda jobs where they were probably able to do us a lot of harm.' Smollett, later exposed as a Comintern spy, is suspected of being the Ministry of Information official who persuaded Cape against accepting *Animal Farm*. The head of the IRD was delighted by Orwell's offer and asked for the list, with reasons attached. Rees sent the notebook from Barnhill and Orwell copied 35 names from a list of 135 together with comments, some of them no doubt libellous, as he had thought. In a letter to Rees he discussed the basis on which the list was compiled: 'It seems to me very important to attempt to gauge people's *subjective* feelings, because otherwise one can't predict their behaviour in situations where the results of certain actions are clear even to a self-deceiver . . . The whole difficulty is to decide where each person stands, & one has to treat each case individually.'[27] The list sent on to Celia and submitted to the IRD has never been published so what remarks he put against each name, as opposed to those on his longer list, are as yet unknown.

The US publication of *Nineteen Eighty-Four* was now imminent. What Orwell did not know was that on 22 April, Eugene Reynal, the vice-president at Harcourt Brace, sent an advanced copy of his book to J. Edgar

Hoover at the FBI, seeking his endorsement and urging him to bring it to the attention of the American people, saying pointedly, 'The book leaves the reader with the shocked feeling that there is not a single horrible feature of the world of 1984 that is not present, in embryo, today.'[28] Hoover replied that he did not endorse books. But it was now in the hands of one of the most powerful people backing the war in the US against 'Un-American Activities'.

Orwell had weakened again. He now found it impossible to write because of an awful feeling of 'heaviness and clumsiness, as well as [an] inability to concentrate for more than a few seconds'.[29] When Powell sent news of the death of Hugh Kingsmill, it found him in depressive mood. 'I have been beastly ill, on & off. I can't make any firm plans . . . It looks as if I may have to spend the rest of my life, if not actually in bed, at any rate at the bath-chair level . . . At present I can do nothing, not even a book review.'[30] And when David Astor proposed a profile of him for the *Observer* he commented, 'It really wouldn't surprise me if you had to change that Profile into an obituary.'[31]

Friends continued to make the long journey from London. One 'wintry' day in early spring, Tosco and Mary Fyvel visited him. The sanatorium seemed to them a bleak place and Orwell looked more wretched, thinner and frailer, than they had expected. 'True, mentally he seemed in perfect control,' wrote Tosco, 'but in body, there he lay flat on his back in bed, looking terribly emaciated, his face drawn and waxen pale – without doubt he was dangerously ill. Constrained by the shock, I tried to tell him how much I had liked his book. He commented a little sadly that because of his illness, the book might have turned out duller and more pessimistic than intended.' When Mary recalled his earlier poverty and mentioned 'all that lovely money coming in from *Animal Farm*', he simply said, 'It may look like it, Mary, but it's all fairy gold, fairy gold,' meaning that more than half of it had gone already in tax.[32]

In early May Sonia Brownell reappeared on the scene. She was just back from Paris where a passionate affair with the existentialist philosopher Maurice Merleau-Ponty had recently broken up. It seems that she informed Warburg that she intended to visit Cranham, and he asked her to report back to him on Orwell's condition. Her relationship with Warburg was crucial to the events that later unfolded.

However, Orwell's health suddenly deteriorated, and he had to put off Sonia's visit. He told Warburg, 'I am in the most ghastly health, & have been for some weeks.' X-rays showed that both lungs had deteriorated badly. 'I asked the doctor recently whether she thought I would survive, & she wouldn't go further than saying she didn't know.' He hinted that he might be ready now to see Morland. 'They can't *do* anything, as I am not a case for operation, but I would like an expert opinion on how long I am likely to stay alive. I do hope people won't now start chasing me to go to Switzerland, which is supposed to have magical qualities. I don't believe it makes any difference where you are, & a journey would be the death of me.'[33] Sadly, this hope would not be realised.

Now more anxious for his author than ever, Warburg arranged for Morland to travel down to Cranham on 22 May. 'He was quite nice and encouraging,' reported Orwell afterwards. 'He says – & the latest x-ray apparently confirms this – that I have quite a good chance of staying alive for some years, but that it is necessary to stay still and do no work for what may be a long time, possibly as much as a year or two years. I don't think I could stick . . . not working for two years, but could manage one year if absolutely necessary.' He said that meant he would have nothing for Warburg in 1950 though the time would then be ripe for a second volume of essays for which the publisher had been pressing.[34] Morland reported directly to Warburg. The patient had a severely diseased left lung but only a relatively slight amount to his right one, he told him. His progress that year had been 'slow but undulating'. If he stopped trying to get well and attempted another book he would certainly relapse. Although a cure was unlikely, 'he might well reach a stage at which he could do several hours writing a day combined with physical rest . . . the stage which we call the "good chronic" i.e. able to potter about and do a few hours sedentary work.' His breakdown after Hairmyres he thought almost certainly due to him having 'foolishly over-exercised'.[35] Warburg in turn asked Morland 'how best to handle this difficult patient', and raised the possibility of getting him to a London hospital. He then reported the gist of the consultant's letter to Orwell, holding out the hope that before long he would be able to do several hours' work each day, provided he also took long rests. Then, echoing Morland's note of caution, he added, 'For God's sake don't start working until you are given the all-clear'.[36]

A combination of factors – Morland's encouraging report, the approaching publication of his book, the good advance notices, and perhaps also the impending visit of the lovely Sonia – seem to have brightened him. *Nineteen Eighty-Four* appeared in the bookshops on 8 June, a first edition of 25,575 copies, with further printings of 5000 plus in the following March and August. This was a major publishing event by any measure, and reviews only went to confirm that an important work had been launched, not just onto the literary scene but into the cultural imagination. When Warburg came to see him a few days after publication, he left him in no doubt that earnings from this novel would far outstrip those for *Animal Farm*, would pay off his tax debts, pay for his treatment and still keep him going for the next three years. Suddenly the money mentioned seemed rather more substantial than fairy gold. Warburg questioned him about his next work – a novella of thirty to forty thousand words with a Burmese setting, he was told. But as there was no immediate prospect of that being written, he was pleased to get Orwell's agreement to a new collection of essays for publication in 1950.

The appearance of *Nineteen Eighty-Four* confirmed Orwell as a major British writer, and yet as a novelist he was not particularly well-regarded. The *Spectator*'s reviewer, Robert Kee, considered that it failed as both a satire and a thriller. However, it was 'a remarkable book' marked by 'the passionate force' of Orwell's own feelings.[37] V. S. Pritchett, in a highly perceptive review for the *New Statesman*, dubbed Orwell 'a great pamphleteer' and saw the hand of the religious dissident behind the novel. 'He is like some dour Protestant or Jansenist who sees his faith corrupted by the "doublethink" of the Roman Catholic Church, and who fiercely rejects the corrupt civilizations that appear to be able to flourish even under this dispensation.'[38] The imprimatur of the literary establishment came from Harold Nicolson in the *Observer*. Although he thought much in it taxed the reader's credulity, he found that the 'Inferno atmosphere' was 'cunningly created and well maintained' and found the whole book 'impressive' and Orwell's thesis 'excellent'.[39]

Undoubtedly the cleverest, most subtle review came in the *TLS* from Julian Symons, drawing a significant parallel between *Nineteen Eighty-Four* and *Burmese Days*, and between Winston Smith and John Flory. It pointed, he said, to 'a curious and interesting journey of the mind'. It also revealed the world according to Orwell, showing that one main aspect of the nightmare depicted in the novel reached back from the suffocating world of Airstrip One to the suffocating world of imperial Burma, in both of which 'free speech is unthinkable'. In Winston telling Julia: 'I hate purity, I hate goodness! I don't want any virtue to exist anywhere,' we saw Flory saying, 'Be as degenerate as you can. It all postpones Utopia.' The main difference lay in the level of sophistication with which the argument was put. Although he revealed a schoolboyish side to his character, especially in the melodramatic torture scenes, one reason why the book had force was that Orwell had presented a future that was recognisable. 'Thanks,' he concluded, 'for a writer who deals with the problems of the world rather than the ingrowing pains of individuals.'[40] 'I must thank you for such a brilliant as well as generous review,' wrote Orwell. 'I don't think you could have brought out the sense of the book better in so short a space. You are of course right about the vulgarity of the "Room 101" business. I was aware of this while writing it, but I didn't know another way of getting somewhere near the effect I wanted.'[41]

Not unexpectedly, the book drew a hostile response from the Communist left. In *Reynolds News*, Arthur Calder-Marshall, one of the few Communists who had liked *The Road to Wigan Pier* and praised *Inside the Whale*, wrote an unpleasantly personal attack on Orwell as a cover for rubbishing the book. He derided his middle-class Etonian background, belittled his association with the POUM and sneered at *Animal Farm*, which 'brought him a fortune from reactionaries in this country and the USA'. *Nineteen Eighty-Four* had been awarded Book of the Month by the right-wing *Evening Standard*, and, he predicted, 'will be used as election propaganda by the Tories'. His conclusion underlined the pettiness of the attack. 'The sooner Comrade Orwell assumes the pen-name of Eric Blair, the better. Except, of course, that Mr Blair, ex-Etonian, ex-civil servant, has no literary reputation at all.' This review epitomised just what the book was attacking, and again, it seems, he had hit his target.[42] Too ill now or perhaps not sufficiently perturbed to respond directly, Orwell simply commented, 'The review in Reynolds's was stupid. My feeling when reading it was that if I was going to smear somebody I would do it better than that.'[43] *Pravda* called it 'squalid . . . a filthy book,' which, if he saw it, would probably have pleased him greatly.[44]

The novel's widest immediate impact was in America where it appeared on 13 June. An initial print run of twenty thousand copies was followed by two more, of ten thousand, on 1 July and 7 September. The Book-of-the-Month Club edition would sell close to two hundred thousand over the next three years. The Signet paperback edition, published the following July, sold over three quarters of a million copies, at 35 cents each, over the following eighteen months. *Reader's Digest* also ran an abridgement,[45] and *Life* magazine carried a summary of the story in strip-cartoon form under the sub-headline, 'An Englishman writes a frightening satire about the cruel fate of man in a regimented left-wing police state which controls his mind and soul.' The *New York Daily News* described it as an attack on the British Labour government. Perturbed by this reading, Orwell issued an official denial stating, 'My recent novel is NOT intended as an attack on Socialism or on the British Labour Party (of which I am a supporter) . . .', which in some form was later printed in *Life*. But this misrepresentation was a clear sign of things to come, and the American right chose to ignore the author. He had been recruited to the great Crusade against Communism, and would be turned to their propaganda ends rather than his own.[46]

Reviews reflected the uncertainty about what Orwell intended. Diana Trilling, writing in the *Nation*, represented the book as 'fantasying the fate not only of an already established dictatorship like that of Russia but also that of Labor England'.[47] Daniel Bell in the *New Leader* mentioned the Labour Government's introduction of wage controls and the creation of the

CIA as indications that the world of *Nineteen Eighty-Four* was already present in 1949. A slightly different tack was taken in the *New York Times Book Review* by Mark Schorer. This was no satire, he thought – the horror was too crushing. It was written out of 'Orwell's irritation at many facets of British socialism, and most particularly, trivial as this may seem, at the drab gray pall that life in Britain today has drawn across the civilized amenities of life before the war'. And although he greeted it as 'the most contemporary novel of the year', he equated Orwell's moral unease with his physical condition, failing thereby to understand the author's fundamental asceticism and the real source of his discontent.[48] However, Philip Rahv at the *Partisan Review*, who knew Orwell as well as any American critic, regarded the book as an object-lesson in power especially aimed at fellow-travellers in thrall to Moscow. It was, he declared, 'the best antidote to the totalitarian disease that any writer has so far produced'. He recommended it particularly to 'those liberals who still cannot get over the political superstition that while absolute power is bad when exercised by the Right, it is in its very nature good and a boon to humanity once the Left, that is to say "our people", takes hold of it'.[49] While this reading comes closer to Orwell's intention than most other American reviews, the book had a far wider focus, and was also aimed at the totalitarianism of the right.

Jacintha, who by now had read most of his novels, found *Nineteen Eighty-Four* deeply morbid and, on a visit to her mother found that the Old Lady had read it, too. 'Sunny day,' she wrote in her diary, 'but still she felt cold.' The implication was that the chilling horror of the book had got to her. Jacintha tried to cheer her by showing her one of Orwell's recent letters ending, 'Nothing ever dies', which seemed to lighten the Old Lady's spirits. But she died three days later, and Jacintha associated the book so closely with her mother's death that she never replied. She had also become worried that he might want to resume their relationship where it had left off in 1922, and cannot have been particularly entranced by Winston's sadistic dreams about Julia. And so Eric the FAMOUS AUTHOR and his first muse finally lost touch. He was never to know what she thought of his final novel, although her silence might have told him all he needed to know.

There was a visit from Evelyn Waugh, a letter of admiration from Franz Borkenau, and one from Lawrence Durrell, then British press attaché in Belgrade at the heart of Tito's newly totalitarian Yugoslavia. It was, he said, 'intellectually the bravest book you've done'. Reading it in Communist Yugloslavia was a profound experience because what Orwell described was happening all around – something his left-wing friends refused to recognise.[50] From his old French teacher Huxley came a letter asserting his book's closeness to and difference from his *Brave New World*.[51] And two old girl-friends surfaced in the wake of his new celebrity – Ruth Graves, his

American friend from Paris, wrote a nostalgic letter offering him any help she could in his illness, and Nancy Parratt, his one-time BBC secretary, now married to an American, wrote saying, 'It must be a pretty strange sensation to be quoted so approvingly by men who, a couple of years ago, would have been on very different ground from you. I must say I at least find it strange to see you turning up so often in such respectable places!'[52] She, at least, knew her old boss and recognised his dilemma.

In June Avril brought Richard from Jura. He was lodged at the Whiteways anarchist commune close to Cranham, where he attended school and visited his father in the afternoons. The permissive atmosphere soon rubbed off on him. 'Richard does nothing now but say "Bugger",' he told Symons.[53] Still anxious not to pass his TB on to his son, Orwell had him x-rayed. Fortunately the results were negative.

Sonia, now recruited as Warburg's go-between, visited Orwell on 25 June, his forty-sixth birthday. This, it seems, was the occasion on which Orwell, probably without much hope of success, again proposed to her. No doubt it was the usual Orwellian proposition. 'I'm not much – a physical wreck in fact – but I would not be jealous if you took lovers, and you might find it interesting to be a writer's widow. What is more, there could well be some kind of income from royalties for a few years.' She did not give him an immediate reply, but obviously there was a considerable difference between being proposed to by a modestly successful if not widely known Orwell in 1945, and a man who, if Warburg was to be believed and if the reviews were any guide, was about to be hailed as a great author, and about to become decidedly no longer poor.

No doubt encouraged by her uncertain response, Orwell hinted to Warburg that he might consider remarrying. In his autobiography, *All Authors Are Equal,* Warburg said that Sonia, still undecided about Orwell's proposal, asked his advice, and he 'pointed out some of the pros and cons' of such a marriage. If she had any doubts about Orwell's stature his publisher would have dismissed them utterly. He also offered her an important role in the salvation of a great and distinguished author – that of Ministering Angel, destined perhaps to save the dying genius. 'With me,' said Warburg, 'the feeling was strong that Orwell had a better chance of recovery with a woman he loved to help him.'[54] Strangely, or perhaps not so strangely, she received the very same advice from Warburg's friend, Morland.[55] It was a role which the guilt-ridden Sonia would have found difficult to resist. No doubt to Orwell's complete surprise, on her next visit she said, 'Yes'. Thus they began, for their own quite different motives, what some came to see as a most extraordinary *danse macabre*. She told Ian Angus: 'When George married me he knew exactly what he was taking on. He knew that I would be downstairs knocking back the wine but he knew that at the right time I would appear with some delicious food and he'd be there in striped pyjamas.' But she also said that 'The reasons why George married me are clear; the reasons why I married him are not clear.'

What Warburg told her he did not reveal, but the disadvantages of marrying Orwell must have included the fact that he was about to die, leaving behind a young stepson to be cared for, and that there would be baleful gossip directed at her especially in literary circles. On the other hand, with her job at *Horizon* about to end, being Orwell's widow offered her an entirely new role and status. With his prospects of large earnings she would be guaranteed an income for the foreseeable future, and a share of the literary fame which would undeniably be coming to him. From her point of view the prospect of security and the independence it offered, must have been extremely attractive. And, according to her friend Anne Dunn, she was very much on the rebound from Merleau-Ponty, the only man she ever truly loved.

Taking on a man in Orwell's plight would also satisfy Sonia's strong drive to be a Good Angel, to take up causes and show generosity. As she later told Hilary Spurling, 'He thought if we married he might live longer – how could I refuse?' From Warburg's point of view the advantages of such a match were considerable. Orwell's literary executor, Rees, was now devoting his time to painting and shuttling between Edinburgh and Jura. If he was to capitalise on Orwell's great success, he would need someone closer to hand with whom to deal. In Sonia Brownell he must have thought he had found his answer. Sonia as Orwell's wife would sideline the distant and preoccupied Rees, and so enable him to deal with someone he probably thought could be easily managed. It must have been quickly evident to him that although she was a highly competent and gifted editor, she had no head whatsoever for business. Orwell had specified that certain of his early novels be suppressed. Warburg knew that Orwell's work would now be in great demand, and there would be large profits in republishing everything. Sonia as a wife would be in a very powerful position to persuade him to change his mind.

But there was a problem. Although, after her discussion with Warburg, she returned to Cranham and told Orwell she had decided to accept his proposal, his condition suddenly worsened, and he now thought that in his desperate state marriage was out of the question. It would be better to wait until he was well enough. However, Sonia had made up her mind. She became a frequent visitor to Cranham, and these strange encounters registered with the staff. One of the nurses, Maude Wright, remembered many years afterwards how the emaciated Orwell received 'regular visits from a well-built blonde lady'.[56] There might even have been, as her friend Janetta Kee seemed to think, some sexual encouragement on her part.

The idea that Sonia married Orwell for his money has been strongly denied by her friends, pointing out that there was no big money until the paperback of *Animal Farm* in 1951. However, Warburg undoubtedly advised her, as he had everyone at Secker & Warburg, that there would be very large royalties from *Nineteen Eighty-Four*, certainly enough to live on for three years and perhaps longer (between £10,000 and £15,000 from UK and US sales for that year alone, he had told Orwell – £14,143, as it turned out). And he must have signalled deals in train for *Animal Farm*. Even so, more likely she saw Orwell as a 'cause', someone she could nurture and take care of in his time of need. As the Angel sent to save the great dying writer she could perhaps assuage her guilt over the boy she had left to drown in Switzerland. On a less exalted note, she had vowed to marry a great man, and Orwell was just about to become a FAMOUS AUTHOR. The job of George Orwell's widow offered an attractive alternative to her limited prospects as a *Horizon* editor. Like one of Gissing's literary wives, she could expect in this way to acquire a reputation by association, an intellectual celebrity of the sort she craved.

No one was under any illusion that she loved George, and even Sonia's best friends knew there could be no future in it. He may have been utterly smitten by her, the fantasy woman he had put into his novel, but he cannot have imagined that she reciprocated. It seems that, as before, he made his proposal a sort of business proposition, and certainly Sonia laid down conditions of her own. It was agreed, for example, that Avril, not she, would bring up Richard, and that she would share Orwell's literary executorship with Rees. He was in the process of making a new will, and to make the prospect more attractive, might well have promised to spare her the attentions of importunate biographers after his death. The request in his will for no biography is said to have come as a complete surprise to her and put her under intolerable pressure thereafter. But it seems unlikely that Orwell would not have discussed the matter with her, as he had previously with Rees.

In July he broke the news to David Astor. 'When I am well & about again I intend getting married again. I suppose everyone will be horrified, but it seems to me a good idea. Apart from other considerations, I think I should stay alive longer if I were married & had someone to look after me. It is Sonia Brownell, the sub-editor of "Horizon".'[57] The words echoed Warburg's,[58] and embodied the idea of Sonia as Ministering Angel. He also told Astor that he was considering moving to a sanatorium closer to London in the care of Morland. He mentioned his plans to few others, though on the 27th he dropped a hint to Jack Common, to whom he sent a loan of £50. 'I haven't ever remarried, though I sometimes think I would if I could get some health back.'[59] In August, although he was feeling ghastly, with high temperatures and so weak he could hardly write, Morland told him he was not doing badly. He had noted no deterioration since he last saw him, he said, and suggested he move to University College Hospital. When Orwell raised the question of his marrying again the doctor said he was very much in favour. This hope held out by Warburg and passed on by Sonia and clung to by Orwell, was now being offered by Warburg's friend, the distinguished Morland.

Unaware that Warburg was almost certainly in the know about all this, Orwell broke the news to him on 22 August. 'As I warned you I might do,' he wrote, 'I intend getting married again (to Sonia) when I am once again in the land of the living, if I ever am. I suppose everyone will be horrified, but apart from other considerations I really think I should stay alive longer if I were married.'[60] Warburg quickly expressed delight. He was now in a position to use Sonia to work on Orwell to change his mind about which of his works he would allow to be published. As she told friends later, she and Warburg together persuaded Orwell that the early novels he wanted suppressed should, after all, go into his uniform edition.[61] And she was useful to Warburg in other ways, becoming a very persuasive reason for Orwell to agree to being moved to Morland's University College Hospital, a short walk from her flat in Percy Street, just off the Tottenham Court Road. On 3 September Orwell was taken to London by what he called 'a luxury ambulance' and admitted to a private ward there.

He now came under increasing pressure to get married. Encouraged, no doubt, by the idea that marriage could prolong his life, and by the 'pros' in favour of marrying George which Warburg had spelled out to her, Sonia now took up the running. As he wrote to David Astor on 5 September,

> Sonia . . . thinks we might as well get married while I am still an invalid, because it would give her a better status to look after me if, eg., I went somewhere abroad after leaving here. It's an idea, but I think I should have to feel a little less ghastly than at present before I could even face a registrar for 10 minutes. I am much encouraged by none of my friends or relatives seeming to disapprove of my remarrying, in spite of this disease. I had had an uneasy feeling that 'they' would converge from all directions & stop me, but it hasn't happened.[62]

It was an almost precise echo of what he wrote to Geoffrey Gorer a few days before marrying Eileen in 1936. And so much for his hope that he would not be pressured into going abroad.

Once settled into a new routine (carefully recorded in his notebook), he could hold sickly court for his friends. 'Sonia comes & sees me for an hour every day, & otherwise I am allowed one visitor for 20 minutes,' he told Rees, adding that Sonia was still insisting that as Mrs Eric Blair she would find it easier to help him. Then Warburg (or so Orwell suspected), with Sonia's compliance, decided to act further to push the matter to a conclusion and earn some cheap publicity in the process. The press was informed, and the *Star* and *Daily Mail* both ran stories on it. Orwell was disgusted, and told Rees, 'Someone, I think Fred Warburg, told the press about this [engagement] & there was some rather nasty publicity.'[63] According to the *Star*,

A specialist's verdict will decide whether fair-haired Miss Sonia Brownell, engaged to novelist George Orwell, will have a bedside marriage . . . Miss Brownell told me today: 'If the doctors say he is well enough we shall be married within a few weeks.' Blue-eyed 30-year-old Miss Brownell, assistant editor of the literary magazine 'Horizon', became engaged to Mr Orwell some two months ago but their engagement was not disclosed until today. They have known one another for five years. In her Bedford-square office today Miss Brownell, in a white lace-work blouse and grey flannel skirt, was wearing her Italian engagement ring of ornamental design with rubies, diamonds and an emerald. She had chosen it herself because she thought it pretty. Her hope is that her husband-to-be – his real name is Eric Blair – will be well enough to leave hospital so that they can go abroad early in the new year.[64]

If he did have pause about encouraging future biographies, this kind of thing with Warburg's hand behind it could well have persuaded him. Sonia told friends that this request was the result of his reading Jessie Conrad's *Joseph Conrad as I Knew Him*, which he tossed to her saying, 'Don't ever do that to me!' Of course that does not sound exactly like a request that *no one* write his biography, but a request that *she* never write about him in the cloying way Conrad's wife had written. It could even have been another allusion to the offending newspaper article.

Sonia had broken the news of her impending marriage to her friends Janetta and Robert Kee while staying with them at Philip Toynbee's house on the Isle of Wight. Kee remembered being flabbergasted. 'She suddenly said to me, "Do you know I'm going to marry George?" And I said, "Who, what?" And she said, "I'm going to marry George Orwell." I was absolutely amazed! I mean, it seemed a most extraordinary development, but her ambition was involved.'[65] That ambition, as Frances Partridge noted, was to marry her 'Great Man'.[66] Muggeridge and Powell thought the news 'intriguing'; Connolly is said to have called it 'a grotesque farce', although Francis

Wyndham remembered him actually encouraging her.[67] (Koestler wrote a letter approving the marriage but privately referred to Sonia as 'frigid', 'lesbian' and completely unappreciative of Orwell's work.) Muggeridge saw the patient in early October and found him in 'good form'. Orwell seemed delighted that he and Sonia were to be married by special licence. 'Deathbed marriages,' he said, rather proudly, 'are not very frequent.' Muggeridge's comment was 'George had developed TB in order to be married by a clergyman which otherwise he'd never have had the face to do.'[68] He asked his friends to get him something to wear for the occasion and Powell bought him a crimson smoking jacket.

In a new mood of optimism perhaps, Orwell renewed his annual membership of PEN and registered to vote. On his next visit Muggeridge found him 'more peaceful', though looking 'inconceivably wasted' with 'the appearance of someone who hasn't very long to live – a queer sort of clarity in his expression and elongation of his features . . . his mind still grinding over the same old political questions'. Then Sonia, who disconcerted him by peering in through the window in the door for quite a long time, came in – 'a large, bouncing girl, quite pleasant', he thought.[69]

In the light of the unwelcome press intrusion following his engagement, Orwell was more anxious than ever to keep his marriage quiet. On 11 October he told Moore, 'I am getting married very unobtrusively this week. It will probably be a long time before I can get out of bed, but if I am equal to travelling by the end of the year the doctor suggests that I should spend the worst of the winter abroad, probably in France.'[70] Marriage while he was still so unwell and travel abroad were exactly what he had been against. It must have taken an extremely subtle combination of Warburg, Morland and Sonia to have wrought so complete a change of mind. Of course, he was hardly in a fit condition to resist.

The marriage took place in Room 65, Orwell's private room in University College Hospital on 13 October. William Braine, the hospital chaplain, conducted them through the Anglican marriage service. David Astor was best man, Sonia's friend Janetta Kee was bridesmaid, and her husband Robert gave the bride away. Janetta found the whole ceremony quite distressing. 'I could hardly watch them being married and I just stared at the bottle of champagne which I supposed we would drink afterwards. It was awfully moving.'[71] According to David Astor, Orwell, although looking like a survivor of Auschwitz, seemed in good spirits; indeed, Janetta remembered him having 'a huge smile on his face'. 'He was,' said Robert Kee, 'obviously potty about Sonia'. As a symbol of hope his fishing rod stood at the foot of the bed. The story of him wearing the crimson smoking jacket could not be verified. Most likely it had not appealed to the bride and had been discarded for the occasion. As an ironic literary footnote, Somerset Maugham, so admired by Orwell, and once himself a TB patient, had written the scene into a short story, 'Sanatorium', about a tubercular marrying on his deathbed. In that story, however, the doctor warns the prospective groom, 'If you get married you'll be dead in six months.'[72]

After that glass of champagne, members of the wedding party were taken by David Astor for lunch at the Ritz, where they were joined by Celia, her sister Mamaine and Robert Kee's publishing partner, James McGibbon. Evelyn Waugh, ever the gossip, sent one of his cryptic postcards to neighbours who knew Orwell: 'Brownell x Blair last Wed in hospital./D. Astor gave bride luncheon leaving groom./Rev. Brain protestant vicar St Pancras officiated./Not asked to luncheon.'[73] Celia, who knew them both, could not imagine any future for the marriage. He had, thought Fyvel, married 'a fantasy'.[74] Frances Partridge, who immediately afterwards found the Kees much moved by the occasion, wrote a few days later, 'Many people regard the Orwell marriage cynically . . . I see it principally as a neurotic one, for a marriage to a bed-ridden and perhaps dying man is as near as no marriage at all as it's possible to get.'[75] Two weeks later the demise of *Horizon* was officially announced.[76]

Anthony Powell reported Orwell 'immensely cheered' by his marriage, and in better form in his hospital room than he had ever known him. 'Sitting up in bed now, he had an unaccustomed epicurean air.' He said that he was sure that one could not die when one had a book inside one, and he had more than one.[77] He told Muggeridge he had five. Two weeks later it looked as if Sonia's angelic ministrations might be having their effect. Writing to Fyvel, thanking him for wedding gifts, he sounded optimistic: 'I am getting along pretty well . . . [and] . . . I enjoy my food very much more than I did, which makes a great difference.'[78] But whatever cause for optimism Morland had given him, privately the doctors knew – and had known since he was admitted – that there was no hope for him.[79] They did not even visit him regularly.

Sonia and George had more in common than meets the eye. Both were lonely, both felt isolated in a hostile world, both were in conflict with their origins and struggled to affirm their individualism, both were critical of the inward-looking tradition of British art and in their own ways looked towards Europe. They shared a deep hostility towards Catholicism no doubt giving them a strong sense of shared understanding. George, still imaginatively in thrall to his childhood, must have certainly recognised the vulnerable child in Sonia. After all, he was at his best with children. But she was also beautiful and intelligent, the sort of woman he found most attractive, and a highly efficient and proven editor. He felt sure that she would be more than capable of handling his literary affairs. He also believed that she would manage his financial affairs with equal efficiency. Undoubtedly she had a certain competence in literary matters, though inclined to depend for advice on others – Warburg, Muggeridge and Fyvel to begin with, Geoffrey Gorer, her agents Cyrus Brooks and Mark Hamilton, and Ian Angus, her co-editor of Orwell's non-fiction, later on. On the financial side, she kept from Orwell the fact that she knew nothing about business and hated dealing with money. However, there, at least, she had the reassurance that his finances were in the hands of an accountant he approved. A meeting of George Orwell Productions took place in Orwell's hospital room on 23 November. Sonia was given a share in the company and a place on the board, of which Jack Harrison, Orwell's accountant, also became a member.

Orwell's reading during these last months of his life reflects a mind infused with a sense of nostalgia and also of an ending to his own story. Just after Sonia's first visit to Cranham he read Maugham's *The Razor's Edge*, the opening paragraph of which reads: 'Death ends all things and so is the comprehensive conclusion of a story, but marriage finishes it very properly too and the sophisticated are ill-advised to sneer at what is by convention termed a happy ending. It is a sound instinct of the common people which persuades them that with this all that needs to be said is said.'[80] Death, of course, was now his ever-present familiar, marriage was meant in some strange way to replace it. He reread Poe's stories – all of them. At times he appears to have been consciously reliving his schooldays. He read a humorous novel by Cyril Alington, his old Eton headmaster, and Connolly's *Enemies of Promise*, with its evocative chapters on Eton and St Cyprian's; he reread Compton Mackenzie's *Sinister Street* over which he and Connolly had been punished by Flip Wilkes; he read two novels by Henry Green, the youngest brother of Philip Yorke whom he thought he had caused to die as a Colleger at Eton. The past was always a powerful presence in Orwell's mind – the source of unforgotten terrors, guilt feelings and resentments. It was also the country from which he felt his greatest sense of exile.

Stephen Spender thought their marriage had produced a strange effect on Sonia. 'I think that her own sense of her virginity has in some way been outraged, despite the fact that George was in hospital. Also she found herself incapable of really loving him, even for the short period of a few weeks before he died. Perhaps she found a whole lifetime of demands being made on her in the few days she had with him – demands which she sometimes refused.' She kept urging Spender to visit George in hospital, which he only managed to do twice. On one of these visits they were discussing one of Morland's earlier patients.

> She came in at about six, and found George talking to me about the death of D. H. Lawrence. George said that D. H. Lawrence died because his philosophy of life had become absolutely untenable. The proof of

this was that one could not imagine Lawrence having any plausible attitude towards events if he were living today. 'Oh, do let's stop talking about this. Let's talk about something cheerful,' said Sonia, suddenly like a bossy hospital nurse. Then she explained that she had to go to a cocktail party, and would not be back that evening. Orwell protested faintly, but she put him off, in her bustling way.[81]

Muggeridge noted something similar. 'Sonia . . . had immediately developed that trait which Tony and I considered characteristic of most matrimonial relationships – i.e. envy rather than jealousy, of her husband. When George's supper was brought in, she said that, after all, he had a wonderful life, waited on hand and foot compared with her struggles with Connolly's bad temper at the offices of *Horizon*.'

His fundamental despondency was captured in his comment to Muggeridge that 'health and beauty' were essential to the good life and that old people should be allowed to commit suicide.[82] He himself was certainly looking very old before his time and by November was losing weight again. He worried about his looks – his false teeth, his greying hair, his 'death's head'. Now he needed glasses for reading. (It was in his last notebook around this time that he wrote, 'At fifty everyone has the face he deserves.') Dr Nicholson, the junior consultant to Morland, noticed how old and wizened he looked sitting out in a chair in the corner of his room.[83] Muggeridge found him 'shrunken and waxen' – the nurses were having difficulty giving him penicillin injections because he had too little meat on his bones for the needle. On Christmas Day he and Powell found him looking 'rather deathly and wretched alone, with Christmas decorations all round'. He talked hopefully about going to Switzerland, but 'there was also a kind of rage in his expression, as though the approach of death made him furious' and 'all the while the stench of death was in the air, like autumn in a garden'.[84] Perhaps he now knew what the more hard-headed doctors already knew. Miracle cures via Switzerland or marriage were illusions.[85]

It was, of course, a profound irony that at the very moment of his sudden celebrity he was sliding towards death in such a wrecked condition. Warburg had been right. He and Orwell, as well as Sonia, knew that he was potentially worth more than any fairy gold imaginable. In America alone *Nineteen Eighty-Four* sold hugely by any standards. It would go on to became one of the all-time best-sellers which by 1970 had sold in excess of eight million copies.[86] In 1984, perhaps unsurprisingly, it topped the US best-seller list. And that was only part of the story.

As the wife of the celebrated George Orwell, Sonia was suddenly something of a celebrity herself. Just after Christmas the distinguished literary editor and critic Desmond MacCarthy wrote to Orwell to say that he considered him 'among the few memorable writers of your generation' who had left 'an indelible mark in English literature'.[87] Finding him too ill to receive visitors, he took Sonia to lunch instead.

Shortly after he had moved from Cranham, George had been persuaded to go to Switzerland – the very place he had hoped he would not be urged to go because he thought the journey would kill him. His decisions to transfer to Morland and marry Sonia were proving expensive. He had worried about the cost of treatment at Cranham; at UCH his fees were higher. Now he had been talked into going to Switzerland, no doubt at even greater expense, and to go by a privately chartered plane and take Anne Dunn's boyfriend Lucian Freud along, too – to help carry him, it was said. The cost of all that would have been astronomical from his point of view. And on top of that he had spent out on what seemed an expensive engagement ring for Sonia.[88] What had happened to turn him from the parsimonious invalid at Cranham, reconciled to a quiet life in Brighton, into the spendthrift ready to roar off to Switzerland with a young woman who did not love him and a young artist he barely knew, can only be imagined. Morland, of course, considered the Swiss climate beneficial, but it might have been thought a place with painful memories for Sonia. No doubt George Orwell Productions coughed up a bonus or two to cover all these unanticipated costs.

That Orwell, the now-famous socialist author of *Animal Farm* and *Nineteen Eighty-Four*, was seriously ill was by this time widely known. On 6 January a letter was sent from the Prime Minister's address, 10 Downing Street, to George Orwell Esq., in the Private Wing, University College Hospital, Gower Street, London W1. Only the envelope has survived, but it looks very likely that Clement Attlee, the Labour leader, sent him a letter wishing him well. Orwell had once written in his diary, 'Attlee reminds me of nothing so much as a recently dead fish, before it has had time to stiffen,'[89] a suitably piscatorial image from a dedicated angler. Now it was Orwell, not Attlee, who was at death's door.

When Stafford Cottman rang and asked to see him, Orwell told him it would be better for him not to – he looked like a skeleton. Cottman was puzzled because he sounded so hale and hearty. Inez and Celia, who did get to see him, found him reading Dante's *Divine Comedy*, preparing himself perhaps for yet another adventure, this time into some 'dark wood'. One unexpected visitor was his old Eton tutor Andrew Gow, who 'happened to be in London' and thought he would just call in. Avril brought Richard to see him but he grew so excited that the nurses became worried about him.[90] And when another visitor, an old LDV comrade, Denzil Jacobs, dropped in, Orwell told him directly that he expected to die at any time.[91] But his mind remained lucid and his interest in current affairs undimmed. As he had once written, 'It is profoundly interesting to know what the mind can still contain in the face of apparently certain death.'[92] Throughout his adult life he had rejected the idea of life after death, and much of his moral enquiry had been directed to the question of why should we behave decently if this is the only life.[93] Now, on the brink of death, he began to speculate hopefully that there was, after all, some form of continuity beyond the grave. During those final months he told many of his friends that with a book inside you you never really died,[94] and he had told Jacintha, 'Nothing ever dies.'

The awareness of death and the need to get his affairs in order no doubt led to the calling of a meeting of George Orwell Productions on 17 January when one share was transferred to Harrison, the accountant. On the 18th he signed his last will and testament, witnessed by a nurse and his solicitor. The following day Muggeridge dropped in to wish him goodbye before he left for Switzerland. In his diary he wrote, 'Doubt very much if I'll ever see him again. He looked at his last gasp.' Harrison returned on the 20th with papers for George to sign. In the course of that meeting, he claimed, George agreed to his being allocated twenty-four more shares, giving him 25 per cent in all, and becoming the company's business manager rather than simply its accountant. Sonia, it appears, left this meeting early and was unaware of all this, something which would come back to haunt her years later. That same day, Celia rang and arranged to see George the following Monday before he left on the Tuesday, and that evening Paul Potts visited, looked into the room, saw Orwell was asleep and left rather than disturb him. He was set to transfer to a sanatorium at Montana Vermala just south-east of Gstaad.[95] But it was not to be. The following morning at around two-thirty he died of a massive haemorrhage; an artery in the damaged walls of his lungs had ruptured and he was suffocated.

He did not die, as he had once feared he might, poverty-stricken in a public ward like the one in Paris where he had envisioned his own death. He died a newly wealthy man in a private ward of one of London's great teaching hospitals in the care of one of the country's most eminent lung specialists. But his death was deeply tragic in its timing. He was in need of strepto-mycin only a year or so before a means of dealing with the side effects was discovered. He died five years before research revealed how damaging smoking was to the lungs. He died before he had the opportunity to enjoy his wealth – it was indeed 'fairy gold' as far as he was concerned, never quite within his reach.

Sonia had arrived back at her Percy Street flat from the hospital the night before, according to her friend Anne Dunn, and she and Lucian

Freud, who were dining at a small nightclub across the street, saw her return and called her over to join them. They sat up through most of the night, discussing the impending trip to Switzerland, so Sonia was not there when the hospital first telephoned. When she learned of George's death early next morning, she was deeply distressed. Janetta remembered her being 'distraught', saying that when she hurried round to the hospital she found his bed unmade and the bedclothes still blood-soaked. There was, of course, also remorse at having, as she thought, let him down when his need was greatest. She may well have shared his hope, confirmed to her by Morland, that marrying her would prolong his life, but he had died suddenly and alone just three months into the marriage. The Ministering Angel had failed to save another who had drowned before help came. No wonder she was both devastated and guilt-stricken.

Morland signed his death certificate giving cause of death as 'Pulmonary Tuberculosis'. Sonia duly informed the authorities. On his certificate of marriage to her he had styled himself 'author', on his death certificate she entered him as 'writer'. At this point she was said not to think very highly of his work, probably not even having read much of it; perhaps the subtle shift in designation indicated this.

Orwell shared the same death date as Lenin, Gorky, Lytton Strachey, George Moore, a novelist he once compared to Gissing, and Cecil B. de Mille, whose Hollywood he despised. And he shared a similar early death from tuberculosis with Keats, Stevenson, Gissing, Lawrence and Katherine Mansfield. He and Gissing died at almost exactly the same age.

Muggeridge was not surprised to hear that George was dead, but saddened because he knew how much he had wanted to live. He was, he wrote, 'a curious character' combining 'intense romanticism with a dry interest in some of the dreariest aspects of life', and he recalled Hugh Kingsmill saying that he sounded like 'a gate swinging on rusty hinges' and 'he only wrote sympathetically about human beings when he regarded them as animals', as in *Animal Farm*. Even so, he thought there was something 'very lovable and sweet' about Orwell, whose writing, like Graham Greene's, expressed 'in an intense form some romantic longing'.[96] Inez, who heard the news on the radio just before an election broadcast by Churchill, wrote, 'Although I saw George only three weeks ago and thought he had not much chance of recovering, yet I was desperately sad and upset. I thought back on all the time we had spent together . . . and my many discussions with Eileen and our lives during the war and George's rather heroic attitude to life . . . Although I thought he would die yet the whole thing came as a shock.'[97] Evelyn Waugh was characteristically cynical, writing to Nancy Mitford: 'G. Orwell is dead and Mrs Orwell presumably a rich woman . . . Will Cyril [Connolly] marry her?'[98]

He had specified in his will that he should be buried (not cremated) in the nearest convenient cemetery according to the rites of the Church of England. Cremation had repelled him ever since witnessing a Hindu funeral in Burma.[99] The problem was that most London graveyards were full, so David Astor undertook the arrangements. His local vicar at Cliveden, the Astors' ancestral home, refused him on the grounds that Orwell was an unbeliever, so he approached the vicar of Sutton Courtenay in Oxfordshire, where he was a regular worshipper. Gordon Dunstan, the incumbent, was cautious enough first to get the approval of his churchwardens. One, a farmer, he persuaded by showing a copy of *Animal Farm*. Muggeridge commented sardonically: 'George died on Lenin's birthday [he meant death-day], and is being buried by the Astors, which seems to cover the full range of his life.'[100]

It was decided that a funeral service be held in London, which Powell and Muggeridge would organise. Astor arranged for it to take place at Christ Church in Albany Street, where he knew the vicar, William Rose. Powell was to choose the Bible readings. The day before the event, Muggeridge and Powell had Sonia to lunch and found her in a very poor way. 'Felt sorry for her but not sympathetic,' wrote Muggeridge. 'We wondered what [she] would now do with herself. Tony said that she was "a painter's girl". I saw what he meant.'[101]

The day of the funeral was overcast and rainy, lending the occasion a gloomy aspect. John Carter, an Etonian contemporary of Orwell's, remembered Warburg standing at the church door welcoming the arrivals as if to a grand literary occasion, saying, 'How good of you to come.'[102] The congregation was a strange, heterogeneous assemblage, mostly comprising unbelievers and Jews, for whom the Anglican funeral service meant little. A children's choir from Notting Hill had been brought in for the occasion, but the hymn-singing was rather ragged and Mr Rose, who officiated, was rather rattled by the apparent lack of piety. Muggeridge found it 'a rather melancholy and chilly affair'. Warburg and his family had taken the front pew and behind that 'a row of shabby-looking relatives of George's first wife, whose grief seemed to me practically the only real element in the whole affair'. The coffin-bearers, thought Muggeridge, looked 'remarkably like Molotov's bodyguard' and the sight of the long coffin, reminding everyone of George's height, was very moving and poignant.[103] The occasion struck Powell slightly differently. As well as the readings he had chosen the hymns – 'All people that on earth do dwell', 'Guide me, O thou great Redeemer', and 'Ten thousand times ten thousand'. 'The Lesson was from Ecclesiastes, the grinders in the streets, the grasshopper a burden, the silver cord loosed, the wheel broken at the cistern.' For some reason he found it 'one of the most harrowing [funerals] I have ever attended'.[104]

Orwell's niece, Jane, there with Avril, Humphrey and Aunt Nellie, thought it an odd and inappropriate funeral for George – pompous, formal, unsubtle and dark. According to her the family were highly suspicious of the woman who had married him on his deathbed. As she recalled it, 'We were very scandalised with Eric suddenly upping and marrying Sonia, because nobody had really ever heard of her, and he hadn't written to Avril and said, "I'm thinking of getting married"; it was just a bolt from the blue. [She] more or less totally and utterly ignored us. I don't think she realised that Eric had any sort of family at all. But she was very upset at the funeral – lots of mascara running and weeping and so on. I mean, she must have known that he was very very ill but it's still a shock, isn't it?'[105] Afterwards there was a wake at Powell's house in Regent's Park.

The Anglican funeral service was scrupulously observed, which means that Orwell had two funerals. The funeral of George Orwell, attended by a large if disparate congregation, took place in Christ Church in Albany Street, and merited a paragraph in *The Times*. The funeral of Eric Blair, with just four people and the pall-bearers present, took place in the quiet village of Sutton Courtenay, and passed unnoticed by all papers, local and national. Gordon Dunstan also followed the strict order of the Anglican Burial Service from the Prayer Book and Eric Blair was duly interred in an English churchyard, in the manner requested.

There is something strangely symbolic about his final resting place. He was buried in the Thames Valley where he had spent the Golden Age of his childhood, laid to rest between Herbert Asquith, the great Liberal Prime Minister who took Britain into the First World War, and a family of local gypsies – taking in the compass range of his whole being: the Edwardian liberal on the one hand and the travellers and hop-pickers on the other. Symbolically, too, inside the beautiful medieval church, there was a magnificent fifteenth-century frieze representing St George and the Dragon. In 1931 he had told Brenda Salkeld, 'If I ever get time to compose my epitaph I shall take care to make it an amusing one. Funerals also ought to be comic . . . I mean death would cease to be horrible if one could see it as something funny.'[106] He did get time to compose it, but in the event there was no attempt at humour. Death had been too close to laugh at any more. The stone was inscribed simply, 'Eric Blair 1903–1950'. On the plot, at his request, a single Polyantha rose was planted to match the one he had planted for Eileen. David Astor marked their great friendship by planting a grove of yew trees in the churchyard in his honour, and instructed his gardener to tend to the plot from time to time.

It is somehow appropriate that Eric Blair should be buried obscurely while George Orwell lives on. It is strange to note that again, following the formal shape of his novels, he had come full circle. Having broken free from religion as a schoolboy, and lived his life as an atheist, faced with the inevitability of death he found himself, figuratively at least, back in the arms of the Anglican Church, for which the old affection lingered.

Strange coincidences marked his passing. On the day he was buried, India was declared a republic. Within a month the Attlee government would suffer a major electoral set-back. Both were prophetic failures for Orwell. One – an India fully independent of Britain, which he thought impossible, had been born; the other – the onward march of socialism, which he had thought unstoppable – was about to be checked and would in time be turned back.

His will remains a mystery. Did Orwell really want to be an UNPERSON, like Winston Smith, a man without a past who had never existed? It seems unlikely that he wanted to do Big Brother's work and have himself air-brushed from literary history. But if what he wrote in his will had been adhered to that might have been the fate of the obscured Eric Blair, and the invented George Orwell would have been known solely through his work. However, any biographer in pursuit of George Orwell will be led inevitably to disinter Eric Blair. The alternative would be to take Dorian Gray or Dr Jekyll at face value.

He did once say that 'one of the most difficult problems of a writer's life [is] the conflict between the literary and the private personality', and with him at times that difficulty clearly became acute. In putting his affairs in order, he had to arrange for the disposal of both characters. George Woodcock wrote, 'From what I remember of Orwell . . . he felt that though Blair would die, Orwell might not. The private man would be no more; the literary personality could carry on, sustained on the wings of his own creation.'[107]

What of E. A. Blair, the FAMOUS AUTHOR and the uniform edition he had dreamed of in the Golden Age of his youth? The Golden Age had gone and so, to all intents and purposes, had E. A. Blair. The uniform edition, launched with the reprint of *Coming Up For Air* in 1948 and projected in detail in his 'Notes to My Literary Executor', would stand as the epitaph to the FAMOUS George Orwell while the wretched, guilt-ridden and disease-ridden Blair would lie in an inconspicuous grave in an obscure churchyard, disposed of and long forgotten. He cannot have believed this entirely because he would have known that biographies would be written, and he preserved notebooks, diaries, a mountain of correspondence, and wrote autobiographical essays with some such possibility in mind.

He died just short of his 'most detestable month' of February, as if not wanting to experience another. It is ironic that in an article published exactly four years earlier, he had written, 'The most recent figures of deaths from tuberculosis . . . are the lowest ever recorded.' Technically of course it may not have been the tuberculosis that killed him, but without it he would certainly have lived.

Aunt Nellie outlived her nephew by exactly five months, dying in June 1950 aged seventy-nine and George Kopp soon followed, dying in Marseilles of a heart attack in 1951. Avril married Bill Dunn and died aged seventy in 1978. Brenda died in 2000 aged ninety-eight and Mabel Fierz lived to be a hundred. Richard did not go to Westminster but to the Scottish public school near Edinburgh which Bill Dunn had attended, and went on to a career as a farmer and then a farm equipment salesman. To that extent the Blair dynasty Orwell would like to have produced himself continued, but his personal heritage, of course, resides in his work.

Chapter 20

Life After Death

'Death cancels everything but truth; and strips a man of everything but genius and virtue. It is a sort of natural canonisation.'

Hazlitt, 'The Spirit of the Age'

It is perhaps a truism to say that biography begins at the moment of death – 'In our end is our beginning.' But death means that, whatever a person of consequence may instruct in a will, however many manuscripts, letters and diaries are burnt, attempts will be made to reconstruct that person's life from public documents, carefully saved letters, memoirs (however conflicting) and other biographical traces scattered in his or her wake. Biography is a means of resurrecting the dead, of making them available to be pilloried or admired, a means of identifying a past life with present lives and learning something from the re-creative process. Often, keepers of the flame, literary widows such as Sonia Orwell, believe that a biography will damage a writer's reputation, unaware that most people are well able to distinguish between what Orwell called a writer's 'literary persona' and 'private personality'. Learning that Céline was a Nazi collaborator should not mean that readers cannot enjoy the power of his prose; as Orwell himself acknowledged, knowing that Dickens acted atrociously towards his wife takes nothing away from the delight he affords most readers; discovering that Orwell had a sadistic side, pounced on women and on occasions paid for sex when the urge came upon him, matters little to those who are drawn to the writer of genius who turned political writing into an art. Orwell himself recognised this when he wrote about the lives of Stendhal, Melville, Dickens, Dali and Pound. Dali was 'a disgusting human being' but at the same time a great draughtsman.[1] Pound disseminated evil anti-Semitic ideas but he is still generally considered a great poet.[2]

Posthumous biography, of course, begins with the obituary. Orwell had condemned *The Times* for its mean-minded, censorious obituaries of both

Lawrence and Joyce, but could hardly have complained about the one they ran for him, which began,

> Mr George Orwell, a writer of acute and penetrating temper and of conspicuous honesty of mind, died on Friday in hospital in London at the age of 46. Though he made his widest appeal in the form of fiction, Orwell had a critical rather than imaginative endowment of mind and he has left a large number of finely executed essays. In a less troubled, less revolutionary period of history he might perhaps have discovered within himself a richer and more creative power of imagination, a deeper philosophy of acceptance. As it was he was essentially the analyst, by turns indignant, satirical and prophetic, of an order of life and society in rapid dissolution. The analysis is presented to a large extent, in autobiographical terms; Orwell, it might fairly be said, lived his convictions. Much of his early work is a direct transcription of personal experience, while the later volumes record, in expository or allegorical form, the progressive phases of his disenchantment with current social and political ideals. The death of so searching and sincere a writer is a very real loss.[3]

The *Observer* obituary came from Arthur Koestler, who said, 'To meet one's favourite author in the flesh is mostly a disillusioning experience. George Orwell was one of the few writers who looked and behaved exactly as the reader expected him to look and behave . . . The urge of genius and the promptings of common sense can rarely be reconciled; Orwell's life was a victory of the former over the latter.'[4] Stephen Spender called him 'an Innocent, a kind of English Candide of the twentieth century . . . He was perhaps the least Etonian character who has ever come from Eton.'[5] Bertrand Russell was more guarded. 'He preserved an impeccable love of truth, and allowed himself to learn even the most painful lessons. But he lost hope. This prevented him from being a prophet for our time.'[6] E. M. Forster was appreciative of Orwell's great courage as both a man and a writer. 'We part company with a man who has been determined to see what he can of this contradictory world and to follow its implications into the unseen – and anyhow to follow them round the corner.'[7] And V. S. Pritchett famously called him 'the wintry conscience of a generation' and 'an Old School Tie [who] had "gone native" in his own country'.[8] In a mostly factual obituary in the *New York Times*, a widespread American misconception was at least corrected. 'Although many reviewers read into Mr Orwell's novel [*Nineteen Eighty-Four*] a wholesale condemnation of left-wing politics, he considered himself a Marxist and member of the non-Communist left wing of the British Labor Party.'[9]

The deeply cynical Malcolm Muggeridge felt sufficiently detached to see in these various tributes the creation of a legend. For example, to say that Orwell was not given to self-pity, he wrote, was simply false. 'It was of course his dominant emotion.'[10] The legend of Saintly George, however, would survive for many years, diligently defended by his over-protective widow, and promoted by the ideologists who had conscripted Orwell to their Cold War cause.[11]

Orwell's reputation certainly benefited from the advent of the Cold War, guaranteeing him a huge readership throughout the world. (A recent estimate puts sales of *Animal Farm* and *Nineteen Eighty-Four* in excess of forty million sold in sixty different translations.)[12] (Behind the Iron Curtain it is said that Communist leaders took it as a blueprint of how to run their oppressive domains, while dissidents were amazed to find that Orwell had never been to Eastern Europe and experienced at first hand the system he described so vividly.)[13] And yet his reputation has survived the Cold War and he still seems to speak to us today. He cannot therefore be written off solely as a lucky beneficiary of world events. Even if we discount the rhetorical claims about Orwell the Saint, the warrior for truth, the conscience of his generation, he has to be recognised as a significant moralist, concerned above all to find a morality suitable for a post-Christian age. When he claimed that all hope rested with the proles, it was because he saw the working class as a repository of the old 'decencies' – Christian morality minus the dogma. He was also a visionary who directed us towards the wider picture – the kestrel-eye view of systems, to show who benefits and who suffers from them – and to point to the great threat of politics and science devoid of morality. If his message was pessimistic it was because he wanted to warn of dangers ahead.

Three weeks after Orwell was buried, Muggeridge and Tosco Fyvel went with Sonia to discuss with Fredric Warburg the future publication of his work. The meeting, at which Warburg presided, agreed that the next George Orwell book should be a collection of essays to be called *Shooting An Elephant* – his idea, according to Muggeridge.[14] Sonia's part in the discussion was not recorded. Richard Rees, it seems, although named as joint literary executor in Orwell's will was not present. What Sonia was not to know was that Muggeridge and Fyvel, through their wartime intelligence work, had contacts with the CIA, and shortly afterwards, with Warburg, would be involved in the CIA-backed Congress for Cultural Freedom, which was busily recruiting the non-Communist left for its anti-Soviet propaganda war. (Koestler was an early and much-valued recruit.) To members of the Congress *Animal Farm* and *Nineteen Eighty-Four* were valuable Cold War ammunition. Later Warburg would become even more involved with this shadowy organisation when he published and distributed *Encounter* magazine secretly funded by the CIA. With these influential advisers helping Sonia decide what happened to Orwell's work from early on, it is not difficult to see how decisions were made which served the interests of Secker and Warburg, and the ideological aims of her three advisers, as much as the literary estate, and affected the author's reputation.

Orwell's two last novels soon became weapons in the hands of anti-Communist defenders of capitalism opposed to even the democratic socialism for which he himself stood. The fate of these two books at the hands of CIA-backed Hollywood production companies, which Frances Stonar Saunders exposed in her book *Who Paid the Piper?*,[15] has been blamed on Sonia. She has been charged with allowing his works to be mis-represented in the service of the right-wing Cold War cause, while all the time it appears that Warburg and others were guiding her in that direction. Orwell himself had been alive to these dangers and would have avoided them, as he had in standing up to the Book-of-the-Month Committee and complaining about the misrepresentation of *Nineteen Eighty-Four* in *Life* magazine. But Sonia was politically naive and, once film rights were sold, control of any resulting script and film would have been out of her hands.

In her book, Stonar Saunders notes that Warburg took a close interest in the screenplays of both *Animal Farm* and *Nineteen Eighty-Four*.[16] This seems to point to his hand being somewhere in the deal with Howard Hunt, the CIA man who bought the film rights of the former from Sonia shortly after Orwell's death, and helped set up the first film production of the latter. It is not possible to verify the story that she agreed to sell the rights of *Animal Farm* in return for a meeting with her favourite film star, Clark Gable – possibly Sonia's joke, her friends think. Warburg's main purpose would have been the effect of the huge film publicity on his sales (in 1954 he published an edition of *Animal Farm* with illustrations from the CIA-backed Halas & Bachelor cartoon), though he had also come to commit himself to the Cold War offensive, and was fully aware of the true funding behind *Encounter*. Later, Sonia quarrelled with Warburg, but at the outset of her literary executorship (from which Rees seems to have been simply excluded either by the 'bustling' Sonia or the calculating Warburg) she must have put her trust in the publisher's judgement and that of advisers such as Fyvel and Muggeridge.

Inevitably, the takeover of the film rights of Orwell's last two books pro-duced movies tailored to ideological ends. In the cartoon version of *Animal Farm* the banquet at which the pigs become indistinguishable from their human oppressors was changed. Orwell's pessimistic intention was thereby obscured and the message that the tyrannical Stalinist pigs are no different from the cruel capitalist farmers was lost. In the Hollywood *Nineteen*

Eighty-Four the pessimistic conclusion – that Winston, the spark of individualism snuffed out, is reduced to loving Big Brother and awaiting the bullet in the back of the neck – was again replaced by the optimistic message that the individual is uncrushable, and Winston dies with the cry of 'Down with Big Brother!' on his lips. Among the critics who damned the cartoon *Animal Farm* when it appeared was David Sylvester, Orwell's old *Tribune* contributor, who called it 'a failure aesthetically, imaginatively and intellectually . . . The essential weakness of the film lies, not in the realisation of detail . . . but in its wilful misinterpretation of Orwell's central intention.'[17] The right-wing press, on the other hand, was mostly encomiastic. To her credit, when Sonia saw the *Animal Farm* film at a Hollywood preview, she hated it and blocked an attempt later to make it available to schools and colleges.[18] Francis Wyndham remembers her being very bitter about it and feeling that once again she had let George down.[19]

The request in Orwell's will for no biography came to haunt Sonia and bring her much grief. She gained a bad reputation for frustrating scholarship, especially among prospective biographers. Even before George's death, her impatience with biographical enquiries is evident in her abrupt note to Yvonne Davet who had requested a few details about him for an article she was writing. 'As for your article,' she wrote, 'he has absolutely nothing interesting to say about his life . . . '[20] That is the voice of Sonia rather than George. He had never been reticent in providing details about himself and, had he been well and in control of his own life, would have readily supplied what Davet wanted. As to 'nothing interesting to say about his life', he had spent most of his writing career saying things about himself in his heavily autobiographical books and in a number of important autobiographical essays, notably 'Such, Such Were the Joys' and 'Why I Write'. Time and again he wrote approvingly of literary biographies. In 1946, for example, he wrote, 'Polarisations, selections, anthologies, and critical biographies, treacherous and misleading as they frequently are, are necessary if one wants to be reasonably well informed.'[21] He enjoyed reviewing biographies, thought biographies valuable in understanding writers and their work, offered himself to write at least one biography (of Mark Twain), and was deeply fascinated by the biographies of the writers he admired – Baudelaire, Swift and Dickens. He called for definitive lives of Conan Doyle and Conrad to be written, willingly supplied information to a biographer of L. H. Myers, and made efforts to have Trotsky's biography of Stalin published in Britain. He was even prepared to read aspects of an author's biography directly from his fiction – seeing Pip's attitude towards Magwitch in *Great Expectations* as 'obviously the attitude of Dickens himself'.[22] (It is curious that in Winston Smith Orwell produced an anti-biographer – a man whose job it is to falsify the past partly in order either to discredit Unpersons or render them invisible to history.)

Despite that final request for no biography, there is no evidence of such a provision in earlier wills, and no mention of this in his March 1945 'Notes for my Literary Executor'. On that very question, he wrote to his first literary executor, Rees, in 1946, leaving him to decide who might be a suitable biographer and allowed to see his letters and papers. He also told Rees that he intended leaving a list of dates and places to assist the person chosen. And he made no effort to destroy letters, diaries and notebooks, as a genuine biography-hater (a Kafka or a Philip Larkin) would have done. More likely, his final will was the outcome of some agreement with Sonia – among the conditions on which she agreed to marry him. This would have been quite characteristic of the man who, after Eileen's death, approached a number of young women with offers of marriage sounding more like proposals for company mergers than unions of heart, mind and body. She seems to have intimated to Tosco Fyvel that she had discussed the contents of this will with him when he was drawing it up. It appears to have been agreed that Sonia would share the literary executorship with Rees, and that she would not be expected to care for Richard. She was, however, quite eager, it seems, to take on the role of literary widow, but it would no doubt have been on her own terms. Not to have to face pressures from biographers would have seemed a reasonable demand in the circumstances. She is said to have been determined that this provision in the will be respected at all costs and his papers defended from invading biographers. She told her agent that even if a biographer were appointed she would never talk to him about George. There was an early enquiry from Woodcock, and seemingly from Julian Symons, but she fended them off by appointing Malcolm Muggeridge (with whom at some point she seems to have become emotionally entangled) as Orwell's 'official' biographer. Privately she said that she considered him too slothful ever to finish the job, and in this case her judgement proved sound. After a few years of gathering material in a desultory fashion, Muggeridge, true to form, grew bored and gave up.[23] One of Sonia's friends thinks it foundered when her relationship with Muggeridge ended.[24]

In the fifties would-be Orwell biographers such as Christopher Hollis, Lawrence Brander and John Atkins were thus restricted to writing memoirs or critical works. While these enhanced Orwell's reputation at home, some were highly sceptical, perhaps recognising that he was being boosted, often for the wrong reasons. After Hollis's 1956 *A Study of George Orwell* appeared, Rupert Hart-Davis wrote to George Lyttleton, Orwell's old English teacher from Eton: 'Orwell is of no importance from a literary point of view, but for some I dare say he . . . was a sort of barometer of the Thirties and early Forties, going through and writing about *all* the experiences of young left-wing intellectuals during those troubled years.' Lyttleton agreed, noting 'How a small persistent clique can bolster up a writer's reputation.'[25]

In the early sixties two Americans, Peter Stansky and William Abrahams – seemingly encouraged by Rees (who appears to have been ready to ignore Orwell's will) – began work on a life only to be rebuffed by Sonia and denied permission to quote Orwell. In an effort to forestall further biographical attempts, together with Ian Angus she edited Orwell's *Collected Essays, Journalism and Letters* in four volumes, hoping that 'it would stand in for a biography' and declaring disingenuously that 'he left no personal papers: there is nothing either concealed or spectacularly revealed in his letters'.[26] (There is a curious footnote to this collection. Sir Steven Runciman came across the letter Eric had sent to him about his first tramping adventure in 1920 and asked Sonia's permission to publish it in *Encounter*. She refused on the grounds that it would harm Orwell's reputation. Later, without reference to Runciman, and to his irritation, she included it in the four-volume collection.)[27] However, despite Sonia's efforts, in 1972 Stansky and Abrahams managed to produce the first part of a two-volume 'unofficial' biography of Orwell, minus quotations.

At this point, Sonia was galvanised to appoint someone 'official' who would embark on the job seriously (Orwell's testamentary request was thus consigned to history). Her first choice, Richard Ellman, declined having just undertaken his biography of Oscar Wilde. Julian Symons was then considered but rejected on Geoffrey Gorer's advice.[28] 'Other names have been mentioned - Koestler, Michael Meyer, Dwight Macdonald and John Wain are said to have been approached by Orwell's agents and by his American publishers - only to be declined or rejected. Finally Sonia chose Bernard Crick, a political scientist, whose review of Miriam Gross's *The World of George Orwell* she had liked. Although, when she read Crick's manuscript, she tried to stop its publication, his *George Orwell: A Life* remains the most exhaustive biography to date. The subsequent biographies, by Michael Shelden and Jeffrey Meyers, written since Sonia's death, have offered fresh interpretations to the life and added newly unearthed facts to the story. The way of biographical research on Orwell had finally opened up.

In the 1970s Sonia became entangled in a convoluted lawsuit to recover the copyrights to Orwell's work from George Orwell Productions over which she had lost control – a lawsuit with all the hallmarks of Jarndyce versus Jarndyce. It was certainly the 'Bleak House' chapter of Orwell's posthumous life. Sonia cannot be blamed entirely for this situation, except for failing to inform Orwell that she had a phobia about money and being too willing to trust such matters to others. As her life became evermore complicated – another marriage, a divorce, editor of a highly respected Paris-based arts magazine, a life as a minor celebrity in French literary circles – she took her eye off the ball and allowed the business to be taken from her (voted off the board of GOP in her absence).[29] Unable to continue with the litigation because of ill-health, just prior to her death from cancer in 1980 she settled out of court, reacquiring the Orwell copyrights for a quarter of a million pounds and leaving herself penniless, but at least ensuring that Richard Blair came into his proper inheritance.

Sonia was a highly controversial character, loved and loathed in equal measure. She made enemies among those who did not appreciate her caustic tongue, her pretentiousness and cultural arrogance. (Discerning friends noted that she talked at great length without ever saying much, and Lucian Freud, once viewing her extensive library at her flat in her absence, wondered to a companion how many she had actually opened.)[30] She was volatile and, as time went on, became obnoxious when drunk. Not that she was unaware of this. After one such occasion she told David Plante, 'I did it again. I put on my act, my widow of George Orwell act. Was I awful?'[31] But her friends remained extremely loyal, defending her stoutly against charges of squandering much of the vast income from the books (she lived on a fixed income from George Orwell Productions and spent much of her money helping impoverished writers), and of being impossible to deal with in matters concerning George's estate (she took her responsibility too seriously and always feared letting George down). Anne Dunn disputed the charge that she had deserted him on his deathbed to spend the night at a club with her and Lucian Freud; Diana Cooke (Witherby) and Francis Wyndham attacked the idea that she had married for money; Ian Angus had to rebut the accusation that she had not done her share of the work in co-editing his *Collected Essays, Journalism and Letters*; and Hilary Spurling wrote a whole book putting her life into context, showing Sonia for the first time in three dimensions.[32] She has been accused of calling herself Sonia Orwell when in fact she was first Sonia Blair and then (on remarriage) Sonia Pitt-Rivers. But it seems that Anne Dunn persuaded her to adopt the Orwell name because of its cachet when she wrote for the Paris-based magazine *Art and Literature*, which they edited together with John Ashbery and Rodrigo Moynihan in the 1960s. And she was, after all, doing no more than Orwell himself in adopting a nom de plume.

Sonia's guardianship of the Orwell literary inheritance seems to have been initially at least somewhat cavalier. In June 1952 she sold the one surviving Orwell novel manuscript – of *Nineteen Eighty-Four* – at a charity auction for £50. On another occasion a page from one of his notebooks was torn out and sold under similar circumstances. And, strangely one might think, hardly any letters from his many girlfriends have survived. Sonia said she had received two love letters from Orwell which she destroyed. No doubt, like his letter to Celia Kirwan, they were couched in fairly graphic language, and might have been thought to damage his memory.[33] However, she did Orwell's reputation a considerable favour in ensuring that all his books were published in the Secker and Warburg uniform edition, and in bringing out his *Collected Essays, Journalism and Letters* when she did. The latter certainly boosted interest in his genius for journalism, a side of Orwell that was comparatively forgotten. It also went a long way to rescuing him from the clutches of the Cold War ideologists and presenting him to the world afresh. Although the collection has been criticised for failing to fully reflect Orwell's political writing (Sonia told Ian Angus she wanted it 'to read like a novel'), the influence of that collection on a new generation of journalists cannot be underestimated.[34] For that she will always deserve credit, along with the archivists at University College, London (notably Ian Angus), who began salvaging and collecting his material in the early 1960s.

Orwell was no saint; he was a flawed human being, full of contradictions and strange tensions – a faithful and gentle friend, yet a man with a poor attitude towards women, an enemy of state torturers with his own streak of sadistic violence, a champion of human decency yet a secret philanderer, a man with an ambiguous attitude towards Jews and homosexuals. He kept much of this darker side of himself hidden behind the façade of the goodly George Orwell, but could still act as a beacon for honesty and truth. This he achieved by working to create a crystal-clear prose, and by hammering away at issues which have remained central to our own age. What constitutes moral behaviour in a godless age? Can individual freedom survive in the face of collective power? How can we protect ourselves from unscrupulous manipulators of language? How can social democracy be achieved and defended against unprincipled totalitarians on the one hand and unprincipled capitalists on the other? How is the unbottled genie of science to be controlled?

As a prophet he had some small successes – predicting that Russia could be attacked and come over to our side against Hitler, and that our defence of Greece in 1940 was half-hearted and would end in failure, and foreseeing 'muzak' ('Its function is to prevent thought and conversation, and to shut out any natural sound, such as the song of birds').[35] But some were monumentally wrong – that private advertisements would disappear from the walls within a year of the war breaking out, that laissez-faire capitalism was dead in England, and that some novels of Charles Reade would outlive those of George Eliot.[36] Forster, in calling him a prophet, referred to the sense of awareness he created that progress was an illusion, and that the enemies of human decency had become more cunning, ruthless and better armed than their predecessors, thanks to science. His religious attitude towards a secular morality also lent him that prophetic air. Politics without morality was to him the great modern evil. His mind was constantly focused on the social consequences of present trends. In that he was genuinely possessed of a sociological imagination.

Orwell's influence on younger writers has been well-catalogued, especially the young 'angry' writers of the 1950s – Kingsley Amis, John Wain, John Osborne and, beyond them, Philip Larkin, Alan Sillitoe, Anthony Burgess, Norman Mailer, Tom Stoppard, Mary McCarthy, Truman Capote, Paul Theroux and Günther Grass.[37] In journalism the influence has been widespread. David Astor insisted that all his young journalists should read 'Politics and the English Language',[38] and hardly a day goes by without Orwell being cited in the press. He pioneered Cultural Studies (greatly influencing Richard Hoggart and Raymond Williams), although whether he foresaw the growth and direction of such work is doubtful. Above all, he left his mark on the language and the culture.

The most notable post-1984 Orwell controversy blew up with the revelation of his having handed over his list of suspected crypto-communists and fellow-travellers to Celia Kirwan and the IRD. When the story broke in 1993, Orwell was accused of betraying his friends, of betraying the left, and of hypocritically acting against every principle of free thought which he advocated publicly. But while he accepted the oft-quoted adage attributed to Voltaire about defending freedom of expression, he also believed that when civilisation was threatened some censorship was tolerable (as he had tolerated it at the BBC). He also said (despite his earlier spat with Kingsley Martin at the *New Statesman*) that no journal could be expected to include views to which it was opposed in principle, and that in wartime 'no government can afford to leave its enemies in key positions'.[39] Just as, in the early forties, he had thought up a list of Nazi sympathisers he thought should be removed from positions of influence, it was perfectly logical that in 1949, feeling that Britain was threatened by a new totalitarian enemy (one which probably had him down for elimination), he should have thought it dangerous for that enemy's supporters to be employed by a government agency designed to resist it. The list was not aimed at banning anyone from being published (as writers were banned in Nazi Germany and Soviet Russia) but from passing as democrats when they were secretly anti-democratic and tools of a hostile country's foreign policy. It was idiotic, he thought, to have people in powerful positions whose sympathies were essentially with the enemy and potential quislings in the event of an occupation. The strange comments he placed against names listed in his notebook are idiosyncratic, and whether these were the comments he sent to the IRD is as yet unknown.

While he defended freedom of speech and expression through

Woodcock's Freedom Defence Committee, the right to threaten western social democracy and western civilisation in time of war was one freedom Orwell clearly thought should be restricted. When Woodcock accused him of inconsistency in supporting freedom but being prepared to see it 'stored away' in times of crisis (in the case of conscription, for example), he replied, 'I have my reasons for arguing like that.'[40] He had his reasons, presumably, for sending in his list to the IRD. When it came to defending what he believed in Orwell was no pacifist, and in 1943 in the midst of war he made clear just how far he was prepared to go: 'To say "X is a gifted writer, but he is a political enemy and I shall do my best to silence him" is harmless enough. Even if you end up silencing him with a tommy-gun you are not really sinning against the intellect. The deadly sin is to say "X is a political enemy: therefore he is a bad writer."'[41] He was not passing a literary judgement on those he named. As he wrote, 'In politics one can never do more than decide which of two evils is the less, and there are some situations from which one can only escape by acting like a devil or a lunatic.'[42]

Had he sent in his list of suspected Nazi sympathisers in 1941 not an eyelid would have blinked or a voice been raised against him. Clearly his critics did not share his view that in 1949 the Russians were threatening to enslave Western democracies as they had enslaved the East European democracies. 'We are faced,' he wrote in 1948, 'with a world-wide political movement which threatens the existence of Western civilization, and which has lost none of its vigour because it has become in a sense corrupt.'[43] He had no illusion whatever about what sort of people he was up against. In Spain they had imprisoned, tortured and murdered his friends without compunction. Anyone who did not fight Stalinism deserved whatever came to them. In 1945, writing about the left-wing intelligentsia, he said, 'The Russian myth is there, and the corruption it causes stinks.' Writers who gave themselves over to it were 'literary prostitutes'.[44] Those who criticised Orwell had no idea how strongly he felt, how powerful was his paranoia. He did not hand in his list on a whim or to please a girlfriend (although the fact that it was Celia who asked him must have been a factor, too), or because he was still living inside his novel; he had lived that nightmare since Spain and what he did was wholly consistent with how he had felt since 1937. It might seem irrational (lunatic or mad), even treacherous, to others, but not to Orwell. Faced with the bestiality of totalitarian rule he found it impossible to remain objective. The cruellest and most memorable image in *Nineteen Eighty-Four* was taken from a poster he saw in Spain, and is brutally articulated by O'Brien: 'If you want a picture of the future, imagine a boot stamping on a human face – for ever.'[45]

He was opposed, however, to banning Communist parties, as advocated by James Burnham in America, since that involved using the suppressive powers the Communists themselves used against their opponents. If one were fighting for one's life and some strong organisation was clearly acting on behalf of the enemy it might be justified to crush it. 'But to suppress the Communist Party now, or at any time when it did not unmistakably endanger national survival, would be calamitous. One has only to think of the people who would approve!'[46] Therein lay his dilemma. In identifying Russian Communism as the enemy and being prepared to fight it, he found himself fighting beside those he also hated.

He seemed unable to grasp that a list sent in to a secret government agency, under whatever compelling circumstances, might be used against such people on a wider front and severely damage their careers. In time, under Conservative governments (which Orwell probably could not have envisaged in 1949) the IRD moved into the field of black propaganda, becoming closer to the CIA and involved in undermining foreign governments unfavourable to Britain. It was wound up finally in 1977 largely for that reason.[47]

Like certain other of his contemporaries, notably Eliot, Orwell has been accused of anti-Semitism, despite his often powerful attacks on it. He was one of the first English journalists, for example, to learn about the holocaust and speak out against it. He saw it as an evil expression of nationalism, which he deplored. He was, however, against a separate Jewish state in Palestine, believing that the Arab case had simply not been heard, and he objected to British soldiers being murdered by Zionist terrorists. If that constituted anti-Semitism then he was guilty. Even so, the Jewish friends with whom he differed over this, Warburg, Koestler and Fyvel, never openly accused him of the vice, although Koestler in a letter after Orwell's death wrote that 'the emotional bias was unmistakably present'.[48] Orwell himself was well aware that in such cases historical context mattered. In defending Eliot, whom Fyvel had attacked as 'anti-Semitic', he argued that,

> One has to draw a distinction between what was said before and what after 1934. Of course all these nationalistic prejudices are ridiculous, but disliking Jews isn't intrinsically worse than disliking Negroes or Americans or any other block of people. In the early twenties, Eliot's anti-Semitic remarks were about on a par with the automatic sneer one casts at Anglo-Indian colonels in boarding houses. On the other hand if they had been written after the persecutions began they would have meant something quite different . . . Some people go round smelling after anti-Semitism all the time. I have no doubt Fyvel thinks I am anti-Semitic. More rubbish is written about this subject than any other I can think of.[49]

There is no doubt that Orwell had a poor attitude to women (although there were some women writers he enjoyed and admired – Charlotte Brontë, Lousia M. Alcott and Katherine Mansfield among them). The many shrewd women who knew him, even while being deeply fond of him and recognising his brilliance, almost invariably referred to his 'sadism', his seeing women as inferior, or his seeing them as sexually necessary but of little worth beyond that. Here again such an attitude was a product of his age and particular upbringing, something he was never able sufficiently to shake off, even though he was married to one highly intelligent and witty woman from whom he probably learned a great deal, and an intelligent woman with whom he probably empathised more than is imagined.

Orwell's 'anti-feminism' (symbolised perhaps by the Anti-Sex League sash – the 'sash' once worn by Suffragettes) probably stems from early childhood. He refers to his mother and her Suffragette friends denouncing men as 'brutes' and 'beasts', fantasised about nuns being raped and came to loath Flip Wilkes, the personification of feminine guile. The only females from his youth of whom he wrote well were those he associated with an early sexual experience – the plumber's daughter and Elsie from the convent, and Jacintha for whom he had harboured lustful desires. He wanted to be attractive to women but found he was not, and seems to have been punishing them for that for the rest of his life.

The charge of homophobia sometimes levelled against Orwell does not stick as neatly as might be imagined. He enjoyed the company of men, and numbers of his friends and acquaintances were either gay or inclined that way – Lehmann, Gorer, Spender, Rees, Senhouse, Forster, and even Gow for whom he retained an attachment. If he had been as homophobic as he is sometimes depicted, he would have kept such people at a long arm's length. He said he found the bodies of young Burmese men extremely attractive and Michael Sayers even found him 'homoerotic'. Among the last books he read were two on the trials of Oscar Wilde and the playwright's apologia, *De Profundis*; indeed, he told George Woodcock that he had 'always been very pro-Wilde',[50] and remarked that to defend homosexuality in Wilde's day would have required a great deal of courage. He railed against 'nancy poets' and claimed to find homosexual approaches repulsive, but was tolerant of homosexuality between tramps and young soldiers denied contact with women. Spender thought Orwell's occasional homophobic outbursts were part of his rebellion against the public school, but Orwell also hinted in his last notebook that he thought men who are loudly homophobic are often concealing their own debaucheries. It reads like a last-minute confession.

On Europe, another area of contention which has grown in importance since Orwell's death, he thought Britain had isolated herself from the continent for far too long, and that this was reflected in her literature and culture. Those English writers who had come to favour other countries (France or Russia) in the thirties were not embracing a wider perspective but rather were turning their back on their own society and culture. The choice, as he saw it, was between absorption into the Soviet Empire, absorption into the American orbit or becoming part of a new United States of Europe. He favoured the latter, but a democratic socialist Europe not a Europe dominated by either totalitarians or capitalists.

As a novelist Orwell had his shortcomings. He was insufficiently interested in individuals to be able to explore character, except his inevitably autobiographical central character. What he lacked was the insight into others he ascribed to Lawrence who, he wrote, could produce lyrical poetry 'by just looking at some alien, inscrutable human being and suddenly experiencing an intense imaginative vision of his inner life'.[51] He could do it by looking in the mirror but not by looking outwards.

As an essayist he was supreme. He could turn out a short article on a slight topic such as toads or Woolworth roses, which not only shone forth as crystalline prose pieces but also affirmed his enduring humanity. He could produce essays of substance and power in which his prose was both persuasive and forceful. And yet, as a thinker there were those who thought he lacked depth. H. G. Wells, for example, considered his views on English character and on the future of socialism to be ill thought-out. His friend Woodcock also thought him too full of contradictions and uncertainties, and, except for a belief in honesty and fair play, lacking in general principles. This, of course, was probably Orwell's strength rather than his weakness. His ideas were an awkward combination of idealism and practicality, which failed to satisfy either the idealist or the pragmatist. He attacked the left from the right and the right from the left. His lack of ideology did, of course, leave him open to misinterpretation on all sides, but in many ways reflected a peculiar English version of commonsense and decency, which is why his work has survived while that of the many theoreticians of his time is forgotten.

Ever since Eton, Orwell had a fascination with language. Jingoist propaganda during the Great War so horrified him that by 1916 he became repelled by the patriotic game, or so he said. In the late twenties he showed his contempt for the swindling language of advertising, and the mendacity of the capitalist press. As the thirties progressed he saw how old propaganda methods were being revived to distort the truth (especially over Spain), and began to warn against deceitful lines spun by totalitarian parties intent on enslaving minds. Some of his most powerful and enduring essays are aimed at countering the dishonest use of language in politics and in his last two novels the theme is central, most especially in *Nineteen Eighty-Four*. It may be his greatest and most enduring contribution to our political and cultural life. His search for a window-pane prose was directed mainly to political ends – to make it harder for swindlers to swindle, liars to lie, and manipulators to manipulate. Propagandists, advertisers, publicists and spin-doctors were his sworn enemies. As long as the idea of democracy survives Orwell's message can only live on and the term 'Orwellian' remain a warning cry.

When it comes to Orwell's inner world, we are mostly dependent on his own words. We have little other choice. Other minds cannot be read directly, but as he invites us to do, we can look for hints, clues, even confirmations in his creative work, where allusions and figures in the carpet reveal patterns of emotions and movements of the mind which may be otherwise concealed. There is ample evidence of nightmare and paranoia, of his feelings of self-hate, of his sadistic inclinations, of his struggles always with a powerful urge to revenge driven by spite and malice. These hidden aspects of Orwell are glimpsed also in his characters and in the character of writers he admired. What we can achieve is a reading of the inner narrative and the mental landscape, an interpretation that makes sense. There can be no photographic record or 'true version', just a version coinciding with what we know about the life history and the work. Therein lies the source of the emotional daemon that drove him.

There are also, of course, his autobiographical essays and passing references in reviews and occasional articles, in which he seems to lay bare both his political and creative motives. Such motives, however, are rarely simple. When he said that he wrote books like *A Clergyman's Daughter*, *Keep the Aspidistra Flying* and *The Road to Wigan Pier* simply for money we know that this only partially accounts for a complex state of mind and the meandering progress of an internal narrative. Money might have been a more salient motive in these cases than in others, although it would be deeply ironic to think that Gordon Comstock, that vitriolic enemy of the 'money-god', was himself the money-god's own creation. He was not of course. Just like Dorothy Hare, he sprang from something deeper in Orwell than the mere need to survive. The motive to express a set of evolving ideas, to assess his own life as it seemed at the time of writing, to air grievances and work at his style were all involved to some degree. His wish to suppress these books was more a rejection of certain discarded selves, roles and performances past, attitudes relinquished. To have been persuaded, on his deathbed and against his better judgement, to agree to their being republished suggests that he was not, after all, averse to his past being raked over. This only makes his stated wish for no biography all the more puzzling. George Woodcock believed he understood the request, assuming, as he did, that the wish was entirely Orwell's. He was, thought Woodcock, obsessively secretive, guarding his private life jealously, keeping his social life in compartments, isolating one set of friends from others. Warburg also commented on his secretiveness. But for a man who wished to conceal his alternative selves he did little to destroy the evidence and cover over the clues.

Orwell's genius does not lie, as does that of Joyce or Proust, in the novel – the main source of his celebrity – but in the creation of genres and the brilliance with which he combined an acute sociological imagination with great economy and clarity of style. Cultural studies; what he called 'the political book'; his expressions of literary intelligence combining a Marxian perspective with an appreciation of fine writing – these are both innovative and highly characteristic. His very particular perspective on the world, his ability to see how whole systems function and the threat they pose, and to portray them in the most limpid of prose in all their comedy and horror – that vision is instantly recognised as 'Orwellian'. Therein lies the genius of George Orwell.

Orwell was the enemy of mealy mouths and weasel words intended to mislead or manipulate. He revealed in the starkest way the threat which not only totalitarianism offers to individual freedom and thought (and literature, its finest expression) but also science unconstrained by morality. Even as the great political issues that formed the background to his greatest novels have faded, other great threats have taken their place – religious totalitarianism and the rise of global plutocracy among them – and the critical tension between science and morality continues to plague the human conscience.

Notes

Chapter 1: The Inheritance

1. 'How the Poor Die', *Now*, [n. 5.], No. 6, [November 1946], CW18, p. 463 [3104].
2. *NEF*, CW9, p. 282.
3. 'Benefit of Clergy: Some Notes on Salvador Dali', intended for *Saturday Book* 4, [1944], CW16, p. 234 [2481].
4. *TLATU*, 19 February 1941, CW12, p. 401.
5. 'Tobias Smollett: Scotland's Best Novelist', *Tribune*, 22 September 1944, CW16, p. 408 [2552].
6. Jean Giraudoux, *Duel of Angels*, Methuen, London, 1958, Act 1.
7. Jacintha Buddicom, *Eric and Us*, Leslie Frewin, London, 1974, p. 14.
8. *BD*, CW2, p. 37.
9. *BD*, CW2, p. 127.
10. 'Rudyard Kipling', *Horizon*, February 1942, CW13, pp. 150–62 [948].

Chapter 2: 'The Golden Age'

1. Daniel Defoe, *A Tour Through the Whole Island of Great Britain*, Peter Davis, London, 1927, p. 301.
2. SSWTJ, CW19, p. 376 [3409].
3. *The English People*, 1947, CW16, p. 216 [2475].
4. Ruth Pitter in *OR*, p. 71.
5. *CUFA*, CW7, p. 27.
6. Quoted in 'How the Poor Die', CW18, p. 465 [3104].
7. GO–Andrew S. F. Gow, 13 April 1946, CW18, pp. 241–3 [2972].
8. *BD*, CW2, p. 283.
9. 'Bare Christmas for the Children,' *Evening Standard*, 1 December 1945, CW17, pp. 409–11 [2809].
10. 'As I Please', 9, *Tribune*, 28 January 1944, CW16, p. 81 [2412].
11. 'Charles Reade', *New Statesman and Nation*, 17 August 1940, CW12, p. 232 [671].
12. 'Just Junk – But Who Can Resist It?', Saturday Essay, *Evening Standard*, 5 January 1946, CW18, p. 19 [2842].
13. 'Why I Write', *Gangrel*, [No. 4, Summer] 1946, CW18, p. 316 [3007].
14. *NEF*, CW9, p. 142.
15. 'Why I Write', *Gangrel*, [No. 4, Summer] 1946, CW18, p. 315 [3007].
16. Mabel Fierz, BBC *Omnibus* 1970; *OR*, p. 98.
17. *HTC*, CW6, p. 140.
18. Review of *The Forge* by Arturo Barea, *Horizon*, September 1941, CW13, pp. 34–5 [852].
19. Review of *Naval Occasions* by Bartimeus, *New English Weekly*, 5 March 1936, CW, pp. 445–7 [290].
20. 'My Country Right or Left', *Folios of New Writing*, No. 2, Autumn 1940, CW12, p. 270 [694].
21. *CUFA*, CW7, pp. 75–6.
22. The so-called 'Anglican convent' mentioned in previous biographies does not appear in local records for Henley, nor was such a place ever registered with the Oxford Diocese. However, the Ursuline convent *was* registered by the Roman Catholic Church in London. Source: Jane Morgan, Oxford Diocese Registrar, Catholic Central Library, London.
23. SSWTJ, CW19, p. 366 [3409].
24. GO–Julian Symons, 20 April 1948, CW19, p. 321 [3386].
25. SSWTJ, CW19, p. 370 [3409].
26. *ACD*, CW3, p. 294.
27. GO–Brenda Salkeld, [July 1931], CW10, p. 206 [107].
28. SSWTJ, CW19, p. 373 [3409].

29. *CUFA*, CW7, p. 41.
30. Humphrey Dakin in *OR*, p. 128.
31. SSWTJ, CW19, p. 373 [3409].
32. *RTWP*, CW5, p. 117.
33. *RTWP*, CW5, p. 118.
34. *RTWP*, CW5, p. 117.
35. *DAOIPAL*, CW1, p. Ch. 36.
36. 'Notes on the Way', *Time and Tide*, 6 April 1940, CW12, p. 123 [604]. The image of the bisected wasp had occurred years before in his review of Henry Miller's *Tropic of Cancer*; see p. 175.
37. *CUFA*, CW7, p. 58.
38. *CUFA*, CW7, p. 76.
39. 'Bare Christmas for the Children,' *Evening Standard*, 1 December 1945, CW17, pp. 410–11 [2809].
40. GO–Herbert Read, 5 March 1939, CW11, pp. 340–1 [536].
41. 'Rudyard Kipling', *New English Weekly*, 23 January 1936, CW10, pp. 409–10 [265].
42. 'Riding Down from Bangor', *Tribune*, 22 November 1946, CW18, p. 943 [3123].
43. GO–Mrs Belloc-Lowndes, 31 July 1945, CW17, p. 235 [2711].
44. 'Books v Cigarettes', *Tribune*, 8 February 1946, CW18, p. 96 [2892].
45. GO–Mother (Ida Blair), 1 October [1911], CW10, p. 6 [2A].
46. *RTWP*, CW5, p. 117.

Chapter 3: Pathos and Nightmare

1. 'Voice', 3: A Magazine Programme (BBC Eastern Service), 6 October 1942, CW14, p. 80 [1547].
2. Gavin Maxwell, *The House of Elrig*, Longmans Green, London, 1965, p. 90.
3. SSWTJ, CW19, p. 369 [3409].
4. Hugo Vickers, *Cecil Beaton: The Authorized Biography*, Weidenfeld & Nicolson, London, 1985, pp. 16–17.
5. SSWTJ, CW19, p. 377 [3409].
6. *KTAF*, CW4, p. 44.
7. *RTWP*, CW5, pp. 114–15.
8. SSWTJ, CW19, p. 357 [3409].
9. SSWTJ, CW19, p. 358 [3409].
10. E. H. W. Meyerstein, *Of My Early Life*, Neville Spearman, London, 1957, p. 31.
11. Cyril Connolly, *Enemies of Promise*, Penguin, Harmondsworth, 1961, p. 175.
12. SSWTJ, CW19, p. 376 [3409].
13. Peter Stansky and William Abrahams, *The Unknown Orwell*, Constable, London, 1972, p. 32.
14. SSWTJ, CW19, p. 359 [3409].
15. SSWTJ, CW19, p. 359 [3409].
16. SSWTJ, CW19, p. 384 [3409].
17. SSWTJ, CW19, pp. 377–8 [3409].
18. SSWTJ, CW19, p. 361 [3409].
19. SSWTJ, CW19, pp. 370–1 [3409].
20. SSWTJ, CW19, p. 362 [3409].
21. SSWTJ, CW19, p. 376 [3409].
22. SSWTJ, CW19, p. 366 [3409].
23. 'Wells, Hitler and the World State', *Horizon*, August 1941, CW12, p. 540 [837].
24. Gavin Maxwell, *The House of Elrig*, p. 79.
25. SSWTJ, CW19, p. 368 [3409].
26. *CUFA*, CW7, pp. 39–40.

27. 'Songs We Used to Sing', Saturday Essay, *Evening Standard*, 19 January 1946, CW18, p. 50 [2868].
28. Jacintha Buddicom, *Eric and Us*, p. 135.
29. Orwell's Last Literary Notebook, CW20, p. 206 [3725].
30. GO–Mamaine Koestler, 24 January 1947, CW19, p. 27 [3159].
31. GO–Mother (Ida Blair), 8 December 1912, CW10, p. 19 [22].
32. SSWTJ, CW19, p. 368 [3409].
33. Crick gives Richard's pension as £438 10s per annum but based on salary rules of half final pay he would more likely have been earning £600.
34. Jane Morgan–GB interview, 31 March 2000.
35. Ruth Pitter in *OR*, p. 71.
36. SSWTJ, CW19, p. 379 [3409].
37. SSWTJ, CW19, p. 383 [3409].
38. Jane Morgan–GB interview, 31 March 2000.
39. 'My Country Right or Left', *Folios of New Writing*, No. 2, Autumn 1940, CW12, p. 269 [694].
40. 'As I Please', 47, *Tribune*, 3 November 1944, CW19, p. 451 [2573].
41. GO–Mother, 25 February 1912, CW10, p. 12 [11A].
42. Sir John Grotrian, quoted in Bernard Crick, *George Orwell: A Life*, Penguin, Harmondsworth, 1992, p. 77.
43. Gavin Maxwell, *The House of Elrig*, p. 75.
44. Jerome K. Jerome passed Shiplake with his companions on their journey up river from Kingston to Oxford, *Three Men in a Boat*, Penguin, Harmondsworth, 1957, p. 133.
45. Jacintha Buddicom, *Eric and Us*, p. 11.
46. Jacintha Buddicom, *Eric and Us*, p. 38.
47. Jacintha Buddicom, *Eric and Us*, p. 76.
48. Jacintha Buddicom, *Eric and Us*, p. 39.
49. 'As I Please', 49, *Tribune*, 24 November 1944, CW16, pp. 472–3 [2581].
50. Jacintha Buddicom, *RO*, p. 14.
51. Avril Dunn, 'My Brother, George Orwell', *Twentieth Century*, March 1961; *OR*, p. 26.
52. 'My Country Right or Left', *Folios of New Writing*, No. 2, Autumn 1940, CW12, p. 269 [694].
53. War-time Diary, 1 June 1940, CW12, p. 175 [632].
54. 'Awake! Young Men of England', *Henley and South Oxfordshire Standard*, 2 October 1914, CW10, p. 20 [23].
55. *AF*, CW8, pp. 7–8.
56. *Henley and South Oxfordshire Standard*, 18 September 1914, p. 3.
57. Michael Holroyd, *Bernard Shaw*, Vol. 2: *The Pursuit of Power*, Chatto & Windus, London, 1989, p. 348.
58. Wilfrid Owen, 'Dolce et Decorum Est', in Jon Stallworthy (ed.), *Anthem for Doomed Youth*, Constable & Robinson, London, 2002, p. 109.
59. *St Cyprian's Chronicle*, August 1918.
60. *St Cyprian's Chronicle*, August 1914.
61. Cyril Connolly, *Enemies of Promise*, p. 178.
62. GO–Julian Symons, 10 May 1948, CW19, p. 336 [3397].
63. Compton Mackenzie, *Sinister Street*, Martin Secker, London, 1913.
64. Cyril Connolly, *Enemies of Promise*, p. 179.
65. G. K. Chesterton, *Manalive*, Thomas Nelson, London, 1915, p. 208.
66. Peter Stansky and William Abrahams, *The Unknown Orwell*, p. 82.
67. Cyril Connolly, *Enemies of Promise*, p. 179.
68. Cyril Connolly, *Enemies of Promise*, p. 178.

69. Cyril Connolly ms, Tulsa University Special Collections.

70. *Henley and South Oxfordshire Standard*, 21 July 1916, p. 3.

71. Review of *Chu Chin Chow* in *Time and Tide*, 13 July 1940, CW12, p. 215 [656].

72. Valentine Cunningham, *British Writers of the Thirties*, Oxford University Press, Oxford, 1988, pp. 113–15.

73. Richard Rees, 'George Orwell', *Scots Chronicle*, 1951, p. 7.

74. Ruth Pitter in *OR*, p. 71.

75. SSWTJ, CW19, p. 379 [3409].

76. Records of Eastbourne Union Workhouse, 1922–28.

Chapter 4: 'Absorbing Wisdom Unawares'

1. Cyril Connolly, *Enemies of Promise*, p. 242.

2. Conrad Noel, *An Autobiography*, Dent, London, 1945, p. 14–15; General Sir Ian Hamilton, *When I Was a Boy*, Faber & Faber, London, 1939.

3. Quoted in Peter Stansky and William Abrahams, *The Unknown Orwell*, p. 73.

4. Jacintha Buddicom, *Eric and Us*, p. 57.

5. Michael Meyer, *Not Prince Hamlet*, Secker and Warburg, London, 1989, p. 65.

6. Jacintha Buddicom, *Eric and Us*, p. 58.

7. Jacintha Buddicom, *Eric and Us*, p. 59.

8. Jacintha Buddicom, *Eric and Us*, p. 66.

9. SSWTJ, CW19, p. 379 [3409].

10. Thomas Gray, 'Ode on a Distant Prospect of Eton College', *Oxford Anthology of English Literature*, Vol. 1, Oxford University Press, 1973, p. 2203.

11. Denys King-Farlow, 'At Eton with George Orwell', GO Archive: Rayner Heppenstall, 'George Orwell', BBC, 2 November 1960, BBC Written Archives.

12. E. A. Caroe quoted in King-Farlow, 'At Eton with George Orwell'.

13. George ('Dadie') Rylands–GB, 12 June 1997.

14. Denys King-Farlow: 'At Eton with George Orwell'.

15. Sir Steven Runciman–GB, 1 April 2000.

16. Film review of *Quiet Wedding*, *Time and Tide*, 8 February 1941, CW12, p. 386 [759].

17. Daniel Defoe, *A Tour Through the Whole Island of Great Britain*, p. 313.

18. Review of *Eton Medley* by B. J. Hill, *Observer*, 1 August 1948, CW19, p. 412 [3431].

19. Ronnie Watkins–GB, 22 August 2000; Cyril Connolly, *Enemies of Promise*, p. 196.

20. Ronnie Watkins–GB, 22 August 2000.

21. Sir Steven Runciman–GB, 1 April 2000 (and in subsequent correspondence).

22. Orwell's Last Literary Notebook, CW20, p. 202 [3725].

23. Christopher Hollis, *A Study of George Orwell*, Hollis & Carter, London, 1956, p. 15.

24. Christopher Hollis, *A Study of George Orwell*, p. 17.

25. Tom Hopkinson, 'George Orwell – Dark Side Out', *Cornhill*, 166 (1953), p. 453.

26. Richard Rees, *George Orwell: Fugitive from the Camp of Victory*, Secker and Warburg, London, 1961, p. 44.

27. Roger Mynors in *RO*, p. 19.

28. John Wilkes in *RO*, p. 11.

29. *KTAF*, CW4, p. 45.

30. Jacintha Buddicom, *Eric and Us*, p. 141.

31. Denys King-Farlow, 'At Eton with George Orwell'.

32. Anthony Powell, *To Keep the Ball Rolling*, Vol. I: *Infants of the Spring*, Heinemann, London, 1976, p. 129.

33. Quoted in Bernard Crick, *George Orwell: A Life*, p. 104.

34. *KTAF*, CW4, p. 44.

35. Christopher Eastwood in *RO*, p. 18.

36. Richard Walmsley Blair's Army Record, Public Record Office, Kew.

37. 'My Country Right or Left', *Folios of New Writing*, No. 2, Autumn 1940, CW12, p. 269 [694].

38. 'London Letter', 15 January 1944, *Partisan Review*, Spring 1944, CW16, pp. 64–70 [2405].

39. *RTWP*, CW5, p. 114.

40. *College Days*, 24 March 1919.

41. 'The Art of Donald McGill', *Horizon*, September 1941, CW13, pp. 23–31 [850].

42. Sir Steven Runciman–GB, 1 April 2000.

43. David Cecil–Tim Russell, 24 January 1980.

44. Sir Steven Runciman–GB, 1 April 2000.

45. 'The Re-discovery of Europe', 'Literature Between the Wars', BBC Eastern Service, 10 March 1942; *The Listener*, 19 March 1942, CW13, p. 212 [1014].

46. Review of *The Brothers Karamazov* and *Crime and Punishment* by Fyodor Dostoevsky, *Observer*, 7 October 1945, CW17, p. 296 [2760].

47. GO–Stanley J. Kunitz and Howard Haycraft, 17 April 1940, CW12, p. 147 [613].

48. *BD*, CW2, p. 65.

49. Jacintha Buddicom, *Eric and Us*, p. 122.

50. 'Why I Write', *Gangrel*, [No. 4, Summer] 1946, CW18, p. 317 [3007].

51. Review of *The Prussian Officer and Other Stories* by D. H. Lawrence, *Tribune*, 16 November 1945, CW17, p. 385 [2796].

52. 'Imaginary Interview: George Orwell and Jonathan Swift', *The Listener*, 26 November 1942, CW14, pp. 154–63 [1637].

53. *Eton College Chronicle*, 15 March 1917.

54. 'On the Vileness of Being Commonplace', *Eton College Chronicle*, 24 June 1920, Editorial: '. . . A suburban villa, built and fitted throughout in what is technically known as the "suburban" style, is the inmost shrine of the commonplace.'

55. *Eton College Chronicle*, 14 July 1918.

56. *Eton College Chronicle*, 14 February 1918, Editorial.

57. 'Is There Any Truth in Spiritualism?', *College Days*, No. 5, 9 July 1920, CW10, p. 71 [52].

58. 'Songs We Used to Sing', Saturday Essay, *Evening Standard*, 19 January 1946, CW18, pp. 49–51 [2868].

59. Harold Acton, *More Memoirs of an Aesthete*, Hamish Hamilton, London, 1986, p. 152.

60. David Pryce-Jones, *Cyril Connolly: Journal and Memoir*, William Collins, London, 1983, p. 45.

61. GO–Prosper Buddicom, 19 January 1921, CW10, p. 79 [59].

62. David Pryce-Jones, *Cyril Connolly: Journal and Memoir*, p. 44.

63. *ITW*, CW12, pp.95–4 [600]

64. Jacintha Buddicom, *Eric and Us*, p. 71.

65. *Eton College Chronicle*, 4 July 1918.

66. *CUFA*, CW7, p. 127.

67. *KTAF*, CW4, p. 48.

68. Review of *The Martyrdom of Man* by Winwood Reade, *Tribune*, 15 March 1946, CW18, p. 152 [2930].

69. Anthony Powell, *Infants of the Spring*, p. 74.

70. Jacintha Buddicom, *Eric and Us*, p. 142.

71. Denys King-Farlow, 'At Eton with George Orwell'.

72. *Eton College Chronicle*: Review of *College Days*, No. 3, 29 November 1919.

73. Peter Stansky and William Abrahams, *The Unknown Orwell*, p. 94.

74. Ruth Pitter in *OR*, p. 69.

75. Jacintha Buddicom, *Eric and Us*, p. 197.

76. GO–Prosper Buddicom, 19 January 1921, CW10, pp. 78–9 [59].

77. GO-Steven Runciman, [August] 1920, CW10, p. 76 [56].

78. Christopher Eastwood, taped interview with Stephen Wadhams, CBC.

79. *Eton College Annals*, 2 November 1918 (Eton College Library).

80. John Lehmann, *In My Own Time*, Little Brown, Boston, 1969, p. 60.

81. *Eton College Chronicle*, 30 November 1921.

82. Edward Marjoribanks's retrospective 1917–1918, *Eton College Annals*.

83. *Eton College Chronicle*, 13 October 1921, p. 102.

84. Sir Steven Runciman–GB, 1 April 2000.

85. Peter Stansky and William Abrahams, *The Unknown Orwell*, p. 182.

86. Mabel Fierz, interview with Stephen Wadhams, CBC.

87. Jeffrey Meyers, *George Orwell: The Wintry Conscience of a Generation*, Norton, New York, 2000, p. 43.

88. Bernard Crick, *George Orwell: A Life*, p. 135.

89. Jacintha Buddicom, *Eric and Us*, p. 152; CW20, p. 44 [3551].

90. Daniel Defoe, *A Tour of the Whole Island of Great Britain*, p. 56.

91. *ACD*, CW3, p. 11.

92. *St Cyprian's Chronicle*, August 1922, p. 6.

93. 'Why I Write', *Gangrel*, [No. 4, Summer] 1946, CW18, p. 316 [3007].

94. Sir Steven Runciman–GB, 1 April 2000.

95. Christopher Hollis, *A Study of George Orwell*, p. 26.

96. Review of *A Passage to India* by E. M. Forster, *New English Weekly*, 24 September 1936, CW10, p. 499 [325].

Chapter 5: 'The Pain of Exile'

1. Martin Wynne (ed.), *On Honourable Terms: The memoirs of some Indian Police Officers, 1915–1948*, British Association of Cemeteries in South Asia, London, 1985, p. 5.

2. 'As I Please', 68, *Tribune*, 3 January 1947, CW19, p. 5 [3146].

3. 'Marrakech', *New Writing*, New Series No. 3, Christmas 1939, CW11, p. 418 [579].

4. *BD*, CW2, p. 98.

5. 'As I Please', *Tribune*, 20 October 1944, CW16, p. 434 [2566].

6. P. E. S. Finney quoted in Martin Wynne (ed.), *On Honourable Terms*, p. 6.

7. *BD*, CW2, p. 98.

8. 'Notes on the Way', *Time and Tide*, 30 March and 6 April 1940, CW12, p. 121 [604].

9. Review of *The Good Earth* by Pearl S. Buck, *Adelphi*, June 1931, CW10, pp. 205–6 [106].

10. *DAOILP*, CW1, p. 118.

11. W. Somerset Maugham, *The Gentleman in the Parlour*, Avon Publications, New York, 1947, p. 15.

12. W. Somerset Maugham, *The Gentleman in the Parlour*, p. 12.

13. W. Somerset Maugham, *A Writer's Notebook*, Heinemann, London, 1949, p. 218.

14. Roger Beadon in *OR*, p. 63.

15. GO–Brenda Salkeld, 7 May [1935], CW10, p. 385.

16. 'Raffles and Miss Blandish', *Horizon*, October 1944, CW16, p. 355 [2538].

17. *TLATU*, 19 February 1941, CW12, p. 405 [763].

18. *BD*, CW2, p. 198.

19. Richard Curle, *Into the East*, Macmillan, London, 1923, p. 48.

20. Kay Ekevall in *RO*, p. 59.

21. Malcolm Muggeridge, Introduction to *Burmese Days*, Time Incorporated, New York, 1962, p. xi.

22. Martin Wynne (ed.), *On Honourable Terms*, p. 17.

23. Roger Beadon in *OR*, p. 63.

24. *BD*, CW2, p. 2.

25. *DAOIPAL*, CW1, p. 169.

26. *BD*, CW2, p. 296.
27. Review of *A Modern De Quincey* by Captain H. R. Robinson, *Observer*, 13 September 1942, CW14, pp. 34–5 [1481].
28. 'Rudyard Kipling', *Horizon*, February 1942, CW13, p. 153 [948].
29. Harold Acton, *More Memoirs of an Aesthete*, p. 153.
30. Peter Stansky and William Abrahams, *The Unknown Orwell*, p. 158.
31. *RTWP*, CW5, p. 41.
32. *RTWP*, CW5, pp. 132–3.
33. Orwell's Last Literary Notebook, CW20, p. 206 [3725].
34. 'Romance', CW10, pp. 89–90 [65].
35. Arthur Koestler–Ian Angus interview, 30 April 1964.
36. 'The Lesser Evil', CW19, p. 98 [62].
37. Orwell's Last Literary Notebook, CW10, p. 190 [3722].
38. *Eton College Chronicle*, 11 October 1917.
39. GO–Tennyson Jesse, 7 March 1946, CW18, p. 128 [2911].
40. 'Extract, A Rebuke to the Author, John Flory', CW10, pp. 103–4 [75].
41. *RTWP*, CW5, pp. 113–34.
42. 'My Country Right or Left', *Folios of New Writing*, No. 2, Autumn 1940, CW12, p. 270 [694].
43. Anthony Powell, *Infants of the Spring*, p. 132.
44. *BD*, CW2, p. 29.
45. 'Shooting an Elephant', *New Writing*, No. 2, Autumn 1936, CW10, p. 502 [326].
46. L. H. Marrison in O*R*, p. 66.
47. *BD*, CW2, p. 186.
48. *BD*, CW2, p. 66.
49. *BD*, CW2, p. 65.
50. GO–Jack Common, 12 October 1938, CW10, p. 223 [496].
51. Christopher Hollis, *A Study of George Orwell*, pp. 27, 28.
52. Christopher Hollis, *A Study of George Orwell*, p. 28.
53. Steven Runciman, *A Traveller's Alphabet: Partial Memoirs*, Thames & Hudson, London, 1991, pp. 193–4.
54. 'George Orwell in Burma', *Asian Affairs*, 57 [NS Vol. 1, Pt 1], pp. 19–28.
55. *BD*, CW2, p. 70.
56. Roger Beadon in O*R*, pp. 64–5.
57. W. H. J. Christie: 'St Cyprian's Days', *Blackwood's Magazine*, May 1971, p. 391.
58. 'John Flory: My Epitaph [1926–30]', CW10, p. 95 [71]. In the manuscript the words 'married women' are replaced by 'stupid women'.
59. A similar atmosphere is achieved in Jack London's 'The Chinago', about the guillotining of the wrong man, which Orwell featured in a radio programme on London in 1945: CW17, pp. 297–306.
60. *BD*: CW2, p. 89.
61. Bernard Crick, *George Orwell: A Life*, p. 589.
62. *BD*, CW2, p. 86.
63. GO–Brenda Salkeld, Friday [Jan/Feb 1933], unpublished.
64. 'Shooting an Elephant', CW10, p. 501 [326].
65. *BD*, CW2, p. 87.
66. 'Shooting an Elephant', CW10, pp. 505–6 [326].
67. George Stuart interview, Orwell Archive.
68. *RTWP*, CW5, p. 101.
69. Review of *Indian Mosaic* by Mark Channing, *Listener*, 15 July 1936, CW10, p. 488 [319].
70. *BD*, CW2, p. 99.

71. *BD*, CW2, p. 70.

72. *RTWP*, CW5, p. 135.

73. George Stuart interview, Orwell Archive.

74. Review of *Paris Gazette* by Leon Feuchtwanger, *Tribune*, 26 April 1940, CW12, p. 154 [616].

75. *BD*, CW2, p. 70.

76. Review of *Zest for Life* by Johann Wöller, *Time and Tide*, 17 October 1936, CW10, p. 508 [328].

77. Review of *The Civilization of France* by Ernst Robert Curtius, translated by Olive Wyon, *Adelphi*, May 1932, CW10, p. 245 [125].

78. *BD*, CW2, p. 86.

Chapter 6: Picking up the Thread

1. *RTWP*, CW5, pp. 136–9.

2. *RTWP*, CW5, p. 140.

3. Avril Dunn, 'My Brother, George Orwell', *Twentieth Century*, March 1961; *OR*, p. 27.

4. Vera Buckler–Ian Angus interview, 28 July 1965.

5. Jane Morgan–GB interview, 31 March 2002.

6. *KTAF*, CW4, pp. 52–3.

7. Avril Dunn, 'My Brother, George Orwell', *Twentieth Century*, March 1961; *OR*, p. 28.

8. Jacintha Buddicom, *Eric and Us*, p. 145.

9. George Bumstead–GB, 28 September 1998; Nancy Fox in *RO*, p. 27.

10. Vera Buckler–Ian Angus, 28 July 1965.

11. Daniel Defoe, *A Tour of the Whole Island of Great Britain*, p. 55.

12. GO–Denys King-Farlow, 9 June 1936, CW10, p. 485 [316].

13. T. E. B. Howarth, *Cambridge Between Two Wars*, William Collins, London, 1978, p. 61.

14. *KTAF*, CW4, p. 6.

15. GO–Eleanor Jaques, Wed. night [19 October 1932], CW10, p. 271 [145].

16. Ruth Pitter in *OR*, p. 69.

17. Ruth Pitter in *OR*, p. 70.

18. Ruth Pitter, BBC talk, 3 January 1956, BBC Written Archives.

19. 'As I Please', 26, *Tribune*, 26 May 1944, CW16, p. 231 [2478].

20. Ruth Pitter in *OR*, p. 70.

21. 'Clink', CW10, p. 255 [135].

22. *DAOIPAL*, CW1, p. 161.

23. Richard Rees, *George Orwell: Fugitive from the Camp of Justice*, Secker and Warburg, London, 1961, p. 44.

24. Peter Stansky and William Abrahams, *The Unknown Orwell*, p. 185.

25. Information from Christopher Date, British Library.

26. 'The Re-discovery of Europe', 'Literature Between the Wars,' I, BBC Eastern Service, 10 March 1942, CW13, p. 214 [1014].

27. Rate Record of Chelsea and Kensington Council.

28. Louis Bannier in *RO*, p. 36.

29. GO–Celia Kirwan, 27 May 1948, CW18, p. 344 [3405].

30. Review of *The Civilization of France* by Ernst Robert Curtius, *Adelphi*, May 1932, CW10, pp. 244–5 [125].

31. 'London Letter', [15 January 1944], *Partisan Review*, Spring 1944, p. 66 [2405].

32. Ruth Graves–GO, 23 July 1949, Orwell Archive.

33. Robert McAlmon and Kay Boyle, *Being Geniuses Together*, 1920–1930, North Point Press, San Francisco, 1984.

34. *ITW*, CW12, p. 86 [600].

35. 'As I Please', 37, *Tribune*, 11 August 1944, CW16, p. 329 [2530].

36. Cyril Connolly, *Previous Convictions*, Hamish Hamilton, London, 1963, p. 271.
37. L. I. Bailey–GO, 19 February 1929, Orwell Archive.
38. Preston Hall record, recovered from hospital archivist by Michael Shelden.
39. Albert Camus, *Notebooks 1942–1951*, New York, Alfred Knopf, 1965, p. 129. This institution still exists in Paris, but bears no resemblance to the place that Orwell and others witnessed in the 1920s. Seventy years later it is a first-class hospital and recognised as such.
40. 'How the Poor Die', CW18, p. 466.
41. Review of *Glimpses and Reflections* by John Galsworthy, *New Statesman and Nation*, 12 March 1938, CW11, p. 126.
42. 'As I Please', 70, *Tribune*, 24 January 1947, CW19, p. 25 [3158].
43. L. I. Bailey–GO, 23 April 1929, Orwell Archive.
44. Mabel Fierz, BBC *Arena*, 1984; *OR*, p. 95.
45. Michael Shelden first brought to light Orwell's comments about *Down and Out* scribbled in the margins of a copy he gave to Brenda Salkeld. See Shelden, *Orwell: The Authorized Biography*, Heinemann, London, 1991, p. 9.
46. *DAOIPAL*, CW1, p. 17.
47. Jon Kimche, interview with Stephen Wadhams, CBC.
48. GO–Editor, *Commentary*, 3 September 1945, 2740A, pp. 278–9.
49. *ITW*, CW12, pp. 97–9 [600].

Chapter 7: Getting a Footing
1. Steven Runciman, *A Traveller's Alphabet: Partial Memoirs*, p. 53.
2. *DAOIPAL*, CW1, p. 23.
3. *DAOIPAL*, CW1, p. 127.
4. 'Why I Write', *Gangrel*, [No 4, Summer] 1946, pp. 316–21 [3007].
5. *ACD*, CW3, p. 224.
6. Dennis Collings in *OR*, p. 79.
7. GO–Sacheverell Sitwell, 6 July 1940, CW12, pp. 308–9 [653].
8. Review of *Poltergeists* by Sacheverell Sitwell, *Horizon*, September 1940, CW12, p. 247 [681].
9. *RTWP*, CW5, p. 106.
10. Mabel Fierz, BBC *Omnibus*, 1970; *OR*, p. 95.
11. Review of *Herman Melville* by Lewis Mumford, *New Adelphi*, March–May 1930, CW10, p. 183 [96].
12. 'As I Please', 15, *Tribune*, 10 March 1944, CW16, p. 118 [2432].
13. Richard Peters–GB interview, 9 May 1999.
14. Fredric Warburg, *All Authors Are Equal*, Hutchinson, London, 1973, p. 57.
15. GB interviews with Maurice Peters, 22 May 1999; Richard Peters, 9 May 1999.
16. Maurice Peters–GB interview, 22 May 1999.
17. Richard Peters–GB interview, 9 May 1999.
18. Review of Mumford's *Melville*, CW10, p. 183 [96].
19. 'Pleasure Spots', *Tribune*, 11 January 1946, CW18, pp. 31–2 [2854].
20. Dennis Collings in *RO*, p. 38.
21. Dorothy Plowman–Ian Angus, 13 November 1959.
22. Dennis Collings in *RO*, p. 37.
23. *KTAF*, CW4, pp. 227–8.
24. *KTAF*, CW4, p. 138.
25. Humphrey Dakin quoted in T. R. Fyvel, *George Orwell: A Personal Memoir*, Hutchinson, London, 1982, p. 48.
26. 'The Cost of Letters', *Horizon*, September 1946, CW18, p. 384 [3057].
27. T. R Fyvel: *George Orwell: A Personal Memoir*, Weidenfeld & Nicolson, London, 1982, pp. 11–12.

28. Preface to the Ukrainian Edition of *Animal Farm*, March 1947, CW19, p. 88.
29. Review of *Angel Pavement* by J. B. Priestley, *Adelphi*, October 1930, CW10, p. 188 [98].
30. Anthony Powell, *Infants of the Spring*, p. 134.
31. Stephen Spender in *RO*, p. 106.
32. Ruth Pitter, BBC talk, 3 January 1956, BBC Written Archives.
33. Review of *Persephone in Hades* by Ruth Pitter, *Adelphi*, September 1932, CW10, pp. 262–3 [139].
34. Review of *The Spirit of Catholicism* by Karl Adam, *New English Weekly*, 9 June 1932, CW10, pp. 246–8 [127].
35. GO–Brenda Salkeld, 27 July 1934, CW10, p. 344 [202].
36. Brenda Salkeld in *RO*, p. 40.
37. GO–Brenda Salkeld, 13 May 1931, unpublished.
38. GO–Max Plowman, 1 November 1930, CW10, p. 189 [100].
39. GO–Brenda Salkeld, [7 July 1931?], unpublished.
40. 'Why I Write', *Gangrel*, [No. 4, Summer] 1946, pp. 316–21 [3007].
41. 'The Spike', *Adelphi*, April 1931, CW10, p. 202 [104].
42. GO–Brenda Salkeld, 21 October 1931, unpublished.
43. Richard Rees, *George Orwell: a Fugitive from the Camp of Victory*, p. 116.
44. GO–Brenda Salkeld Friday night [Late June 1931], unpublished.
45. GO–Brenda Salkeld, [18 July 1931] pmk, unpublished.
46. Stephen Spender, interview with Stephen Wadhams, CBC.
47. GO–Brenda Salkeld, [8 July 1931?], unpublished.
48. GO–Brenda Salkeld, Sunday night, [July] 1931, CW10, pp. 206–7 [107].
49. Ruth Pitter, BBC talk, 3 January 1956, BBC Written Archives.
50. 'The Spike', *Adelphi*, April 1931, CW10, p. 198.
51. 'Hop-picking Diary', 25 August 1931, CW10, pp. 220–1 [111].
52. Review of *Gypsies* by Martin Block, *Adelphi*, December 1938, CW11, p. 247 [508].
53. 'Hop-picking Diary', 8 October 1931, CW10, p. 230 [113].
54. GO–T. S. Eliot, 30 October 1931; CW10, p. 235.
55. GO–Brenda Salkeld, Saturday night [October 1931], CW10, p. 237 [118].
56. GO–Brenda Salkeld, [9 November or December 1931], unpublished.
57. GO–Brenda Salkeld, [September 1932], CW10, p. 268 [142].
58. T. S. Eliot–GO, 19 February 1932, Orwell Archives.
59. Mabel Fierz in *RO*, p. 46.
60. Bernard Crick, *George Orwell: A Life*, p. 221.
61. 'The Proletarian Writer', BBC broadcast, 6 December 1940, CW12, p. 296 [715].
62. GO–S. Moos, 16 November 1943, CW15, p. 308 [2356].
63. GO–Brenda Salkeld, [10 November or December 1931], unpublished.

Chapter 8: The Invention of George Orwell

1. *TLATU*, 19 February 1941, CW12, p. 408 [763].
2. GO–Eleanor Jaques, Tuesday [14? June 1932], CW10, p. 249 [129].
3. *CUFA*, CW7, p. 9.
4. John Betjeman, *Poetry of the Thirties*, Penguin, Harmondsworth, 1964, p. 74.
5. Geoffrey Stevens–GB interview, 2 October 1998.
6. GO–Brenda Salkeld, Sunday [September? 1932] CW10, p. 268 [142].
7. GO–Eleanor Jaques, Tuesday [14? June 1932] CW10, p. 249 [129].
8. *ACD*, CW4, p. 235.
9. 'Boys' Weeklies', *Horizon*, 11 March 1940, CW12, p. 63 [598].
10. GO–Eleanor Jaques, Tuesday [14? June 1932], CW10, p. 249 [129].
11. Review of *Further Extracts from the Notebooks of Samuel Butler*, *Adelphi*, April 1934, p. 340 [197].

12. *KTAF*, CW4, p. 230.
13. GO–Eleanor Jaques, Monday [19 September 1932], CW10, p. 269 [143].
14. *ACD*, CW3, p. 8.
15. Quoted by Bernard Crick, *George Orwell: A Life*, p. 224.
16. Sheila Hodges, *Gollancz: The Story of a Publishing House*, Gollancz, London, 1978, pp. 58–9.
17. GO–Leonard Moore, 26 April 1932, CW10, p. 242 [124].
18. Mabel Fierz–GO, Friday [1932?], Orwell Archives.
19. Adrian Fierz–GB interview, 18 December 1999.
20. GO–Eleanor Jaques, Monday [19 September 1932], CW10, p. 269.
21. Maurice Peters–GB interview, 22 May 1999.
22. Mabel Fierz in *OR*, p. 96.
23. GO–Brenda Salkeld, Tuesday night [August 1932 or later], unpublished.
24. Review of *Byron and the Need of Fatality* by Charles du Bos, *Adelphi*, September 1932, CW10, pp. 263–5 [140].
25. Review of Gogol by Boris de Schloezer, Adelphi, April 1933, CW10, pp. 310–11 [168].
26. GO–Leonard Moore, [25 March 1933], CW10, p. 309 [167].
27. Orwell's Last Literary Notebook, CW20, p. 215 [3725].
28. Malcolm Muggeridge, BBC *Arena*, 1984; *OR*, 1984.
29. SSWTJ, CW19, p. 374 [3409].
30. Review of *The Spirit of Catholicism* by Karl Adam, *New English Weekly*, 9 June 1932, CW10, p. 246 [127].
31. GO–Editor, *New English Weekly*, 5 May 1932, CW10, p. 246 [126].
32. GO–Brenda Salkeld, [beginning of September 1932], unpublished.
33. GO–Eleanor Jaques, Wed. night [19 October 1932], CW10, p. 271 [145].
34. GO–Brenda Salkeld, (Sunday)[November 1932], unpublished.
35. Introduction to the French Edition of *Down and Out in Paris and London*, 15 October 1934, CW10, pp. 353–4 [211].
36. Review of *Further Extracts from the Notebooks of Samuel Butler*, *Adelphi*, April 1934, CW10, p. 339 [197].
37. John Ruskin, *Modern Painters*, 1903, Vol. 3, Pt 4, Chapter 14.
38. GO–Jack Common, [22 May 1938], CW11, p. 149 [443].
39. See Lists of Paris residents at 6 rue du Pot de Fer 1927 and 1930, Archive de Paris.
40. Avril Dunn, 'My Brother George Orwell', *Twentieth Century*, March 1961; *OR*, p. 29.
41. Cecil Day Lewis, *Adelphi*, February 1933, p. 382.
42. W. H. Davies, *New Statesman and Nation*, 18 March 1933, pp. 338–40.
43. *TLS*, 12 January 1933, p. 22.
44. *Listener*, 8 March 1933, p. 368.
45. Compton Mackenzie, *Daily Mail*, 12 January 1933; J. B. Priestley, *Evening Standard*, 12 January 1933.
46. Humbert Possenti–Editor, *Times*, 31 January 1933, p. 6.
47. *Times*, 11 February 1933, CW10, pp. 303–4 [10].
48. GO–Brenda Salkeld, [3? February 1933], unpublished.
49. GO–Brenda Salkeld, Friday night [10? March 1933], CW10, pp. 307–8 [165].
50. GO–Brenda Salkeld, Saturday [? June 1933], CW10, pp. 316–18 [176].
51. Review of *Criticisms and Opinions of the Works of Charles Dickens* by G. K. Chesterton, *Adelphi*, December 1933, CW10, p. 325 [185].
52. GO–Brenda Salkeld, Friday night [10? March 1933], CW10, p. 108 [165].
53. GO–Brenda Salkeld, Friday night [10? March 1933], CW10, p. 307 [165].
54. Nellie Limouzin–GO, 3 June 1933, CW10, p. 314 [174].
55. GO–Brenda Salkeld, Saturday, [? June 1933], CW10, p. 317 [176].

56. *Adelphi*, March 1933, CW10, p. 306 [164]; *Adelphi*, May 1933, CW10, p. 312 [171]; *Adelphi*, October 1933, CW10, p. 322 [182].
57. Henry Stapley–GB interview, 7 November 1998.
58. GO–Eleanor Jaques, 7 July 1933, CW10, p. 319 [178].
59. Jack Denny in *RO*, p. 30.
60. Mme Prent–Ian Angus interview, 6 August 1971.
61. GO–Eleanor Jaques, [6 June 1933], CW10, p. 316 [175].
62. GO–Brenda Salkeld, Saturday [? June 1933], CW10, pp. 316–18 [176].
63. *Nation*, 6 September 1933, p. 279.
64. *New Republic*, 11 October 1933, p. 257.
65. GO–Eleanor Jaques, Thursday [20 July 1933], CW10, p. 320 [179].
66. *ITW*, 11 March 1940, p. 96 [600].
67. Henry Stapley–GB interview, 7 November 1998.
68. GO–Leonard Moore, Sunday [26 November 1933], CW10, p. 324 [184].
69. Avril Dunn, 'My Brother, George Orwell', *Twentieth Century*, March 1961; OR, p. 28.

Chapter 9: Tory Anarchist Meets James Joyce

1. GO–Leonard Moore, Saturday [27 January 1934], CW10, p. 334 [190].
2. GO–Brenda Salkeld, Sunday [10? December 1933], CW10, p. 329 [186].
3. Review of *Criticisms and Opinions of the Works of Charles Dickens* by G. K. Chesterton, *Adelphi*, December 1933, CW10, pp. 324–6 [185].
4. *BD*, CW2, p. 76.
5. Jeffrey Meyers, *George Orwell: The Wintry Conscience of a Generation*, pp. 329–30.
6. Preface to the Ukrainian Edition of *Animal Farm*, CW19, p. 110.
7. Review of *Critique of Poetry* by Michael Roberts, *Adelphi*, March 1934, CW10, pp. 336–7 [196].
8. Review of *The Aesthetic of Stéphane Mallarmé* by Hasye Cooperman, and *Baudelaire: The Tragic Sophist* by G. T. Clapton, *Adelphi*, July 1934, CW10, pp. 342–3 [201].
9. GO–Brenda Salkeld, 27 July 1934, CW10, p. 344 [202].
10. GO–Brenda Salkeld, 27 July 1934, CW10, p. 345 [202].
11. GO–Brenda Salkeld, Tuesday night [Late August? 1934], CW10, p. 347 [204].
12. GO–Brenda Salkeld, Wed. night [early September? 1934], CW19, p. 348 [205].
13. Peter Stansky and William Abrahams, *The Unknown Orwell*, p. 232.
14. GO–Brenda Salkeld, [11? September 1934], CW10, p. 350 [207].
15. GO–Leonard Moore, 3 October 1934, CW10, pp. 351–2 [209].
16. Review of *The Prussian Officer and Other Stories* by D. H. Lawrence, *Tribune*, 16 November 1945, CW17, p. 386 [2796].
17. Quoted in Crick, *George Orwell: A Life*, p. 258.
18. Jon Kimche in *RO*, p. 55.
19. GO–Brenda Salkeld, 16 February 1935, CW10, p. 374 [235]; 14 November 1934, unpublished.
20. GO–Leonard Moore, 14 November 1934, CW10, p. 358 [215].
21. *New York Herald Tribune*, 28 October 1934, p. 3; *New York Times Book Review*, 28 October 1934, p. 7; *Boston Evening Transcript*, 1 December 1934, p. 3. Source: Peter Stansky and William Abrahams, *The Unknown Orwell*, p. 228.
22. 'Bookshop Memories', *Fortnightly*, November 1936, CW10, pp. 510–13 [330]; GO–Brenda Salkeld, 14 November 1934, unpublished.
23. GO–Brenda Salkeld, Tuesday night [late August? 1934], CW10, pp. 346–8 [204].
24. Quoted by Sheila Hodges, *Gollancz: The Story of a Publishing House*, p. 106.
25. GO–Victor Gollancz [Ltd.], 17 December 1934, CW10, p. 363 [219].
26. Jeffrey Meyers, *George Orwell: The Wintry Conscience of a Generation*, pp. 111–13.
27. 'St Andrew's Day, 1935', *Adelphi*, November 1935, CW10, p. 403 [261].

28. Kay Ekevall, interview with Stephen Wadhams, CBC.
29. GO–Brenda Salkeld, 16 February 1935, CW10, p. 374 [235].
30. GO–Brenda Salkeld, 16 February 1935, CW10, p. 375 [235].
31. GO–Brenda Salkeld, 16 February 1935, CW10, p. 375 [235].
32. Kay Ekevall–GB interview, 14 October 1999.
33. Rayner Heppenstall, *Four Absentees*, Barrie & Rockliffe, London, 1960, p. 51.
34. Orwell's Notes on His Books and Essays, CW20, p. 387 [3728].
35. GO–Brenda Salkeld, CW10, 7 March 1935, p. 384 [242].
36. L. P. Hartley, *Observer*, 10 March 1935, p. 6.
37. V. S. Pritchett, *Spectator*, 22 March 1935, p. 504.
38. Peter Quennell, *New Statesman and Nation*, 23 March 1935, p. 422.
39. Leonard P. Moore–GO, 9 May 1935, Orwell Archive.
40. Geoffrey Stone, *Commonweal*, 18 June 1935, p. 220.
41. Elisaveta Fen, *A Russian's England*, Paul Gordon, Warwick, 1976, p. 345.
42. Kay Ekeval in *RO*, p. 58.
43. Lettice Cooper, 'George Orwell's First Wife', *PEN Broadsheet*, 16, Spring 1984, p. 19.
44. Eileen Blair–GO, 21 March 1945, CW17, p. 99 [2638].
45. GO–Rayner Heppenstall, Tuesday night [24 September 1935], CW10, p. 393 [252].
46. GO–Rayner Heppenstall, 5 October 1935, CW10, p. 399 [275].
47. Kay Ekeval in *RO*, p. 58.
48. T. R. Fyvel, *George Orwell: A Personal Memoir*, Hutchinson, London, 1982, p. 104.
49. GO–Julian Symons, 10 May 1948, CW19, p. 336 [3397].
50. Review of *Flowers of Evil: A Life of Charles Baudelaire* by Edwin Morgan, *Observer*, 31 December 1944, CW16, p. 509 [2596].
51. GO–Rayner Heppenstall, 5 October 1935, CW10, pp. 399–400 [275].
52. Review of *The Proceedings of the Society* by Katharine M. Williams, *Adelphi*, August 1935, CW10, p. 391 [249].
53. *KTAF*, CW4, p. 125. Poem attributed to Villon translated by Cecily Mackworth.
54. E. M. Forster, *Two Cheers for Democracy*, Edward Arnold, London, 1951, p. 72.
55. *Times*, 16 July 1935, p. 219.
56. Cyril Connolly, *New Statesman and Nation*, 6 July 1935, p. 18.
57. Cyril Connolly, 'George Orwell: Some Letters', *Encounter*, 18, January 1962, p. 56.
58. Cyril Connolly, BBC *Omnibus*, 'The Road to the Left', 1970.
59. Geoffrey Gorer, BBC *Omnibus*, 'The Road to the Left', 1970.
60. GO–Geoffrey Gorer, Sat. [23 May 1936], CW10, p. 482 [311].
61. Lydia Shiel–GO, 6 September 1935, Orwell Archive.
62. Michael Sayers, *Adelphi*, August 1935, pp. 316–17.
63. Michael Meyer–GB interview, 5 April 2002; Meyer, *Not Prince Hamlet*, p. 69; Michael Sayers–GB conversation, 18 June 2002.
64. Rayner Heppenstall, *Four Absentees*, p. 63.
65. Elisaveta Fen, *A Russian's England*, p. 347.
66. Michael Sayers–GB interview, 23 September 2000.
67. Review of *Tropic of Cancer* by Henry Miller, *New English Weekly*, 14 November 1935, CW10, p. 405 [263].
68. Michael Sayers–GB interview, 23 September 2000.
69. Cyril Connolly, *Enemies of Promise*, p. 10.
70. GO–Stanley J. Kunitz and Howard Haycraft, 17 April 1940, CW12, p. 148 [613].
71. Rayner Heppenstall, *Four Absentees*, p. 82.
72. Rayner Heppenstall, *Four Absentees*, pp. 86–7.
73. Michael Sayers–GB interview, 23 September 2000.
74. GO–Leonard Moore, 8 November 1935, CW10, p. 403 [262].
75. Peter Davison's calculations.

76. *RTWP*, CW5, p. 213.
77. *KTAF*, CW4, Textual Note, pp. 279–87.
78. Orwell's Rudyard Kipling Obituary, *New English Weekly*, 23 January 1936, CW10, p. 409 [265].
79. *RTWP*, CW5, pp. 90–1.

Chapter 10: Journeys of Discovery
1. *RTWP*, CW5, p. 3.
2. *RTWP*, CW5, p. 5.
3. *RTWP*, CW5, p. 6.
4. *RTWP*, CW5, p. 10.
5. *RTWP*, CW5, p. 13.
6. *RTWP*, CW5, p. 14.
7. *RTWP*, CW5, p. 14.
8. 'The Road to Wigan Pier Diary', CW10, p. 431 [282].
9. Joe Kennan, BBC *Omnibus*, 'The Road to the Left', 1970; *OR*, p. 132.
10. *RTWP*, CW5, p. 38.
11. *RTWP*, CW5, pp. 30–1.
12. 'The Road to Wigan Pier Diary', CW10, p. 444 [282].
13. War-time Diary, 15 April 1941, CW12, p. 479 [788].
14. 'The Road to Wigan Pier Diary', CW10, p. 466 [282].
15. Richard Rees, BBC *Omnibus*, 'The Road to the Left', 1970.
16. GO–Jack Common [16? April 1936], CW10, p. 471 [300].
17. GO–Brenda Salkeld, 2 May 1936, unpublished.
18. Lettice Cooper in *RO*, pp. 117–18.
19. 'As I Please', 7, *Tribune*, 21 January 1944, CW16, pp. 76–9 [2410]. (The rose continues to flourish today [2003].)
20. GO–Richard Rees, 20 April 1936, CW10, p. 474 [304].
21. GO–Jack Common, 3 April 1936, CW10, pp. 468–9 [298].
22. GO–Brenda Salkeld, 2 May 1936, unpublished.
23. William Plomer, *Spectator*, 24 April 1936, p. 768.
24. Cyril Connolly, *New Statesman and Nation*, 25 April 1936, p. 635.
25. GO–Brenda Salkeld, 2 May 1936, unpublished.
26. Geoffrey Gorer–GO, 21 April 1936, Orwell Archive.
27. Edith Sitwell–Richard Jennings, [29 June 1937], Richard Greene (ed), *Selected Letters of Edith Sitwell*, Virago Books, London, 1998, p. 202.
28. Anthony Powell, *Infants of the Spring*, p. 301.
29. GO–Geoffrey Gorer, [23 May 1936], CW10, p. 482 [311].
30. GO–Brenda Salkeld, 2 May 1936, unpublished.
31. GO–John Lehmann, 27 May 1936, CW10, p. 483 [312].
32. GO–Denys King-Farlow, 9 June 1936, CW10, p. 485 [316].
33. GO–Brenda Salkeld, 10 June 1936, unpublished.
34. Elisaveta Fen, *A Russian's England*, p. 348.
35. Lettice Cooper in *OR*, p. 162.
36. Vera Buckler–Ian Angus interview, 28 July 1965.
37. GO–Brenda Salkeld, 2 May 1936, unpublished.
38. Elisaveta Fen, *A Russian's England*, p. 419.
39. GO–Jack Common, 12 October 1938, CW11, p. 222 [496].
40. Humphrey Dakin, BBC *Omnibus*, 'The Road to the Left', 1970; interview with Stephen Wadhams, CBC.
41. Review of *The Rock Pool* by Cyril Connolly, *New English Weekly*, 23 July 1936, CW10, p. 491 [321].

42. Randall Swingler, 'The Right to Free Expression', Annotated by George Orwell, *Polemic*, 5, September–October 1946, CW18, (3090), p. 443.

43. *RTWP*, CW5, p. 161-162.

44. Henry Miller–GO, [August 1936?], Orwell Archive.

45. GO–Henry Miller, 26–27 August 1936, CW10, pp. 495–6 [323].

46. Review of *Black Spring* by Henry Miller, *New English Weekly*, 24 September 1936.

47. Orwell's Last Literary Notebook, CW20, pp. 204–5 [3725].

48. Review of *A Song of the Tide* by Ernest Raymond, *New Statesman and Nation*, 16 November 1940, CW12, p. 285 [705].

49. Elisaveta Fen, *A Russian's England*, p. 349.

50. Cyril Connolly in BBC *Omnibus*, 'The Road to the Left', 1970.

51. Jon Kimche, *RO*, p. 140.

52. 'A happy vicar I might have been', *Adelphi*, December 1936, CW10, pp. 524–5 [335].

53. *RTWP*, CW5, p. 201.

54. Fredric Warburg, *An Occupation for Gentlemen*, Houghton Mifflin, Boston, 1960, p. 229.

55. *RTWP*, CW5, p. 215.

56. '*The Road to Wigan Pier* Diary', 15 February 1936, CW10, p. 427 [278].

57. Anthony Quinton, 'A Sense of Smell', BBC Third Programme, 19 January 1954, BBC Written Archives.

58. Review of *Men and Politics* by Louis Fischer, *Now and Then*, Christmas 1941, CW13, p. 101 [908].

59. 'Culture and Democracy', 22 November 1941, CW13, p. 72 [885]. Never published by Orwell. Talk given to Fabian Society, which was later published from notes (in a version he disowned) as *Victory or Vested Interest*, Routledge, London, 1942.

60. 'The Proletarian Writer' from BBC series 'The Writer in the Witness-Box, *Listener*, 19 December 1940, CW12, pp. 294–301 [715].

61. 'Notes on the Spanish Militias', CW11, p. 136 [439].

62. Anthony Powell, *Infants of the Spring*, p. 36.

63. Elisaveta Fen, *A Russian's England*, p. 417.

64. 'Notes on the Spanish Militias', CW11, p. 136 [439].

65. Orwell's Notes on His Books and Essays, CW20, pp. 223–31 [3728].

Chapter 11: The Spanish Betrayal

1. 'Notes on the Spanish Militias', CW11, p. 136 [439].

2. *HTC*, CW6, p. 186.

3. 'As I Please', 42, *Tribune*, 15 September 1944, CW16, p. 403 [2549].

4. *ITW*, 11 March 1940, CW12, p. 106 [600].

5. Alfred Perlès, *My Friend Henry Miller*, Belmont Books, New York, 1962, pp. 129–31.

6. *HTC*, CW6, p. 183.

7. *HTC*, CW6, pp. 2–3.

8. *HTC*, CW6, pp. 1–2.

9. GO's poem in 'Looking Back on the Spanish War', [1942?], CW12, pp. 510–11 [1421].

10. PRO/HW 17/27, 25 August 1936, Public Record Office, Kew.

11. PRO/HW 17/27, 25 August 1936.

12. PRO/HW 17/27, 25 August 1936.

13. PRO/HW 17/27, 8 January 1937.

14. Dr Kenneth Sinclair-Loutit–GB, 17 January 2001.

15. *HTC*, CW6, p. 8.

16. *HTC*, CW6, p. 10.

17. John McNair–Ian Angus, April 1964.

18. *HTC*, CW6, pp. 12–13.

19. *HTC*, CW6, p. 21.

20. *HTC*, CW6, p. 20.
21. *HTC*, CW6, p. 17.
22. Bert Govaerts, 'Georges Kopp', *Vrij Nederland*, 24 August 1985.
23. *HTC*, CW6, p. 28.
24. *HTC*, CW6, p. 32.
25. *HTC*, CW6, pp. 29, 35.
26. Robert Edwards in Rayner Heppenstall, *George Orwell*, BBC Third Programme, 2 November 1960, BBC Written Archives.
27. Stafford Cottman in *RO*, p. 81.
28. Walter Tapsell Report on the British ILP Contingent to Communist HQ in Albacete, Marx Memorial Library.
29. Jon Kimche, interview with Stephen Wadhams, CBC.
30. *RTWP*, CW5, p. 131.
31. *HTC*, CW6, p. 59.
32. Robert Edwards in Rayner Heppenstall, *George Orwell*, BBC Third Programme, 2 November 1960, BBC Written Archives.
33. *HTC*, CW6, pp. 45–6.
34. Ruth Dudley Edwards, *Victor Gollancz, A Biography*, Gollancz, London, 1978, p. 238.
35. Charles Orr, 'Homage to Orwell – as I Knew Him in Catalonia', unpublished paper, International Institute of Social History, Amsterdam.
36. Jack Branthwaite in *RO*, p. 84.
37. Stafford Cottman in *RO*, p. 81.
38. Eileen Blair–Leonard Moore, 12 April 1937, CW10, p. 17 [365].
39. Robert Edwards, interview with Stephen Wadhams, CBC.
40. 'Caesarian Section in Spain', *The Highway*, March 1939, CW11, p. 334 [534].
41. Walter Tapsell Report on ILP Contingent, Barcelona 1937, Marx Memorial Library.
42. *HTC*, CW6, p. 74.
43. John 'Paddy' Donovan–Ian Angus, 27 April 1967.
44. 'Looking Back on the Spanish War', [1942?], CW12, p. 501 [1421].
45. Dr Kenneth Sinclair-Loutit–GB, 17 January 2001.
46. PRO/HW 17/27, Public Record Office, Kew.
47. David Crook–Jimmy, 24 January 1937, in Marcel Acier (ed.), *Spanish Trenches: Recent Letters from Spain*, Modern Age Books, New York, 1937.
48. David Crook-Carolyn Wakeman [n.d. but late 1990s].
49. Bernard Crick, *George Orwell: A Life*, p. 332.
50. Eileen Blair–Marie O'Shaughnessy, 22 March 1937, CW11, p. 14 [363].
51. Richard Rees, *George Orwell: Fugitive from the Camp of Victory*, p. 147.
52. Rosalind Obermeyer–Ian Angus, 30 January 1967.
53. Victor Gollancz, Preface to George Orwell's *The Road to Wigan Pier*, Left Book Club, Gollancz, London, 1936.
54. GO–Victor Gollancz, 9 May 1937, CW11, p. 22 [368].
55. Harold Laski, *Left News*, March 1937, pp. 275–6.
56. Arthur Calder-Marshall, *Time and Tide*, 20 March 1937, p. 382.
57. Douglas Goldring, *Fortnightly*, April 1937, pp. 505–6.
58. Cyril Connolly–GO, 13 October 1937, Orwell Archive.
59. Harry Pollitt, review of *The Road to Wigan Pier*, *Daily Worker*, 17 March 1937.
60. *HTC*, CW6, p. 116.
61. Walter Tapsell Report on ILP Contingent, Barcelona 1937, Marx Memorial Library.
62. *HTC*, CW6, p. 132.
63. GO–Cyril Connolly, 8 June 1937, CW11, p. 28 [371].
64. Review of *The Clash* by Arturo Barea, *Observer*, 24 March 1946, CW18, p. 168 [2944].
65. Frank Frankford, BBC *Arena*, 1984.

66. *HTC*, CW6, pp. 128–9.
67. Fredric Warburg, *An Occupation for Gentlemen*, p. 137.
68. KGB File: David Crook Report, Alba Collection.
69. Paul Crook-GB 20 July 2000
70. David Wickes File, Alba Collection.
71. Jack Branthwaite, *RO*, pp. 89–90.
72. Frank Frankford, BBC *Arena*, 1984.
73. *HTC*, CW6, p. 137.
74. Harry Milton in *RO*, p. 90.
75. *HTC*, CW6, p. 148.
76. *HTC*, CW6, p. 152.
77. Eileen Blair–Laurence O'Shaughnessy, [*c.* 10 June 1937], Orwell Archive.
78. Anthony Powell, *Infants of the Spring*, p. 132.
79. *HTC*, CW6, p. 151.
80. KGB file: David Crook Report, Alba Collection.
81. *HTC*, CW6, p. 128.
82. *HTC*, CW6, p. 165.
83. *HTC*, CW6, p. 170.
84. *HTC*, CW6, p. 171.
85. George Kopp, 'Account of events related to my discovery of a file containing various documents on Bob Smillie's case', Greenwich, 30 January 1939, Orwell Archive.
86. Townsend Ludington, *Dos Passos: A Twentieth Century Odyssey*, Dutton, New York, 1980, pp. 362–409.
87. David Crook–Carolyn Wakeman.
88. GO–Heppenstall, 31 July 1937, CW11, p. 53 [381].
89. Review of Mary Low and Juan Brea, *Red Spanish Notebook*, *Time and Tide*, 9 October 1937, CW11, p. 87 [401].
90. John McNair–Ian Angus, April 1964; Fredric Warburg, *An Occupation for Gentlemen*, pp. 236–7.
91. *HTC*, CW6, p. 186.
92. GO–Stanley J. Kunitz and Howard Haycraft, 17 April 1940, CW12, pp. 147–8 [613].
93. *HTC*, CW6, p. 84.
94. Review of *An Interlude in Spain* by Charles d'Ydewalle, *Observer*, 24 December 1944, CW16, p. 502 [2593].
95. *Review of Russia under Soviet Rule*, by N. de Basily, *New English Weekly*, 12 January 1939, CW11, p. 317 [524].
96. Review of *The English Revolution: 1640*, edited by Christopher Hill, *New Statesman and Nation*, 24 August 1940, CW12, p. 245.
97. Tribunal of Espionage and High Treason document translated by Catherine Rylance. (First published in (translation by Stephen Schwartz) Victor Alba and Stephen Schwartz, *Spanish Marxism Versus Soviet Communism: A History of the POUM*, Transaction Books, New York, 1988.)
98. 'Looking Back on the Spanish War', [1942?], CW13, pp. 508–9 [1421].

Chapter 12: The Road to Morocco
1. *HTC*, CW6, pp. 186–7.
2. 'Eye-Witness in Barcelona', *Controversy: The Socialist Forum*, Vol. 1, No. 11, August 1937, CW11, p. 549 [382].
3. GO–Charles Doran, 2 August 1937, CW11, p. 65 [386].
4. 'Orwell's List of Crypto-Communists and Fellow-Travellers', CW20, p. 250 [3732].
5. 'Eye-Witness in Barcelona', *Controversy: The Socialist Forum*, 1, No. 11, August 1937, CW11, pp. 54–60 [2593].

6. 'Spilling the Spanish Beans', *New English Weekly*, 29 July and 2 September 1937, CW11, pp. 41–6 [378].
7. GO–Victor Gollancz, 9 May 1937, CW11, p. 23 [368].
8. Victor Gollancz–GO, 6 July 1937, Orwell Archive.
9. GO–Editor of *Time and Tide*, 5 February 1938, CW11, p. 115 [422].
10. Fredric Warburg–GO, 6 July 1937, Orwell Archive.
11. Georges Kopp–Eileen Blair, 8 July 1937, CW11, p. 50 [378A].
12. GO–Amy Charlesworth, 1 August 1937, CW11, p. 62 [384].
13. GO–Charles Doran, 2 August 1937, CW11, p. 65 [386].
14. GO–Victor Gollancz, 20 August 1937, CW11, p. 72 [390].
15. GO–Rayner Heppenstall, 31 July 1937, CW11, p. 53 [381].
16. GO–Jack Common, 16 February 1938, CW11, p. 122 [427].
17. GO–Nancy Cunard, [3–6 August 1937], CW11, p. 66 [386A].
18. GO–Amy Charlesworth, 1 August 1937, CW11, p. 62 [384].
19. GO–Rayner Heppenstall, 31 July 1937, CW11, p. 54 [381].
20. Jack Branthwaite, *RO*, pp. 100–1.
21. Introduction to the Ukrainian Edition of *Animal Farm*, CW8, p. 113.
22. The 1936–7 Electoral Register names him as Inns, but Orwell always spelt his name Innes. ('John Innes' disembowelled, of course, gives us 'Jones'.)
23. Rayner Heppenstall, *Four Absentees*, p. 146.
24. Dan Pinnock–GB interview, 1 June 1997.
25. GO–Charles Doran, 2 August 1937, CW11, p. 65 [386].
26. Editor, *International Literature*–GO, 25 August 1937, Orwell Archive.
27. GO–Geoffrey Gorer, 15 September 1937, CW11, p. 81 [397].
28. GO–Editor, *Manchester Guardian*, 22 September 1937, CW11, p. 82 [398].
29. Frank Frankford interview with Stephen Wadhams, CBC.
30. 'That Mysterious Cart: George Orwell Replies to F. A. Frankford', *New Leader*, 24 September 1937, CW11, p. 85 [399].
31. Fredric Warburg, *An Occupation for Gentlemen*, p. 232.
32. 'Why I Write', *Gangrel*, [No. 4, Summer] 1946, CW18, pp. 316–21 [3007].
33. Review of *Men and Politics* by Louis Fischer, *Now and Then*, Christmas 1941, CW12, pp. 101–2 [908].
34. Quoted in Peter Stansky and William Abrahams, *Orwell: The Transformation*, Constable, London, 1979, p. 190.
35. Stephen Schwartz–GB, 18 July 2001.
36. Cyril Connolly, BBC *Arena*, 1984 (but from earlier BBC programme by Malcolm Muggeridge).
37. Bill Alexander, 'George Orwell and Spain', in Christopher Norris (ed.), *Inside the Myth: Orwell: View from the Left*, Lawrence & Wishart, London, 1984, p. 97.
38. GO–Stephen Spender, 2 April 1938, CW11, p. 130 [434].
39. Review of *Assignment in Utopia* by Eugene Lyons, *New English Weekly*, 9 June 1938, CW11, p. 159 [451].
40. Desmond Young, *Try Anything Twice*, Hamish Hamilton, London, 1963, p. 189.
41. GO–Cyril Connolly, [1 December 1937], CW11, p. 100 [411].
42. Stephen Spender, interview with Stephen Wadhams, CBC.
43. GO–Cyril Connolly, 27 April 1938, CW11, p. 146 [440].
44. Review of *Spanish Testament* by Arthur Koestler, *Time and Tide*, 5 February 1938, p. 113 [421].
45. Publication of *Homage to Catalonia*, CW11, p. 135 [438].
46. *Observer*, 20 May 1938, p. 8.
47. *Manchester Guardian*, 14 June 1938, p. 8.
48. Philip Mairet, *New English Weekly*, 26 May 1938.

49. Geoffrey Gorer, *Time and Tide*, 30 April 1938, pp. 599–600.
50. Geoffrey Gorer, interview with Stephen Wadhams, CBC.
51. Review of *The Great Dictator*, *Time and Tide*, 21 December 1940, CW12, p. 315 [727].
52. Herbert Read–GO, 9 June 1938, Orwell Archive.
53. J. R. Ackerley in the *Listener*, 16 June 1938.
54. CW11, p. 122, note 2 [426].
55. Eileen Blair–Jack Common, Monday [Monday–Tuesday, 14–15 March 1938?], CW11, p. 128 [432].
56. Eileen Blair–Jack Common, Monday [Monday–Tuesday, 14–15 March 1938?], CW11, p. 129 [432].
57. Preston Hall Medical Report, 1936, Orwell Archive (originally unearthed by Michael Shelden).
58. GO–Stephen Spender, 2 April 1938, CW11, p. 131 [434].
59. GO–Geoffrey Gorer, 18 April 1938, CW11, p. 134 [436].
60. GO–Leonard Moore, 6 December 1937, CW11, p. 100 [412].
61. Eileen Blair–Leonard Moore, 30 May 1938, CW11, p. 154 [447].
62. Elisaveta Fen, *A Russian's England*, p. 349.
63. GO–Jack Common, Sunday [22 May 1938], CW11, p. 149 [443].
64. GO–Jack Common, 29 September 1938 CW11, pp. 211–12 [489].
65. Stephen Spender, *RO*, p. 106.
66. GO–Stephen Spender, [15? April 1938], CW11, p. 132 [435].
67. Elisaveta Fen, *A Russian's England*, p. 419.
68. 'Why I Joined the ILP', *New Leader*, 24 June 1938, CW11, pp. 167–9 [457].
69. Review of *Assignment in Utopia* by Eugene Lyons, *New English Weekly*, 9 June 1938, CW11, pp. 158–60 [451].
70. Eileen Blair–Ida Blair, 15 September 1938, CW11, p. 198 [481].
71. Tony Hyams–GB interview, 4 December 1998.
72. Eileen Blair–Ida Blair, 15 September 1938, CW11, p. 199 [481].
73. Eileen Blair–Ida Blair, 15 September 1938, CW11, p. 199 [481].
74. GO–Jack Common, 26 September 1938, CW11, p. 204 [486].
75. Eileen Blair–Marjorie Dakin, 27 September 1938, CW11, p. 206 [487].
76. Eileen Blair–Marjorie Dakin, 27 September 1938, CW11, p. 206 [487].
77. GO–Cyril Connolly, 14 December 1938, CW11, p. 253 [512].
78. Eileen Blair–Geoffrey Gorer, 4 October 1938, CW11, p. 217 [493].
79. GO–Jack Common, 12 October 1938, CW11, p. 222 [496].
80. GO–Jack Common, 29 September 1938, CW11, p. 212 [489].
81. GO–Leonard Moore, 1 October 1938, CW11, p. 215 [491].
82. Eileen Blair–Geoffrey Gorer, CW11, p. 218 [493].
83. GO–Charles Doran, 26 November 1938, CW11, p. 239 [504].
84. GO–John Sceats, 24 November 1938, CW11, p. 237 [504].
85. GO–George Woodcock, 28 September 1946, CW18, p. 411 [3087]
86. Eileen Blair–Mary Common, 5 December 1938, CW11, pp. 248–50 [510].
87. 'Marrakech', *New Writing*, New Series No. 3, Christmas 1939, CW11, pp. 416–21 [579].
88. GO–Jack Common, 28 December 1938, CW11, p. 259 [516]; 12 January 1939, CW11, p. 318 [525].
89. GO–Herbert Read, 4 January 1939, CW11, p. 314 [522].
90. GO–Geoffrey Gorer, 20 January 1939, CW11, p. 321 [528].
91. T. R. Fyvel, *George Orwell: A Personal Memoir*, p. 109.
92. Morocco Diary, 27 January 1938, CW11, p. 325 [530].
93. Harold Acton, *More Memoirs of an Aesthete*, p. 153.
94. Lettice Cooper, *OR*, p. 164.
95. GO–Lydia Jackson, 1 March 1939, CW11, p. 336.

96. GO–Jack Common, Sunday [9 April 1939], CW11, p. 350 [544].
97. GO–Lydia Jackson, [11] April 1939, CW11, p. 351 [345A].
98. Elisaveta Fen, *A Russian's England*, p. 431.
99. GO–Richard Rees, 31 March 1949, CW20, p. 73 [3584].
100. *CUFA*, CW7, p. 166.
101. *TLS*, 17 June 1939, p. 152.
102. *The Times*, 23 June 1939, p. 3.
103. *Spectator*, 21 July 1939, p. 106.
104. Max Plowman-GO, 19 June 1939.
105. GO–Leonard Moore, 14 July 1939 [4 July?], CW11, p. 365 [555].
106. Richard Rees, *George Orwell: Fugitive from the Camp of Victory*, p. 145.
107. GO–Brenda Salkeld, 25 June 1940, unpublished.
108. 'In Front of One's Nose', *Tribune*, 22 March 1946, CW18, p. 163 [2940].

Chapter 13: One Character in Search of a War

1. Orwell's Last Literary Notebook, CW20, p. 204 [3725].
2. Cyril Connolly in BBC *Omnibus*, 'The Road to the Left', 1970.
3. Elisaveta Fen, *A Russian's England*, p. 431.
4. Elisaveta Fen, *A Russian's England*, p. 432.
5. Fredric Warburg, *All Authors Are Equal*, p. 97.
6. 'My Country Right or Left', *Folios of New Writing*, Autumn 1940, CW12, pp. 271–2 [694].
7. 'The Limit to Pessimism': Review of *The Thirties* by Malcolm Muggeridge, *New English Review*, 25 April 1940, CW12, p. 151 [615].
8. GO–Jack Common, 23 February 1939, CW11, p. 331 [533].
9. Ethel Mannin–GO, 20 September 1939, Orwell Archive.
10. Ethel Mannin–GO, 30 October 1939, Orwell Archive.
11. Victor Gollancz–GO, 1 January 1940, Orwell Archive.
12. GO–Victor Gollancz, 8 January 1940, CW12, p. 5 [583].
13. GO–Geoffrey Gorer, 10 January 1940, CW12, p. 7 [585].
14. Paul Laity (ed.), *Left Book Club Anthology*, Victor Gollancz, London, 2001.
15. GO–Geofrey Gorer, 10 January 1940, CW12, p. 7 [585].
16. T. R. Fyvel, *George Orwell: A Personal Memoir*, p. 99.
17. T. R. Fyvel, *George Orwell: A Personal Memoir*, p. 107.
18. GO–Geoffrey Gorer, 3 April 1940, CW12, p. 137 [607].
19. 'Charles Dickens', CW12, p. 55 [597].
20. 'Charles Dickens', CW12, p. 56 [597].
21. 'Literary Criticism: The Frontiers of Art and Propaganda', *Listener*, 29 May 1941, CW12, p. 486 [792].
22. Review of *The Development of William Butler Yeats* by V. K. Narayan Menon, *Horizon*, January 1943, CW14, p. 279 [1791].
23. 'Boys' Weeklies', CW12, p. 58.
24. Fredric Warburg, *All Authors Are Equal*, p. 57.
25. GO–Geoffrey Gorer, 3 April 1940, CW12, p. 137 [607].
26. 'Frank Richards Replies to George Orwell,' *Horizon*, May 1940, CW12, p. 81 [599].
27. GO–Geoffrey Trease, 1 May 1940, CW12, pp. 156–7 [618].
28. *ITW*, 11 March 1940, CW12, p. 91 [600].
29. 'English Writing in Total War', *New Republic*, 14 July 1941, CW12, p. 530 [831].
30. *ITW*, 11 March 1940, CW12, p. 112 [600].
31. Arthur Calder-Marshall, *Time and Tide*, 9 March 1940, pp. 257–8.
32. Philip Mairet, *New English Weekly*, 14 March 1940, pp. 307–8.
33. *TLS*, 20 April 1940, p. 192.

34. Q. D. Leavis, *Scrutiny*, September 1940, pp. 173–6.

35. *The Dickensian*, 25 May 1940, CW12, p. 167.

36. War-time Diary, 20 June 1940, CW12, p. 188 [639].

37. GO–Stanley J. Kunitz and Howard Haycraft, 17 April 1940, CW12, pp. 147–8 [613].

38. GO–Humphry House, 11 April 1940, CW12, p. 141 [609].

39. *NEF*, CW9, p. 72.

40. Review of *The Great Dictator*, *Time and Tide*, 21 December 1940, CW12, p. 315 [717].

41. Review of *Film Stories* by H. G. Wells, *Tribune*, 21 June 1940, CW12, p. 190 [640].

42. GO–Stanley J. Kunitz and Howard Haycraft, 17 April 1940, CW12, pp. 147–8 [613].

43. Elisaveta Fen, 'George Orwell's First Wife', *Twentieth Century*, August 1960, p. 122.

44. T. R. Fyvel, *George Orwell: A Personal Memoir*, p. 105.

45. T. R. Fyvel, *George Orwell: A Personal Memoir*, p. 135.

46. *TLATU*, 19 February 1941, CW12, p. 413 [763].

47. War-time Diary, 14 June 1940, CW12, p. 184 [637].

48. 'Our Opportunity', *Left News*, January 1941, CW12, pp. 344–6 [737].

49. GO–Brenda Salkeld, 25 June 1940, unpublished.

50. War-time Diary, 17 September 1940, CW12, p. 263 [689].

51. War-time Diary, 24 September 1940, CW12, p. 268 [693].

52. War-time Diary, 3 March 1941, CW12, p. 443 [772].

53. War-time Diary, 6 May 1941, CW12, p. 490 [796].

54. War-time Diary, 8 April 1941, CW12, p. 468 [786].

55. War-time Diary, 30 June 1940, CW12, p. 201 [646].

56. War-time Diary, 21 and 24 June 1940, CW12, pp. 192, 196 [641, 644].

57. Patricia Donahue in *RO*, p. 119.

58. GO–Editor, *Time and Tide*, 22 June 1940, CW12, pp. 192–3 [642].

59. War-time Diary, on Balbo: 30 June 1940, CW12, p. 202 [646]; on Chiappe: 1 December 1940, CW12, p. 294 [713].

60. Arthur Koestler–Ian Angus, 30 April 1964.

61. Review of *The Lady in Question*, *Time and Tide*, 30 November 1940, CW12, p. 291 [709].

62. Review of *The Gay Mr Trexel*, *Time and Tide*, 7 December 1940, CW12, p. 304 [719].

63. Review of *Applause*, *Time and Tide*, 7 September 1940, CW12, p. 253 [684].

64. War-time Diary, 17 June 1940, CW12, p. 187 [639].

65. Orwell's BBC Record, BBC Written Archives.

66. War-time Diary, 28 June 1940, CW12, p. 199 [644].

67. War-time Diary, 24 June 1940, CW12, p. 197 [644].

68. Review of *Till the Day I Die* by Clifford Odets, *Time and Tide*, 17 August 1940, CW12, p. 235 [672].

69. War-time Diary, 23 August 1940, CW12, p. 241 [677].

70. War-time Diary, 25 July 1940, CW12, p. 220 [660].

71. GO–John Lehmann, 6 July 1940, CW12, p. 208 [652].

72. 'My Country Right or Left', *Folios of New Writing*, Autumn 1940, CW12, p. 272 [694].

73. 'English Writing in Total War', *New Republic*, 14 July 1941, CW12, p. 527 [831].

74. Review of *An Epic of the Gestapo* by Sir Paul Dukes, *Tribune*, 13 September 1940, CW12, p. 258 [686].

75. War-time Diary, 29 and 31 August 1940, CW12, p. 246 [680].

76. 'The Proletarian Writer', Draft Introduction, 12 November 1940, CW12, pp. 282–4 [704].

77. 'The Proletarian Writer', discussion between George Orwell and Desmond Hawkins, BBC broadcast 6 December 1940; *Listener*, 19 December 1940, CW12, p. 297 [715].

78. A. S. F. Gow, *Letters from Cambridge*, Cape, London, 1945, pp. 54, 98.

79. Review of *Darkness at Noon* by Arthur Koestler, *New Statesman and Nation*, 4 January 1941, CW12, pp. 357–9 [741].
80. Inez Holden Diary, 11 August 1941, in private hands.
81. *TLATU*, 19 February 1941, CW12, p. 392 [763].
82. *TLATU*, 19 February 1941, CW12, p. 401 [763].
83. *TLATU*, 19 February 1941, CW12, p. 405 [763].
84. *TLATU*, 19 February 1941, CW12, p. 432 [763].
85. *Listener*, 6 March 1941, p. 349.
86. V. S. Pritchett, 'Current Literature', *New Statesman and Nation*, 1 March 1941, p. 216.
87. Christopher Hollis, 'Men and Movements', *Tablet*, 8 March 1941, p. 194.
88. Roger Senhouse Diaries, 21 January 1941, Eton College Archive.
89. War-time Diary, 18 May 1941, CW12, p. 501 [803].
90. Inez Holden–Ian Angus, 26 May 1967.
91. 'Fascism and Democracy', Victor Gollancz (ed.), *The Betrayal of the Left*, Gollancz, London, 1941. Also CW12, p. 380 [753].
92. Inez Holden Diary, 11 August 1941.
93. John Craxton–GB interview, 25 September 1999.
94. Inez Holden Diary, 16–17 April 1941.
95. Inez Holden–Ian Angus, 4 November 1966.
96. War-time Diary, 22 April 1941, CW12, p. 480.
97. War-time Diary, 11 May 1941, CW12, p. 496 [799].
98. 'Literary Criticism IV: Literature and Totalitarianism', BBC broadcast 21 May 1941; *Listener*, 19 June 1941, CW12, p. 504 (see Note) [804].
99. *Cherwell*, 22 May 1941.
100 War-time Diary, 3 July 1941, CW12, p. 522 [826].
101 War-time Diary, 23 June 1941, CW12, p. 518 [820].
102 War-time Diary, 3 July 1941, CW12, p. 522 [826].
103 'London Letter', 17 August 1941, *Partisan Review*, November–December 1941, CW12, p. 549 [843].
104 'London Letter', 17 August 1941, *Partisan Review*, November–December 1941, CW12, p. 553 [843].
105 'London Letter', 1 January 1942, *Partisan Review*, March–April 1942, CW13, p. 108 [913].
106 Roger Senhouse Diaries, 21 August 1941, Eton College Archive.
107 Anthony Powell, *Infants of the Spring*, p. 131.

Chapter 14: War of Words

1. Arthur Koestler, in *OR*, p. 169.
2. 'London Letter', 15 April 1941, *Partisan Review*, July–August 1941, CW12, p. 472 [787].
3. R. A. Rendall, Internal memo, 25 June 1941, BBC Written Archives.
4. Leonard P. Moore–D. Pearson Smith (BBC), 25 August 1941.
5. Sir Arthur Keith–D. Pearson Smith (BBC), 28 August 1941.
6. Obituary of Hetta Empson, *Times*, 4 January 1997, p. 19.
7. William Empson in Miriam Gross (ed.), *The World of George Orwell*, Simon and Schuster, New York, 1971, p. 94.
8. Henry Swanzy in *OR*, p. 123.
9. Martin Esslin, 'Television and Telescreen', in *On Nineteen Eighty-Four*, edited by Peter Stansky, Stanford Alumni Association, Stanford, California, 1983, p. 128.
10. War-time Diary, 28 August 1941, CW13, p. 23.
11. Stevie Smith, *The Holiday*, Virago Press, 1979, p. 29.
12. Stevie Smith, *The Holiday*, p. 68.
13. Una Marson–GO, 2 April 1949, Orwell Archive.

14. Rosalind Obermeyer–Ian Angus interview, 30 January 1967.
15. GO–Anne Popham, 18 April 1946, CW18, p. 249 [2978].
16. Mary Treadgold–GB interview, 30 July 1999.
17. Martin Esslin, 'Television and Telescreen', p. 122.
18. 'London Letter', 1 January 1942, *Partisan Review*, March–April 1942, CW13, p. 113 [913].
19. 'Money and Guns', 'Through Eastern Eyes', BBC Eastern Service broadcast, 20 January 1942, CW13, p. 132 [927].
20. 'Orwell's List of Crypto-Communists and Fellow-Travellers', CW20, p. 246 [3732].
21. L. F. Rushbrook Williams–R. A. Rendall, Memo, 17 October 1941, BBC Written Archives.
22. GO–Rayner Heppenstall, 16 April 1940, CW12, pp. 146–7 [612].
23. GO–L. P. Garrod, 3 August 1943, CW15, p. 181 [2214].
24. Review of *Beggar My Neighbour* by Lionel Fielden, *Horizon*, September 1943, CW15, p. 211 [2257].
25. 'Wells, Hitler and the World State', *Horizon*, August 1941, CW12, pp. 536–41 [837].
26. Inez Holden Diary, 30 August 1941.
27. Inez Holden, 'Orwell or Wells?', *Listener*, 24 February 1972.
28. Lettice Cooper, *Black Bethlehem*, Gollancz, London, 1947, p. 154.
29. 'Room 101,' CW13, pp. 57–8 [870]; Dr Maurice O'Regan–BBC, 22 October 1941, BBC Written Archives.
30. 'Culture and Democracy', CW13, p. 78 [885].
31. David Astor–GB interview, 2 December 1999.
32. 'London Letter', 1 January 1942, *Partisan Review*, March–April 1942, CW13, p. 113 [913].
33. *ITW*, CW12, p. 98 [600].
34. 'London Letter', 1 January 1942, *Partisan Review*, March–April 1942, CW13, p. 111 [913]; 'Looking Back on the Spanish Civil War', [1942?], CW13, p. 509 [1421].
35. 'Rudyard Kipling', *Horizon*, February 1942, CW13, pp. 150–162 [948].
36. 'The End of Henry Miller', *Tribune*, 4 December 1942, CW14, p. 217 [1715].
37. 'Looking Back on the Spanish War', [1942?], CW13, p. 504 [1421].
38. War-time Diary, 27 April 1942, CW13, pp. 288–9 [1124].
39. Inez Holden, 'Orwell or Wells?', *Listener*, 24 February 1972.
40. 'The Re-discovery of Europe', 'Literature Between the Wars: I', BBC Eastern Service, 10 March 1942, CW13, pp. 209–21 [1014]; slightly edited version in *Listener*, 19 March 1942.
41. John Craxton–GB interview, 25 September 1999.
42. Sunday Wilshin interview with Stephen Wadhams, CBC.
43. Henry Swanzy interview with Stephen Wadhams, CBC.
44. Rachel Clapton–GB interview, 21 July 2000.
45. R. F. Rushbrook Williams 17/7/42/ countersigned G. C. Willams 22/7/42, BBC Written Archives.
46. War-time Diary, 14 March 1942, CW14, p. 229 [1025].
47. War-time Diary, 5 October 1942, CW14, p. 76 [1546].
48. GO–Eastern Service Director, Memo, 15 October 1942, CW14, pp. 100–1 [1571].
49. Memo from J. B. Clark to I.A.C. (OS)/2. E.S.D./ [Staff Private], BBC Written Archives.
50. Henry Dakin–GB interview, 30 March 2000.
51. Anthony Powell, *Infants of the Spring*, p. 137.
52. David Astor–GB interview, 21 December 1999.
53. Inez Holden, *It Was Different At The Time*, John Lane The Bodley Head, London, 1943.
54. George Woodcock–GO, 14 November 1942, Orwell Archive.
55. Vera Buckler–Ian Angus interview, 28 July 1965.

56. 'Not Enough Money: A Sketch of George Gissing', *Tribune*, 2 April 1943, CW13, pp. 215–17 [1987].

57. Review of *The Development of William Butler Yeats* by V. K. Narayana Menon, *Time and Tide*, 17 April 1943, CW15, p. 69 [2017].

58. Michael Meyer, *Not Prince Hamlet*, p. 60.

59. GO–G. H. Bantock, [Late 1945–early 1946], CW18, p. 456 [2825].

60. Poetic exchanges between Alex Comfort and GO: 'Letter to an American Visitor' by 'Obadiah Hornbooke' (Alex Comfort), *Tribune*, 4 June 1943, CW15, pp. 138–40 [2137]; 'As One Non-Combatant to Another (A Letter to 'Obadiah Hornbooke')', *Tribune*, 18 June 1943, CW15, pp. 142–5.

61. GO–Alex Comfort, Sunday [11? July 1943], CW15, p. 166 [2183].

62. CW15, p. 179 n. 1.

63. L. F. Rushbrook Williams, Confidential Report of Head of Dept, BBC Written Archives.

64. Memo from Indian Programme Organiser (IPO) (L. A. Bokhari–E.S.D: Subj: Mr Blair's Outside Activities), 17 August 1943, BBC Written Archives.

65. Memo EB–OSEA THROUGH ESD. [22/8], 20 August 1943, BBC Written Archives.

66. GO–Rayner Heppenstall, 24 August 1943, CW13, p. 206 [2247].

67. GO–L. F. Rushbrook Williams, 24 September 1943, CW15, p. 250 [2283].

68. L. F. Rushbrook Williams 20/11/43, BBC Written Archives.

69. Elizabeth Knight interview, BBC *Arena*, 1984.

70. 'As I Please', 44, *Tribune*, 13 October 1944, CW16, p. 428 [2562].

71. Medical Report, 22 October 1943, BBC Written Archives.

72. William Empson in Miriam Gross (ed.), *The World of George Orwell*, p. 95.

73. David Astor–GB interview, 21 December 1999.

74. Anthony Powell, *Infants of the Spring*, p. 140.

Chapter 15: Tribune of the People

1. *Tribune*, 26 November 1943, p. 5.

2. Peter Vansittart–GB interview, 6 September 1999.

3. Margaret Crosland–GB interview, June 2000.

4. David Sylvester–GB interview, 20 March 2000.

5. Paul Potts, *RO*, p. 139.

6. John Morris, 'That Curiously Crucified Expression', *Penguin New Writing*, No. 40, September 1950; OR, pp. 171–6.

7. 'As I Please', 71, *Tribune*, 31 January 1947, CW19, p. 37 [3107].

8. Julian Symons in *RO*, p. 146.

9. Julian Symons in *RO*, pp. 146–7.

10. Michael Foot in BBC *Omnibus*, 'The Road to the Left', 1970; T. R. Fyvel, *George Orwell: A Personal Memoir*, p. 140.

11. 'As I Please', 60, *Tribune*, 8 November 1946, CW18, p. 462 [3108].

12. Review of *Arrival and Departure* by Arthur Koestler, *Manchester Evening News*, 9 December 1943, CW16, p. 19 [2389].

13. GO–Leonard Moore, 9 January 1944, CW16, p. 59 [2403].

14. Michael Meyer, *Not Prince Hamlet*, pp. 65–9.

15. Lettice Cooper, *RO*, p. 131.

16. J. R. R. Tolkien, 'On Fairy Stories', *Tree and Leaf*, Unwin Books, London, 1964, p. 20.

17. GO–Dorothy Plowman, 19 February 1946, CW18, p. 115 [2903].

18. Review of *An Unknown Land* by Viscount Samuel, *Listener*, 24 December 1942, CW14, p. 254.

19. 'As I Please', 10, *Tribune*, 4 February 1944, CW16, p. 89 [2416].

20. GO–Gleb Struver, 17 February 1944, CW16, p. 99 [2421].

21. Michael Meyer, *Not Prince Hamlet*, p. 72.

22. Review of *The Heart of the Matter* by Graham Greene, *New Yorker*, 17 July 1948, pp. 405–6 [3424].

23. GO–Anthony Powell, 25 June 1948, CW19, p. 313 [3416].

24. GO–Leonard Moore, 19 March 1944, CW16, pp. 126–7 [2436].

25. GO–Victor Gollancz, 19 March 1944, CW16, p. 127 [2437].

26. Victor Gollancz–GO, 23 March 1944, Orwell Archive.

27. GO–Victor Gollancz, 25 March 1944, CW16, p. 135 [2442].

28. Victor Gollancz–GO, 2 April 1944, CW16, p. 142 [2448n].

29. Michael Meyer, *Not Prince Hamlet*, pp. 65–9.

30. *AF*, CW8, p. 95.

31. V. S. Pritchett, Review of *Critical Essays*, *New Statesman and Nation*, 16 February 1946, p. 124.

32. Michael Sayers–GB interview, 23 September 2000.

33. Review of *Faith, Reason and Civilization* by Harold Laski, submitted to but not used by the *Manchester Evening News*, 13 March 1944, CW16, p. 123 [2434].

34. 'London Letter', 17 April 1944, *Partisan Review*, Summer 1944, CW16, p. 159 [2425].

35. Jonathan Cape–Leonard Moore, 16 June 1944, Orwell Archive.

36. GO–Leonard Moore, 9 May 1944, CW16, p. 182 [2466].

37. T. S. Eliot–GO, 13 July 1944, Orwell Archive.

38. 'Arthur Koestler', 11 September 1944, CW16, p. 394 [2548].

39. GO–Dwight MacDonald, 4 April 1945, CW17, p. 120 [2652].

40. Review of *Four Quartets* by T. S. Eliot, *Manchester Evening News*, 5 October 1944, CW16, p. 422 [2559].

41. Diane Athill, *Stet: A Memoir*, Granta Books, London, 2000, p. 32.

42. GO–Leonard Moore, 23 February 1946, CW18, p. 123 [2908].

43. Review of *'42 to '44: A Contemporary Memoir upon Human Behaviour During the Crisis of the World Revolution* by H. G. Wells, *Observer*, 21 May 1944, p. 198 [2474].

44. David Astor–GB interview, 2 December 1999.

45. 'Benefit of Clergy: Some Notes on Salvador Dali', intended for *Saturday Book*, 4, 1944, CW16, pp. 232–40 [2481].

46. 'Raffles and Miss Blandish', *Horizon*, October 1944, CW16, pp. 345–8 [2538].

47. 'Decline of the English Murder', *Tribune*, 15 February 1946, CW18, pp. 108–10 [2900]; 'As I Please', 52, *Tribune*, 29 December 1944, CW16, pp. 505–6 [2595].

48. 'Arthur Koestler', CW16, p. 393 [2548].

49. 'Catastrophic Gradualism', *C.W. Review*, November 1945, CW17, p. 343 [2778].

50. 'Marx and Russia', *Observer*, 15 February 1948, CW19, p. 269 [3346].

51. Anthony Powell, *Infants of the Spring*, p. 134.

52. Bernard Crick, *George Orwell: A Life*, pp. 464–5.

53. Michael Shelden, *Orwell: The Authorized Biography*, p. 419.

54. Lettice Cooper, *RO*, pp. 130–1.

55. Inez Holden, 'Summer Journal', *Leaves in the Storm* (edited by Stephen Schimanski and Henry Treece), Lindsay Drummond, London, 1947, p. 248; see CW16, p. 283n.

56. 'Just Junk – But Could You Resist It?', *Evening Standard*, 5 January 1946, CW18, p. 16 [2841].

57. T. R. Fyvel, *George Orwell: A Personal Memoir*, p. 147.

58. Paul Potts, 'Don Quixote on a Bicycle', *London Magazine*, 4 March 1957, p. 40.

59. 'As I Please', 66, *Tribune*, 20 December 1946, CW18, p. 518 [3137].

60. 'As I Please', 50, *Tribune*, 1 December 1944, CW16, p. 487 [2586].

61. 'As I Please', 57, *Tribune*, 2 February 1945, CW17, p. 38 [2613].

62. 'As I Please', 40, *Tribune*, 1 September 1944, CW16, p. 362 [2541].

63. 'As I Please', 40, *Tribune*, 1 September 1944, CW16, p. 371 [2541].

64. 'As I Please', 41, *Tribune*, 8 September 1944, CW16, p. 387 [2547].

65. 'As I Please', 41, *Tribune*, 8 September 1944, CW16, pp. 385–91 [2547].

66. 'As I Please', 54, *Tribune*, 12 January 1945, CW17, p. 19 [2603].

67. Lettice Cooper, interview with Stephen Wadhams, CBC.

68. Eileen Blair–GO, 21 March 1945, CW17, p. 99 [2638]: 'It would be better to find somewhere with more space because you and Richard would be too much for the cottage very soon and I don't know where his sister could go.'

69. 'As I Please', 58, *Tribune*, 9 February 1945, CW17, p. 43 [2616].

70. 'Funny, But Not Vulgar', [1 December 1944], *Leader Magazine*, 28 July 1945, CW16, pp. 482–7 [2585].

71. 'As I Please', 51, *Tribune*, 8 December 1944, CW16, p. 495 [2590].

72. 'As I Please', 57, *Tribune*, 2 February 1945, CW17, p. 39.

73. Stephen Spender in *RO*, p. 106.

Chapter 16: The Dark Side of Solitude

1. Review of *The Condemned Playground* by Cyril Connolly, *Observer*, 2 December 1945, CW17, p. 413.

2. GO–Duchess of Atholl, 15 November 1945, CW17, p. 384 [2795].

3. 'As I Please', 58, *Tribune*, 9 February 1945, CW17, p. 43 [2616].

4. 'Notes for My Literary Executor', signed 31 March 1945, CW17, p. 113 [2648].

5. Harold Acton, *More Memoirs of an Aesthete*, pp. 152–3.

6. A. J. Ayer interview with Stephen Wadhams, CBC.

7. 'In Defence of P. G. Wodehouse', *Windmill*, No. 2, [July] 1945, CW17, pp. 51–63 [2624].

8. P. G. Wodehouse–Denis Macail, 11 August 1951, in Frances Donaldson (ed.), *Letters of P. G. Wodehouse*, Hutchinson, London, 1990, pp. 191–2.

9. Ernest Hemingway–Harvey Breit, 16 April–1 May 1952, University of Tulsa, Special Collections.

10. GO–Celia Kirwan, 29 January 1948, CW19, p. 258 [3332].

11. 'Paris Puts a Gay Face on her Miseries', *Observer*, 25 February 1945, CW17, p. 64 [2625A] [Appendix to *Collected Works*].

12. GO–Leonard Moore, 29 November 1945, CW17, p. 402 [2806].

13. Review of *Huis Clos* by Jean-Paul Sartre, *Tribune*, 30 November 1945, CW17, p. 406 [2808].

14. Albert Camus, *Notebooks 1942–1951*, Knopf, New York, 1965, p. 150.

15. GO–Christy & Moore, 20 September 1947, CW19, p. 207 [3275A].

16. Eileen Blair–GO, 21 March 1945, CW17, p. 99.

17. Eileen Blair–GO, 21 March 1945, CW17, p. 97 [2638].

18. Eileen Blair–Lettice Cooper, 23 March 1945, CW17, p. 105 [2640].

19. Eileen Blair–Leonard Moore, 22 March 1945, CW17, p. 104 [2639].

20. A. J. Ayer, interview with Stephen Wadhams, CBC.

21. Inez Holden Diary, 5 April 1945.

22. Paul Potts in *OR*, p. 145.

23. Susan Watson in *RO*, p. 157.

24. Nellie Limouzin–Marjorie Dakin, 16 April 1945, CW17, p. 128 [2659].

25. Stephen Spender in *RO*, p. 145.

26. Edna Bussey–Ian Angus, 19 September 1968.

27. Lettice Cooper, interview with Stephen Wadhams, CBC.

28. Anne Popham, 18 April 1946, CW18, p. 249 [2978].

29. GO–Dorothy Plowman, 19 February 1946, CW18, p. 115 [2903].

30. Eileen's death certificate.

31. GO–Anthony Powell, 13 April 1945, CW17, p. 124 [2656].

32. Fredric Warburg–GO, 6 April 1945, CW17, p. 121 [2653].

33. GO–Anne Popham, 18 April 1946, CW17, p. 250 [2978].

34. Bernard Crick, *George Orwell: A Life*, p. 700.
35. 'London Letter', *Partisan Review*, Summer 1945, CW17, pp. 164–5 [2672].
36. Susan Watson in *OR*, pp. 217–18.
37. Inez Holden Diary, 26 June 1945.
38. Roger Senhouse Diary, 24 July 1945, Eton College Library.
39. Malcolm Muggeridge, *Like it Was* [Diaries], William Collins, London, 1981, p. 195.
40. John Craxton–GB interview, 25 September 1999.
41. Review of *Mind at the End of Its Tether*, by H. G. Wells, *Manchester Evening News*, 8 November 1945, CW17, p. 359 [2784].
42. Cyril Connolly, *Horizon*, September 1945, pp. 215–16.
43. Kingsley Martin, *New Statesman and Nation*, 8 September 1945, pp. 165–6.
44. Graham Greene, *Evening Standard*, 10 August 1945, p. 6.
45. Reginald Reynolds–GO, 22 August 1945, Orwell Archive.
46. Dwight MacDonald–GO, 31 December 1945, Orwell Archive.
47. Extract of letter from Malcolm Muggeridge to Orwell, 13 September 1945, CW17, p. 289 [2752].
48. GO–Dwight MacDonald, 3 January 1946, CW18, p. 11 [2839].
49. William Empson–GO, 24 August 1945, Orwell Archive.
50. Michael Davie (ed.), *The Diaries of Evelyn Waugh*, Weidenfeld & Nicolson, 1976, Penguin, Harmondsworth, 1979, p. 633.
51. Evelyn Waugh–GO, 30 August 1945, Mark Amory (ed.), *The Letters of Evelyn Waugh*, Penguin, Harmondsworth, 1982, p. 211.
52. 'You and the Atom Bomb', *Tribune*, 19 October 1945: CW17, p. 321 [2770].
53. 'The Prevention of Literature', *Polemic*, No. 2, January 1946, *The Atlantic Monthly*, March 1947, CW17, pp. 376, 374 [2792].
54. Fredric Warburg, *All Authors Are Equal*, p. 55.
55. GO–Leonard Moore, 22 January 1946, CW18, p. 54 [2871].
56. GO–Geoffrey Gorer, 22 January 1946, CW18, p. 53 [2870].
57. Yvonne Davet–GO, 22 March 1946, CW18, p. 172 [2949].
58. Michael Sayers–GB interview, 12 July 2000.
59. GO–Ruth Fischer, 21 April 1949, CW20, p. 94 [3603].
60. See Orwell on Zamyatin's *We* in 'Freedom and Happiness', *Tribune*, 4 January 1946, CW18, pp. 13–17 [2841].
61. Sonia Brownell–Daniel Bronda interview, 20 May 1963, Orwell Archive.
62. Arthur Koestler–Ian Angus, 30 April 1964.
63. John Russell–GB interview, 28 June 2000.
64. Hilary Spurling, *The Girl from the Fiction Department*, Hamish Hamilton, London, 2002.
65. Michael Meyer–GB interview, 5 April 2000.
66. Quoted in Michael Shelden, *Friends of Promise*, Hamish Hamilton, London 1989, p. 160.
67. Review of *Twilight Bar* by Arthur Koestler, *Tribune*, 30 November 1945, CW17, p. 409 [2808].
68. Arthur Koestler quoted by T. R. Fyvel, *George Orwell: A Personal Memoir*, p. 146.
69. T. R. Fyvel, *George Orwell: A Personal Memoir*, p. 209.
70. GO–Dorothy Plowman, 15 February 1946, CW18, p. 116 [2903].
71. Celia Kirwan–Mamaine Koestler, 28 January 1946, Private hands.
72. Celia Goodman (Celia Kirwan), *RO*, p. 164.
73. GO–Brenda Salkeld, 15 February 1946, unpublished.
74. Fredric Warburg, *All Authors Are Equal*, p. 93.
75. Evelyn Waugh, *The Tablet*, 6 April 1946, p. 176.
76. V. S. Pritchett, *New Statesman and Nation*, 16 February 1946, p. 124.

77. GO–Anne Popham, 15 March 1946, CW18, pp. 153–4 [2931].
78. GO–Anne Popham, 18 April 1946, CW18, pp. 248–50 [2978].
79. 'George Gissing', [May–June 1948?], CW19, p. 349 [3406].

Chapter 17: The Man Who Loved Islands
1. GO–Leonard Moore, 22 March 1946, CW18, p. 166 [2942].
2. GO–Stafford Cottman, 25 April 1946, CW18, pp. 257–8 [2984].
3. Fredric Warburg internal memorandum, Secker and Warburg, 14 January 1946, CW18, p. 38 [2861].
4. 'Confessions of a Book Reviewer', *Tribune*, 3 May 1946, CW18, p. 350 [2992].
5. 'Some Thoughts on the Common Toad', *Tribune*, 12 April 1946, CW18, pp. 238–9 [2970].
6. 'Some Thoughts on the Common Toad', *Tribune*, 12 April 1946, CW18, p. 240 [2970].
7. John Betjeman–GO, 18 April 1946, Orwell Archive.
8. T. R. Fyvel, *George Orwell: A Personal Memoir*, p. 162; War-time Diary, 9 August 1940, CW12, p. 229 [667].
9. GO–Humphrey Dakin, 8 May 1946, CW18, p. 309 [2998].
10. Jane Morgan–GB interview, 21 March 2000.
11. George Kopp–GO, 20 March 1946, Orwell Archive.
12. GO–Celia Kirwan, 20 January 1948, CW19, p. 258 [3332].
13. 'The Prevention of Literature', *Polemic*, No. 2, January 1946; *Atlantic*, March 1947, CW17, p. 377 [2792].
14. 'As I Please', *Tribune*, 29 November 1946, CW18, p. 504 [3126].
15. Martin Martin, *A Description of the Western Islands of Scotland*, 1703, Eneas Mackay, Stirling, 1934, p. 267.
16. Margaret Fletcher, *RO*, p. 170.
17. Michael Meyer, *Not Prince Hamlet*, p. 72.
18. GO–George Woodcock, 2 September 1946, CW18, p. 385 [3085].
19. GO–Brenda Salkeld, 30 June 1946, unpublished.
20. Inez Holden's Diary, 16 August 1947.
21. GO–Sonia Brownell, 12 April 1947, CW19, pp. 123–4 [3212].
22. GO–Helmut Klöse, 26 September 1946, CW18, p. 407 [3083].
23. GO–Gwen O'Shaughnessy, 1 January 1948, CW19, p. 247 [3324].
24. Avril Blair–Humphrey Dakin, 1 July 1946, CW18, p. 337 [3025].
25. Paul Potts, *RO*, p. 182.
26. Avril Blair–Humphrey Dakin, 1 July 1946, CW18, p. 337 [3025].
27. Jeffrey Meyers, *Orwell: Wintry Conscience of a Generation*, p. 259.
28. David Holbrook–GB interview, 6 December 2000.
29. GO–George Woodcock, 12 August 1946, CW18, p. 373 [3048].
30. 'Vogue Spotlight' by Allene Talmey, *Vogue* (New York), 15 September 1946, CW18, p. 396 [3068].
31. GO–Gleb Struve, 25 February 1948, CW18, p. 276 [3354].
32. Edmund Wilson, *New Yorker*, 7 September 1946, p. 89.
33. Isaac Rosenfeld, *Nation*, 7 September 1946, pp. 273–4.
34. Orville Prescott, 'Outstanding Novels', *Yale Review*, Vol. 26, No. 2, December 1946, p. 381.
35. Edward Weeks, 'The Atlantic Bookshelf', *Atlantic*, Vol. 178, No. 3, September 1946, p. 142.
36. GO–Dwight MacDonald, 5 December 1946, CW18, p. 506 [3128].
37. GO–Richard Rees, 5 July 1946, CW18, p. 340 [3028].
38. 'Why I Write', *Gangrel*, [No. 4, Summer] 1946, CW18, p. 318 [3007].
39. Domestic Diary, 29 September 1946, CW18, pp. 411–12 [3088].

40. 'How the Poor Die', *Now*, [n.s.], No. 6 [November 1946], CW18, pp. 459–67 [3104].
41. GO–George Woodcock, 28 September 1946, CW18, p. 411 [3087].
42. Anthony Powell, *Infants of the Spring*, p. 138.
43. 'Politics vs. Literature', *Polemic*, No. 5, September–October 1946, CW18, p. 430.
44. GO–Leonard Moore, 23 October 1946, CW18, p. 453 [3100].
45. Fredric Warburg, *All Authors Are Equal*, p. 92.
46. 'London Letter', *Partisan Review*, Summer 1946, CW18, p. 291 [2990].
47. 'Lear, Tolstoy and the Fool', *Polemic*, No. 7, March 1947, CW19, pp. 54–67 [3181].
48. Rodney Phillips–GB interview, 30 November 1999.
49. Introduction to *British Pamphleteers*, Vol. 1, edited by George Orwell and Reginald Reynolds [written Spring 1947?; published 15 November 1948], CW19, p. 115 [3206].
50. 'Why I Write', *Gangrel*, [No. 4, Summer] 1946, CW18, p. 319 [3007].
51. GO–Julian Symons, 2 January 1948, CW19, p. 250 [3325].
52. Fredric Warburg, *All Authors Are Equal*, p. 48.

Chapter 18: The Nightmare and the Novel
1. John Russell–GB interview, 28 June 2000.
2. GO–Sonia Brownell, 12 April 1947, CW19, pp. 123–4 [3212].
3. GO–F. D. Barber, 15 April 1947, CW19, p. 126 [3214].
4. Domestic Diary, 13 May 1947, CW19, p. 142 [3227].
5. Domestic Diary, 21 May 1947, CW19, p. 145 [3227].
6. Bill Dunn, *RO*, p. 184.
7. 'As I Please', 14, *Tribune*, 3 March 1944, CW16, p. 112 [2429].
8. *NEF*, CW9, p. 142.
9. 'Arthur Koestler', 11 September 1944, CW16, pp. 394, 399 [2548].
10. 'As I Please', 22, *Tribune*, 28 April 1944, CW16, pp. 172–3 [2460].
11. 'Toward European Unity', *Partisan Review*, July–August 1947, CW19, p. 163 [3244].
12. GO–T. R. Fyvel, 31 December 1947, CW19, pp. 240–1 [3322].
13. GO–Julian Symons, 29 October 1948, CW19, p. 461 [3481].
14. GO–Fredric Warburg, 4 May 1946, CW18, p. 305 [2994].
15. GO–Fredric Warburg, 31 May 1947, CW19, p. 149 [3232].
16. Review of *The Collected Stories of Katherine Mansfield*, *Observer*, 13 January 1946, CW18, p. 35 [2858].
17. 'Toward European Unity', *Partisan Review*, July–August 1947, CW19, p. 163 [3244].
18. Anthony West, *New Yorker*, 28 January 1956, pp. 86–92.
19. Review of *Barbarians and Philistines: Democracy and the Public Schools* by T. C. Worsley, *Time and Tide*, 14 September 1940, CW12, pp. 261–2 [688].
20. T. R. Fyvel, Letter to the Editor, *Spectator*, 14 September 1956, p. 351.
21. Domestic Diary, 12 June 1947, CW19, p. 155 [3240].
22. GO–Leonard Moore, 28 July 1947, CW19, p. 178 [3251].
23. Jane Morgan–GB interview, 31 March 2000.
24. GO–Anthony Powell, 8 September 1947, CW19, p. 200 [3267].
25. GO–Julian Symons, 2 January 1948, CW19, p. 249 [3325].
26. GO–Dwight MacDonald, 7 March 1948, CW19, p. 281 [3359].
27. GO–John Middleton Murry, 20 February 1948, CW19, p. 273 [3350].
28. GO–Humphrey Dakin, 3 January 1948, CW19, p. 251 [3326].
29. GO–Leonard Moore, 7 December 1947, CW19, p. 234 [3313].
30. GO–Celia Kirwan, 7 December 1947, CW19, p. 233 [3312].
31. GO–Frederick Tomlinson, 23 December 1947, CW19, p. 235 [3315].
32. GO–Fredric Warburg, 4 February 1948, CW19, p. 264 [3339].
33. GO–Julian Symons, 26 December 1947, CW19, p. 237 [3318].

34. GO–Helmut Klöse, 12 January 1948, CW19, p. 256 [3330].

35. Dr James Williamson, *RO*, p. 198.

36. GO–David Astor, Monday [9 February 1948], CW19, p. 266 [3342].

37. GO–George Woodcock, 4 January 1948, CW19, p. 254 [3329].

38. GO–Celia Kirwan, 20 January 1948, CW19, p. 257 [3332].

39. David Astor–Bruce Dick, 19 February 1948, Orwell Archive.

40. GO–Fredric Warburg, 22 February 1948, CW19, p. 275 [3353].

41. GO–Anthony Powell, 8 March 1948, CW19, p. 283 [3360].

42. GO–Julian Symons, 20 April 1948, CW19, pp. 321–2 [3386].

43. 'Writers and Leviathan', *Politics and Letters*, Summer 1948, CW19, p. 288 [3364].

44. Diary Entry, 24 March 1949, CW19, p. 310 [3378].

45. Dr J. Williamson, BBC *Arena*, 1984.

46. GO–Dwight MacDonald, 7 March 1948, CW19, p. 282 [3359].

47. GO–Roger Senhouse, 19 April 1948, CW19, p. 320 [3385].

48. GO–Julian Symons, 20 April 1948, CW19, pp. 321–2 [3386].

49. GO–Lydia Jackson, 24 May 1948, CW19, p. 341 [3402A].

50. GO–Celia Kirwan, 27 May 1948, CW19, p. 344 [3405].

51. 'George Gissing', May–June 1948?, CW19, p. 347 [3406].

52. 'George Gissing', May–June 1948?, CW19, p. 352 [3406].

53. Review of *Great Morning* by Osbert Sitwell, *Adelphi*, July–September 1948, CW, p. 397 [3418].

54. GO–George Woodcock, 12 July 1948, CW19, p. 402 [3421].

55. Fredric Warburg–GO, 19 July 1948, CW19, p. 409 [3426].

56. GO–George Woodcock, 12 January 1949, CW20, p. 16 [3521].

57. Avril Dunn, 'My Brother, George Orwell', *Twentieth Century*, March 1961, p. 260.

58. Bruce Dick–David Astor, 5 January 1949, CW20, p. 13 [3518].

59. GO–David Astor, 9 October 1948, CW19, p. 451 [3467].

60. GO–Fredric Warburg, 22 October 1948, CW19, pp. 456–7 [3477].

61. Peter Davison note, CW20, p. 19 n3 [3525].

62. Eileen O'Shaughnessy, 'End of the Century, 1984', *Sunderland Church High School for Girls Chronicle*, June 1934, pp. 81–2.

63. GO–Julian Symons, 29 October 1948, CW19, pp. 460–1 [3481].

64. Roger Senhouse–GO, 2 November 1948, CW19, p. 463 [3483].

65. GO–David Astor, 19 November 1948, CW18, pp. 468–9 [3490].

66. Fredric Warburg–GO, 26 November 1948, CW19, p. 472 (note 3) [3495].

67. Avril Dunn, 'My Brother, George Orwell', *Twentieth Century*, March 1961, p. 260.

68. Avril Blair–Humphrey Dakin, 14 December 1948, Orwell Archive.

69. 'Fredric Warburg's Report on *Nineteen Eighty-Four*', 13 December 1948, CW19, pp. 479–81 [3505].

70. See e.g. 'Looking Back on the Spanish War', [1942?], CW13, p. 504 [1421].

71. *NEF*, CW9, p. 17.

72. L. F. Rushbrook Williams, Confidential Report of Head of Dept, 7 August 1943, BBC Written Archives.

73. Richard Rees–Malcolm Muggeridge, 8 March 1955, in Miriam Gross (ed.), *The World of George Orwell*, p. 167.

74. 'Notes on the Way', *Time and Tide*, 30 March and 6 April 1940, CW12, p. 127 [604]; *ITW*, 11 March 1940, CW12, p. 105 [600].

75. *NEF*, CW9, pp. 265–7.

76. *NEF*, CW9, p. 80.

77. 'The Prevention of Literature', *Polemic*, No. 2, January 1946, CW17, p. 380 [2792].

78. GO–Fredric Warburg, 21 December 1948, CW19, p. 486 [3511].

79. GO–Roger Senhouse, 26 December 1948, CW19, pp. 487–8 [3513].

80. Domestic Diary, 5 December 1948, CW19, p. 479 [3504].
81. Avril Dunn, 'My Brother, George Orwell', *Twentieth Century*, March 1961, p. 261.
82. GO–David Astor, 21 December 1948, CW19, p. 485 [3510].
83. 'Why I Write', *Gangrel*, [No. 4, Summer] 1946, CW18, p. 320 [3007].

Chapter 19: The End of the Beginning

1. GO–Jacintha Buddicom, 14 February 1949, CW20, p. 42 [3550].
2. Dr Bruce Dick–David Astor, 5 January 1949, CW19, p. 13 [3518].
3. GO–Herbert Read, 26 February 1949, CW20, p. 48 [3554].
4. GO–Fredric Warburg, 17 January 1949, CW20, p. 18 [3524].
5. GO–Richard Rees, 18 January 1949, CW20, p. 23 [3529].
6. Fredric Warburg, *All Authors Are Equal*, pp. 107–8.
7. Fredric Warburg, *All Authors Are Equal*, pp. 108–9.
8. GO–Richard Rees, 28 January 1949, CW20, p. 30 [3536].
9. GO–Julian Symons, 2 February 1949, CW20, p. 31 [3538].
10. GO–Jacintha Buddicom, 14 February 1949, CW20, p. 42 [3550].
11. GO–Jacintha Buddicom, Tuesday [15 February 1949], CW20, p. 44 [3551].
12. Malcolm Muggeridge, *Like it Was*, pp. 324–5.
13. Malcolm Muggeridge, *Like it Was*, p. 324.
14. Malcolm Muggeridge, *Like it Was*, p. 330.
15. T. R. Fyvel–H. Fink, 18 October 1962, Ian Angus files.
16. GO–Anthony Powell, 2 February 1949, CW20, p. 31 [3537].
17. GO–Rees, 28 January 1949, CW20, p. 30 [3536].
18. Fredric Warburg, *All Authors Are Equal*, p. 110.
19. GO–Leonard Moore, 17 March 1949, CW20, pp. 66–7 [3575].
20. Eugene Reynal–J. Edgar Hoover, 22 April 1949, CIA files.
21. GO–Richard Rees, 8 April 1949, CW20, p. 82 [3593].
22. GO–William Philips, 8 June 1949, CW20, p. 130 [3644].
23. GO–Richard Rees, 17 April 1949, CW20, p. 88 [3600].
24. GO–Gwen O'Shaughnessy, 17 April 1949, CW20, p. 91 [3601].
25. Diary Entry, Last Literary Notebook, 17 April 1949, CW20, p. 92 [3602].
26. GO–Celia Kirwan, 6 April 1949, CW20, p. 322 [3590B].
27. GO–Richard Rees, 2 May 1949, CW20, p. 105 [3617].
28. Eugene Reynal–J. Edgar Hoover, 22 April 1949, CIA files.
29. GO–Richard Rees, 25 April 1949, CW20, p. 97 [3607].
30. GO–Anthony Powell, 11 May 1949, CW20, p. 109 [3622].
31. GO–David Astor, 9 May 1949, CW20, p. 108 [3621].
32. T. R. Fyvel, *George Orwell: A Personal Memoir*, p. 162.
33. GO–Fredric Warburg, 16 May 1949, CW20, p. 116 [3626].
34. GO–Fredric Warburg, Friday [27 May 1949], CW20, pp. 121–2 [3635].
35. GO–Fredric Warburg, [27 May 1949]; Andrew Morland–Fredric Warburg, 25 May 1949, CW20, pp. 121–2 [3635].
36. Fredric Warburg, *All Authors Are Equal*, p. 113.
37. Robert Kee, *Spectator*, 17 June 1949, p. 834.
38. V. S. Pritchett, *New Statesman and Nation*, 18 June 1949, pp. 645–8.
39. Harold Nicolson, *Observer*, 12 June 1949, p. 7.
40. Julian Symons, *TLS*, 10 June 1949, p. 380.
41. GO–Julian Symons, 16 June 1949, CW20, p. 137 [3647].
42. Arthur Calder-Marshall, *Reynolds News*, 12 June 1949, p. 4.
43. GO–Mr Shaw, 20 June 1949, CW20, p. 137 [3650].
44. Gillian Fenwick, George *Orwell Bibliography*, St Paul's Bibliographies, Winchester, 1998, p. 131.

45. Publication of *Nineteen Eighty-Four*, CW20, p. 127 [3643].
46. Fredric Warburg, *All Authors Are Equal*, pp. 118–19; John Rodden, *The Politics of Literary Reputation: The Making and Claiming of 'St George' Orwell*, Oxford University Press, New York, 1989, p. 26.
47. Diana Trilling, *Nation*, 25 June 1949, pp. 716–17.
48. Mark Schorer, *New York Times Book Review*, 10 June 1949, p. 2.
49. Philip Rahv, *Partisan Review*, July 1949, p. 749.
50. Lawrence Durrell–GO, June/July 1949, Orwell Archive.
51. Aldous Huxley–GO, 21 October 1949, Orwell Archive.
52. Ruth Graves–GO, 23 July 1949, CW20, p. 150 [3664]; Nancy Parratt–GO, 8 December 1949, CW20, p. 183.
53. Julian Symons, 'Orwell, a Reminiscence', *London Magazine*, September 1963, p. 47.
54. Fredric Warburg, *All Authors Are Equal*, p. 120.
55. Francis Wyndham–GB interview, 5 August 2000.
56. Maude Locke–GB, 13 May 1999.
57. GO–Astor, 18 July 1949, CW20, p. 147 [3661].
58. Fredric Warburg, *All Authors Are Equal*, p. 120.
59. GO–Jack Common, 27 July 1949, CW20, p. 152 [3666].
60. GO–Fredric Warburg, 22 August 1949, CW20, p. 159 [3678].
61. Hilary Spurling, *The Girl from the Fiction Department*, p. 100.
62. GO–David Astor, 5 September 1949, CW20, p. 165 [3686].
63. GO–Richard Rees, 17 September 1949, CW20, p. 169 [3692].
64. 'Star Man's Diary', *Star*, 17 September 1949, CW20, pp. 169–70 [3693].
65. Robert Kee–GB interview, 4 December 1999.
66. Frances Partridge, *Everything To Lose: Diaries 1945–1960*, Little, Brown, Boston, 1985, p. 98.
67. Quoted by Michael Shelden, 'The Merry Widow', *The Age*, 13 July 2002; Francis Wyndham–GB interview, 5 August 2000.
68. Malcolm Muggeridge, *Like it Was*, p. 354.
69. Malcolm Muggeridge, *Like it Was*, pp. 353–4.
70. GO–Leonard Moore, 11 October 1949, CW20, pp. 174–5 [3700].
71. Janetta Parladé–GB interview, 25 November 1999.
72. W. Somerset Maugham, 'Sanatorium', *The Complete Short Stories*, Vol. 2, Heinemann, London, 1951, p. 928.
73. Frances Donaldson, *Evelyn Waugh: Portrait of a Country Neighbour*, Weidenfeld & Nicolson, London, 1968, p. 26.
74. T. R. Fyvel, *George Orwell: A Personal Memoir*, p. 152.
75. Frances Partridge, *Everything to Lose*, p. 98.
76. Malcolm Muggeridge, *Like it Was*, p. 359.
77. Anthony Powell, *Infants of the Spring*, pp. 141–2.
78. GO–T. R. Fyvel, 25 October 1949, CW20, p. 177 [3705].
79. Dr Howard Nicholson–GB interview, 12 May 2000.
80. W. Somerset Maugham, *The Razor's Edge*, Heinemann, 1944, Mandarin, London 1994, p. 1.
81. Stephen Spender, *Journals 1939–1983*, Faber and Faber, London, 1985, pp. 108–9.
82. Malcolm Muggeridge, *Like it Was*, pp. 357–8.
83. Dr Howard Nicholson–GB interview, 12 May 2000.
84. Malcolm Muggeridge, *Like it Was*, p. 368.
85. Dr Harold Nicholson–GB interview, 12 May 2000.
86. Nicholas Parsons, *The Book of Literary Lists*, Sigwick and Jackson, London, 1985, p. 67; Fredric Warburg, *All Authors Are Equal*, p. 114–15.
87. Desmond MacCarthy–GO, 29 December 1949, Orwell Archive.

88. Michael Shelden says that Orwell gave Sonia a blank cheque to buy this expensive item; Francis Wyndham, *London Review of Books*, 7 November 1971, p. 4, says it was inexpensive.

89. War-time Diary, 19 May 1942, CW13, p. 331 [1182].

90. Audrey Dawson, interview with Stephen Wadhams, CBC.

91. Denzil Jacobs–GB interview, 30 September 1999.

92. Review of *A Modern De Quincey* by Captain H. R. Robinson, *Observer*, 13 September 1942, CW14, p. 34 [1481].

93. 'Lear, Tolstoy and the Fool', *Polemic*, No. 7, March 1947, CW19, p. 64 [3181].

94. Anthony Powell, *Infants of the Spring*, p. 142; Malcolm Muggeridge, *Like it Was*, p. 263.

95. Malcolm Muggeridge, *Like it Was*, p. 374.

96. Malcolm Muggeridge, *Like it Was*, p. 375.

97. Inez Holden Diary, 22 January 1950.

98. Evelyn Waugh–Nancy Mitford, January [1950], *The Letters of Evelyn Waugh*, Penguin, Harmondsworth, 1980, p. 320.

99. *DAOIPAL*, CW1, p. 169.

100. Malcolm Muggeridge, *Like it Was*, p. 375.

101. Malcolm Muggeridge, *Like it Was*, p. 376.

102. John Carter–Ian Angus, 1967.

103. Malcolm Muggeridge, *Like it Was*, p. 376.

104. Anthony Powell, *To Keep the Ball Rolling*, Vol. III: *Faces in my Times*, Heinemann, London, 1980, pp. 220–1.

105. Jane Morgan-GB interview, 31 March 2000.

106. GO–Brenda Salkeld, [October 1931], CW10, p. 236 [118].

107. George Woodcock, 'Orwell, Blair and the Critics', *Sewanee Review*, 83, 1975, p. 525.

Chapter 20: Life After Death

1. 'Benefit of Clergy: Some Notes on Salvador Dali', [1944], CW16, p. 237 [2481].

2. 'A Prize for Ezra Pound', *Partisan Review*, May 1949, CW20, pp. 100–2 [3612].

3. *The Times*, 23 January 1950, p. 7.

4. Arthur Koestler, *The Trail of the Dinosaur*, Vintage, London, 1994, pp. 47–8.

5. Stephen Spender, Review of *Homage to Catalonia*, *World Review*, 16, June 1950, p. 51.

6. Bertrand Russell, 'George Orwell', *World Review*, 16, June 1950, pp. 5–7.

7. E. M. Forster, *Two Cheers for Democracy*, Edward Arnold, London, 1951, p. 74.

8. V. S. Pritchett, *New Statesman and Nation*, 28 January 1950, p. 96.

9. *New York Times*, 22 January 1950, p. 77.

10. Malcolm Muggeridge, *Like it Was*, p. 376.

11. John Rodden, *The Politics of Literary Reputation*, p. 21.

12. John Rodden, *The Politics of Literary Reputation*, pp. xii–xiii, 6, 44–6.

13. Cezslaw Milosz, *The Captive Mind*, Farrar, Straus, Giroux, New York, 1984.

14. Malcolm Muggeridge, *Like it Was*, p. 389.

15. Frances Stonar Saunders, *Who Paid the Piper?: The CIA and the Cultural Cold War*, Granta Books, London, 1999, pp. 293–8.

16. Frances Stonar Saunders, *Who Paid the Piper?*, p. 294.

17. David Sylvester, 'Orwell on the Screen', *Encounter*, Vol. IV, No. 3, March 1955, p. 35.

18. Minutes of Meeting of Directors of George Orwell Productions Limited, 17 July 1978; in private hands.

19. Francis Wyndham–GB interview, 5 August 2000.

20. Sonia Blair–Yvonne Davet, 6 January 1950, CW20, p. 185 [3716].

21. Review of *The Formative Years* by David Mathew, *Tribune*, 29 March 1946, CW18, p. 176 [2952].

22. 'Charles Dickens', 11 March 1940, CW12, p. 36 [597].

23. Ian Angus–GB conversation, February 2000.

24. Anne Dunn–GB, 23 December 1999.

25. *The Lyttleton–Hart-Davis Letters*, edited by Rupert Hart-Davis, Vol. 2: 1956–57, John Murray, London, 1979, pp. 21, 23.

26. John Rodden, *The Politics of Literary Reputation*, p. 148.

27. Sir Steven Runciman–GB, 1 April 2000.

28. Ian Angus–GB conversation, February 2000.

29. Hilary Spurling, *The Girl from the Fiction Department*, pp. 172–3.

30. Anne Wollheim; John Russell–GB interview, 28 June 2000.

31. David Plante, *Difficult Women*, Gollancz, London, 1983, p. 97.

32. Hilary Spurling, *The Girl from the Fiction Department*.

33. Sonia Orwell, 'Unfair to George', *Nova*, June/July 1969.

34. John Rodden, *The Politics of Literary Reputation*; Timothy Garton Ash, 'On the Shelf', *Sunday Times*, 26 June 1998.

35. 'Pleasure Spots', *Tribune*, 11 January 1946, 18 CW18, p. 31 [2854].

36. Predictions: Hitler would attack Russia and the Greek campaign would go the way of the Norwegian: CW12, p. 444; laissez-faire capitalism was dead in England: CW12, p. 475; in the war advertisements would disappear within a year: CW12, p. 469; Charles Reade would outlive George Eliot, CW12, pp. 232–4.

37. Jeffrey Meyers, *George Orwell: Wintry Conscience of a Generation*, Chapter 17.

38. David Astor–GB interview, 2 December 1999.

39. 'Freedom of the Park', *Tribune*, 7 December 1945, CW17, p. 417 [2813].

40. George Woodcock, *The Crystal Spirit*, Penguin, Harmondsworth, 1970, p. 39.

41. 'Literature and the Left', *Tribune*, 4 June 1943, CW15, p. 126 [2120].

42. 'Writers and Leviathan,' *Politics and Letters*, Summer 1948, CW19, p. 292 [3364].

43. 'Marx and Russia', *Observer*, 15 February 1948, CW19, p. 270 [3346].

44. 'The Prevention of Literature', *Polemic*, No. 2, January 1946; *The Atlantic Monthly*, March 1947, CW17, p. 379 [2792].

45. *NEF*, CW9, p. 280.

46. 'Burnham's View of the Contemporary World Struggle', *New Leader* (New York), 29 March 1947, CW19, pp. 102–3 [3204].

47. BBC, 'The Third Room' (Orwell and the IRD), BBC Radio 4, May 1999.

48. Arthur Koestler–Mr Walton, 6 July 1977, Orwell Archive.

49. GO–Julian Symons, 29 October 1948, CW19, p. 461 [3481].

50. GO–George Woodcock, 18 June 1947, CW17, pp. 157–8: [3241].

51. Review of *The Prussian Officer and Other Stories* by D. H. Lawrence, *Tribune*, 16 November 1945, CW17, p. 386 [2796].

Bibliography

Works by George Orwell
Down and Out in Paris and London, Gollancz, London, 1933
Burmese Days, Gollancz, London, 1934
A Clergyman's Daughter, Gollancz, London, 1935
Keep the Aspidistra Flying, Gollancz, London, 1936
The Road to Wigan Pier, Gollancz, London, 1937
Homage to Catalonia, Secker and Warburg, London, 1937
Coming Up For Air, Gollancz, London, 1939
Inside the Whale, Gollancz, London, 1940
The Lion and the Unicorn, Secker and Warburg, London, 1941
Animal Farm, Secker and Warburg, London, 1945
Nineteen Eighty-Four, Secker and Warburg, London, 1949
The Collected Essays, Journalism and Letters of George Orwell (4 volumes), edited by Sonia Orwell and Ian Angus, Secker and Warburg, London, 1968; Penguin, Harmondsworth, 1970
Complete Works of George Orwell (20 volumes), edited by Peter Davison, assisted by Ian Angus and Sheila Davison, Secker and Warburg, London, 1998

Works about Orwell
Atkins, John, *George Orwell: A Literary Study*, Calder & Boyars, London, 1954
Brander, Laurence, *George Orwell*, Longmans Green, London, 1954
Buddicom, Jacintha, *Eric and Us*, Leslie Frewin, London, 1974
Coppard, Audrey and Crick, Bernard (eds), *Orwell Remembered*, Ariel Books, London, 1984
Crick, Bernard, *George Orwell: A Life*, Secker and Warburg, London 1980; Penguin, Harmondsworth, 1982
Davison, Peter, *George Orwell: A Literary Life,* Macmillan, London, 1998
Fenwick, Gillian, *George Orwell: A Bibliography*, St Paul's Bibliographies, Winchester, 1998
Fyvel, T. R., *George Orwell: A Personal Memoir*, Macmillan, London, 1982
Gross, Miriam (ed.), *The World of George Orwell*, Weidenfeld & Nicolson, London, 1971
Heppenstall, Rayner, *Four Absentees*, Barrie & Rockcliff, London, 1960
Hitchens, Christopher, *Orwell's Victory*, Allen Lane, Penguin Press, London, 2002

Hollis, Christopher, *A Study of George Orwell*, Hollis & Carter, London, 1956

Hopkinson, Tom, *George Orwell*, Longmans Green, London, 1953

Lewis, Peter, *George Orwell: The Road to 1984*, Heinemann, London, 1981

Meyers, Jeffrey, *A Reader's Guide to George Orwell*, Thames & Hudson, London, 1975

Meyers, Jeffrey (ed.), *Orwell: The Critical Heritage*, Routledge and Kegan Paul, London, 1975

Meyers, Jeffrey, *Orwell; Wintry Conscience of a Generation*, Norton, New York and London, 2000

Meyers, Valerie, *George Orwell*, Macmillan, London, 1991

Rees, Richard, *George Orwell: A Fugitive from the Camp of Justice*, Secker and Warburg, London, 1961

Rodden, John, *The Politics of Literary Reputation: The Making and Claiming of 'St George' Orwell*, Transaction Publishers, Oxford, New York, 1989

Shelden, Michael, *Orwell: The Authorized Biography*, Heinemann, London, 1991

Stansky, Peter and Abrahams, William, *The Unknown Orwell*, Constable, London, 1972

Stansky, Peter and Abrahams, William, *Orwell: The Transformation*, Constable, London, 1979

Thompson, John, *Orwell's London*, Fourth Estate, London, 1984

Wadhams, Stephen (ed.), *Remembering Orwell*, Penguin, Harmondsworth, 1984

Woodcock, George, *The Crystal Spirit*, Jonathan Cape, London, 1969; Penguin, Harmondsworth, 1970

Other works

Acton, Harold, *More Memoirs of an Aesthete*, Methuen, London, 1970

Amis, Kingsley, 'The Roads to Airstrip One', *Spectator*, 197, 3 August 1956

Connolly, Cyril, *Enemies of Promise,* Routledge and Kegan Paul, London, 1938

Hopkinson, Tom, 'George Orwell: Dark Side Out', *Cornhill*, 166, pp. 453–4, 1953

Hollis, Christopher, 'George Orwell and his Schooldays', *Listener*, 51, 4 March 1954

Lehmann, John, *In My Own Time: Memoirs of a Literary Wife*, Little, Brown, Boston, 1969

Owen, James, 'A Meeting With Steven Runciman', *Spectator*, 280, 15 August 1998

Peters, R. S., 'A Boy's View of George Orwell,' *Psychology and Ethical Development*, pp. 461–3, Allen & Unwin, London, 1974

Pick, J. B., 'A Bed at Hairmyers', *Scots Magazine,* 121, April 1984

'Profile of George Orwell', *Vogue*, 15 September 1946

Ratcliffe, Roger, 'The Dream Island Where Orwell Had His Nightmare Vision,' *Sunday Times*, p. 5, 22 May 1883

Simmons, Michael, 'Beauty and the Bleak', *Guardian*, p. 62, 16 October 1993

Acknowledgements

In the process of researching and writing this book I have to acknowledge the help of the following people who knew Orwell or moved in the same circles: Victor Alba, Mulk Raj Anand, David Astor, Anne Olivier Bell, Rosamond Bernier, Richard Blair, George Bumstead, John Craxton, Margaret Crosland, Henry Dakin, Lucy Dakin, Anne Dunn, Revd Prof. Gordon Reginald Dunstan, the late Kay Ekevall, the late Martin Esslin, Fay Evans, Adrian Fierz, Michael Foot, the late David Gascoyne, the late Celia Goodman, the late Desmond Hawkins, David Holbrook, Leonard Hymans, Denzil Jacobs, Robert Kee, Michel Kopp, Quentin and Liz Kopp, Cecily Mackworth, Maude Locke, the late Gwen Marsh, Jane Morgan, the late Michael Meyer, Catherine Moncure (O'Shaughnessy), Douglas Moyle, Dr Howard Nicholson, Janetta Parladé, Frances Partridge, Professor Richard Peters, the late Captain Maurice Peters, Rodney Phillips, Dan Pinnock, Kathleen Raine, the late Vernon Richards, the late Sir Steven Runciman, John Russell, the late George Rylands, Michael Sayers, Dr Kenneth Sinclair-Loutit, Lady Natasha Spender, Henry Stapley, Geoffrey Stevens, J. H. Souchard, the late David Sylvester, Mary Treadgold, Peter Vansittart, the late Ronnie Watkins, Anne Wollheim, Ingeborg Woodcock, the late George Woodcock, Francis Wyndham. I owe a special debt to Peter Davison and Ian Angus for the magnificent work they have done in preserving and making Orwell's work so readily available, and especially for *The Complete Works of George Orwell*. Both have been unstinting in their help and advice in the preparation of this book. I am grateful also to the following biographers, scholars, contacts, journalists, translators, witnesses and local historians: David Archibald, Laura Badell and Eva Carnicer of Barcelona, Tim

Brennan, Alice Carnwath, Rachel Clapton, Paul Crook, Rob Evans (*Guardian*), Beatrice Dennis, Mike Grundey (*Worcester Evening News*), Dr John Haffenden, Professor James K. Hopkins, Phyllis Kirk, Revd D. Nichol (Powick), Mrs Moriarty (Beauchamp Court), Professor John Rodden, Patrick Curry, Catherine Rylance, Frances Stonar Saunders, Stephen Schwartz, Brian and Doris Southam, Hilary Spurling, John Squires, John Surtees, Dr Susana Tavera of Barcelona University, Professor Jeremy Treglown, Stephen Wadhams (CBC), Carolyn Wakeham, Colin Ward, Sylvia Westley, John Yorke. The following individuals and staff of institutions need also to be thanked for their help and assistance: Jill Furlong and staff of the Orwell Archive, Manuscripts Department, University College, London; Lori Curtis, Head of Special Collections, Tulsa University; Gail Malmgreen, Taniment Institute Library, New York University; Tara Wenger and Richard B. Watson, Harry Ransom Humanities Research Center, University of Texas at Austin; David C. Greenbaume, Lilly Library, Indiana University; Jean Archibald, Edinburgh University Library; Ann Aldridge, Librarian, Goldsmiths' College, University of London; Jeff Walden and Neil Somerville, BBC Written Archives, Caversham; Michael Meredith (College Librarian), Nick Baker (Photographic Curator) and Penny Hadfield (School Archivist), Eton College; Tina Craig, Deputy Librarian, Royal College of Surgeons; Deborah Quare, Librarian, St Hugh's College, Oxford; Jayne Ringrose, Archivist, Pembroke College, Cambridge; Sylvia Minto, Sunderland High School for Girls; the Headmaster and Jayne Barnett, Secretary, of St Felix Girl's School, Southwold; Elizabeth Brown, Librarian, Hairmyres Hospital; Andrew L. Bowen, Church of England Records Centre; John Rees, Oxford Diocese Registrar; Catholic Central Library, London; Family Record Centre, London; India and Oriental Collection, British Library; International Institute of Social History, Amsterdam; Iowa University Library; Yale University Library; The Berg Collection, New York Public Library; The Huntington Library, Los Angeles; Dwight D. Eisenhower Library, Abilene; John F. Kennedy Library, Boston; La Bibliothèque Nationale, Paris; Hôpital Cochin, Paris; Les Archives départmentales de Paris; Public Record Office, Kew; The London Library; Marx Memorial Museum Library; The Workers' Educational Association; Henley Public Library; Eastbourne Public Library; East Sussex Records Office, Lewes; Hillingdon Central Library; Westminster Central Library; Kensington & Chelsea Public Library; Dr Jim Hoyland, Janet Whitton, Kate Searle (local historian, Cranham); B. Browett (local historian, Southwold), John Chinnery (local historian, Hayes).

Kind thanks must also go to the Provost and Fellows of Eton College; to Bill Hamilton of A. M. Heath, and to the Estate of the late Sonia Brownell Orwell for permission to use copyright material.

In the production of this book much is owed to Alan Samson and Catherine Hill, my editors at Little, Brown; to Garrett Kiely, Farideh Koohi-Kamali, and Roee Raz at Palgrave Macmillan; to the meticulous work of John English, the copy editor; and to David Baldeosingh Rotstein for the remarkable cover he designed for the book. Finally, for guidance through the quiet waters and heavy seas of three biographies, I have to thank my agent, Anthony Goff, and his assistant, Georgia Glover.

Index